HOW TO PAINT

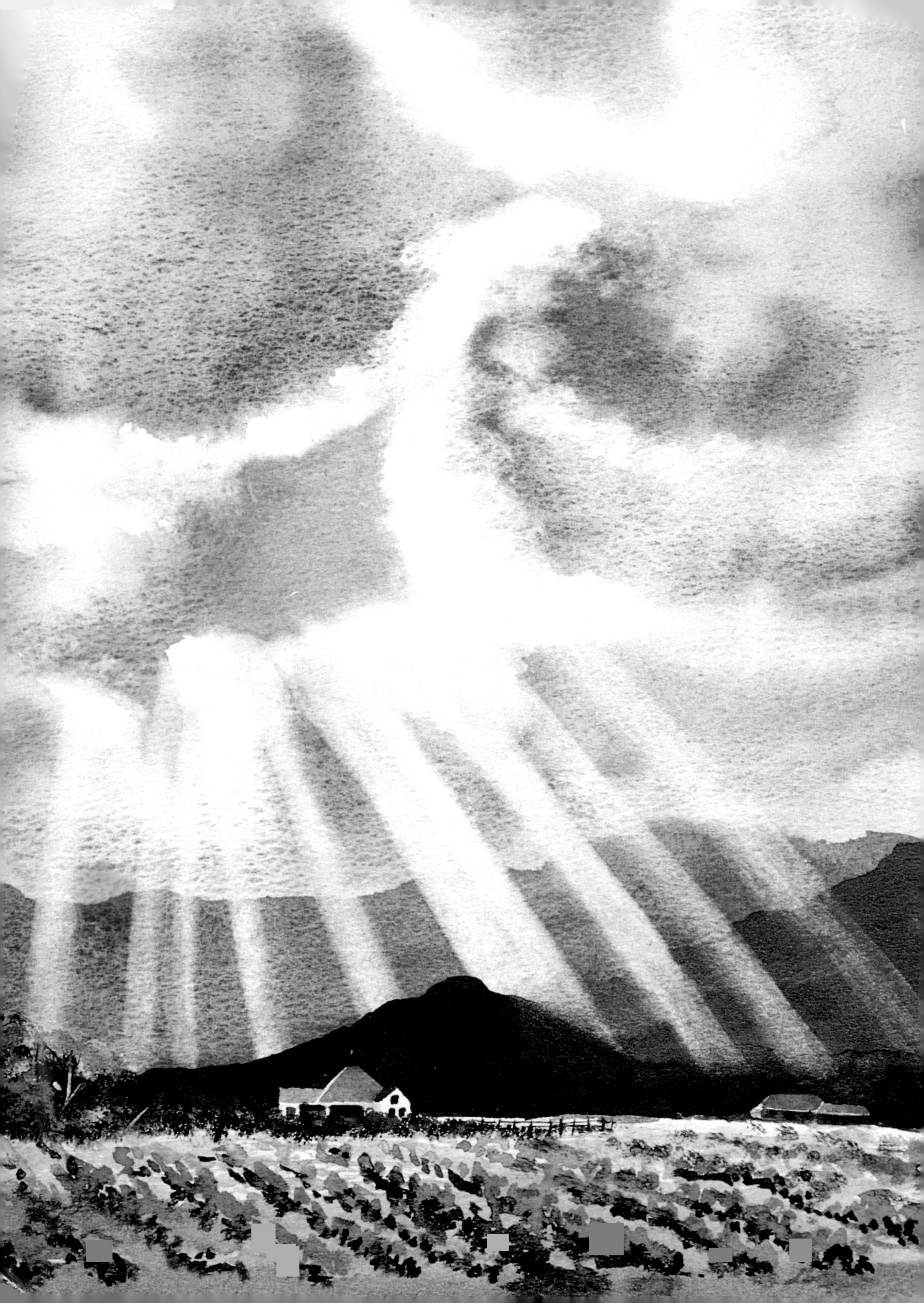

HOW TO PAINT

A complete step-by-step guide for beginners covering watercolours, acrylics and oils

■

ANGELA GAIR AND IAN SIDAWAY

NEW HOLLAND

Published in 2005 by
New Holland Publishers (UK) Ltd
London • Cape Town • Sydney • Auckland
www.newhollandpublishers.com

Garfield House, 86-88 Edgware Road
London W2 2EA
United Kingdom

80 McKenzie Street
Cape Town 8001
South Africa

14 Aquatic Drive
Frenchs Forest, NSW 2086
Australia

218 Lake Road
Northcote, Auckland
New Zealand

ISBN 1 84537 087 2 (PB)

10 9 8 7 6 5 4 3 2 1

Printed by Craft Print International,
Singapore

Contents

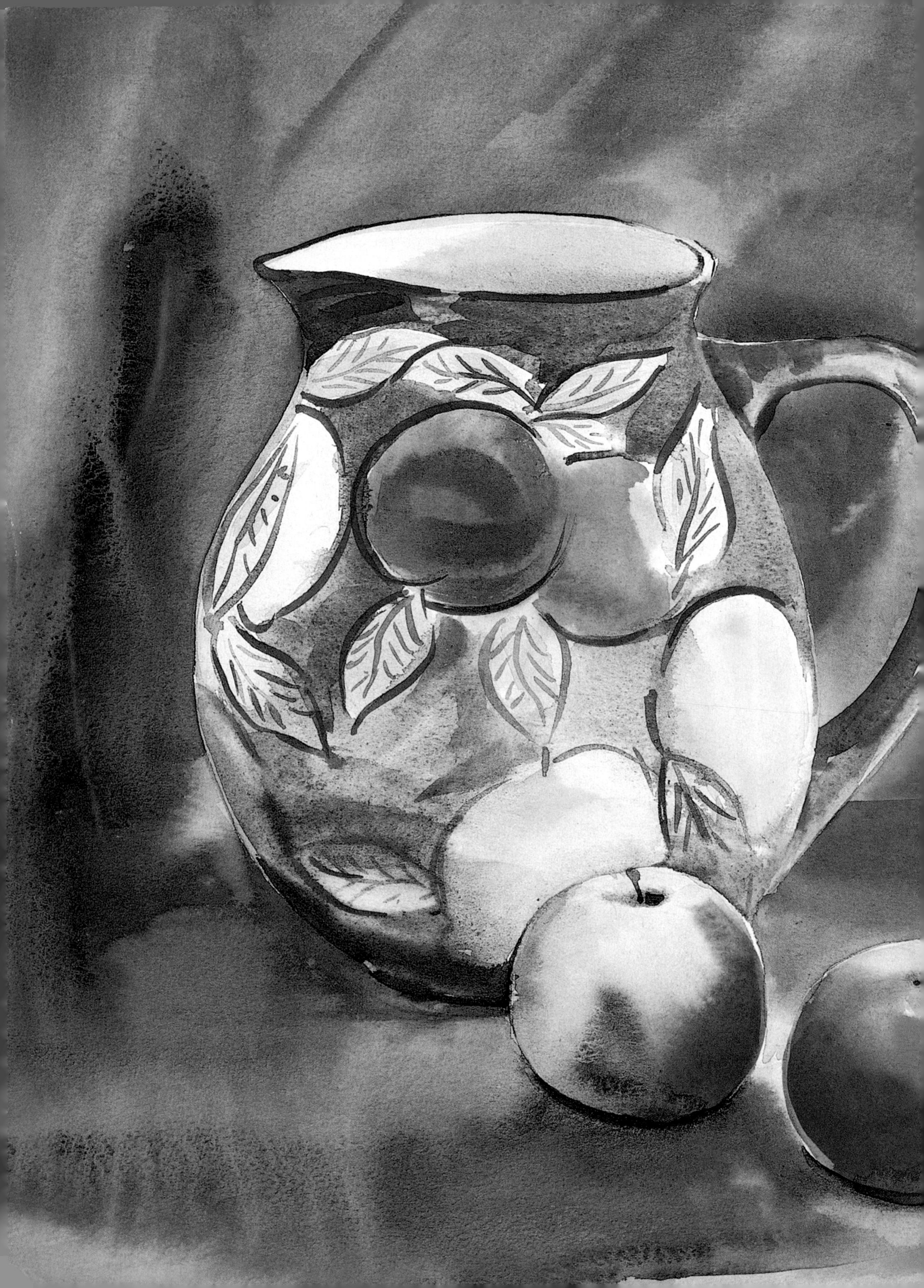

Watercolours

ANGELA GAIR

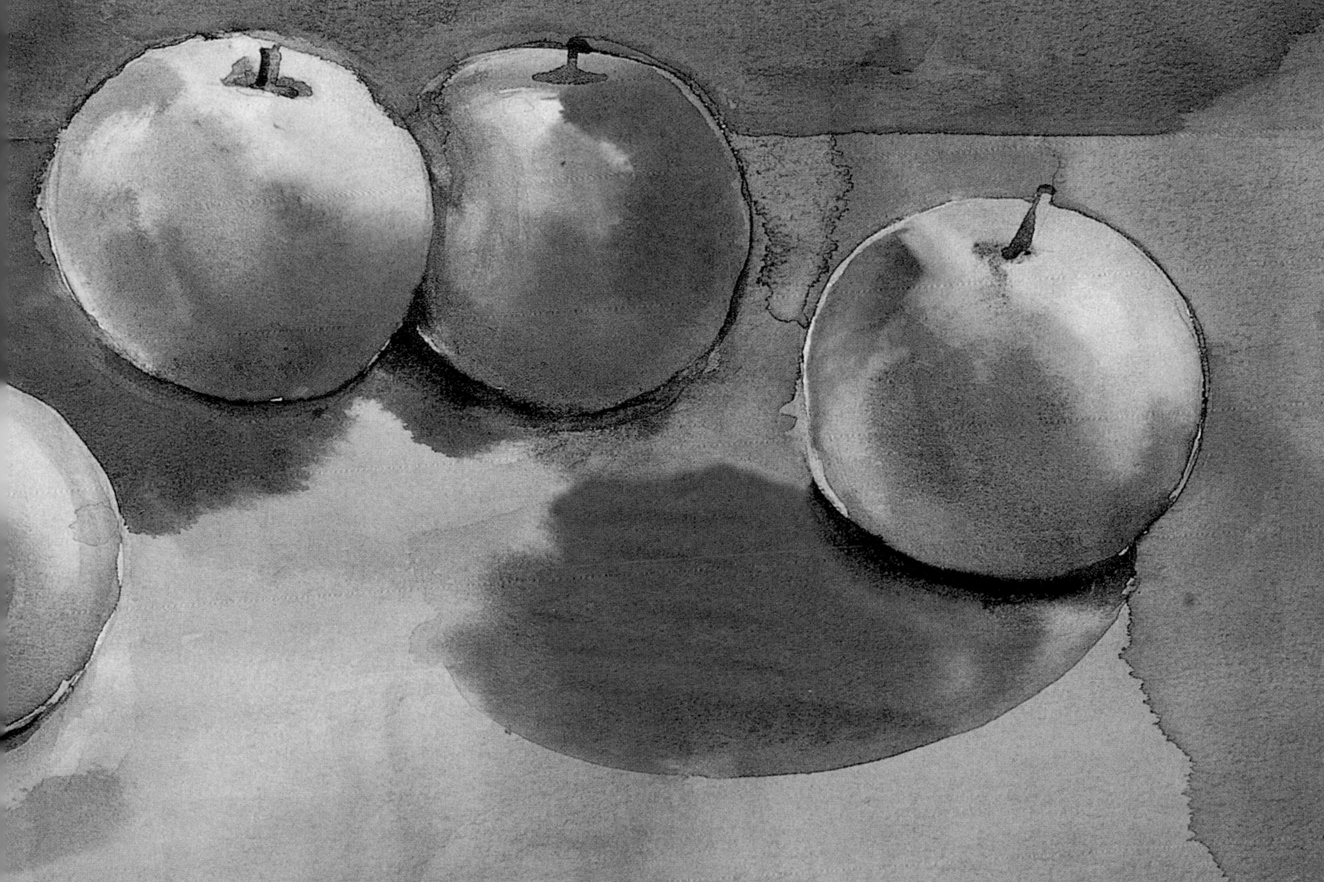

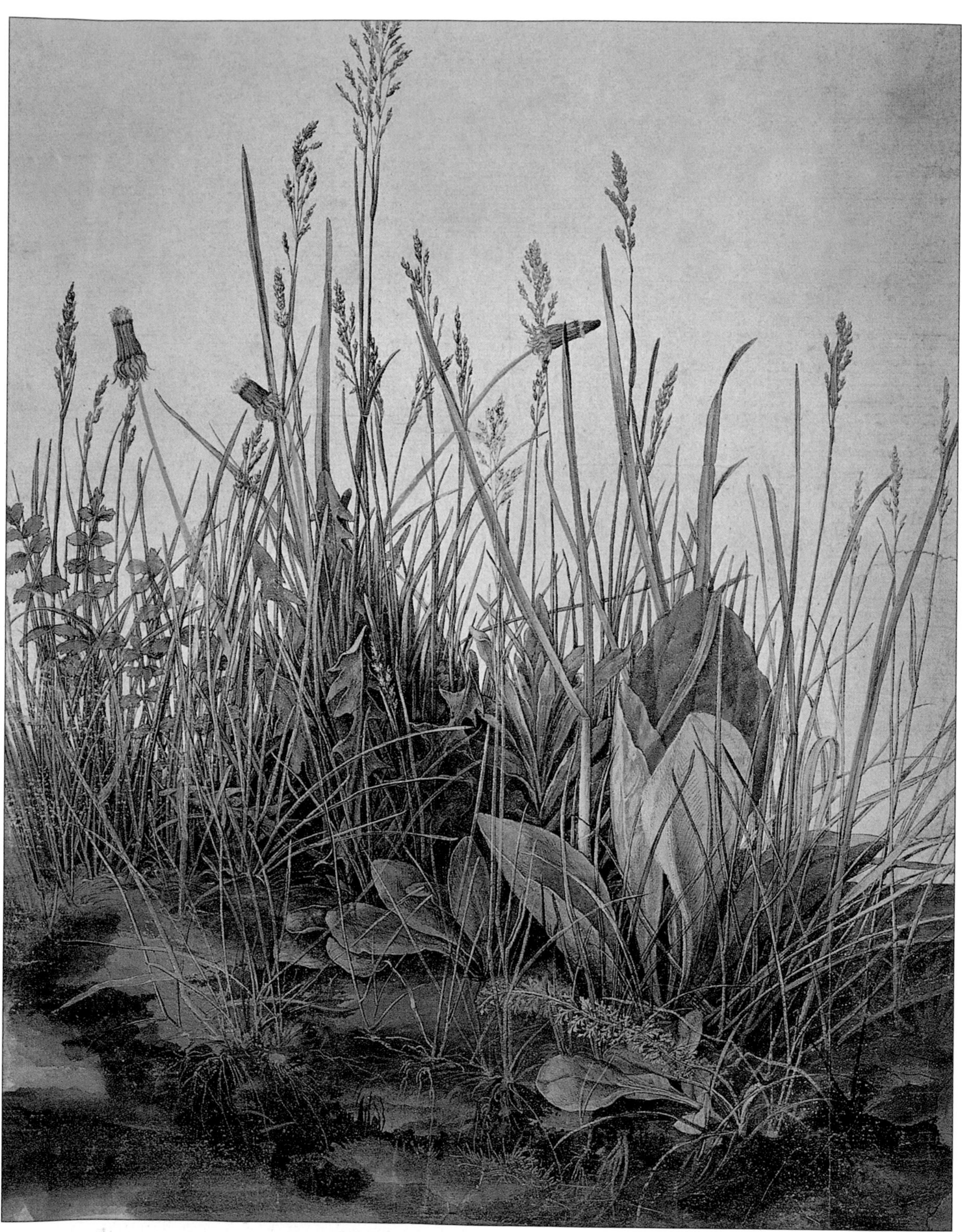

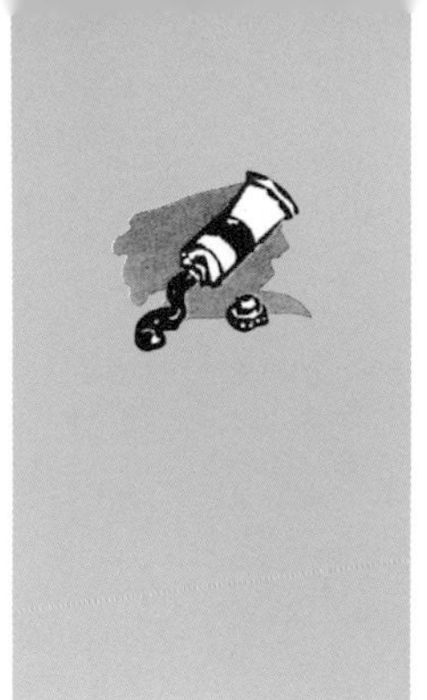

INTRODUCTION

There can be few things which are more unpredictable or satisfying than working in watercolour. The unique freshness and delicacy of the medium, its ability to produce breathtaking images with just a few brief strokes, have fascinated painters for centuries.

Water-based paint has its origins in prehistoric times. Stone Age man depicted animals and hunting scenes on the walls of cave-dwellings using pigments mixed from natural earth colours – yellow and red ochres, and black made from carbon – which were bound with animal fat and diluted with water.

Ancient Egyptian artists used water-based pigments on plaster to paint decorative reliefs on the walls of their palaces and tombs. They used mainly red, blue, green, black and white pigments, derived from minerals which were ground in water and bound with starch or honey. The colours are as fresh and intense today as they were thousands of years ago.

Water-based paints rose to prominence with the fresco paintings of the Renaissance artists of fifteenth- and sixteenth-century Florence. Fresco painting involved applying pigments mixed with water directly onto wet plaster. As the plaster dried, the colour was bonded into it and became part of the wall, instead of lying on the surface. The ceiling of the Sistine Chapel, painted by Michelangelo (1475–1564), is one of the largest and grandest frescoes ever painted.

The German Renaissance artist Albrecht Dürer (1471–1528) painted meticulous studies of plants, flowers and animals. As was the practice at the time, he used opaque watercolour to give his botanical works substance and clarity. But he was also one of the first painters to exploit the transparency of watercolour. Among his numerous paintings are delicate landscapes composed of thin layers of colour applied in swift, spontaneous brush strokes. These have a wonderfully

The Great Piece of Turf *Albrecht Dürer*

Dürer was the first European artist to exploit the transparent qualities of watercolour. His technical skill as an engraver is reflected in this meticulously detailed watercolour study of a clump of grass and wild flowers, which combines thin washes of colour, pen-and-ink line, and touches of body colour.

A City on a River at Sunset *J M W Turner*

This small study is one of many that Turner produced in preparation for a series of engravings to illustrate the "Great Rivers of Europe". Breathtakingly economical in its evocation of place and atmosphere, it is painted in transparent watercolour and body colour on blue paper.

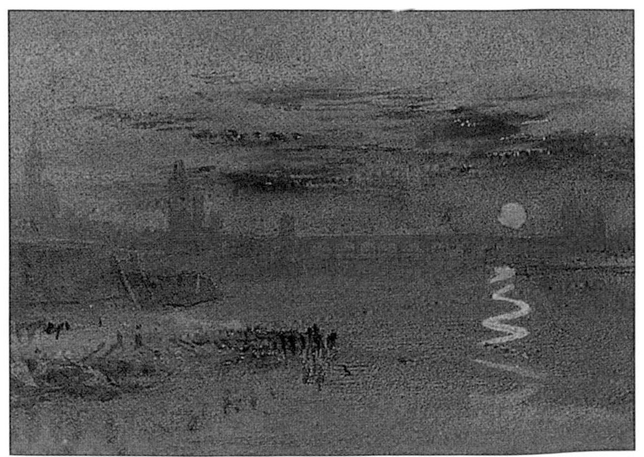

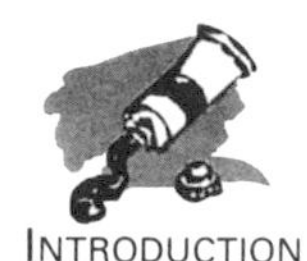

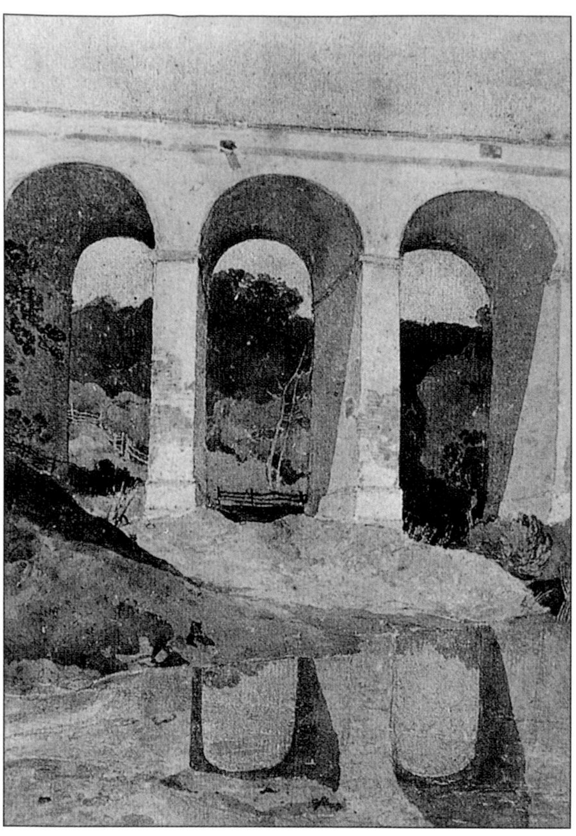

Chirk Aqueduct *John Sell Cotman*

This image leaves an indelible imprint on the mind, such was Cotman's skill in balancing and controlling colour, line, tone and mass. Laying down crisp washes of clear, luminous colour, he created a pattern of simple, interlocking areas of light and dark tone that effectively convey the weight and bulk of the enormous structure.

free quality which anticipates by several centuries the work of watercolour masters such as Turner and Cézanne.

Inexplicably, watercolour fell into obscurity after Dürer's death, and throughout the sixteenth and seventeenth centuries it was mainly used for making preliminary studies, roughs and sketches for oil paintings.

During the eighteenth century watercolour at last began to be recognized as a medium in its own right. By the late eighteenth and nineteenth centuries watercolour painting had become enormously popular and something of a British speciality, due in part to the emergence of "The Grand Tour". As Britain grew more prosperous and outward-looking, it became fashionable for the sons of wealthy families to travel through continental Europe in order to broaden their education. These young tourists often took watercolour painters along with them to paint the classical ruins and picturesque scenes they visited.

The two greatest watercolour painters of the eighteenth century were Thomas Girtin and JMW Turner. Girtin (1755–1802) broke away from the accepted conventions of watercolour painting, in which preliminary outlines were "filled in " with a grey underpainting, over which washes of colour were carefully laid. Girtin painted directly onto white paper, thus allowing light to reflect off the paper and enhance the transparent brilliance of the colours. He used a strictly limited palette of five basic colours – yellow ochre, burnt sienna, light red, monastral blue and ivory black – with which he created subtle harmonies of tone. Girtin was one of the first watercolourists to paint directly from nature, braving all conditions in his desire to capture the transient and fluctuating effects of light and weather.

Joseph Mallord William Turner (1775–1851) was another iconoclast, who opened the way for artists to interpret their own sensations before nature. Turner explored the dynamic and sensuous elements of nature – storm and wreck, wind, sky and water, the shimmering light of Venice, misty mountains, rivers and lakes at sunset. In his preoccupation with colour and light he splashed, dragged, scratched and pushed the wet paint around, literally bending the medium to his will.

The golden age of British watercolour painting continued well into the nineteenth century with the work of such notable luminaries as John Sell Cotman (1782–1842), John Varley (1778–1842), Samuel Palmer (1805–1881) and others too numerous to mention.

Meanwhile, watercolour painting was also flourishing in America. Winslow Homer (1836–1910) and Thomas Eakins (1844–1916) are synonymous with the realist tradition, continued in the twentieth century by Edward Hopper (1882–1967). Some of the more avant-garde artists left America for Europe, where they exerted considerable influence. James Abbott McNeill Whistler (1834–1903) was a master of the technique known as "wet-into-wet", in which colours are flooded onto the paper and fuse together into semblances of water, sky or trees. Influenced by Japanese art, he captured the essentials of a scene with breathtaking skill and economy of means. John Singer Sargent (1856–1925) showed equal skill in his use of expressive brush strokes to capture the shifting effects of sunlight and shadow.

The artist who revolutionized modern watercolour painting was Paul Cézanne (1839–1906). Although loosely associated with the Impressionists, Cézanne was less interested in the ephemeral effects of nature than in its solidity and permanence. Believing that drawing and colour are inseparable, he interwove colour and line, applying one over the other for a unity of effect. In his later career he turned increasingly to watercolour, exploiting its qualities to describe the volume of objects with successive washes of pure colour and using the direction of the brushmarks to "sculpt" their contours.

During the twentieth century watercolour has played its part in the numerous experimental art movements that have evolved over the decades. In particular, abstract and expressionist painters including Wassily Kandinsky (1866–1944), Emil Nolde (1867–1956) and Paul Klee (1879–1940) found the unpredictable quality of watercolour an ideal medium for expressing their highly personal visions.

Watercolour continues to flourish in the traditional vein, but at the same time has escaped the strict confines of the purist approach formulated in the eighteenth century. Today, watercolour may be combined with other media – gouache, acrylics, pastel, collage – without raising a disapproving eyebrow. Infinitely versatile and adaptable, it appeals to die-hard traditionalists and avant-garde sophisticates alike. Its future as a leading paint medium is assured.

The Waterfan *Winslow Homer*

In his later career, Homer painted extensively in the Bahamas and Bermuda. In his seascapes and landscapes he recorded both the ethereal light of the tropical storms and the vibrant colour present on clear days.

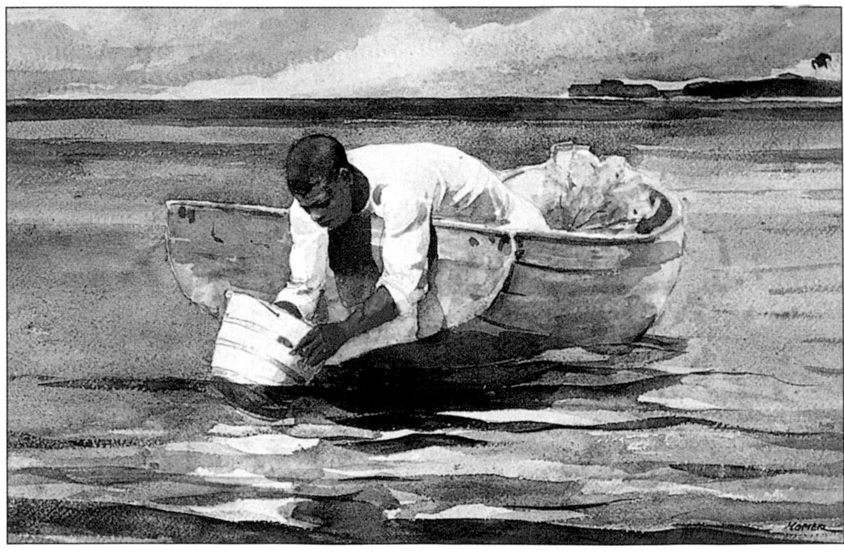

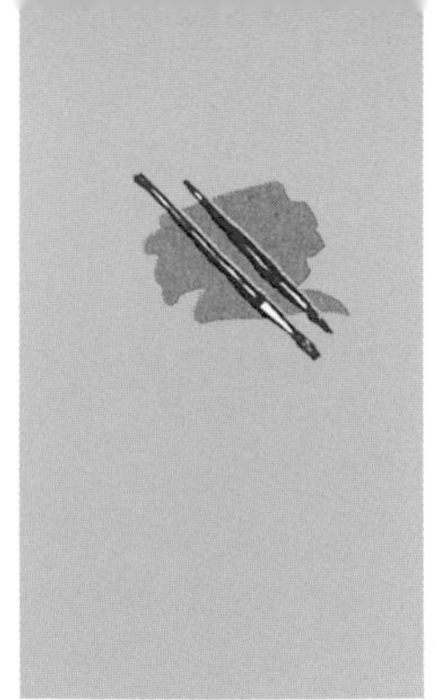

Materials and Equipment

The range of watercolour paints and equipment on display in art supply stores is quite daunting. Yet one of the advantages of watercolour painting is that it requires few materials – many a masterpiece has been created with just a few colours, a couple of brushes, a jar of water and a sheet of paper. This section outlines all the paints and equipment you will need when you first start.

Paints

Watercolour paints are available in tubes of creamy paint and in small blocks of semi-moist colour called "pans". There are two grades – "artist's" and "student's". The student's range is cheaper, but you will get better results from the artist's range, which contains finer quality pigments.

Tube colour is richer than pan colour and is useful for creating large areas of wash quickly; simply squeeze the paint onto a palette and mix it with water. The only disadvantage is that the paint can leak and solidify if the cap is not replaced properly after use.

Pans can be bought individually as well as in special paintboxes with slots to hold the pans in place and a lid which opens out to form a convenient mixing palette. They are economical to buy and useful for outdoor work as they are easily portable. However, it takes a little effort to lift enough colour onto the brush to make a large wash.

Gouache is an opaque type of watercolour made by binding the pigments with gum arabic and combining them with white chalk. The paint dries to an opaque, matt (flat) finish, quite different to the delicate transparency of pure watercolour, yet watercolour and gouache can be used together in the same painting with great success.

Suggested Palette

You do not need a large number of colours to paint expressive pictures. Most artists use a basic palette of pigments that forms the backbone of their work, augmented by additional pigments if they are needed for a particular subject. Keeping to a small range of pigments encourages you to mix them together to create a range of subtle hues, while at the same time achieving a harmonious painting.

There is no definitive basic palette; every artist will, of course, have their own special favourites. However, the colours described and illustrated on page 13 should meet most requirements.

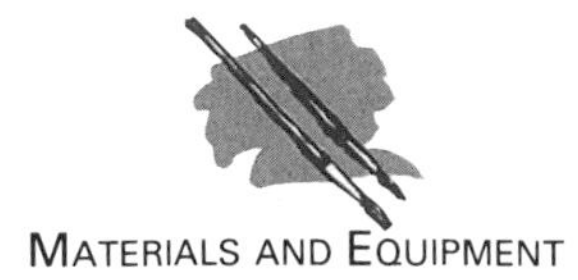

SUGGESTED PALETTE

Cadmium yellow pale
A strong bright warm yellow, very useful in mixes. When mixed with viridian it produces soft, warm greens.

Cadmium red pale
A warm, intense red. Produces good pinks and purples when mixed with other colours.

Alizarin crimson
A cool, slightly bluish red; diluted it creates delicate pinks. Mixed with ultramarine, it produces a pure violet.

Cobalt blue
Gentler and more subtle than French ultramarine, it is wonderful for skies.

French ultramarine
A dark, subdued blue with a faint hint of violet. Mixes well with yellow to form a rich variety of greens and with brown to form interesting greys.

Viridian
This deep, rich green retains its brilliance, even in mixes. Ideal for cooling reds, it also mixes well with burnt sienna to create a useful shadow colour.

Sap green
A lovely, resonant green that provides a wide range of natural greens and browns in mixes — ideal for landscape colours.

Yellow ochre
A soft yellow, very useful in landscape painting. Produces soft, subtle greens when mixed with blues.

Burnt sienna
A gentle, dark and transparent brown. Mixes well with other pigments to create muted, subtle colours.

Burnt umber
A rich and versatile brown, ideal for darkening colours.

Payne's grey
Made from a mixture of blue and black, this is a good all-round colour. In mixes, it produces intense shadows that are still full of colour.

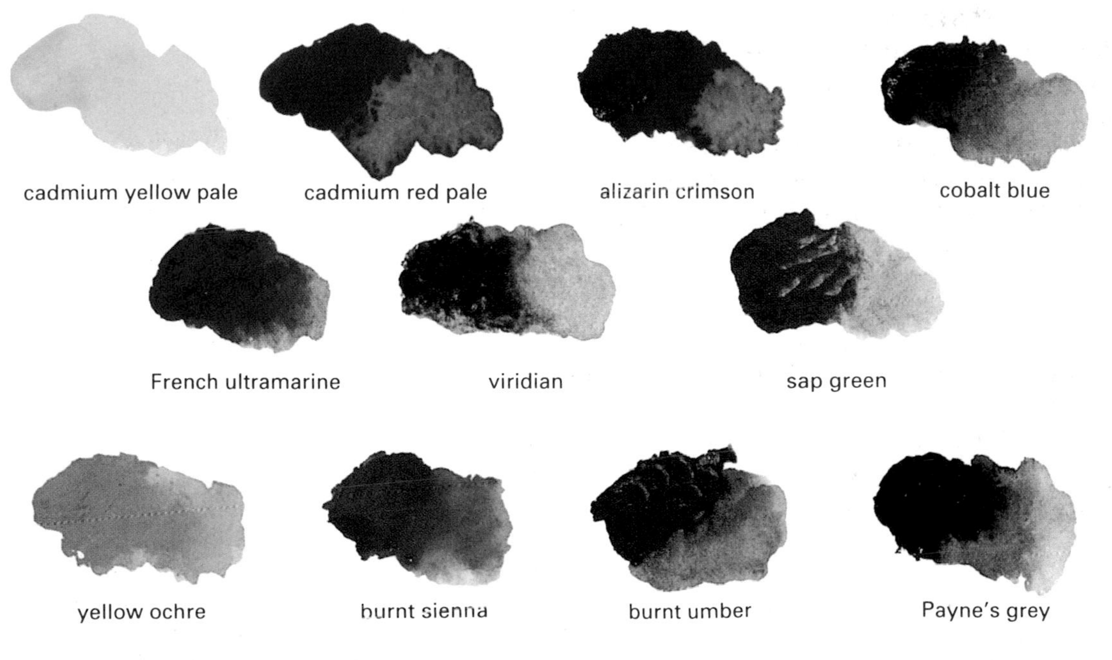

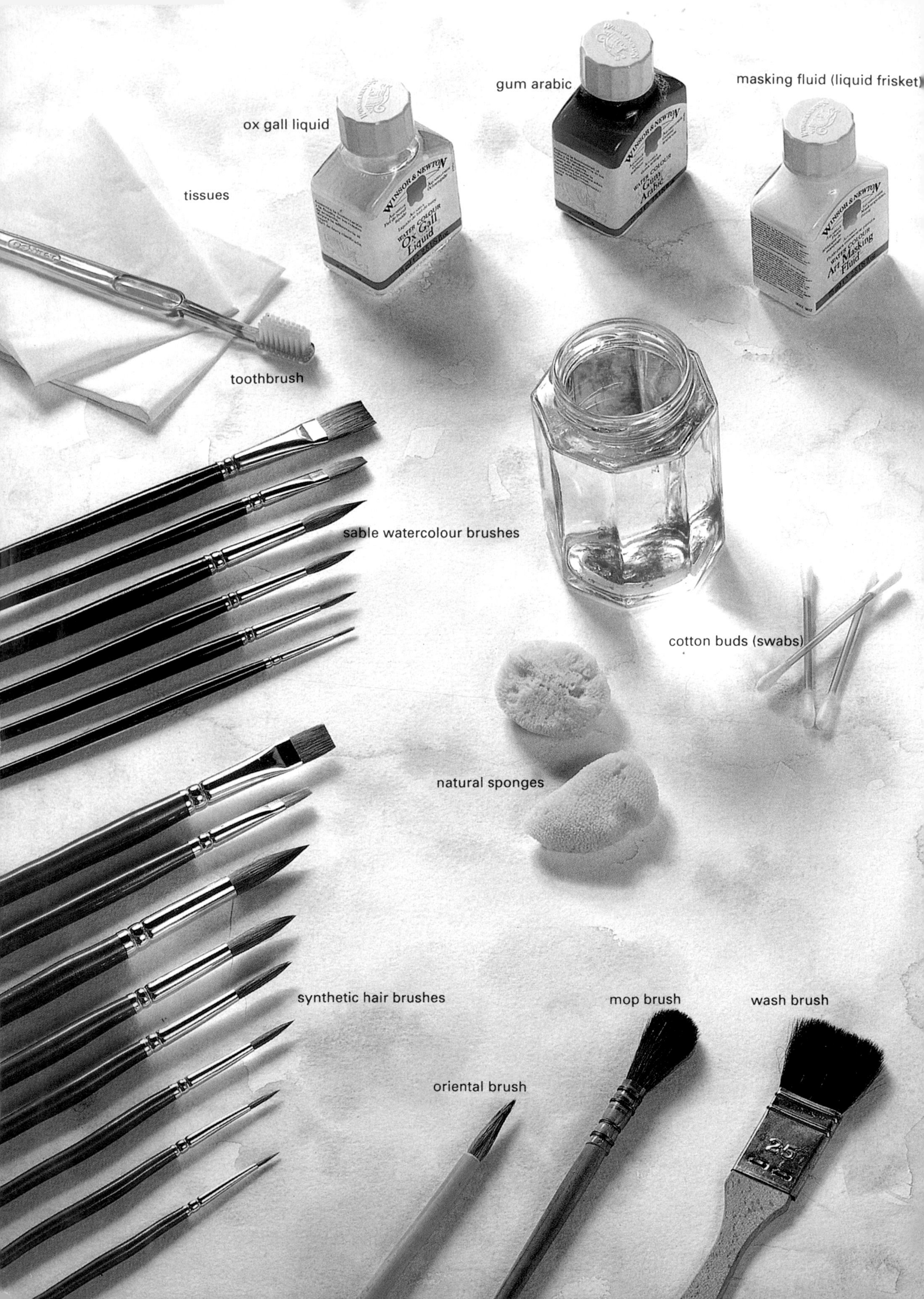
gum arabic
masking fluid (liquid frisket)
ox gall liquid
tissues
toothbrush
sable watercolour brushes
cotton buds (swabs)
natural sponges
synthetic hair brushes
mop brush
wash brush
oriental brush

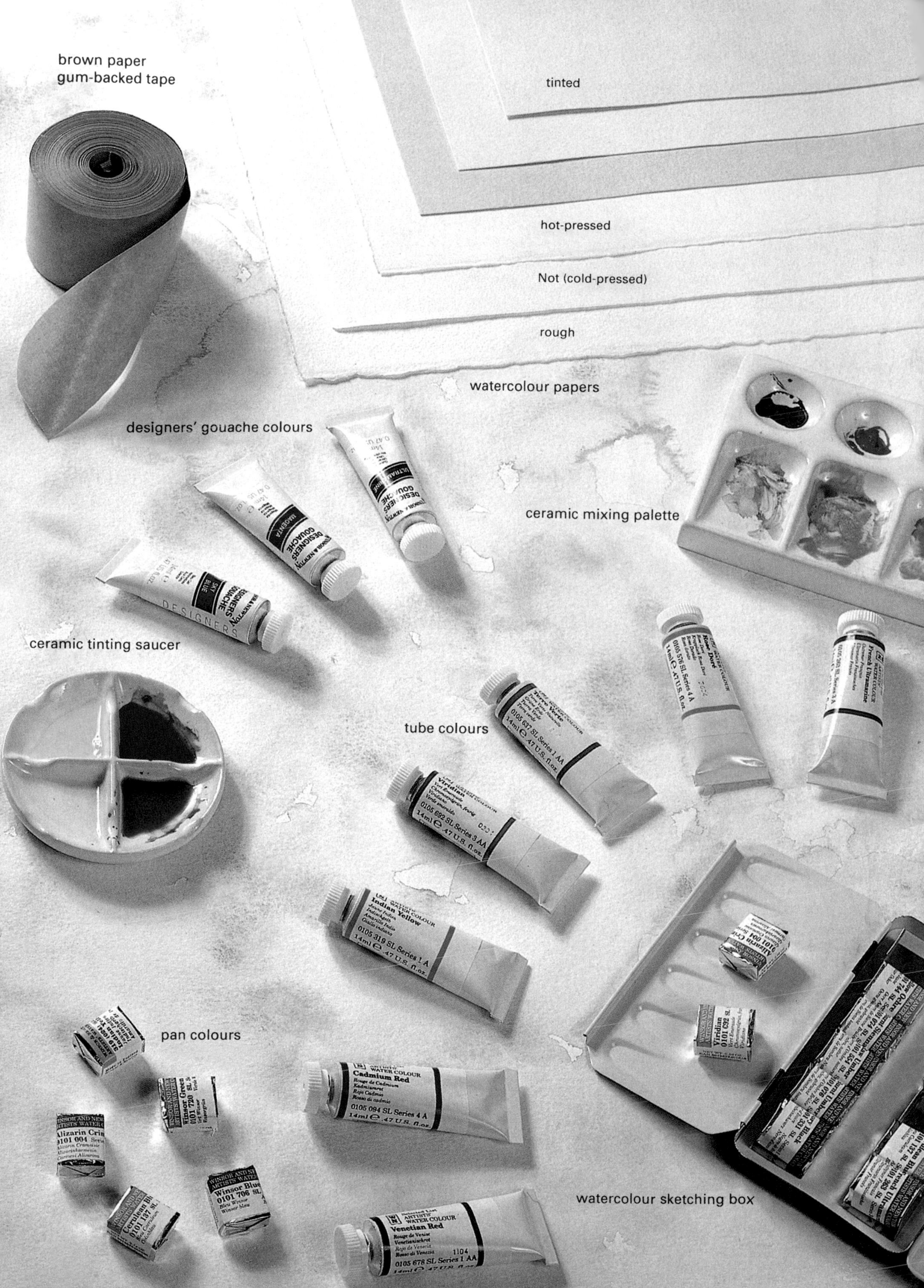
brown paper
gum-backed tape
tinted
hot-pressed
Not (cold-pressed)
rough
watercolour papers
designers' gouache colours
ceramic mixing palette
ceramic tinting saucer
tube colours
pan colours
watercolour sketching box

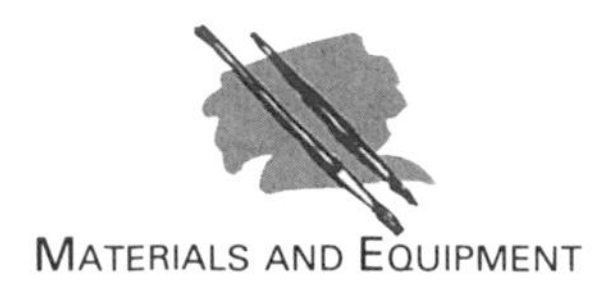

BRUSHES

Brushes are especially important in watercolour painting, so it is worth buying good quality ones. Sable brushes are expensive, but they give the best results and will last for many years. They are resilient, hold their shape well, do not shed their hairs, and have a springiness which results in lively, yet controlled brush strokes.

Sable blends – sable mixed with other hairs such as squirrel, ox hair or synthetic fibres – are a less expensive alternative that will give you perfectly good results. Bamboo-handled Oriental hog's hair brushes are inexpensive and versatile; the full-bodied head holds plenty of paint and also points well for painting fine details.

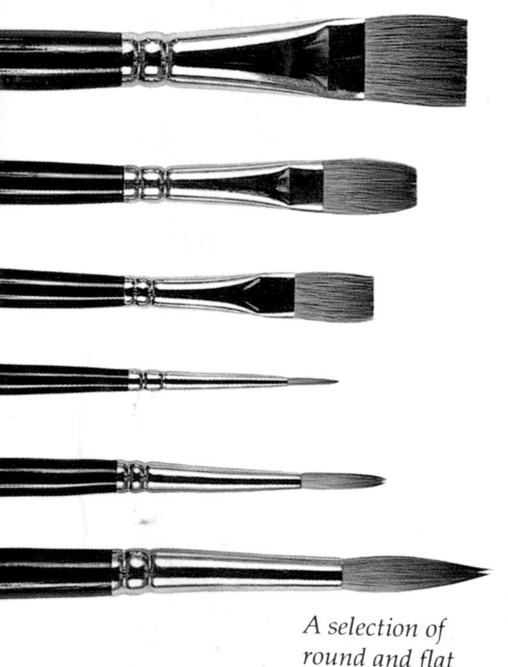

A selection of round and flat sable brushes in a range of sizes.

Brush Shapes

There are two basic shapes for watercolour brush heads: rounds for painting small areas and detail; and flats for applying broad washes.

Rounds are bullet-shaped brushes that come to a fine point. By moving the broad side of the brush across the paper you can paint sweeping areas of colour, and with the tip you can paint fine details. Flats are wide and square-ended. They are ideal for spreading water rapidly over the paper to create a wash. The flat edge is useful for making clean-cut lines.

Brush Sizes

Brushes are graded according to size, ranging from as small as 0000 to as large as 14. The size of flats generally denotes the width of the brush, measured in millimetres or inches.

Three or four brushes are enough to start with; choose a small round for fine detail, a large flat for laying washes, and a medium-sized round and flat for general work.

Brush Care

Look after your brushes and they will last a long time. When painting, try not to leave brushes standing in water as this can ruin both the hairs and the handles. When you have finished painting, rinse brushes in running water, making sure that any paint near the metal ferrule is removed.

After cleaning, shake out the excess water and gently reform the brushes to their original shapes, then either lay them flat or place them head-upwards in a jar to dry. If you store wet brushes in an airtight container, mildew will develop. Moths are very keen on sable brushes, so if you need to store brushes for any length of time, use some mothballs to act as a deterrent.

PAPER

A wide variety of watercolour paper is available, both in single sheets and, more economically, in pads and blocks. The choice of paper depends largely on the subject, the technique used, and the effect required. Paper varies in surface texture and in weight (thickness). The surface texture of paper is known as its "tooth". There are three kinds of surface:

Hot-pressed (HP) is very smooth, with almost no "tooth". It is suitable for finely detailed work, but most artists find its surface too slippery for pure watercolour painting.

Not, meaning not hot-pressed (cold-pressed), is the most popular type of surface, and is ideal for less experienced painters. Its medium-textured surface is good for both large, smooth washes and for fine brush detailing.

Rough paper has a pronounced "tooth" which catches at the brush and causes watercolour strokes and washes to break up. The paint sinks into the pitted surface and leaves speckles untouched, producing a luminous sparkle.

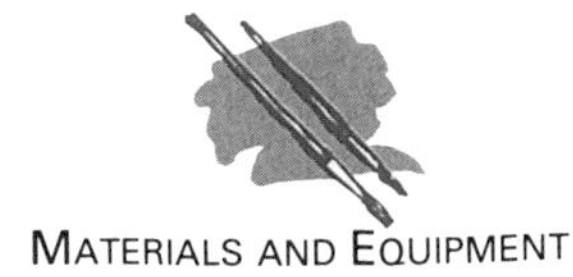

Traditionally, the weight of paper is measured in pounds (lb) per ream (480 sheets). The equivalent metric measure is grams per square metre (gsm). As a guide, the lightest watercolour paper is 150gsm (70lb), while a heavier grade is 300gsm (140lb). The heaviest paper weighs 640gsm (300lb). Paper tends to cockle (buckle or warp) when wet, and the lighter the paper, the more it cockles. This problem is avoided by stretching it before use (see pages 20-21).

Prepared boards consist of thin watercolour paper ready-mounted on thick cardboard, which is convenient as stretching is unnecessary.

Watercolour blocks consist of sheets of paper stuck together on the edges of all four sides to prevent cockling. They are very useful when you do not want the bother of stretching paper or when you are working outdoors. When the painting is finished you simply tear off the top sheet.

Palettes

If you are using pan colours, the box in which they are kept doubles as a palette, because the inside of the lid has wells for mixing colour. You can buy recessed palettes for tube colours with separate mixing wells which slant so that the paint collects at one end ready for use. Tinting saucers are useful for mixing large amounts of colour; these are small ceramic dishes, either divided into four compartments for laying out separate colours or undivided for a single colour. You could also try improvising with an old white china plate, which will give you plenty of room for mixing.

Accessories

You will need a soft pencil (3B or 2B) for drawing; a kneaded putty eraser for erasing pencil lines without spoiling the surface of the paper; soft tissues or a natural sponge for mopping up excess water and lifting out colour, and also for applying paint when you want a textured effect; cotton buds (swabs) for lifting small areas of colour; jars for water; a drawing board; brown paper gum-backed tape for stretching paper; and masking fluid (liquid frisket) for reserving light or white areas in a painting.

A china hors d'oeuvres dish is an excellent alternative to recessed palettes or tinting saucers, especially if mixing large amounts of paint; separate colours or tones can be mixed in each section.

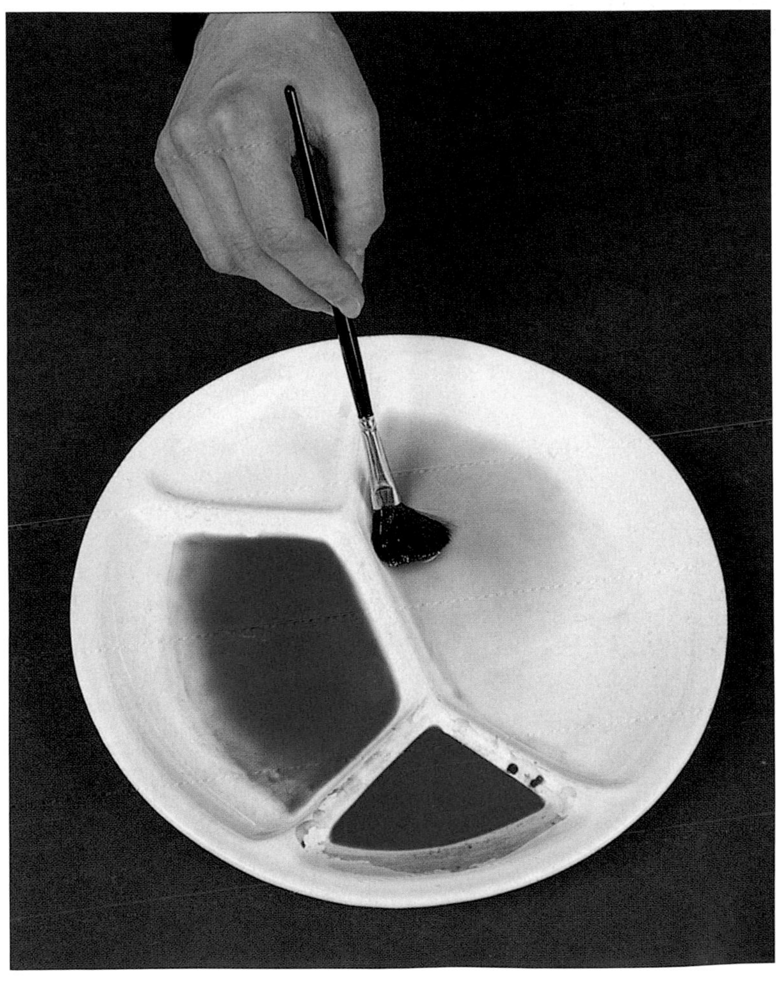

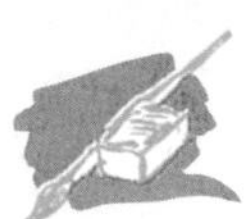

Basic Techniques

Mixing Paint

You can use almost any non-absorbent white surface as a palette for watercolour paint; in fact, when mixing a wide range of colours you may find an old white china plate gives you more room than a standard watercolour palette.

Watercolour paint always dries lighter on the paper than it appears when wet, so mixing is often a matter of trial and errror. It is impossible to tell by looking at the paint on a palette whether the colour or shade is right: the colour must be seen on the paper. Therefore, when mixing, you should always have a spare piece of the selected paper ready for testing the colours before committing them to the actual painting.

Always mix more paint than you think you will need; it is surprising how quickly it is used up. This applies particularly to watercolour washes, which need a lot of paint; it is frustrating to run out of colour half-way through an expansive sky wash, for example. And if you run out of a particular mixed colour, you may find it

If you find a certain colour mixture successful for a particular subject, keep a note of it for future reference. This test piece relates to the project painting shown on page 60. It provides a useful – and very attractive – visual record of the colours used for various elements of the painting.

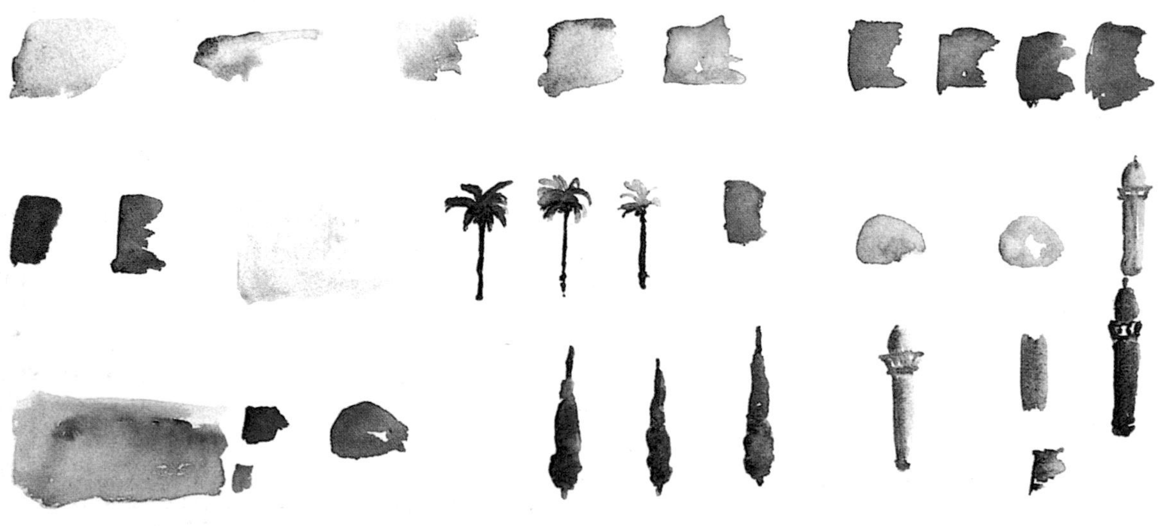

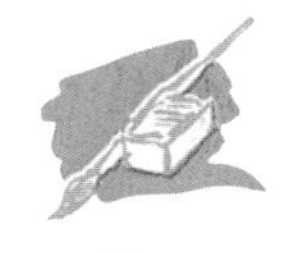

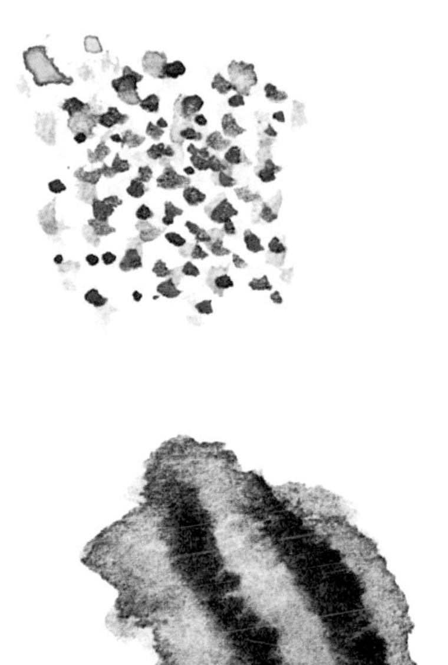

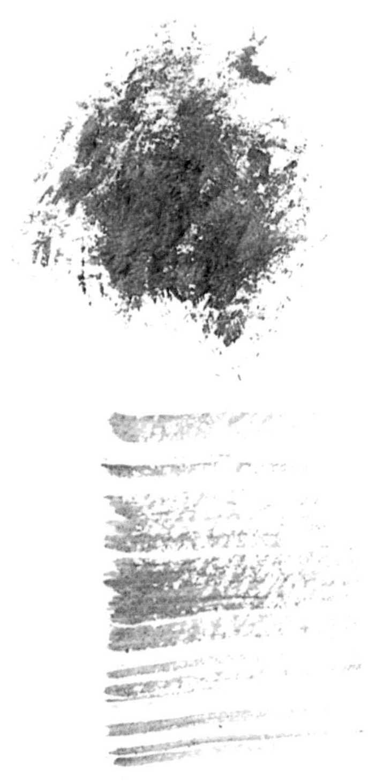

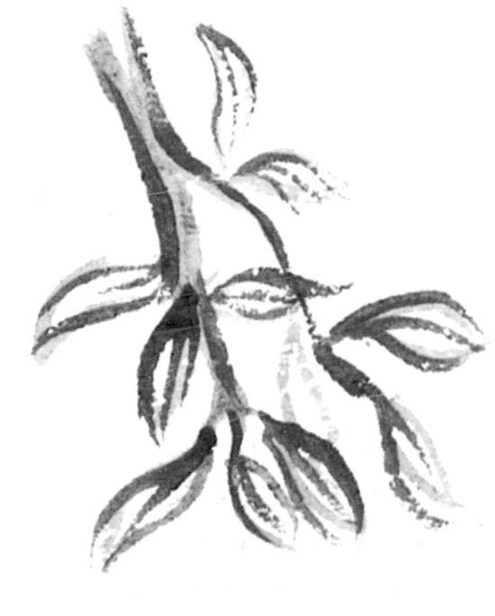

Make a page of brush marks to discover what your brushes are capable of. These marks were made with a round brush (top row) and a flat brush (bottom row).

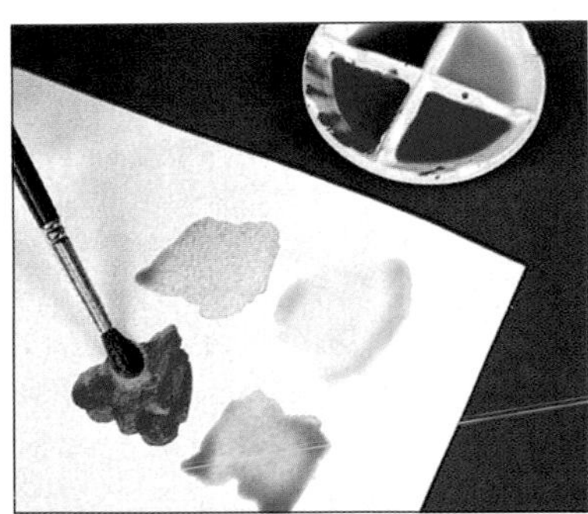

Watercolour dries lighter than it appears when wet, so test each colour on spare paper before applying it to the actual picture.

extremely difficult to match the exact colour again.

When using tube colours, squeeze a small quantity of paint onto the palette. Then pick up a little of the paint on the brush, transfer this to the mixing dish and add water, a little at a time, until you have achieved the required strength of colour. With pan colours, moisten the paint with a brush to release the pigment, then transfer the colour to the palette (or use the wells set in the inside lid of the paintbox) and mix it with water to the strength required.

Try to keep your colours fresh and clean at all times. Rinse your brush each time you use a new colour, and replace the water in your jar frequently as dirty water contaminates the colours and mutes their brilliance.

Brush Strokes

In oil and acrylic painting the thick paint is normally applied with stiff bristle brushes in a series of choppy strokes. The watercolour technique is quite different, requiring fluid, gliding movements to form continuous strokes. Unless you are painting fine details, move your whole arm to create flowing strokes. Keeping your painting hand relaxed, hold the brush around the middle of the handle. If you paint from the wrist as though you were writing with a pen, the strokes will be stiff and cramped.

Try out different brush techniques using both round and flat brushes, like those illustrat-

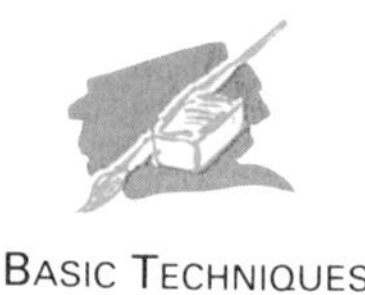

ed here. The pressure exerted with the brush controls the width of the stroke. For fine strokes, the tip of the brush should glide across the paper. To make wider strokes, press down with the brush.

As well as short strokes, try making long, flowing ones. Painting a long stroke is similar to a follow-through in golf or tennis. Keep your hand and arm moving before, during and after the brush stroke.

You will find that the texture and absorbency of the paper will influence the marks you make. The surface of rough paper produces friction which breaks up the stroke, producing a lively, sparkling effect (see drybrush painting, pages 82–89). Conversely, a smooth paper will yield smooth lines because the brush glides easily over its surface.

Stretching Paper

Most papers will cockle (buckle or wrinkle) when they become wet with watercolour paint. This can be avoided by stretching paper before starting to work on it. The paper is first soaked in water, allowing it to expand, and is then fastened down securely to a board so that it dries taut.

Have ready a drawing board, a sheet of watercolour paper, trimmed all round to about 2.5cm (1in) smaller than the drawing board, a sponge, and four strips of brown paper gum-backed tape, cut 5cm

Stretching Watercolour Paper

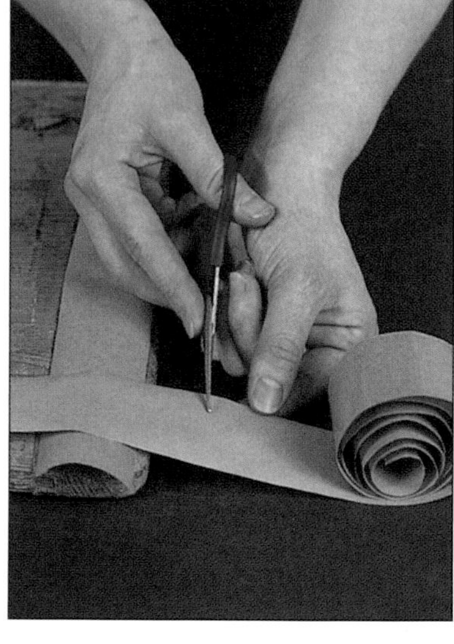

1
Cut four strips of brown paper gum-backed tape to length.

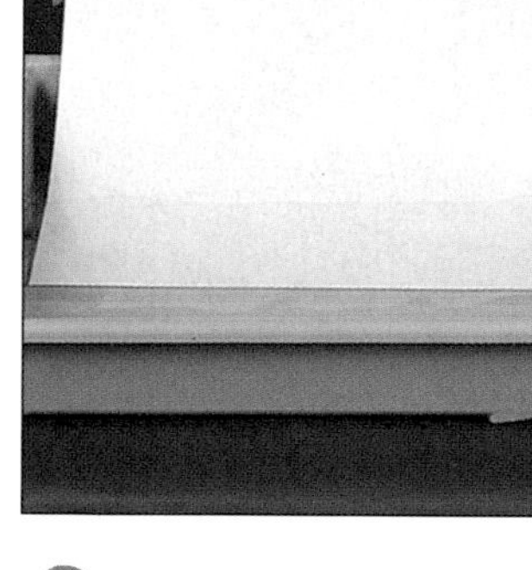

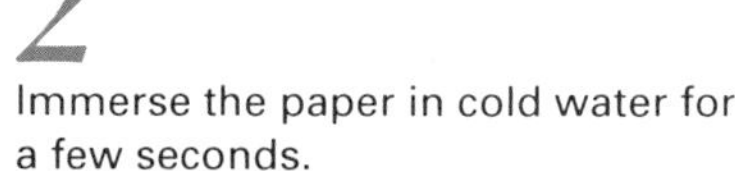

2
Immerse the paper in cold water for a few seconds.

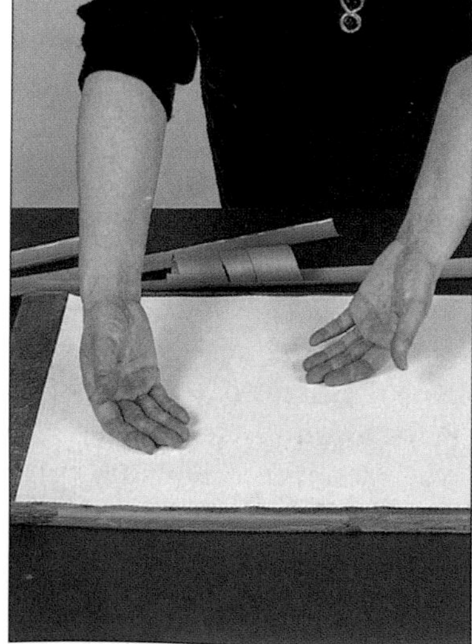

3
Lay the paper flat on the board. Smooth it out from the centre using the backs of your hands.

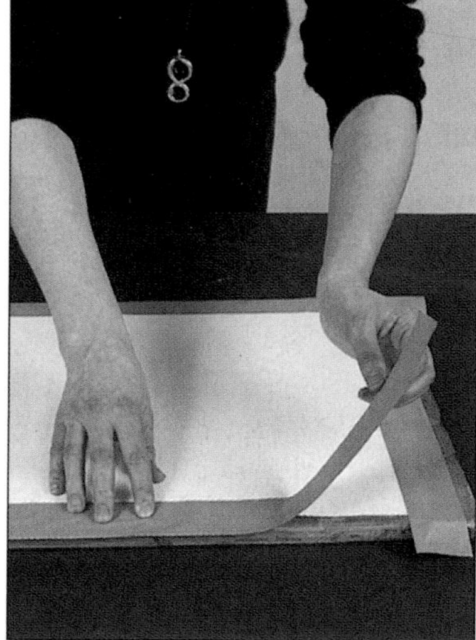

4
Stick down the edges of the paper with the strips of gummed tape and leave to dry.

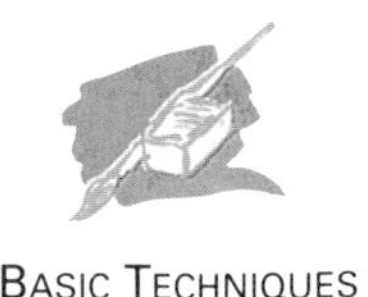

Laying Flat Washes

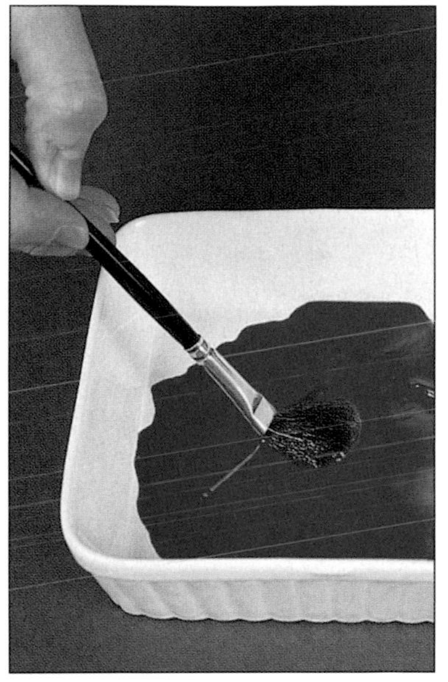

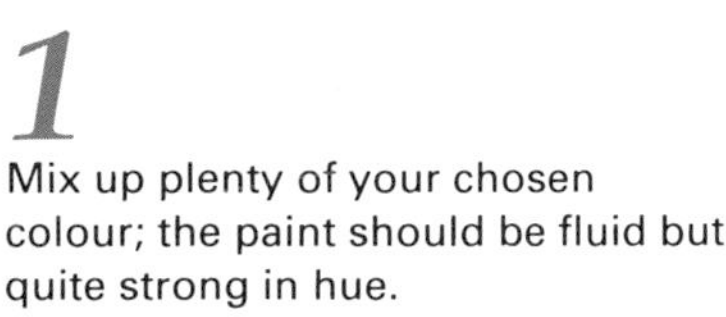

Mix up plenty of your chosen colour; the paint should be fluid but quite strong in hue.

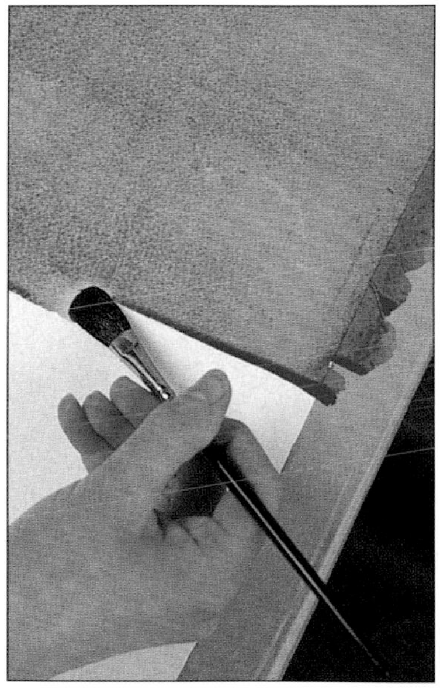

2

Tilt the board slightly. Lay a band of colour across the top of the paper. Then continue down the paper with overlapping strokes, working in alternate directions and picking up the excess paint from the previous stroke each time.

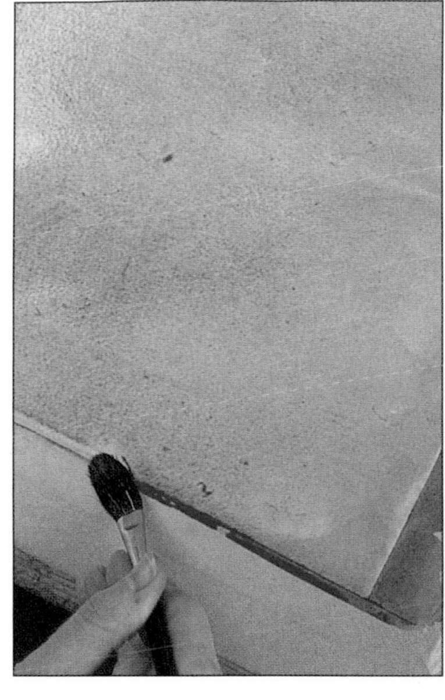

3

Finally squeeze out the brush and soak up the excess colour at the base of the wash. Leave the wash to dry in the same tilted position.

(2in) longer than each side of the paper.

Immerse the paper in cold water — you can do this in a sink, a bath or a photographer's developing tray. The soaking time depends on the weight (thickness) of the paper; lightweight papers will require no more than a minute, heavier papers perhaps a couple of minutes. Hold the paper by one corner and shake off the surplus water gently. Lay the paper on the drawing board, smoothing it out carefully from the centre to make sure it is perfectly flat.

Working quickly, moisten the gummed paper strips with a wet sponge and stick them along each edge of the paper so that two-thirds of their width is attached to the drawing board and one-third to the paper. This ensures that the paper will not pull away from the board as it dries. Tape one side of the paper first, then the two adjacent sides, and finally the remaining side, opposite to the first strip.

Allow the paper to dry flat, away from direct heat, for several hours. As the paper dries, it will shrink and become taut. Do not use until it is completely dry. When working with a lot of water the paper may still cockle slightly; don't worry, it will dry smooth again.

Laying Washes

There are three basic types of wash: the flat wash, the gradated wash and the variegated wash. All of these can be applied on either a dry or a

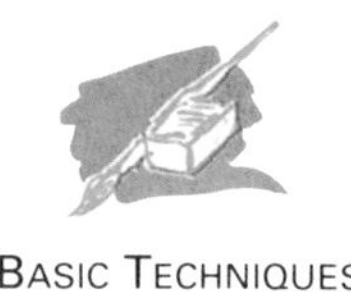

damp surface, although the latter helps the wash to flow more evenly.

Washes must be applied quickly and in one go, so mix up plenty of paint – you always need more than you think. The colour should be fluid, but quite strong, to compensate for the fact that it will dry much lighter on the paper. Tilt the board slightly to allow the wash to flow downwards.

Flat Wash

A flat wash is so called because it is all the same tone. To lay a flat wash, first moisten the stretched paper. Then load a large flat or round brush with paint and take it across the paper in one stroke. A bead of paint will form along the bottom of the stroke.

Load your brush again and, working in the opposite direction, lay another stroke beneath the first, slightly overlapping it and picking up the bead of colour. The excess paint will reform along the base of the second stroke. Continue working down the paper in alternate directions until the whole area is covered. Then squeeze the excess paint out of the brush with your fingers and stroke the bottom band again lightly to pick up the excess colour.

Let the wash dry in the same tilted position, otherwise the paint will flow back and dry leaving an ugly tidemark. The wash should be flat, transparent and consistent in both tone and colour.

Gradated Wash

A gradated wash starts with strong colour at the top, gradually lightening towards the bottom. The method of application is exactly the same as for a flat wash, except that with each successive stroke, the brush carries more water and

Laying Gradated Washes

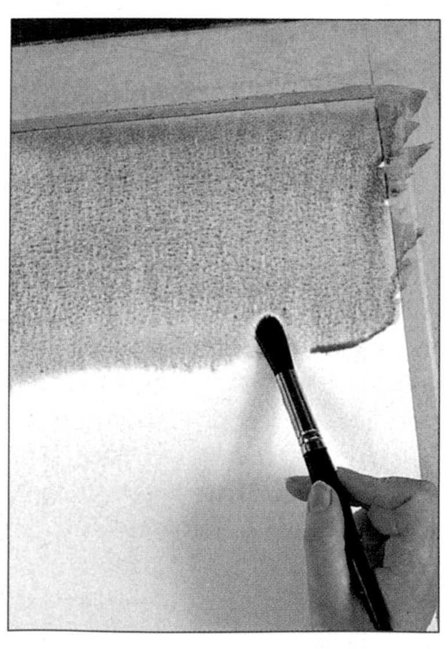

1
Lay a band of full-strength colour across the top of the paper. Lighten the colour with more water and lay another band under the first, picking up the paint at the bottom of the first band.

2
Continue in this way, applying increasingly diluted tones until you reach the bottom of the paper.

3
Leave the wash to dry in a tilted position.

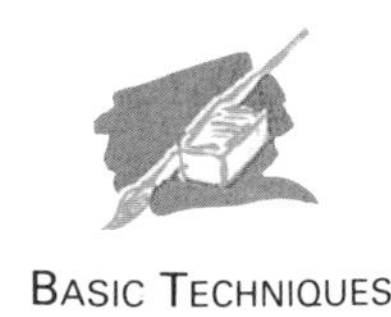

less pigment. Gradated washes are very useful when painting skies, where the colour is most intense at the zenith and fades gradually towards the horizon.

It takes a little practice to achieve an even gradation with no "stripes". The secret is to keep the paint as fluid as possible so that each brush stroke flows into the one below.

Moisten the area to be painted, and tilt the board at a slight angle. Load a large brush with paint at full strength and lay a band of colour across the top of the paper, taking care not to lift the brush until you reach the end of the stroke. Don't hesitate. Quickly add more water to the paint in the palette and run the brush under the first line of colour, picking up the paint which has run down to the base of the first band. Repeat this process. Each succeeding stroke will get weaker by adding increasing amounts of water and the wash will become paler as it reaches the bottom of the paper.

Variegated washes are similar to gradated washes, except that several different colours are used instead of just one. This technique is very effective in skies and landscapes as demonstrated in the project commencing on page 76.

Squaring Up

You may wish to base a watercolour painting on a small sketch or a photographic image; but it is often difficult to maintain accuracy when enlarging a reference source to the size of your working paper. A simple method of transferring an image in a different scale is by squaring up (sometimes called scaling up).

Using a pencil and ruler, draw a grid of equal-sized squares over the sketch or photograph. The more complex the image, the more squares you should draw. If you wish to avoid marking the original, make a photocopy of it and draw the grid onto this. Alternatively, draw the grid onto a sheet of clear acetate placed over the original, using a felt-tip pen.

Then construct an enlarged version of the grid on the sheet of watercolour paper, using light pencil marks. This grid must have the same number of squares as the smaller one. The size of the squares will depend on the degree of enlargement required: for example, if you are doubling the size of your reference material, make each square twice the size of the squares on the original.

When the grid is complete, transfer the image that appears in each square of the original to its equivalent square on the new paper. The larger squares on the new paper serve to enlarge the original image. You are, in effect, breaking down a large-scale problem into smaller, manageable areas.

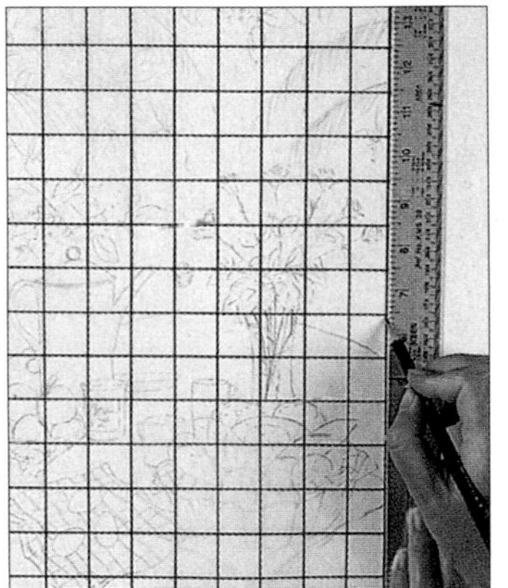

1

Draw a grid of squares onto a sheet of tracing paper laid over the reference sketch.

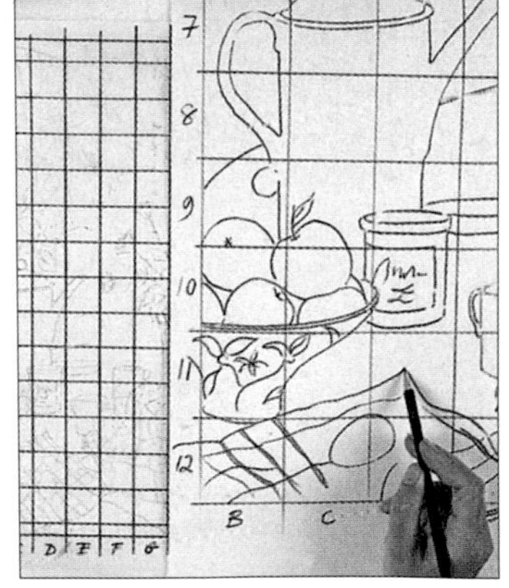

2

Lightly draw a grid of larger squares onto the watercolour paper and transfer the detail, square by square.

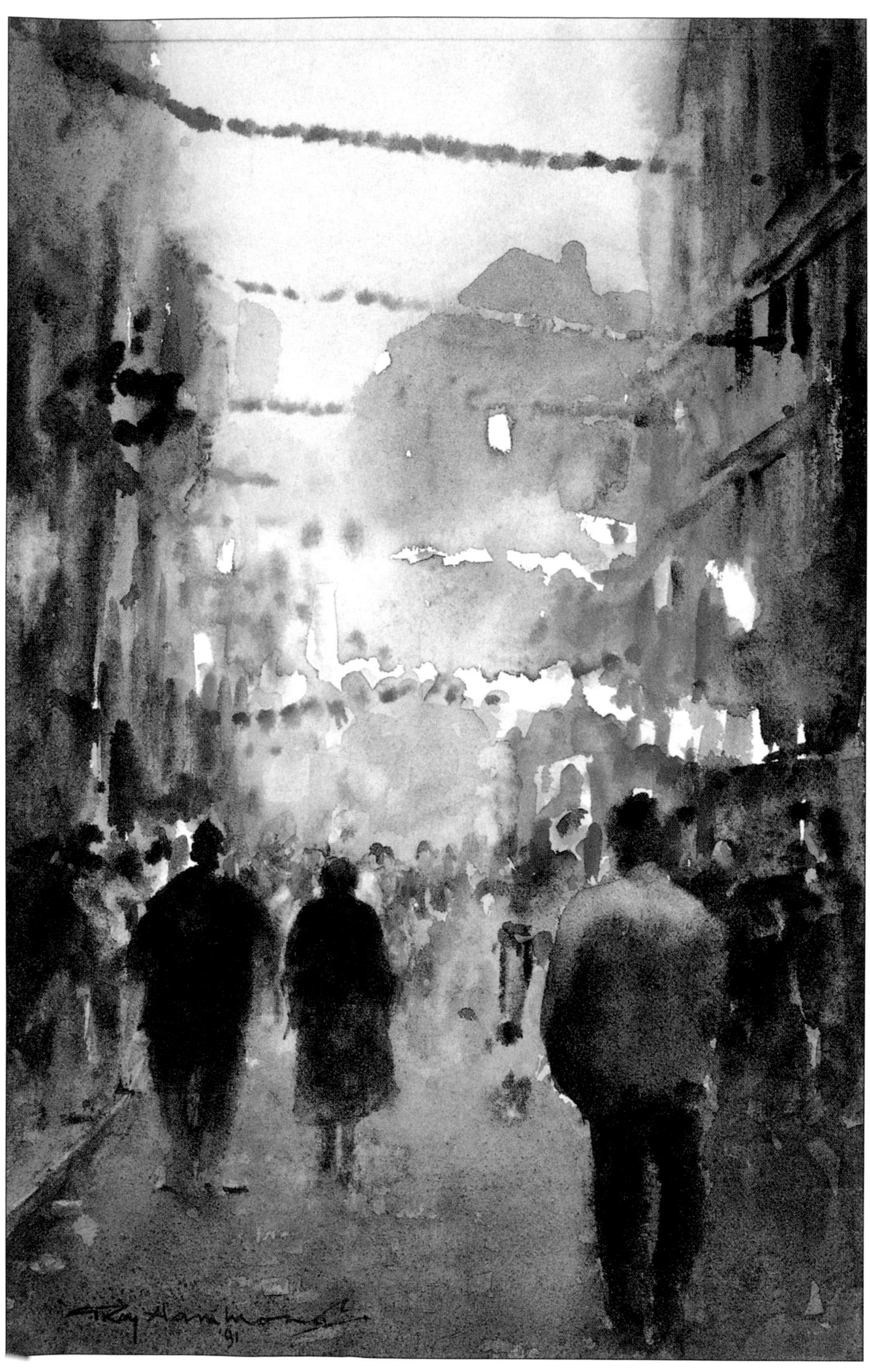

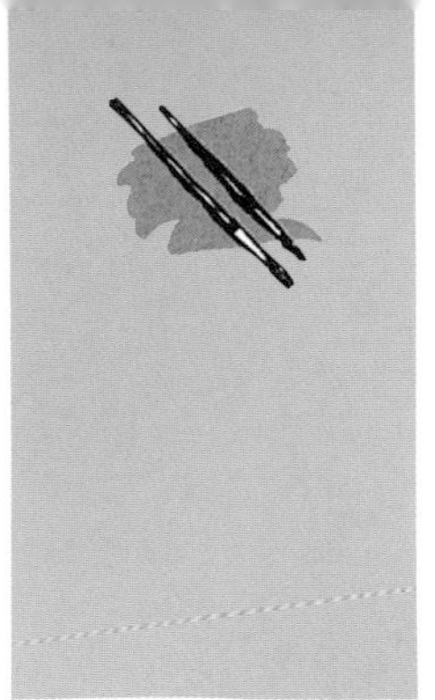

GALLERY

Watercolour is such a responsive and versatile medium that no two artists need use it in exactly the same way. On the next few pages you will find a selection of watercolour paintings by contemporary artists, which have been chosen to illustrate the diversity of artistic expression that can be achieved. The paintings encompass a broad range of techniques, which are fully explained and demonstrated in the step-by-step projects that follow.

It is always interesting and instructive to study the work of other artists, and analysing their methods can act as a stimulus in developing your own artistic language. After all, we should not be surprised to learn that all of the great masters of art were themselves inspired and influenced by the work of previous masters.

~

Street Party to Celebrate the Sardine Season, Lisbon

Roy Hammond

25 x 17cm (10 x 6½in)

Hammond has concentrated on the light in this scene, capturing the moment when the day ends and night is about to fall. He conveys the soft, hazy twilight by working almost entirely wet-into-wet, with a few small details added at the dry stage. The gaily coloured electric lights gain luminosity by contrast with the cool, shadowy tones in the street below.

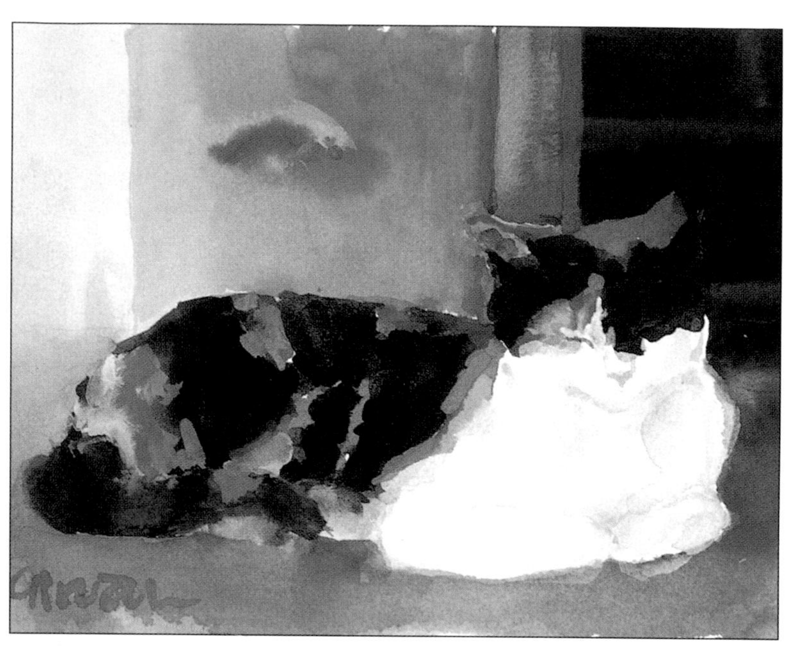

Afternoon Sun

Geraldine Girvan

18 x 27cm (7 x 10½in)

It takes courage to plunge straight into a watercolour painting without first making an underdrawing. Girvan, however, enjoys the knife-edge thrill of working directly onto dry paper with wet washes, unconstrained by a pencil outline. With this intuitive approach she has captured the essential character of her cat basking in the sun.

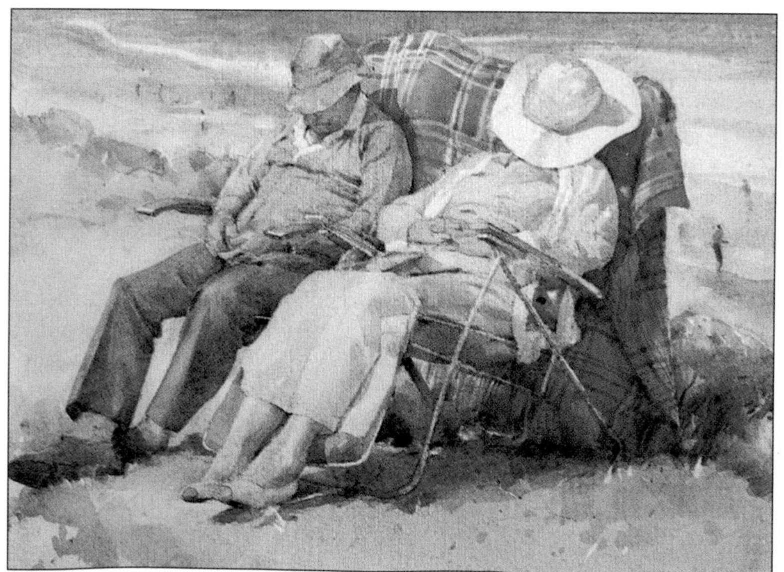

Fred and Edna

David Curtis

25 x 20cm (10 x 8in)

This expressive and amusing portrait is based on a drawing done on site. It has a fresh, spontaneous feel, yet it was painted using the classical watercolour technique of methodically building up glazes and washes over a careful underdrawing, using a limited palette. To preserve the clear brilliance of the colours, it is important to allow each wash to dry before applying the next.

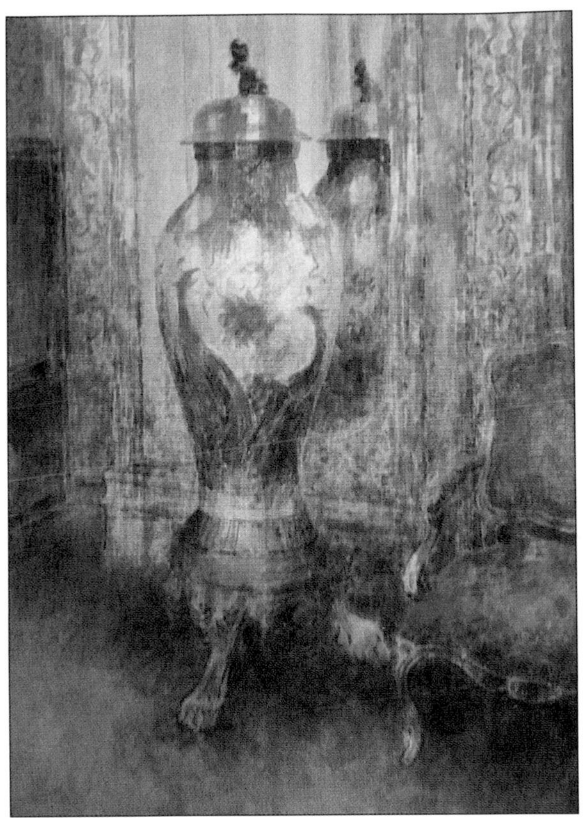

In the Ballroom, Polesden Lacey

Pauline Fazakerley

53 x 34cm (21 x 13½in)

The all-enveloping atmosphere of light in this painting is achieved by floating on many washes of thin colour. As the work progresses, the washes become smaller, finally ending in tiny overlaid dabs. As in the painting below, the impression of light is derived solely from the white paper glowing through the transparent layers of pigment, and no body colour is used.

Jug and Bowl

Sue Read

30 x 38cm (12 x 15in)

This painting has a mood of stillness and calm, of quiet introspection, engendered by the beautifully balanced composition, the neutral, almost monochromatic colours and the cool, subdued light. Read works very closely from her subject, observing every nuance of tone and colour. No body colour is used here – the colours are applied in transparent layers, with the highlights left as untouched paper.

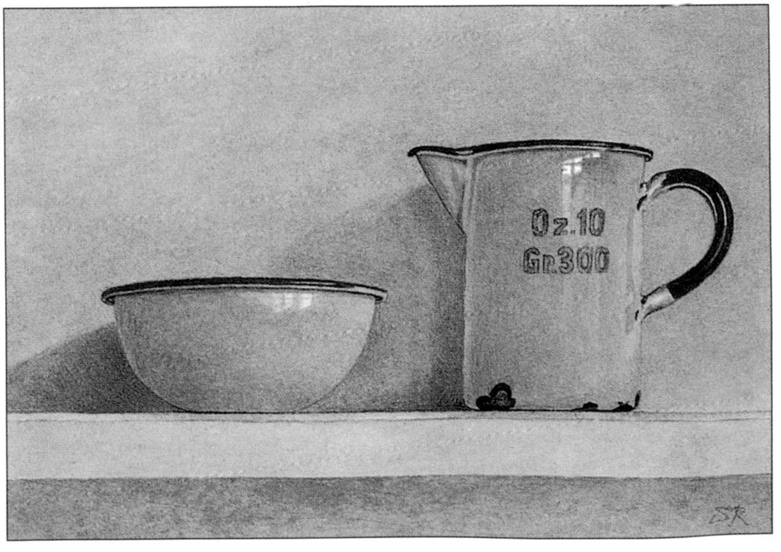

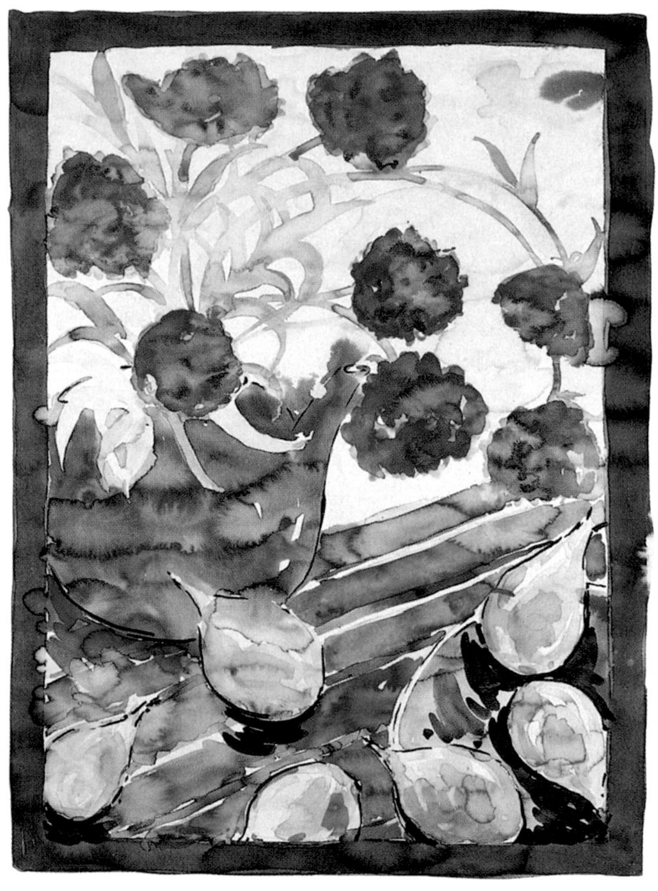

Peonies and Pears

Annie Wood

80 x 56cm ($31\frac{1}{2}$ x 22in)

The fluid, quicksilver nature of watercolour is exploited to the full in this still-life painting. Wood works rapidly and on a large scale, brushing great pools of colour onto damp paper without waiting for one wash to dry before applying the next. Some washes have run together, creating blotched marks known as backruns, and these are deliberately used to suggest texture and pattern.

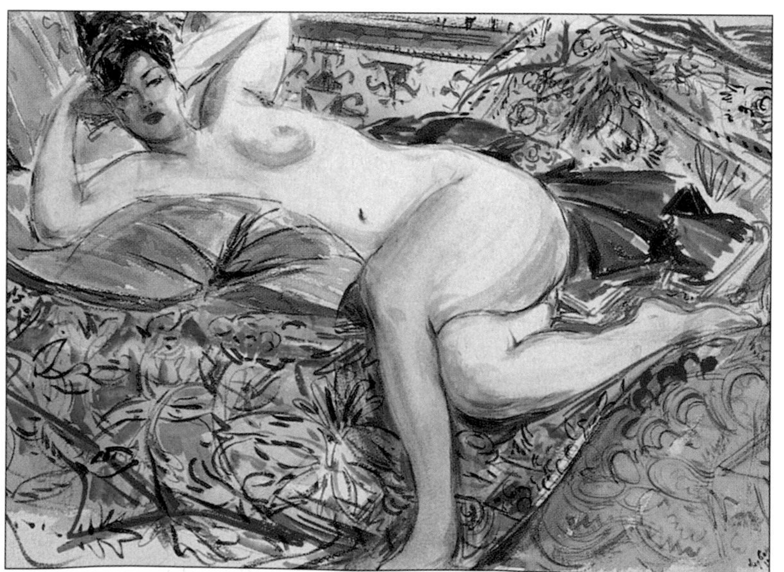

Mattia on a Kashmiri Shawl

Kay Gallwey

38 x 56cm (15 x 22in)

This decorative composition of a nude reclining on a couch has an elegance and exuberance reminiscent of the Fauve painters Henri Matisse and Raoul Dufy. The voluptuous form of the nude is in strong contrast to the Oriental pattern of the shawl, which Gallwey suggests with animated lines rapidly drawn with the tip of the brush.

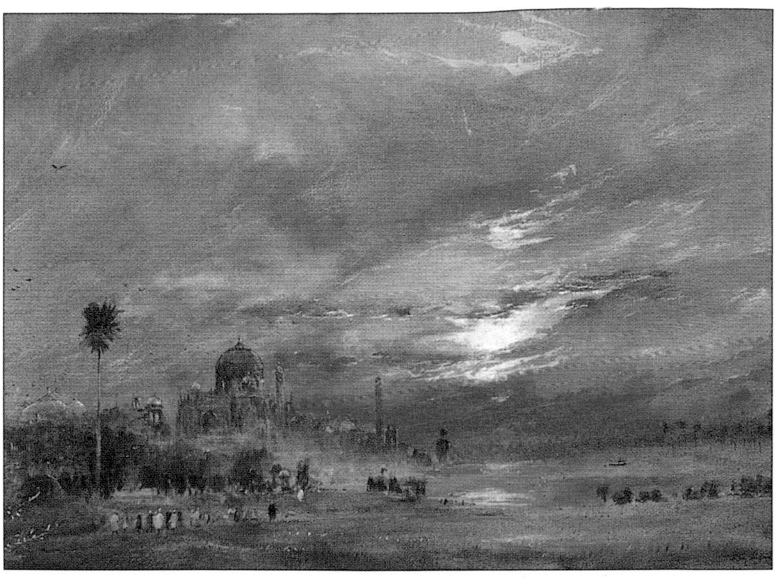

The Taj Mahal, Agra (1905), Souvenir of Albert Goodwin

Roy Hammond

36 x 53cm (14 x 21in)

When Hammond is in need of inspiration, he turns to his favourite 19th-century artists. This beautiful sunset is an interpretation in watercolour of an oil painting by the painter Albert Goodwin (1845–1932). The dark tones in the landscape counterpoint the brilliant colours in the sky, while the brightest area of all – the setting sun – is suggested by small patches of untouched paper.

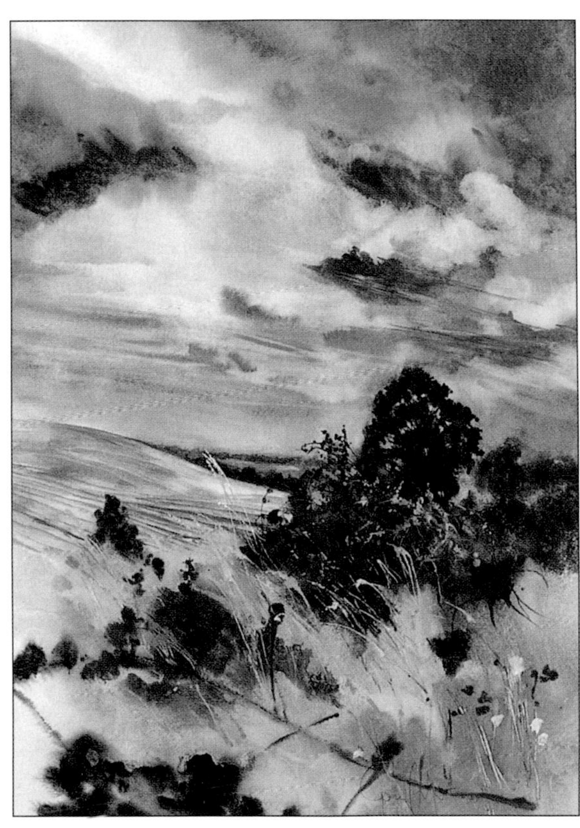

Stubble Fields and Brambles

Tony Porter

57 x 37cm (22½ x 14½in)

Porter deliberately seeks out the wild and empty places, eery under the cold northern light and buffeted by the coastal winds, of his native East Anglia. He always paints on location, flooding his colours onto very wet hot-pressed paper and allowing the paint itself to express, with great eloquence, the spirit of the place.

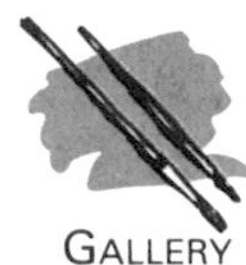

The River Tweed at Melrose

Ronald Jesty

34 x 57cm (13½ x 22½in)

A "drop gate" – used to prevent cattle wandering from one field into another by wading through the shallows – is the subject of this bold composition. Jesty has worked up from the lightest to the darkest tones with a series of carefully planned, minutely executed washes. The control and subtlety exercised here – the drop gate was painted without the aid of masking techniques – indicate the considerable technical skill of the artist.

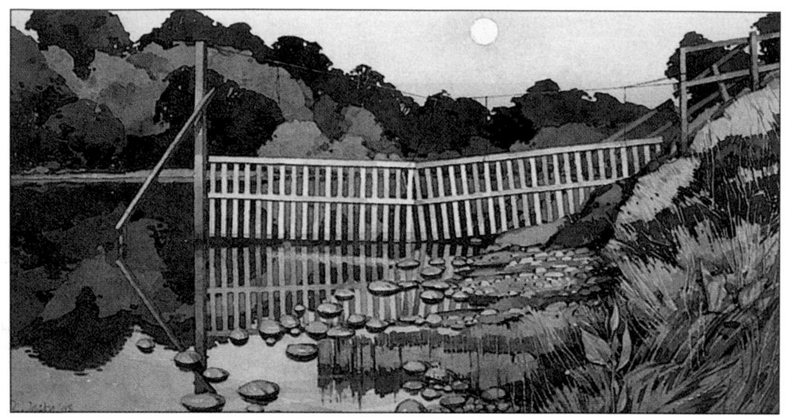

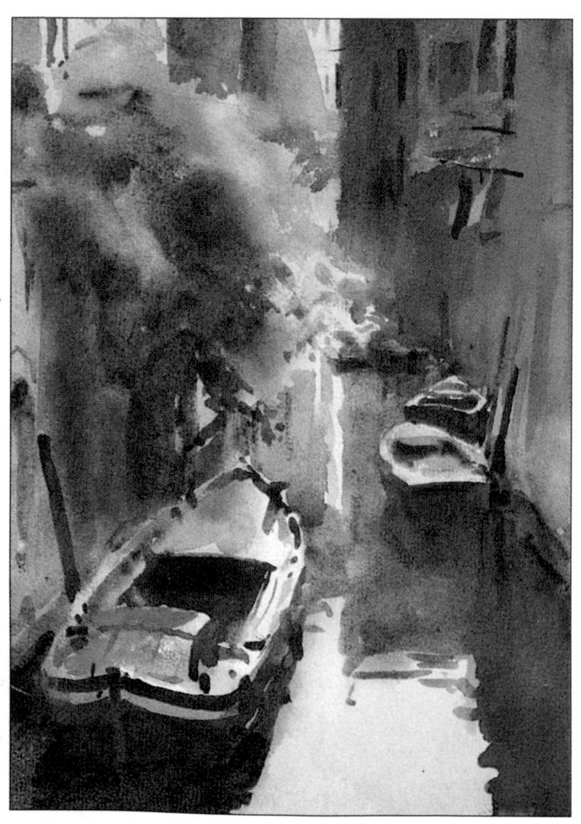

Venetian Barge

Trevor Chamberlain

25 x 17cm (10 x 6½in)

Chamberlain is particularly interested in the effects of atmosphere and light, and always works from life in the open air. The still calm of late afternoon is beautifully described by means of limpid washes that melt softly into each other, and the mood is underlined by the restrained harmony of the colour values.

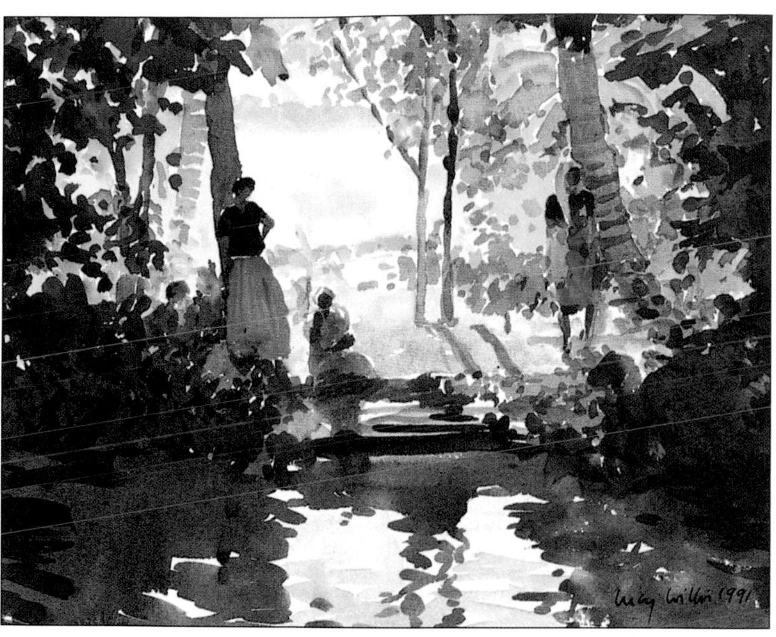

Women by the Water

Lucy Willis

25 x 34cm (10 x 13½in)

Freshness and clarity are the keynotes of this lovely painting. Willis keeps her colours fresh and clear by allowing her brush strokes and washes to settle undisturbed, and this means establishing the tonal and colour values in advance so that they can be applied with confidence. The impact of this image stems from the contrast of the small sunlit area, surrounded and emphasized by the dark tones of the trees and water.

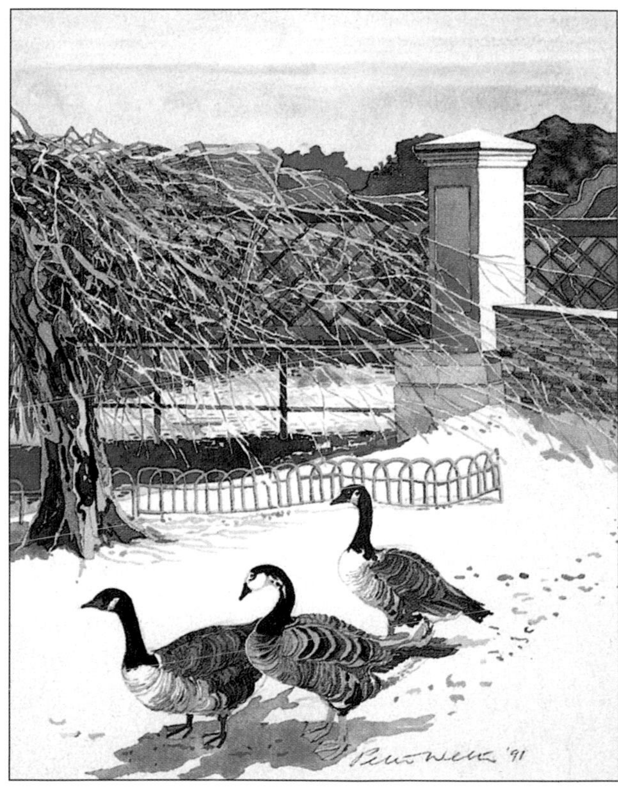

Geese Wintering in Regents Park

Peter Welton

29 x 22cm (11½ x 8½in)

Welton has his own highly individual style of painting. He never pre-draws outlines, preferring to feel his way into the painting and invent it as he goes along; this painting was based on various photographs of the geese, the bridge and the tree, taken at different times. He applies the paint very thin and very wet, literally staining the paper with coloured water. Far from appearing weak, the colours derive a clarity and brilliance from the light-reflecting surface of the paper beneath. To maximize the potential of juxtaposed colours, each one is allowed to dry before its neighbour is applied, and not a sliver of white paper is allowed to appear between them.

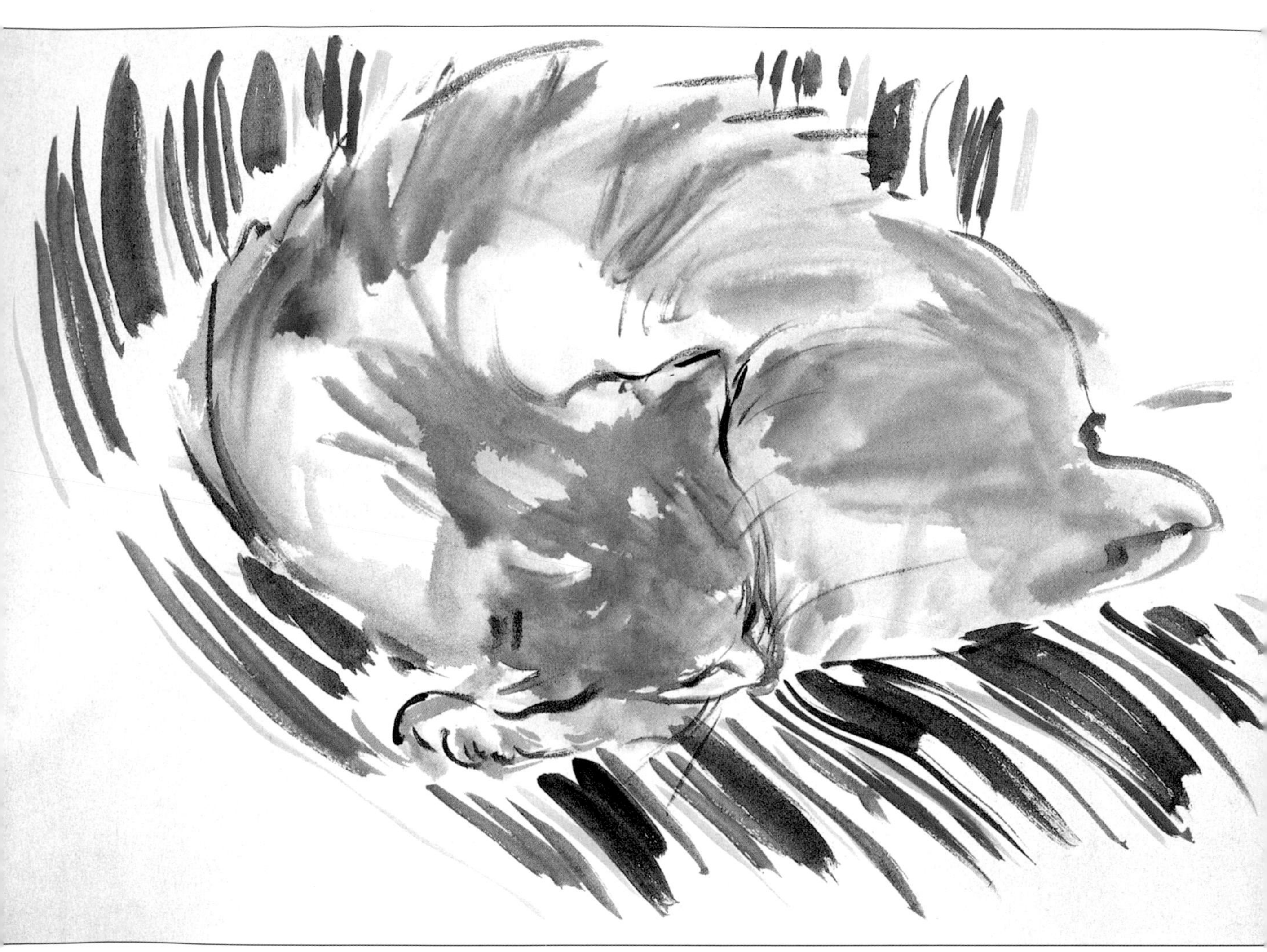

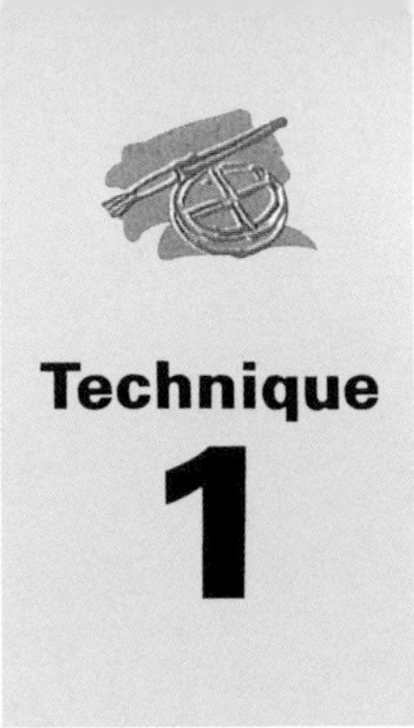

Technique

1

PAINTING WITH RAGS

There is no rule that says you have to paint with a brush. Fascinating and unexpected results can be achieved using less orthodox painting implements – sponges, rags, even a finger dipped in paint. Although for some people these methods of painting have connotations of primary school art lessons, they do have a valuable part to play in stimulating visual ideas. More importantly, they are an excellent way of loosening up and developing confidence with the watercolour medium.

This lively portrait of the artist's cat was painted literally in minutes using a piece of rag dipped in paint. The languid grace of a feline cries out to be captured in paint – but cats, being cats, are liable to yawn, stretch and walk away at just the wrong moment, so you have to work quickly. In a sense this can be an advantage, because it forces the artist to concentrate on the essential details and the finished painting has a rhythm and vitality which conveys a personal response to the subject.

Kay Gallwey
Mr Bill Asleep
38 x 58cm (15 x 23in)

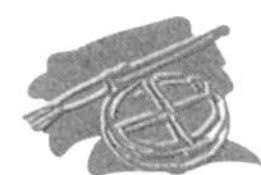

Using Rags

Working on a large sheet of paper with a rag dipped in watercolour paint and then wrapped around your finger or crumpled into a wad is a liberating experience. The fingers are sensitive tools, and because they are more or less in direct contact with the paper, you will find yourself working more boldly and intuitively, making fluid and decisive marks.

Irregular, mottled textures and patterns can be obtained by dabbing paint onto the paper with a sponge or a crumpled piece of rag. You can use this effect to paint weathered rocks, for example, or to give textural interest to an empty foreground. And by smearing the paint on you can create soft marks suitable for painting skies and water, flowers or animal fur.

Rags and sponges are also useful for the rapid application of paint over large areas and for the smooth blending of tones and colours. As the following project demonstrates, this facility can be used expressively in a line and wash painting. The texture and markings of the cat's fur are built up with paint smeared on with a rag, and then brush lines are used to define the form of the cat and to suggest the background.

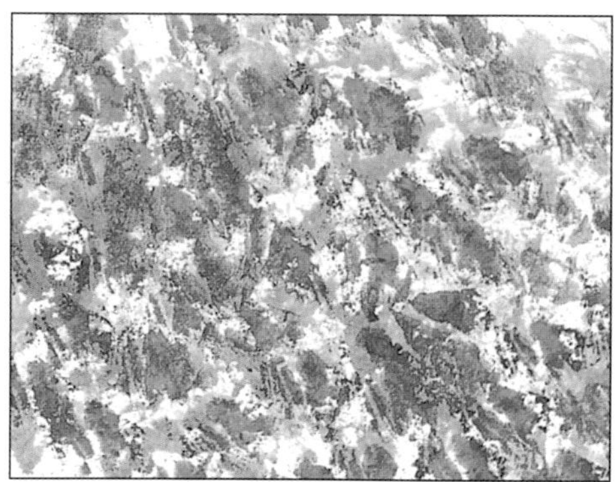

Try using a crumpled rag to suggest natural textures such as summer foliage or weathered rocks. Dampen the rag and squeeze it into a ball. Dip it into a pool of colour, then press it gently onto the paper and lift it cleanly away. A natural sponge can be used in the same way.

Mr Bill Asleep

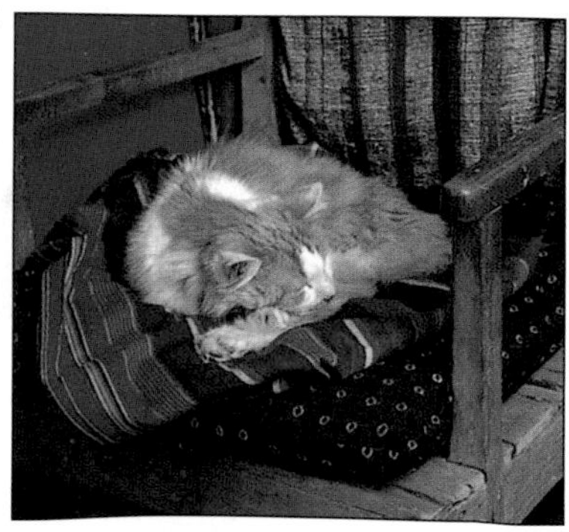

Left: The artist painted the cat from life, choosing an opportune moment when he was taking a nap after lunch.

Materials and Equipment

• SHEET OF 300GSM (140LB) HOT-PRESSED WATERCOLOUR PAPER, STRETCHED • WATERCOLOURS: CADMIUM ORANGE, CADMIUM YELLOW, CADMIUM RED, PAYNE'S GREY, IVORY BLACK, BURNT UMBER AND MAGENTA • COTTON RAG • FINELY TAPERED WATERCOLOUR BRUSH

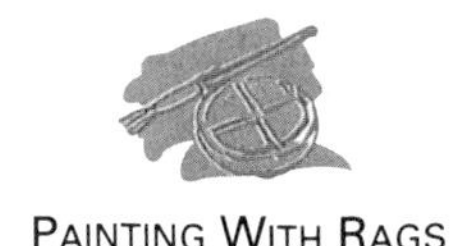

1

Roughly wet the paper with a damp rag. Mix fluid washes of cadmium orange and cadmium yellow on your palette (a white plate is useful as you can use the central area for mixing the colours). Crumple a piece of cotton rag between your fingers, dip it into the cadmium orange wash and quickly draw the outline of the cat. Build up the colour and texture of the fur with pale tints of cadmium orange and cadmium yellow, smearing the paint on with the rag using broad marks that follow the form of the cat.

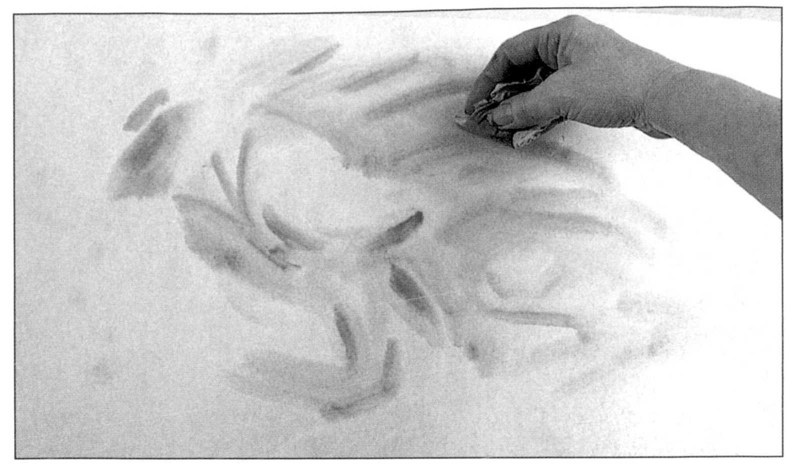

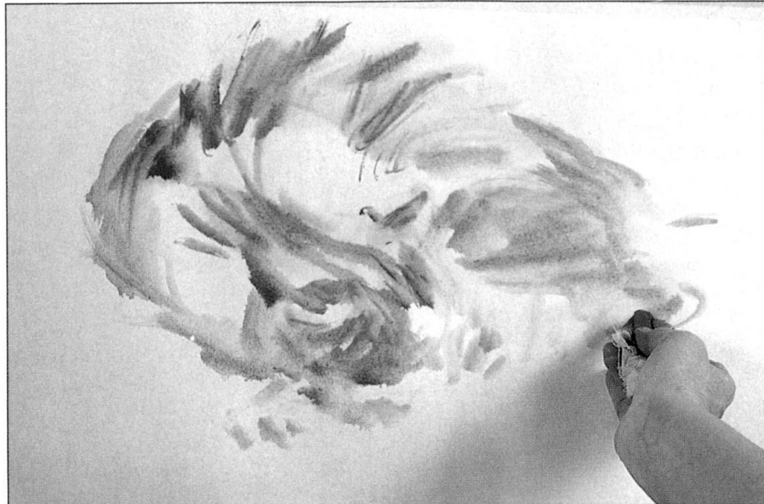

2

Using stronger colours now, continue to work up the form of the cat. Wrap the rag around your finger, dip it into the paint and make swift, gestural marks with it. The aim is to define the shape and posture of the cat, at the same time suggesting the texture and markings of the fur, so refer constantly to your subject. Vary the colour by adding touches of cadmium red to deepen it, particularly on the head, so as to bring it forward in the picture plane. Use soft, pale marks of Payne's grey for the shadow areas and to define the area of the eyes and nose.

3

Having established the underlying form, continue building up the ginger colour of the fur with stronger, deeper tones of cadmium orange mixed with cadmium red. Leave to dry. Paint the cushion with magenta, ivory black and cadmium yellow stripes. Finally, use a finely tapered brush to define the shape of the head and features with delicate lines of ivory black and burnt umber applied loosely and lightly.

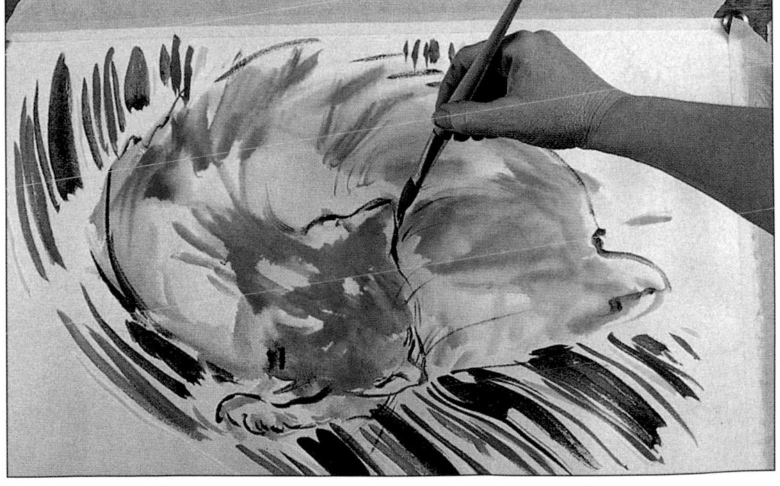

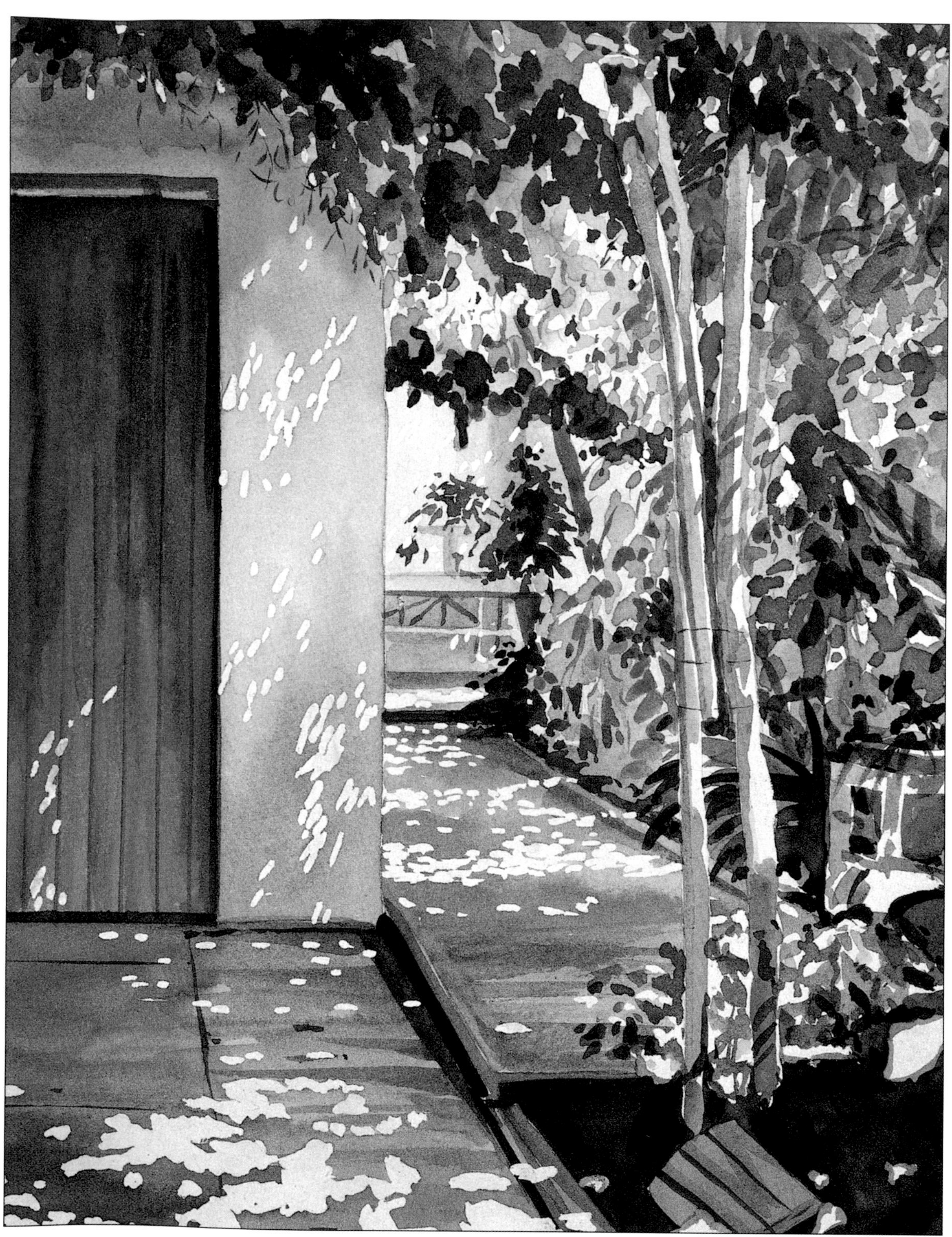

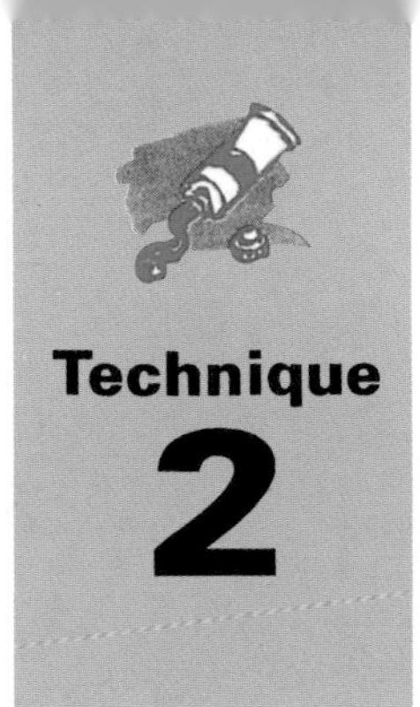

Technique

2

Masking Out

Because watercolour is transparent, it is impossible to paint a light colour over a dark one; you have to decide in advance where your white areas are going to be and then paint around them. Leaving small or detailed areas white can, however, be tricky because it inhibits the flow of the surrounding washes. The solution is to use masking fluid (liquid frisket) to seal off the white areas, allowing the rest of the surface to be painted over freely.

In this atmospheric courtyard scene, dappled sunlight filtering through the trees plays on every surface. The artist painted these highlights with masking fluid to preserve them and then laid the washes on top. When the painting was completed the masking fluid was removed to reveal the white "negative" shapes, which were modified by further pale washes to create an impression of warmth and sunlight.

~

Mark Topham
Summer Courtyard
28 x 22cm (11 x 8½in)

~

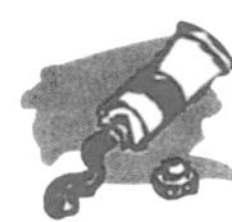

Using Masking Fluid

Masking fluid (liquid frisket) is a dilute rubber solution. It is sold in bottles and is slightly tinted so that you can see where it has been applied. When brushed onto the paper it dries quickly to form a water-resistant film, protecting the area underneath while you finish the rest of the painting.

Simply brush the fluid over the areas which are to remain white. Once it is dry, you can ignore the white shapes completely and paint around them. When the painting is completely dry, remove the rubbery mask by rubbing gently with a fingertip, revealing the untouched paper beneath.

If you intend using masking fluid, choose a paper with a medium surface (known as Not or cold-pressed), from which the rubbery solution is easily removed; it is not suitable for use on rough papers as it sinks into the indentations and cannot be peeled off completely. On smooth (hot-pressed) papers the danger is that the surface will be spoiled by the action of rubbing away the mask.

Always use an old brush to apply masking fluid, and wash it in warm, soapy water immediately after use to prevent the fluid from drying hard on the bristles.

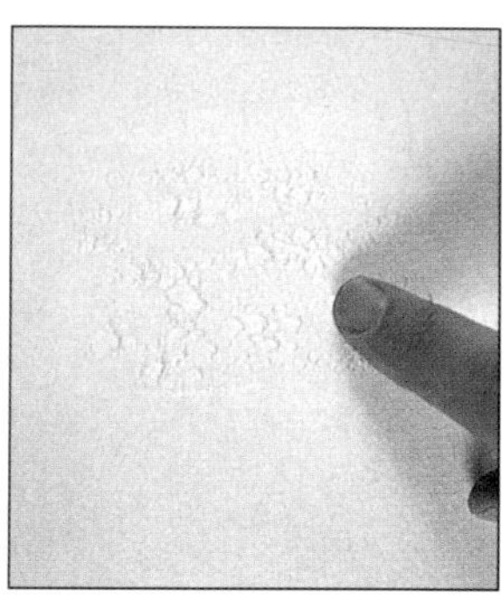

Masking fluid can be used to create weathered textures in a landscape painting. Here the fluid is applied and then partially rubbed away just before it dries.

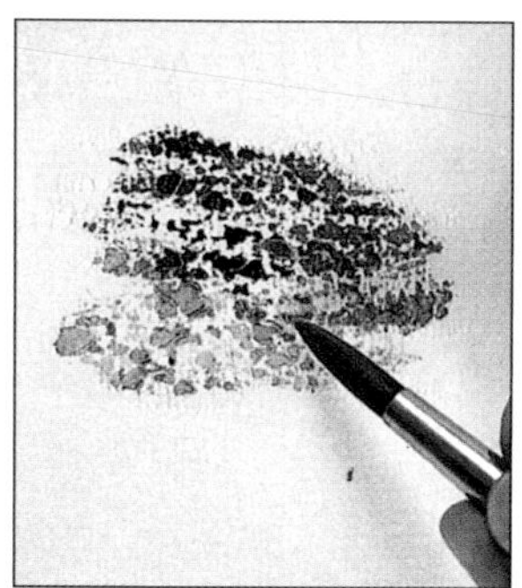

When the mask is dry washes of colour are applied over the area; the mask resists the wash, but the colour sinks into the tiny patches which have been rubbed away.

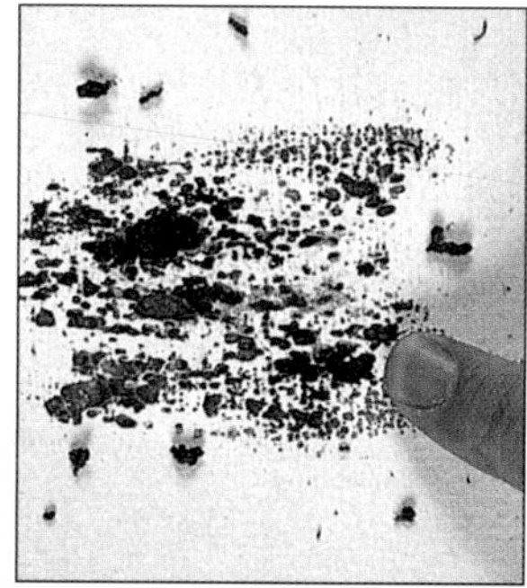

When the paint is totally dry the mask is gently removed by rubbing with the fingertip. This reveals a mottled texture which could be used to suggest tree bark or old stone.

Summer Courtyard

Materials and Equipment

• Sheet of 300gsm (140lb) NOT (cold-pressed) surface watercolour paper, stretched • Soft pencil • Ruler • Old watercolour brush for applying masking fluid (liquid frisket) • Masking fluid • Watercolour brushes: large and medium-sized rounds • Watercolour paints: burnt sienna, yellow ochre, sap green, aureolin, French ultramarine, Payne's grey, viridian • Tissues

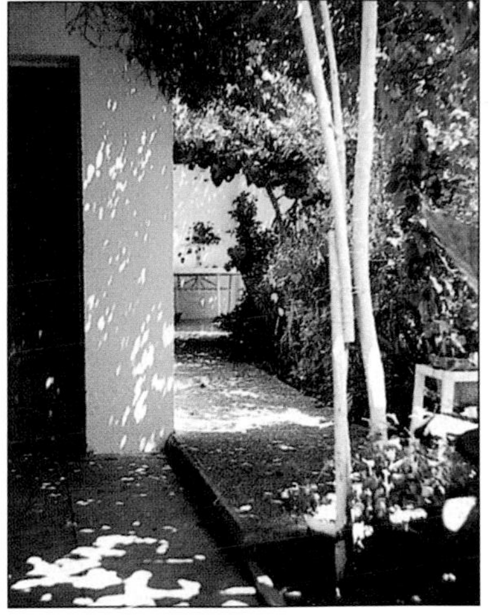

Left: While visiting friends, the artist painted this view of their patio garden. The confetti-like patterns of light falling through the trees and the vine-covered pergola made an attractive subject.

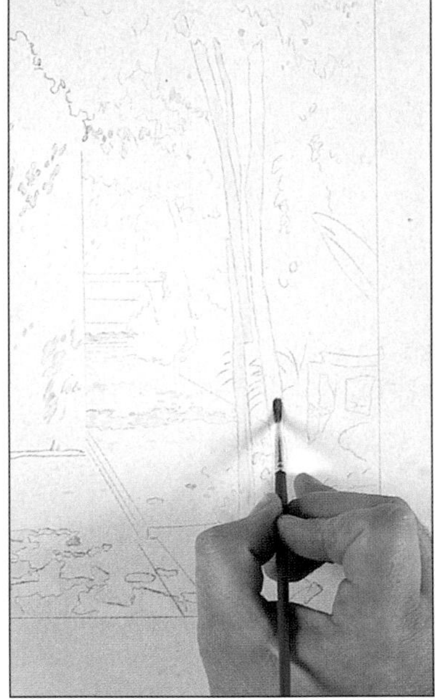

1

Start by making a careful line drawing of the subject, taking care that the lines are light enough not to show through the watercolours. Using an old paintbrush, paint masking fluid (liquid frisket) over those areas of the image which are to be left white. Wash the brush out immediately and leave the fluid to dry hard.

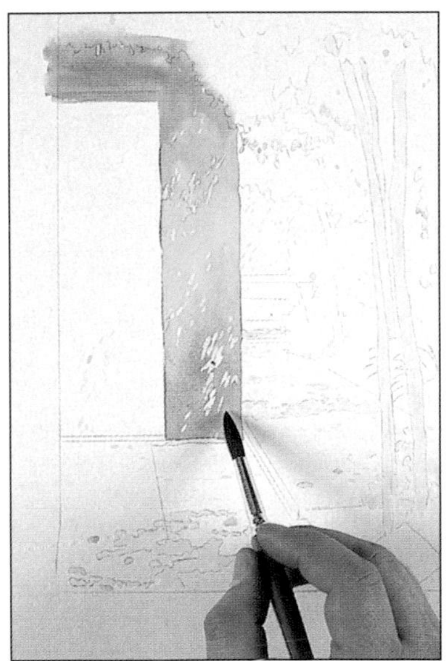

2

Apply clean water to the wall of the building on the left. When the shine has left the paper, paint the wall with a pale, variegated wash (see pages 76–81), starting with burnt sienna at the top, then yellow ochre, sap green, aureolin and finally ultramarine at the base. Use a large round brush and allow the colours to fuse wet-into-wet (see pages 68–75) on the paper.

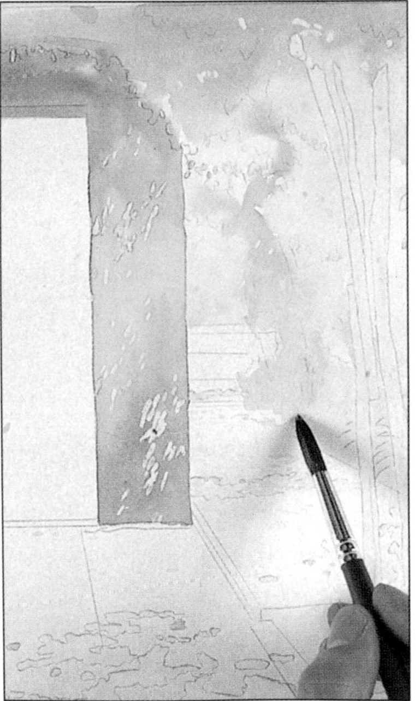

3

Wash in the background area with a pale mixture of aureolin and a little sap green. While the paint is still damp, drop in a little yellow ochre here and there to indicate light-struck areas and ultramarine to indicate cool, shadowy areas.

4

Using the same colours as in step 3, but less dilute, paint the foliage with a medium-sized round brush. Use small, dabbing strokes and vary the tones of green from light to dark. Use mixtures of Payne's grey, burnt sienna and ultramarine for the dark foliage at the top left.

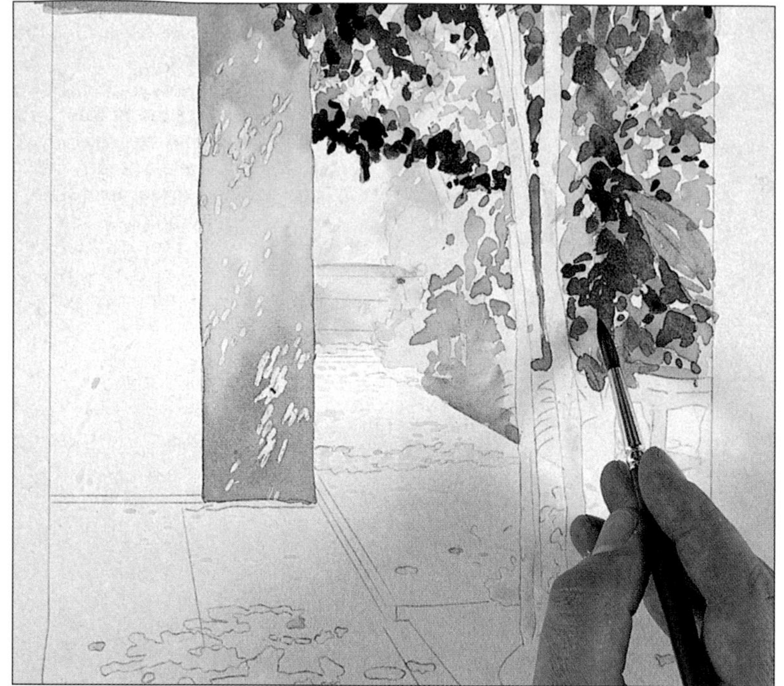

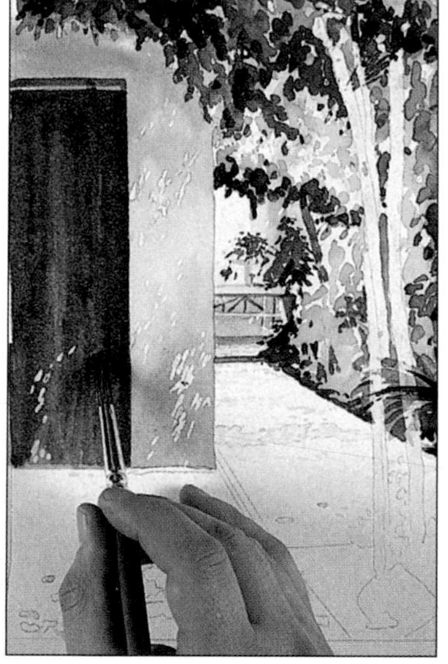

5

Paint the wooden door with a mixture of viridian and Payne's grey, lightening the tone with more water near the base. Add a spot of sap green at the bottom to give an impression of reflected light from the courtyard outside.

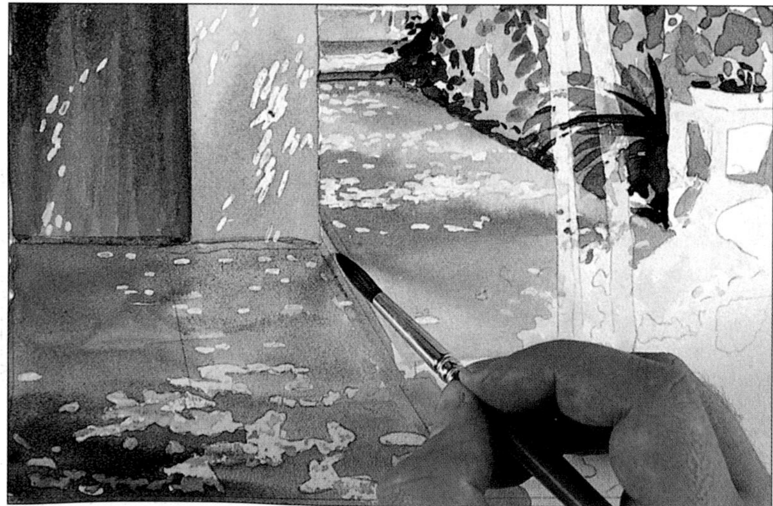

6

Paint the paving stones using various mixtures of Payne's grey, yellow ochre, burnt sienna, sap green and ultramarine. Keep the tones pale and light in the background, and stronger and darker in the foreground. This helps to create a sense of perspective and distance.

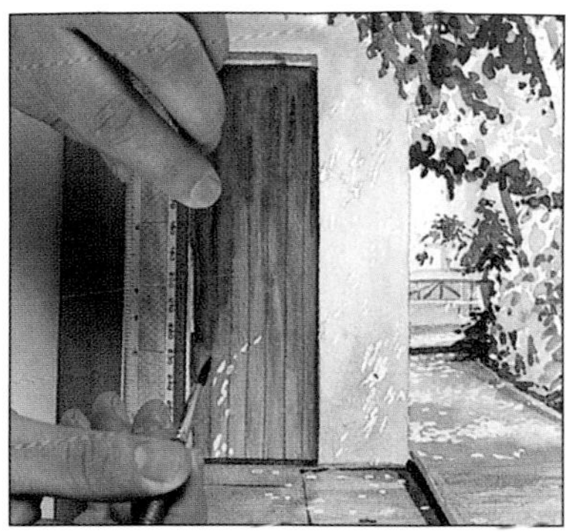

7

When the paint has dried, use a mixture of Payne's grey and burnt sienna and a finely pointed brush to indicate the wooden panels of the door. If you don't have a steady hand you may find a ruler useful here; bunch your fingers underneath the ruler so it doesn't touch the paper, then draw the brush along the ruler with the ferrule resting on its edge.

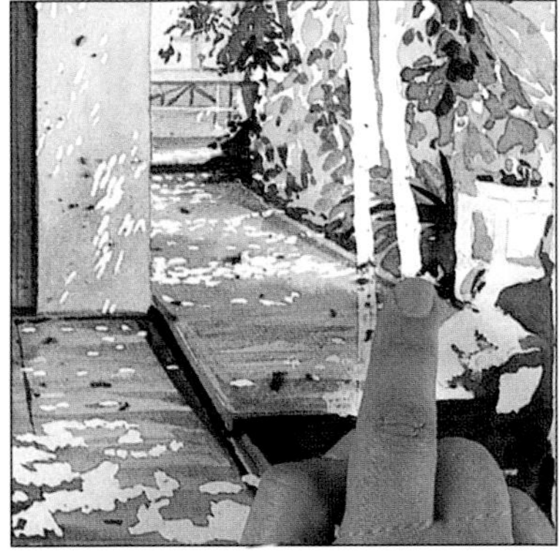

8

When the painting is thoroughly dry – and not until – remove all the masking fluid by rubbing gently with a fingertip; all the highlights are now revealed, perfectly preserved.

9

The masked areas appear rather stark, so warm them up with just a hint of colour. Mix aureolin and a touch of burnt sienna to a very pale tint and apply this to the patterns of dappled light, dabbing the colour off with a tissue if it looks too strong.

Add shadows to the white-painted support posts of the pergola on the right with a pale wash of ultramarine. This helps to recreate the warm, sunny atmosphere of the setting. Finally, paint the terracotta pot on the right with burnt sienna.

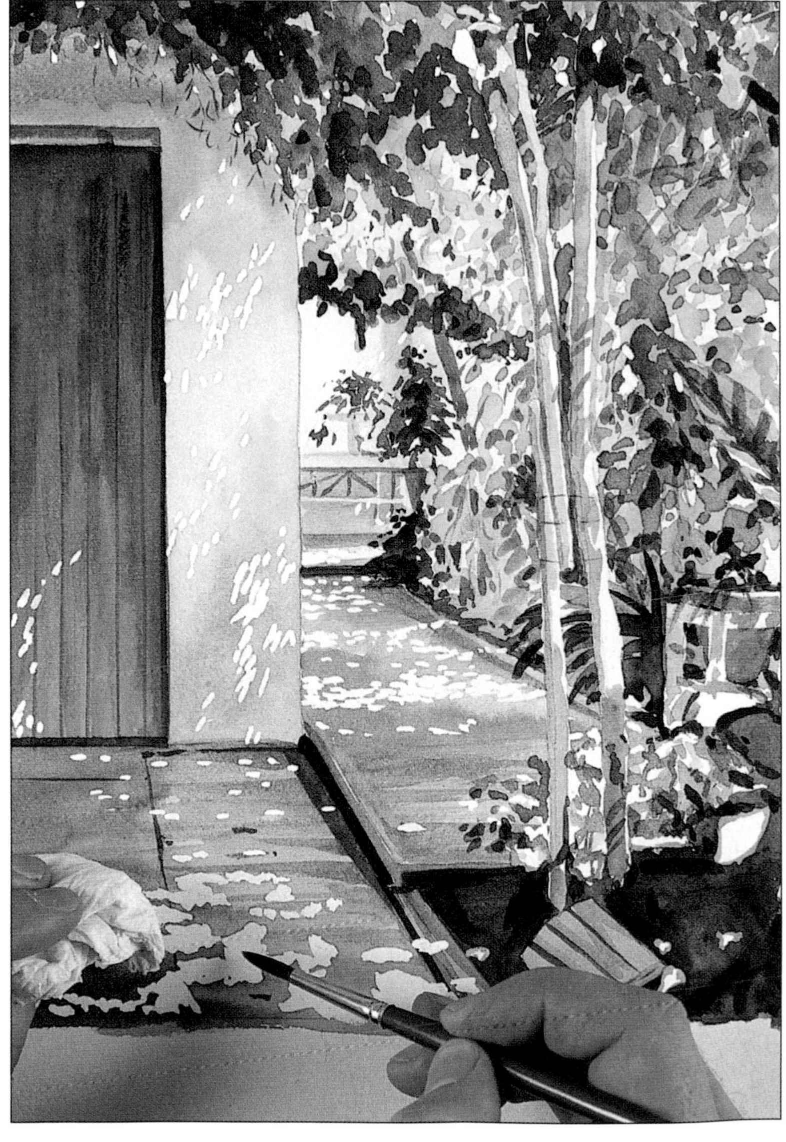

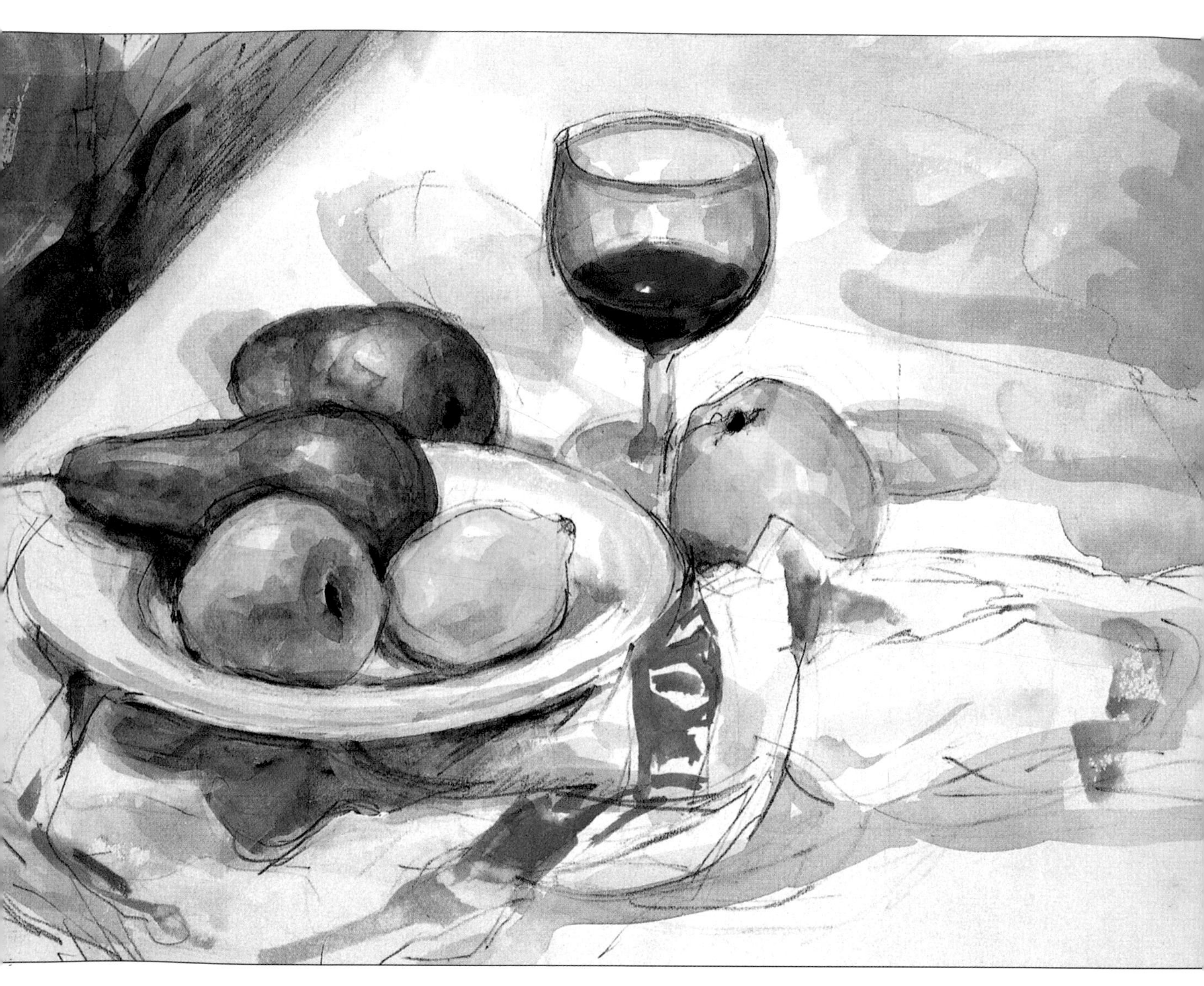

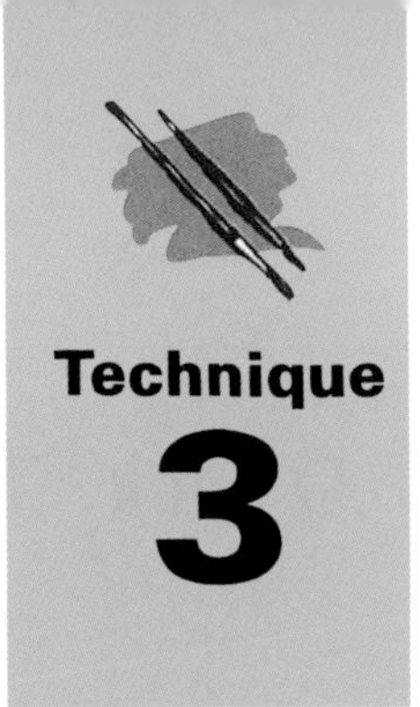

WORKING FROM LIGHT TO DARK

Working from light to dark is the classical method of building up a watercolour painting; the artist starts with the palest of washes and builds up the tones and colours very gradually to the density required. This structured method of using watercolour is sometimes called "wet-on-dry", and is especially useful for modelling the forms of objects to suggest volume.

In this informal still life the artist applies crisp strokes and washes of transparent colour, one on top of the other, to suggest the firm but rounded forms of the fruits.

~

Elizabeth Moore
Still Life
28 x 38cm (11 x 15in)

~

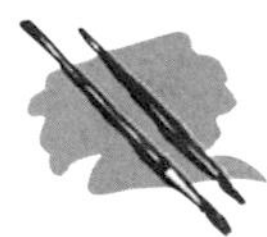

Light To Dark Technique

Because watercolour is transparent, light colours cannot be painted over dark ones; the dark areas have to be built up gradually by overlaying colours in successive layers. Working on dry paper, the lightest tones are applied first and left to dry; then progressively darker tones are built up where required, leaving the lightest areas intact. This process results in richer, more resonant passages than can be achieved by painting with a single, flat wash of dense colour.

This technique requires a little patience, because it is essential to allow each layer of paint to dry before applying the next; if you do not, the colours will simply mix and the crispness and definition will be lost. To speed up the process, you can use a hairdryer on a cool-to-warm setting. Remember also that the characteristic freshness and delicacy of the medium is lost if too many washes are allowed to build up, so always test your colours on scrap paper before applying them to the painting; a few layers, applied with confidence, will be more successful than colours muddied by constant reworking.

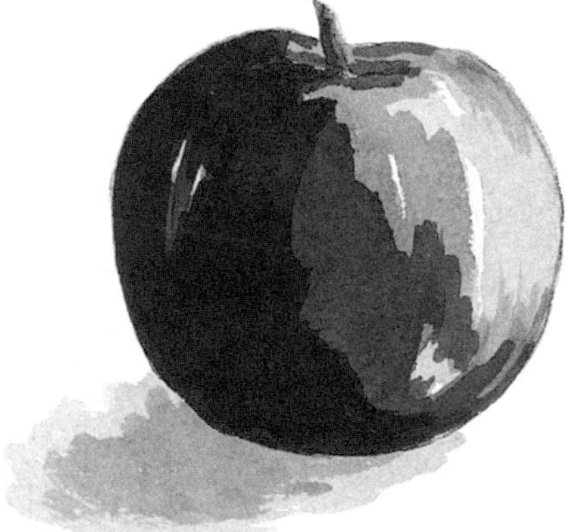

This simple image demonstrates how to build up overlapping washes of colour from light to dark and create a convincing sense of three-dimensional form.

Still Life

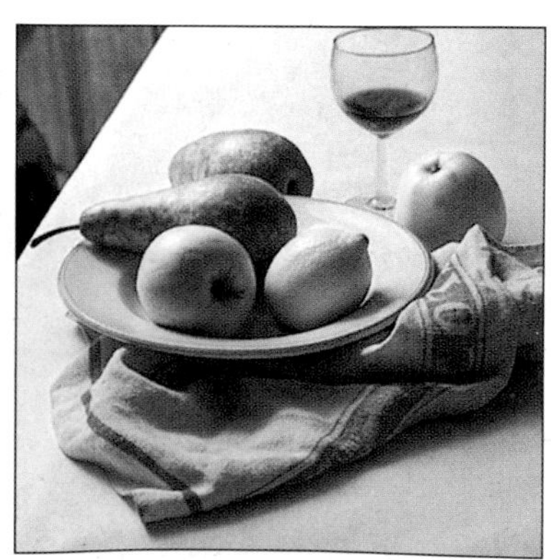

Left: A lamp was placed above and to the left of the still-life group; this powerful light source creates strong shadows that help to define the forms of the fruit.

Materials and Equipment

• SHEET OF 300GSM (140LB) HOT-PRESSED WATERCOLOUR PAPER, STRETCHED • SOFT PENCIL • KNEADED PUTTY ERASER • WATERCOLOUR BRUSH: MEDIUM-SIZED ROUND • WATERCOLOUR PAINTS: ALIZARIN CRIMSON, LEMON YELLOW, SAP GREEN, RAW UMBER, CADMIUM RED, PAYNE'S GREY

1

Make a light pencil drawing of the group. Begin with the lightest tones, keeping all your colours pale and transparent. Note where the brightest highlights are and indicate them by leaving the paper white.

Using a medium-sized round brush, paint the wine with alizarin crimson. Paint the lemon and the apple on the right with lemon yellow; the apple on the plate with sap green, and the pears with varied tones of raw umber and sap green. Indicate the bowl of the wine glass and the cast shadows on the cloth with Payne's grey. Paint the pattern on the cloth with cadmium red.

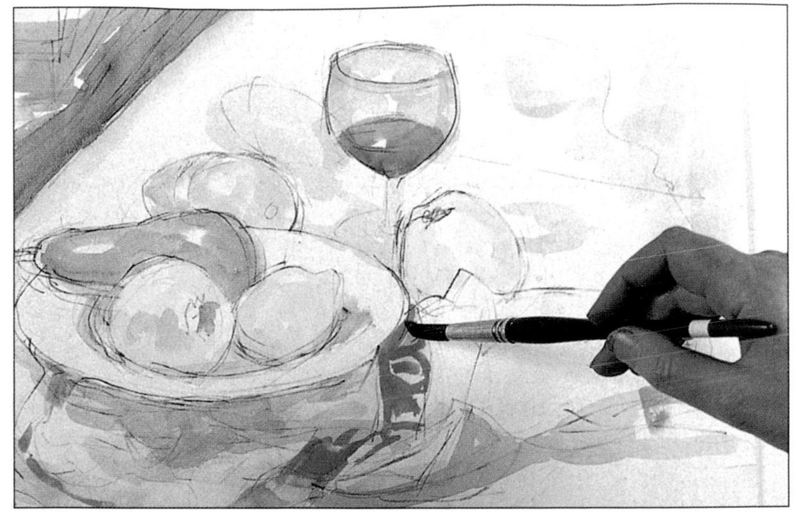

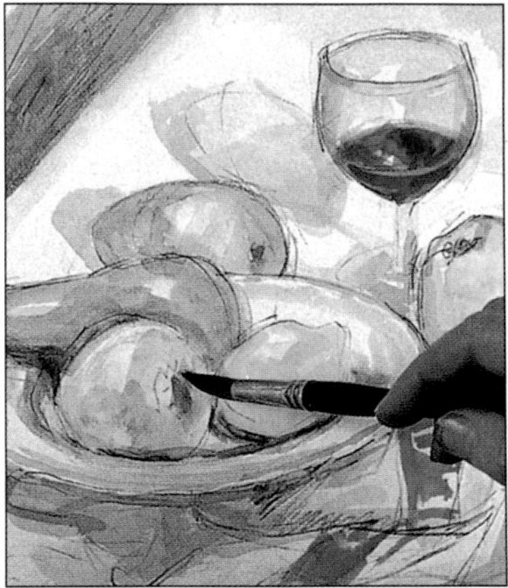

2

Prepare slightly stronger mixes of your colours and add the mid-tones, working around the highlights and paler tones. Add strokes of alizarin and cadmium red to the wine. For the pears, apply overlaid washes of raw umber and sap green, using curved strokes that convey the rounded forms of the fruits. Model the apples with strokes of sap green and lemon yellow, and strengthen the colour of the lemon with overlaid washes of lemon yellow. Paint the rim of the plate with sap green.

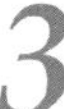

3

Continue developing the mid-tones and shadows, leaving the highlights intact. Add hints of pure colour here and there to add "zing". The subtle modulations of colour and tone are achieved by overlaying strokes of delicate, transparent pigment, like so many layers of tissue paper. Observe, too, how the brush strokes are left largely unblended to create textural interest.

Finally, darken and strengthen the tones in the wine glass, the fruits and the shadow beneath the plate.

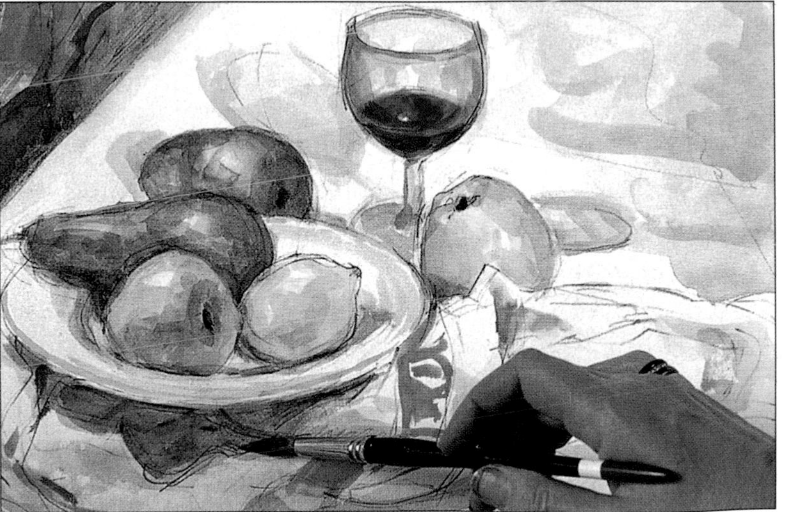

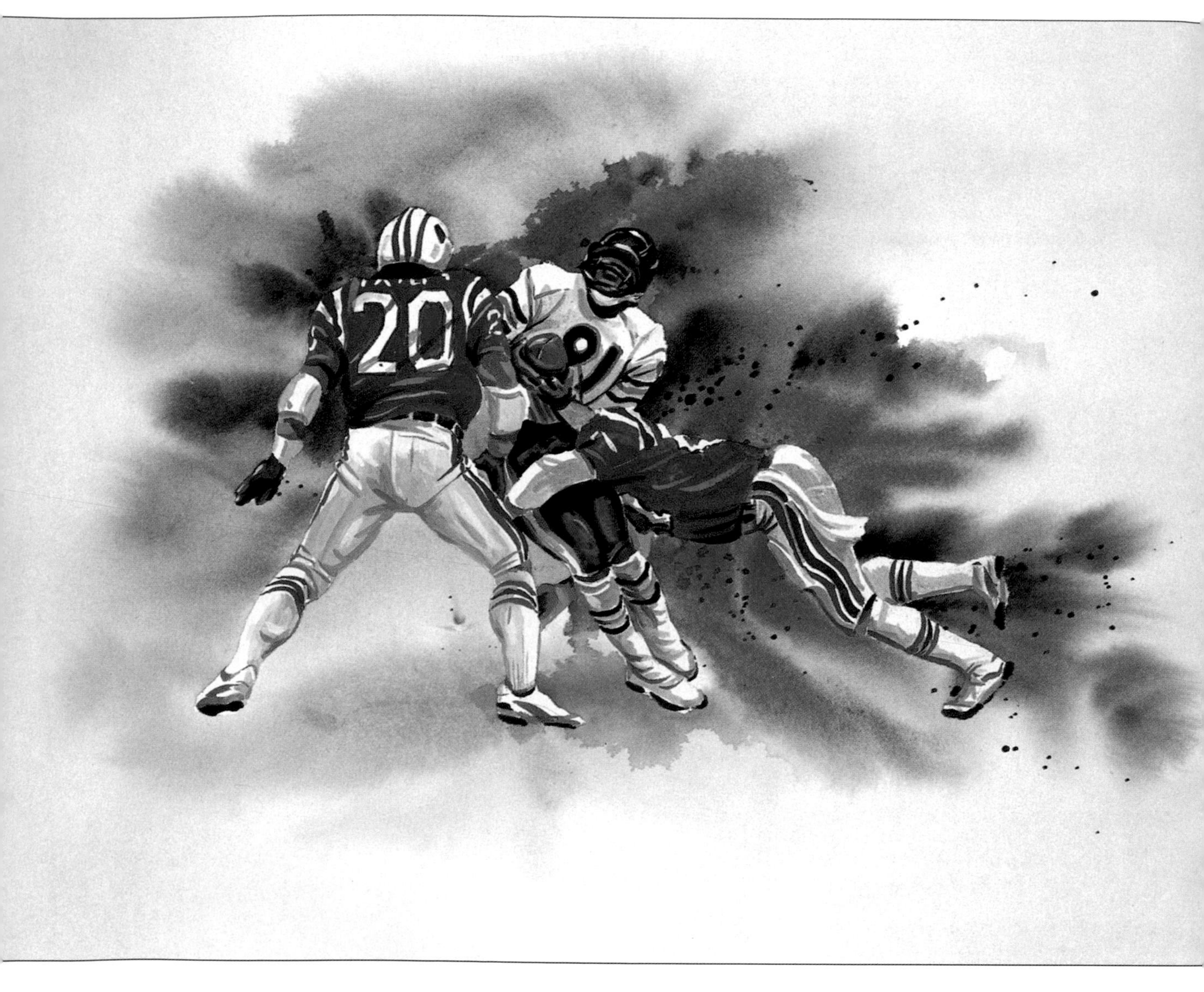
20

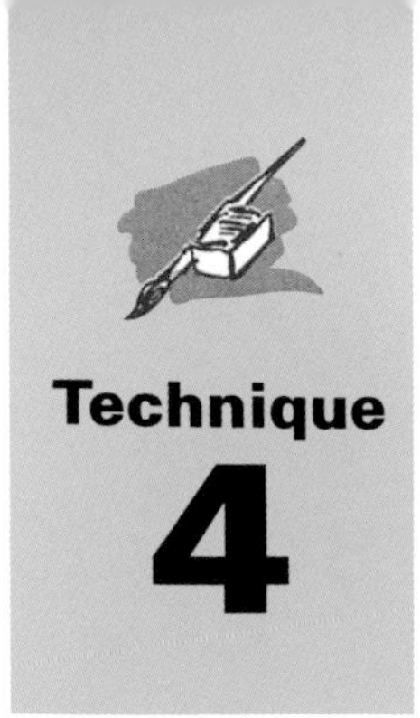

Technique

4

Body Colour

Portraying a moving subject is one of the greatest challenges facing an artist, and it is all too easy to end up with stilted figures and trees that look like cardboard cut-outs. But when it comes to capturing movement, a fluid medium like watercolour almost does the work for you; a watercolour wash, applied to wet paper, will spread, streak and blur of its own accord, and these expressive marks have an inherent energy of their own.

In this painting the artist exploits the physical contrast between thin and thick paint to capture the drama and fast pace of a game of American football. The strong, graphic qualities of gouache accentuate the bright colours and the sheer bulk of the heavily padded figures, while the streaks and blurs of watercolour in the background capture the momentum of the tackle.

~

Mark Topham
American Football
30 x 41cm (12 x 16in)

~

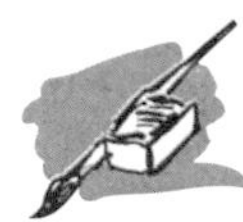

USING BODY COLOUR

The term "body colour" refers to opaque water-based paint such as gouache. The term is also applied when Chinese white watercolour paint, which is opaque, is used to add highlights in an otherwise transparent watercolour painting.

Some "purists" reject the idea of using body colour because it destroys the delicacy which is the hallmark of transparent watercolour. Yet many great artists, including Turner and Picasso, have mixed transparent washes with body colour to achieve particular effects. Watercolour and gouache are, after all, made up of the same basic ingredients, and they can work well together in the same painting, the opacity of gouache enhancing the transparency of watercolour.

If you have not used gouache paints before, it is a good idea to experiment with them before embarking on a painting. Gouache may be used thick, but still wet, or it can be thinned down so that it resembles pure watercolour. Unlike watercolour, it is possible to work from dark to light with gouache, adding white to lighten the colours rather than thinning them with more water.

The only disadvantage of gouache paints is that they remain soluble even when dry, which means that brushing a layer of wet paint over another layer tends to muddy the colours. However, this problem can be overcome by mixing acrylic glaze medium — available in tubes from art supply stores — into the paints. The acrylic glaze medium acts as a sealant, allowing you to build up successive washes without disturbing the layers beneath.

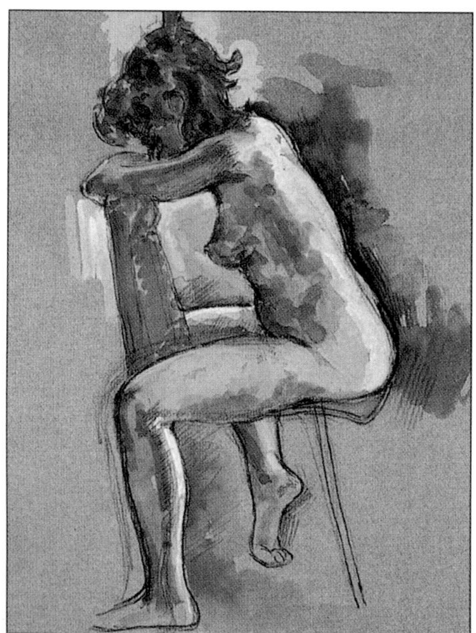

Body colour is particularly effective on tinted papers. In this nude study the buff paper forms the mid-tones, while the highlights on the figure's back and legs are accentuated by adding Chinese white to the transparent colours.

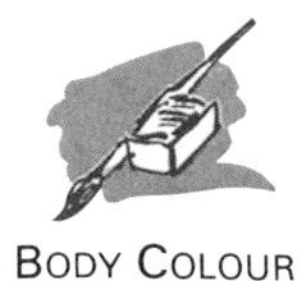

American Football

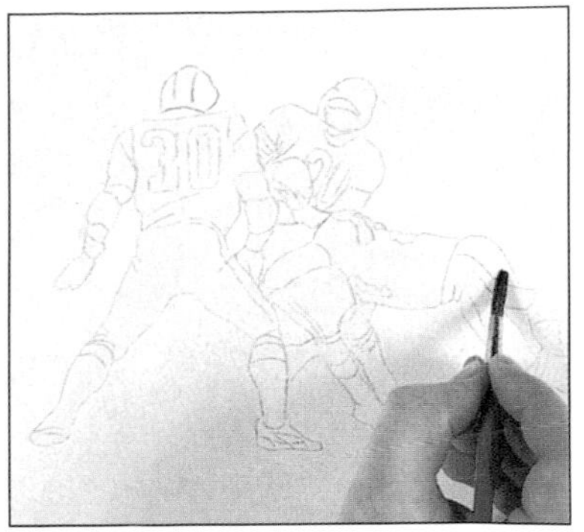

1

Make a careful outline drawing of the figures and the details of their clothing. Using an old paintbrush, fill in the shapes of the figures with masking fluid (liquid frisket) and leave to dry.

Materials and Equipment

• SHEET OF 300GSM (140LB) NOT (COLD-PRESSED) SURFACE WATERCOLOUR PAPER, STRETCHED • SOFT PENCIL • KNEADED PUTTY ERASER • OLD WATERCOLOUR BRUSH FOR APPLYING MASKING FLUID (LIQUID FRISKET) • MASKING FLUID • WATERCOLOUR BRUSHES: LARGE AND SMALL ROUNDS, MEDIUM-SIZED FLAT • WATERCOLOUR PAINTS: NEUTRAL TINT, INDIGO, ALIZARIN VIOLET, SAP GREEN AND FRENCH ULTRAMARINE • GOUACHE PAINTS: CADMIUM RED, HAVANNAH LAKE, SAP GREEN, ULTRAMARINE, BURNT SIENNA, GOLDEN YELLOW, YELLOW OCHRE AND ZINC WHITE • ACRYLIC GLAZE MEDIUM

2

Start by painting the background with transparent watercolour. On separate areas of your palette, mix dilute washes of neutral tint, indigo and alizarin violet watercolours. Using a large round brush, saturate the entire painting area with clean water.

When the shine has left the paper, paint the background around the figures with fast, spontaneous strokes of the three colours using a medium-sized flat brush. Let the colours merge wet-into-wet (see pages 68–75) where they meet, at the same time using the brush to guide the colours outwards from the figures so that they fade out into the background. Indicate the grass with sap green.

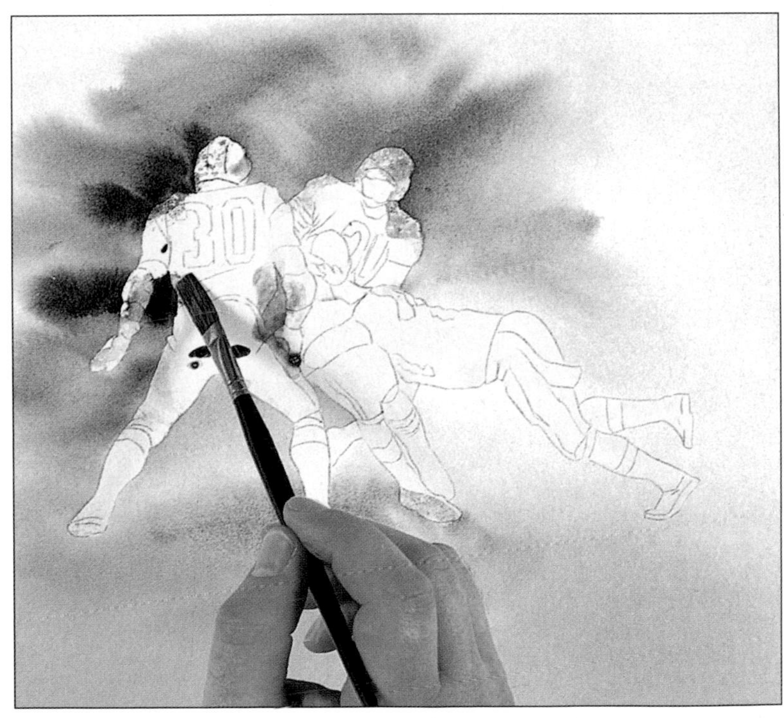

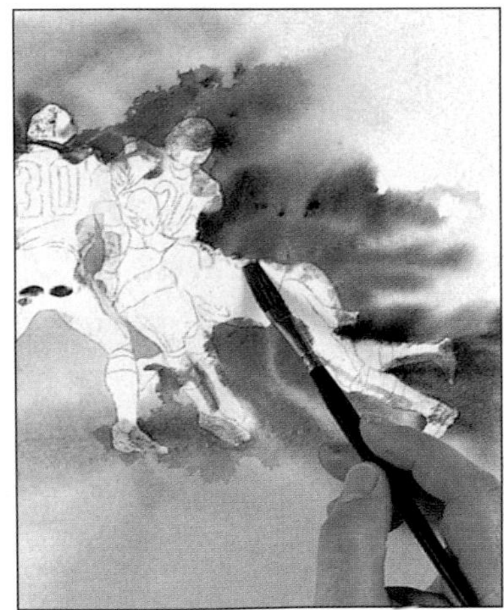

3

To emphasize the movement of the "flying" figure on the right, apply strokes of French ultramarine and neutral tint behind him, again allowing the colours to spread outwards. Leave to dry.

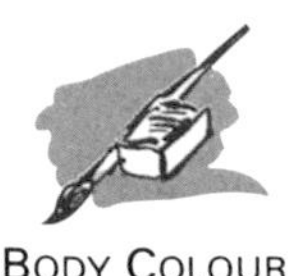

4

To give an impression of dirt being kicked up by the players' feet, use the spattering technique. Load the brush with a dark wash of neutral tint, then hold it at a shallow angle about 2.5cm (1in) above the paper. Gently tap the brush with a forefinger to release a shower of drops onto the paper. If necessary, use a hairdryer to dry the spattered area and prevent the colour from soaking into the paper.

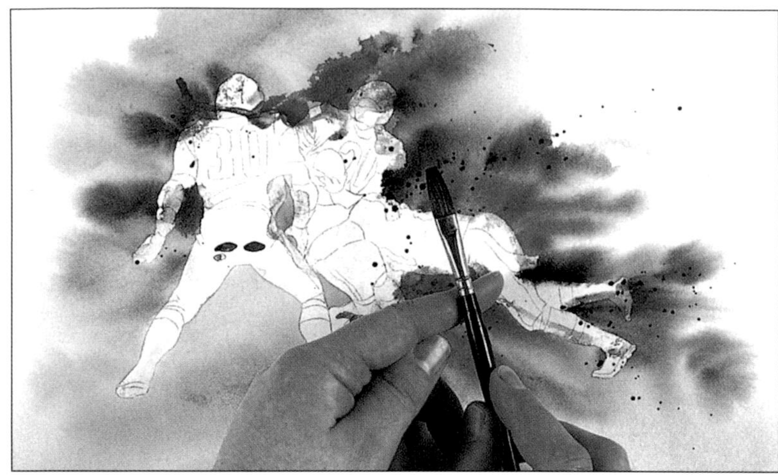

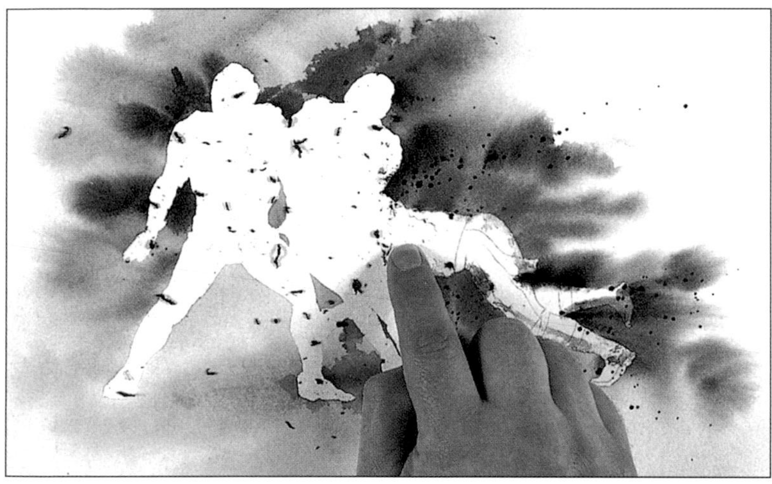

5

When the background is completely dry, remove the masking fluid from the figures by rubbing with a clean fingertip. You may have to reinstate the pencilled details on the clothes as they may have been rubbed away with the dried mask.

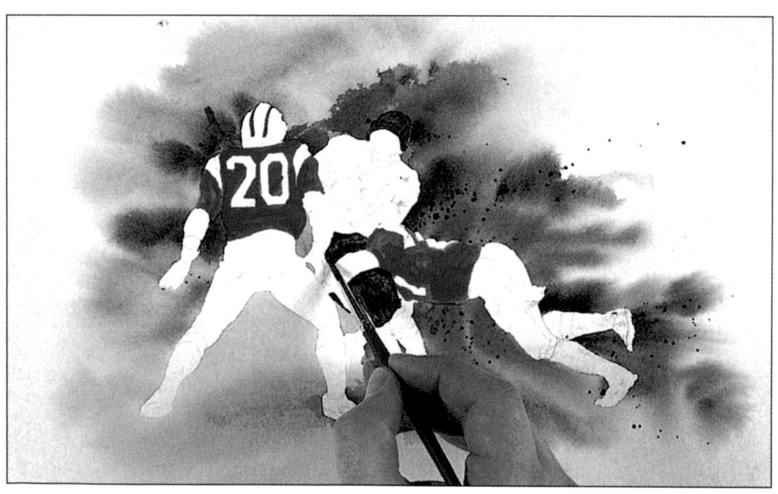

6

Then paint the figures using gouache, remembering to add a little acrylic glaze medium to the initial colours. Using a small round brush, paint the jerseys with cadmium red, darkened with a touch of Havannah lake in the shadow areas. Paint the green helmet and pants with sap green, darkened with ultramarine in the shadows.

7

Using gouache, paint the football with a mix of burnt sienna and cadmium red, then paint the stripes and number on the central figure with golden yellow and sap green darkened with ultramarine. For the stripes on the other two figures, use cadmium red and ultramarine. Apply strokes of burnt sienna to the soles of the boots. Leave to dry.

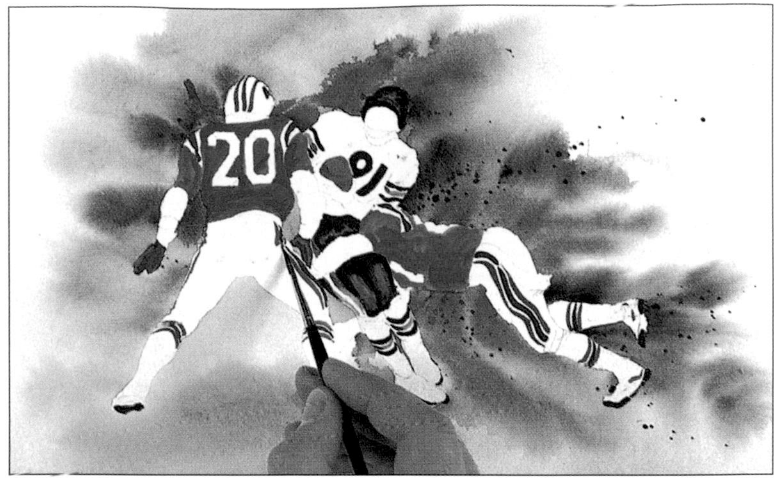

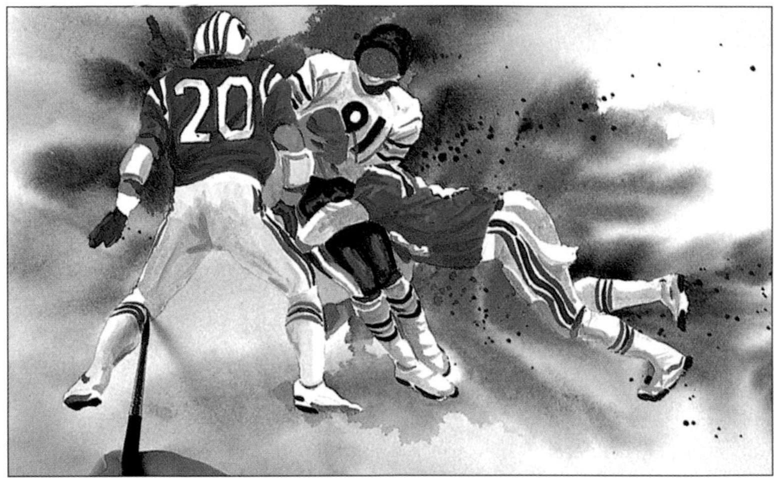

8

Block in the flesh tones of the figures using mixes of burnt umber, yellow ochre and zinc white. Use zinc white as the base for all the white parts of the players' clothing, mixing into it touches of alizarin violet watercolour, plus yellow ochre, ultramarine and cadmium red gouache for the shadows. It is these subtle hints of colour that help to describe the forms of the figures and create a sense of light.

Paint the folds and creases in the red jerseys using cadmium red darkened with ultramarine, and on the white jersey using neutral tint watercolour and zinc white.

9

Then all that remains is to paint the final details with fine brush strokes. Work all over the picture adding definition to the figures and clothing. For example, add more dark creases to the clothing and a few highlights with drybrush strokes (see pages 82–89) of zinc white. Paint the creases on the left-hand figure's pants with a mix of sap green and white gouache, and the highlights with pure white. Suggest the facial features on the central figure, then complete his helmet and visor.

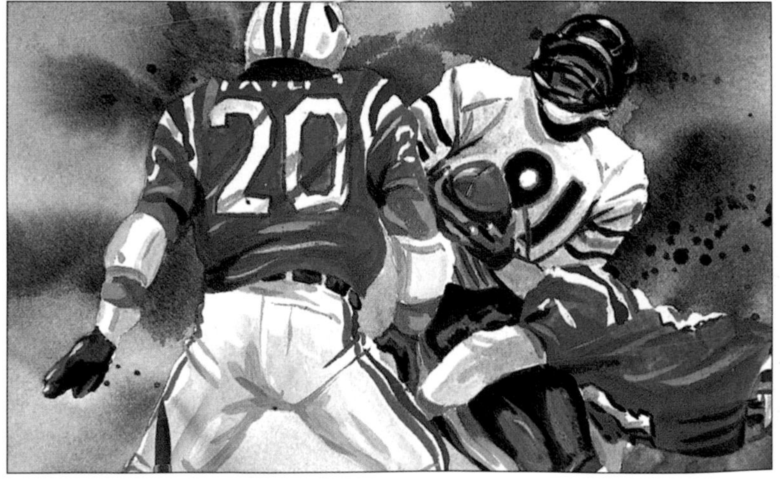

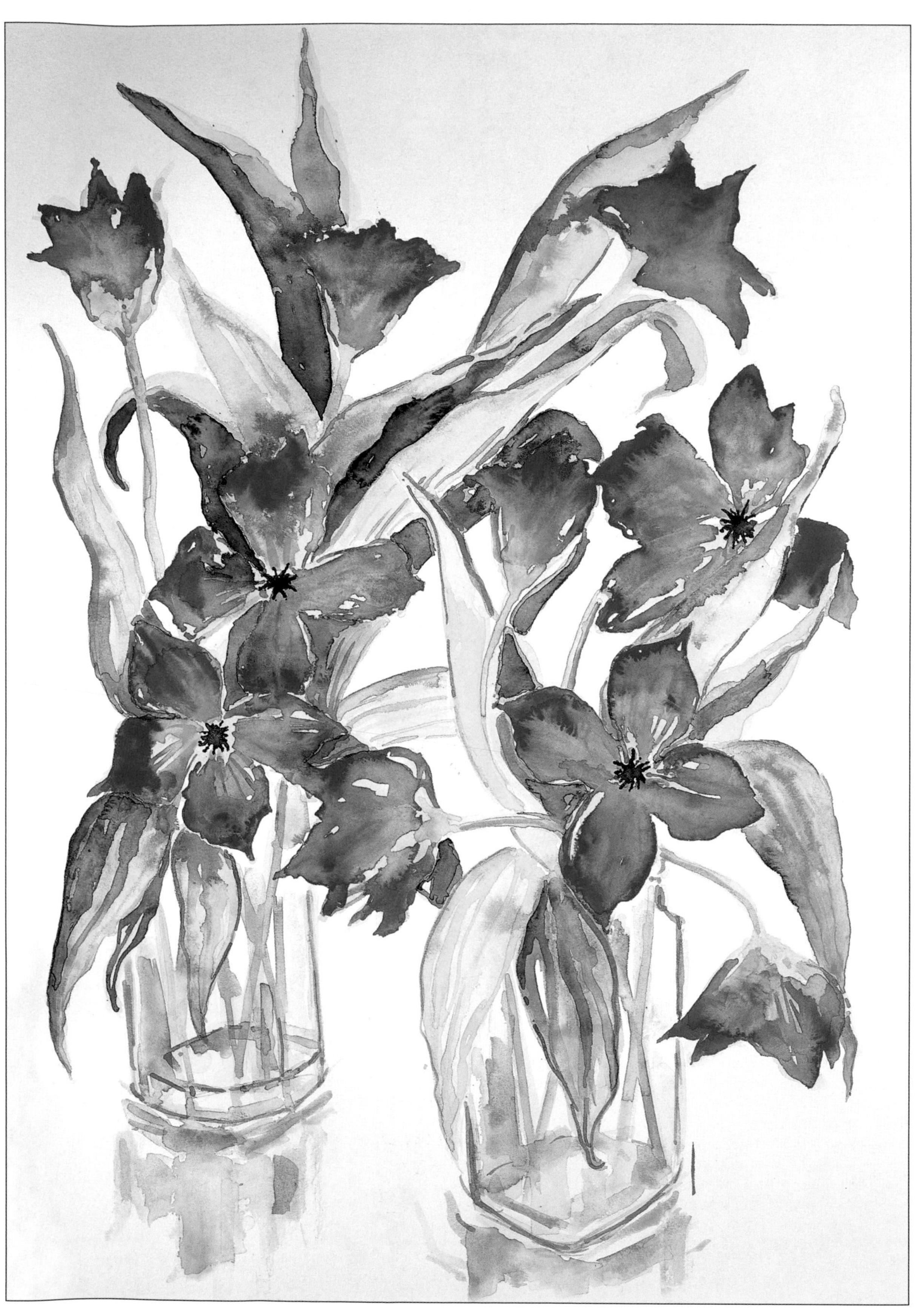

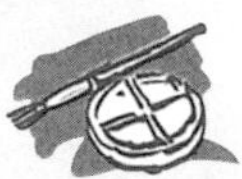

Technique

5

BACKRUNS

This painting was executed very quickly as the artist wanted to concentrate primarily on capturing the energetic shapes and gestures of the tulips and their foliage. In some areas wet washes were deliberately applied on top of still-damp ones to create marks and blotches known as "backruns", which not only add form and texture but also contribute to the spontaneity of the finished piece.

Some varieties of tulip make more appealing subjects to paint after they have been standing in water for a day or two, when the petals begin to open out and the leaves and stems bend and curl to form graceful shapes. The so-called "parrot" tulips are particularly interesting, with their frilled petals and vibrant striped markings.

~

Annie Wood

Parrot Tulips

74 x 53cm (29 x 21in)

~

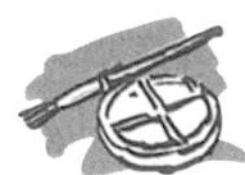

USING BACKRUNS

Backruns, also known as "blooms", are those dreaded hard-edged blotches that sometimes appear in a watercolour wash just when you least want them. A backrun forms when one wash is flooded into another before the first wash has completely dried; as the second wash spreads out it dislodges some of the paint particles beneath, and these particles collect at the edge of the wash as it dries, creating a dark, irregular line.

Backruns can, however, be used quite deliberately to create textures and effects that are difficult to obtain using normal painting methods. For example, a series of small backruns creates a mottled pattern suggestive of weathered, lichen-covered stone; in landscapes, backruns can represent amorphous shapes such as distant hills, trees and clouds, or ripples on the surface of a stream; and they add texture and definition to the forms of leaves and flowers. Certainly part of the attraction of backruns is their power to suggest, encouraging the viewer to use their imagination.

It takes a little practice to create deliberate backruns (unwanted, accidental ones are much easier!). Backruns are more likely to occur on smooth papers than on absorbent or rough-textured papers.

Apply the first wash and allow it to dry a little. When the second is applied, the first should be damp rather than wet; if it is too wet, the washes will merge together without a backrun, as they do in the wet-into-wet technique (see pages 68–75). Small, circular backruns are formed by dropping paint from the end of a brush into the damp wash. Pale backruns can also be created by flooding or dropping clear water into a wash.

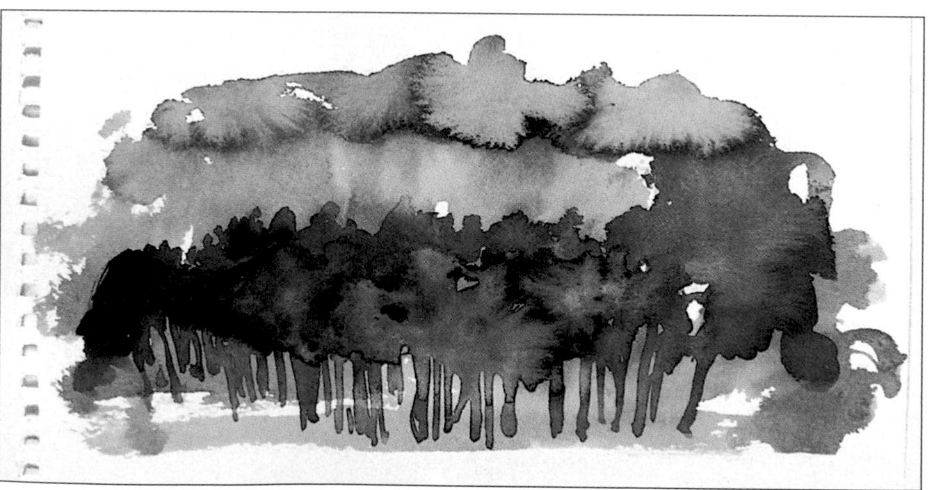

Here backruns have been deliberately created by dripping water into the wet paint; this pushes the pigment particles outwards, creating interesting mottled patterns suggestive of trees, clouds and swirling mist.

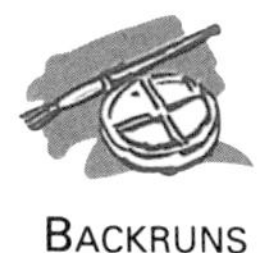

PARROT TULIPS

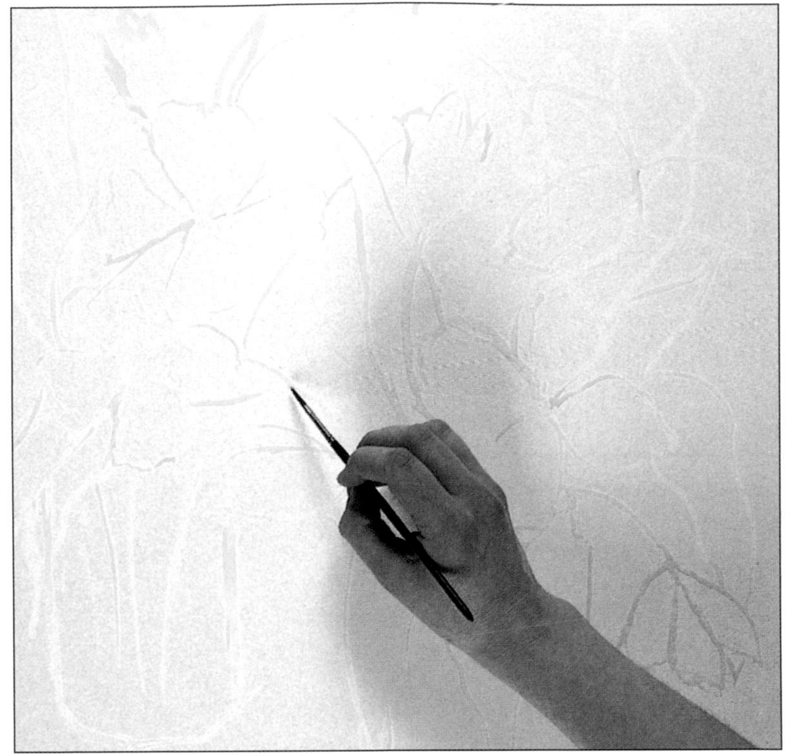

Materials and Equipment

• SHEET OF 410GSM (200LB) NOT (COLD-PRESSED) SURFACE WATERCOLOUR PAPER, STRETCHED • WATERCOLOUR BRUSHES: SMALL AND MEDIUM-SIZED ROUNDS • WATERCOLOUR PAINTS: LEMON YELLOW, SCARLET LAKE, CADMIUM YELLOW PALE, CHROME GREEN YELLOW PALE, CHROME GREEN LIGHT, VIRIDIAN, CERULEAN, CARMINE AND ALIZARIN

1

Mix a large wash of lemon yellow and, using a small round brush, lightly draw the outlines of the flowers and the vases.

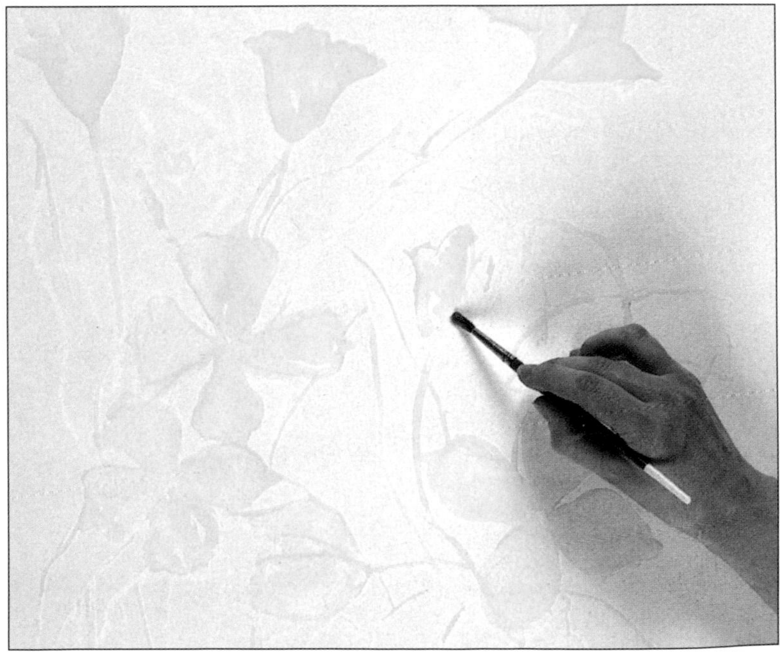

2

With a medium-sized round brush, fill in the shapes of the flowers (but not the leaves) with lemon yellow. As you work, go back to the flowers already painted and drop in some clean water from the end of the brush to keep the paint wet.

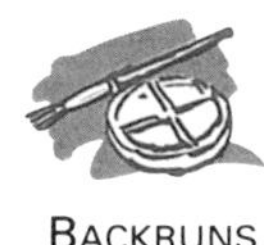

3

Mix cadmium yellow pale and a touch of scarlet lake to make a pale orange. Apply this colour to the base of the petals and allow it to spread a little.

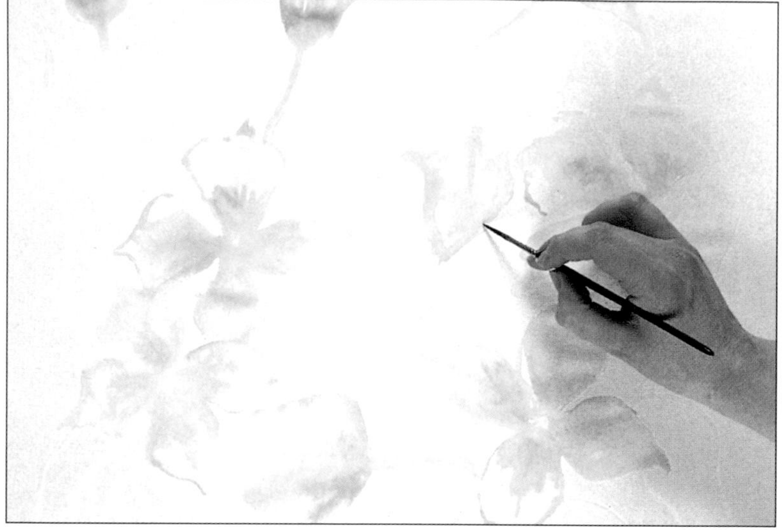

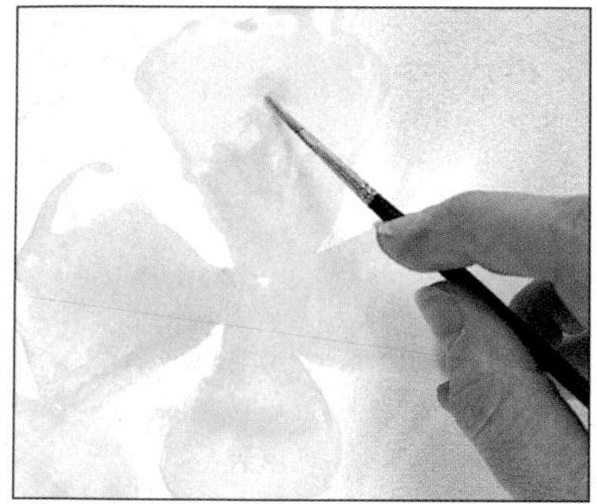

4

Use a small round brush and gently guide the orange pigment upwards slightly, allowing the colour to fade gradually into the wet underlayer of yellow. At the same time, take the colour around the outlines of the petals to define them.

5

Fill in the leaf shapes with lemon yellow, strengthened with cadmium yellow pale in places. While the paint is still wet, paint the mid-tones in the leaves with chrome green light. Lightly indicate the flower stalks and the shadows in the clear glass vases.

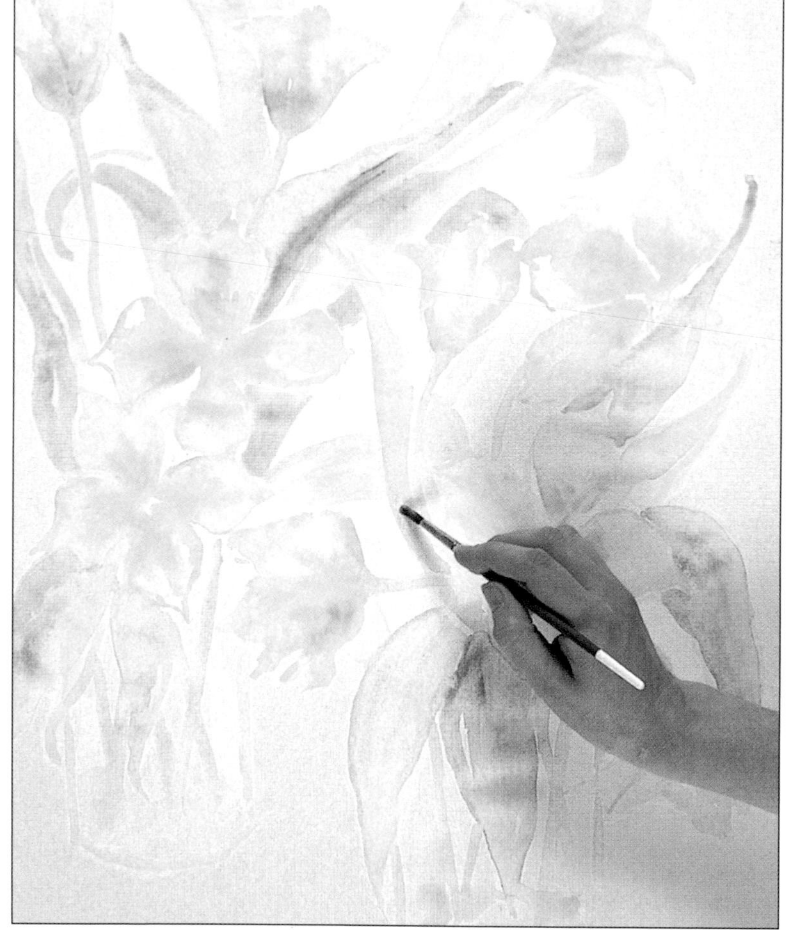

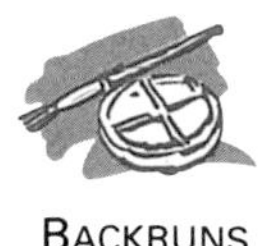

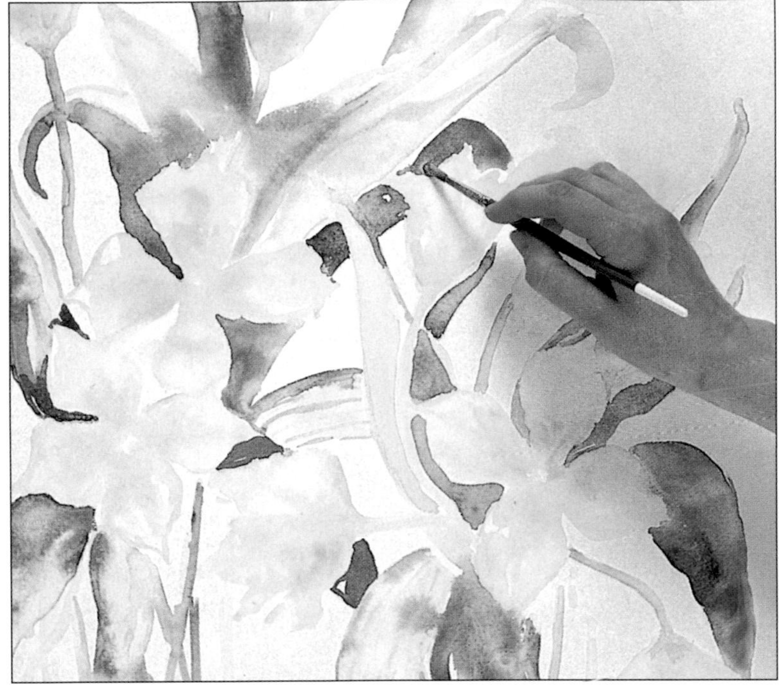

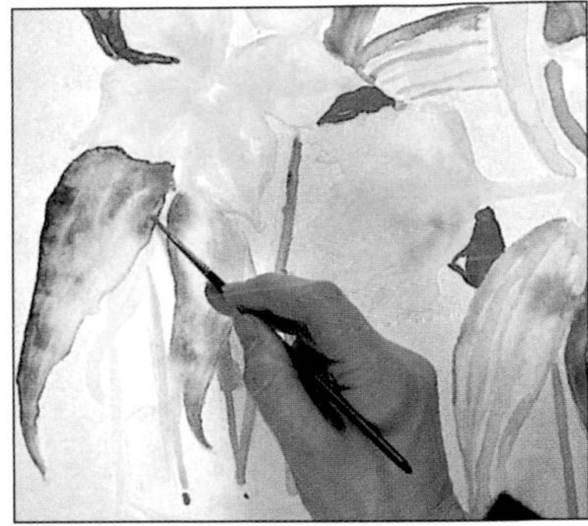

Above: In this detail you can see the effect of dropping wet paint into a semi-wet wash; the second colour seeps out into the first, creating little "blooms" and blotches that add interesting texture.

6

Allow the paint to dry a little, then paint the darker shadows and striping on the leaves with viridian.

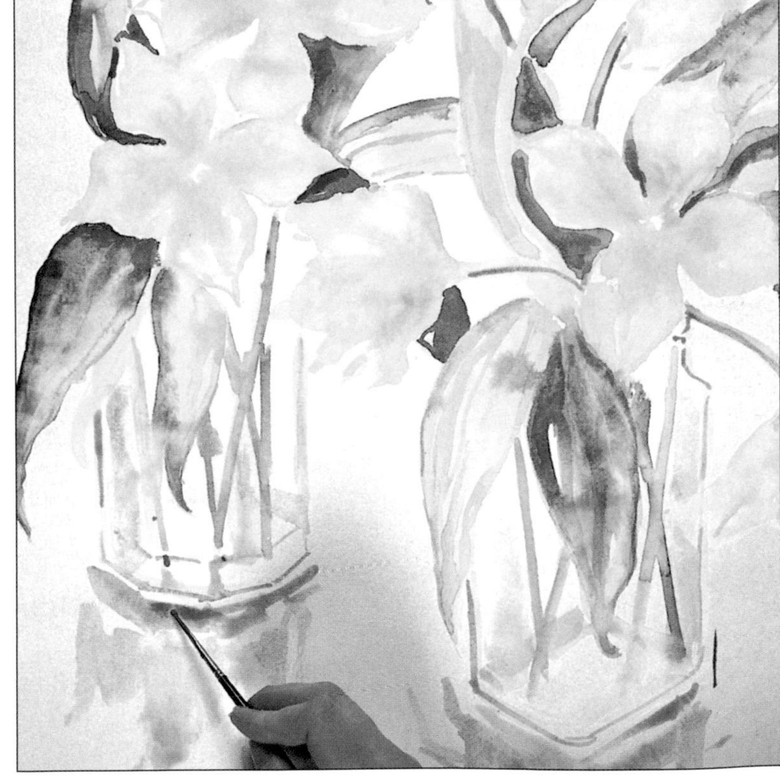

7

Add definition to some of the details on the leaves with cerulean, this time using the paint a little more thickly. Use cerulean, diluted to a pale tint, to indicate the forms of the vases. Also indicate the reflections of the vases on the shiny surface of the table, gradually fading out the colour as you move downwards.

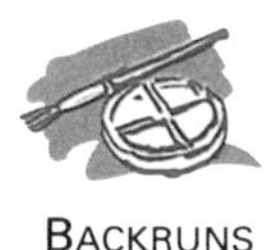

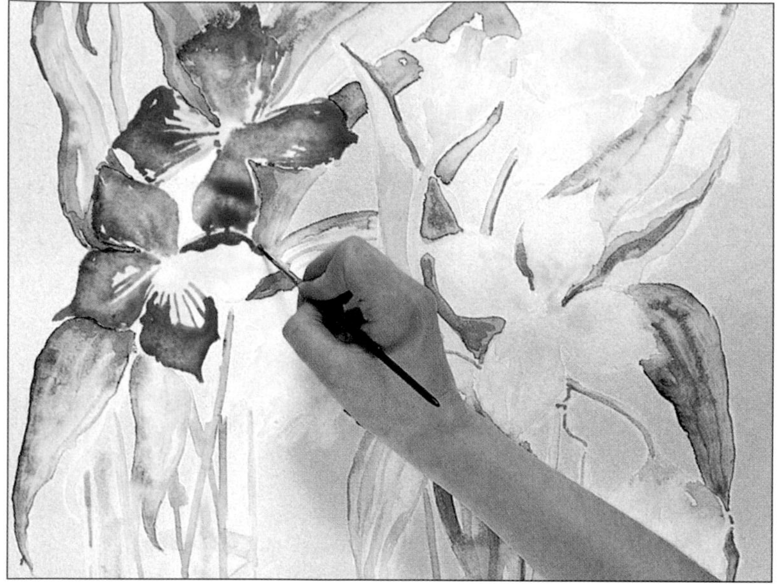

8

If the flower forms have dried, re-wet them and dab off any excess water with a tissue. Using a small brush, outline each petal with a fairly strong mix of carmine and then quickly guide the paint in from the edges and leave it to spread and diffuse of its own accord. Do not cover the yellow paint entirely, but paint the striped patterns on some of the flowers.

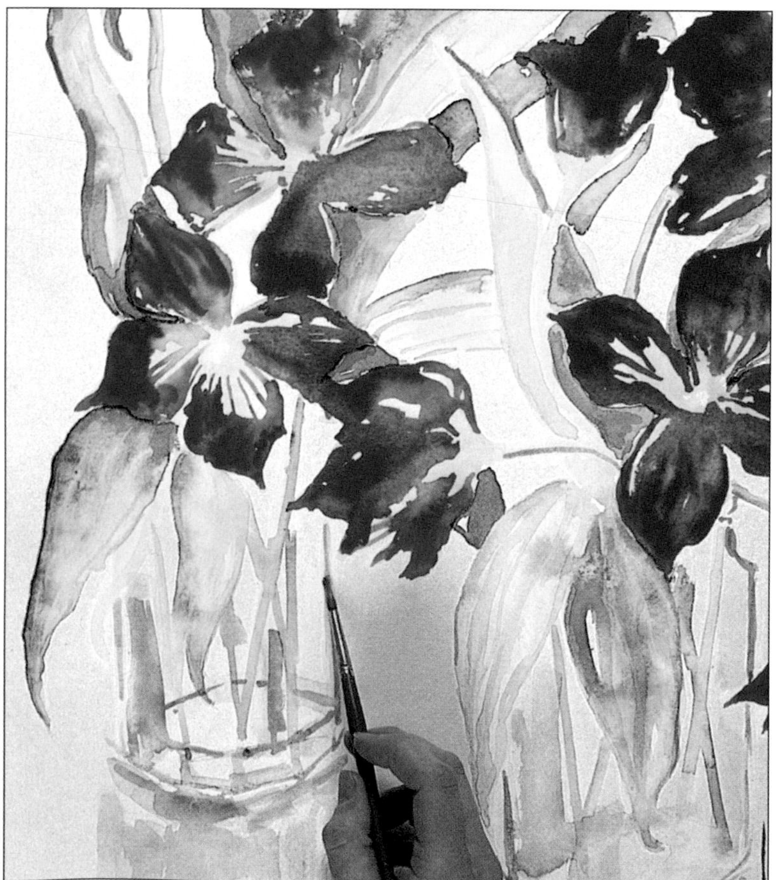

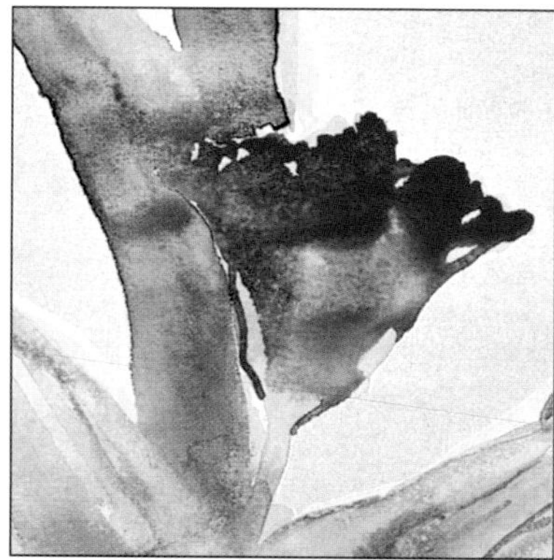

Above: This close-up detail shows the lovely gradations of colour that occur when the second colour bleeds into the wet paint beneath. Even if the colour runs back into the leaves in places, do not worry; it is "happy accidents" like these that lend poetry to a watercolour painting.

9

Continue painting the flowers, then add further detail to the vases and their reflections using carmine diluted to a pale tint.

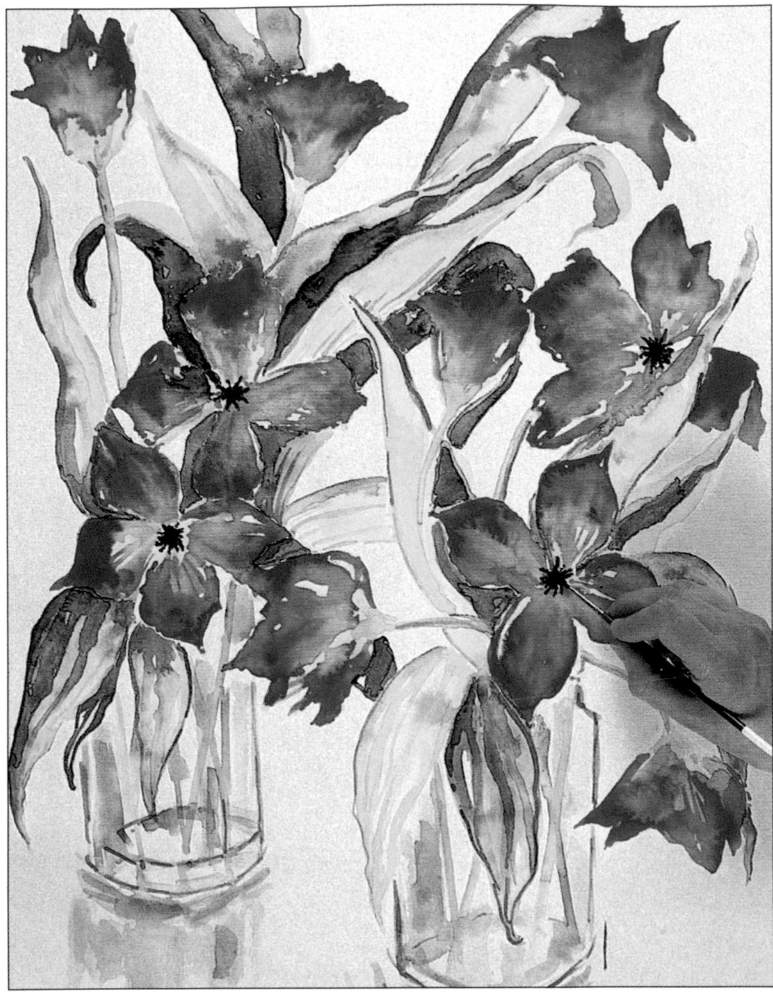

10

Using a strong mix of viridian, redefine the darks in the leaves. Then mix viridian and alizarin crimson to make a browny black and paint the stamens in the open flowers. Leave the painting to dry flat.

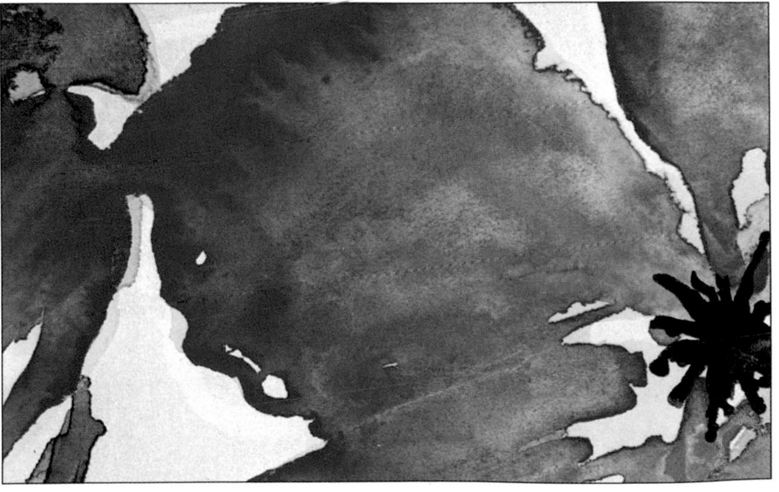

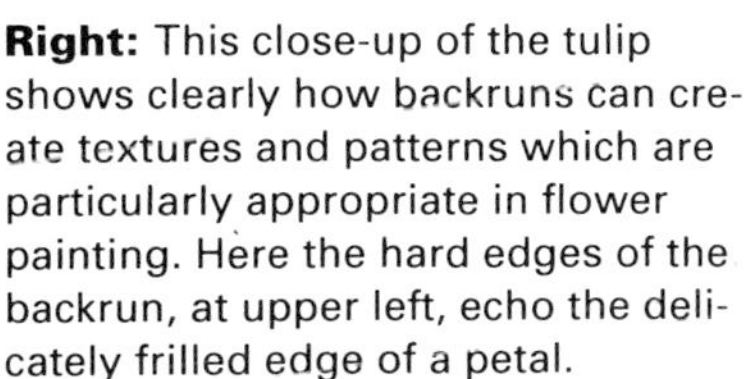

Right: This close-up of the tulip shows clearly how backruns can create textures and patterns which are particularly appropriate in flower painting. Here the hard edges of the backrun, at upper left, echo the delicately frilled edge of a petal.

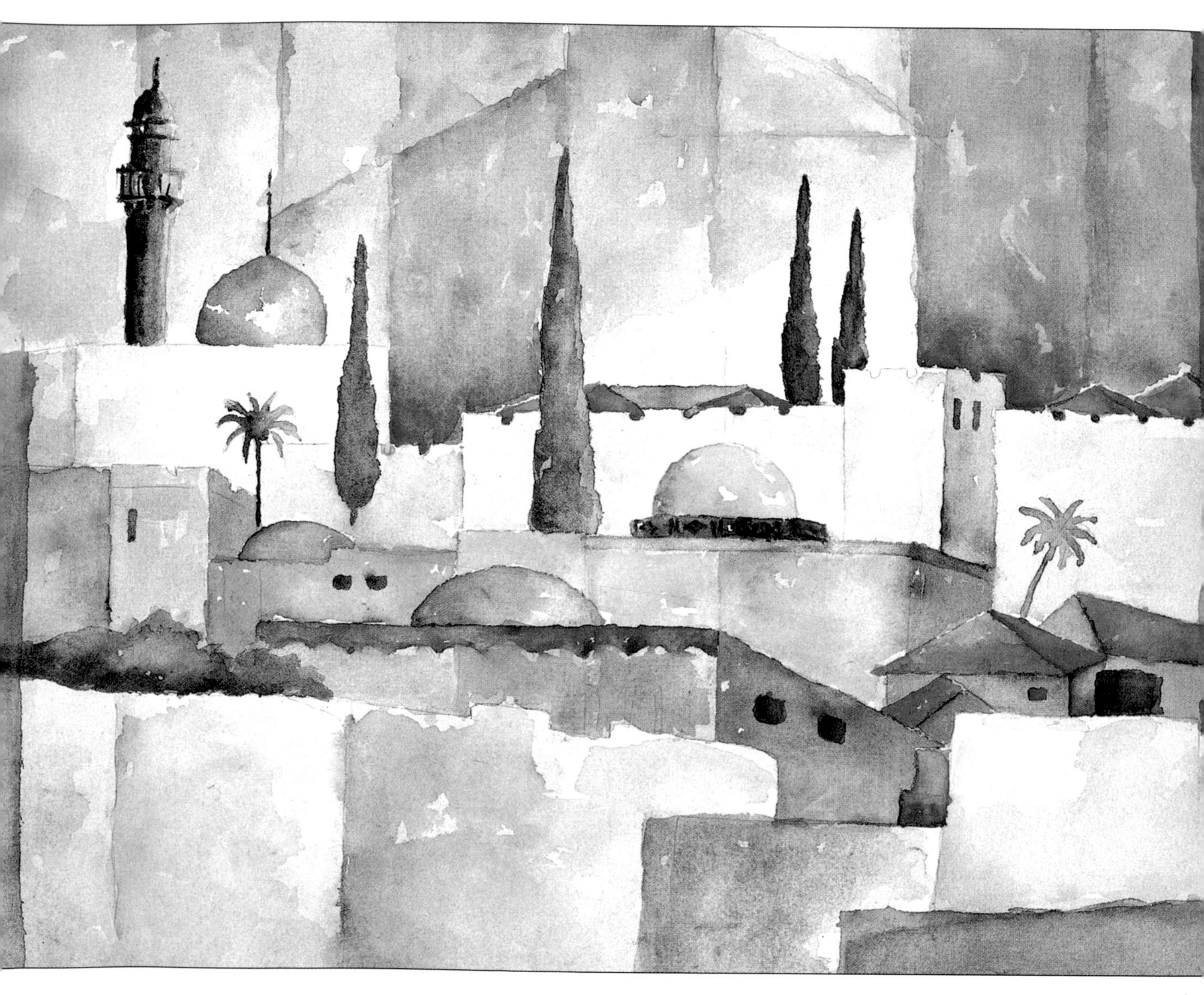

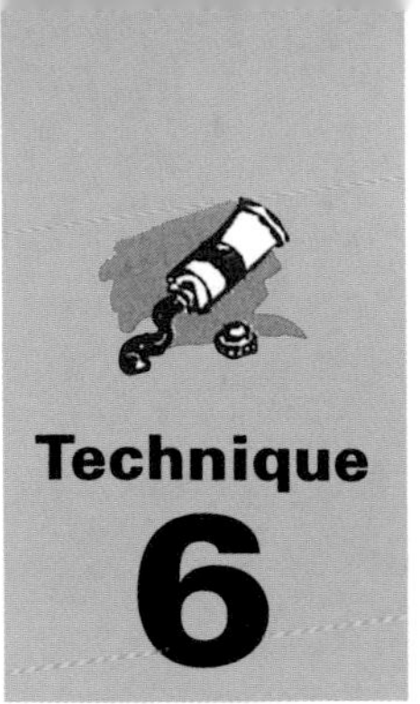

GLAZING

Glazing is a time-honoured technique usually associated with oil painting. The principle is to apply a thin transparent wash over another colour so that the underlying colour shows through. Glazed colours have an incredible richness and luminosity, seeming to glow from within.

In this semi-abstract painting, the artist has used coloured glazes to create fragmented planes of transparent colour that convey a lively impression of the architecture and strong sunlight of Jerusalem. The structural elements - the domes of mosques, flat-roofed buildings, palm trees, even the sky - are broken down into crystalline forms, creating a unified pattern of intersecting crescents and verticals.

~

Rivka Sinclair
Old Jerusalem
28 x 38cm (11 x 15in)

~

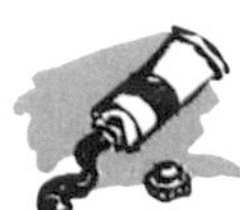

GLAZING TECHNIQUE

The chief characteristic of watercolour is its transparency, and in using the glazing technique this is exploited to the full. Glazing watercolours means applying the paints in dilute, transparent layers over one another, each layer being allowed to dry before the next is added, thus building up thin veils of colour. Because each layer is transparent, light is able to travel through to the white paper beneath and reflect back up through the colours. The result is rich and glowing, suggestive of the subtle and ephemeral qualities of light.

Glazing, otherwise known as the "wet-on-dry" method, is ideal for painting objects with precise shapes or hard, crisp edges. The dry surface "holds" the paint, so that brush strokes will not distort or "bleed".

It is interesting to experiment with glazing as a way of mixing colour. For example, try glazing a wash of blue over a dry wash of yellow to create green. Then mix the same two colours together on a palette and apply the colour to a sheet of paper; the glazed colour has a certain resonance and luminosity that the physically mixed colour lacks. This is because the incomplete fusion of the glazed colours produces a flickering optical sensation, so the surface of the picture seems to palpitate with light.

When glazing, always apply the palest colours first, so that light is allowed to reflect off the white paper. It is vital to allow one glaze to dry completely before applying the next, otherwise the clarity of the glaze is lost as the two colours will partially mix and become muddy. Remember, too, that dirty water will contaminate the colours, so change the water in the jar frequently, and rinse the brush thoroughly between colours.

Avoid applying more than two or three layers of colour when glazing in watercolour - any more and the delicate, transparent nature of the medium is lessened.

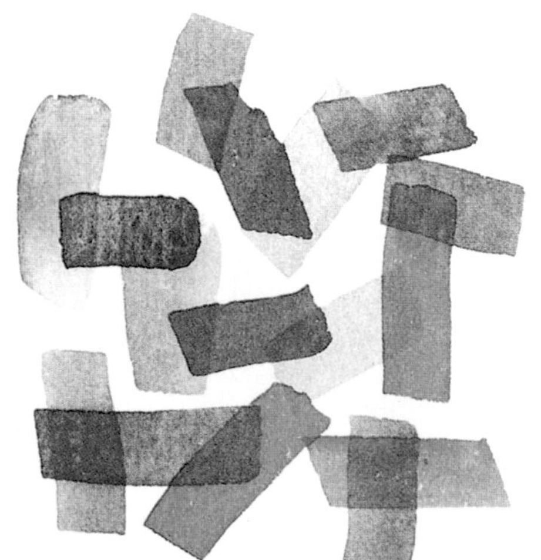

Glazing demonstrates the transparency and depth of watercolours. Try applying different-coloured glazes one on top of the other to create varied tones and hues.

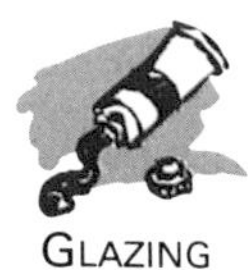

OLD JERUSALEM

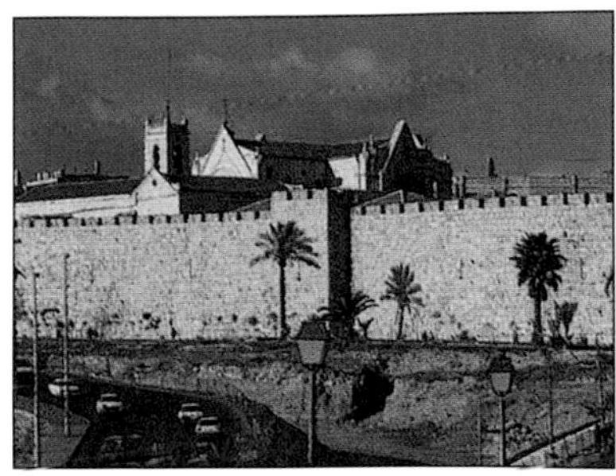

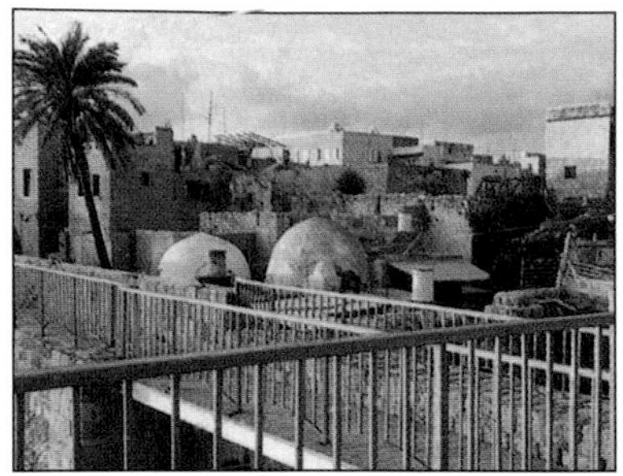

Above: This painting was done mainly from imagination and memory, with photographs of Jerusalem providing references for some of the details.

Materials and Equipment

• SHEET OF 300GSM (140LB) NOT (COLD-PRESSED) SURFACE WATERCOLOUR PAPER, STRETCHED • SOFT PENCIL • KNEADED PUTTY ERASER • WATERCOLOUR BRUSHES: 25MM (1IN) AND 13MM (½IN) FLATS, SMALL ROUND • WATERCOLOUR PAINTS: YELLOW OCHRE, NAPLES YELLOW, RAW UMBER, CHARCOAL GREY, FRENCH ULTRAMARINE, PURPLE, PAYNE'S GREY, ANTWERP BLUE, WINSOR BLUE, CERULEAN, BURNT SIENNA, WARM SEPIA, NEW GAMBOGE, RAW SIENNA, INDIGO, HOOKER'S GREEN NO.2, DARK GREEN, ALIZARIN CRIMSON, CADMIUM YELLOW

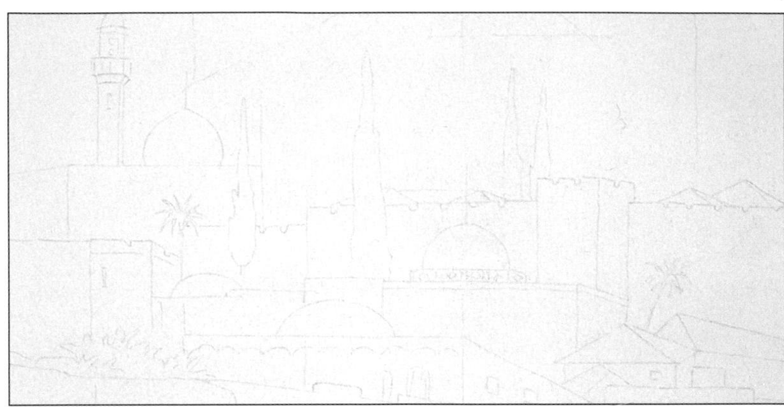

1

Draw the outlines of the subject using a soft pencil. Keep the lines light so that they will not show through the paint layers.

2

Mix yellow ochre and Naples yellow for the lighter walls of the buildings, and raw umber and charcoal grey for the darker walls. Use very pale tints of these colours so that the white of the paper shines through them. Hold the 25mm (1in) flat brush at a low angle to the paper and use the square end of the brush to block in the colours.

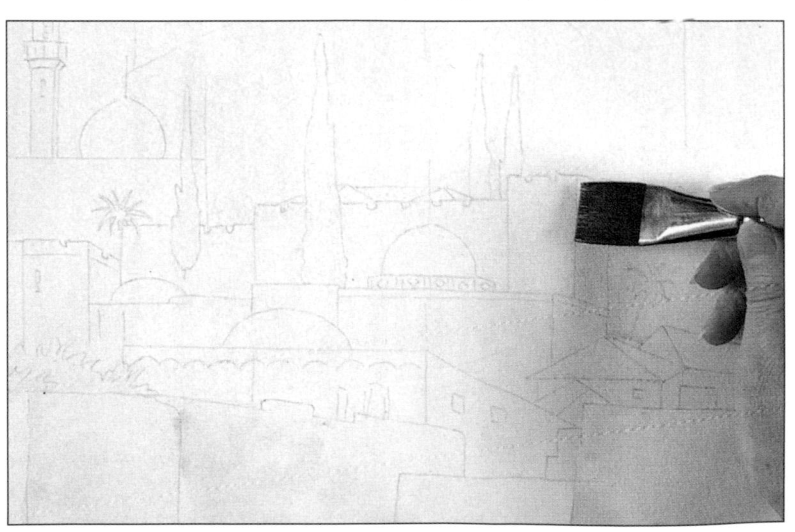

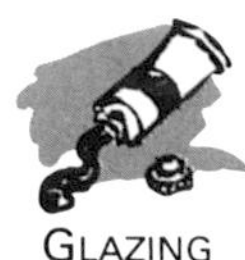

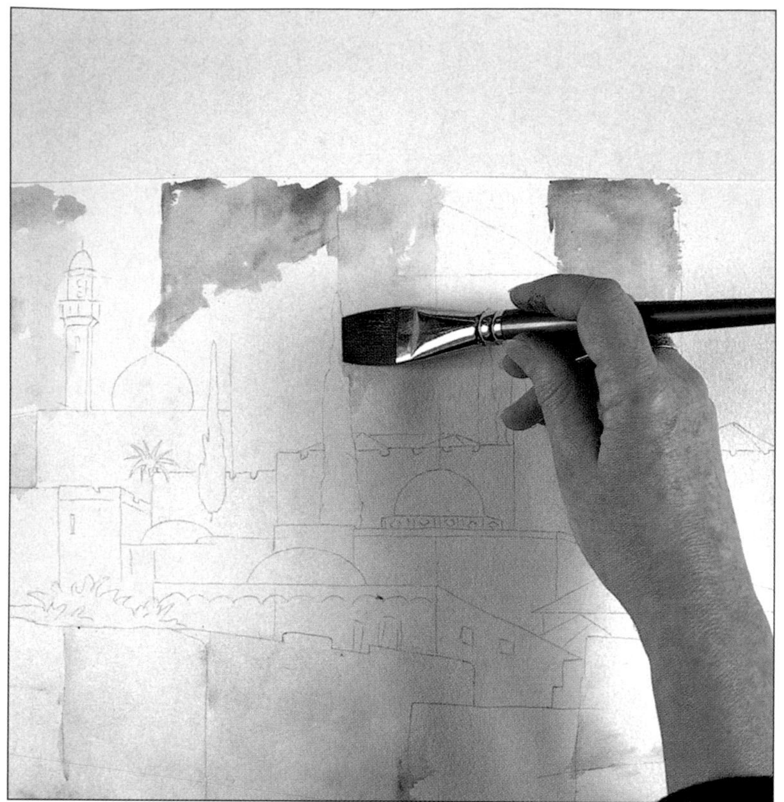

3

Mix a range of blues on a palette for the sky. Moving across from left to right, the artist has used the following mixtures: ultramarine, purple, Payne's grey and Antwerp blue; Winsor blue, cerulean and a touch of Payne's grey; cerulean and a touch of Payne's grey; and ultramarine, purple and a touch of Payne's grey. Apply the colours thinly, in separate "blocks" as shown.

4

With the smaller flat brush add further glazes of colour to the walls in the centre of the painting using various mixtures of burnt sienna, yellow ochre and warm sepia, still keeping the colour very diluted. Paint the blue domes with cerulean, purple and Payne's grey, leaving tiny flecks of white to indicate sunlight reflecting off them. Paint the rooftops using new gamboge and raw sienna, and burnt sienna and warm sepia. Paint the yellow dome with new gamboge and raw umber.

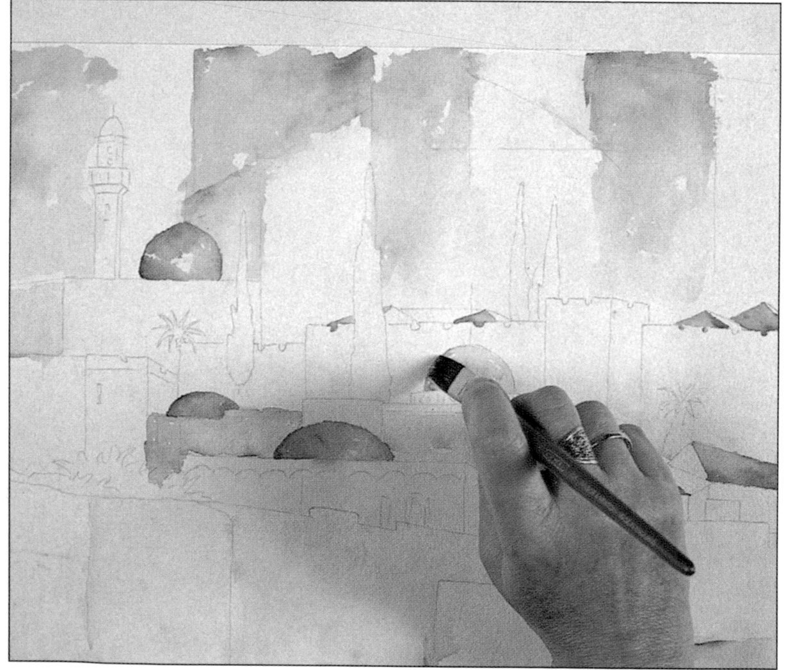

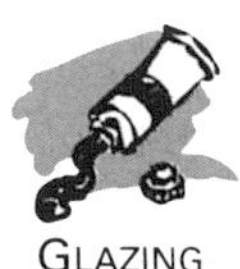

5

Mix ultramarine, purple and Payne's grey and fill in the darker areas of the sky, varying the intensity of the blue in each section so that they do not appear too uniform.

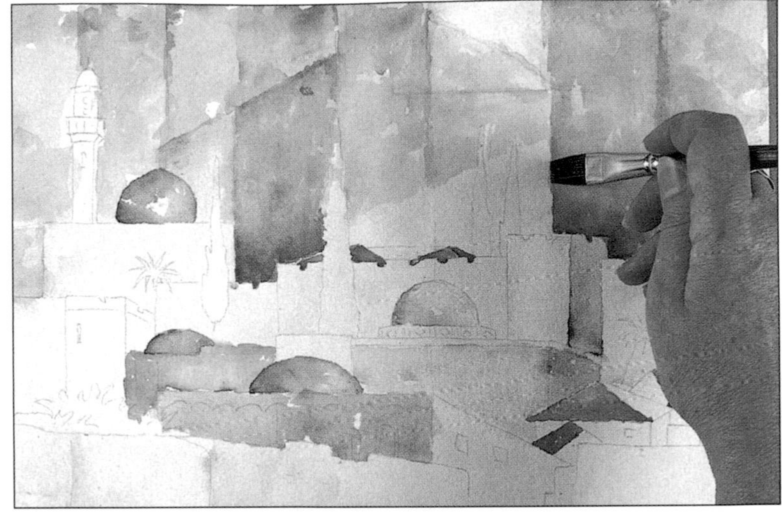

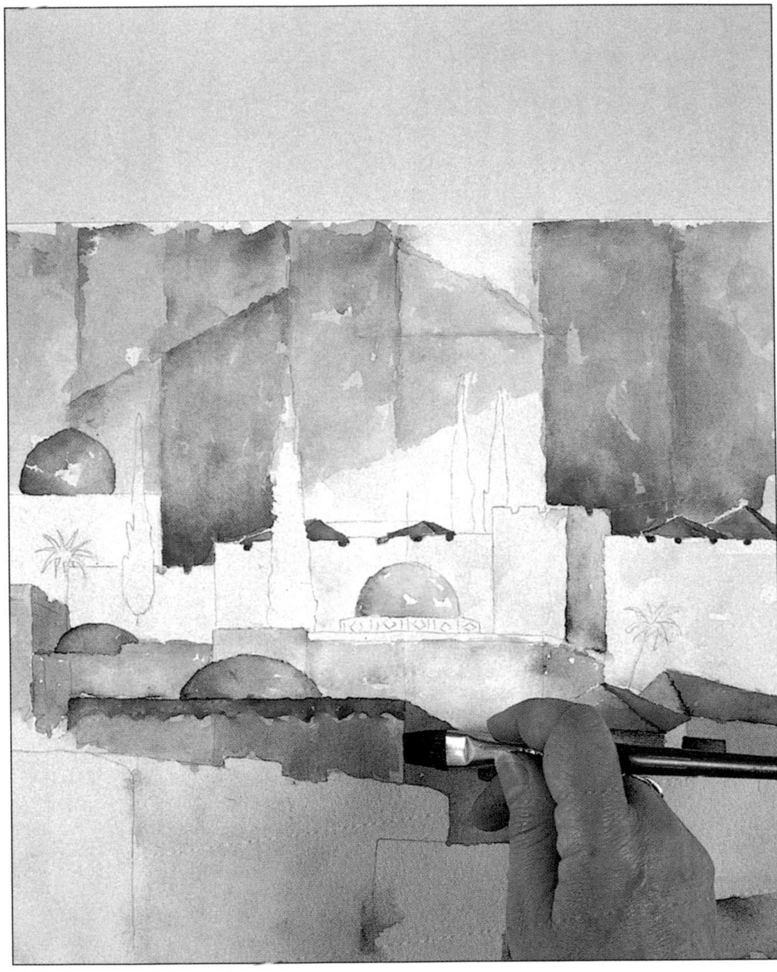

6

Paint the blue walls of the central building with purple, ultramarine and a hint of Payne's grey, strengthen the shadow side with indigo and ultramarine and use the same colour for the decoration along the top of the wall. Paint the other blue walls with similar blues.

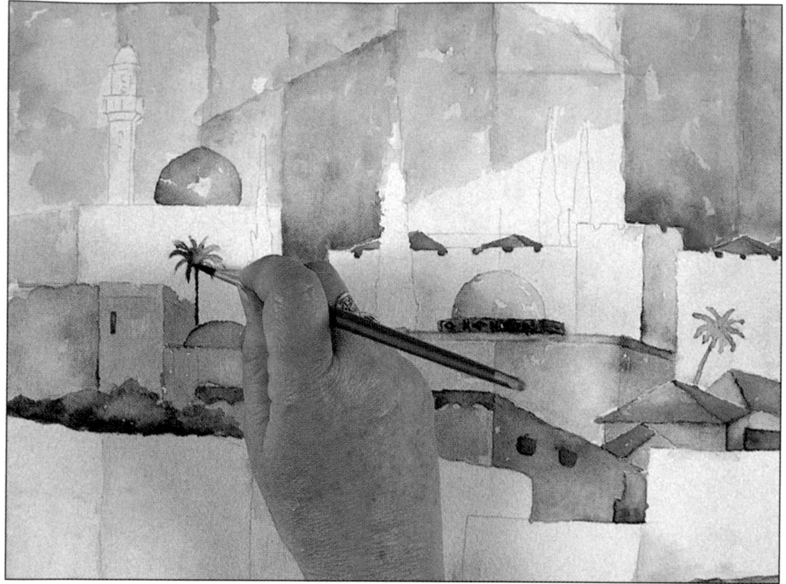

7

Using the small round brush paint the windows in the blue buildings with ultramarine and purple, and the decorative wall beneath the yellow dome with indigo and ultramarine. Paint the foliage on the left with Hooker's green no.2 and raw umber, darkened at the base with warm sepia. Paint the palm trees with a mixture of yellow ochre, Hooker's green no.2, dark green and alizarin crimson.

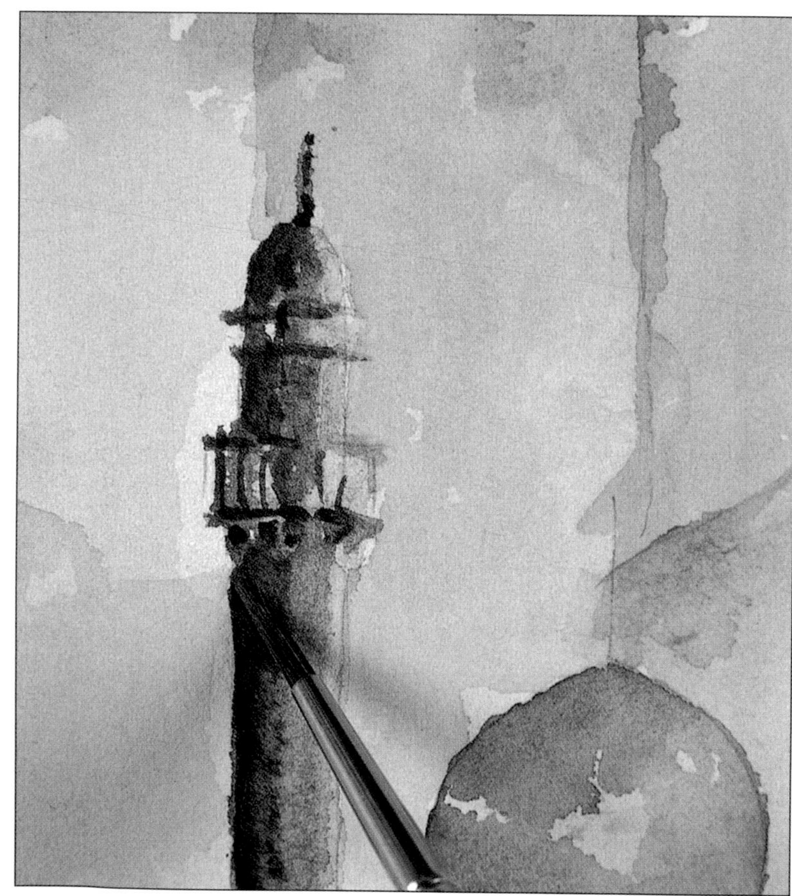

8

Paint the minaret with varied tones of cadmium yellow, raw umber and dark green. Observe here how the tones gradate from dark on the left to light on the right, indicating the rounded form of the tower. Mix a darker tone from raw umber and dark green and use the tip of the brush to lightly draw in the architectural features at the top of the minaret.

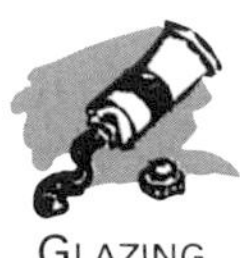

9

Paint the tall cypress trees with Hooker's green no.2 and yellow ochre, glazed over with Hooker's green no.2 and raw umber. For the cypress trees in the distance use dark green and cadmium yellow overlaid with dark green and raw umber. Strengthen the colours in the walls at the base of the picture with glazes of burnt sienna in some sections and ultramarine in others. Use a tissue to lighten any colours which look too strong.

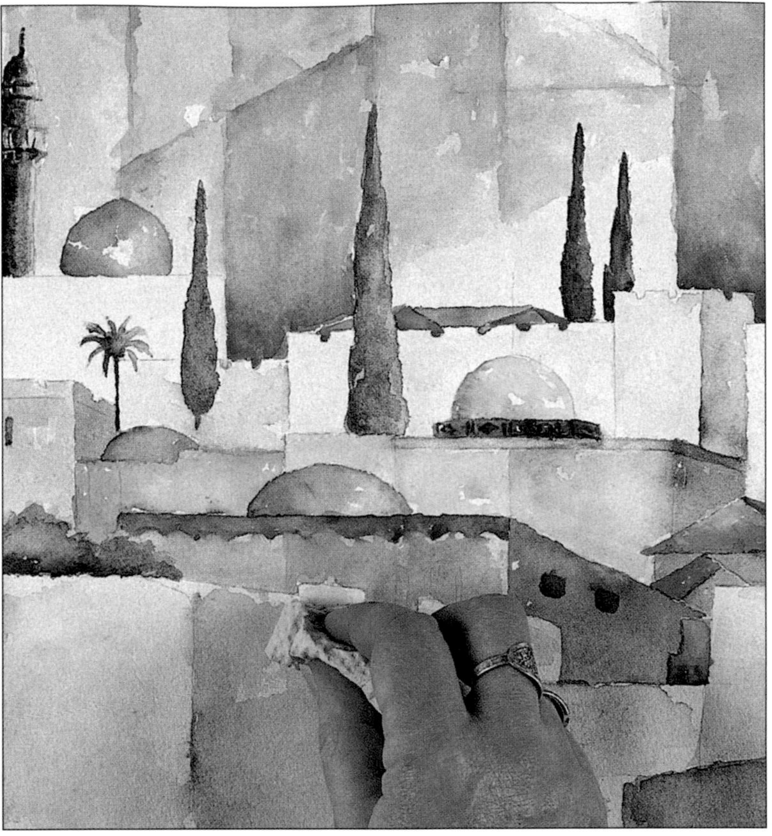

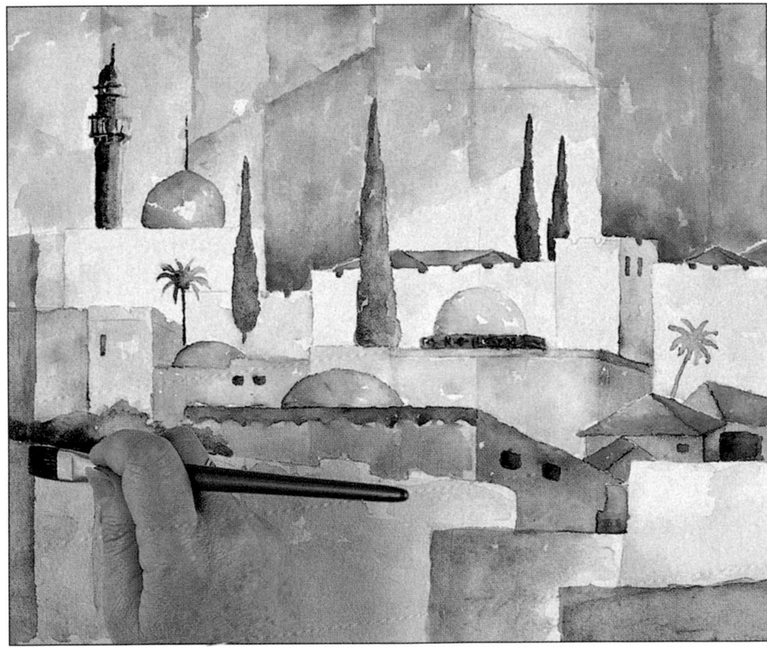

10

Paint the remaining windows with warm sepia and burnt sienna. Finally, mix a thin, transparent wash of indigo and ultramarine and apply broad, vertical strokes on the left and right sides of the painting.

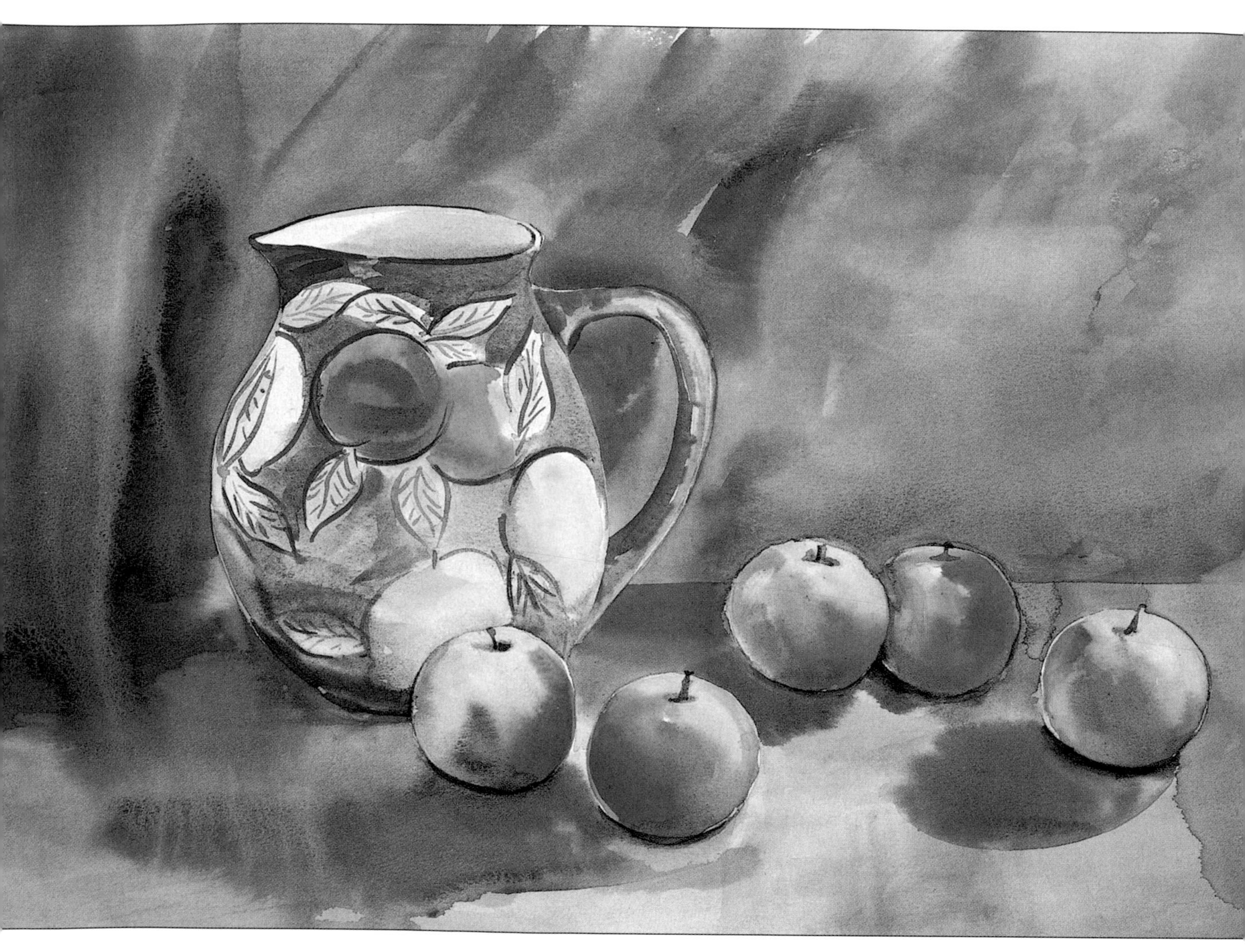

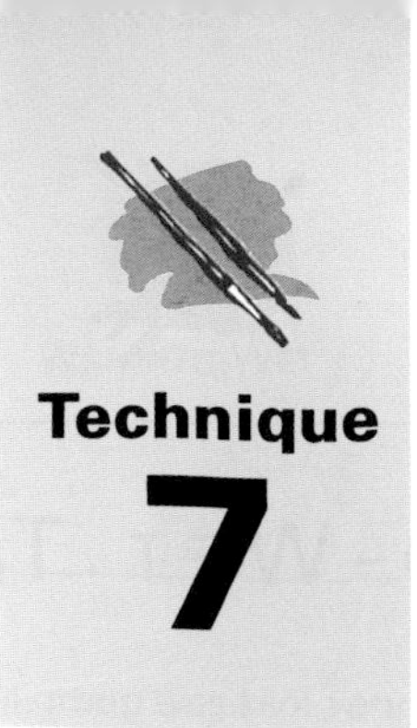

Technique

7

Wet-Into-Wet

This still-life painting is a wonderful example of the interaction of water, paint and paper that is unique to the watercolour medium. The artist worked rapidly and intuitively, flooding the background colours onto wet paper and controlling the direction of the flow by tilting the board in different directions. The apples were painted while the background was still wet so as to create a slightly suffused effect. The result is more of a lyrical impression of the subject than a literal interpretation.

Penelope Anstice
Apples and Jug
38 x 56cm (15 x 22in)

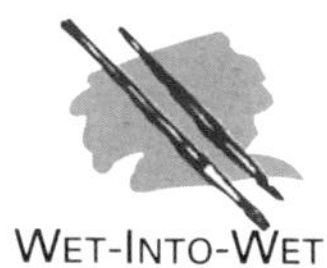

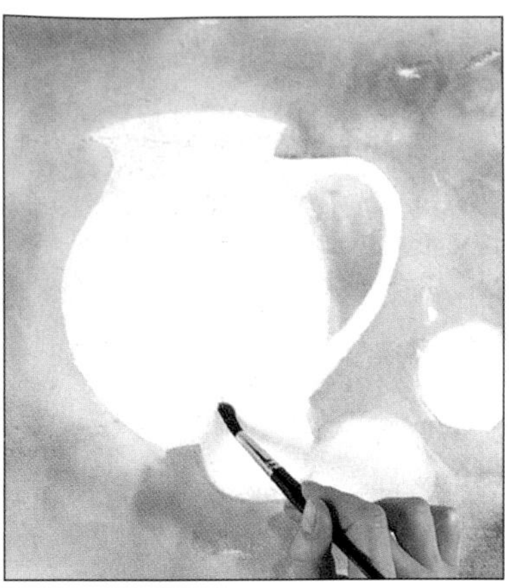

3

While the background is still damp, use a large round brush to paint the apples with a pale wash of cadmium yellow pale and a little Naples yellow.

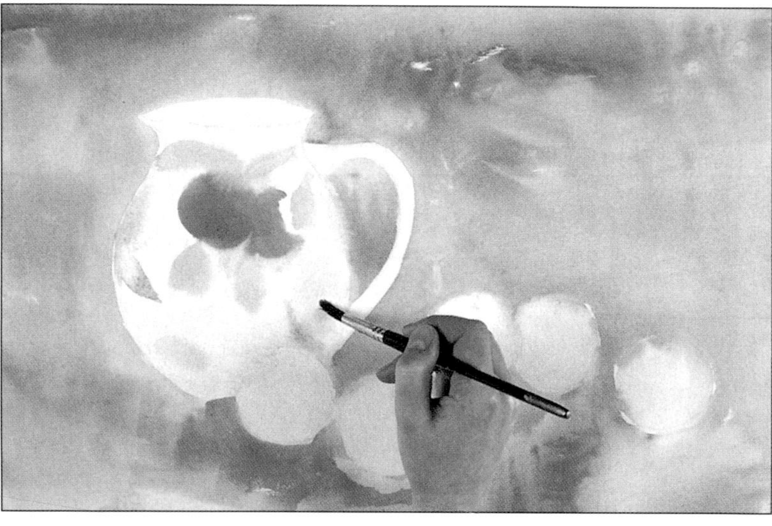

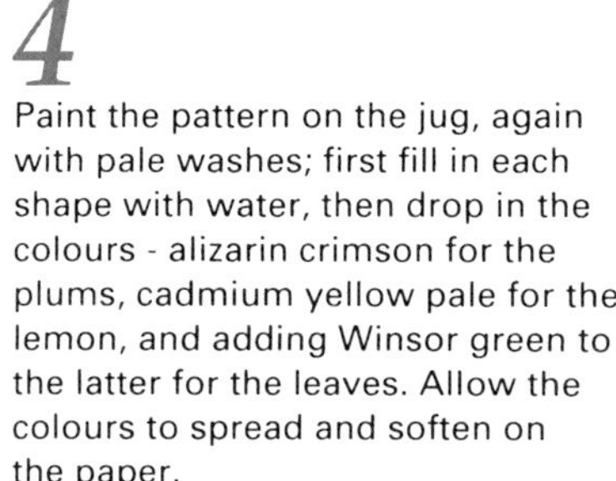

4

Paint the pattern on the jug, again with pale washes; first fill in each shape with water, then drop in the colours - alizarin crimson for the plums, cadmium yellow pale for the lemon, and adding Winsor green to the latter for the leaves. Allow the colours to spread and soften on the paper.

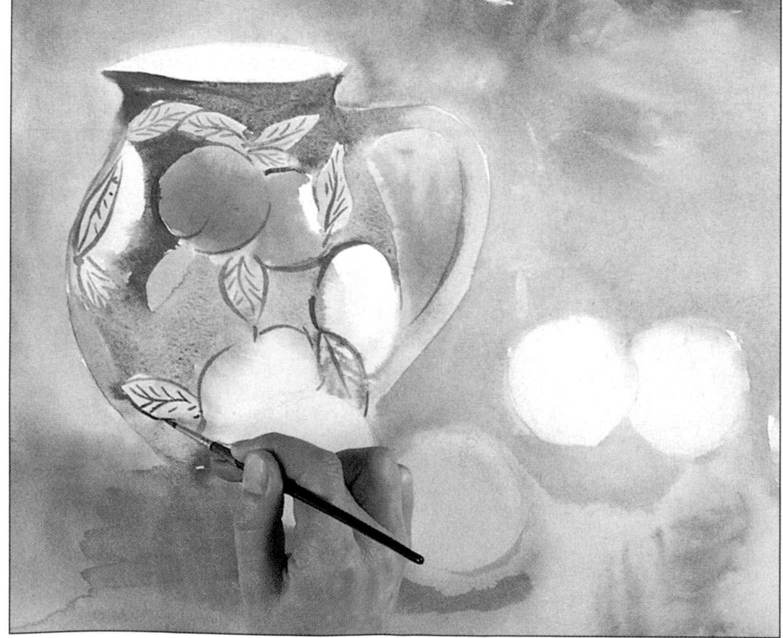

5

Fill in the background colour of the jug with diluted French ultramarine. With a small, well-pointed round brush, paint the outlines of the leaves and fruit with a darker mix of ultramarine.

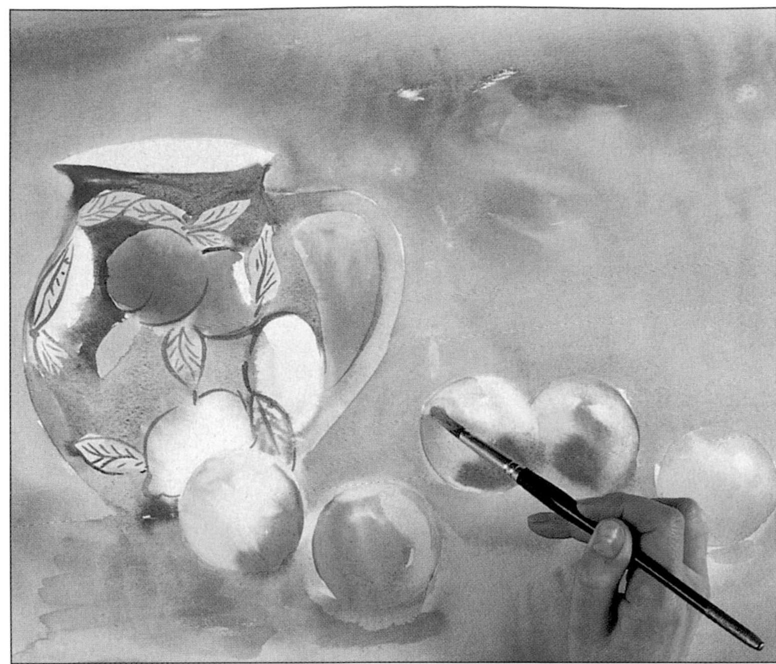

6

Exploit the wet-into-wet method to depict the apples (except for the one on the extreme right) with a variety of reds and greens. For the reds, use various mixtures of alizarin crimson, vermilion and yellow ochre; for the greens, a pale wash of cadmium yellow pale with a touch of Prussian blue. Moisten each apple with clean water, then apply the colours and allow them to fuse slightly. This gradual merging of the two colours creates a natural-looking, rounded contour.

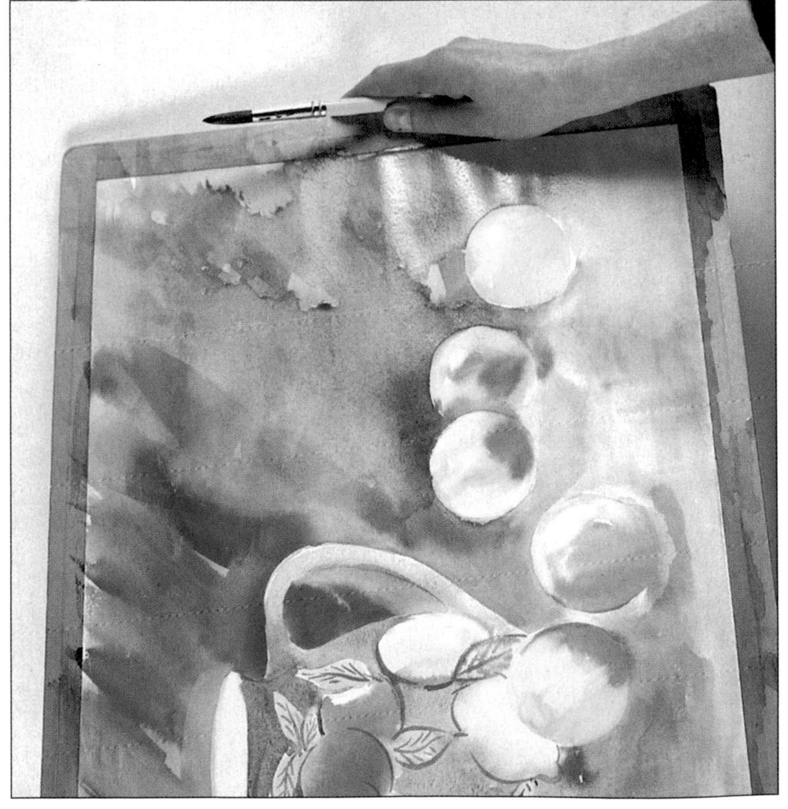

7

Make sure the background wash is completely dry. Mix a large wash of Prussian blue and magenta, this time slightly stronger than the first wash. Re-wet the background with clear water, then apply the paint with broad, loose strokes, leaving patches of the undertone showing through in places. Use a smaller brush to apply colour in the gaps between the apples.

Tilt the board in various directions to encourage the paint to move around and do interesting things; for example, where wet paint flows back into damp paint, it will dry with a hard edge which adds texture and interest to the large expanse of background area. Leave to dry.

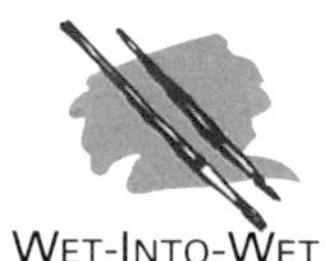

8

Wet the left half of the background and apply a third wash of Prussian blue and magenta, this time much darker than before. Use the same colour to paint the shadows on the table; first wet the shadow shapes, then fill them with paint and allow the paint to bleed softly into the surrounding areas, but use the brush to guide the paint away from the edges of the apples to keep them crisply defined. To anchor the apples to the table, darken the shadows directly beneath them with a touch of Payne's grey.

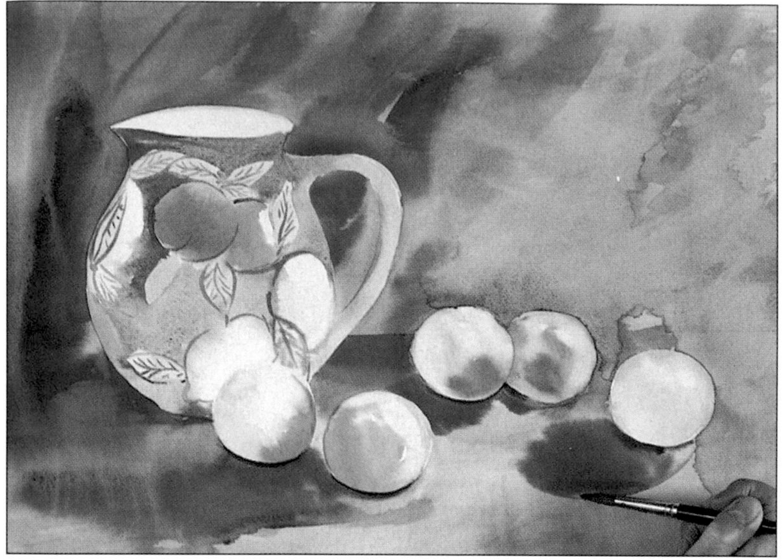

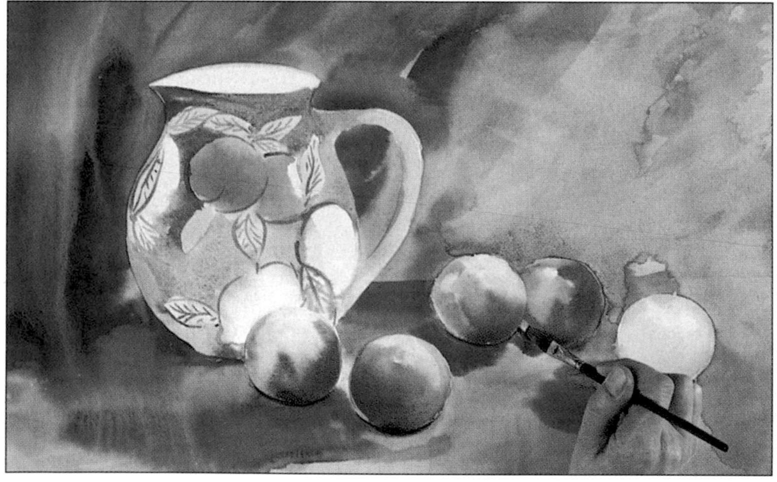

9

Mix yellow ochre and Prussian blue and apply this to the darkest areas of the apples while they are still wet, allowing the colour to merge into the red and green.

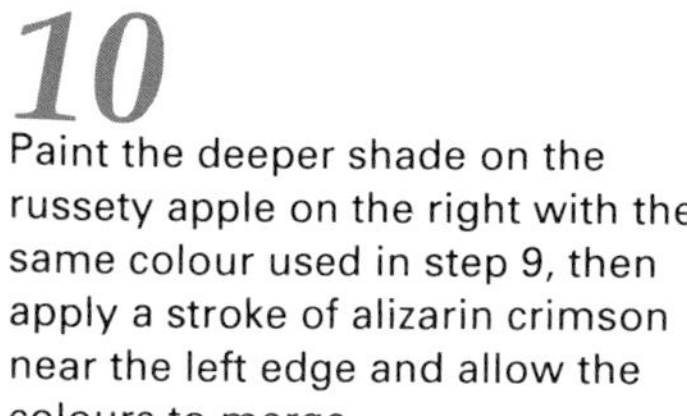

10

Paint the deeper shade on the russety apple on the right with the same colour used in step 9, then apply a stroke of alizarin crimson near the left edge and allow the colours to merge.

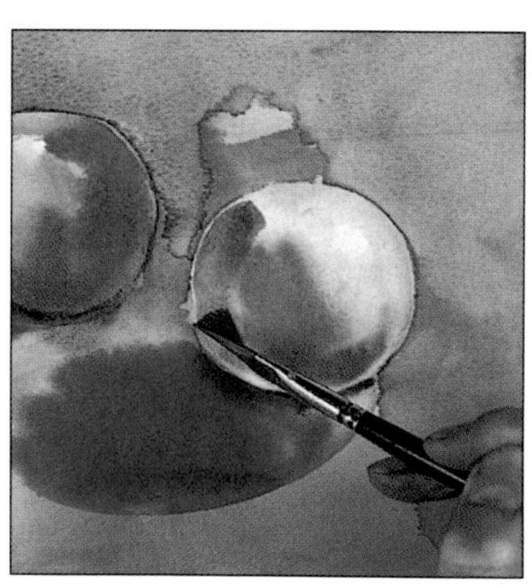

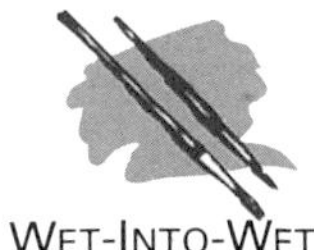

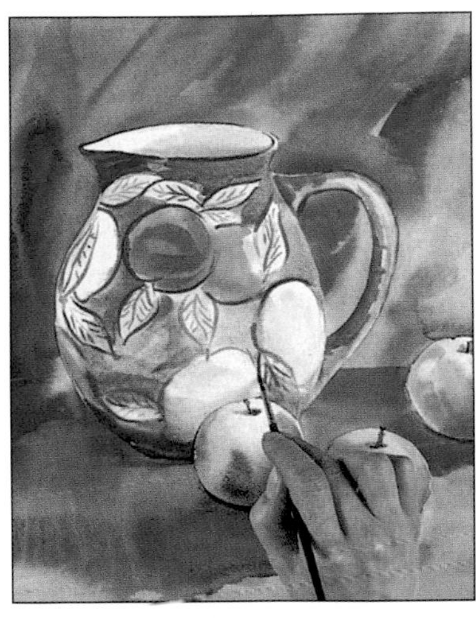

11

Paint the apple stalks with burnt umber and Payne's grey. Paint the darker tones on the jug and its handle with a deeper shade of ultramarine. Wet the shadow shape inside the jug and apply a wash of Naples yellow, darkened with a touch of ultramarine at the base of the shadow. Deepen the colours on the jug's pattern with further washes of the same colours used in step 4. Leave to dry, then use a strong tone of ultramarine and a small round brush to define the rim of the jug and sharpen the linear details on the jug's pattern.

12

Finally, re-wet the right-hand side of the background and, using a large flat brush, apply a loose wash of diluted alizarin crimson and magenta.

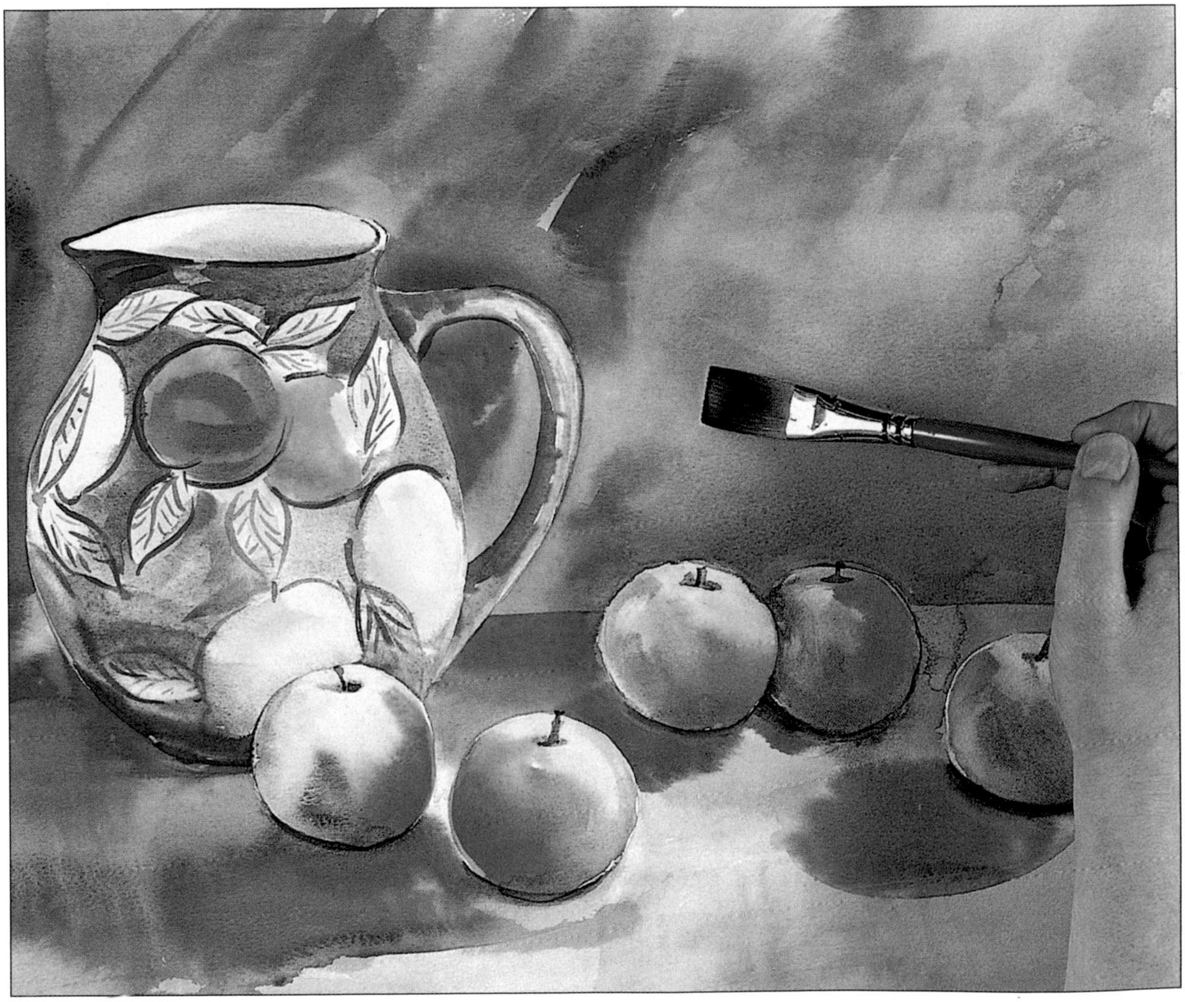

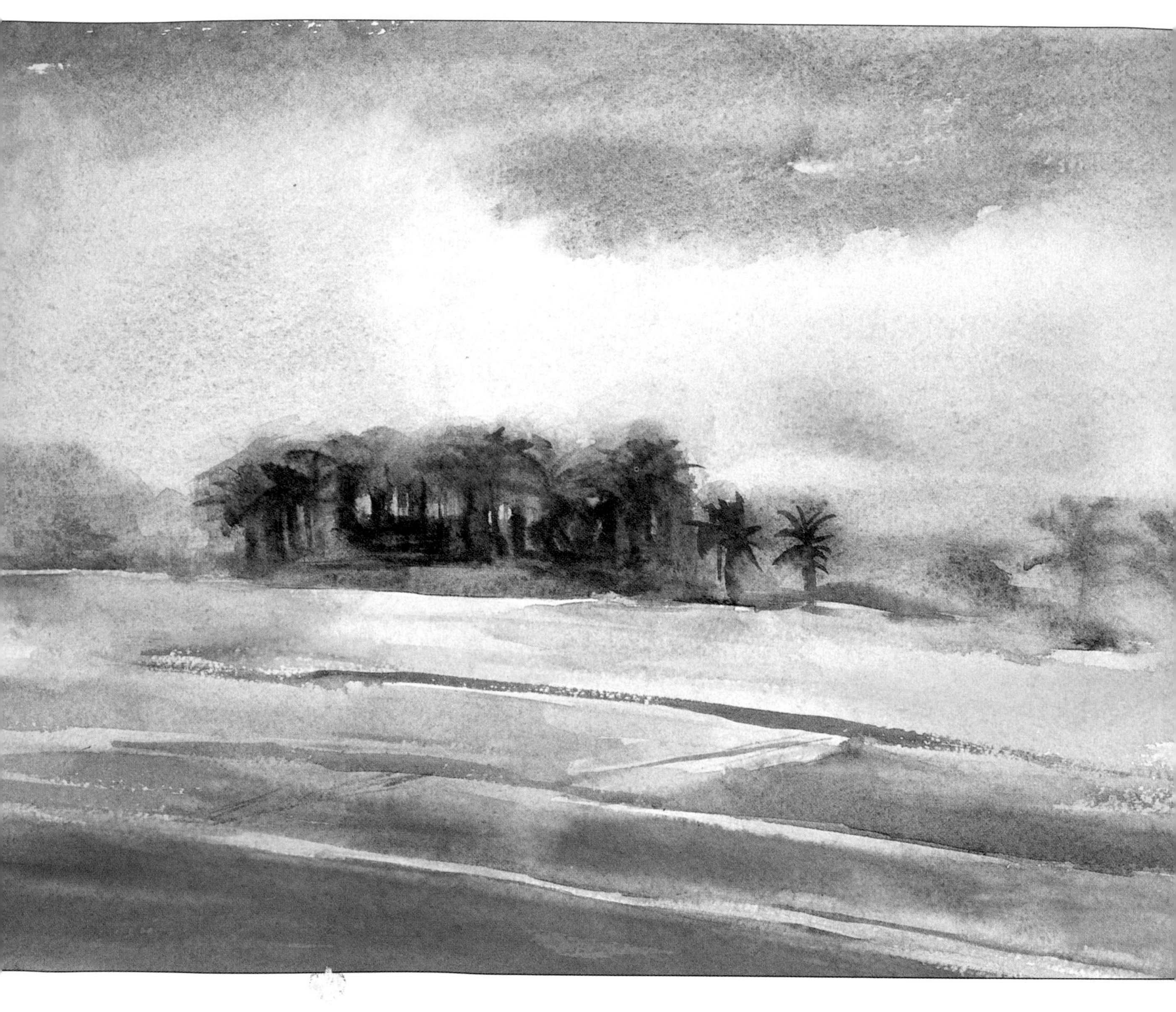

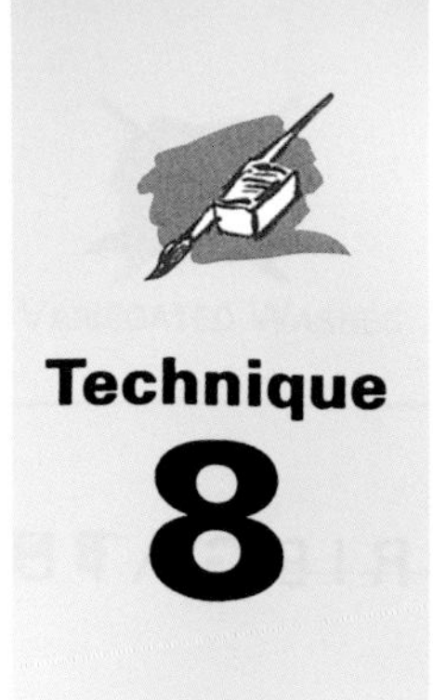
Technique
8

VARIEGATED WASHES

This attractive picture was painted on-the-spot in Goa, India. It relies for its effect on the way each colour blends softly into the next with no hard edges, evoking the steamy atmosphere of a tropical landscape after a monsoon rainstorm. Working on well-dampened paper, the artist applied strokes of variegated colour to the sky and landscape areas and allowed them to spread and diffuse to create the effect of the watery sky and the flooded fields. A heavy stretched paper with a Not (cold-pressed) surface, which would not buckle when heavy washes were applied, was used.

Penelope Anstice
Indian Landscape
28 x 38cm (11 x 15in)

4

Then indicate the marshy fields. Using a medium-sized round brush, sweep a few broad strokes of clean water across the lower half of the picture, leaving tiny slivers of dry paper between the strokes. Mix the following paints on the palette: yellow ochre and Naples yellow; emerald green and cadmium yellow pale; and ultramarine, magenta and Naples yellow. Sweep these three mixes into the wet brush strokes, allowing them to blend and fuse slightly where they meet. Leave to dry completely.

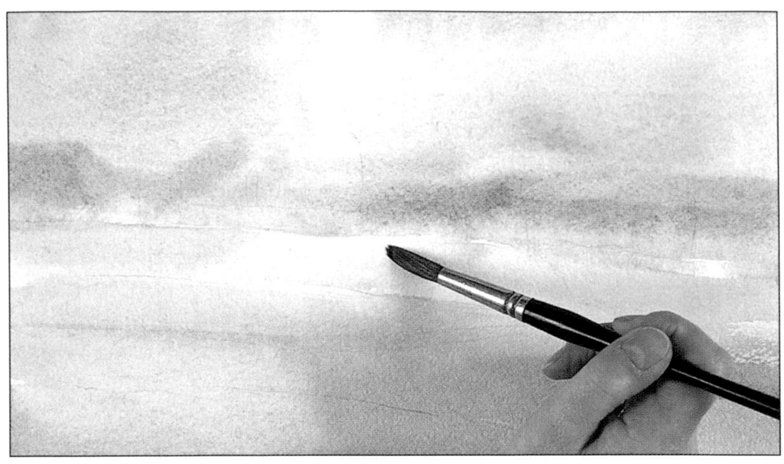

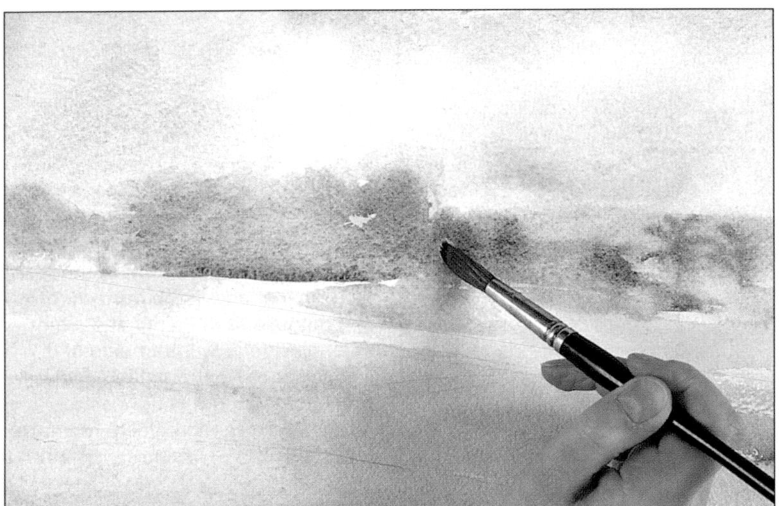

5

Paint the palm trees on the right with a pale tint of magenta and ultramarine. Re-wet the area of the main clump of trees and drop into it a mixture of magenta, ultramarine and yellow ochre. Allow the colours to blend partially.

6

Strengthen the colours in the fields using greys mixed from magenta, ultramarine and Naples yellow, and an earth colour mixed from Indian red and yellow ochre in the immediate foreground. Mix a purplish brown from cerulean, Indian red and yellow ochre and use a small round brush to add a few drybrushed lines (see pages 82–89) to add texture. Observe how the slivers of white paper between the strokes look like pools of water lying on the surface of the fields.

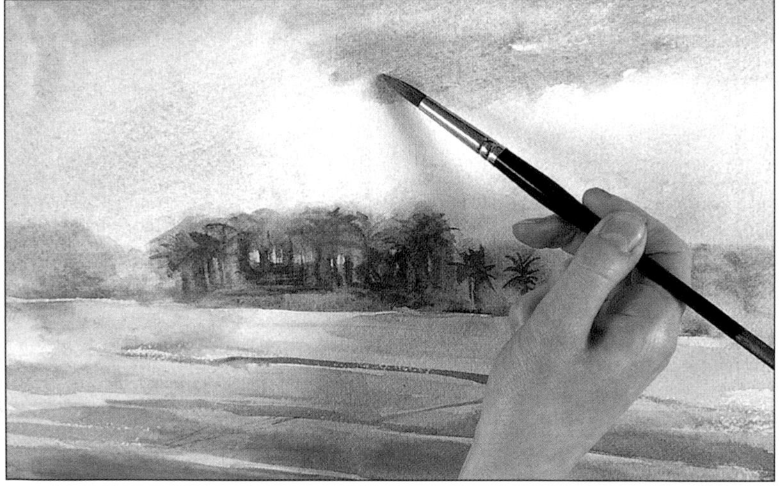

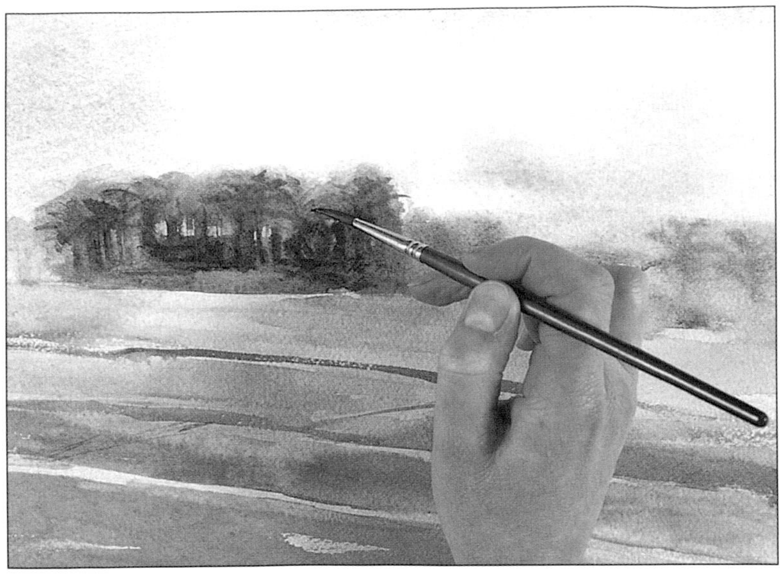

7

Re-wet the main clump of trees and work into it using a small round brush and cerulean, Indian red and yellow ochre. Paint the darker trunks and foliage of the trees with mixtures of viridian, ultramarine and cerulean, but don't overstate them - keep the forms soft and amorphous, otherwise you will lose the impression of mistiness.

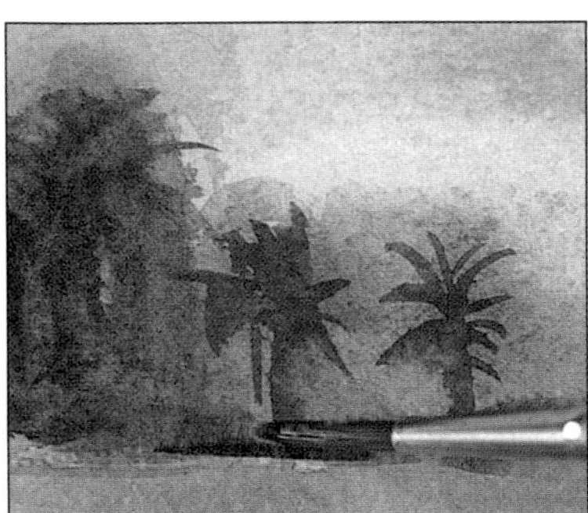

Left: This detail shows how the forms of the trees are softened by lifting out some of the colour using a wet brush.

8

Finally, use a medium-sized round brush and a pale grey mixed from ultramarine and yellow ochre to paint the dark rain cloud near the top of the picture. Leave the painting to dry flat.

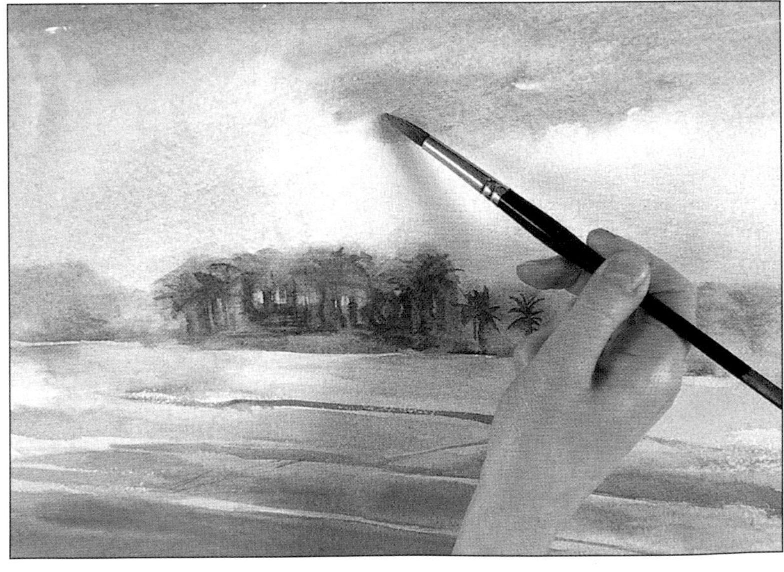

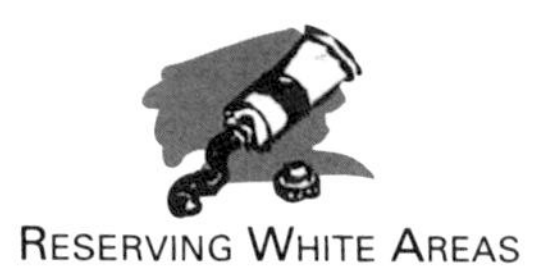

Still Life with Fruit

1

With a soft pencil make a careful outline drawing of the still life, including the pattern on the vase and cloth.

Materials and Equipment

• Sheet of 300gsm (140lb) NOT (cold-pressed) surface watercolour paper, stretched • Soft pencil • Kneaded putty eraser • Watercolour brush: 13mm (1/2in) flat • Watercolour paints: French ultramarine, Payne's grey, indigo, alizarin crimson, Hooker's green no.2, raw umber, new gamboge, burnt sienna, yellow ochre, cadmium red, warm sepia and purple • Soft brush, sponge or tissues

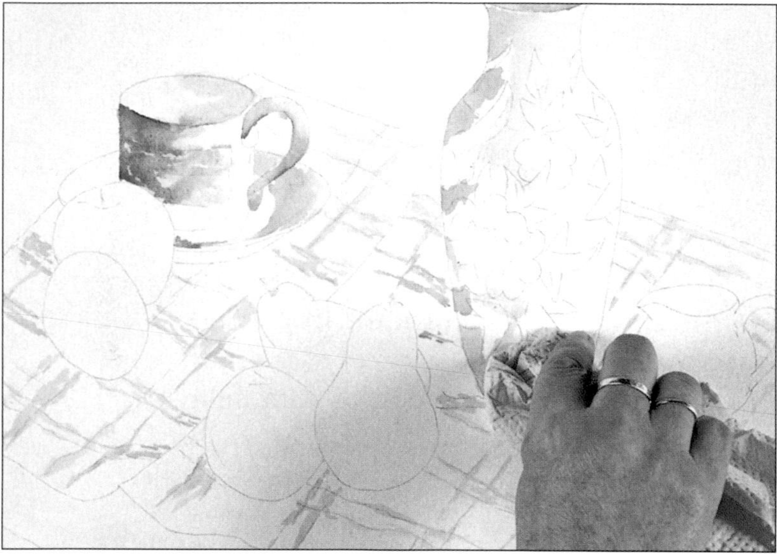

2

Mix a very pale wash of ultramarine and a hint of Payne's grey and begin painting the shadows and the pattern on the cup and saucer. Where the shadows fade out, lift out some of the colour with a clean soft brush, sponge or tissue. Use the same colour for the checked pattern on the tablecloth. Paint the shadows on the vase with indigo and a touch of Payne's grey. Blot the colour with a tissue if it looks too strong.

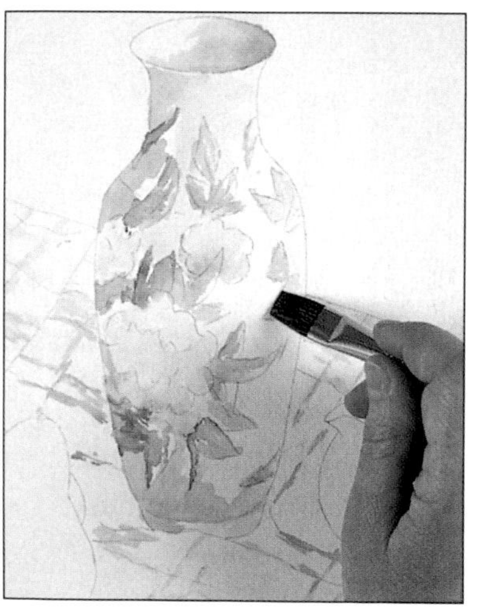

3

Paint the pink flowers on the vase with a pale wash of alizarin crimson. For the dark leaves use Hooker's green no.2, adding a little raw umber to the mix for the lighter greens.

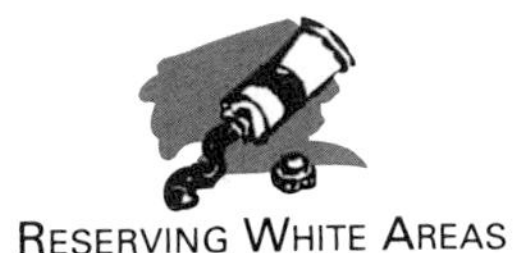

4

Paint the lemon with a pale wash of new gamboge, leaving white highlights on the top surface. Darken the end of the lemon with a hint of burnt sienna. Prepare a slightly darker mix of ultramarine and Payne's grey and deepen some of the shadows on the cup and saucer, taking care to keep the brightest highlights, such as the one inside the cup, clean.

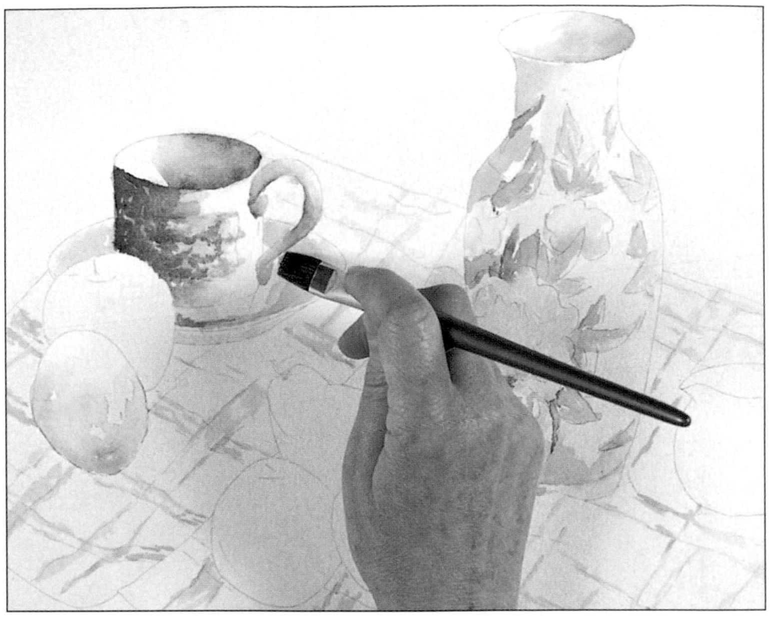

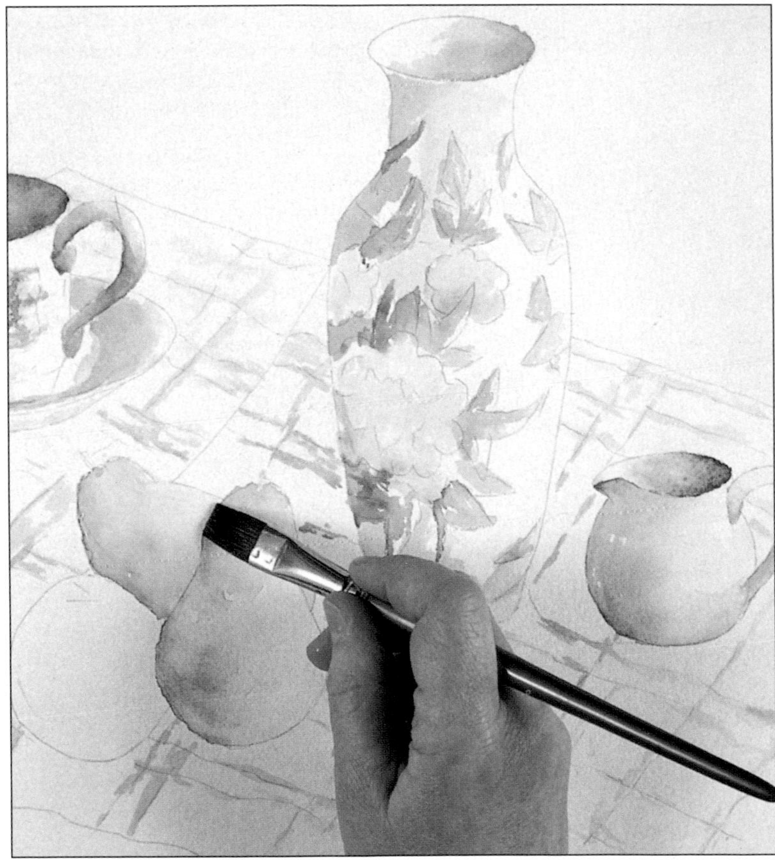

5

Paint the little brown jug on the right with a pale wash of yellow ochre and Payne's grey, darkened with more Payne's grey in the shadow areas. Mix a pale wash of raw umber and paint the pears, working carefully around the sharp highlights. While this wash is still wet, add touches of Hooker's green no.2 in places to vary the tones and suggest the forms of the pears.

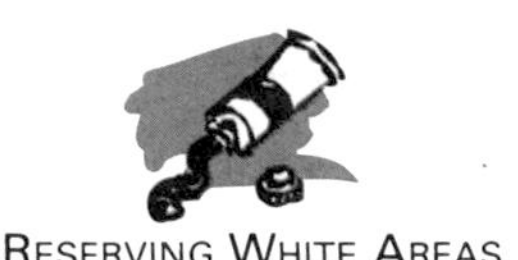

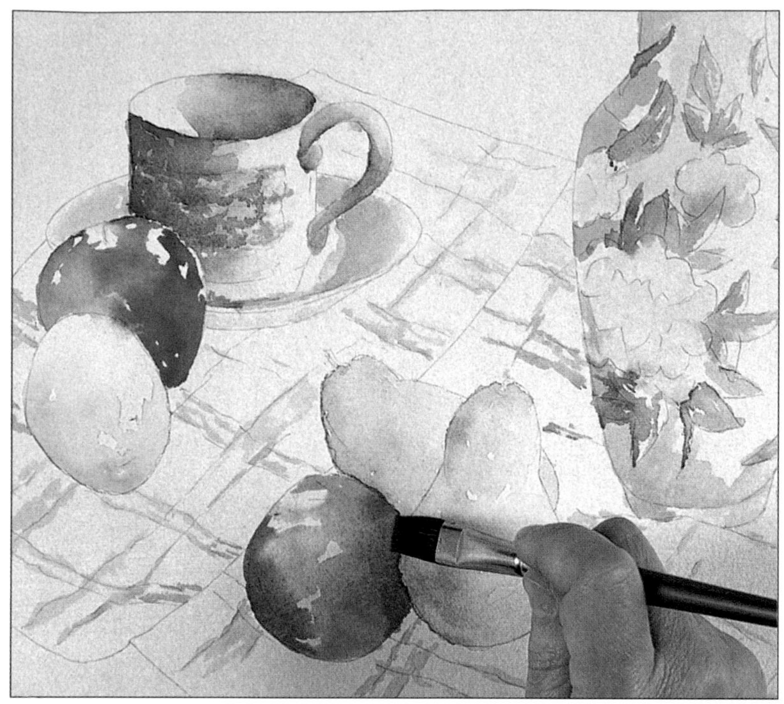

6

When the pears are completely dry, paint the red apples; apply separate strokes of dilute cadmium red and slightly stronger alizarin and allow the two tones to merge where they meet, thus suggesting the rounded forms of the apples. Again, work carefully around the white highlights to keep them clean and sharp.

7

Return to the vase and strengthen the colours in the floral pattern with stronger washes of the same colours used in step 3. Leave to dry. Prepare a wash of indigo, ultramarine and Payne's grey, diluted to a medium tone, and strengthen the shadows on the vase; start at the edge and drag the colour into the body of the vase so that it becomes gradually lighter, suggesting its rounded form.

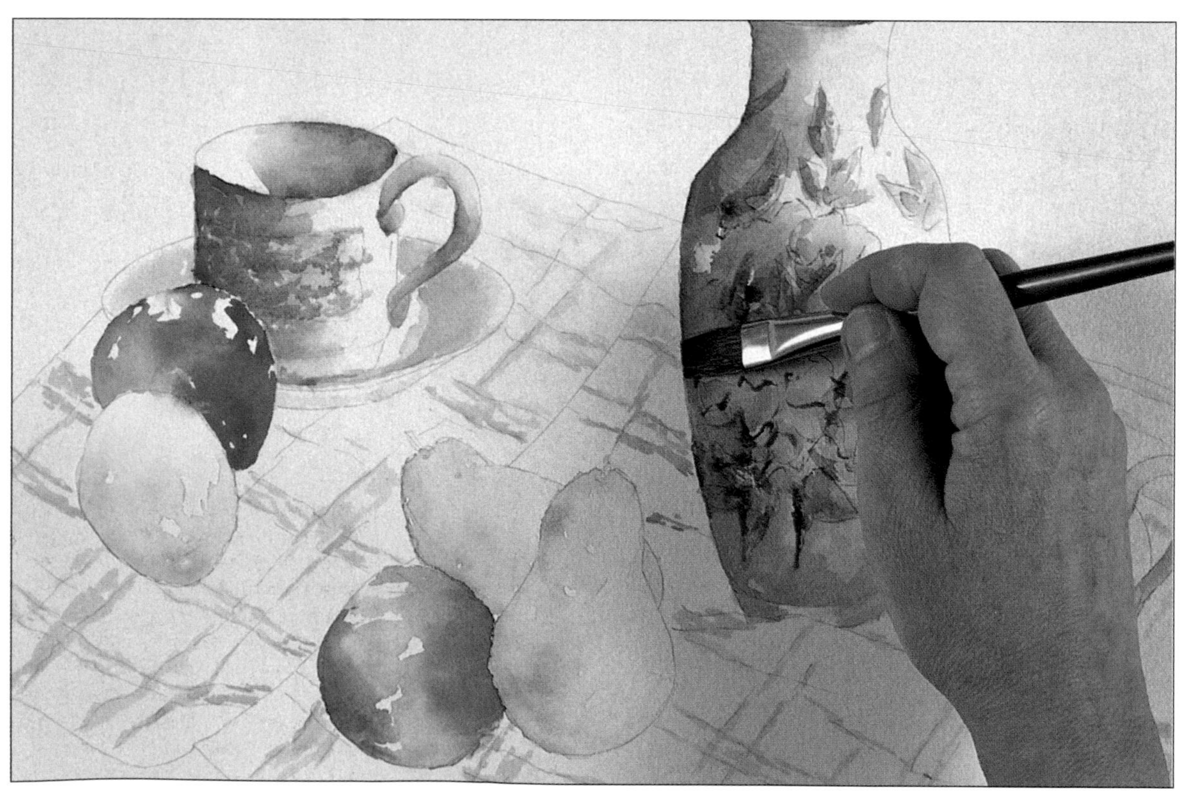

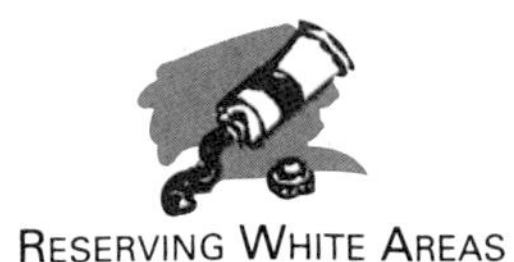

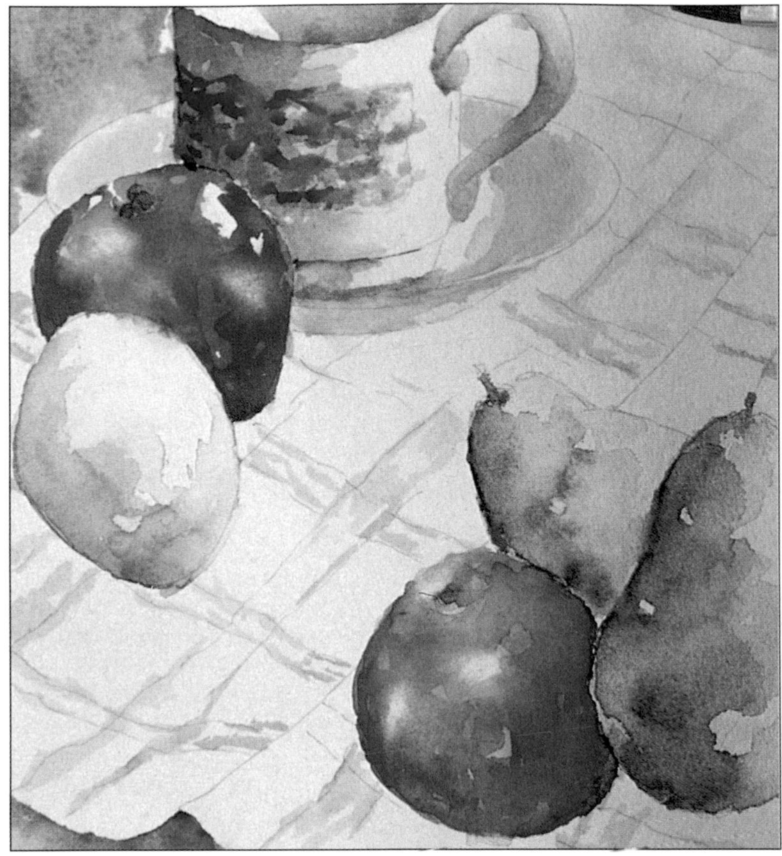

8

Apply further layers of colour to the fruits to build up their forms, allowing each wash to dry before adding the next. Mix burnt sienna and new gamboge for the shadow side of the lemon, adding a hint of Payne's grey for the darkest part. For the apples, apply stronger washes of cadmium red and alizarin; just before the colour dries, lift out one or two soft highlights with a tissue. Strengthen the darks in the pears with washes of Hooker's green no.2, raw umber and ultramarine.

In this close-up detail you can see how the glazes of colour, applied wet-on-dry, suggest the form and volume of the fruits.

9

Strengthen the shadows on the brown jug with washes of warm sepia and Payne's grey. Wash in the background with broad, wet washes carrying alizarin crimson, purple and ultramarine to the right, changing to purple, ultramarine and Payne's grey as you move across to the left. Apply the colours loosely, wet-into-wet (see pages 68-75), and leave tiny speckles of white paper to lend sparkle to the background.

Paint the stalks on the pears with a brown mixed from Hooker's green no.2 and raw umber. Finally, paint the cast shadows on the cloth with a transparent wash of ultramarine, purple and a hint of Payne's grey.

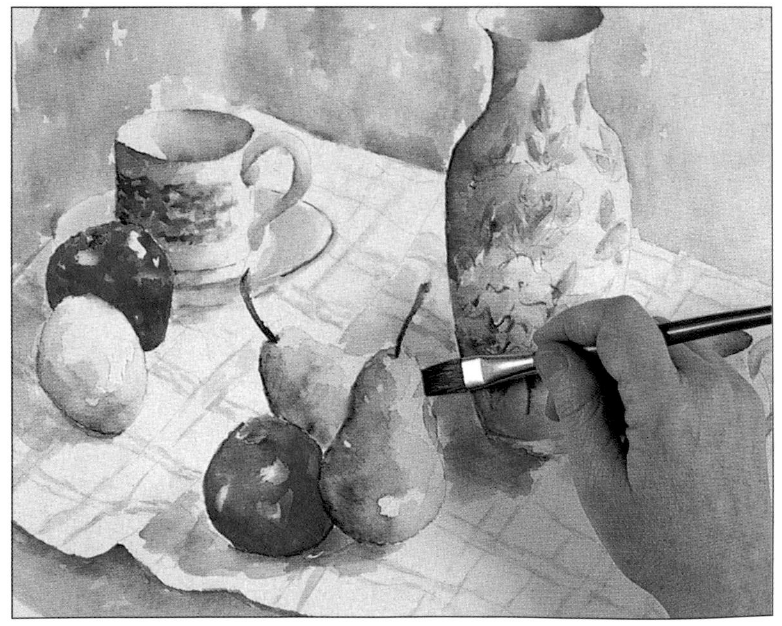

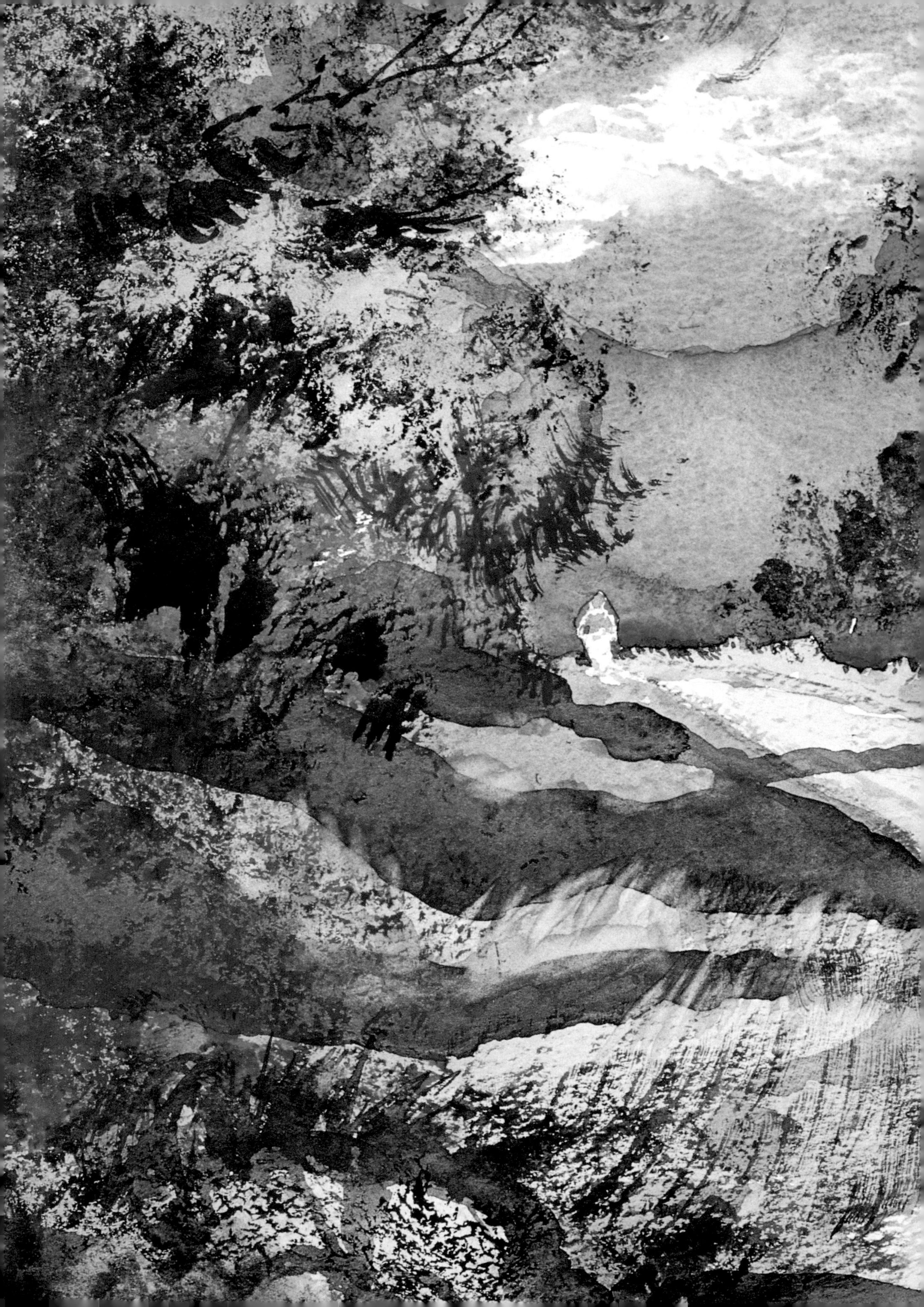

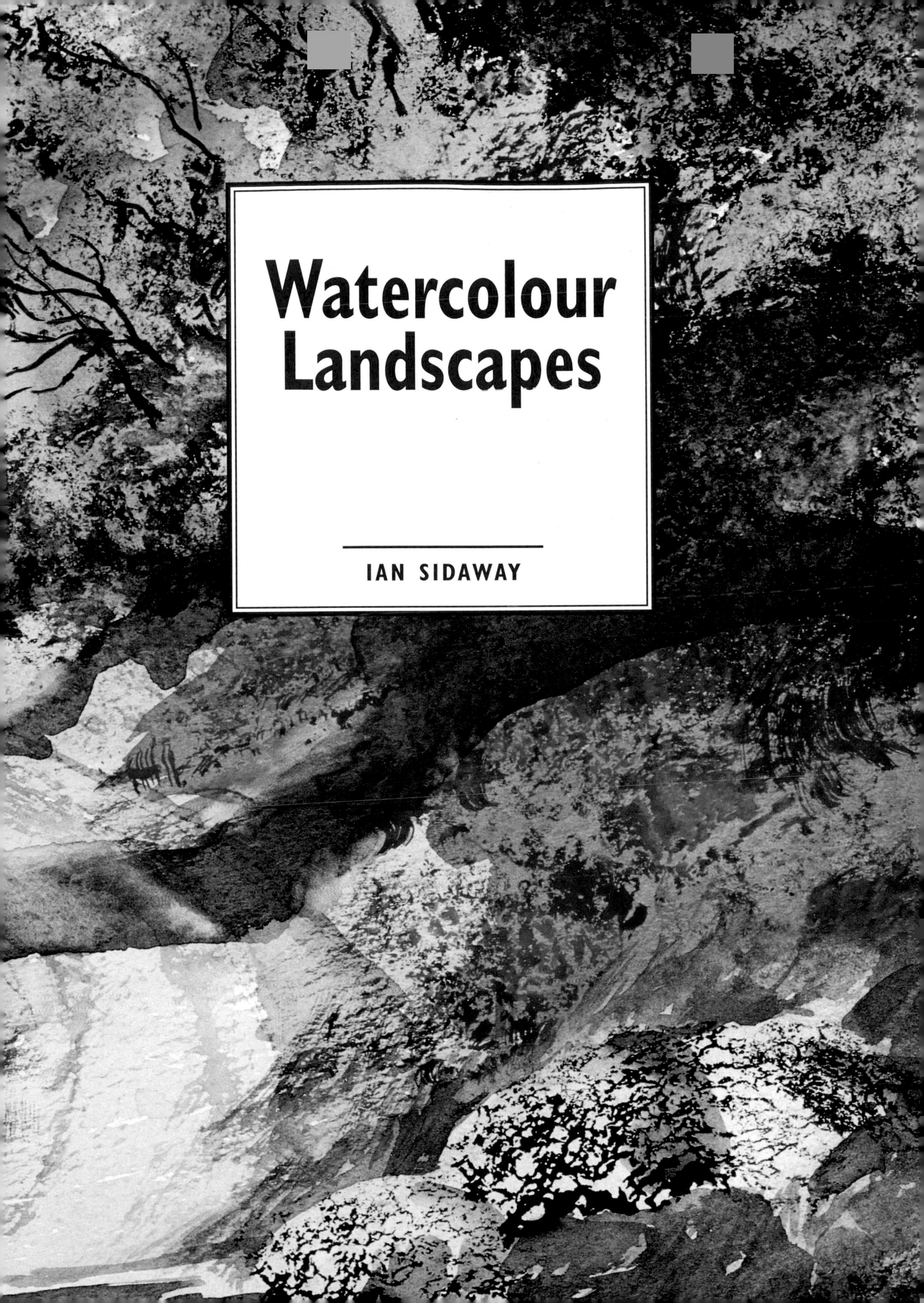

Watercolour Landscapes

IAN SIDAWAY

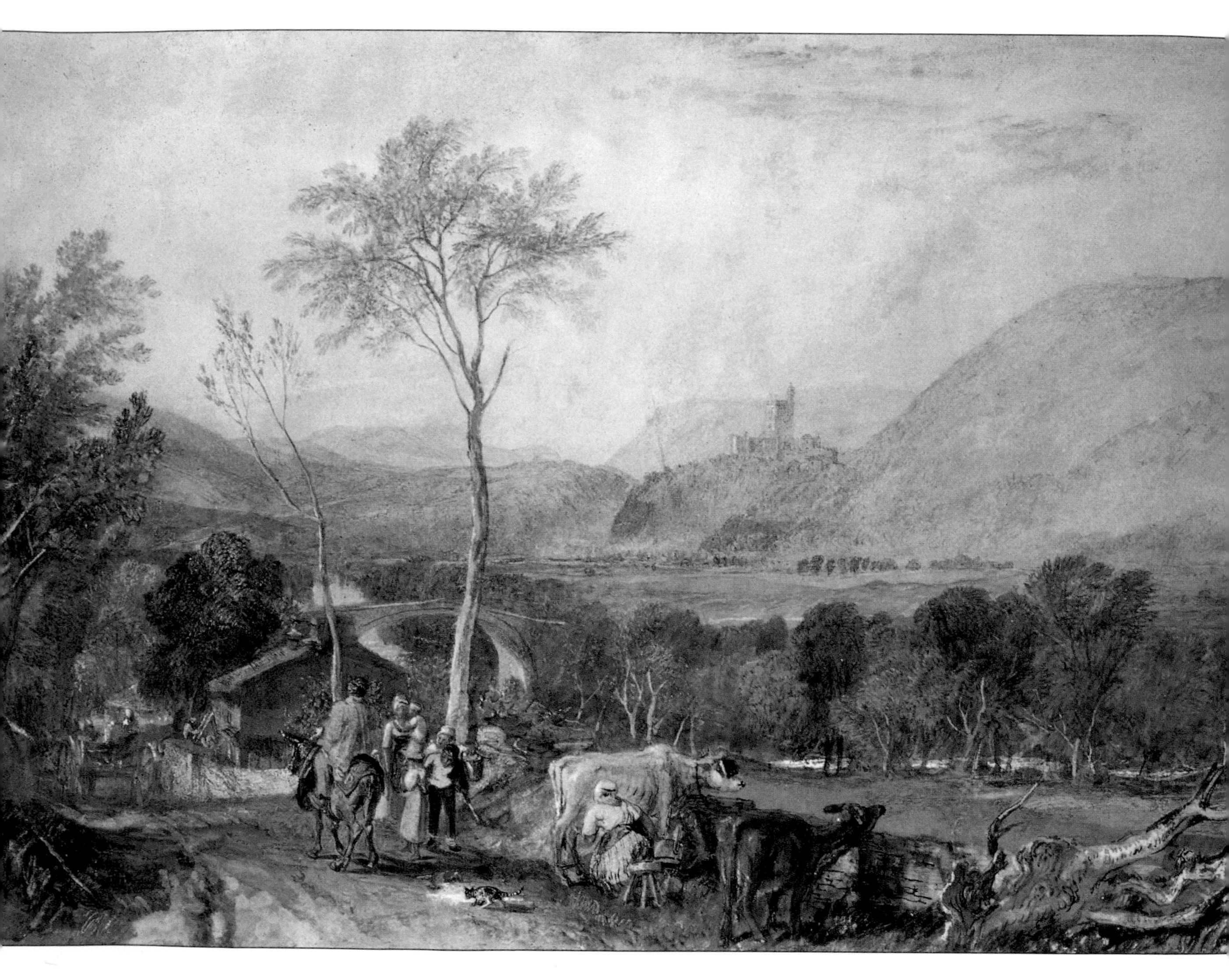

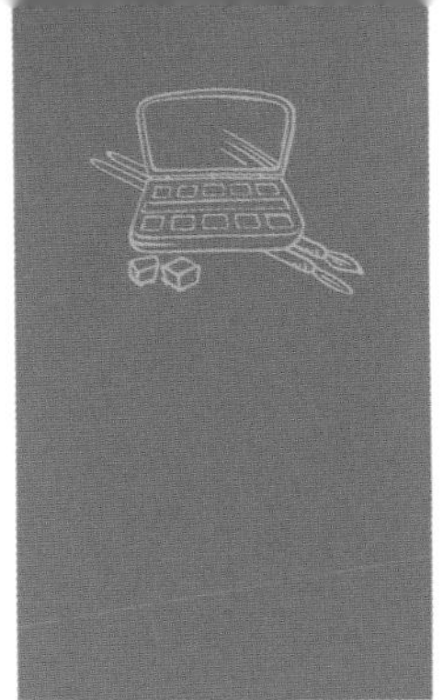

INTRODUCTION

It was in China that the art of painting with brush and watercolour or dilute ink first reached a form that could be described as a fine art. Chinese painting is linked closely with that country's calligraphy; the same materials are used in both, as are many of the brush techniques and visual considerations. Created on silk or paper – both of which were invented in China – many calligraphy works were made as scrolls that were opened and "read" from right to left, a form that perfectly suited landscape subjects.

In Europe the beginnings of the watercolour tradition are more difficult to pin down. Watercolour, or more correctly gouache or body colour, was used to illuminate religious texts and manuscripts. The beginnings of its use in the artist's studio and as a material for painting on a larger scale are not so easily traced. However, it is thought to have first been used by apprentice artists who trained by making tonal drawings using a brush and a mixture of water and a single brown pigment that was made from beech wood soot, known as *bistre.*

Hornby castle
Joseph Mallord William Turner 1775–1851

Turner saw watercolour enter its "Golden Age", as can be seen in this beautifully composed landscape using classic light to dark technique.

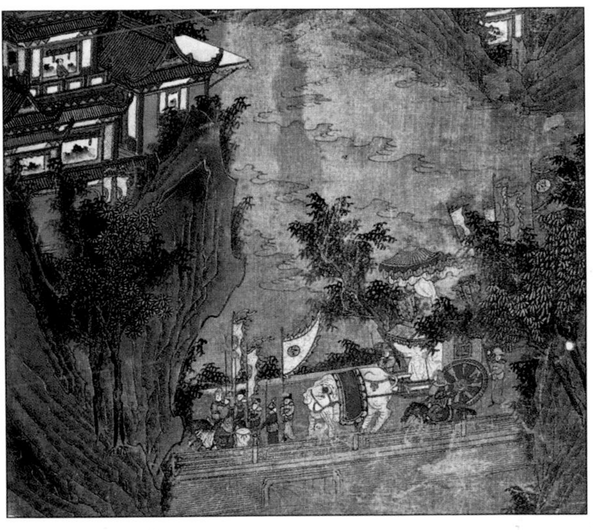

Landscape (detail)
Li Sixun 651–716

This Chinese work on silk already shows a grasp of techniques such as working light to dark.

During the 17th century artists began to make more use of the technique and added sepia, a reddish brown pigment made from the inky secretions of cuttle-fish, to the palette. Full-colour paintings using water-based materials were rare before the 18th

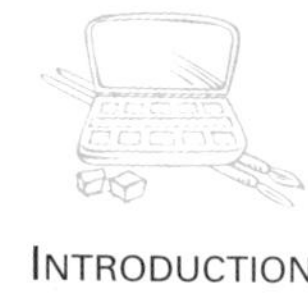

century, although the characteristic fluidity of watercolour lends itself perfectly to landscape and the natural world, something that German artist Albrecht Dürer (1471–1528) had recognised some 300 years earlier.

During the 17th century wash drawings began to be made as finished works, rather than as studies for oil paintings. In Antwerp Peter Paul Rubens (1577–1640) executed a number of watercolour landscapes, as did the Dutch painter Anthony Van Dyck (1599–1641). It was Van Dyck who began the tradition of working on location (*"en plien-aire"*).

An English Landscape
Anthony Van Dyck 1599–1641

With his economic brushwork, Van Dyck manages to give this coastal scene a freshness that a more studied approach would miss.

With many European artists in the 17th and 18th centuries visiting England, and many English patrons collecting foreign artists' works, it was small wonder that watercolour landscape painting became so popular in England. By 1855 a French critic reviewing an exhibition of English watercolour paintings in Paris wrote: "Watercolour is, for the English, a national art".

Paul Sandby (1725–1809), who worked in the military drawing office at the tower of London, was seen as the "father of English watercolour". A founding member of the Royal Academy in London, Sandby worked exclusively in England, Wales and Scotland. His work had great flair, poetry and sense of place. He was not afraid to experiment, using watercolour both as thin transparent washes and as body colour. His exhibitions in London influenced many younger artists

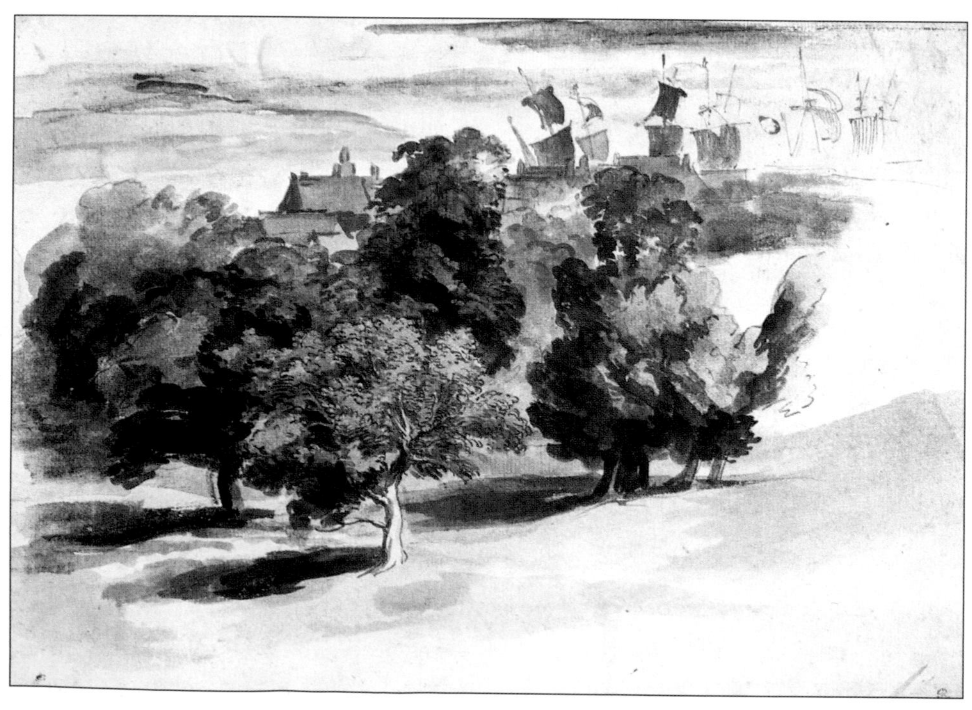

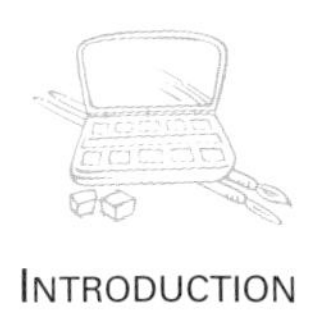

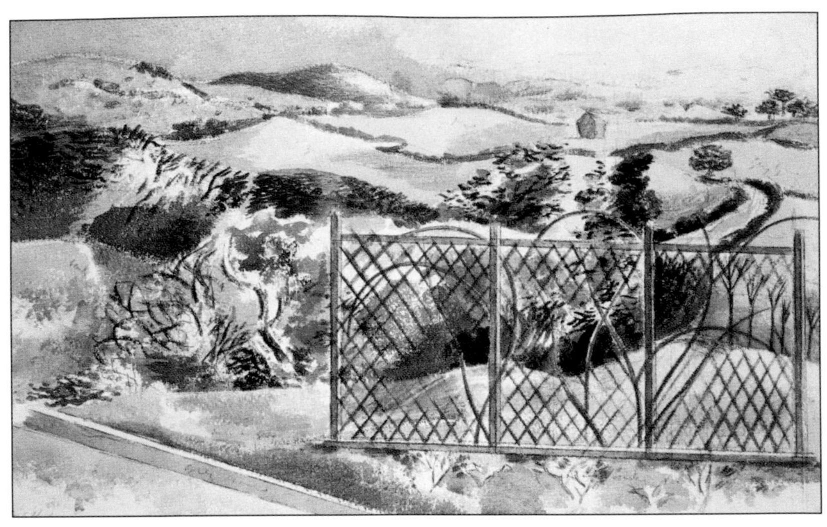

and moved no less an artist than Thomas Gainsborough (1727–1788) to describe him as a genius. Sandby was closely followed by Thomas Girtin (1775–1802) and William Turner (1775–1851). While Girtin died at 27, Turner saw English watercolour landscape painting enter into the 19th century and what was to be called its "Golden Age".

The 1820–30s saw a romantic and mystic view of the landscape emerge in the work of artists such as William Blake (1757–1827) and Samuel Palmer (1805–1881). Two expatriate Americans working in England, James Abbott McNeill Whistler (1834–1903) and John Singer Sargent (1856–1925) pushed the watercolour technique forward in the late 19th century. Across the Atlantic the torch bearer was Winslow Homer (1836–1910). His landscapes of Nassau, in the Bahamas, and Maine are powerful works.

In the early 20th century watercolour found a new set of devotees. These included Englishman Paul Nash (1889–1946), a master interpreter of the rhythm of landscape.

Icknield Way
Paul Nash 1889–1946

Painted in 1935, this work shows Nash's skill at capturing the essence of a landscape, using a limited palette to create a sense of harmony.

The architect Charles Rennie Mackintosh (1868–1928) produced watercolours that are masterpieces of design and contain echoes of art nouveau. While Sir William Russell Flint (1880–1969), showed breathtaking technical ability in his exquisite landscapes.

The last half of the 20th century up to the present day has seen a huge diversity of watercolour work, from the claustrophobic world depicted by American Andrew Wyeth (1917–) to the moody seascapes of the contemporary English artist Len Tabner, and the restful coastal reflections of his compatriot Robert Tilling. The range of vision underlines the versatility of the material, capable as it is of capturing intimate detail and also the grandeur of an intriguing subject.

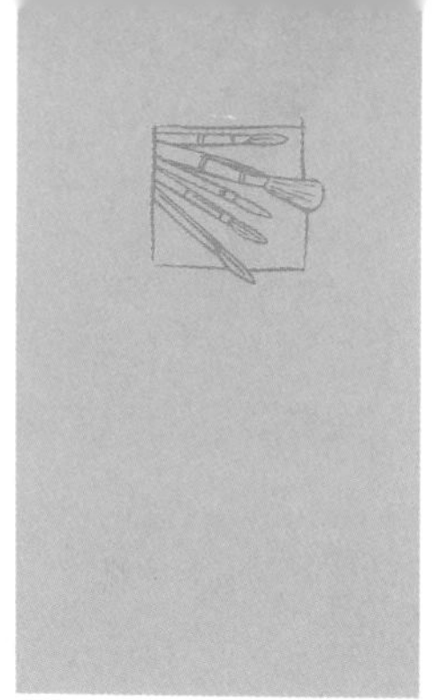

Materials and Equipment

Preparation is the key to creating successful watercolours, and choosing good quality materials and equipment is essential. Start off with a few well-chosen basics, and then experiment with different brushes, colours and papers.

Paper

There are hundreds of watercolour papers from which to choose. Some are easier to work on than others, and each has distinct qualities. By learning a little about their characteristics, you will be able to make an informed choice.

Watercolour paper is either handmade or machine-made. Handmade is more expensive than machine-made, but it is a wonderful surface on which to work. Machine-made paper is made using the same processes, but the sheets are formed on a machine. Though cheaper, it is still good to use and can be the better choice for the beginner.

Watercolour paper is woven: a sheet is formed by coating the mesh surface of a mould with pulp. As the pulp fibres dry, they interlock, giving the sheet its strength. The sheet is then processed to give one of three different surfaces.

Rough Rough paper is made by allowing the felts, dampened cloths placed between the wet sheets as they dry, to leave an imprint on the paper surface. The sheets are not pressed, so the paper texture remains rough. With practice, rough papers can be a good choice for watercolour landscape. Washes can be made to lie flat with consistent strength of colour; it is also possible to create a number of textural effects that give the work vibrancy.

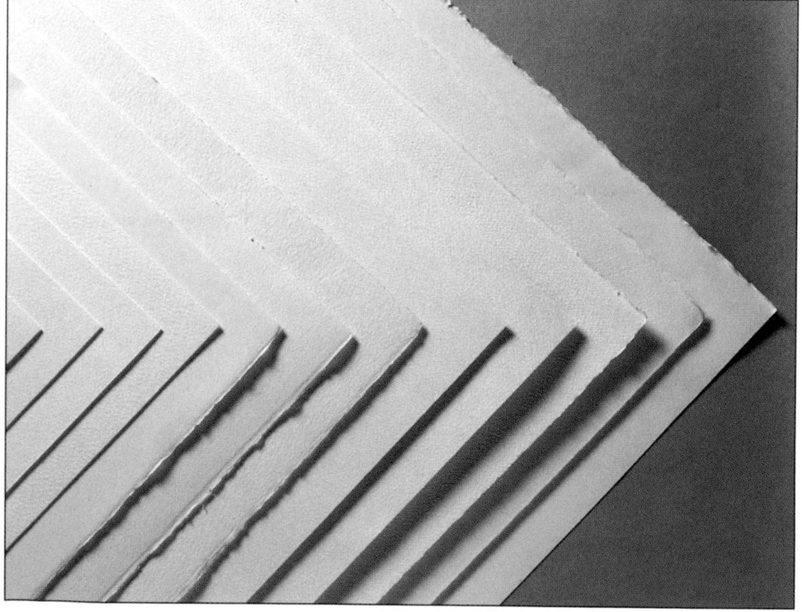

There is an almost dizzying array of papers available. However, once the basic properties of the various types are known, it becomes simple to select the right paper for the job.

Hot Pressed Formed in the same way as rough paper, but laid onto smoother felts, this paper is then pressed between polished steel rollers or plates to remove any surface texture. It is good for drawing and detailed work, but makes washes difficult to control and the finished work may lack depth.

Cold Pressed Cold pressed paper is also known as NOT – for "Not Hot Pressed". The paper receives a moderate pressing but retains a slight texture. Cold pressed paper is the easiest to use; it is smooth enough for detailed work, and has enough texture to allow for lively brush work and textural effects. Colour sits well on the surface and flat washes are easily achieved: this type of paper is the best choice for beginners.

Absorbency Paper is "sized" during manufacture, and the amount and type of "sizing" affects its absorbency. Paper can be internally sized, surface-sized, or both. Internally sized paper allows paint to sink into the fibres. This results in good depth of colour, flat washes are possible, but corrections are difficult. Surface-sized paper absorbs less paint so it is easier to make corrections but flat washes are difficult. Colours may be bright, but lack depth.

Size and Weight Papers are available in a range of sizes. The standard size is 560x760mm (22x30in). Certain brands are available in rolls and large sheets up to 1220x1520mm (48x60in). A paper's weight indicates its thickness, and is described in two ways.

The first is in pounds (lbs) and refers to the weight of a ream (500 sheets of paper). The second is in grams (gsm) and refers to the weight in grams of one square metre of a single sheet. Watercolour paper ranges from around 90lb/200gsm to 400lb/850gsm.

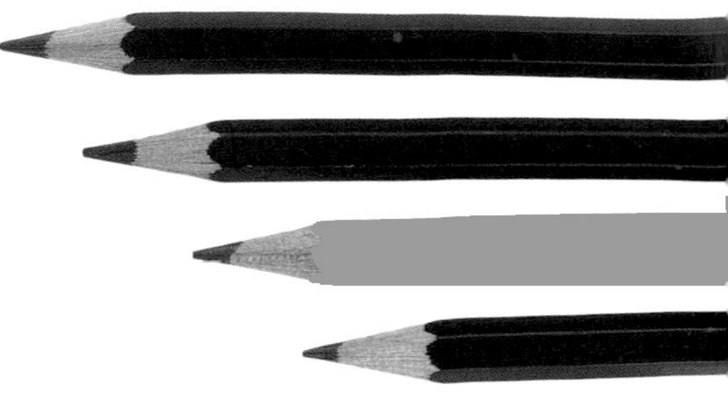

A selection of pencils, varying in hardness. Some artists like their initial sketch to show through in the finished work.

WATERCOLOUR PAINT

Paint is available in semi-moist pans, half pans, tubes and bottles. Bottled colours are strong and vivid, but often fade when subjected to sunlight. Pan colours are easy to use, and enable the artist to mix only a little paint at a time. This allows control of the mixes and is economical. It is easy to use too much tube colour but if a large amount of a wash is needed to cover a large area, tube colour is the better choice.

Choosing a palette of colours to use is a personal choice. However, most artists will use a limited palette from which they can mix a complete range of colours. The limited palette colours are: cadmium red; alizarin crimson; lemon yellow; yellow ochre; cadmium yellow; cobalt blue; cerulean blue; ultramarine blue; burnt umber; raw umber; viridian; oxide of chromium; sap green and Paynes grey.

As artists gain in skill, they tend to use fewer colours. You can produce a complete spectrum with a remarkably small selection of colours. Below are some standard choices for most artists' palettes.

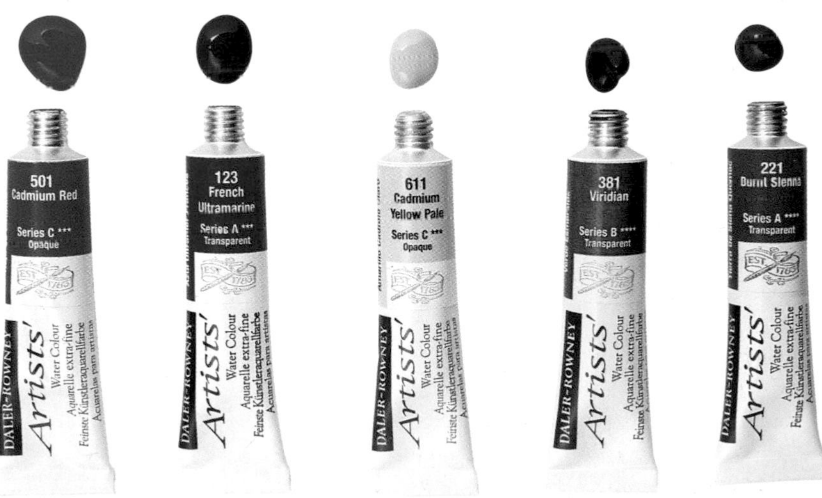

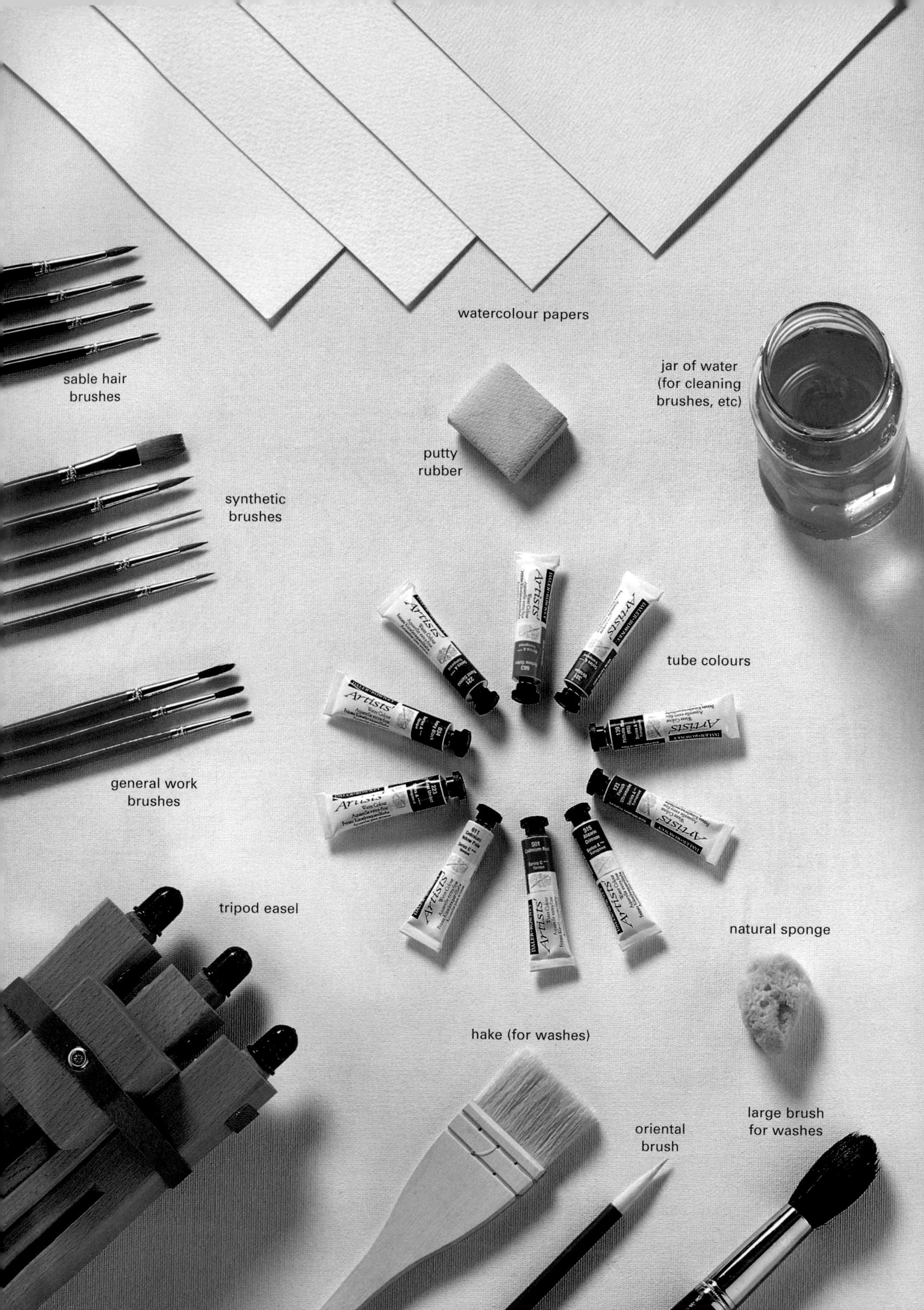
watercolour papers
sable hair brushes
jar of water (for cleaning brushes, etc)
putty rubber
synthetic brushes
tube colours
general work brushes
tripod easel
natural sponge
hake (for washes)
large brush for washes
oriental brush

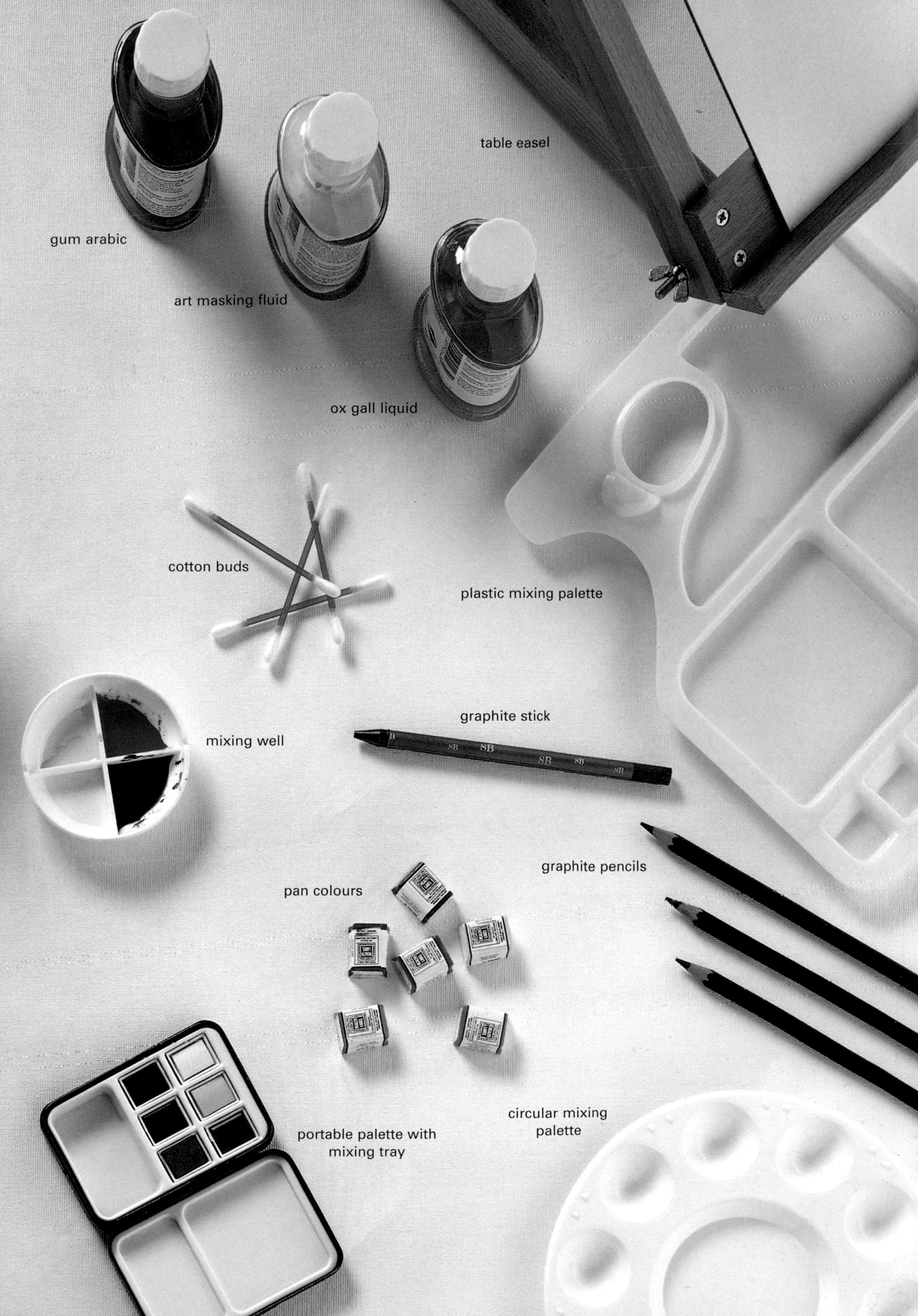
table easel
gum arabic
art masking fluid
ox gall liquid
cotton buds
plastic mixing palette
graphite stick
mixing well
graphite pencils
pan colours
circular mixing
palette
portable palette with
mixing tray

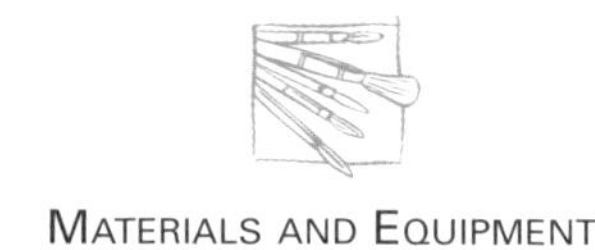

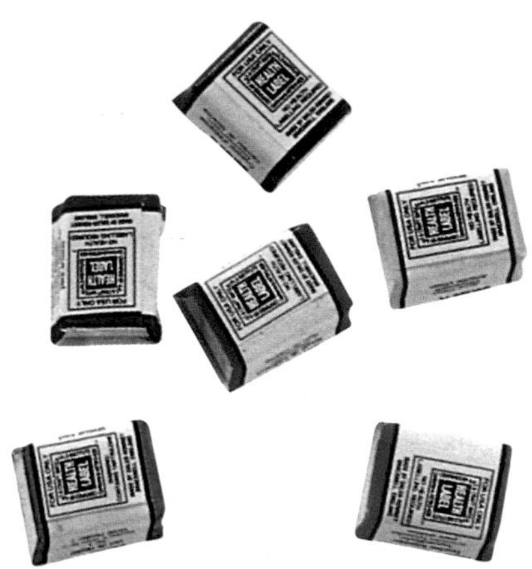

Pan colours are more economical and portable than tube colours. They are sold as cubes of paint.

MEDIUMS & ADDITIVES

Adding mediums and additives to paint alters its behaviour. Gum Arabic, gum water and watercolour medium increase transparency and the brilliance of colours. They also increase the solubility of the paint when it dries, making corrections easy to make by re-wetting the paint.

Ox gall is a wetting agent made from the gall bladder of cattle. Some papers that are heavily sized repel the watercolour washes, making them puddle. A few drops of ox gall lessens the paint's surface tension, making it flow more easily.

Aquapasto and impasto gels are used to add body to watercolour mixes. Texture medium will produce similar effects and can be used to give a layered effect. Blending medium slows the drying time of the watercolour washes and can be very useful when working in the sun or in hot weather.

Granulation medium makes paint granulate, giving it a textured, speckled appearance. Art masking fluid is a liquid rubber solution that resists paint when dry. It is painted onto the work with a brush and then removed when the painting is dry to reveal an unpainted area.

Permanent masking fluid can be used in the same way as art masking fluid but does not need to be removed. Paint can also be added to it, and then when used in the normal way, will repel subsequent washes.

BRUSHES

Brushes for watercolour are made using synthetic polymer, nylon or natural animal hair. The best brushes are made from the tail hair of the sable; they hold a lot of paint and hold their point and shape well. Sable brushes are expensive but if looked after repay the initial expense with years of use. Squirrel, ox, pony and goat hair are used for many larger wash brushes whilst oriental brushes use hair from exotic sources, including wolf.

The most useful brushes are the round, the mop and the flat. These are available in a range of sizes. Round brushes can be used for most jobs, while mop or wash brushes are used for applying washes. Flat brushes can also be used for washes and are easy to control.

Oriental brushes are useful but were intended to be used and held in a different way to brushes made in the West. One

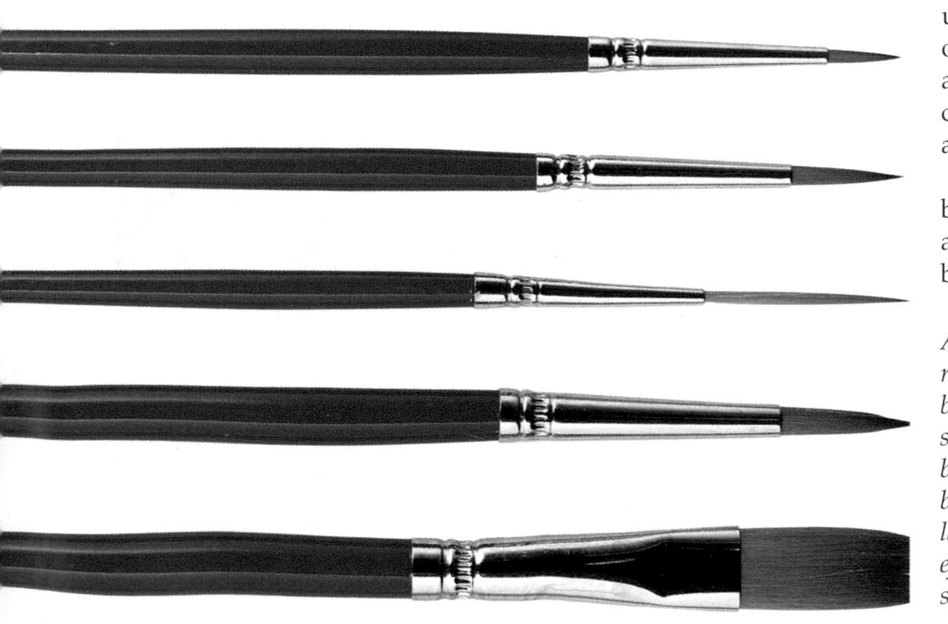

A selection of brushes increases the repertoire of the artist. From top to bottom: a rigger brush for detail; a slightly larger detail brush; a long brush for drawing lines; a medium brush for general work; and a large, flat head brush for painting effective washes. Each artist's style calls for different brushes.

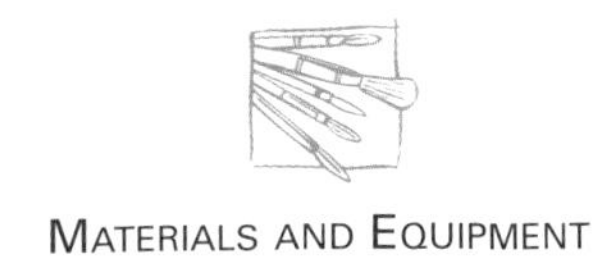

of the most useful is the "hake", this is a flat soft brush which makes an ideal wash brush.

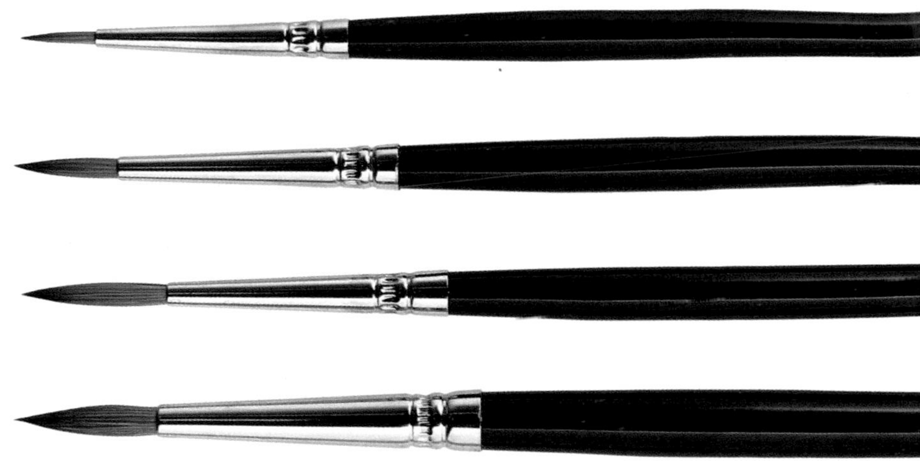

AUXILIARY EQUIPMENT

Drawing boards are needed to stretch paper. Having several boards means that you can stretch several sheets at the same time. You will need a board that will accommodate the largest sheet of paper you are likely to stretch, whilst smaller boards are good for taking with you when working on location. An economical way of making boards is to buy a sheet of medium density fibre (MDF) board and cut it into several boards; this can be done free of charge at DIY stores.

Whilst an easel is by no means vital, it can be beneficial and makes adjusting the angle at which you work easy. Watercolours are invariably worked on flat or at the very most a 40° angle, as otherwise the washes run. Table easels are ideal when working at home since they offer just the right degrees of tilt. If you are working on location you will need an easily transportable easel that will grip your board and paper at the correct angle and is stable enough not to blow over.

You will need one or more palettes in which to mix colours. While palettes inside many watercolour paint boxes are convenient, they are usually too small. A wide range of palettes made from metal, plastic and ceramic are available, each with a different configuration of mixing wells. If you are using large quantities of paint and mixing washes, you will need a palette with deep wells. Old yoghurt pots or tin cans make good mixing wells.

Sponges are useful for painting with, making textures and mopping up paint. Natural sponges have intricate, organic patterns and artists will often collect a few. Finally, keep a roll of paper towel to hand.

Sable brushes are the best-quality brushes available. However, they are expensive and unattractive from an environmental point of view. Synthetic brushes are usually perfectly usable.

It is worth keeping a store of different papers at hand – to create different effects. A desk and tripod easel will also come in handy.

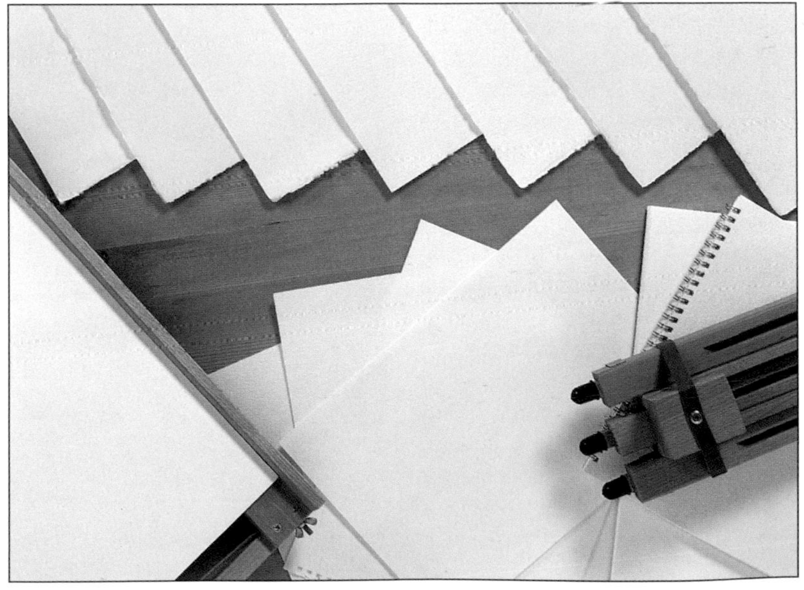

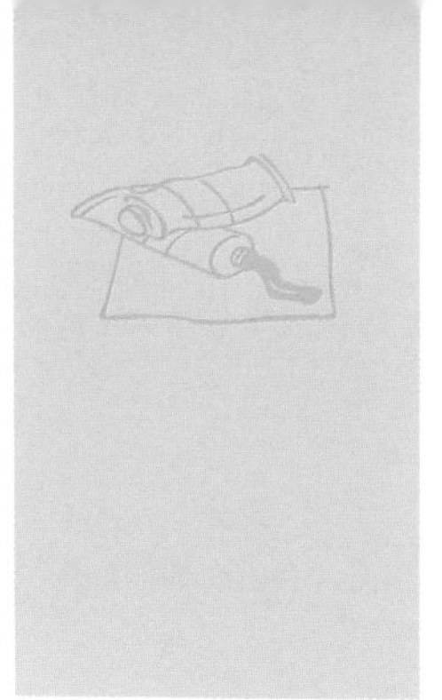

Basic Techniques

Spending some time learning and practising the techniques will give you confidence when you come to paint. It will also strengthen your understanding of the medium's capabilities and the creative effects you can achieve with it.

Having a sound knowledge of the basic techniques is more important when you are using watercolour than when using any other medium. Watercolour has a reputation for being difficult and unpredictable. This is not unfounded; it can sometimes seem to have a mind of its own, which can lead the artist to frustration. Unlike oil and acrylic paint and any of the dry art materials, watercolour does not always stay where it is put. Using wet on dry washes is on the whole controllable but when working wet into wet, making a graded or variegated wash, or when using techniques such as masking or granulation, the paint does not always do quite what was intended.

It is with practice and experience that the watercolour artist learns how to look ahead and take advantage of those chance effects that are a characteristic of watercolours, and are part of the real charm and attraction of this medium.

Mixing Paint

When using the traditional transparent watercolour technique, no white paint is used. Paintings are made on white paper. A colour is made lighter in tone by adding more water. This thins the colour so that when it is applied to the paper in the form of a wash, it absorbs very little light and so allows a high degree of light to reflect back off the white paper surface through the layer of paint.

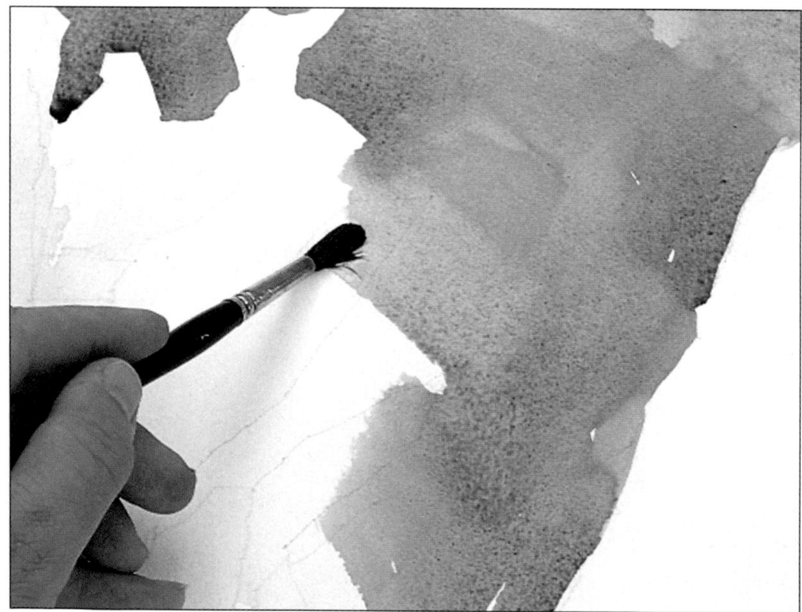

It is important to know how to fill a large area with the same colour. The artist can then add darker or lighter areas to create depth and texture.

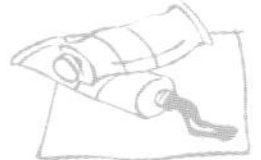

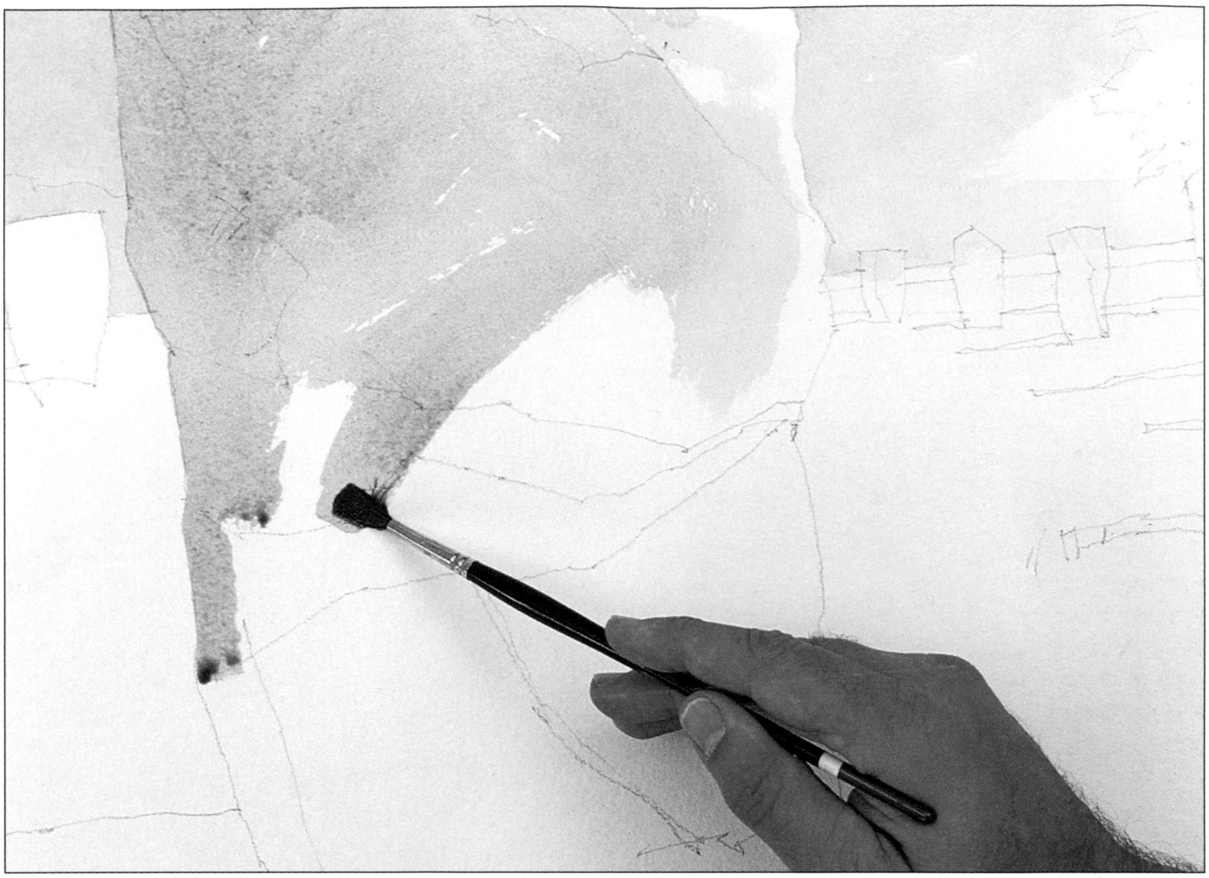

When making a wash it is easiest to bring the paint down from the top of the paper.

A colour can be made darker or more intense by adding more pigment. When this is applied to the paper, it absorbs more light and allows less light to reflect back to the viewer.

Basic Wash Technique

The manipulation and organization of semi-transparent washes is central to good watercolour technique. The ideal is to lay a perfectly flat wash over a sizeable area. In reality a completely flat wash is rarely if ever used, other than when you need to paint a wide expanse of colour, such as a clear blue sky. Even then nuances or brush marks or a change in colour intensity should not be considered as something imperfect or bad. Indeed being able to accommodate and utilize the occasionally fickle behaviour of the paint into the work is all part of good watercolour technique. When it works to the artist's advantage, this has become known as the "happy accident" and is something that experienced watercolour artists incorporate into their work all the time.

You will find that it helps to take a few minutes to prepare your work area prior to beginning your painting. If you are left-handed arrange your paints, palettes and brushes to the left of your support; if you are right-handed arrange everything to the right. This will help to prevent many of the spills, smudges and blots that can happen when you are painting the picture. Try to have two jars of water to hand: one for mixing, and the other for cleaning your brushes. The water can become dirty very quickly and nothing

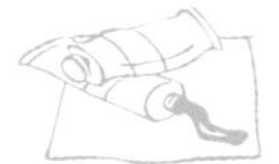

is guaranteed to make your colours look muddy and subdued more than using dirty water. Make sure that you have enough palettes and containers ready to make your mixes in, and always have plenty of paper towels to hand for clearing up those previously mentioned spills and blots, and for making any corrections on the paper.

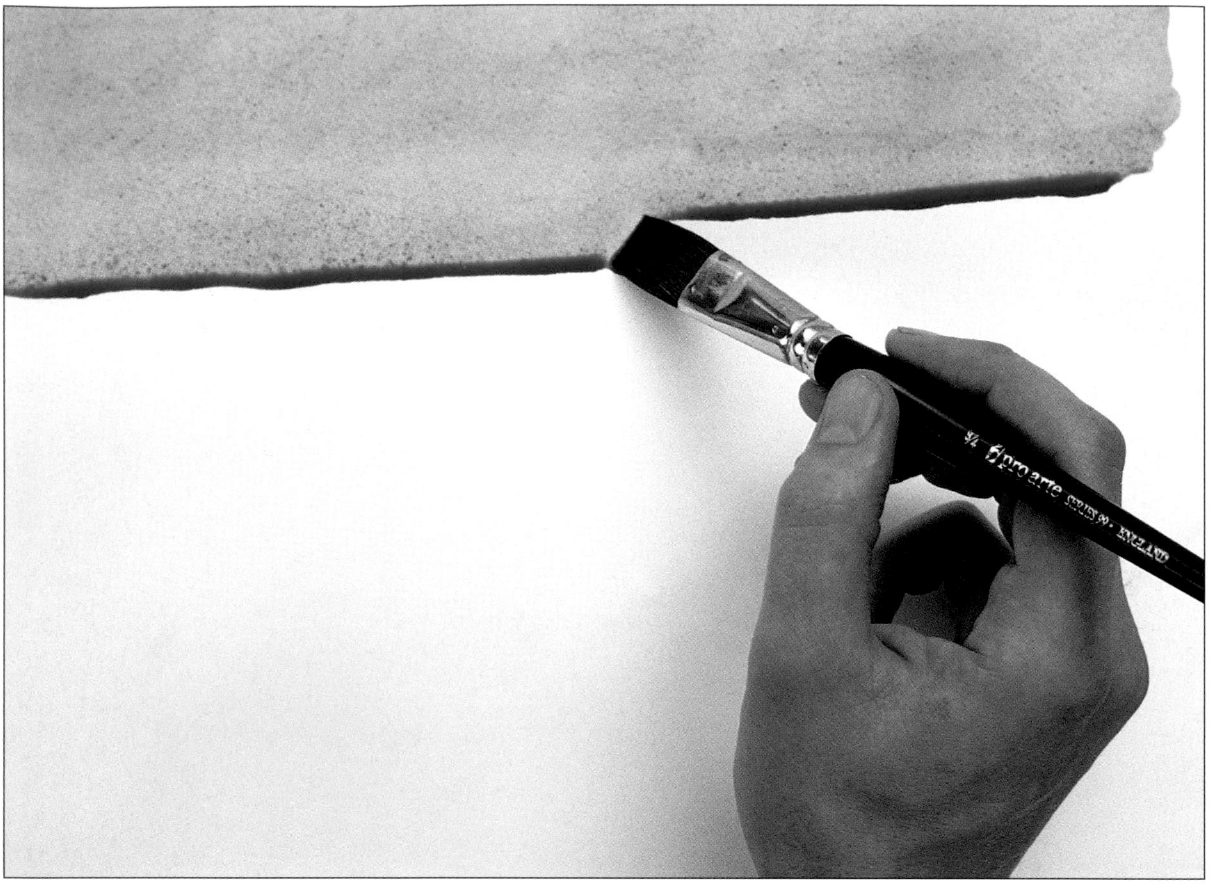

Flat Wash

Whilst being able to lay a flat wash is not always necessary, learning to lay a flat wash is good practice. A flat wash is one where a consistent colour or tone covers a sizeable area. In order to be successful, it needs to be carried out methodically, reasonably quickly and in one go. Mix up plenty of the required colour before you start. Running out halfway through will mean having to mix more. This causes two problems: first, you will find it almost impossible to mix exactly the same tone of colour, and second, the laid wash will start to dry while you are mixing the new colour, which means a mark will result at the point where the work has been resumed.

Choose a large enough brush, which suits the size of the area to be covered and which you can easily manipulate. Remember that a very large brush may hold too much paint, which could result in runs.

Flat washes are useful for learning the behaviour of watercolour paint.

First place your support at a slight angle of around 20°. Some artists like to dampen the area to receive the wash first, using a sponge. This is not necessary, but you may like to experiment with both dry and damp surfaces to see which suits you best. Load the brush with paint and make a steady horizontal

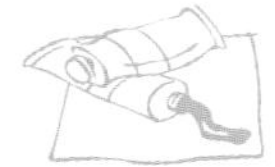

Stretching Watercolour Paper

When a sheet of watercolour paper is wet, the paper fibres swell and the sheet becomes marginally larger, which causes it to buckle. As the sheet dries and shrinks the uneven buckled surface often remains. This makes applying subsequent washes difficult, since the paint collects and puddles in the "valleys". The answer is to stretch the paper onto a drawing board. This forces it to dry flat and tight each time it dries. All papers can be stretched but heavier weight papers of 300lb/640gsm and more tend to stay flat without stretching as their inherent thickness prevents buckling. In order to stretch your paper you will need: a sheet of your chosen paper cut to the size you intend to work, a wooden drawing board that is larger than the sheet of paper being used, gummed paper tape, scissors, a sponge and clean water.

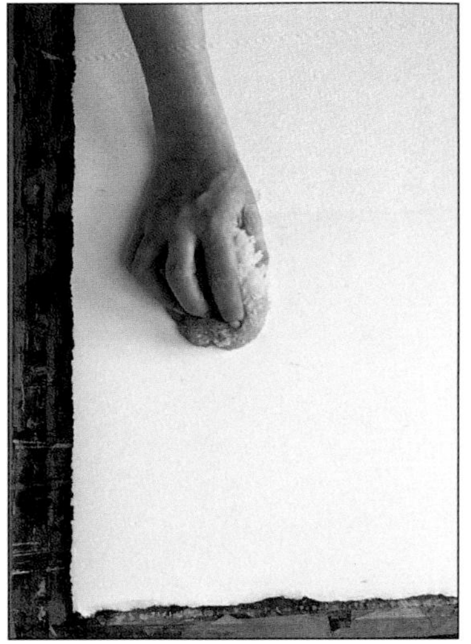

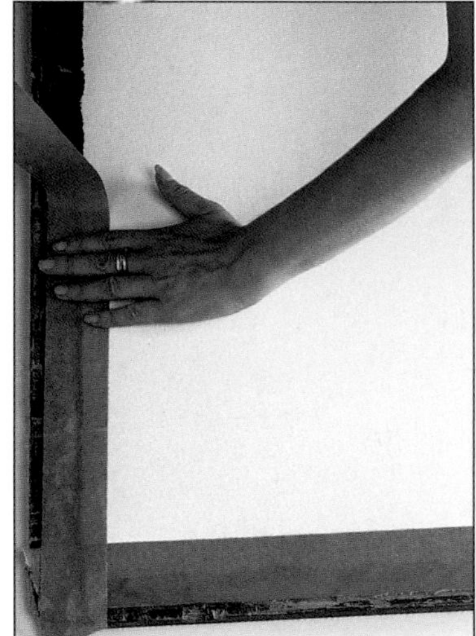

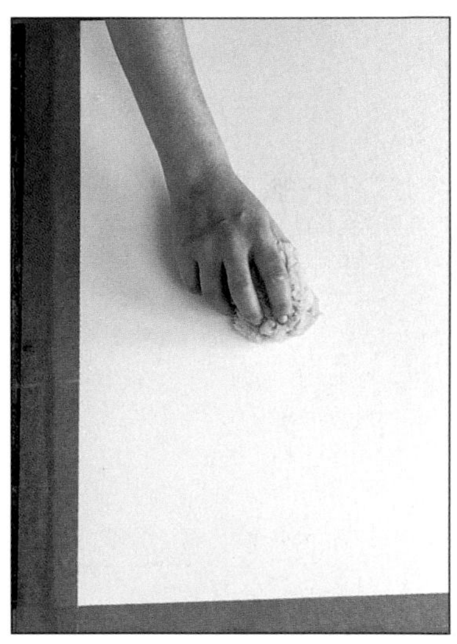

1

Working on a flat surface, place the sheet of watercolour paper onto the centre of the board. Cut four lengths of gummed tape, one for each side of the paper. Using the sponge, wet the paper thoroughly with water. The thicker the sheet, the more water it will need. Some books recommend soaking the paper in a bath, with thicker handmade papers being soaked for prolonged periods of time and then transferred to the board. This is rarely necessary and sponges are fine for all but the thickest of papers. Remove excess water with the sponge.

2

At this point you will need to work quickly as the paper will begin to curl and buckle. If the paper is very thin the degree of curling can be alarming. Wet one length of paper tape using the sponge and apply it along one edge of the paper so that one-third sticks to the paper with the remaining two-thirds sticking to the board. Smooth the tape down using the sponge. If the paper is curling, smooth it out and apply the tape to the other three edges in the same way. If the paper is only marginally smaller than the drawing board, smooth the tape over its edge.

3

The paper may not look flat at this stage, but resist the temptation to fiddle with it. Place the board to one side and let it dry. Drying time depends on how wet and how thick the sheet of paper was, but if you are working in room temperature, most papers should be sufficiently dry in one or two hours. The drying can be speeded up by using a hair dryer. To ensure that the sheet dries in an even manner the dryer must be kept moving, and you need to take care not to allow the dryer to come too close. To remove the painting once it has been completed, use a sharp knife to cut around the edge where the paper tape joins the board.

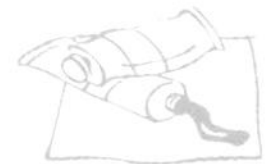

stroke across the top of the paper or area of paper that is to receive the wash.

Once the stroke has been made, notice how the tilt of the board has made the paint collect or puddle along the bottom of the stroke. Refill your brush and make another horizontal stroke in the same direction, slightly overlapping the first. This collects up the puddled paint, which runs down and collects at the bottom of the second stroke.

Repeat the process until the area is covered. Collect any paint that puddles at the bottom of the painted area by carefully touching it with a dry brush or paper towel. Leave the support at the same angle while the wash dries naturally.

Right: Washes are used here early in the picture to build up areas of colour.

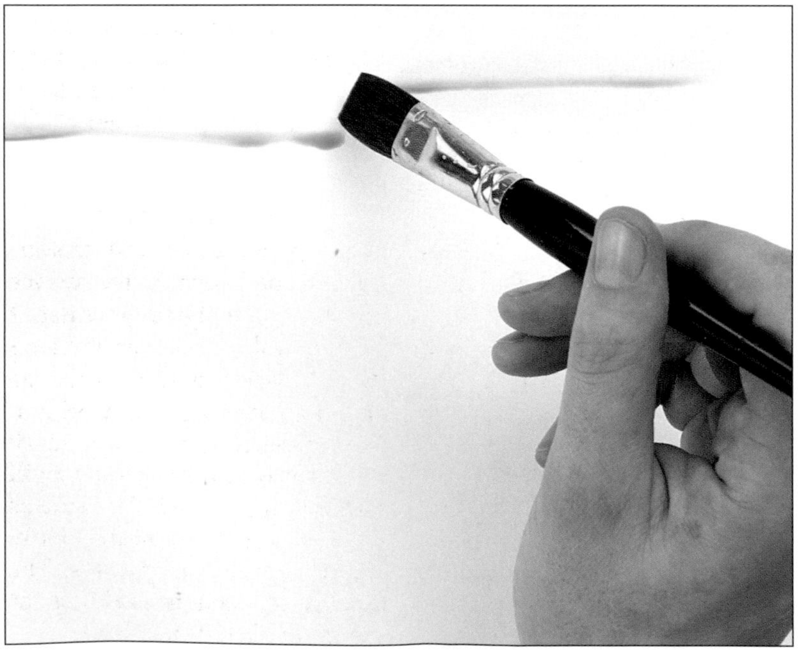

Left: In this graded wash, the paint gradually gets lighter.

Graded Wash

A graded wash is one where the tone of the colour changes over the area, becoming either lighter or darker. A graded wash is made in precisely the same way as a flat wash. The gradation of colour is achieved by adding more water to the wash mix after each one or several horizontal strokes of the brush, so making the colour become gradually lighter down the paper.

Mastering this technique may take some practice. It is a little more difficult to achieve

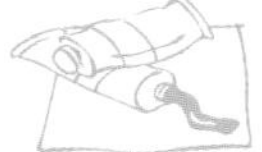

than an ordinary wash as watercolour washes behave and dry at different rates according to how much water or pigment they contain. A variation on the graded wash technique is to use a sponge to wet the lighter portion of the area and bring the wash down into it.

Variegated Wash

The variegated wash has one colour blending into another. It is made in the same way as other washes, but at some point a second colour is introduced. Mix up plenty of both colours before you start and have two brushes, one for each colour. You need to choose the colours carefully because some become muddy and dull when they are mixed together. Begin working as before and when you want to make the transition from one colour to the next, simply switch brushes and colours and carry on. The result may not be a perfect seamless transition but that doesn't matter. Again, you may find the process is easier if you dampen the paper beforehand, using a sponge and water.

Granulated Wash

Certain pigments used in watercolour paint are relatively coarse and tend to separate out when mixed together. As the paint dries this leaves a speckled or granular effect, which for the landscape artist can be very useful. The paint mixtures that work best are the earth colours, which include, burnt umber, raw umber and raw sienna, combined with any blue.

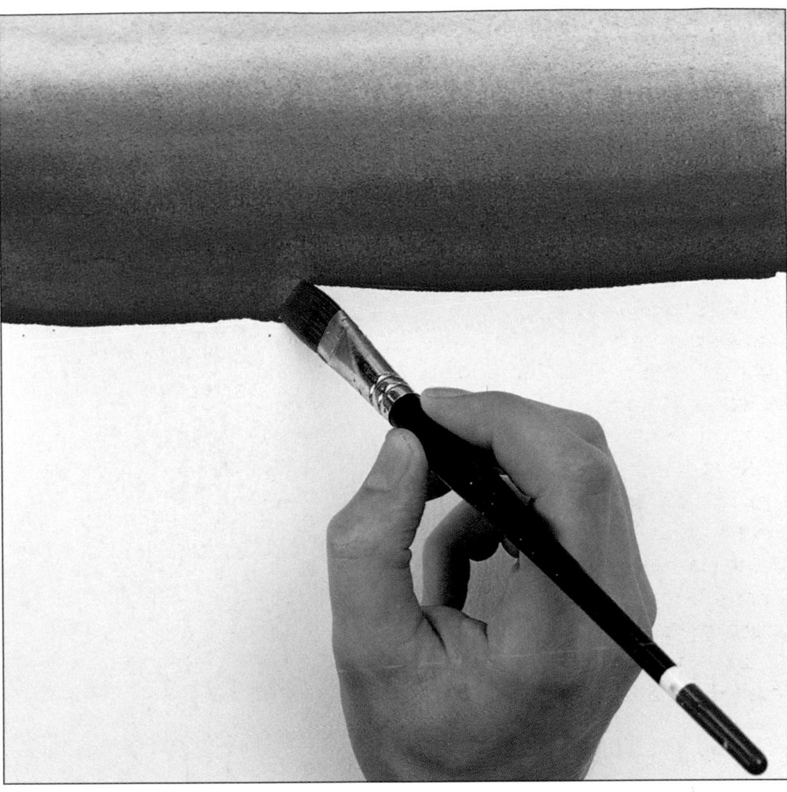

A variegated wash, in which blue has been run into red. This technique is particularly effective for painting the subtle changes of colour in a sunrise or sunset. It takes a bit of practice to perfect.

Certain combinations work better than others and the effect works to a greater or lesser extent depending on the surface texture of the paper used. You can also use special granulation medium which can be mixed into watercolour washes. The more of the medium that is mixed into the wash, the greater the degree of granulation that appears as the paint dries.

Watercolour paint is applied to either a dry or a wet surface and each results in the paint behaving and drying in a distinctly different way. These techniques are known as "wet on dry" and "wet on wet" and can be used either on their own or in combination with one another in the confines of one painting.

Wet on Dry

When a wash or watercolour mark is made onto a dry surface the paint usually stays where it is put, unless the paper being used does not contain much size and is particularly absorbent. The edge quality of the mark will be crisp and the colour will remain pretty much the same as was mixed, becoming only slightly lighter as it dries. The wet on dry technique allows for sharp focus and detail.

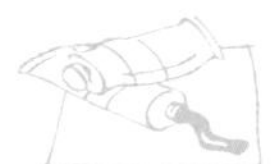

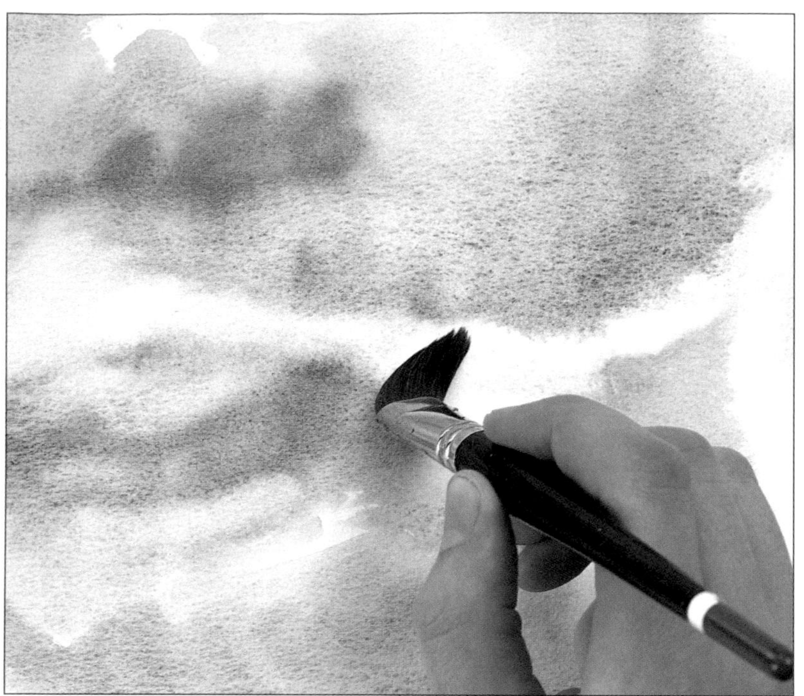

Working wet on wet for a sky area.

MASKING

There are various other techniques that can be employed by the watercolour artist to achieve different effects. One such is masking. This is the practice of using an agent to repel paint – thus preserving white areas of the paper. There are various substances that can be used. The most common is commercially produced masking fluid which is much more controllable than substances such as wax, with the added benefit that it can be easily removed.

ROCK SALT

It can be quite difficult to achieve textural effects with watercolour paint. Artists have therefore devised a number of

WET ON WET

When a watercolour wash or mark is made onto a wet or damp surface, the paint spreads and bleeds in all directions. Depending on the dampness of the support this can be difficult to control, particularly for the beginner. The wet on wet technique results in colours mixing together to create some beautiful effects when dry. The paint will dry with a mixture of soft edges and harder water or drying marks where very wet paint has pushed against paint that is not so wet and then taken longer to dry. This technique is the one you should use when trying to capture atmospheric skies, mists or perhaps swirling water or wet sand.

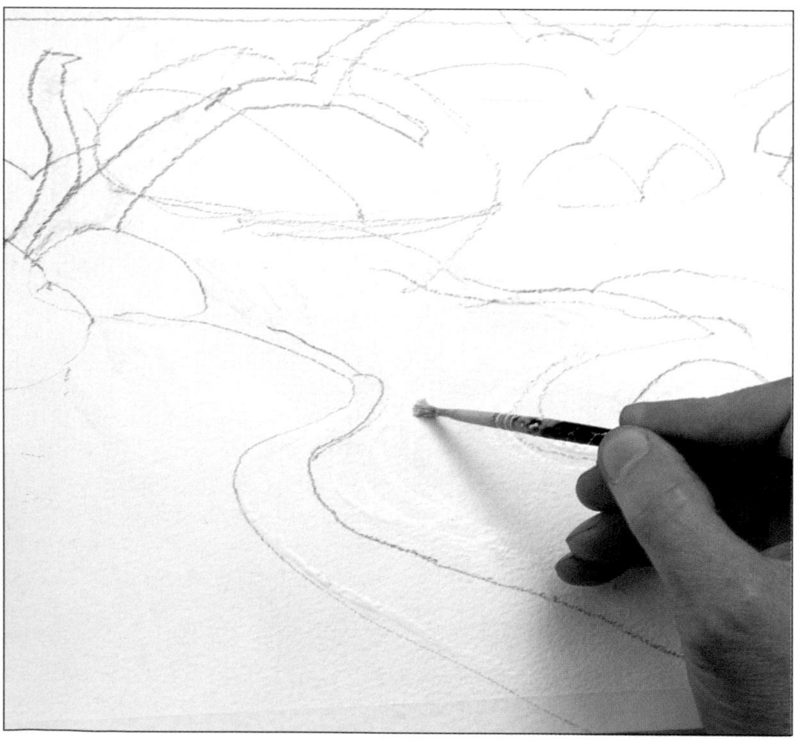

Painting removable masking fluid onto paper.

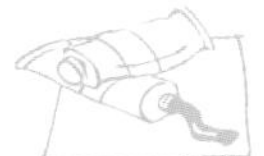

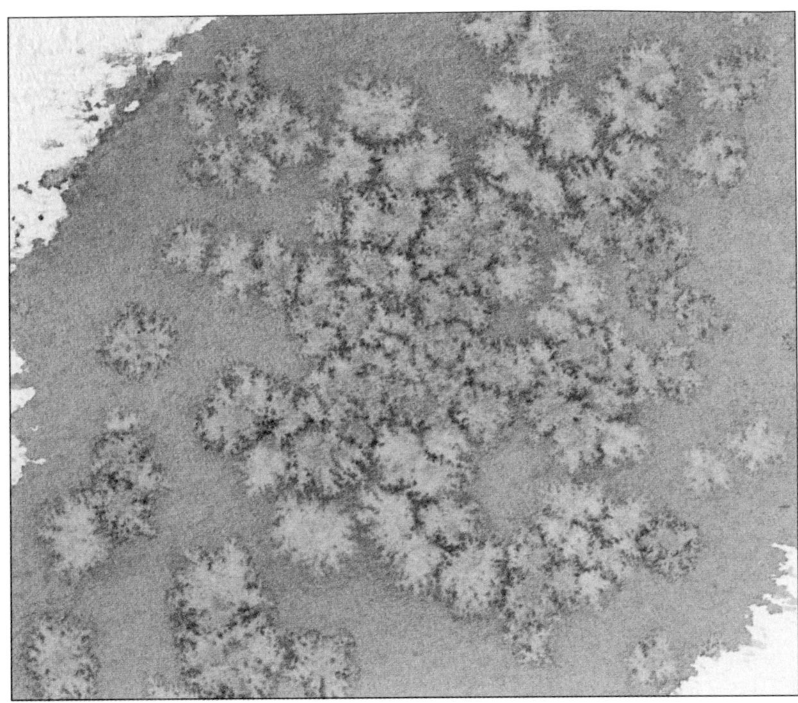

The dappled effect caused by sprinkling salt crystals onto wet paint. Each crystal sucks up the paint immediately surrounding it, making a roughly circular, star-like impression. The absorbency of the paper alters its effectiveness.

"cheats" that can be used to add texture to a picture. One of these is the use of rock salt. When rock salt crystals are sprinkled onto a still-wet area of paint, they immediately start to absorb the paint. When the paint is dry, the salt is removed leaving a dappled effect. This technique is particularly useful for creating rocky or rough watery areas with watercolour paint.

Spattering

Another method for texturing otherwise flat areas of colour is spattering. This involves using the brush to flick paint onto the paper. A toothbrush is especially useful for spattering, allowing for more control over the direction of the paint. Spattering helps to create a speckled appearance, and is used for waves crashing on the shore and rough surface effects.

Spattering is another technique that creates interesting textures in a painting. By levering back the bristles, the artist effectively catapults paint at the page. It need not be hit-and-miss though. Cover areas you do not want to spatter.

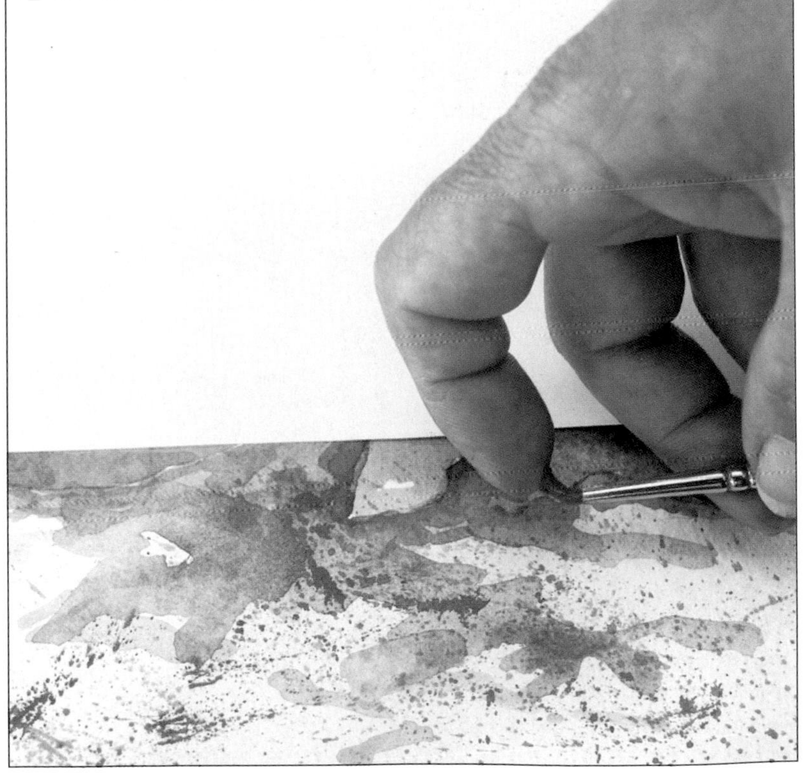

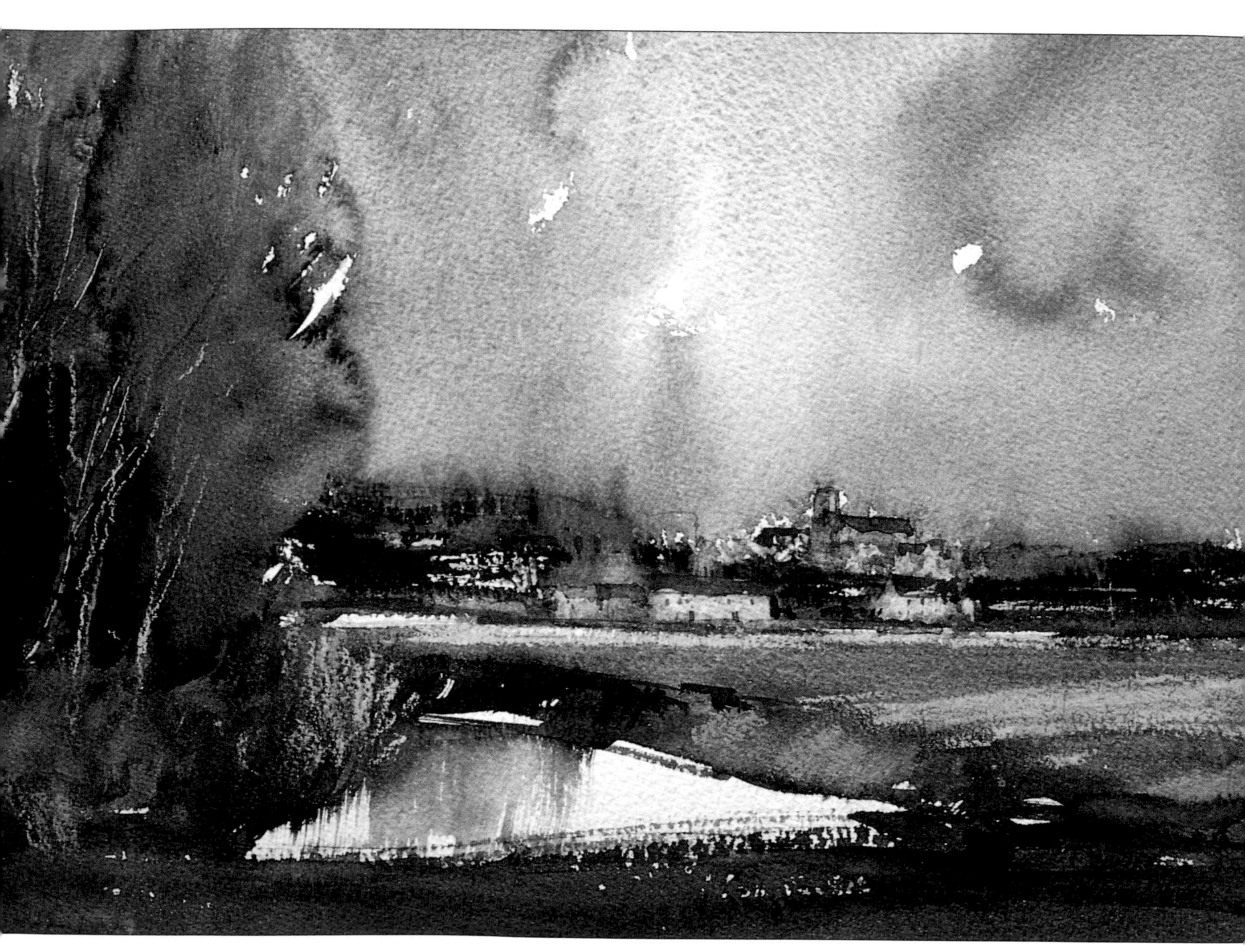

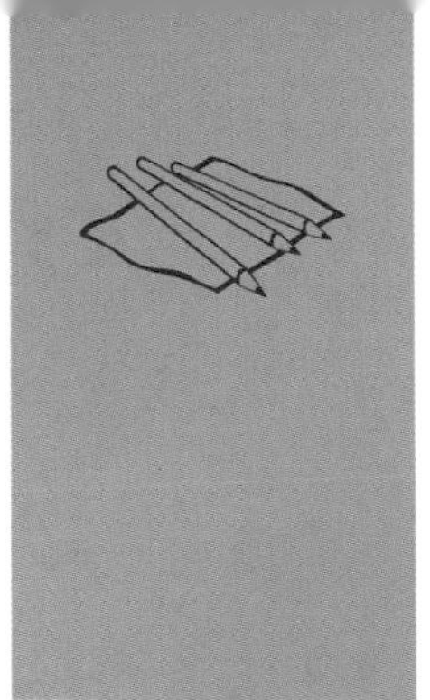

GALLERY

Once a few basic skills have been mastered, watercolour can be used to achieve a range of effects. The watercolour landscapes by contemporary artists on the following pages demonstrate just some of the many different effects that artists can produce using a limited arsenal of painting techniques. Watercolour can be used for shadowy, atmospheric scenes in the depths of wooded areas as well as bright, buoyant landscapes dominated by blue skies.

The key to working in watercolour, demonstrated in the work that follows, is to know basically what you are going to do before you start, and not to overwork the paper. Watercolour landscapes invariably benefit from lightness of touch – a quality that develops with the skill of the artist.

~

Cley Village

Alan Oliver

30 x 40cm (12 x 16in)

Wet into wet washes dry to leave interesting watermarks that read as the foliage of trees and rain falling across the horizon. The fluid brush strokes pick up the texture of the rough paper, adding a certain crispness to the paint work, while the restrained use of a little soft pastel adds colour to the work.

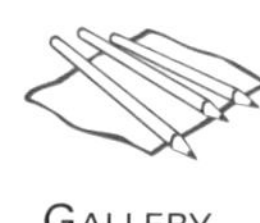

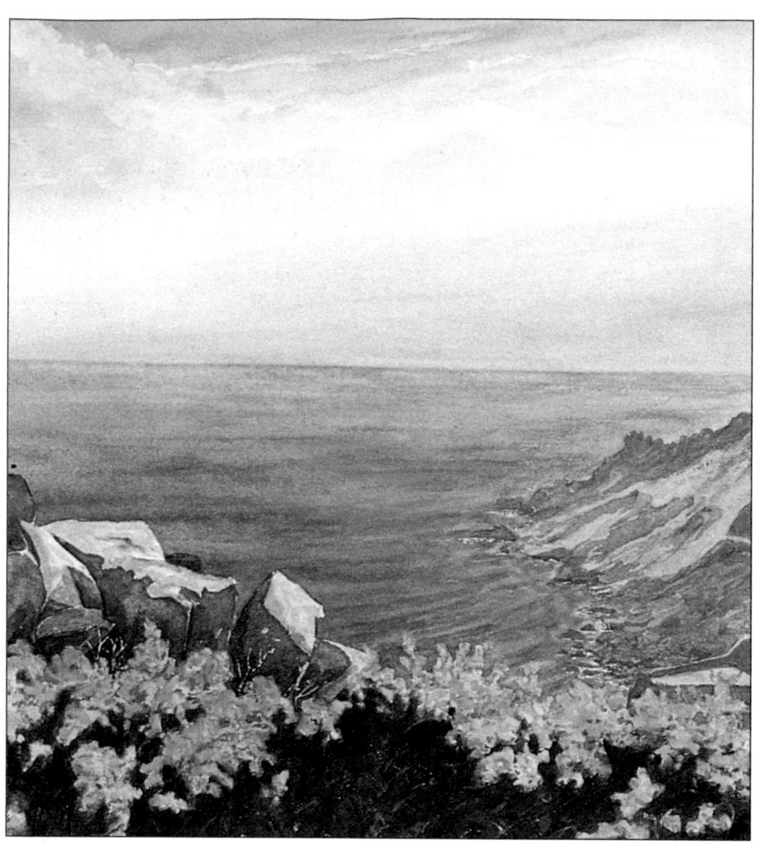

Lamorna

Annette Johnson
35 x 55cm (14 x 22in)

This picture of the Cornish coast in southern England uses predominantly cool colours and an unusual composition, resulting in a an almost palpable sense of space. The crisp detail on the rocks and the yellow flowers create a barrier over which the viewer peers down into the bay below.

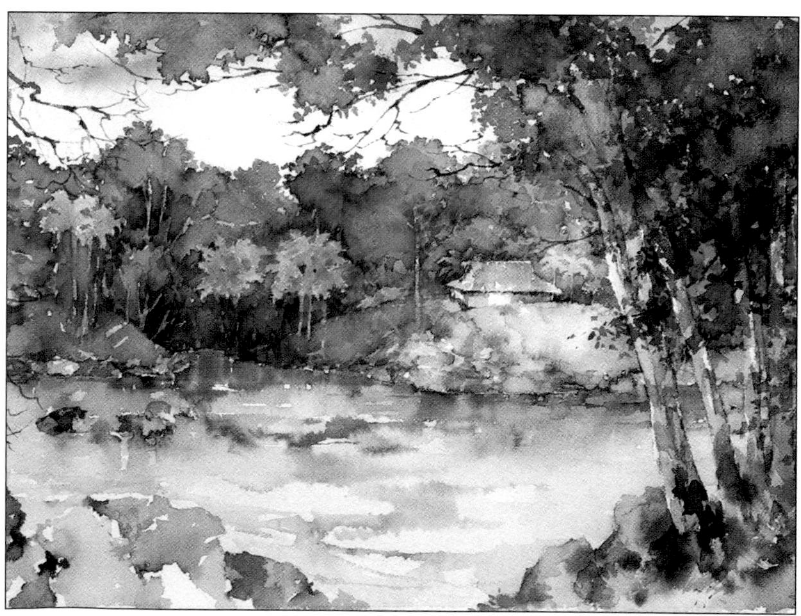

Peter's Island

Shirley Felts
40 x 55cm (16 x 22in)

The surface texture of the paper is exploited beautifully here to give an uneven-edge quality to the brush work. This is consistent with the effects of the leaves and the multi-layered, thick and almost impenetrable undergrowth of this scene in Guyana, South America.

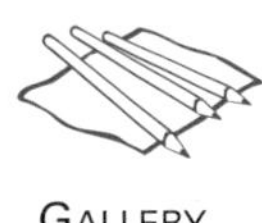

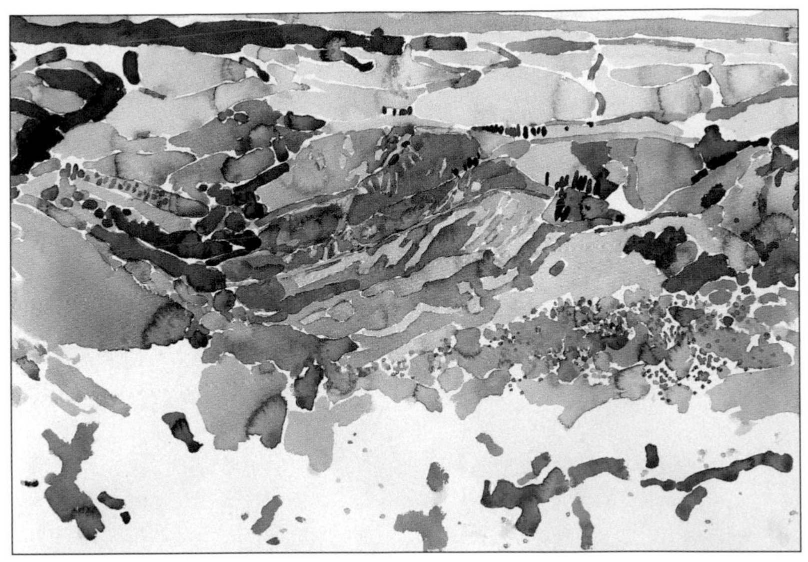

The Balze, Volterra

Katy Ellis
45 x 60cm (18 x 24in)

A patchwork of colours are applied predominantly wet on dry over and next to one another. They link together like a jigsaw to represent a sweeping Italian vista of trees interspersed with rocky outcrops.

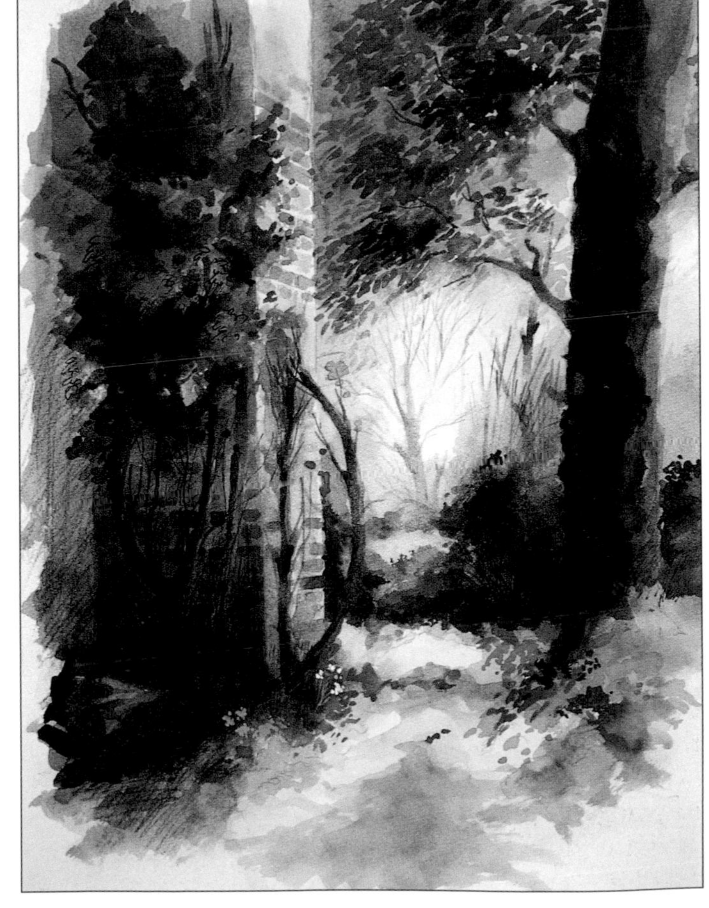

Early Morning at the Dell

John Lidzey
40 x 30cm (16 x 12in)

Early morning sunlight creates a tunnel through the trees that pulls the viewer into this picture, while the small jewel-like patch of blue flowers in the foreground pulls the eye back again.

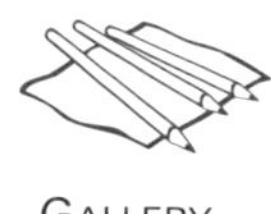

Garden Ruins, Gunnersbury

Roger Hutchins
40 x 30cm (16 x 12in)

The effects of dappled light and shade are achieved here by the clever use of layering wet paint on dry. The shadows are painted in with cooler blues and greys over the warmer reds and browns of the brickwork.

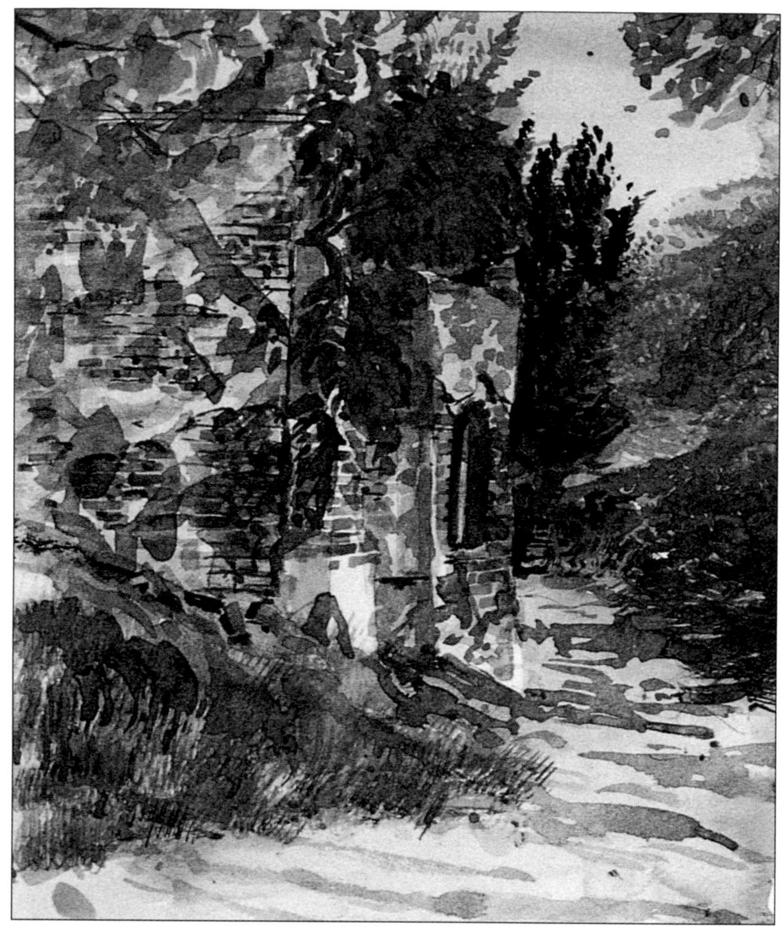

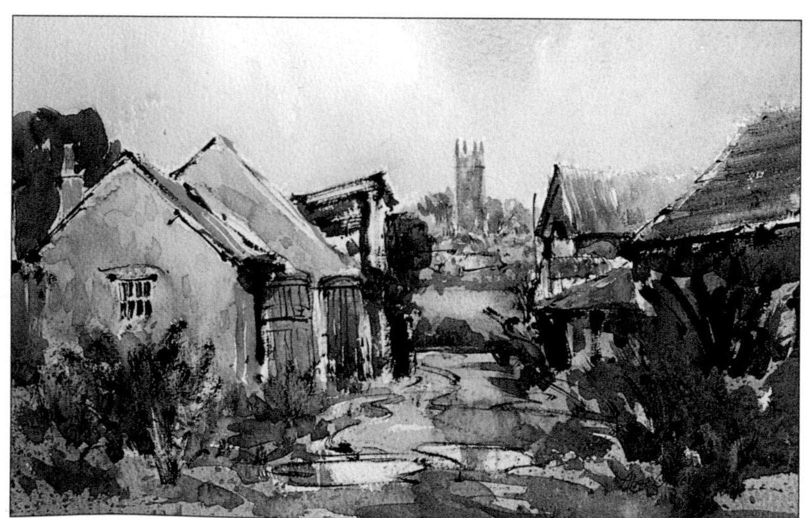

Abandoned Farmyard

Alan Oliver
30 x 40cm (12 x 16in)

A very real sense of distance is achieved by using a combination of linear and aerial perspective. Black paint is used effectively to add definition and detail to the foreground.

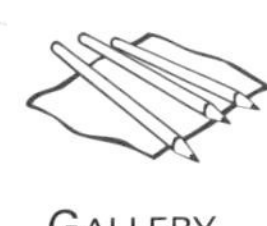

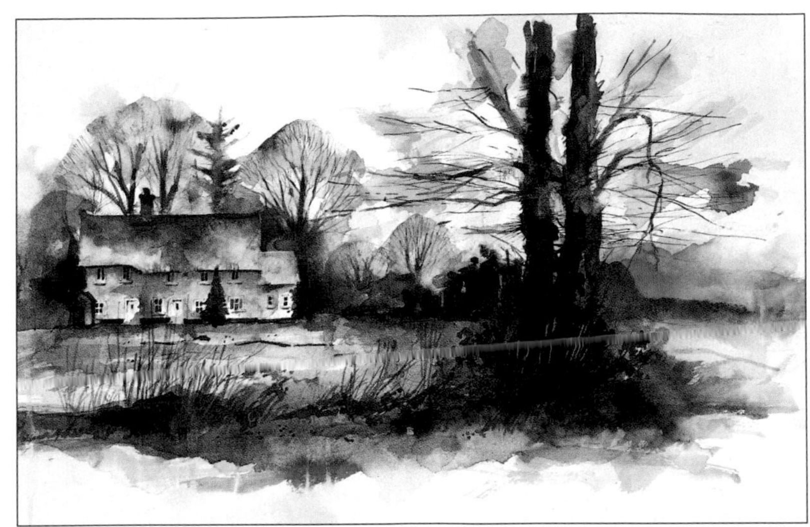

Cottage at Yaxl

John Lidzey

20 x 40cm (8 x 1

The rich colours
autumn are cr
using a combin
yellow and e
the coolness is
suggeste ues and
greys. N te e fine
twigs nd es are
pulle the paint is
wet rom dark tree trunk
st the foreground.

The Old Monastery, Majorca

David Curtis

45 x 65cm (18 x 26in)

Here a mixture of dry brush and wet on wet work recreates a mountain scene. The painting captures the sunlight striking the buildings and people of the village. The artist uses fainter colours to paint the mountains in the distance, creating a great sense of three-dimensional space.

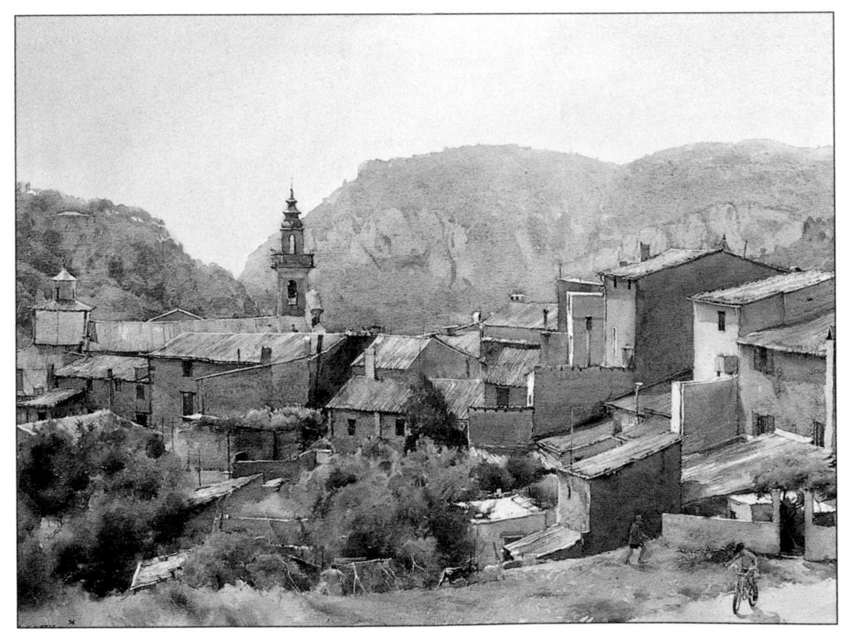

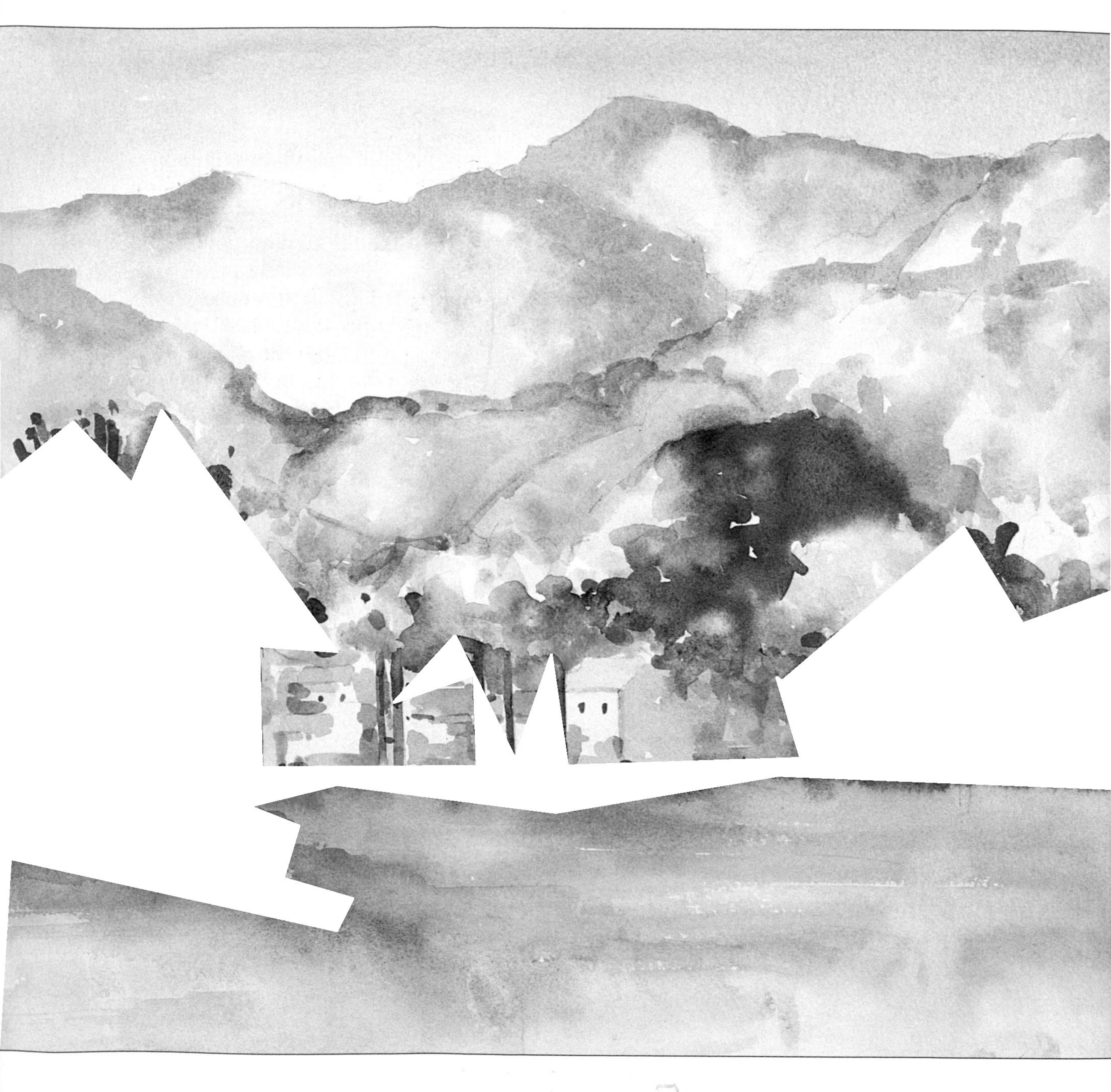

LIGHT TO DARK

Traditional watercolour painting involves building up washes of colour on a white background. An artist will usually work from light to dark, gradually applying darker washes as the painting progresses. This technique is perfect for creating the sense of distance many landscapes require. In this work, the distant hills are washed in at the beginning of the painting and are then left largely unmodified. Stronger colours applied below the hills bring the mid- and foreground closer to the viewer. In the finished picture, the eye is swept back over the field in the foreground, through the woods and the village, and then up into the mountains in the distance.

Barry Freeman
Minorcan Village
40 x 60cm (16 x 24in)

Light to Dark Technique

The darkness of the tone of a colour is governed by the amount of water added. A wash that contains a lot of pigment and relatively little water will be dark and intense, while a wash that contains little pigment and a lot of water will be pale in tone and colour. In areas where a pale wash has been applied a high proportion of the light that falls on the paper is reflected back through the wash. In areas where a dark wash has been used much of the light is absorbed with less reflecting back. Working darker colours over lighter ones means that paintings need to be planned so that the washes proceed in the right order. Before you start a painting, work out the stages into which your painting will be divided.

MINORCAN VILLAGE

Materials and Equipment

- SHEET OF NOT, 600 GSM WATERCOLOUR PAPER, STRETCHED (SEE P. 111)
- 2B PENCIL • ¾IN FLAT BRUSH, MEDIUM-SIZE SOFT HAIR BRUSH
- WATERCOLOUR PAINTS: CERULEAN BLUE, ULTRAMARINE BLUE, ALIZARIN CRIMSON, LIGHT RED, CADMIUM YELLOW, YELLOW OCHRE, VIRIDIAN GREEN
- KITCHEN PAPER TO CATCH MISTAKES

1. ◀

Make a light pencil sketch, marking the principal areas of the scene: the foreground field, the trees, the buildings and the mountains. Using a ¾in flat brush damp the surface down. Apply the first pale wash: ultramarine blue for the sky and distant mountains, light red for the closer ones. Mix some alizarin crimson into the light red as you come forward. For the foreground use yellow ochre, mixing alizarin crimson into the mix to add warmth for the near left-hand corner.

2. ▶

When the previous wash is dry, mix some cerulean blue, ultramarine blue, cadmium yellow and alizarin crimson. Apply this wash to the most distant hill. Add some more alizarin crimson and light red for the closer hills. Use a wash of viridian green and cadmium yellow for the tree foliage. Use more of the same wash for the area in front of the trees and the village. Take care to leave the houses white at this stage. Also try to keep the edges of the washes soft. Running a slightly damp brush along the edge of a wash areas will usually break up any sharp lines that may have formed.

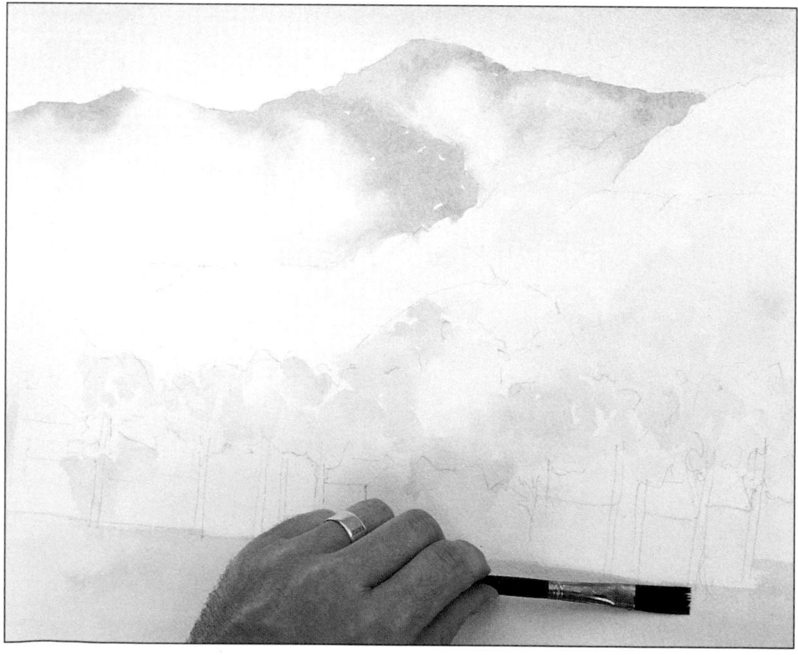

3. ◄
Paint the roof tops with a light red, alizarin crimson and cadmium yellow wash. Mix light red, ultramarine blue and alizarin crimson for the warm areas on the hills. Use pure alizarin crimson for the hillside on the right and pure yellow ochre for the hill on the left.

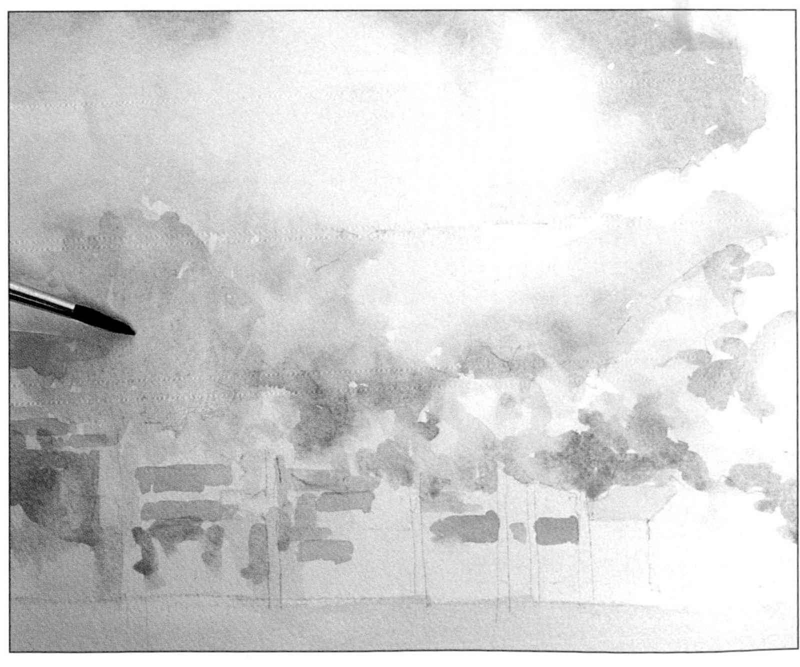

4. ►
Use a cerulean blue and cadmium yellow wash for the darker foliage areas in the trees. Apply pure cerulean blue to contrast with the red of the roofs.

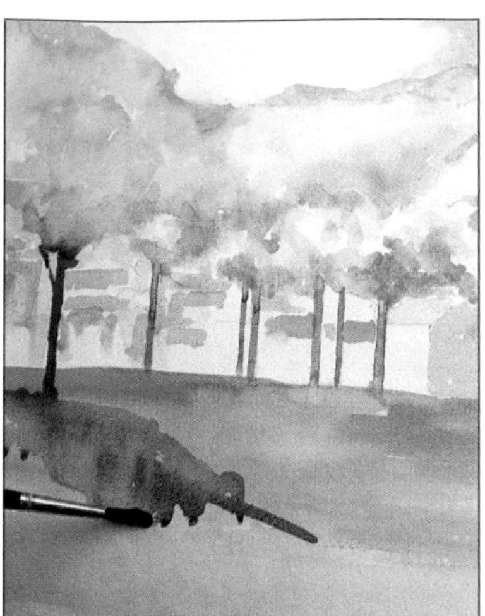

5◄

Mix cerulean blue and yellow ochre for the dark green field areas on the top of the right-hand hill. Use alizarin crimson and viridian green for a dark wash onto the left-hand hills. Make two separate washes for the foreground area. Alizarin crimson and light red, and then yellow ochre and light red. Apply the red mix to the left side of the foreground and the dark orange one to the right – keep them wet and allow the two to merge in the centre. Mark the dark tree trunk and shadow with ultramarine blue, light red and a little viridian green.

6▼

Now add some shadows to the main wooded area with ultramarine blue, cerulean blue and alizarin crimson. Mark in the windows of the houses and the trunks of the trees. Use ultramarine blue and alizarin crimson for the shadow under the tree on the left, and viridian green for the foliage.

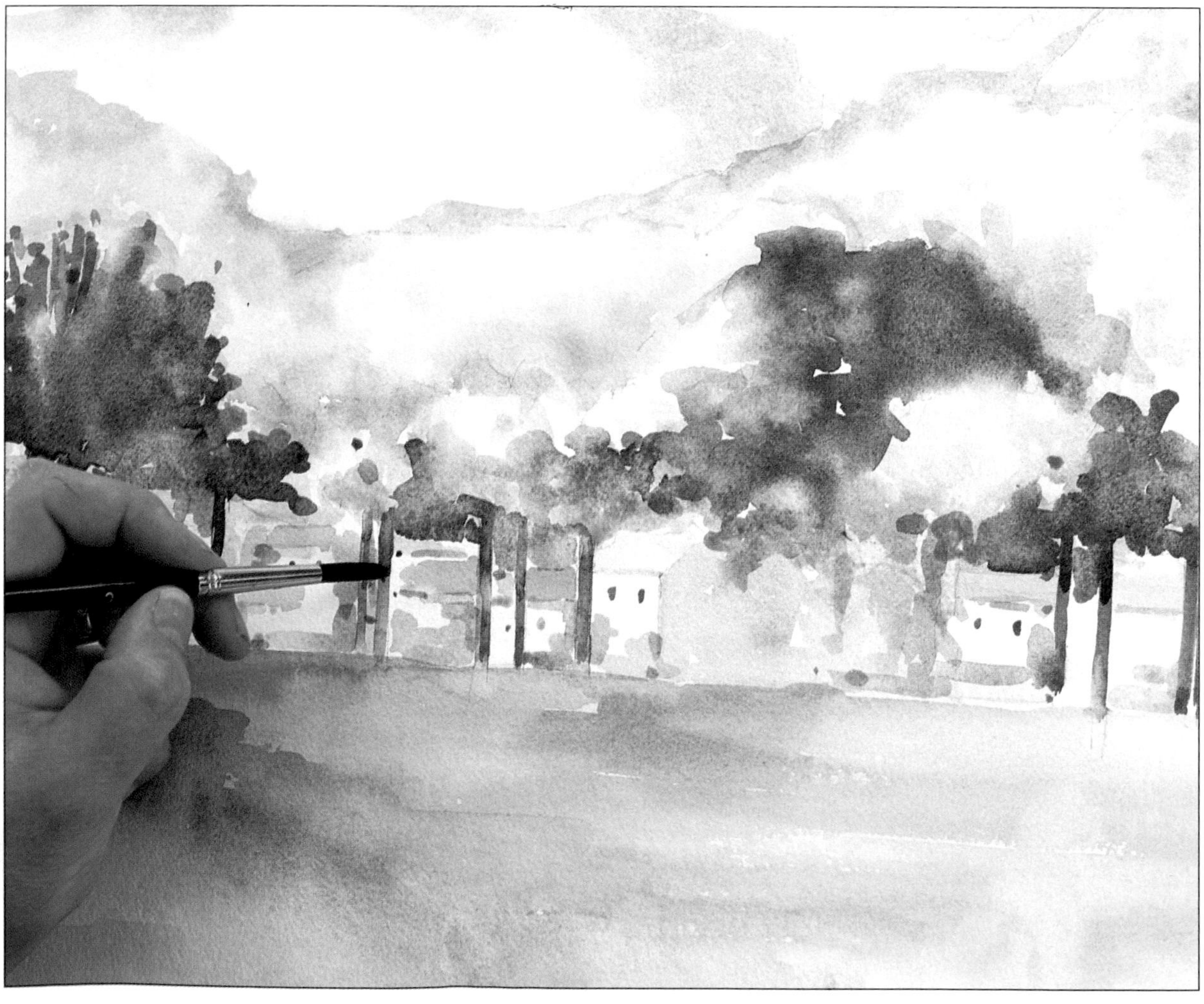

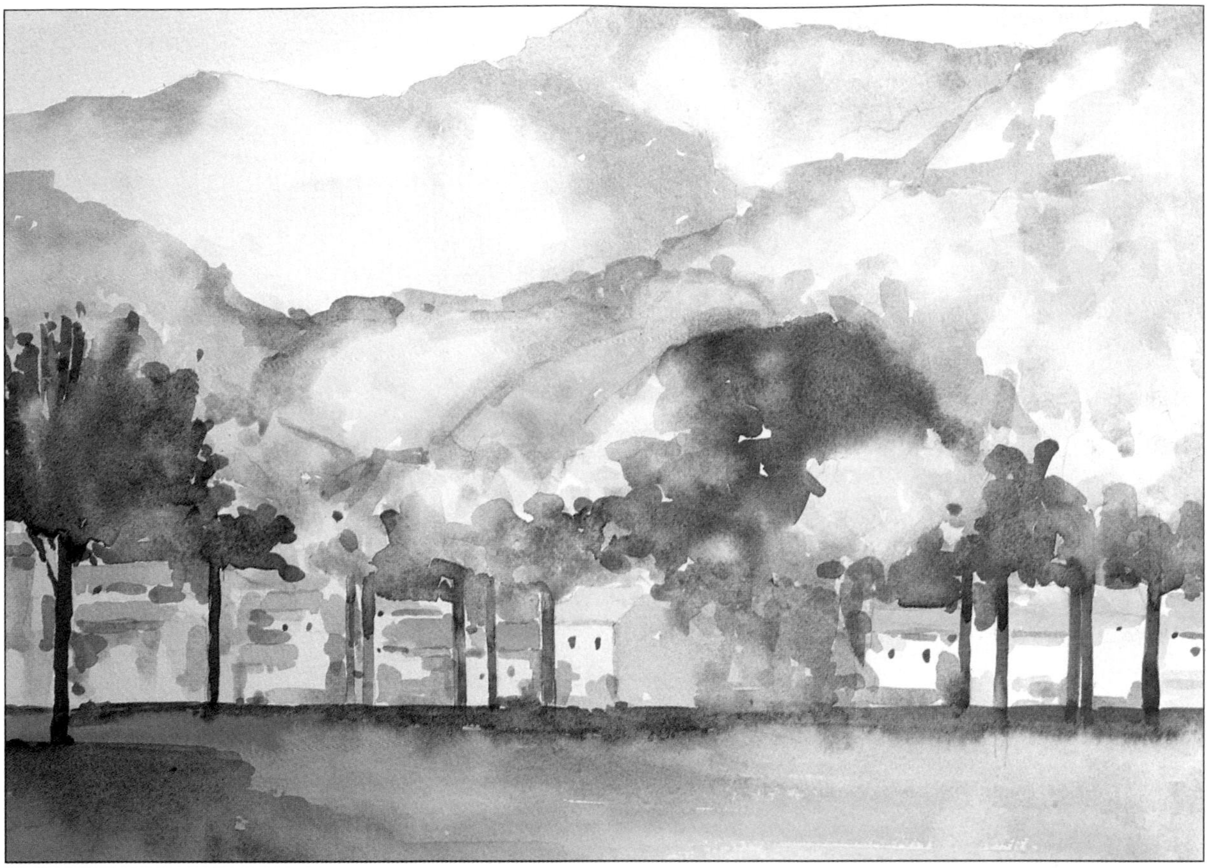

7.▲

Make a strong wash of viridian green, ultramarine blue and light red for the shadow area in front of the trees and the houses. Use this to darken some of the tree trunks on the right end of the wood, bringing them forward in the picture.

8.▶

Finish the painting by adding some more definition to the hills in the middle distance with a wash of cerulean blue, a little alizarin crimson, some cadmium yellow and a touch of yellow ochre. Now apply some cerulean blue to the furthest hillside. This last application of paint should push the hill back rather than bring it forward.

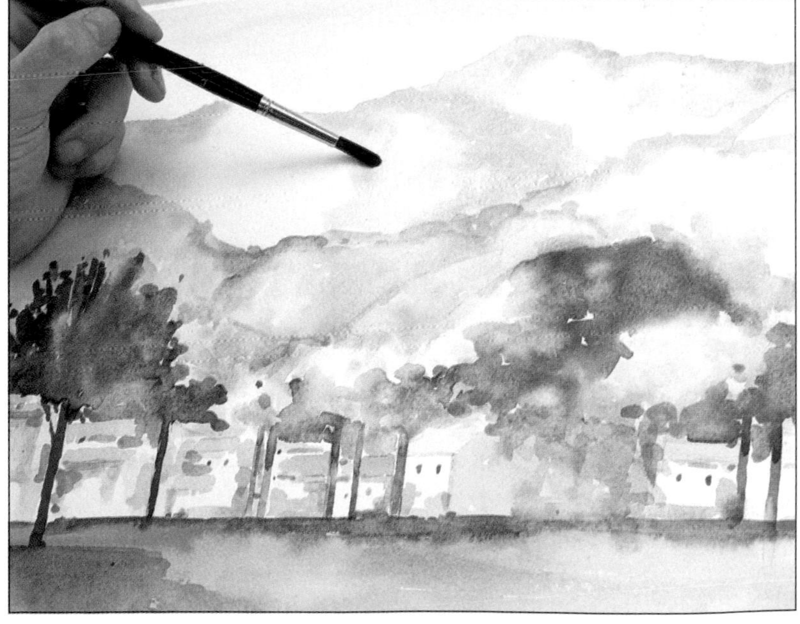

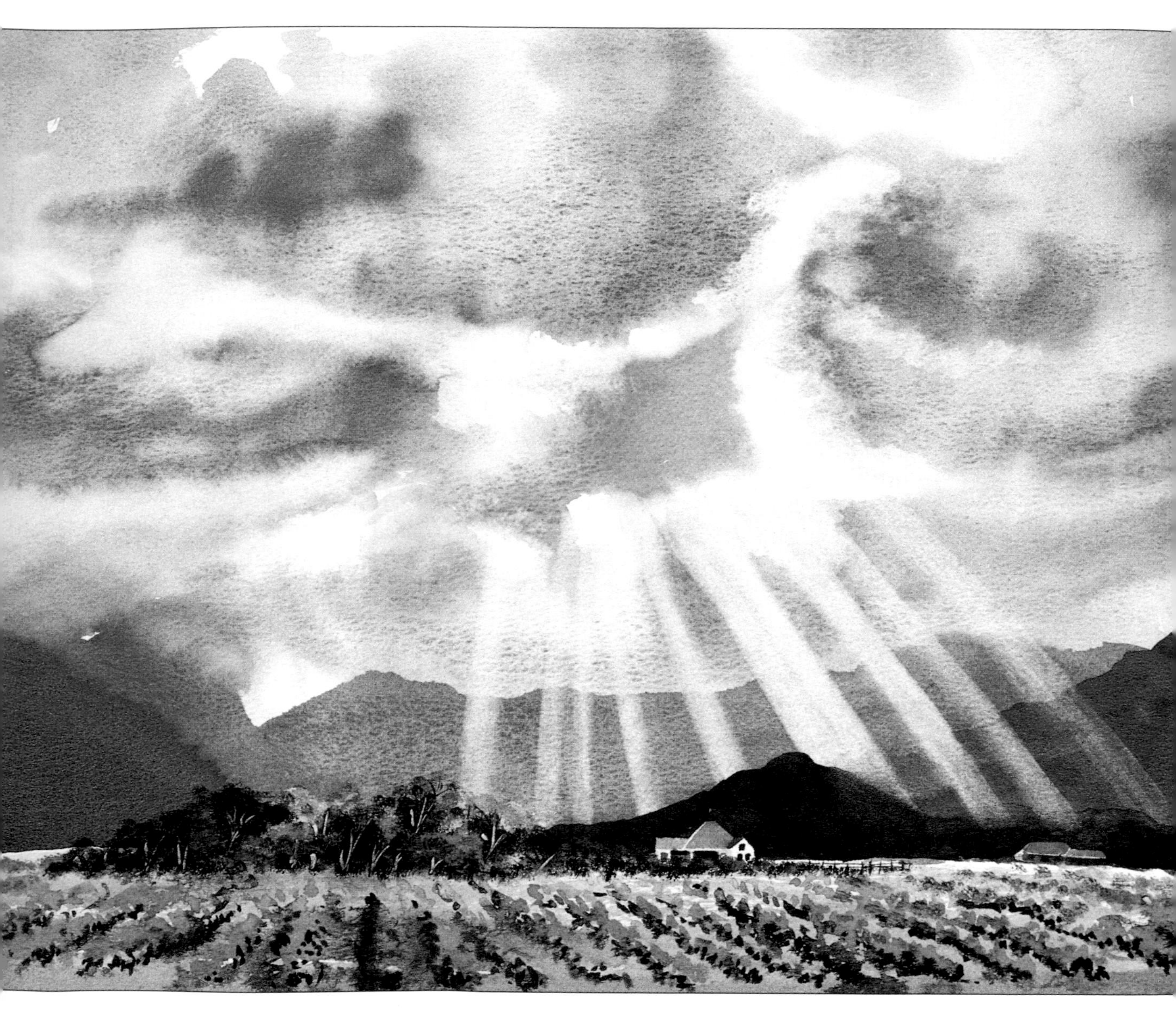

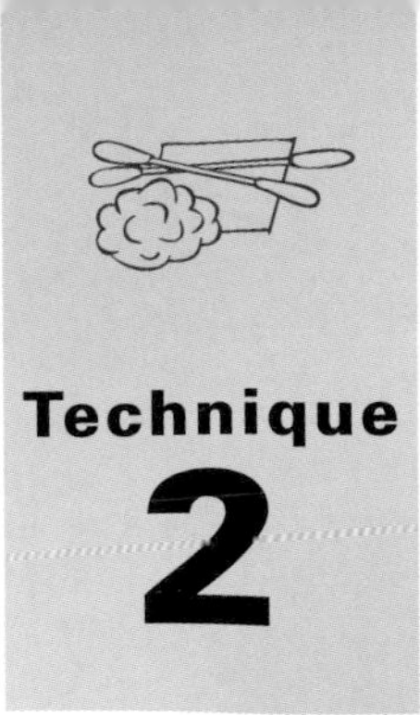

Technique

2

Lifting Out

There are rare moments when landscape, sky and light combine to create a truly dramatic scene. In this painting the artist uses a technique called "lifting out" to create rays of light breaking through the cloudy sky and pouring onto the earth. The sky itself was created using wet on wet painting, taking full advantage of watercolour paint's tendency to blend and merge with other wet areas. This can of course be the bane of many a watercolour artist, but, when controlled, it can also be used to great artistic effect. The calm of the house and the vineyard in the midst of the breathtaking land- and skyscape contributes to the overall impact of the work.

Roger Hutchins
The Vineyard
30 x 40cm (12 x 16in)

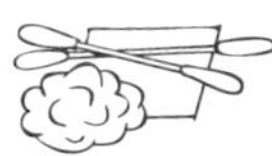

Lifting Out Technique

Although it is not as flexible as oil paint, watercolour paint can be removed from the paper once it has been applied. The simplest way of doing this is with absorbent materials such as blotting paper, tissue paper, kitchen paper, rags or cotton wool buds. These can be used to lift out newly applied paint that is still damp. This technique is perfect for catching mistakes and unwelcome runs of colour. It can also be used creatively, for example to lift out areas of sky for white clouds. Paint may also be removed once it has dried. This entails using a clean damp brush to dissolve the paint once more, and then an absorbent material to lift the paint out. Both these techniques are more effective on less absorbent papers.

THE VINEYARD

Materials and Equipment

• SHEET OF ROUGH, 300 GSM WATERCOLOUR PAPER, STRETCHED (SEE P. 111) • FLAT SOFT HAIR BRUSHES: ¼IN, ¾IN AND ⅝IN • NO.2 RIGGER BRUSH • ZERO BRUSH FOR DETAIL • NO.4 HOG BRISTLE BRUSH • MEDIUM SOFT HAIR BRUSH • WATERCOLOUR PAINTS: CERULEAN BLUE, ULTRAMARINE BLUE, INDIGO, RAW SIENNA, ALIZARIN CRIMSON, INDIAN RED, GAMBOUGE YELLOW, SEPIA, SAP GREEN, VIRIDIAN GREEN • KITCHEN PAPER TO CATCH MISTAKES

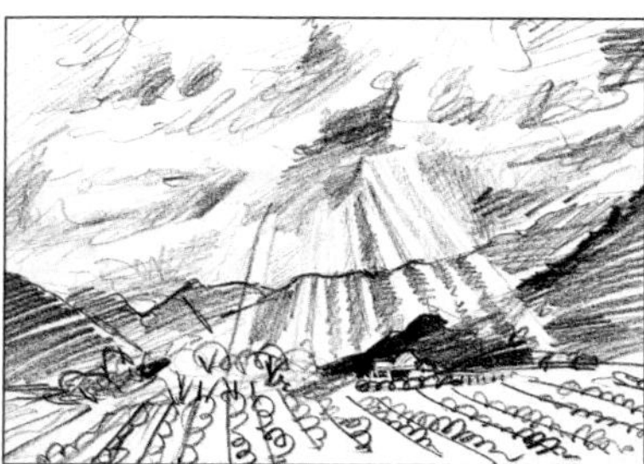

Left: The artist used this quick sketch of a South African vineyard as reference for the painting.

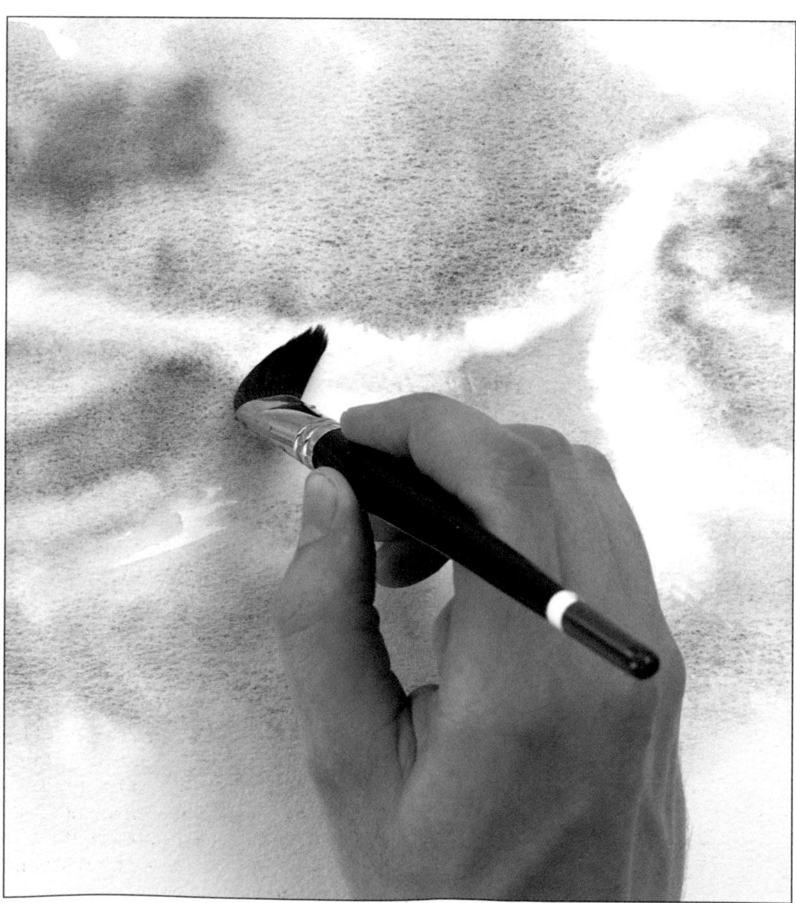

1. ◀ Using a large flat brush, cover the paper with a thin wash of raw sienna. Blot out an area where the break in the clouds will be with kitchen paper. While the wash is still damp, add other colours to the sky; first cerulean blue for the break in the clouds. Now add some darker colours, ultramarine blue, alizarin crimson and Indian red. Allow the colours to run into each other a little. Add touches of indigo to mark dark areas in the cloud. Use a clean damp brush to create lighter areas, washing out the colour and dabbing it off with kitchen paper.

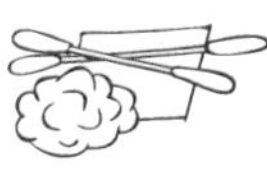

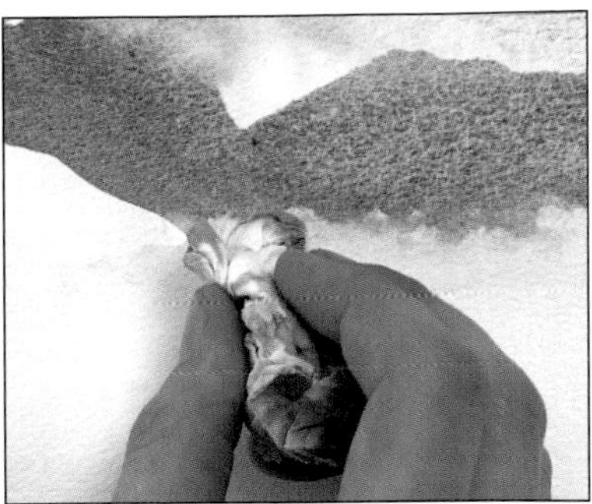

2.

Now start on the hills by giving the area a wash of ultramarine blue and alizarin crimson. Dab away the paint with kitchen paper where the trees are to go.

3.

Use gambouge yellow for the foreground. Mix indigo with ultramarine and Indian red for the closer hills. Use a clean damp hog bristle brush to lift paint for the rays of sunlight. Dab off the moisture with kitchen paper.

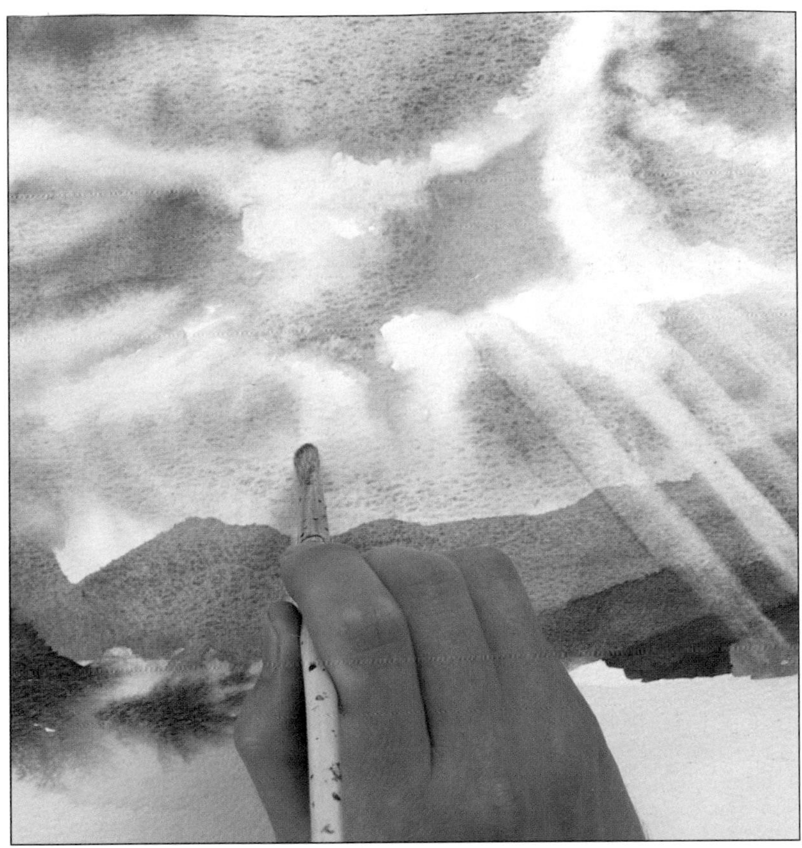

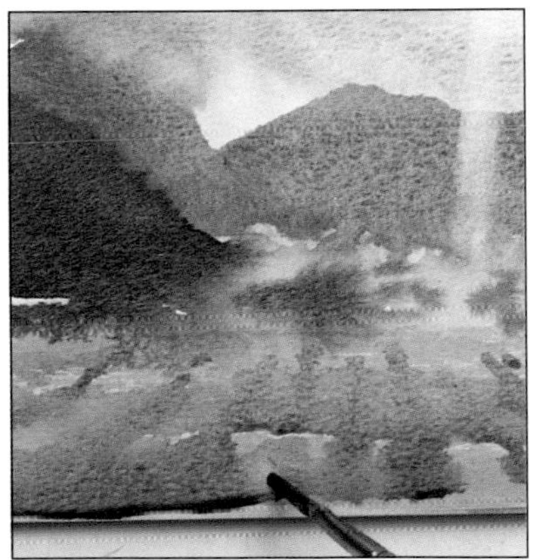

4.

With a ¼in brush add sap green mixed with gambouge yellow for the foreground foliage. Now mix raw sienna and Indian red to establish the lines of the vineyard. The paint should merge slightly.

5.

Use sepia mixed with indigo to add shadow areas to the foreground plants. Mix indigo, Indian red and a little ultramarine blue wash for the near hillside. Be sure to leave blank areas outlining the buildings. Now use the same colour but a smaller brush to add some shadows to the buildings. Build the trees up with neat viridian green. Use the end of the brush to mark the trunks of the trees. Finally, use a zero brush to add detail to the buildings, and use alizarin crimson mixed with viridian and ultramarine blue around the buildings.

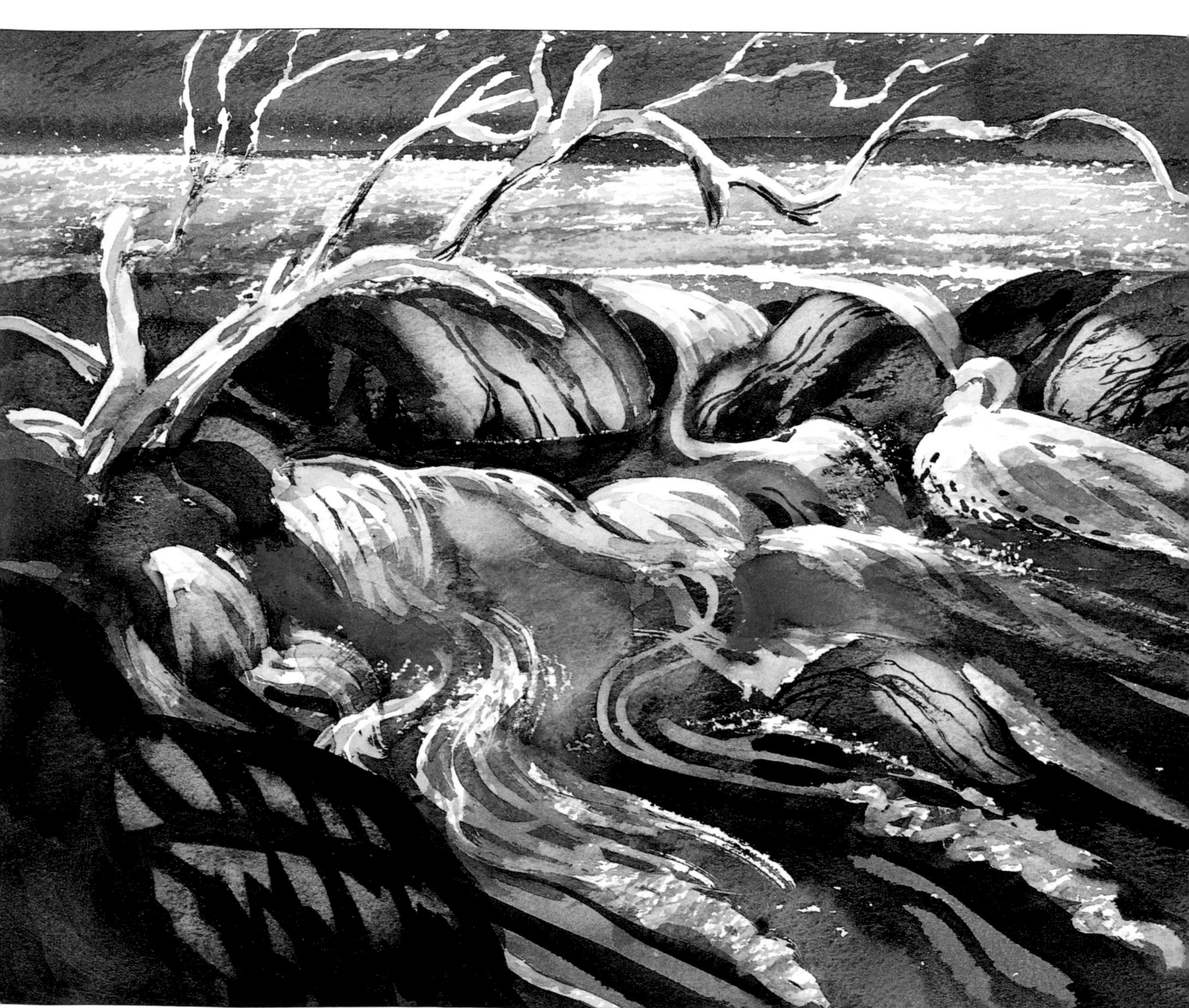

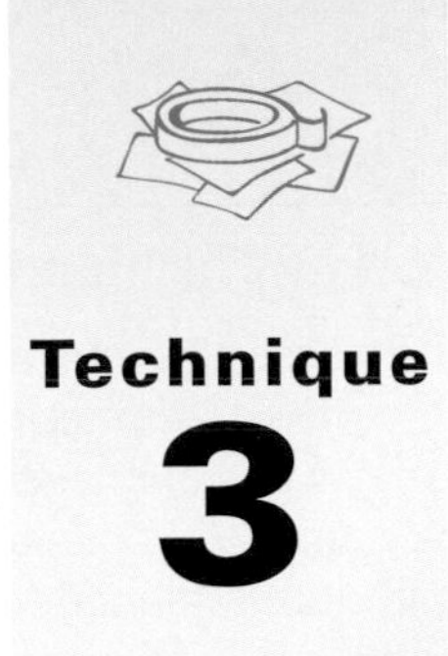

Technique

3

MASKING

Here the artist has used two different methods of masking to create water effects. First he uses art masking fluid to achieve the swirling white surf of the water as it plunges down the rapids. Then he uses a purpose-made stencil to lift out sharp-edged areas on a foreground rock and portray glistening moisture. The first technique needs to be thought out right at the beginning of the painting, as the masking fluid has to be applied early on. The second technique can be carried out at the last moment, as it involves lifting paint off rather than keeping the area white all along. Both serve here to convey the movement and texture of this wild scene.

John Barber
Welsh River Scene
30 x 40cm (12 x 16in)

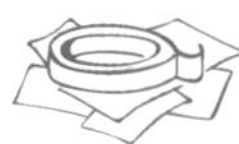

Masking Technique

There are numerous methods for masking areas so that they will show a previous wash or the white of the paper in the finished painting. Art masking fluid is a rubber solution that is painted onto the paper. Washes can then be laid over it. When the masking fluid is finally removed (rubbed off by hand) the previous colour remains. To create sharp edges or straight lines, artists often use masking tape. This can be applied, painted over and then removed to create straight edges. Here John Barber cuts out shapes in a piece of clear plastic to create a stencil for lifting out sharp-edged areas of paint on a rock. All these masking techniques are highly flexible and can be applied in a wide range of painting scenarios.

Welsh River Scene

Materials and Equipment

• SHEET OF ROUGH, 300 GSM WATERCOLOUR PAPER, STRETCHED (SEE P. 111) • PENCIL • FLAT SOFT HAIR BRUSHES: ONE SMALL, ONE MEDIUM, ONE LARGE • OLD BRUSH • WATERCOLOUR PAINTS: CERULEAN BLUE, ULTRAMARINE BLUE, COBALT BLUE, BURNT SIENNA, YELLOW OCHRE, VIRIDIAN GREEN, PAYNE'S GREY, IVORY BLACK • ART MASKING FLUID • KITCHEN PAPER • SCALPEL • SHEET OF THIN, CLEAR PLASTIC (OVERHEAD PROJECTOR SHEET) • CRAYON

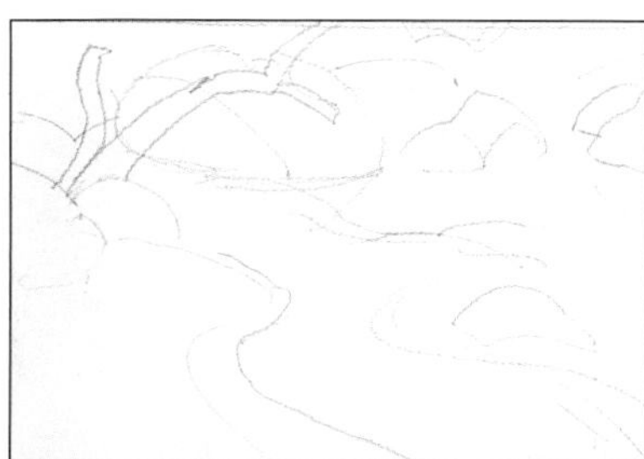

1. First sketch the principal shapes of the picture in pencil. Include quite a detailed outline of the branch over the river. This sketch will act as a guide for applying the art masking fluid in the next stage.

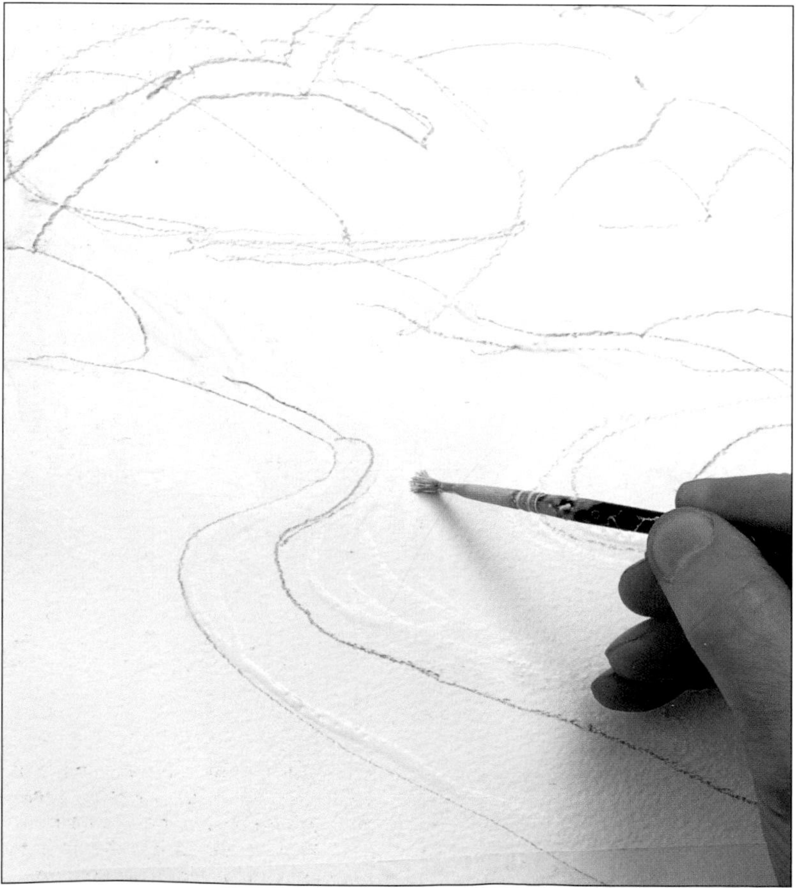

2. Use a small, old brush to apply the art masking fluid to the painting. Shake the bottle before you start. Paint the fluid onto the paper over the areas that you want to appear white in the final picture. Remember that you can always paint over areas if you put too much down – but not vice versa. Fill in the branch, the white water of the rapids and some dappled areas of foam. If you miss areas, do not go over the masking fluid again until it is dry – this usually takes about five minutes. Allow all the masking fluid to dry before continuing with the painting.

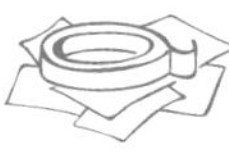

3.▸

Mix viridian, yellow ochre and Payne's grey. Now use a large flat brush to apply a wash of this colour to the area above the horizon of the water. Load the brush well with paint so that you can make the application in one go. As the paint passes over the masking fluid it will form into small droplets. These should be allowed to dry before the fluid is removed. Allow the brush to dry slightly. Apply it lightly over the area below the horizon. As the bristles pass over the bumpy surface of the paper, the paint will miss patches of paper. This should create the dappled effect of distant water.

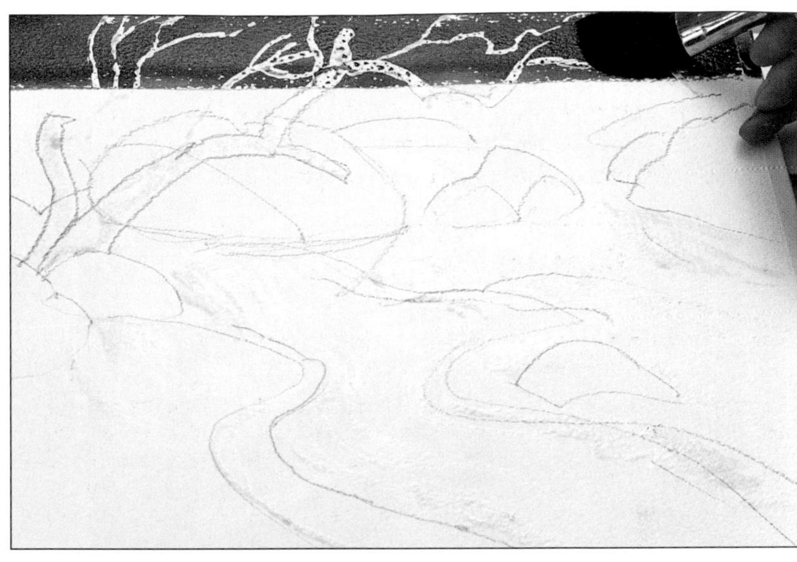

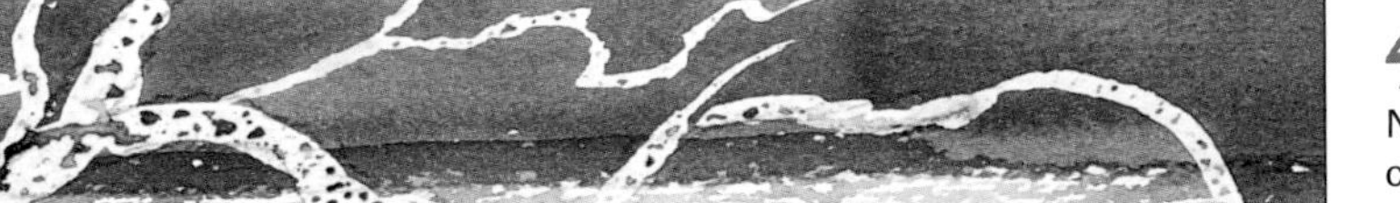

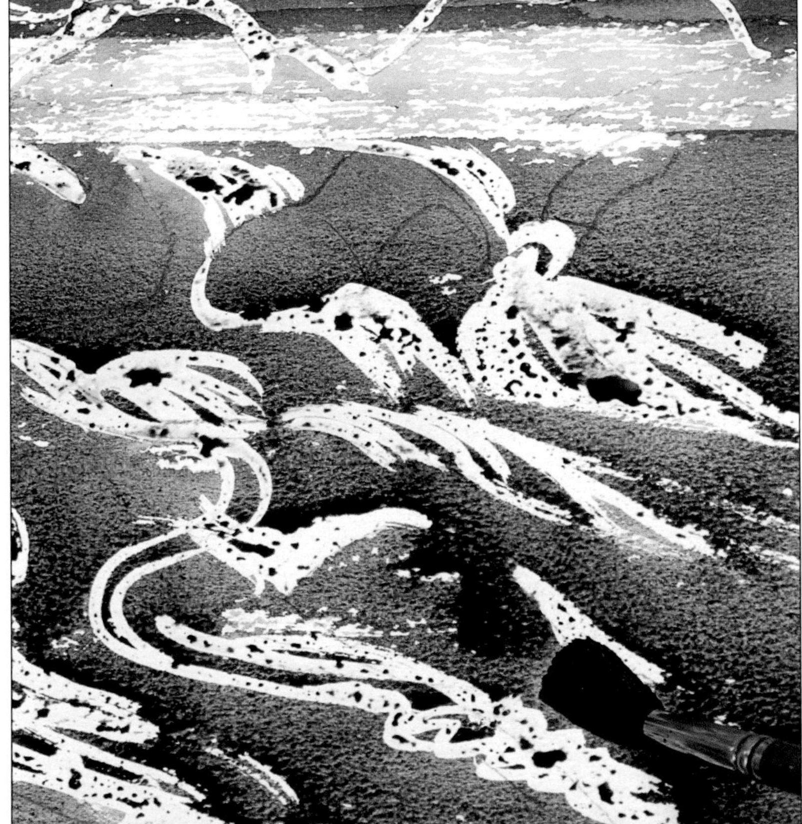

4.◂

Now mix a dark colour using black, cobalt blue and burnt sienna. Then a green with viridian and ultramarine. Apply the first wash to the rest of the picture. Now add areas of the green into the wet paint.

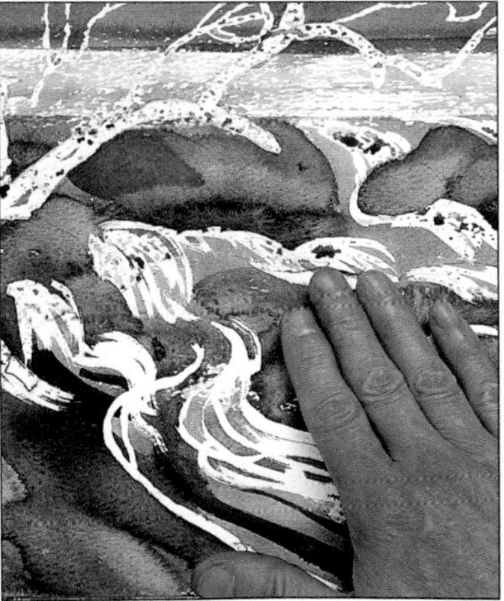

5.▴

Add some yellow ochre to the green wash. Use this to establish the rock shapes. Add black for some dark areas in the water. Allow the paint to dry, then rub off the masking fluid.

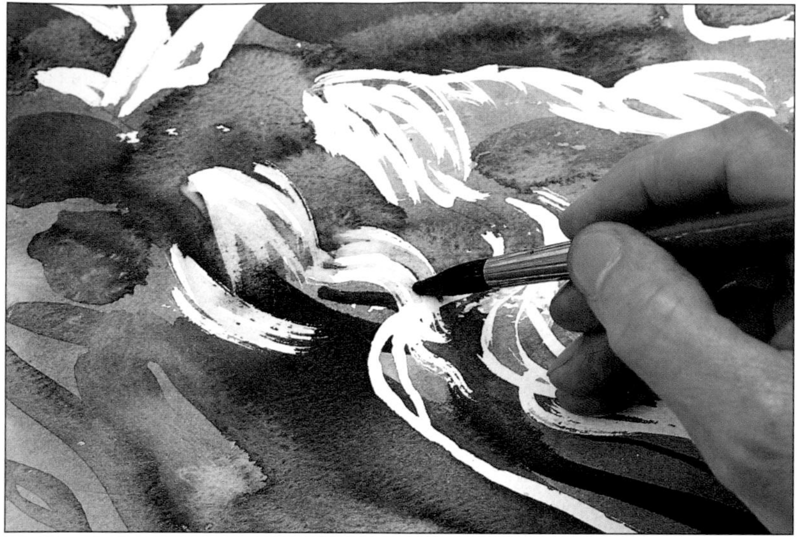

6.◀

The white areas that remain are too strong as they stand. Use a wet brush without paint to introduce some of the background colour to the white areas. Leave only the areas that you want to remain completely white. The background colour will not completely cover up the white areas – they will continue to show up as lighter areas. In the end probably only about 10 per cent of the white areas that you created with the masking fluid will remain untouched in the picture. This is why, as mentioned earlier, you can start with more white areas than you will actually need.

7.▶

The next stage is to create some highlights on the rocks. Do this with a clean, damp brush (without any paint). Rub the paper gently with the brush and some of the paint should lift off, creating the impression of light falling on the rocks.

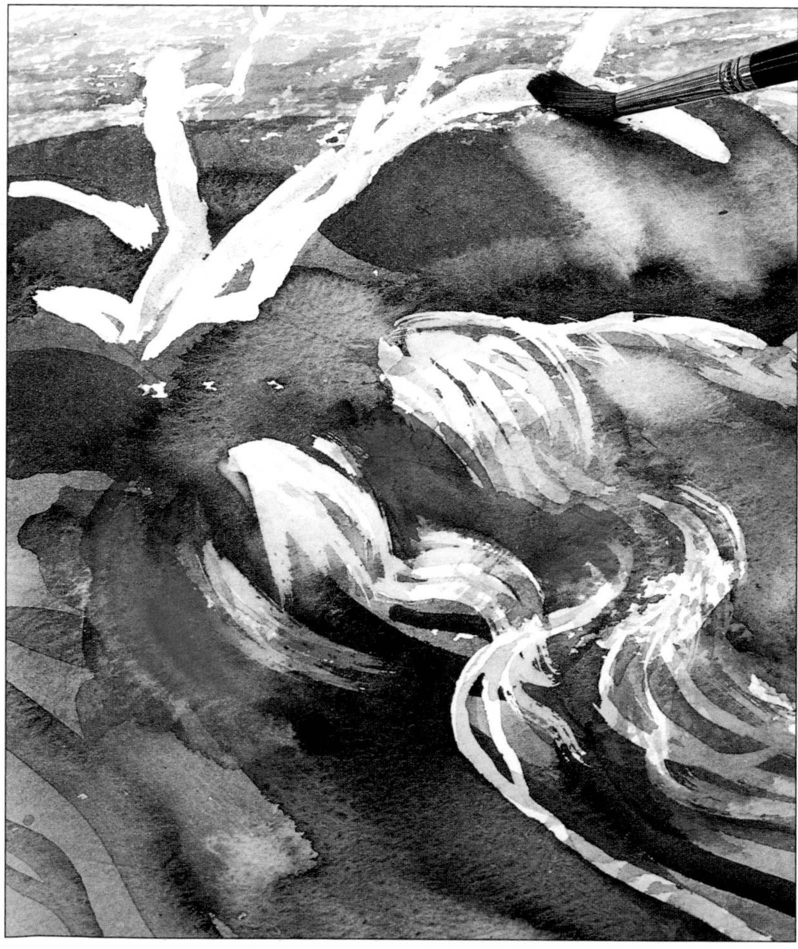

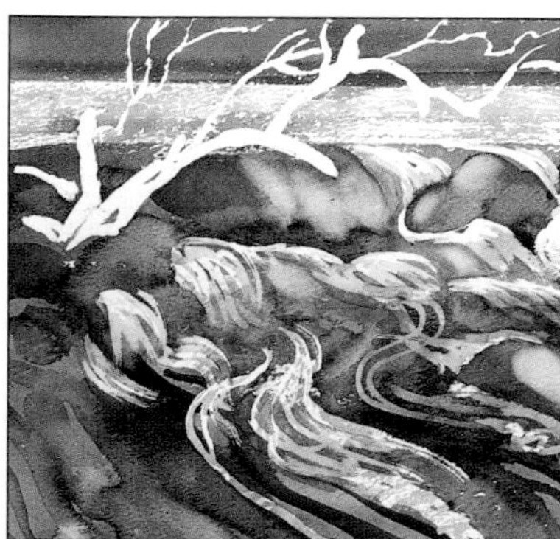

8.▲

Apply some cerulean blue to the river and across the upper water area. Now mix yellow ochre with a little Payne's grey and colour the branch – leaving white highlights.

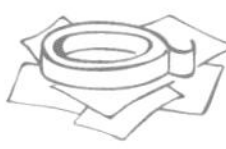

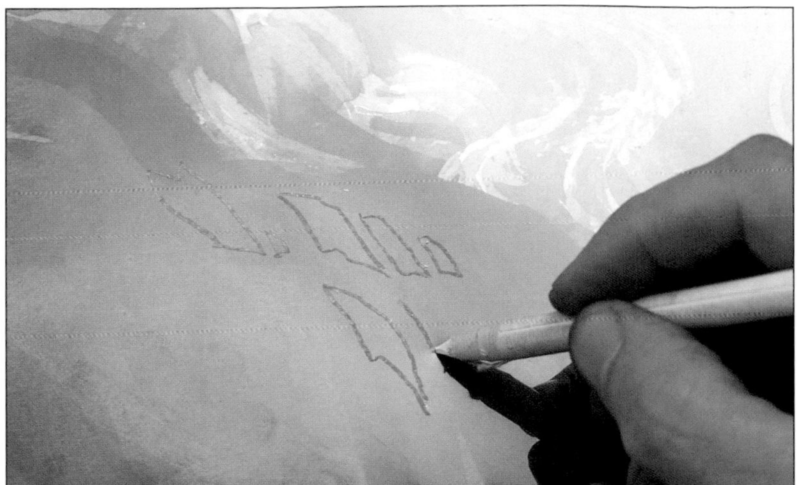

9.

Define the rocks with thin lines of viridian, black and burnt sienna mix. Now add a rock to the lower left corner in black and viridian. Allow this to dry. Place a piece of thin, clear plastic over the rock. Using a pencil or crayon, draw some sharp-edged shapes onto the plastic where you want highlights on the rock. Also draw the outline of the rock.

10.

Remove the plastic from the painting. Using a scalpel, cut out the shapes in the plastic. You will then be left with a custom-made stencil with which to create highlights on the foreground rock.

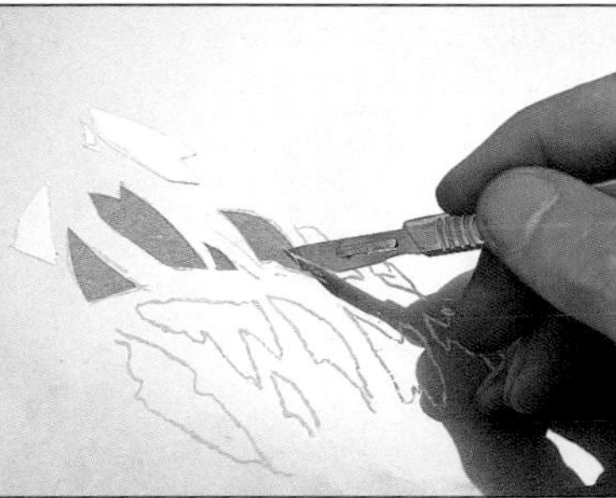

11.

Place the stencil over the rock in the same position as it was when you drew the pencil marks. Use wet kitchen paper to lift off the paint under the stencil, keeping the stencil firmly in place. Dab down rather than from side to side to avoid water running under the stencil. Remove the stencil when the paint has lifted.

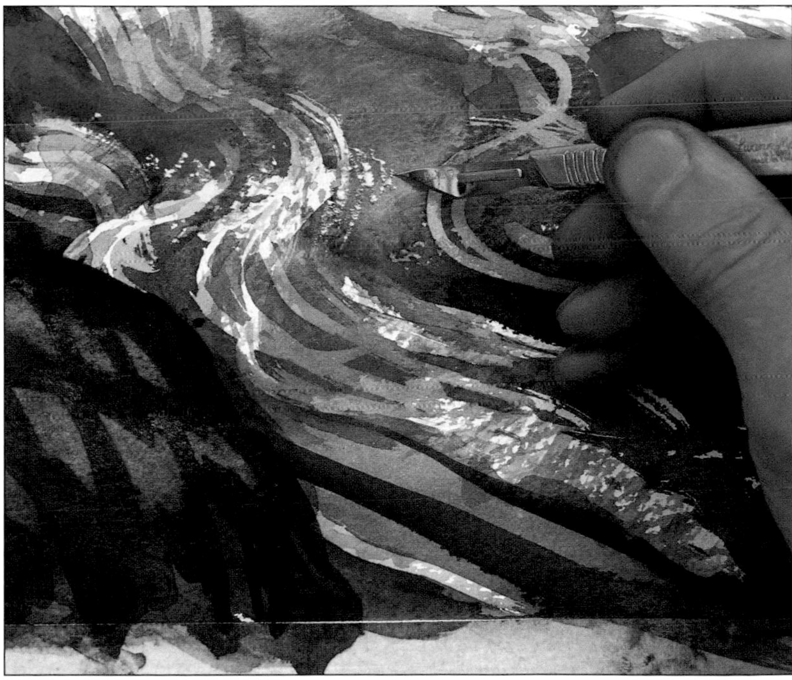

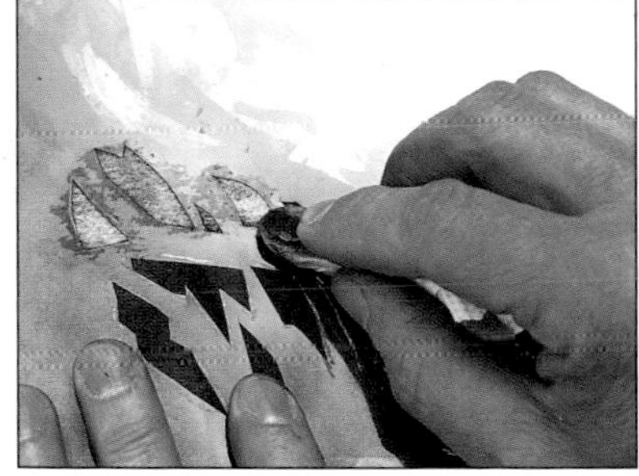

12.

Now add a weak wash of yellow ochre to the rock to warm the colour a little. Finally, use the point of a scalpel to scratch off small flecks of paint and expose the white paper below. Do this around the base of some of the rocks and in the rapids to create bubbling water.

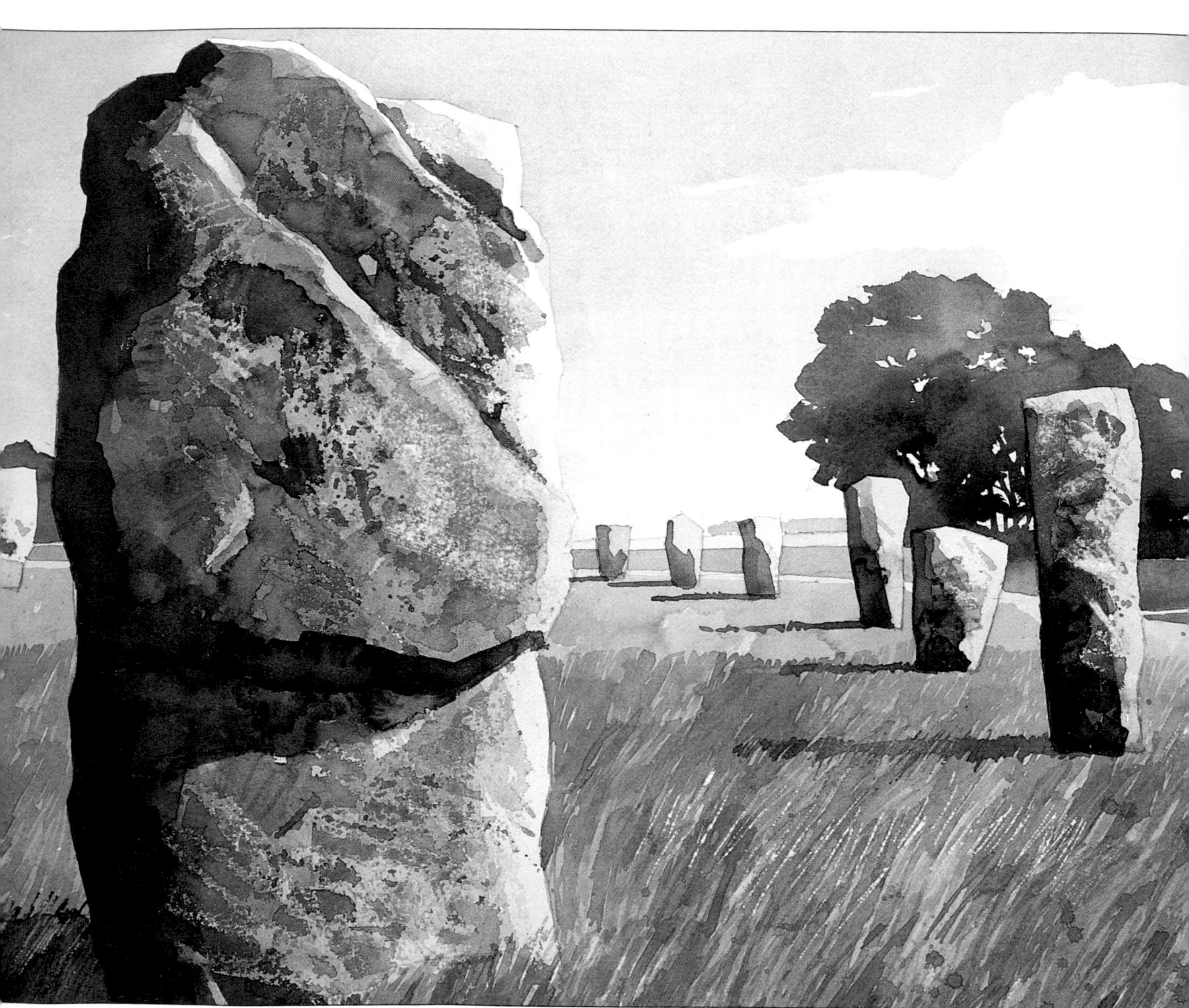

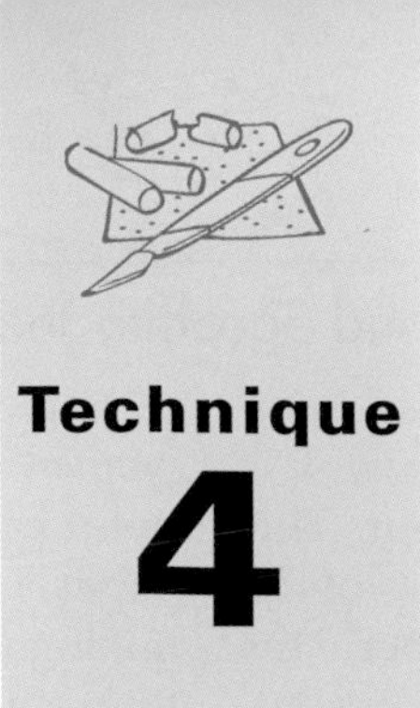

Technique

4

Resist and Sgraffito

This powerful scene has been painted using a number of techniques for creating texture. I have used candle wax on the paper to resist paint layered over it. The result mimics the rough texture of the ancient rocks, covered in lichen and weather-worn. I have also used sgraffito (scratching with a sharp point) to lift out areas of white paper in the grass. I worked by gradually layering up darker colours, allowing the textures to build as the painting progresses. The combined effect is a series of different planes of colour and texture, increasing the visual impact of the whole picture.

Ian Sidaway
Avebury Stone Circle
55 x 75cm (22 x 30in)

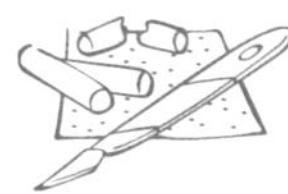

Resist and Sgraffito Technique

For the watercolour artist the term resist is usually reserved for the use of wax. When wax is rubbed onto paper it repels watercolour. This results in a dappled effect, the coarseness of the effect depending on the grain of the paper. This technique is particularly effective for representing rocks, cliffs, pebble beaches, ploughed fields or the bark on trees. Sgraffito, the other technique used here, comes from the Italian *graffiare* (to scratch). This involves using a sharp point or abrasive surface to scratch up white paper. The term also applies to the technique of mixing Gum Arabic to paint and then using a fine point to clear away lines of paint. Both techniques create highlights – and are used here to mimic light falling on uneven surfaces.

Stone Circle

Materials and Equipment

• SHEET OF ROUGH, 600 LBS WATERCOLOUR PAPER, STRETCHED (SEE P. 111) • PENCIL • FLAT SOFT HAIR BRUSHES: ONE SMALL, ONE MEDIUM • WATERCOLOUR PAINTS: CERULEAN BLUE, ULTRAMARINE BLUE, BURNT SIENNA, BURNT UMBER, YELLOW OCHRE, SAP GREEN, PAYNE'S GREY • GUM ARABIC • PALETTE KNIFE • CRAFT KNIFE OR SCALPEL • WHITE WAX CANDLE • KITCHEN PAPER TO CATCH MISTAKES

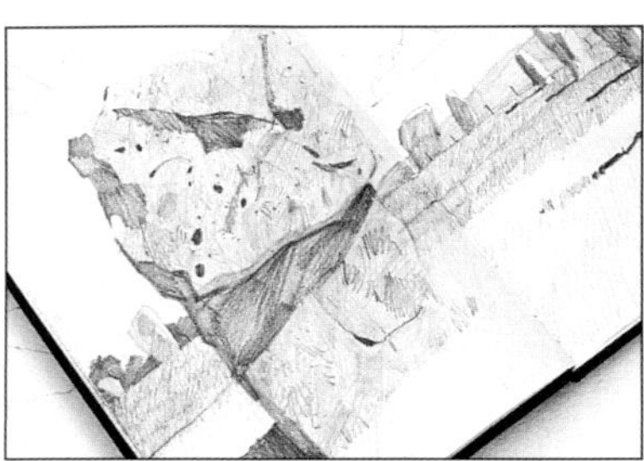

Left: For reference I used a pencil drawing from my sketch book, made on location. The site is the impressive stone circle of Avebury in southern England, a few miles away from the smaller, but more well-known, Stonehenge. The stones have become intricately textured – perfect subjects for resist technique.

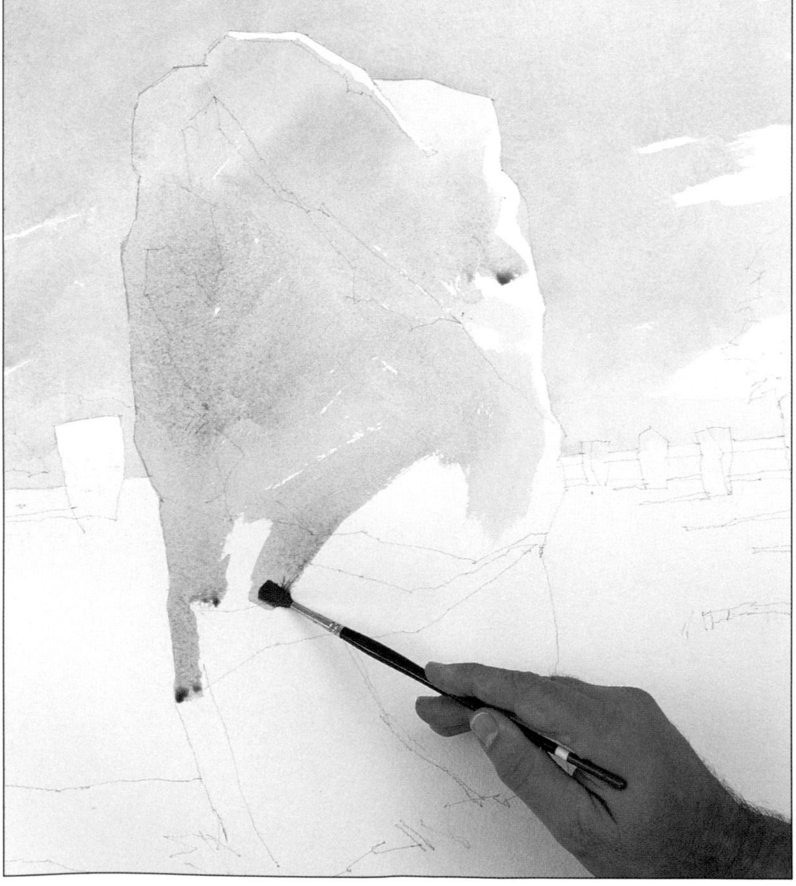

1. ◀ First make a pencil sketch of the principal outlines in the picture. Now use a cerulean blue and ultramarine blue wash for the sky, leaving white areas for clouds. Allow this wash to dry before continuing. Now mix yellow ochre, burnt sienna and Payne's grey. Use a weak wash of this to colour the stones, leaving blank areas for white highlights. Start at the top of the stones and bring the paint down – this allows for far more accurate placing of the paint. The aim is to try to keep the paint within the boundaries of the stones, making a sharp edge.

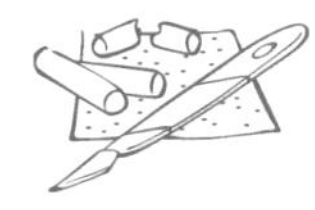

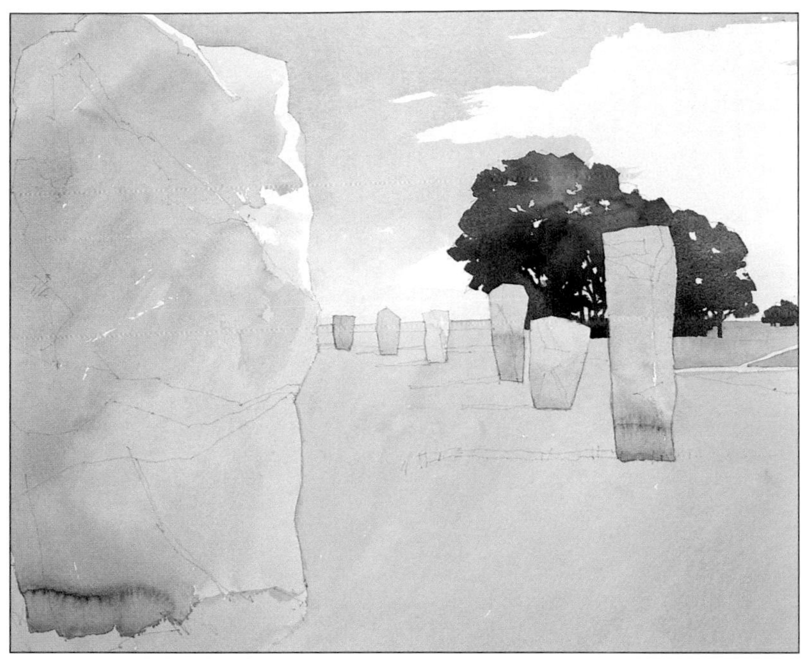

2.

Now make a slightly stronger wash of the same colour and put another layer on the stones – again leaving highlight areas and not covering the previous wash entirely. Mix sap green and yellow ochre for the first wash over the grass. Leave white areas for the chalk paths. Allow this to dry. Mix sap green and burnt umber for the trees. Leave blank areas for the gaps in the foliage as well as the gaps around the trunks. All the main elements of the picture have now received their first application of paint.

3.

Use a diluted wash of the tree mix to paint in the darkened hillside in the middle distance – leaving the paths white. Mix sap green with a little yellow ochre for the grass and apply it with the flat edge of the brush – using the paper texture.

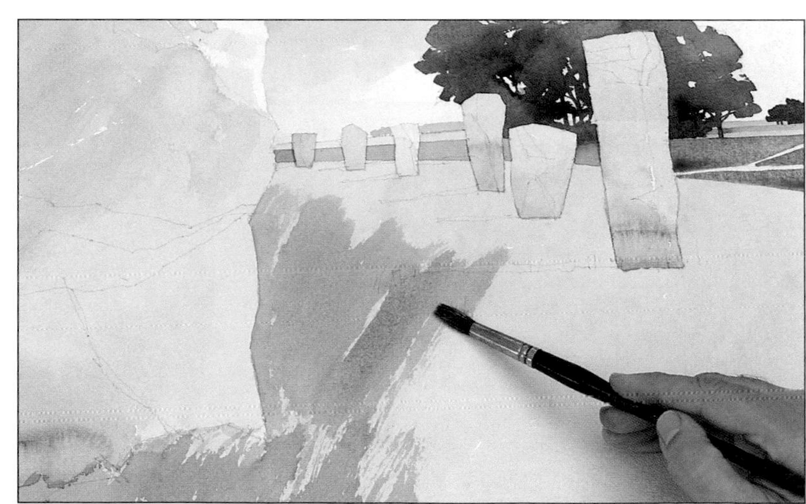

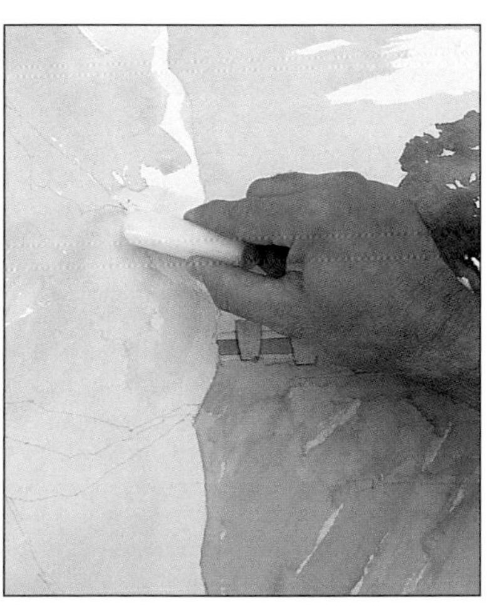

4.

Now is the time for the first use of wax resist. Use a clear candle to rub wax onto the foreground stones. Rub it into areas that you want to attain a dappled effect. Also draw almost parallel lines of wax. As subsequent layers of paint are applied the wax will allow the lighter layers of paint to show through.

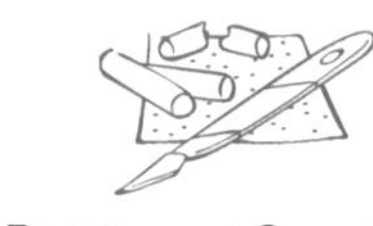

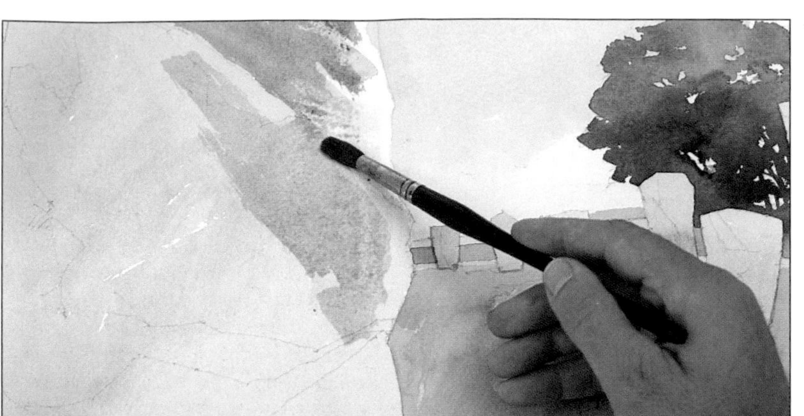

5.

Mix a darker stone wash with Payne's grey and burnt umber. Apply this to the stones – leaving highlight areas. As the colours get darker, they are applied to smaller areas of the stones. The stones reduce in detail as they recede. The most distant ones need only two different tones – light and dark.

6.

Continue to work up the texture of the stones. Gradually apply stronger greys, until eventually adding the final dark shadow areas. Reserve the very darkest colours for the rock in the foreground – this will add to the sense of distance in the work. As well as wax resist, there are other means of creating texture on the rocks. Allowing the darker colours to backrun slightly into the lighter colours gives an effective impression of lichen or moss on the rock. Also try spattering paint onto the paper – again adding to the rough texture of the stone.

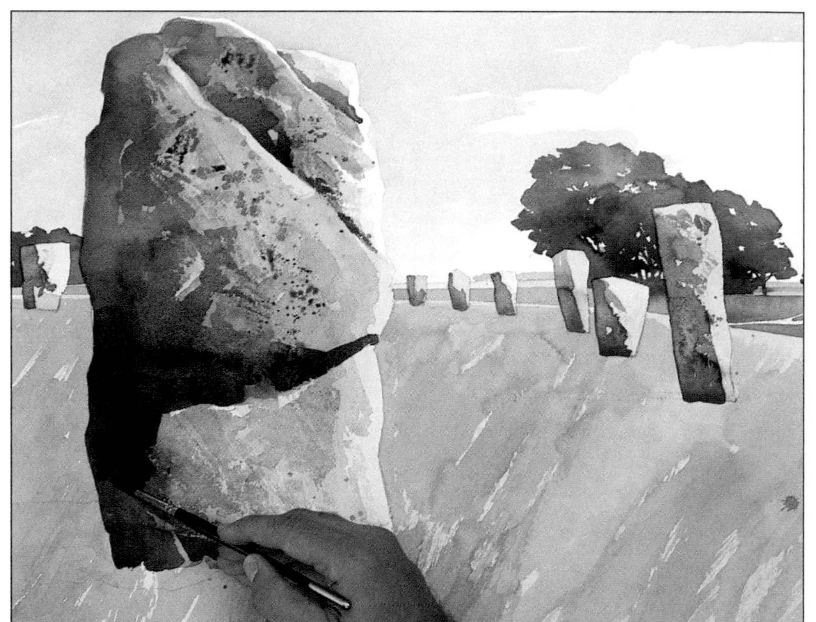

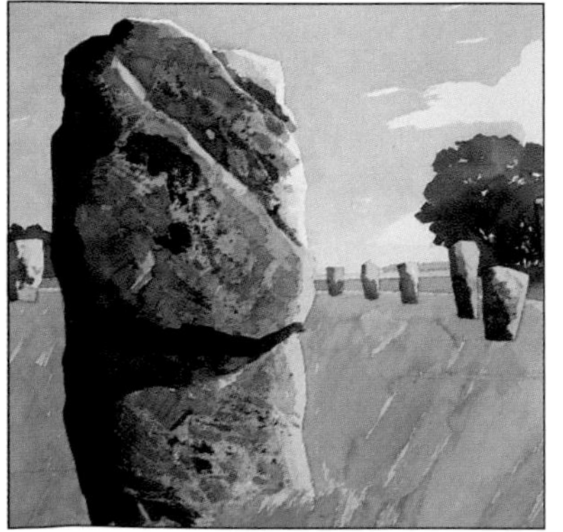

7.

Now step back and take a look at the picture. Most of the definition on the rocks should be complete. However the stones still look as if they are floating above the ground – so the next stage will be to add shadows. These will "ground" the stones, giving the desired impression of weight and solidity. Before this, however, the foreground grass needs some added texture.

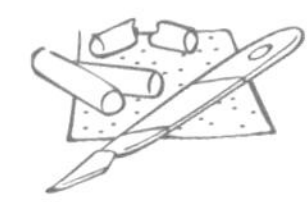

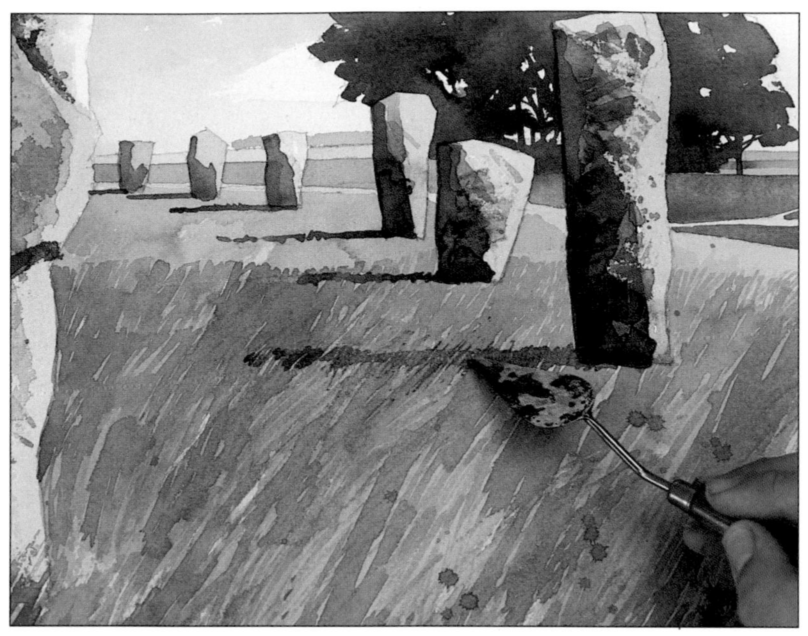

8.

Mix a wash of sap green, yellow ochre and burnt umber. Then use a thin brush in rapid strokes to create the impression of tall grass in the foreground. Allow this to dry. Now mix sap green, Payne's grey and burnt umber with Gum Arabic. Use this for the rock shadows. For the shadows that fall on the tall grass, run a fine edge (such as a palette knife) back and forward through the wet paint. This will create the impression of rippling shadows.

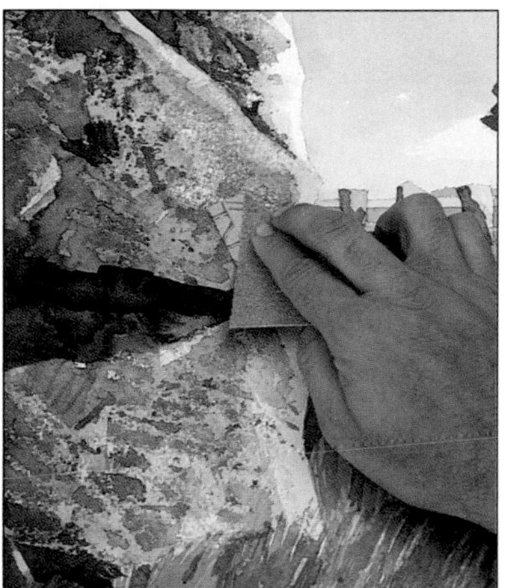

9.

The picture is now complete apart from some finishing touches. Use a piece of coarse sand paper to rub off some paint on the two nearest stones. This will create dappled highlights and enhance the texture.

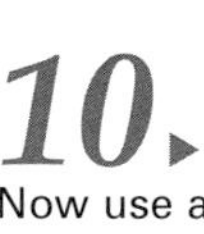

10.

Now use a sharp edge such as a craft knife or a scalpel to scratch a series of parallel lines into the tall grass area. Exposing the white of the paper underneath creates effective highlights – giving the impression of sunlight striking the individual stalks of grass. The angle of the lines should match the surrounding grass – enhancing the illusion of a stiff breeze.

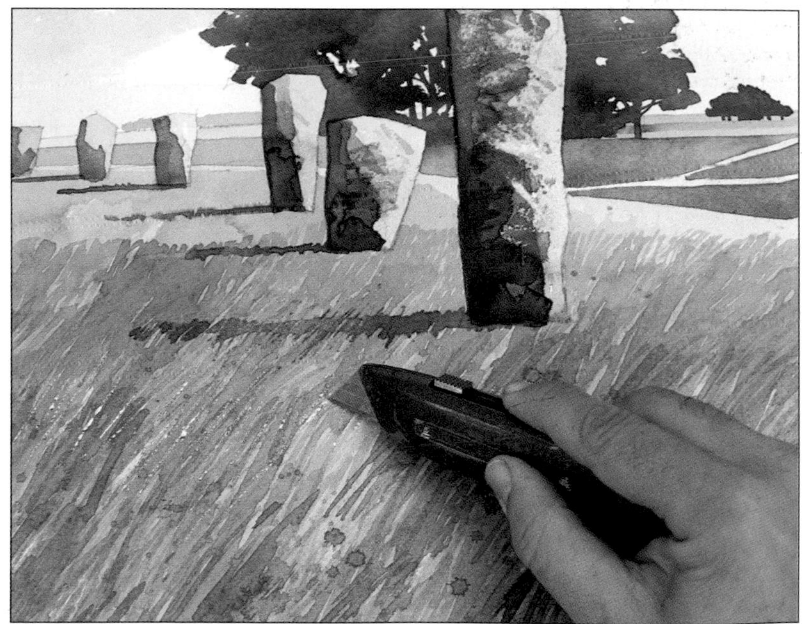

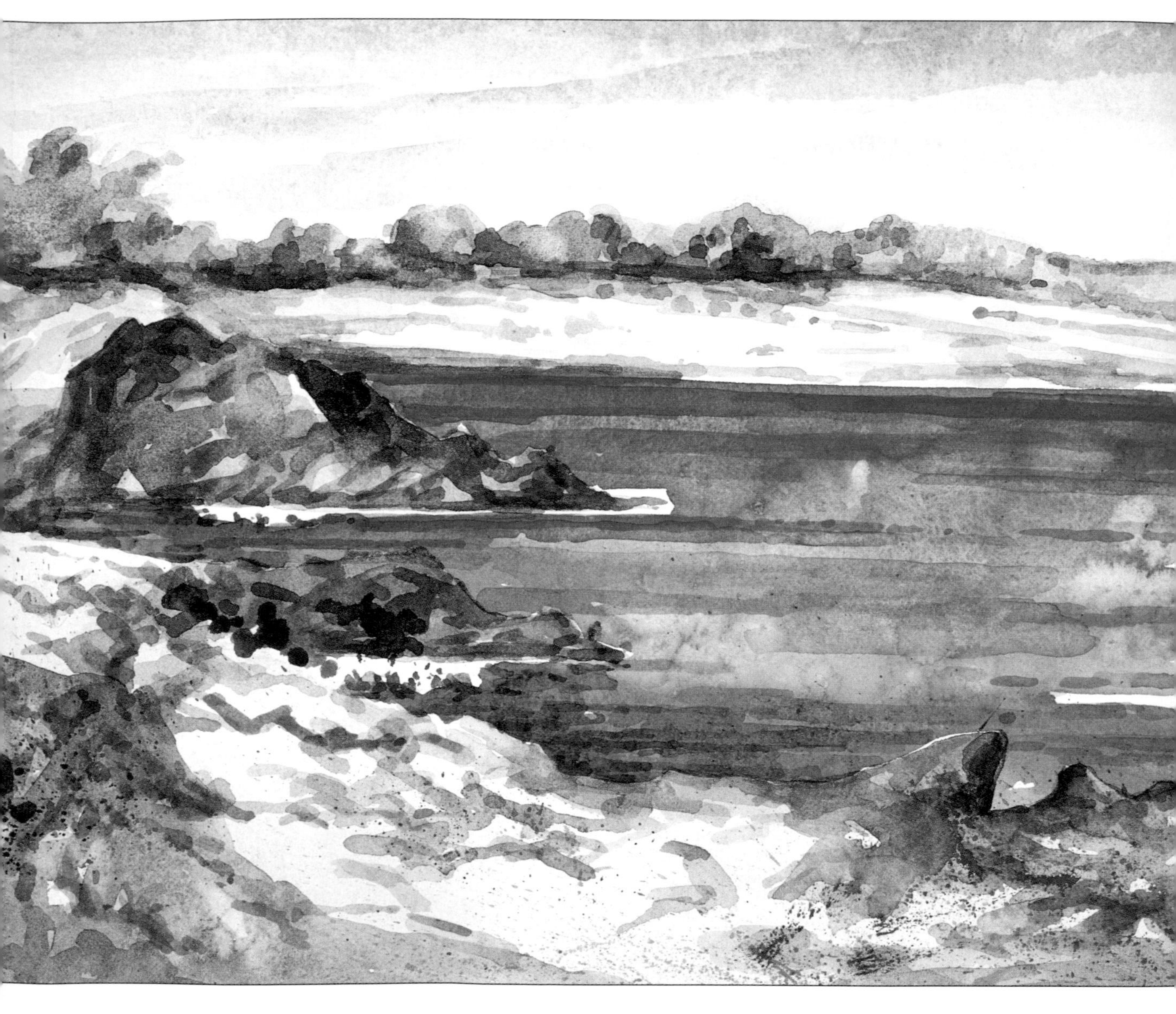

Spattering and Rock Salt

This lively painting captures the freshness of the Mediterranean in springtime. Although the sea is calm, it is not as placid as it is in summer. The artist, James Horton, uses spattering and rock salt to capture the movement of the water – as it meets the rocky shore and as it enters the bay. He also uses the two techniques to enhance the texture of the rocky beach, creating the impression of ragged rocks and scattered pebbles. James' style is liberal and brisk, which creates an immediacy in the image that a more laboured work would not capture. This style also suits on-location painting.

James Horton
Mediterranean Coast
30 x 40cm (12 x 16in)

Spattering and Rock Salt Technique

Flicking paint onto the paper is known as spattering and is a useful technique to liven up flat washes and to create textural effects. Hold the damp (not sodden) brush flat over the work and tap the brush gently to release the paint. More control can be achieved by using a stiff bristle brush such as a toothbrush: pull your thumb over the bristles and allow them to spring forward again. Spattering onto dry and wet paper creates different effects – so try experimenting first to make sure you use the right combination. Another technique used here is the application of rock salt. When this is applied to wet paint, it soaks up the surrounding moisture, creating a dappled effect. This is handy for suggesting uneven surfaces.

MEDITERRANEAN COAST

Materials and Equipment

• SHEET OF ROUGH, 450 LBS WATERCOLOUR PAPER, STRETCHED (SEE P. 111) • FLAT, SOFT HAIR BRUSHES: ONE MEDIUM, ONE SMALL • WATERCOLOUR PAINTS: ULTRAMARINE BLUE, COBALT BLUE, PRUSSIAN BLUE, SCARLET LAKE, ALIZARIN CRIMSON, VERMILLION, CADMIUM RED, CADMIUM ORANGE, BURNT UMBER, BURNT SIENNA, OXIDE OF CHROMIUM, YELLOW OCHRE, LEMON YELLOW, PAYNE'S GREY • ROCK SALT • KITCHEN PAPER TO CATCH MISTAKES

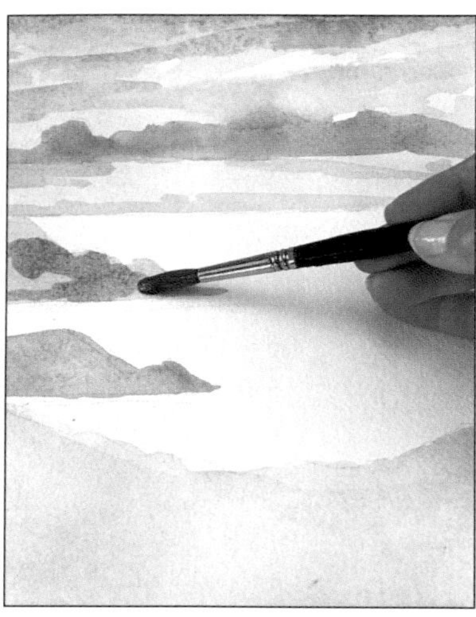

1. Wash in the sky with ultramarine, cobalt blue and alizarin crimson. Use yellow ochre for the distant shore. Add cobalt and vermillion for the two outcrops. Now add cadmium red for the foreground. Mix alizarin crimson, ultramarine, and vermillion for the outcrops. Mix lemon yellow and oxide of chromium for the trees and add ultramarine and yellow ochre for the dark areas in the trees. Use vermillion, cadmium red, and lemon yellow to make dark areas on the distant shore. Add cobalt blue to the sky, and use burnt umber to darken the distant outcrop.

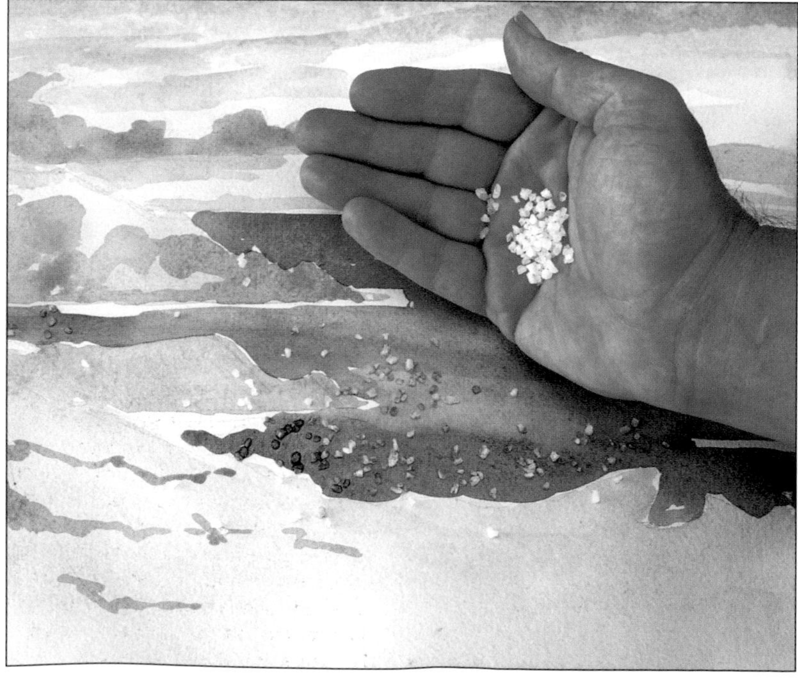

2. Mix vermillion and burnt umber and mark in lines on the near beach. Now mix two washes for the sea: first ultramarine blue and alizarin crimson, and second Prussian blue and cadmium orange. Use the first wash for the distant water and the second in the foreground. Save some of these colours for later. While the sea paint is still wet, sprinkle some rock salt crystals over the area. Leave these in place to take effect while you continue working on other areas.

3.

Using rock salt can be a hit-and-miss affair. Try to scatter the salt so that it is spread evenly over the area that you want the dappled effect to appear on. Break up clumps of crystals. Leave the crystals in place until they are completely dry. This technique is best used indoors – where the salt will not be blown around in the wind.

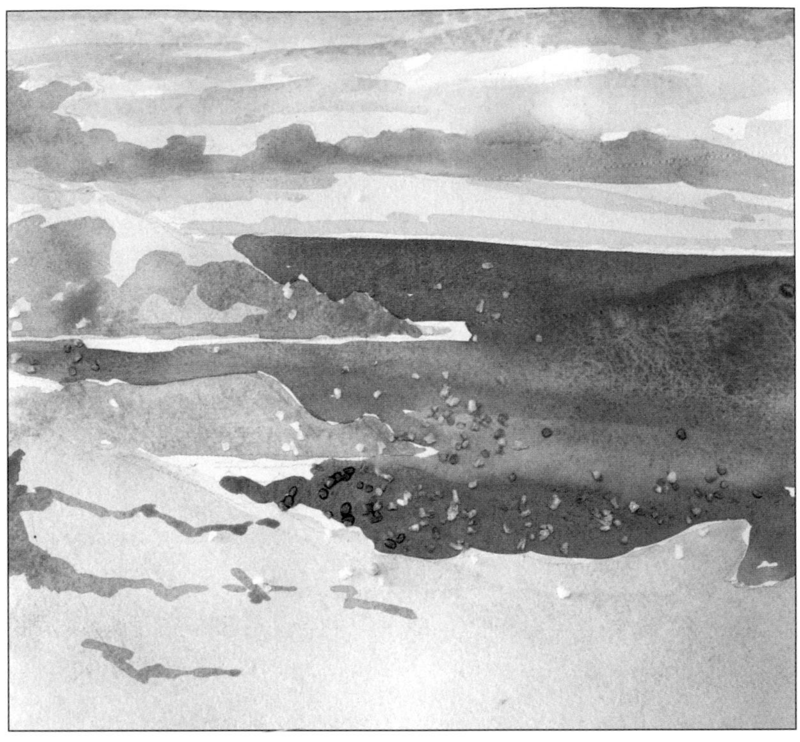

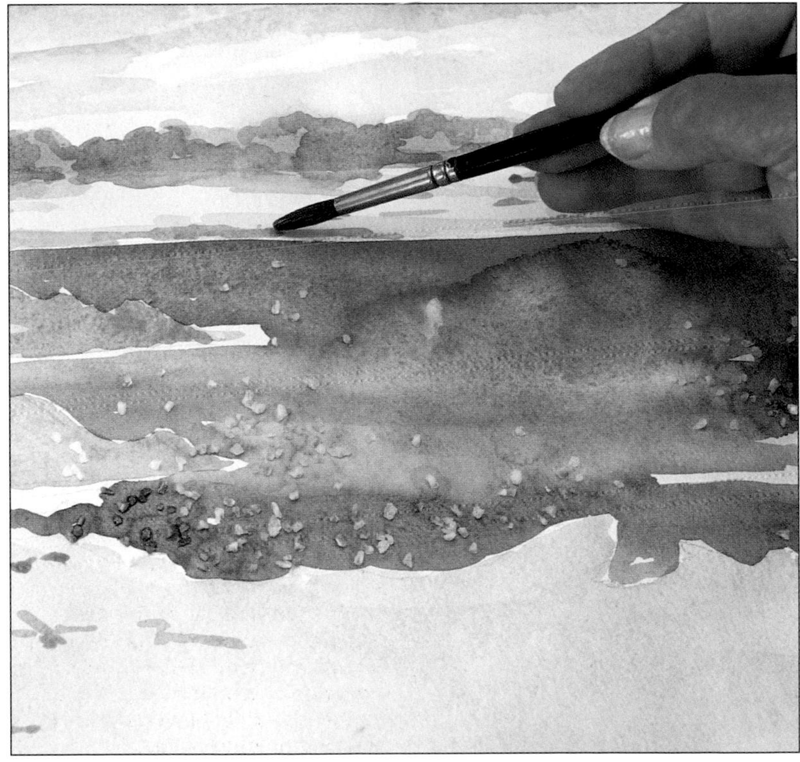

4.

While the rock salt is drying, apply some oxide of chromium into the distant trees. Now mix burnt umber and vermillion and use this to mark in more dark areas on the distant shore. Add some oxide of chromium to some of the distant sea mixture for shade in the trees. Now add scarlet lake to this mixture to mark dark tones on the far outcrop.

5.

Use burnt umber to add darker tones to the nearer outcrop. Use this colour to outline the shore line on the right. Now use burnt sienna to add to the lines on the foreground. Do the same with Payne's grey, and then cadmium red to add another tone. These lines should gradually build to give the impression of the rocks on the beach – but do not overdo it. Now the rock salt should be ready to be removed – check that it is dry. Shake the crystals off into a dustbin. Use some of the sea wash saved from earlier to go over the sea again – to integrate the dappled effect of the salt.

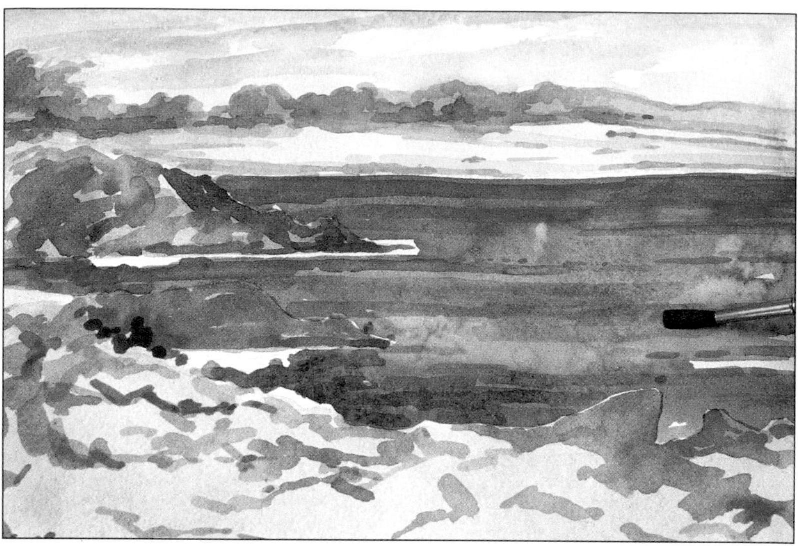

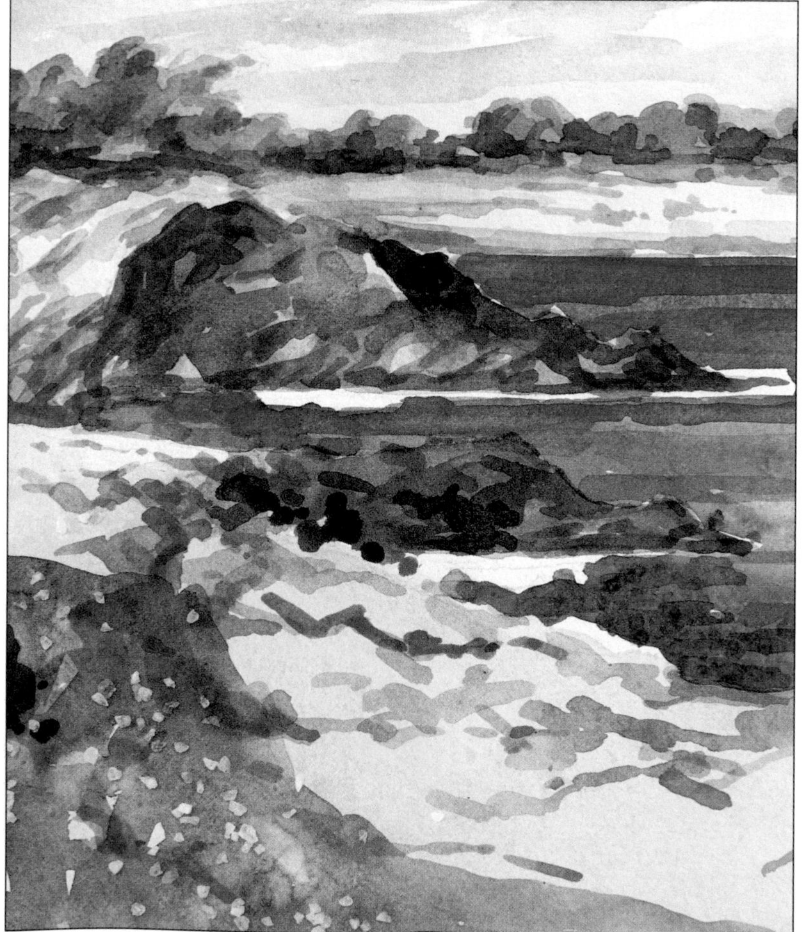

6.

Now use alizarin crimson and vermillion to paint a dark rock into the left corner of the picture. Again, add salt to the wet paint and leave the crystals in place to dry. Use oxide of chromium and a little cobalt blue for more dark areas in the trees. Use alizarin crimson and ultramarine blue mix for the dark areas on the far outcrop.

7.

When it has dried, remove the rock salt from the rock. Mix some vermillion and cadmium orange together and add touches of this into the rock. Now use some alizarin crimson and ultramarine blue for the dark areas in the sea.

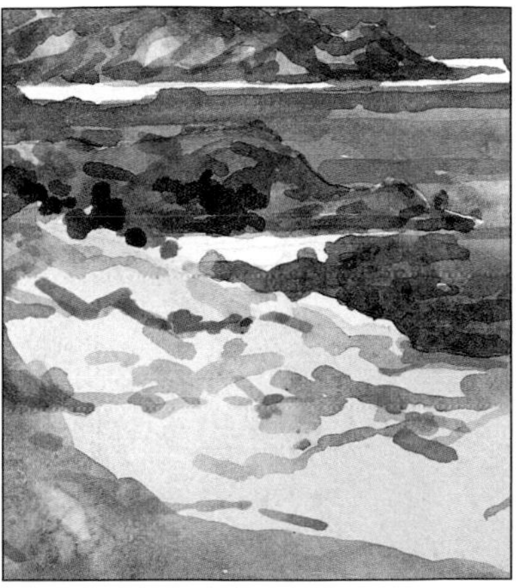

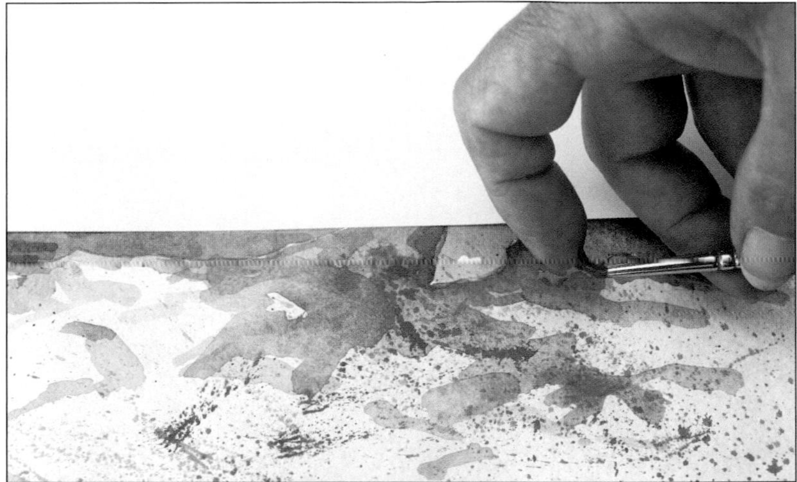

8.

Make a mixture of burnt umber, yellow ochre and vermillion and load it onto a small brush. Now cover the sea area of the painting with a piece of paper for protection. You can now spatter the beach area without getting paint onto the sea.

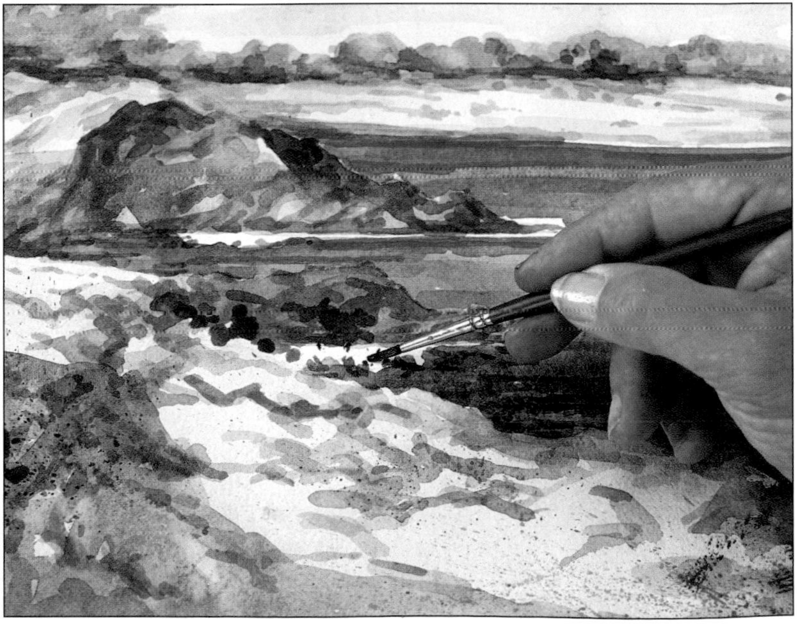

9.

Mix ultramarine blue and scarlet lake to mark some darker areas onto the shore. Use a dark colour to add some definition into the trees. Finish off the sea with the washes used earlier, adding in wave lines. Now load a small brush with ultramarine blue and spatter some spray where the waves hit the shore.

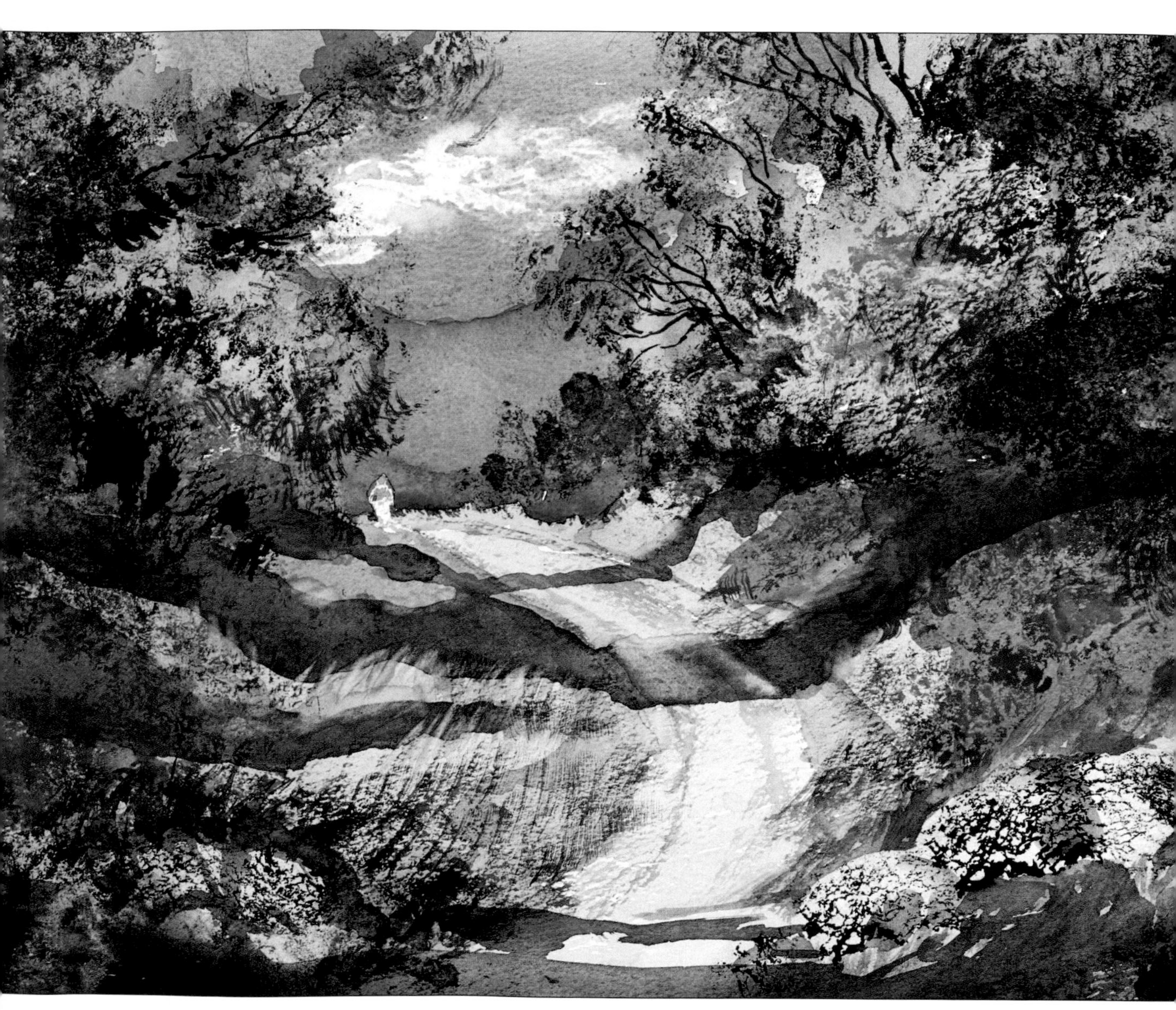

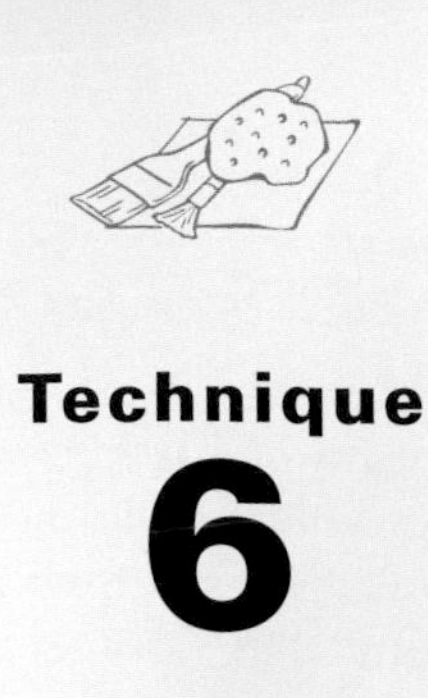

Technique

6

DRY BRUSH AND SPONGES

In this work the artist demonstrates a masterly command of two different techniques. He uses both dry brushes and sponges to create the impression of leaves, ground foliage and rocks. In his careful use of colour and shading, John Barber has also managed to convey the low, crisp light of a fine autumn day. The path with the figure just about to disappear from view adds to the sense of a moment in time captured and preserved – reflecting the fact that the leaves are soon to fall and winter is on the way. This is a fine example of how a painting can trigger an emotional response in the viewer.

John Barber
Autumn Woods
30 x 40cm (12 x 16in)

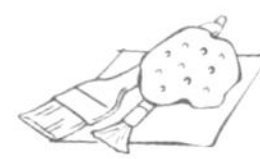

Dry Brush and Sponges Technique

When a brush that is barely damp is dragged across the paper surface the bare minimum of paint is deposited. Far from leaving a solid mark, lines from the individual bristles can be seen. The technique is perfect for creating the impression of grass, rocks, bark or the grain of wood. The brush needs to be fanned out before being applied so that each bristle can make its mark. Sponges are a useful tool for the water-colour artist. When used as a stencil to dab colour onto a surface, they leave the impression of their intricate forms. Natural sponges have a more organic, irregular form, while artificial sponges are more regular. They can be used to effect a range of natural forms, including tree shapes, storm clouds and rock surfaces.

AUTUMN WOOD

Materials and Equipment

- SHEET OF ROUGH, 300 GSM WATERCOLOUR PAPER, STRETCHED (SEE P. 111)
- PENCIL
- FLAT SOFT HAIR BRUSHES: ONE SMALL BRUSH FOR DETAIL, ONE MEDIUM BRUSH, ONE LARGE BRUSH FOR WASHES
- WATERCOLOUR PAINTS: ULTRAMARINE BLUE, BURNT SIENNA, VERMILLION, YELLOW OCHRE, SAP GREEN, VIRIDIAN GREEN, IVORY BLACK
- KITCHEN PAPER
- ARTIFICIAL SPONGE
- NATURAL SPONGE

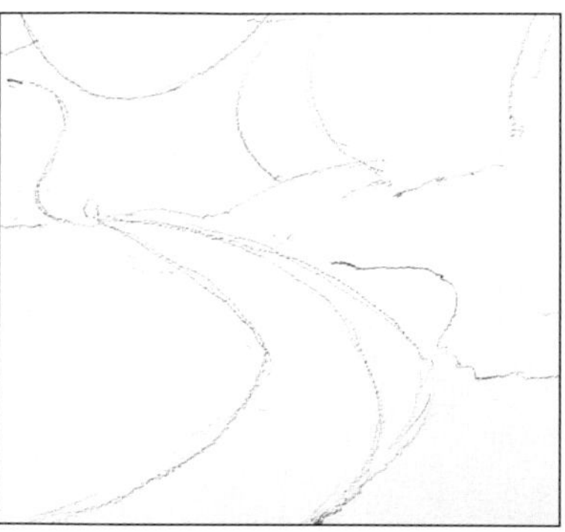

1. Make a pencil sketch. Wash in the sky with ultramarine, bringing the paint down below the level of the trees. Lift out cloud shapes with kitchen paper. Allow this to dry. Add viridian and burnt sienna to the sky wash for the centre area. Leave a white shape for the figure. Use this colour for the overhanging tree on the left and for the far right area.

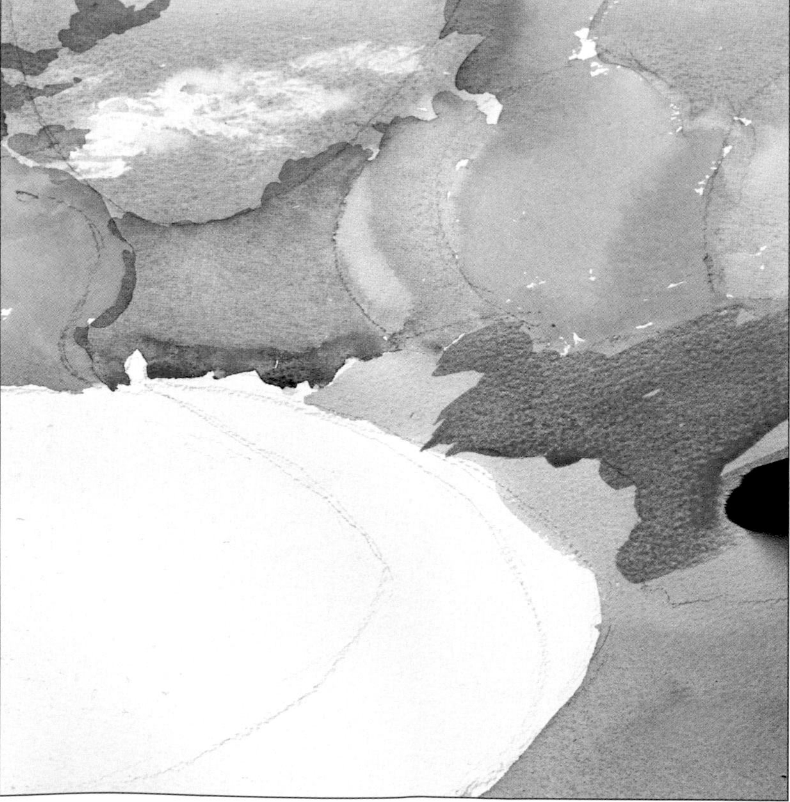

2. Add burnt sienna for a lighter green to the right of the centre. Add yellow ochre and viridian for the golden trees. Use a light wash of this for the grass area on the right, then add a darker area with burnt sienna. Use the same light wash for the grass on the left. Paint the path with yellow ochre. Mix sap green with a little burnt sienna for the grass along the right edge of the path and darken this slightly for the left side. Use yellow ochre with sap green for the lower left corner.

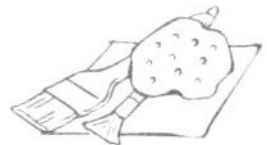

3▸

Use yellow ochre for the bright foliage to the right of the figure. Now mix yellow ochre and burnt sienna for the ferns on the left. Add viridian into the yellow ochre for the green in the near foreground. Paint the shadows with alizarin crimson, ivory black and ultramarine mixture.

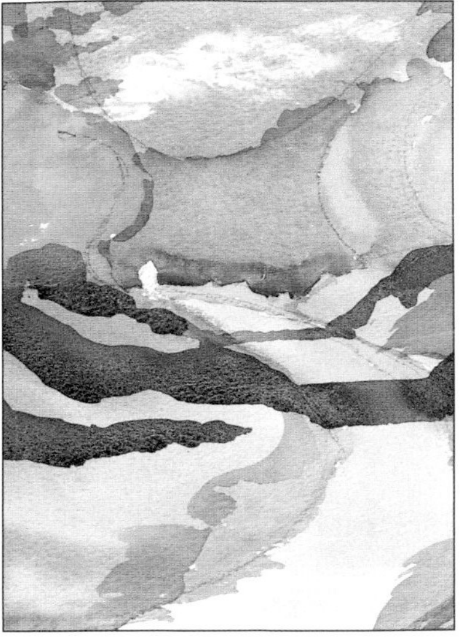

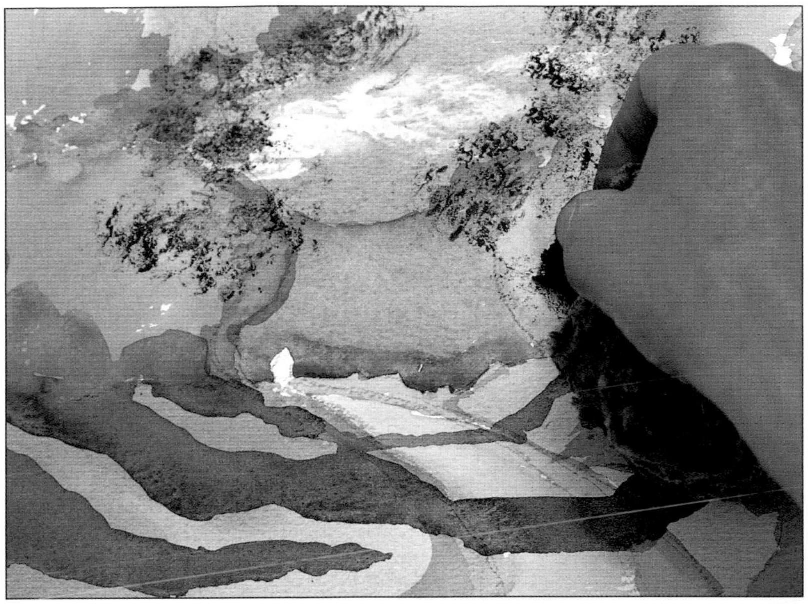

4◂

Allow the shadows to dry. Mix viridian green, burnt sienna and ultramarine. Apply this colour to the trees with a natural sponge, rotating the head so as not to repeat patterns. Use this colour for the lower foreground foliage as well.

5▸

Change the sponge colour to burnt sienna, cadmium yellow and a little ultramarine. Use this to add foliage to the bright golden trees. Now use just burnt sienna and a little ultramarine for the ferns and the nearest branches of the golden trees. Use a damp, clean brush to lighten the shadow areas.

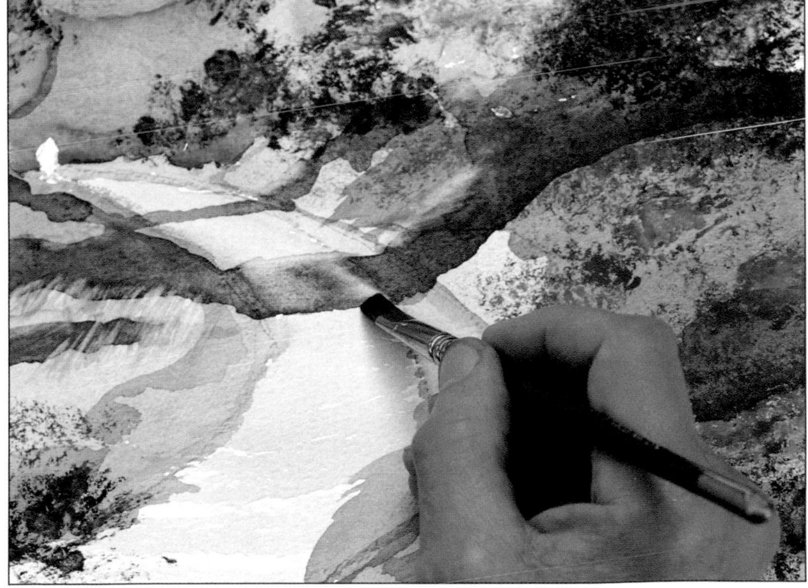

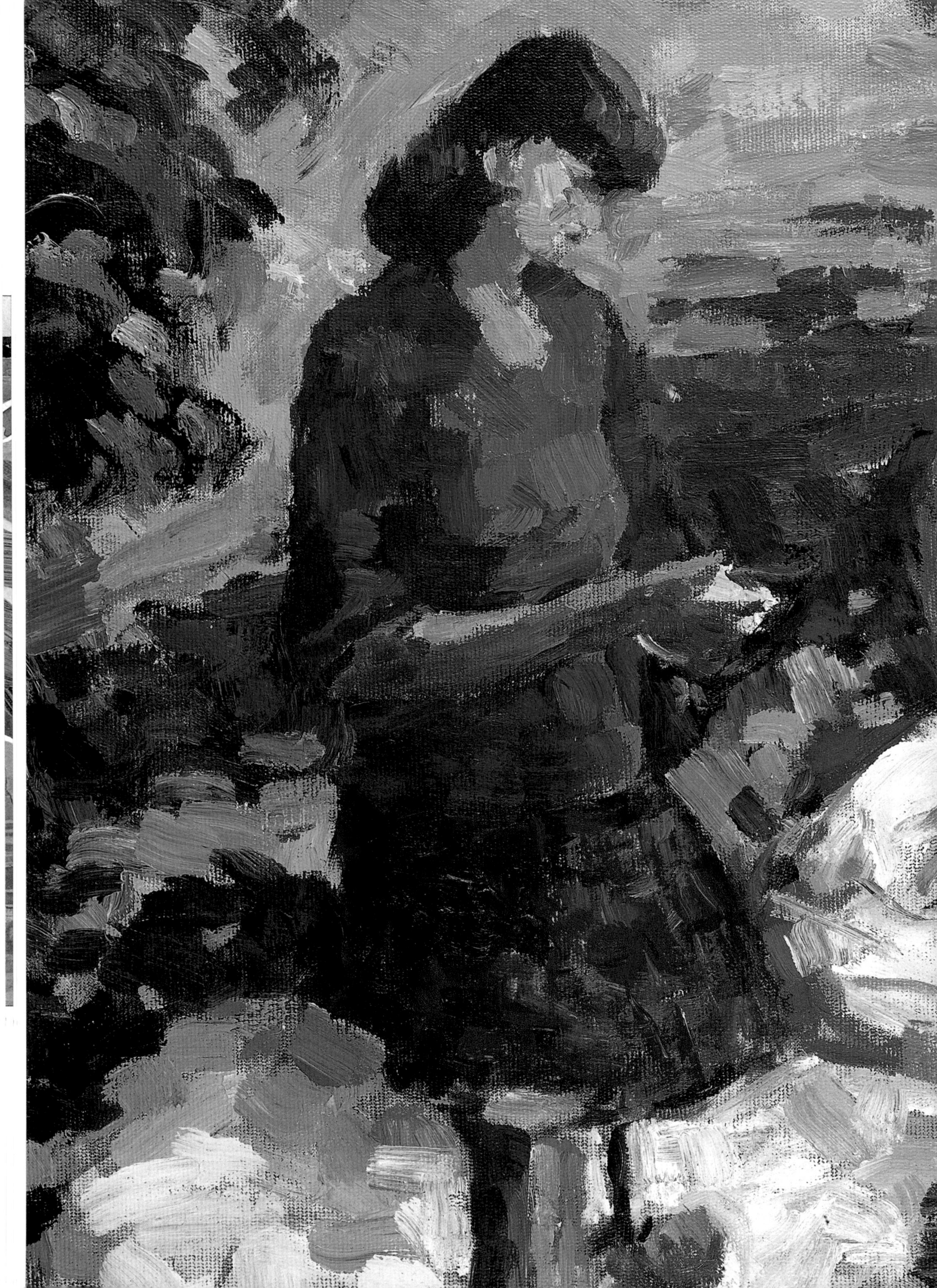

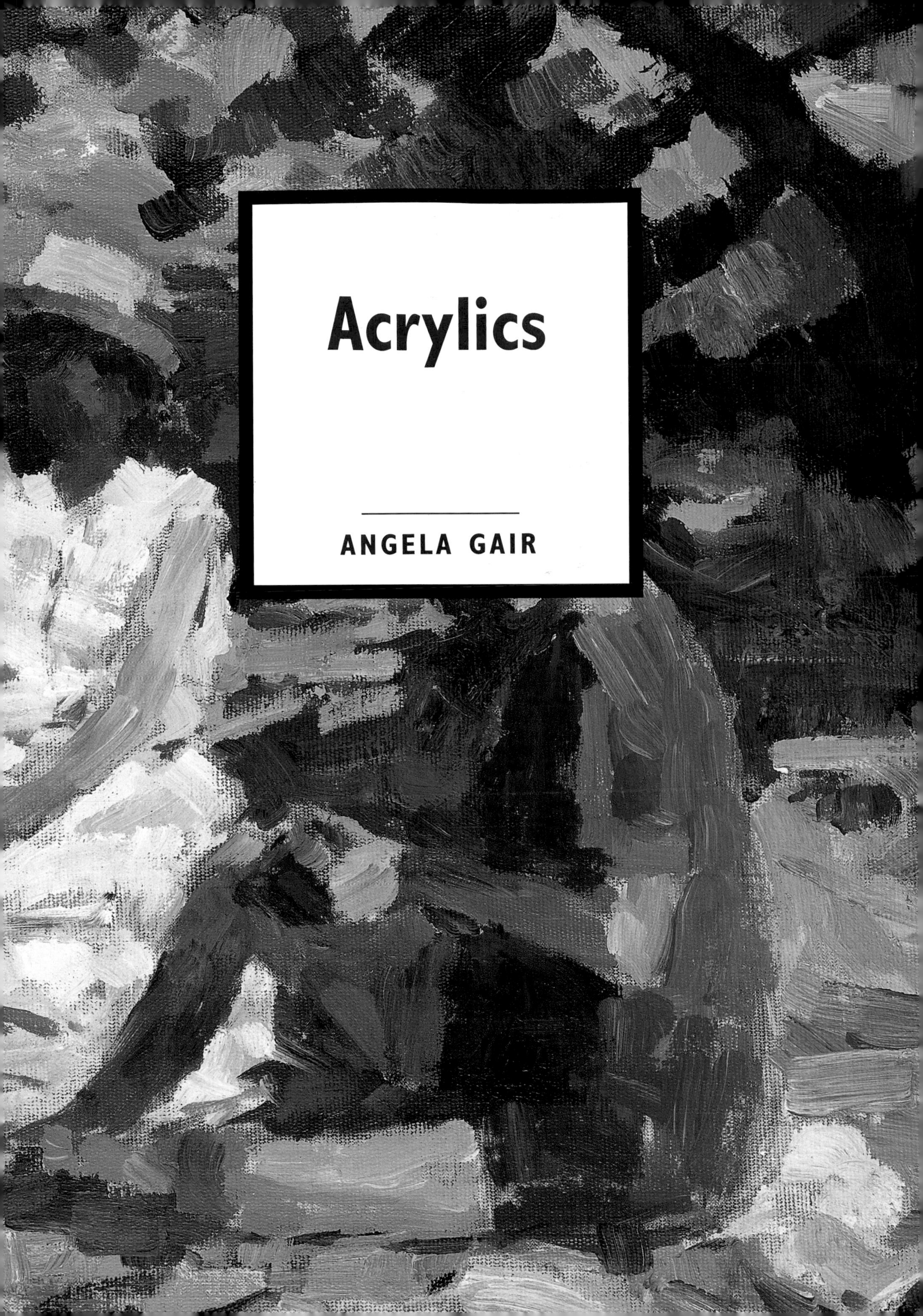
Acrylics
ANGELA GAIR

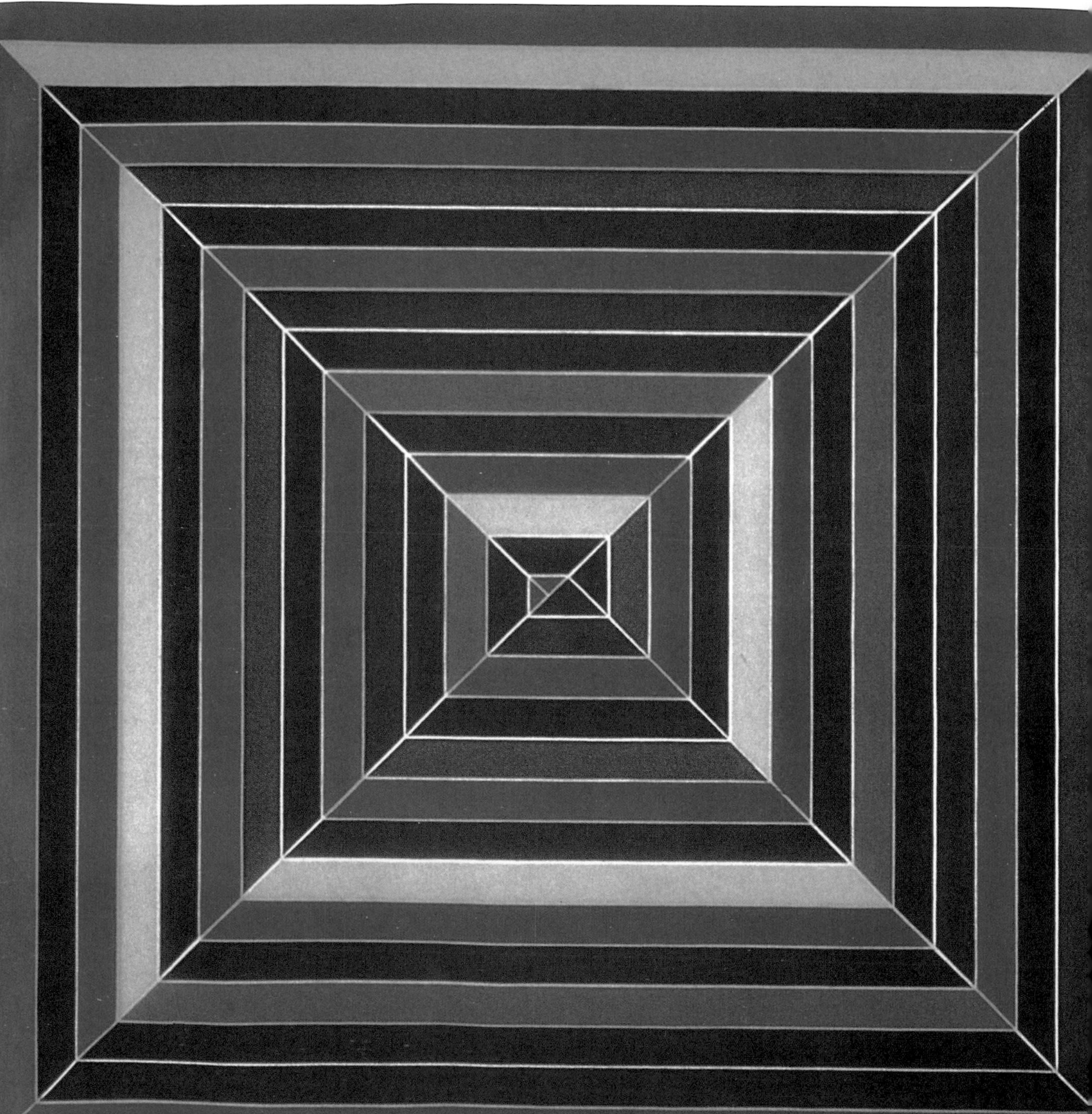

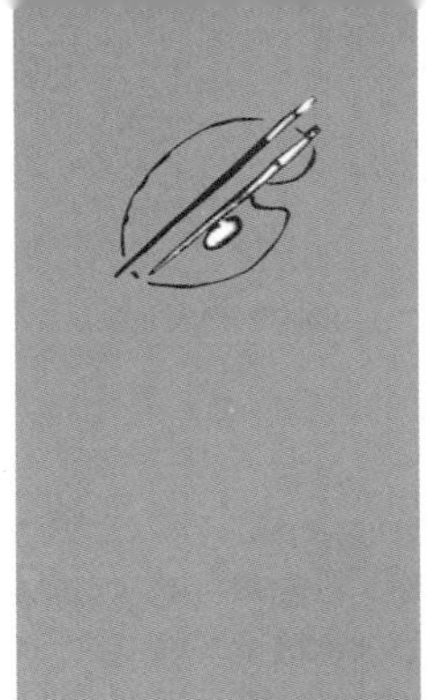

Introduction

Acrylic paint is a synthetic, man-made product of modern science. The coloured pigments are essentially the same as those used in traditional media, but the vehicle is a transparent acrylic polymer. Once applied to the support the paint dries in a matter of minutes, and once dry it forms a tough, flexible film that is insoluble in water and will not rot, discolour or crack. This gives acrylics an advantage over oil paints, which do not remain flexible but become quite brittle, and yellow and darken with age.

Acrylics are an extraordinarily versatile medium. They can be used opaquely, like oils or gouache, or thinned with water to create effects identical to those of watercolour. The most outstanding quality of acrylic paint is the speed with which it dries. The rapid drying time is a problem for some artists – the paint cannot be brushed and moved around on the canvas in the same way as oils – but the advantage is that succeeding layers of colour can be built up rapidly without disturbing the underlying layers, and mistakes can be covered easily, even when painting a light colour over a dark one.

Hyena Stomp *Frank Stella*

Here Stella has created a clockwise "spiral" of vibrantly coloured stripes that set up a strange visual sensation; the picture seems at one moment like a square tunnel, the next like an aerial view of a stepped pyramid. The precise geometry of the square was achieved by brushing colour into areas that had been isolated with strips of masking tape, thus creating razor-sharp edges between each stripe, with a fine line of unprimed canvas between.

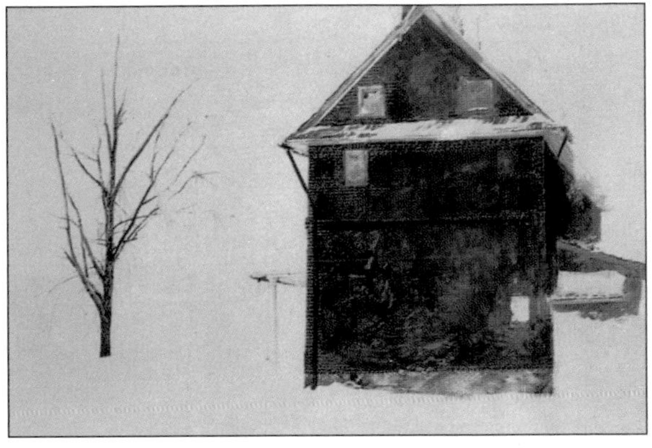

Study for Tenant Farmer *Andrew Wyeth*

Many of Wyeth's paintings depict a lonely rural world, bleak and uncompromising. Here a delapidated farmhouse and a spiky, dead tree stand out starkly against a cold winter landscape, the mood of the scene underlined by the muted palette of browns and greys.

Another advantage of acrylics is that they are insoluble once dry. This means that the traditional technique of building up areas of colour in a series of transparent layers, or glazes, can be achieved in a matter of minutes and without risk of losing the clear brilliance of each colour. Oils are slow-drying, so glazing is a lengthy procedure because each layer must dry before the next is applied.

The development of acrylic paints as a fine art medium came about as an indirect result of technological advances made in the plastics industry in the 1920s. An American firm, Rohm and Haas, invented the first synthetic resins for use

in making a host of products, from household utensils to aircraft windows to false teeth. These early polymers were eventually developed as a base for house paints, providing a durable and weatherproof replacement for distemper.

Meanwhile in Mexico a group of artists, including Diego Rivera (1886–1957) and David Alfaro Siqueiros (1896–1974) were engaged in painting large murals for public buildings. Finding that oil paints were not stable enough to withstand outdoor weather conditions, they experimented with the new acrylic paints and found them quite successful.

These early resin emulsions were not available in saturated colours because they solidified when mixed with a pigment, therefore they were of little use to fine artists. But by the 1950s these problems had been overcome and acrylic artists' paints were available in the United States. By happy coincidence, this was an era of change and experimentation in American art, and the new medium played a pivotal role in the Abstract and Pop Art movements that emerged. Being extremely easy to use, versatile in application, and, most importantly, extremely fast-drying, acrylic paints minimized the artists' involvement with the technical skills of painting, leaving them free to explore the purely creative aspects.

The Abstract Expressionists challenged the notion that a picture was the end result of a planned design. For them the action of applying the paint determined the outcome – hence they became known as "Action painters". The fast-drying quality of acrylic paint was a godsend to such painters, for it allowed them to build up thick layers of paint rapidly and intuitively, knowing that they would dry within a matter of hours or even minutes – something which is impossible with oils.

The most renowned of these painters, Jackson Pollock (1912–1956) placed enormous canvases on the floor and moved rapidly around the picture from all sides, pouring and dripping paint directly from the can, or using sticks to fling it on with whiplash strokes to create a wild tracery of lines and spots of colour.

As a demonstration of acrylic's unique versatility, the medium was adopted just as enthusiastically by Abstract and Hard Edge painters such as Mark Rothko (1903–1970), Frank Stella (born 1935) and Morris Louis (1912–1962). These artists played down personal expression and adopted a more considered approach to the han-

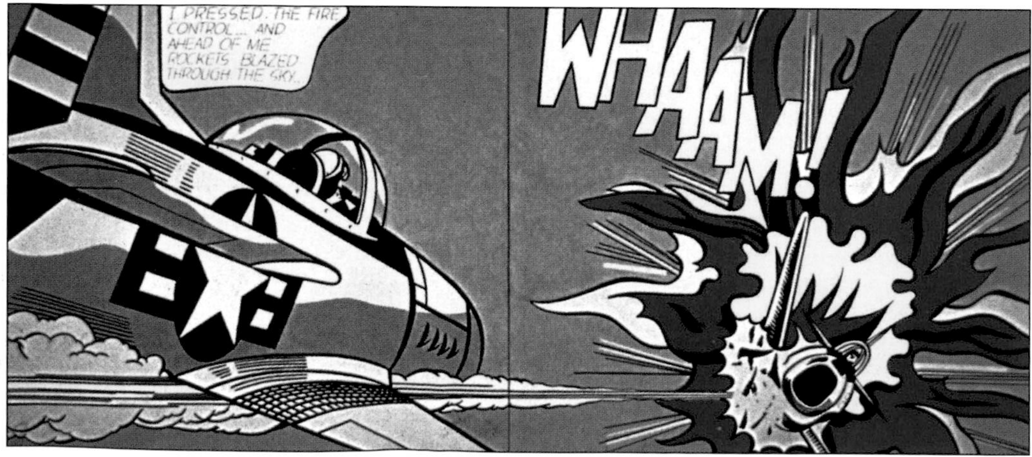

Whaam! *Roy Lichtenstein*

This picture is painted on two separate canvas panels and uses imagery derived from war comics. In some areas of the image Lichtenstein mimics the mechanical printing process of dot shading used in comic-book production; he placed a metal mesh screen on the canvas and brushed paint through the regularly spaced holes with a toothbrush.

A Bigger Splash *David Hockney*

Acrylic paints have a high degree of opacity and are easily brushed out to give flat, level areas of colour. Hockney found these qualities ideal for conveying the intense atmosphere of heat and bright sunlight typical of California. In this picture he applied the large, smooth areas of colour with a paint roller. The splash itself, though it appears random, was very carefully painted with small brushes, and took Hockney two weeks to complete.

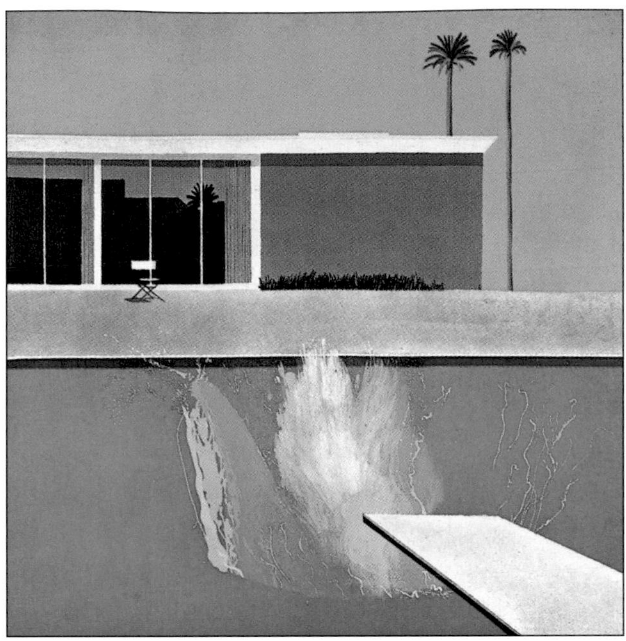

dling of paint; they found that acrylics could be diluted and applied in flat washes of intense, even colour ideally suited to the formal, hard-edged rigour of their images.

In 1953 Morris Louis began using acrylics to explore a new technique of soaking washes of diluted paint into unprimed canvas, relying on the absorbent, softening quality of the canvas weave to obtain subtle, "stained" effects. Whereas with oils it was necessary to size and prime the canvas before applying paint to prevent the oil in the paint from eventually rotting the canvas, acrylics could be applied directly without these preliminaries. Frank Stella's rigid compositions featured perfectly straight bands of intense colour with fine lines of unprimed canvas in between. To create the hard, straight edges, he applied strips of masking tape to the canvas, brushing the paint against their edges. Acrylics were ideal for this style of painting as the paint dried to a flat, even layer which disguised the activity of the brush.

On both sides of the Atlantic the 1960s saw the rise of the so-called "Pop" culture. Economic prosperity meant a surfeit of cheap, "popular" products with instant appeal, designed to be consumed immediately and thrown away after use. Artists like Roy Lichtenstein (born 1923) and Andy Warhol (1930–1987) in America and Peter Blake (born 1932) and Eduardo Paolozzi (born 1924) in Britain took as their inspiration the popular icons of the age – advertising slogans, throw-away packaging, comic-strip images, hot dogs and hamburgers – and used them in their paintings to make an ironic comment on the consumerist ethos of the time. The British artist David Hockney (born 1937) was converted to acrylics when he moved to California in 1964, finding their intense colours ideal for capturing the cloudless skies and vivid light of the West Coast.

The quality of acrylic paints has improved considerably since they were first introduced, and in recent years they have gained popularity not only with students and amateur painters but also with professional artists, some of whom previously dismissed them as an inferior alternative to oil paints. The higher pigment content, the greater flexibility of the latest resins and their longer working time now make acrylics a more serious challenge to traditional media than ever before.

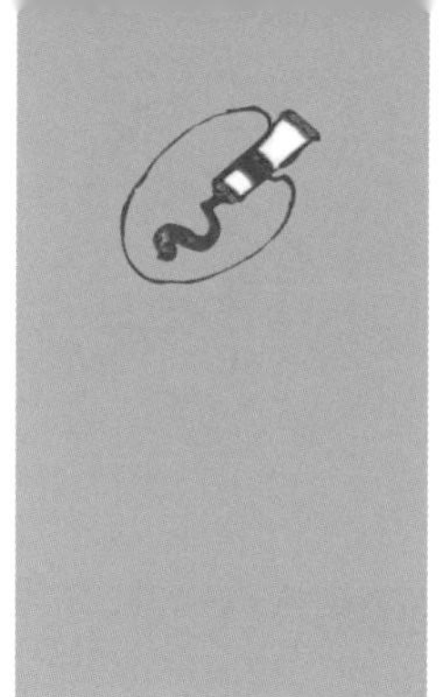

Materials and Equipment

Although acrylic paints are a relatively new painting medium, most of the equipment you will need — brushes, palettes, supports, and so on — is the same as that used with traditional oil paints or watercolours. The paints may be mixed with water or combined with various mediums which alter the character of the paint, producing a range of different effects and finishes.

Paints

Acrylic paints are available in broadly the same traditional colours as oil paints or watercolours, as well as a few synthetic ones with unpronounceable names such as dioxazine purple and quinacridone violet, which are peculiar to acrylics. The paints are sold in tubes, jars and bottles with droppers. Which type you choose depends on the consistency of paint you prefer: tube paint is the thickest, with a consistency similar to oils; paint in jars is more creamy; and the bottled type is very fluid, ideal for covering large areas with intense, transparent washes. Acrylics are available in both "artist's" and "student's" quality. The former contain pure pigments, the latter synthetic ones.

Suggested Palette

Although the manufacturers of acrylic paints offer many inviting hues, few professional painters use more than 12 or 15. Keeping to a narrow range of colours encourages you to mix them together to create a variety of subtle hues, and results in a unified, harmonious painting. The colours described and illustrated on page 175 should meet your requirements initially; you can then expand your palette as you gain more experience.

Mediums

Acrylic tube colours can be thinned with water, but they dry with a rather dull finish. However, there are various painting mediums available which give the colours brilliance and depth, improve the flow and brushability of the paint and produce a range of different effects and finishes. The mediums are milky white in appearance as they come out of the tube, but become transparent when dry.

Gloss medium thins the paint to a creamy consistency: if you add more the paint then turns transparent and allows the underlying colours to shine through, making it ideal for

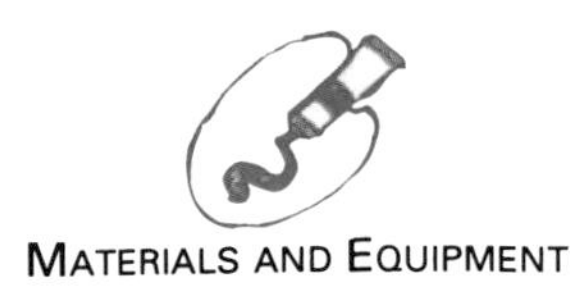

SUGGESTED PALETTE

Cadmium yellow light
A bright, warm yellow. Mixes with blues to form warm yellowish greens and combines well with all reds.

Cadmium red light
A warm, intense red, very dense and opaque.

Naphthol crimson
Produces a range of violets with the blues and delicate pinks with white.

Ultramarine blue
A strong, rich blue. Mixes with yellows to form a variety of greens and with browns to form interesting greys.

Cobalt blue
A subtle blue, excellent for painting skies.

Viridian
A rich, transparent, bluish green. Retains its brilliance, even in mixes.

Titanium white
The only available white in acrylic, titanium has good covering power.

Yellow ochre
A soft yellow which is excellent for covering, mixing or glazing. Produces soft, subtle greens when mixed with blues.

Raw sienna
A warm transparent colour, excellent for glazing.

Burnt sienna
A rich, coppery red, useful for warming other colours. It is transparent and frequently used in glazes and washes.

Burnt umber
A rich and versatile brown, ideal for darkening all colours. In mixes, a little goes a long way.

Payne's grey
An opaque blue-grey with weak tinting strength. Useful for modifying other colours.

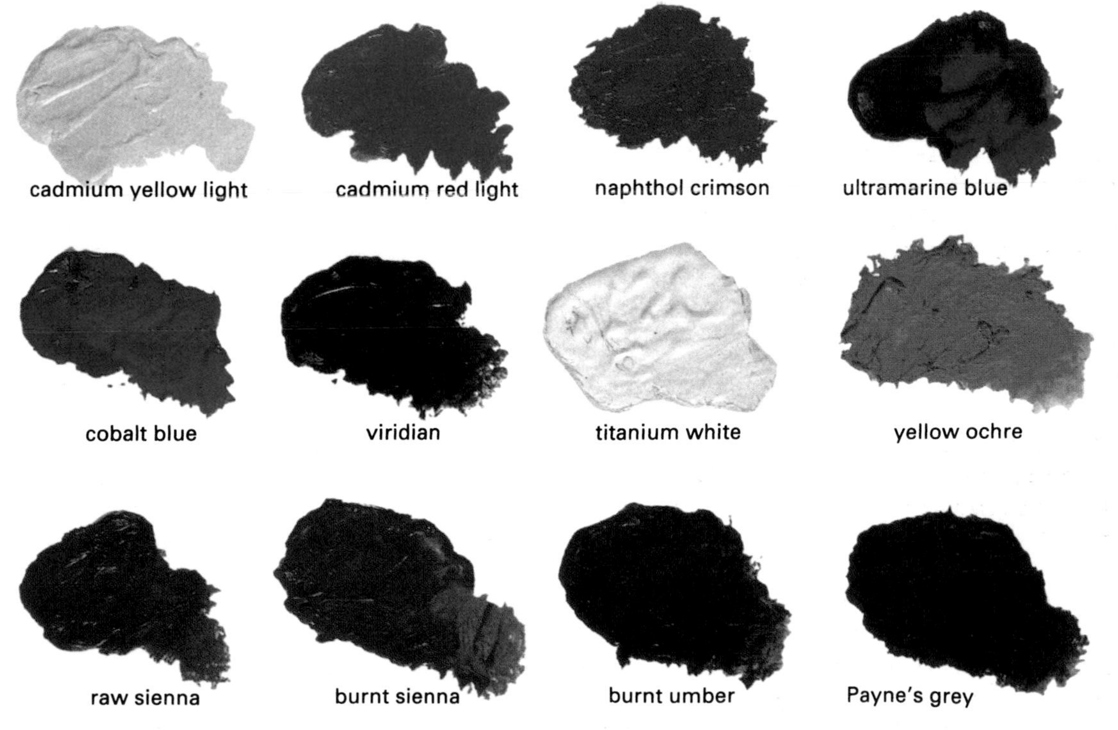

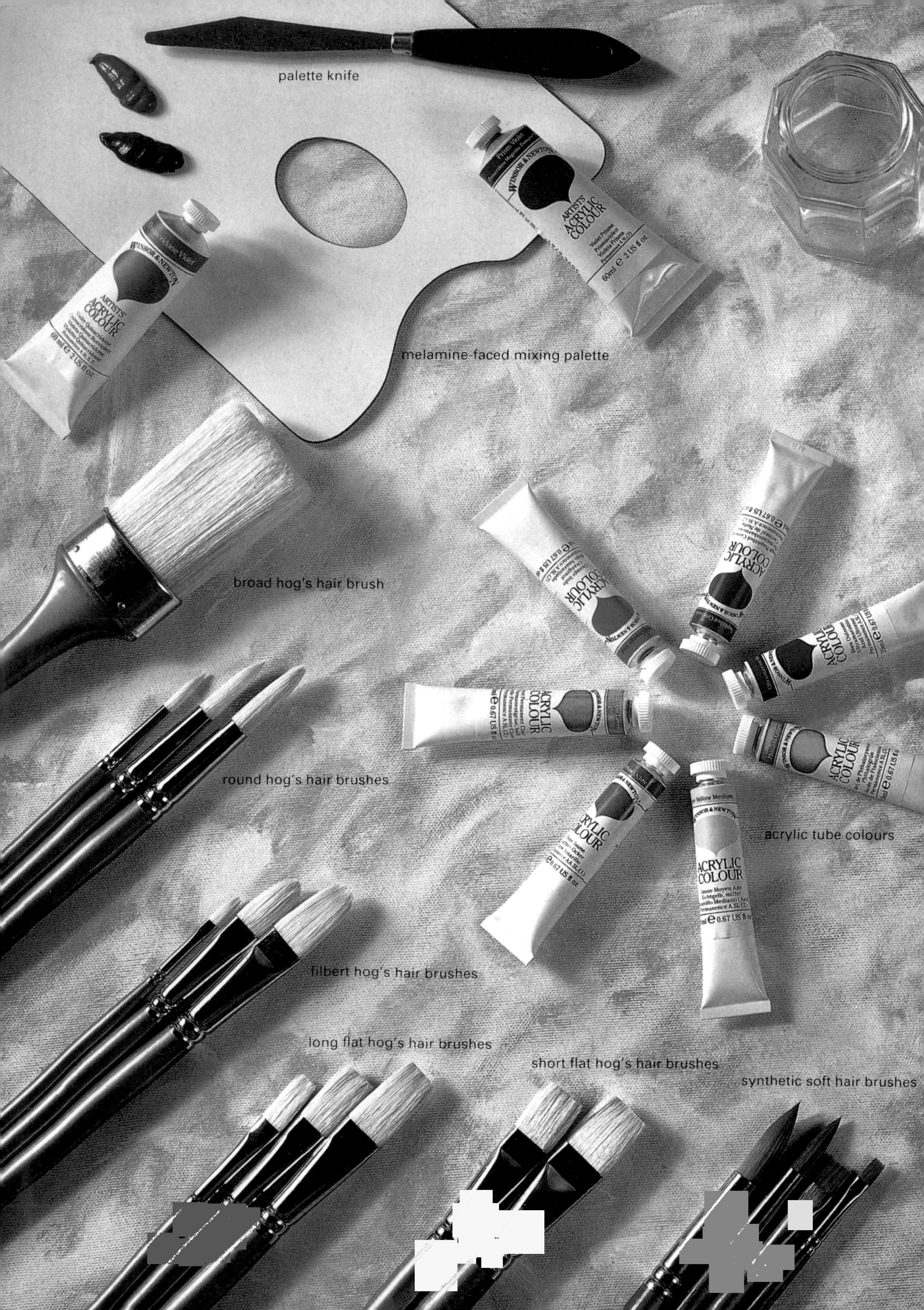
palette knife
melamine-faced mixing palette
broad hog's hair brush
round hog's hair brushes
acrylic tube colours
filbert hog's hair brushes
long flat hog's hair brushes
short flat hog's hair brushes
synthetic soft hair brushes

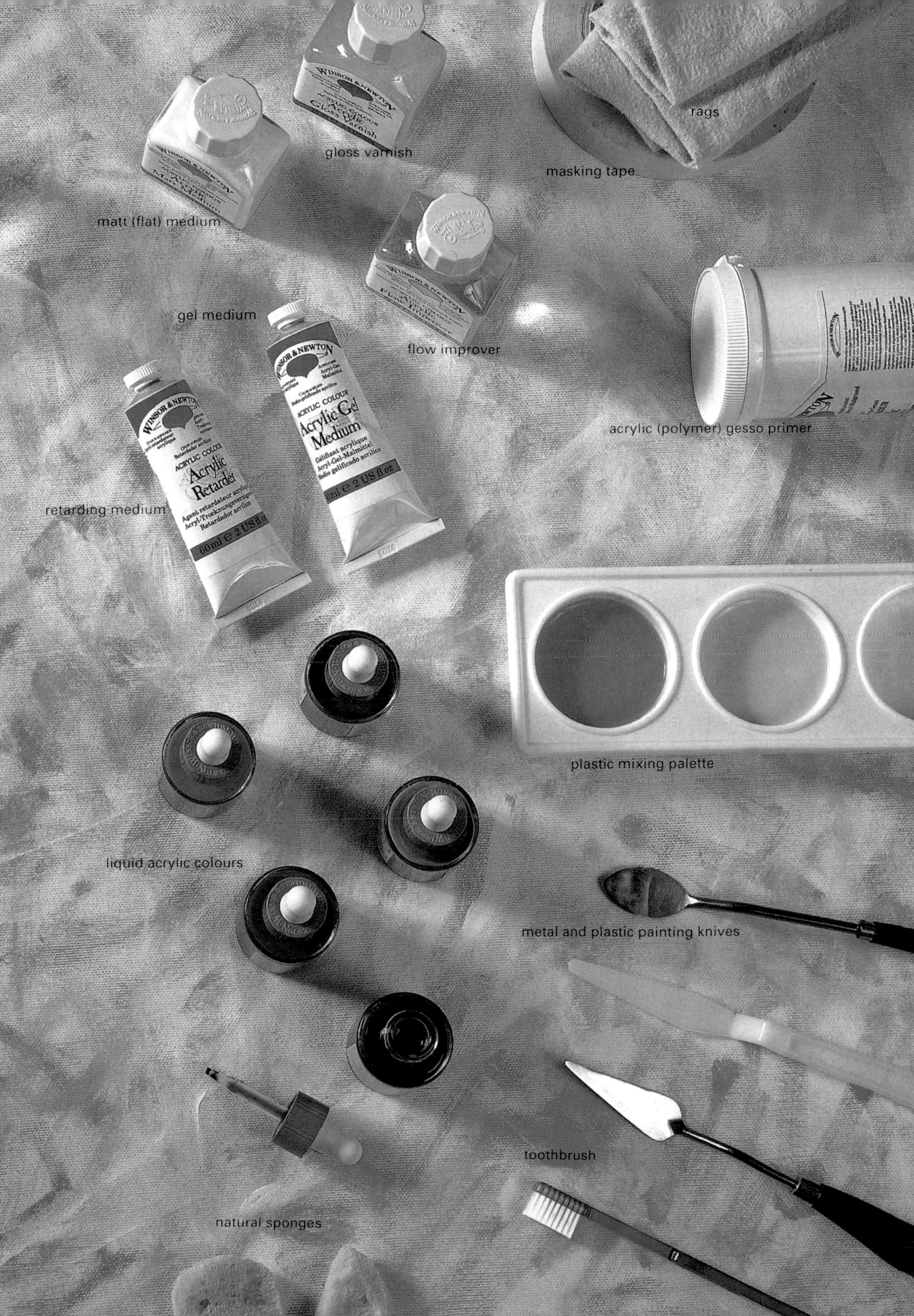

rags
gloss varnish
masking tape
matt (flat) medium
gel medium
flow improver
acrylic (polymer) gesso primer
retarding medium
WINSOR & NEWTON
ACRYLIC COLOUR
Acrylic Retarder
60ml e 2 US fl oz
WINSOR & NEWTON
ACRYLIC COLOUR
Acrylic Gel Medium
Gélifiant acrylique
Acryl-Gel-Malmittel
2 US fl oz
plastic mixing palette
liquid acrylic colours
metal and plastic painting knives
toothbrush
natural sponges

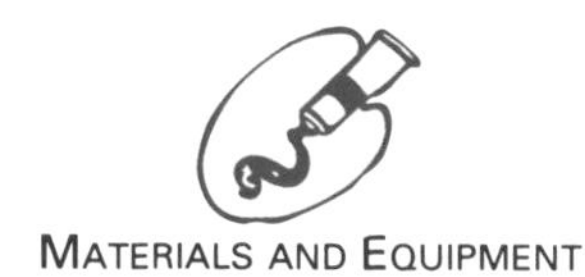

the glazing technique (see pages 232-237). Gloss medium dries to a shiny finish like oil paintings.

Matt (flat) medium can be used in exactly the same way as gloss, but it dries to a satiny finish with no shine. Some artists find that a blend of equal parts of gloss and matt medium produces a pleasing semi-gloss effect.

Gel medium thickens the consistency of the paint to make it suitable for richly textured brush strokes, impasto effects and knife painting.

Retarding medium is a transparent substance which slows down the drying time of the paint considerably, allowing you greater freedom to move the paint around and produce softly blended effects. Mix the retarder in the ratio of one part to six for earth colours, and one part to three for other colours. If too much retarder is added, the paint will become sticky and unpleasant to use.

Primers and Varnishes

Acrylic (polymer) gesso primer is a very thick, white liquid which can be brushed onto an absorbent surface such as hardboard (masonite) or raw canvas to provide a smooth, receptive surface to paint on (see page 180).

Once dry, acrylic paint is tough and durable and can be washed with soap and water, so a protective coat of varnish is not absolutely necessary. However, the surface of the picture can be enhanced by giving it a coat of medium or varnish, both of which are available in either a gloss or matt (flat) finish.

Brushes

Brushes used for oil painting are also suitable for acrylics. If the paint is to be diluted and used like watercolour, use sable or synthetic soft hair brushes, which give a smoother, softer stroke. Brushes previously used with oil paint must be carefully cleaned to remove all traces of oil from the bristles before using them with acrylics.

If you intend buying new brushes, it is worth considering the synthetic ones which have been recently developed specifically for use with acrylics. They are easier to clean than natural bristle brushes, and built to withstand the tough handling demanded by acrylics.

Most manufacturers produce around 12 sizes in any one brush series, 12 usually being the largest and 00, 0 and 1 being the smallest. The scale and style of your paintings will determine which brush sizes you choose, but as a general rule larger brushes are more versatile than smaller ones; they hold more paint and encourage a bolder approach. Paintbrushes are made in a range of shapes:

Flats have long bristles with square tips. They hold a lot of paint and can be used flat, for broad areas and washes, or on their edge for fine lines.

Brights have short, stiff bristles, giving them greater spring and control. They produce strongly textured strokes.

Filberts have slightly rounded tips that make soft, tapered brush strokes.

Rounds have long bristles, tapered at the ends. Use the body of the brush for loosely handled areas, and the tip for fine details.

Riggers have long, thin, flexible hairs. They are used for very fine linear detail such as painting the rigging on boats – hence their name.

Household paintbrushes are inexpensive and useful for applying primer and for staining the canvas prior to painting.

Painting and Palette Knives

Palette knives, made of flexible steel, are used for mixing paint on the palette, while painting knives are specifically designed for applying paint to the canvas to achieve a thick impasto effect (see pages 244-251). Plastic knives are also available specifically for use with acrylics as they are easier to clean.

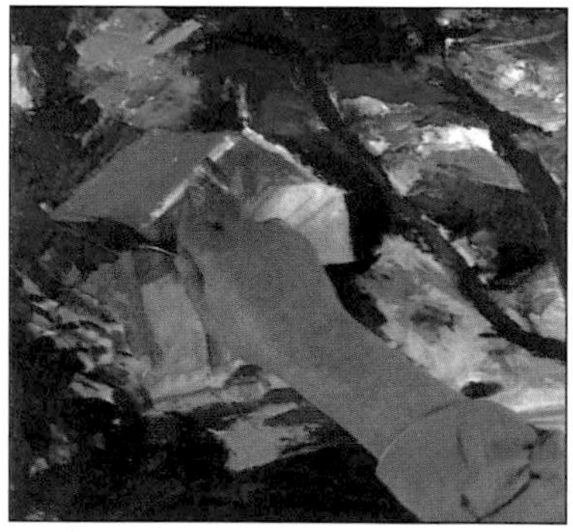

A richly textured painting surface can be built up using a painting knife to apply thick layers of paint.

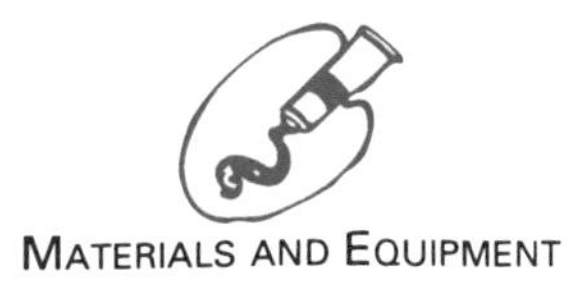

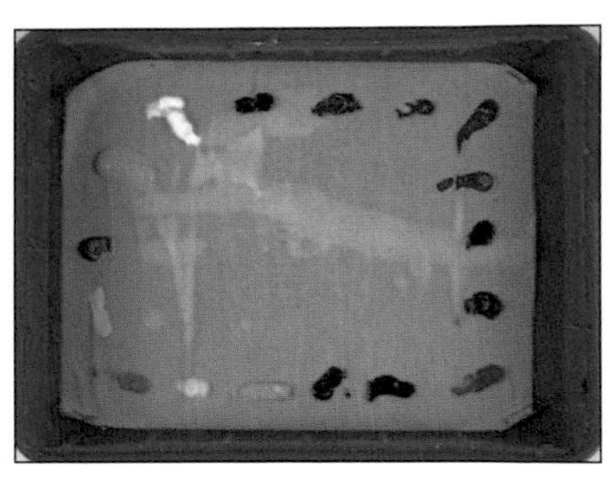

An improvised version of the "staywet" palette, designed to keep paints moist during use.

Palettes

Palettes for acrylic painting are made of plastic, which is easy to clean. A wooden palette is not recommended; the paint gets into the porous surface of the wood and is difficult to remove. Many painters prefer to use improvised palettes, especially for mixing large quantities of colour. Any smooth, non-porous material will do, such as a sheet of white laminated plastic, an offcut of hardboard (masonite) coated with acrylic primer, or a sheet of glass with white paper underneath. For mixing very fluid washes, use disposable plastic containers, paper cups or metal bun trays (muffin pans).

Acrylic paints dry out rapidly on the palette, but a special "staywet" palette is now available which keeps the colours moist for days, even weeks. It is basically a plastic tray lined with wet blotting paper, covered with a sheet of "membrane" paper. The colours are squeezed onto this and absorb moisture from the blotting paper through the membrane. Again, you can improvise your own version using a shallow plastic tray lined with blotting paper and a sheet of membrane paper (these are sold in refill packs for the "staywet" palette).

Supports

Acrylic paints can be applied to virtually any surface that is oil- and grease-free and slightly absorbent. One important point to remember is that acrylics will not adhere to any surface that contains oil or wax. Most canvas and canvas boards are now primed with an acrylic primer, but be careful not to buy those that are prepared specially for oil paint.

Canvas is normally made of linen, jute or cotton duck, and is available in fine, medium and coarse-grained weaves. If your painting style uses bold, heavy brush strokes, a coarse weave is best. For detailed brushwork and soft blending, a finely woven texture is more suitable.

Canvas can be bought ready-primed and stretched on wooden frames in various sizes. The surface of such a canvas is taut but flexible, with a pleasant receptiveness to the stroke of the brush. You can also buy unprimed canvas by the metre (yard) and stretch it yourself. Commercially prepared canvas boards are reasonably priced and are suitable for beginners trying out acrylics for the first time.

An excellent yet inexpensive support for acrylics is hardboard, which you can buy from builders' suppliers. Most artists use the smooth topside of the board but the reverse side is fine if you prefer a rougher texture. It is preferable to prime absorbent surfaces such as hardboard with acrylic gesso (see page 180).

Acrylics are suitable for use on cardboard, artboard or thick paper. It is best to stretch paper, especially if it is lightweight, otherwise the application of wet washes of colour will make it buckle.

Miscellaneous Items

You will also need a drawing board (when working on paper); jars for water; and a soft pencil for drawing. Another useful item is a hand spray of the type used for misting houseplants – spray the paints on your palette from time to time to prevent them from drying out.

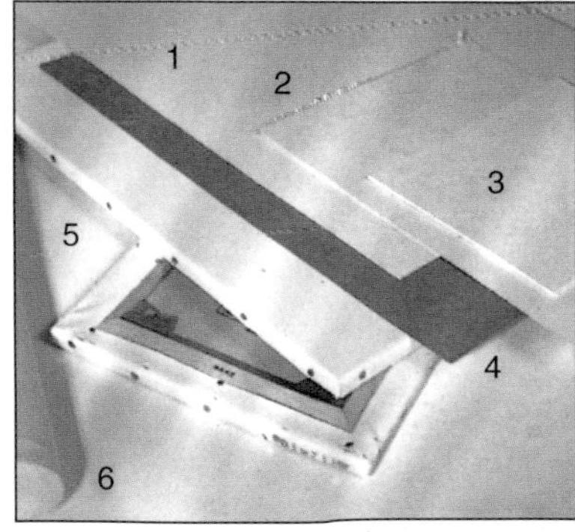

Acrylics can be used on a wide variety of painting surfaces, ranging from thin paper to a tough concrete wall. Shown here are: 1 *illustration board;* 2 *watercolour paper;* 3 *canvas board;* 4 *hardboard (masonite);* 5 *stretched canvas; and* 6 *raw canvas.*

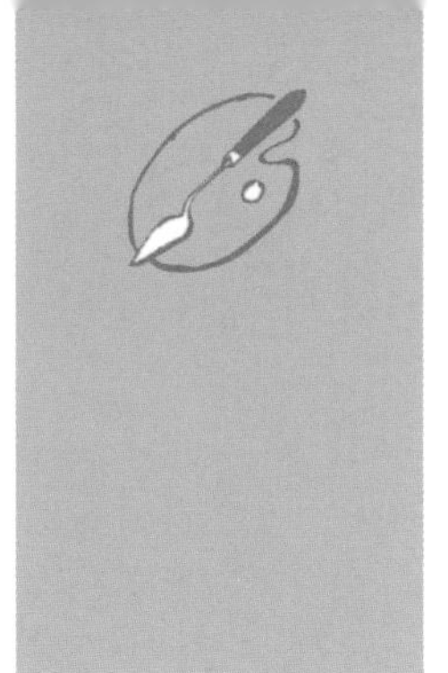

Basic Techniques

Priming with Acrylic (Polymer) Gesso

Acrylic paints can be used on either primed or unprimed surfaces, depending on the effects you seek to achieve. An absorbent surface which is unprimed, such as raw canvas, cloth or plastered walls, will absorb the pigment and dry to an even, matt (flat) finish which some artists find desirable. However, it is usual to prepare surfaces that are absorbent or dark in colour, such as hardboard (masonite), with acrylic gesso primer.

Acrylic primer is simply acrylic medium mixed with inert titanium white, but it is inexpensive to buy ready-made. Brushed onto the support prior to painting, it dries quickly to provide a matt, even surface to which the paint adheres readily. It also provides a luminously bright undercoat which enhances the colours of the painting and gives added translucence to thin washes.

Very smooth surfaces such as hardboard should first be lightly sandpapered before applying the gesso. Using a household paintbrush, apply two or three thin coats, each one at right-angles to the one before. Allow each coat to dry before the next is applied. (The gesso will dry in about 30 minutes.) For a smooth painting surface, dilute the primer to a milky consistency with water. If you prefer a more textured painting surface, use it straight from the jar (or with just a little water) and apply it with rough brush strokes. If priming illustration board, paint an equal number of coats on both sides to prevent warping. Paper does not require priming, though some artists like the smooth surface this provides.

If you do not require a white ground, but want a primed surface rather than an absorbent one, use acrylic medium which makes an excellent transparent primer.

Priming Supports

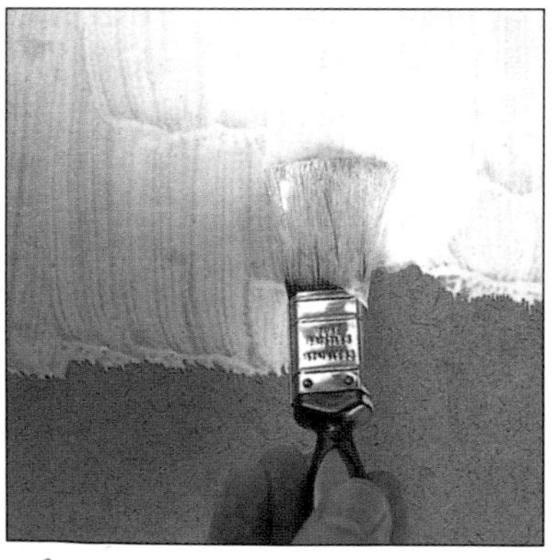

1

Apply a smooth coat of primer, working the brush in one direction only. Allow to dry.

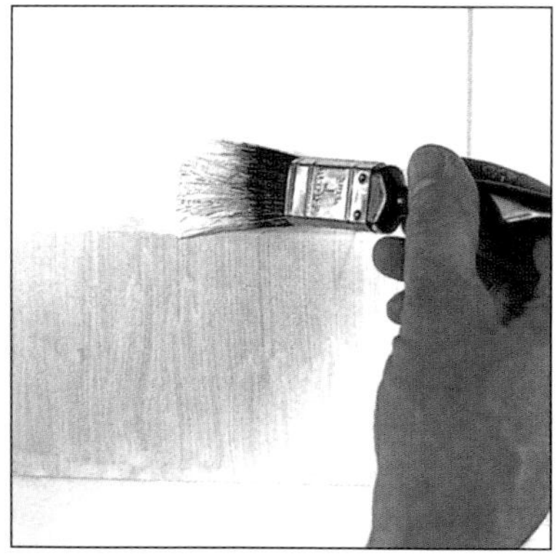

2

Apply a second coat of primer so that the strokes run at right-angles to those laid down in the first coat.

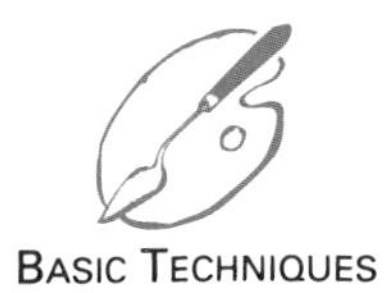

Mixing Paint and Medium

As mentioned earlier, there are various mediums which can be added to the paint to produce particular effects. Acrylic mediums appear milky white when squeezed out of the tube, but dry transparent. Simply squeeze a small pool of medium onto your palette along with your colours. Mix the required colours together with a palette knife, then scoop up some medium and work it into the paint. If desired, the paint can be thinned further by adding water.

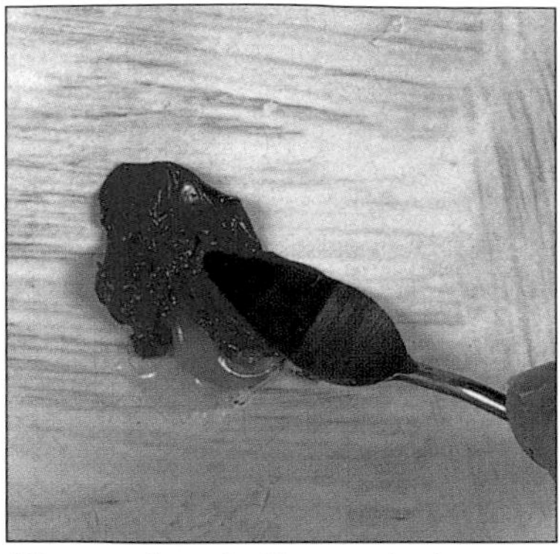

Use a palette knife or painting knife to mix pigment and medium together on the palette.

Brush Strokes

One of the great pleasures of acrylic painting is the way the paint responds to the brush. Each type of brush leaves a different kind of mark in the paint and performs a different task. With practice and experience you will learn just what each brush is capable of and which ones suit your particular painting style.

Paint can be applied rapidly and spontaneously or slowly and methodically; in thick, short strokes and dabs or thin, transparent washes; it can be skimmed over the surface of the canvas to create lively, broken strokes in a technique known as drybrushing, or laid on with a circular scrubbing motion to produce a thin veil of colour called a scumble.

It is important that you feel relaxed and comfortable when painting. First, position yourself so that you are able to see what you are painting as well as the canvas with minimal movement of your head. If you are painting at an easel, do not stand too close to your work; paint with your arm extended so that the movement of the arm from the shoulder, through the elbow and wrist, is fluid, confident and controlled.

Hold the brush where it feels naturally balanced, keeping your hand well back from the ferrule. Holding the brush too tightly, and too close to the ferrule, limits movement to the fingers and results in brush marks that are stilted and monotonous.

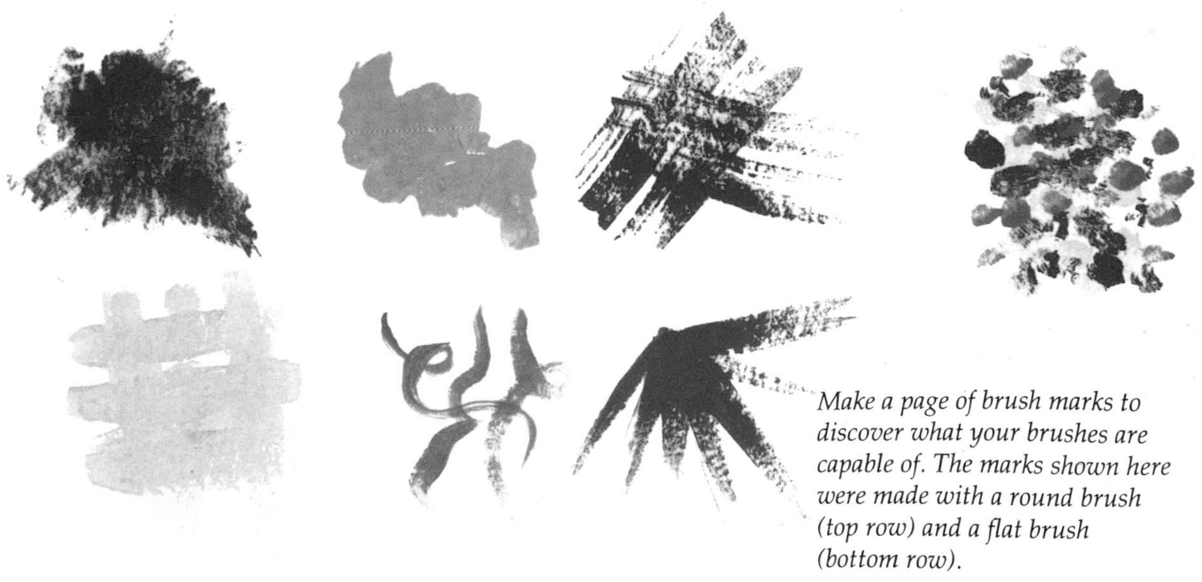

Make a page of brush marks to discover what your brushes are capable of. The marks shown here were made with a round brush (top row) and a flat brush (bottom row).

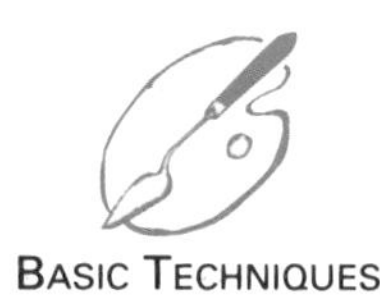

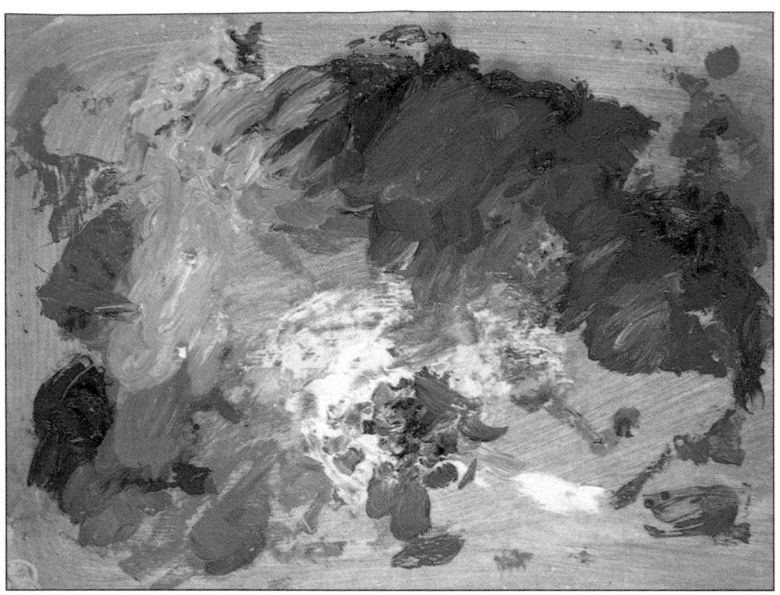

This palette layout follows the order of the spectrum with red, yellow, green, blue and violet across the top and white and neutrals beneath them.

Laying Out your Palette

Arranging colours on a palette is a personal matter. It is important, however, to arrange your colours in a systematic way – and use that same orderly arrangement every time you paint, so that you know where each colour is without having to look. Squeeze the colours onto the palette in generous mounds. Beginners tend to squeeze out little blobs of colour in haphazard fashion, and end up wasting a lot of time trying to find the spot of colour they need and constantly screwing and unscrewing the caps of the paint tubes.

Some artists like to lay out their colours in the order of the spectrum with red, orange, yellow, green, blue and violet across the palette and earth colours down the side. Others prefer to align warm colours (the reds, oranges and yellows) and cool colours (the greens, blues and violets) on opposite sides of the palette.

Precautions

The speed at which acrylics dry is one of their major attractions, but the drawback is that they dry equally quickly on palettes and brushes – and once dry they are impervious to water. With care and a little ingenuity, however, this need not be a problem.

To prevent paint drying on your brushes during a painting session, keep them in a jar of clean water whenever you are not using them. It is even better to lay them flat in a shallow tray of water – that way the bristles will not get distorted. All you need is a plastic tray – the type oven-ready meals come in; cut a notch in one end for the brush handles to rest on. Always be sure to moisten your brushes with water *before* loading them with acrylic paint; otherwise the paint will stick to the dry bristles and gradually build up a stiff film that ruins them.

After use, brushes should be rinsed thoroughly in clean water. To remove paint from the neck of the brush, where the hairs enter the metal ferrule, stroke the brush gently across a bar of soap. Then lather the bristles in the palm of your hand with a gentle circular motion until the last trace of colour comes out in the lather. Rinse again, then shake out the water and re-shape the bristles with your fingers. Leave the brushes to dry upright in a jar.

If brushes do become caked with paint, soak them overnight in methylated spirit. This

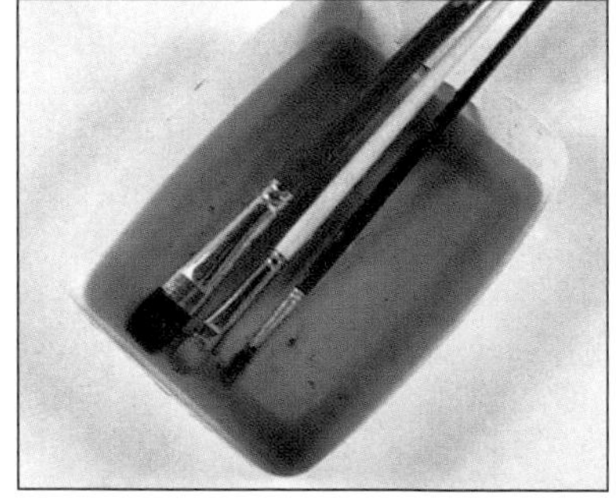

During a painting session, keep brushes immersed in water to prevent paint drying on the bristles. A shallow tray like this one will also prevent distortion of the bristles.

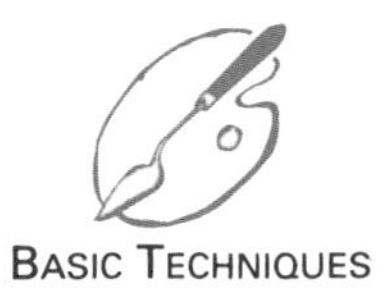

should loosen the paint sufficiently for it to be worked out under running water. Then wash the brushes in mild soap and warm water.

To prevent paints from drying out on the palette, spray them periodically with a mist of water. Special "staywet" palettes are available which keep paints moist for days (see page 179). Use plastic palettes for ease of cleaning, and wash them immediately after use. If paint becomes caked on the palette, leave it to soak in warm water for an hour and then peel or scrape it off.

At the end of the painting session, it is worth making the effort to wipe the tube caps and the screw heads with a damp cloth; otherwise the dried paint will make it difficult to remove the caps next time you paint. (If tube caps are stuck, they can usually be loosened by pouring hot water over them.)

Once dry, acrylic paint is almost impossible to remove from any absorbent surface, so take the precaution of wearing old clothes and shoes when working, and protect surrounding surfaces with sheets of newspaper.

Squaring Up

You may wish to base an acrylic painting on a sketch or photographic image; but it is often difficult to maintain the accuracy of the drawing when enlarging or reducing a reference source to the size of your canvas or paper. A simple method of transferring an image in a different scale is by squaring up (sometimes called scaling up).

Using a pencil and ruler, draw a grid of equal-sized squares over the sketch or photograph. The more complex the image, the more squares you should draw. If you wish to avoid marking the original, make a photocopy of it and draw the grid onto this. Alternatively, draw the grid onto a sheet of clear acetate placed over the original, using a felt-tip pen.

Then construct an enlarged version of the grid on your support, using light pencil lines. This grid must have the same number of squares as the smaller one. The size of the squares will depend on the degree of enlargement required: for example, if you are doubling the size of your reference material, make the squares twice the size of the squares on the original reference drawing or photograph.

When the grid is complete, transfer the image that appears in each square of the original to its equivalent square on the support. The larger squares on the working sheet serve to enlarge the original image. You are, in effect, breaking down a large-scale problem into smaller, manageable areas.

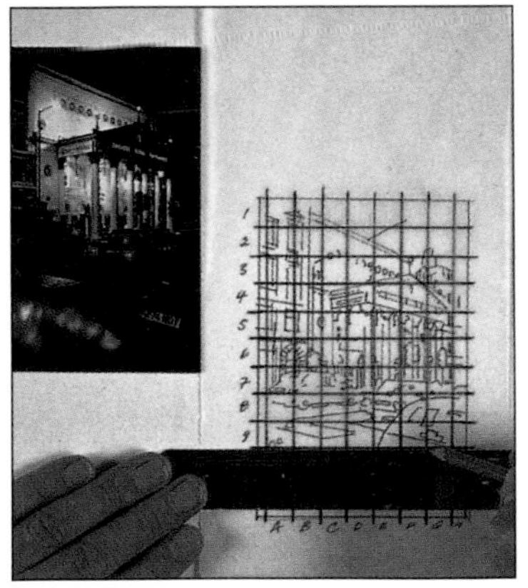

1

Make a sketch from the reference photograph and draw a grid of squares over it.

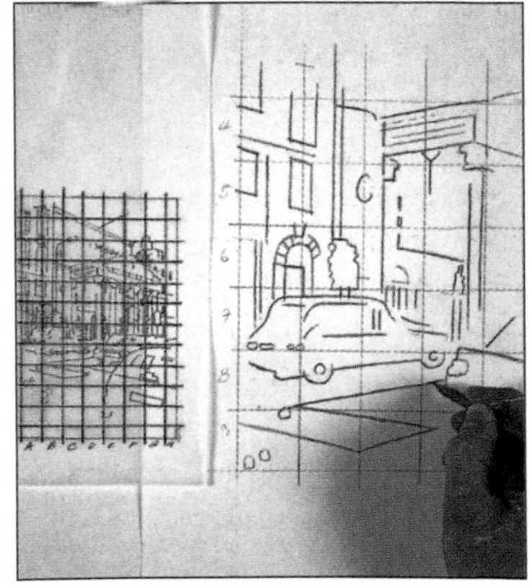

2

Draw a grid of larger squares onto the support and transfer the detail from the sketch, square by square.

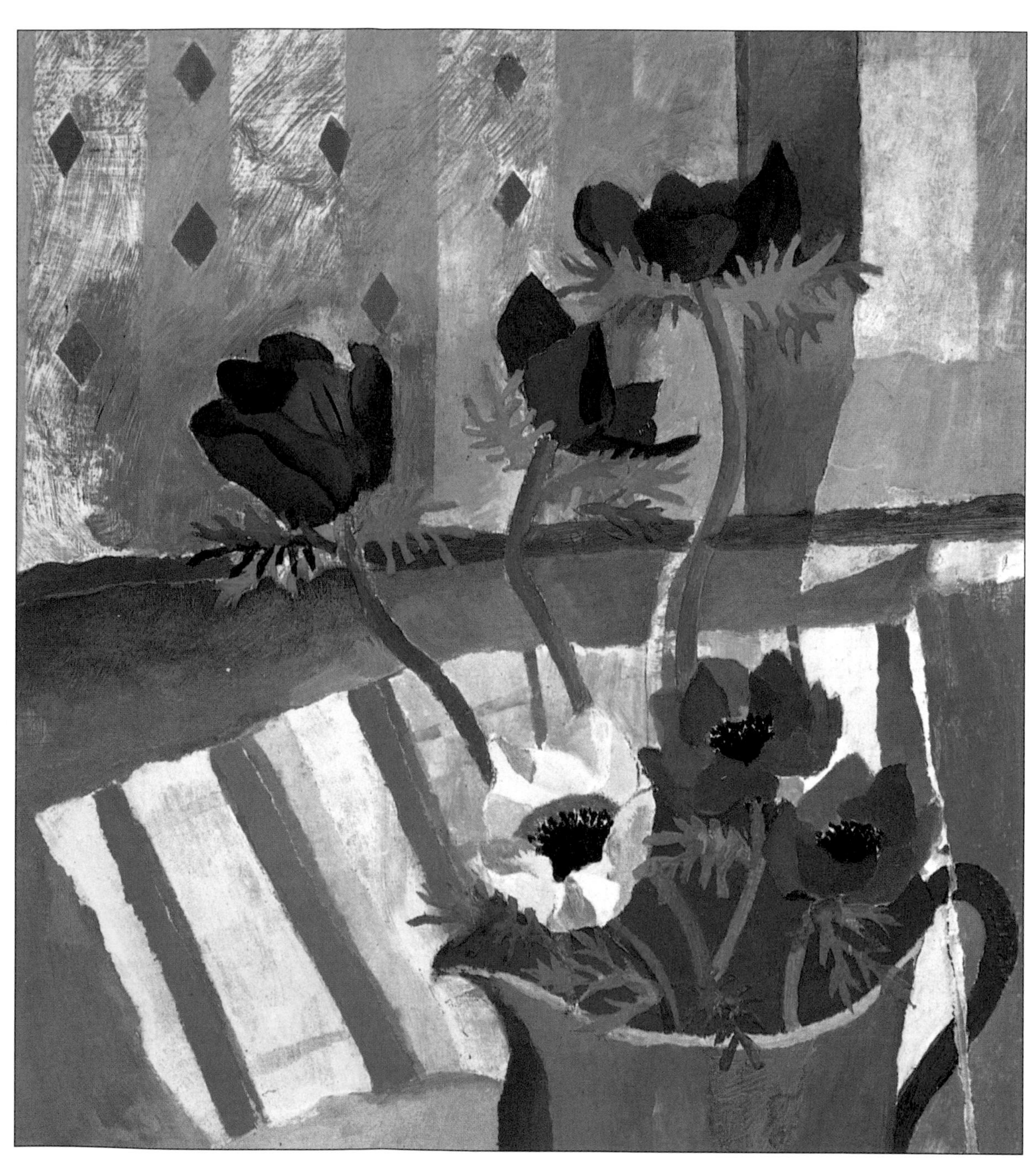

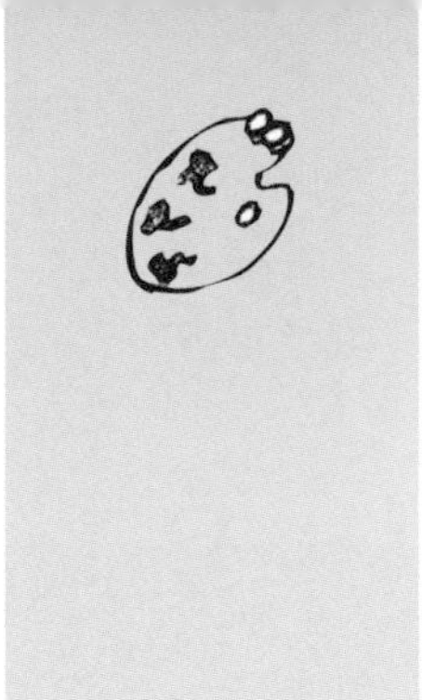

GALLERY

Art – whether painting, music or dance – is a symbiotic relationship between technical skill and originality of vision. While it is true that technical excellence alone will not produce great art, it is also true that knowledge of the basic skills and techniques is the "language" which enables the artist to express his or her personal vision with confidence.

The following pages illustrate the work of several contemporary painters in acrylic. As well as revealing the immense versatility of this exciting medium, these works reflect the diversity of the artists' creative vision. Having learned the basic techniques of acrylic painting, you should feel encouraged to explore the medium further, and to use it to express what you have to say.

~

Anemones

Katie Scampton

25 x 23cm (10 x 9in)

Colour and pattern are the dominant themes in this semi-abstract still life. Torn and cut pieces of masking tape have been used as stencils to achieve the sharp, graphic quality of the patterned elements, and also to define some of the leaves and petals.

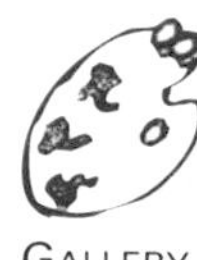

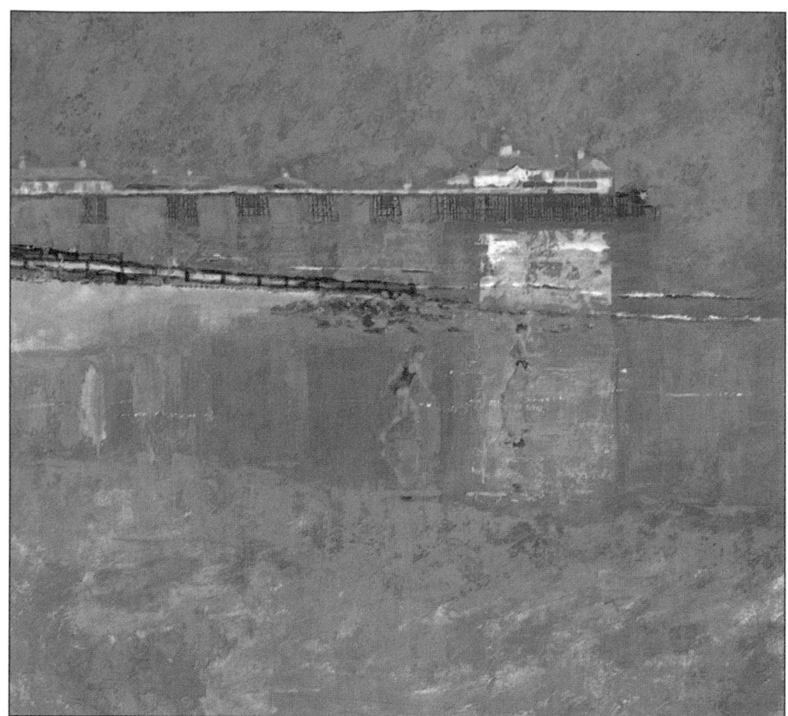

The Beach at Eastbourne

Terry McKivragan

74 x 74cm (29 x 29in)

Subtle and atmospheric, this painting has qualities more usually associated with oils than with acrylics. This is achieved by building up the colours in thin, smoky layers rather than solid blocks of colour. McKivragan starts off with thin washes and applies increasingly thicker layers of paint, allowing the previous layers to come through. The final colours are gently dragged with a painting knife, giving the paint surface an attractive, almost pastel-like quality.

St Martin's

Gary Jeffrey

56 x 67cm (22 x 26½in)

For Jeffrey, the quality of the paint surface is an important element in the painting. He works on thick cartridge (drawing) paper primed with shellac, which not only provides a warm tone on which to paint but also seals the surface. The paint can be moved around on this smooth, non-porous ground, allowing interesting textures and brush marks to be built up.

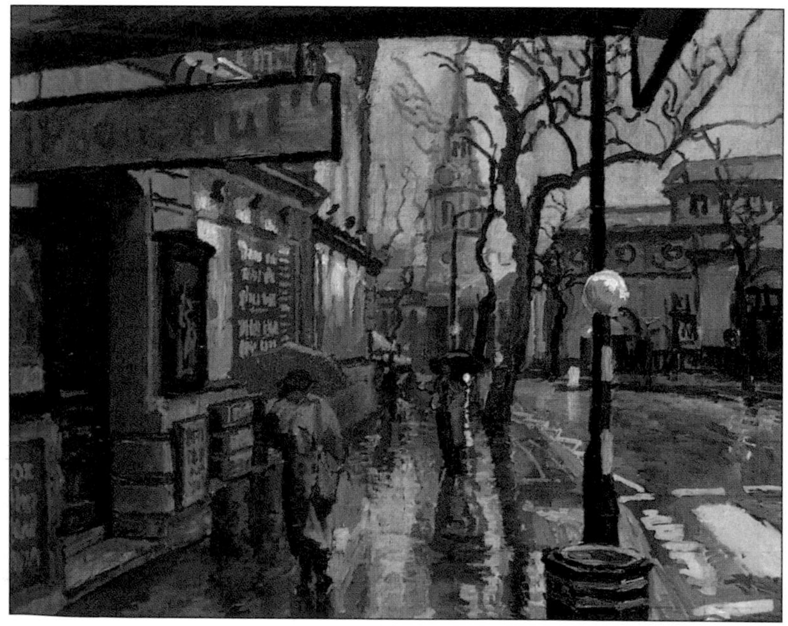

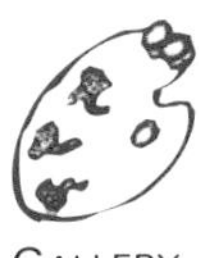

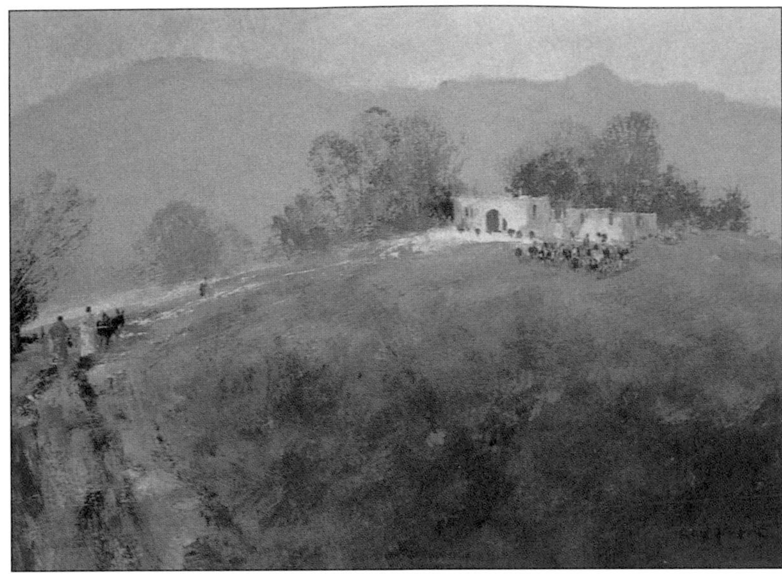

Near Marrakesh

Roy Perry

22 x 30cm (8½ x 12in)

Working on watercolour paper primed with acrylic gesso, Perry has used a limited palette of blues and earth colours for this quiet pastoral scene. The brushwork overall is smooth, with textural interest provided by the delicate touches of drybrush used to suggest the trees, the foreground grass and the rough track leading to the village.

Rustic Study II

Phil Wildman

41 x 51cm (16 x 20in)

Both acrylic paint and acrylic medium are adhesive, and this makes them ideal for collage work. For this semi-abstract image Wildman used a combination of thin washes of acrylic paint and layers of tissue paper, both flat and crumpled, to build up an interesting surface texture which is appropriate to the subject.

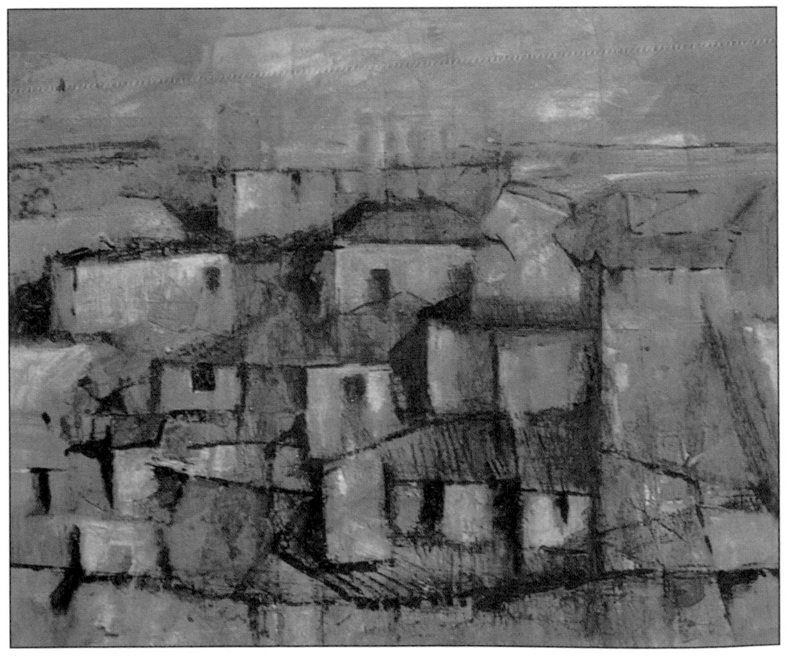

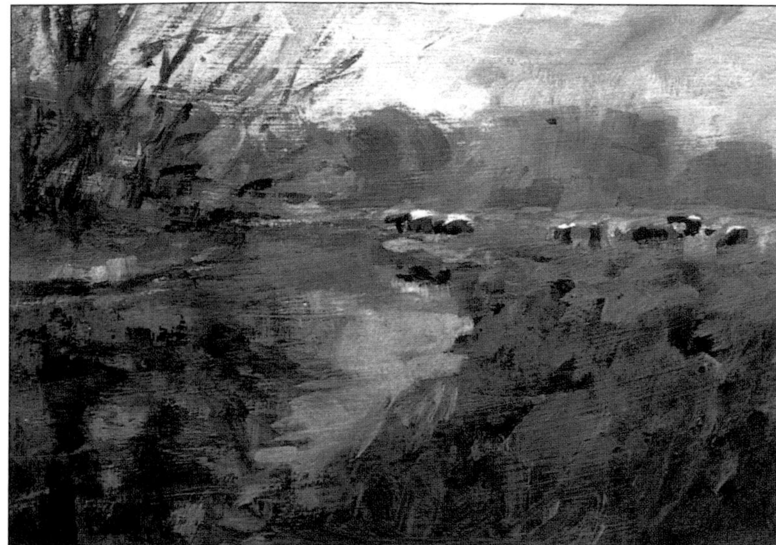

The River Avon

Valerie Batchelor

15 x 23cm (6 x 9in)

Batchelor's paintings are impressionistic, her main concern being to capture the quality of the light on her subjects. She works on smooth paper or board primed with gesso, and always starts by brushing a thin layer of colour – one which contrasts with the dominant colour of the picture – over the support. Here, for example, the ground colour is a warm red. Small patches of the ground remain exposed throughout the picture, their warm colour helping to unify the composition and contrasting with the cool greens and greys.

Provençal Landscape

Ted Gould

64 x 76cm (25 x 30in)

A hillside villa, surrounded by olive trees, provided attractive inspiration for this painting. The influence of Cézanne is evident here: like Cézanne, Gould uses planes of colour to define forms and exploits the visual phenomenon whereby warm colours (reds and yellows) appear to advance, while cool colours (blues and greens) seem to recede. The picture strikes a beautiful balance between realism and abstraction, the repeated arabesques of the paint marks emphasizing the painting's surface unity.

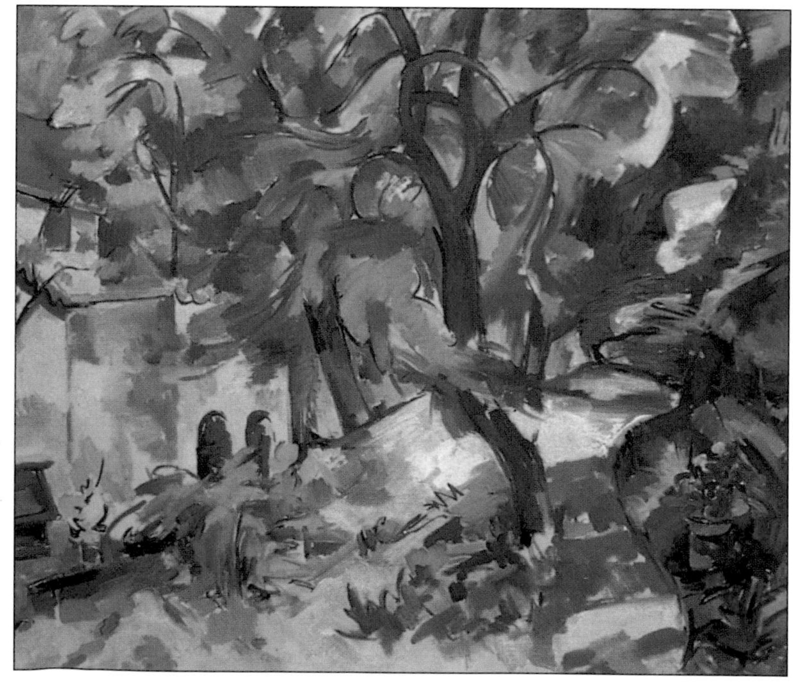

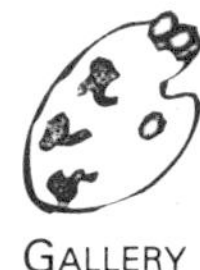

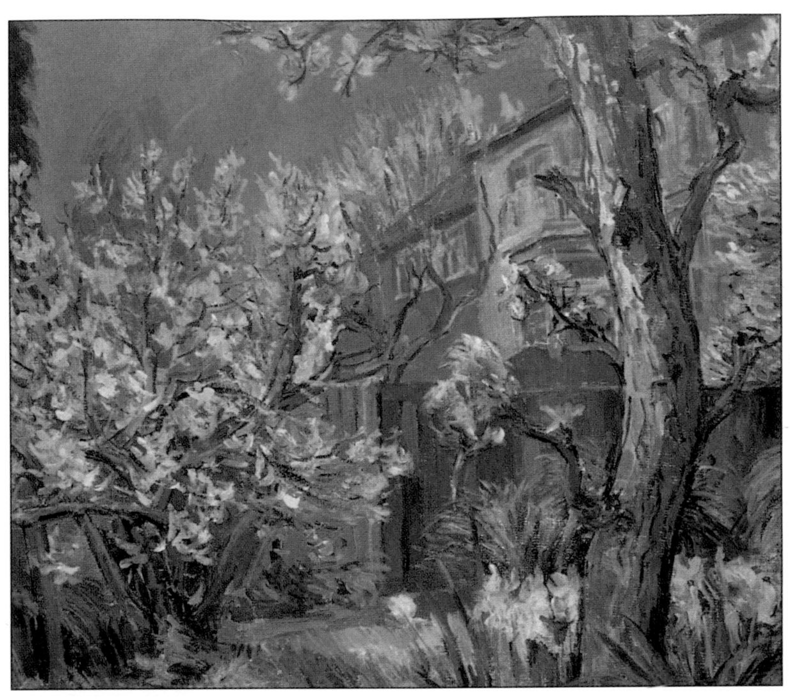

Springtime Garden

Ted Gould

51 x 61cm (20 x 24in)

The fresh, sparkling quality of spring sunshine is beautifully recreated in this painting of a corner of the artist's garden. The broad colour areas were first blocked in with thin colour, overlaid with dabs and strokes of thick, pure colour in the trees and grass. The high-key colour scheme of complementary colours – blue and yellow – creates a scintillating, light-filled image.

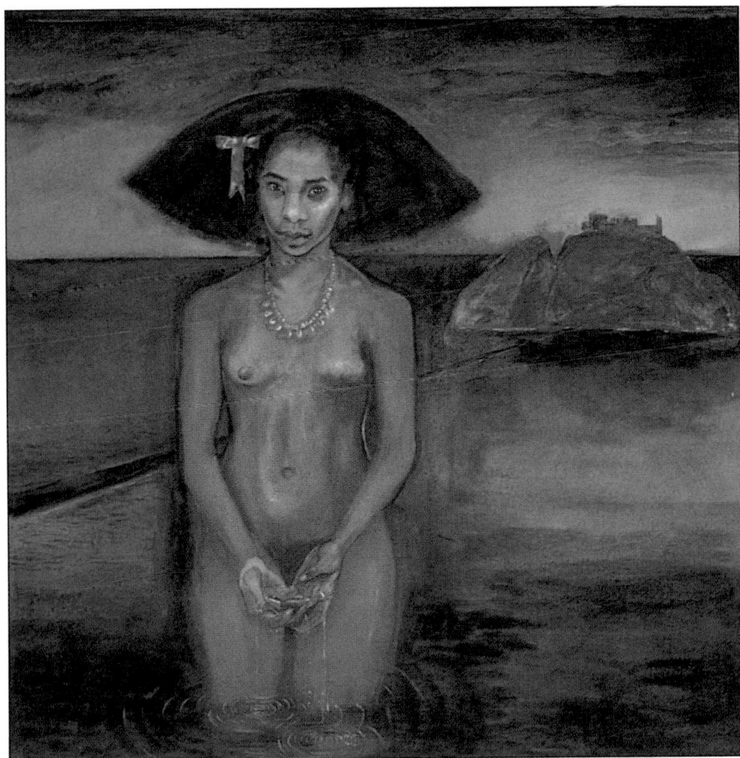

The Girl from the Tower

Barbara Tyrrell

81 x 81cm (32 x 32in)

Everything about this picture — the composition, the way colours and tones are balanced against each other, and the way the paint is applied — contributes to its haunting quality. The luminous depth of the colours is achieved by superimposing multiple glazes of transparent paint.

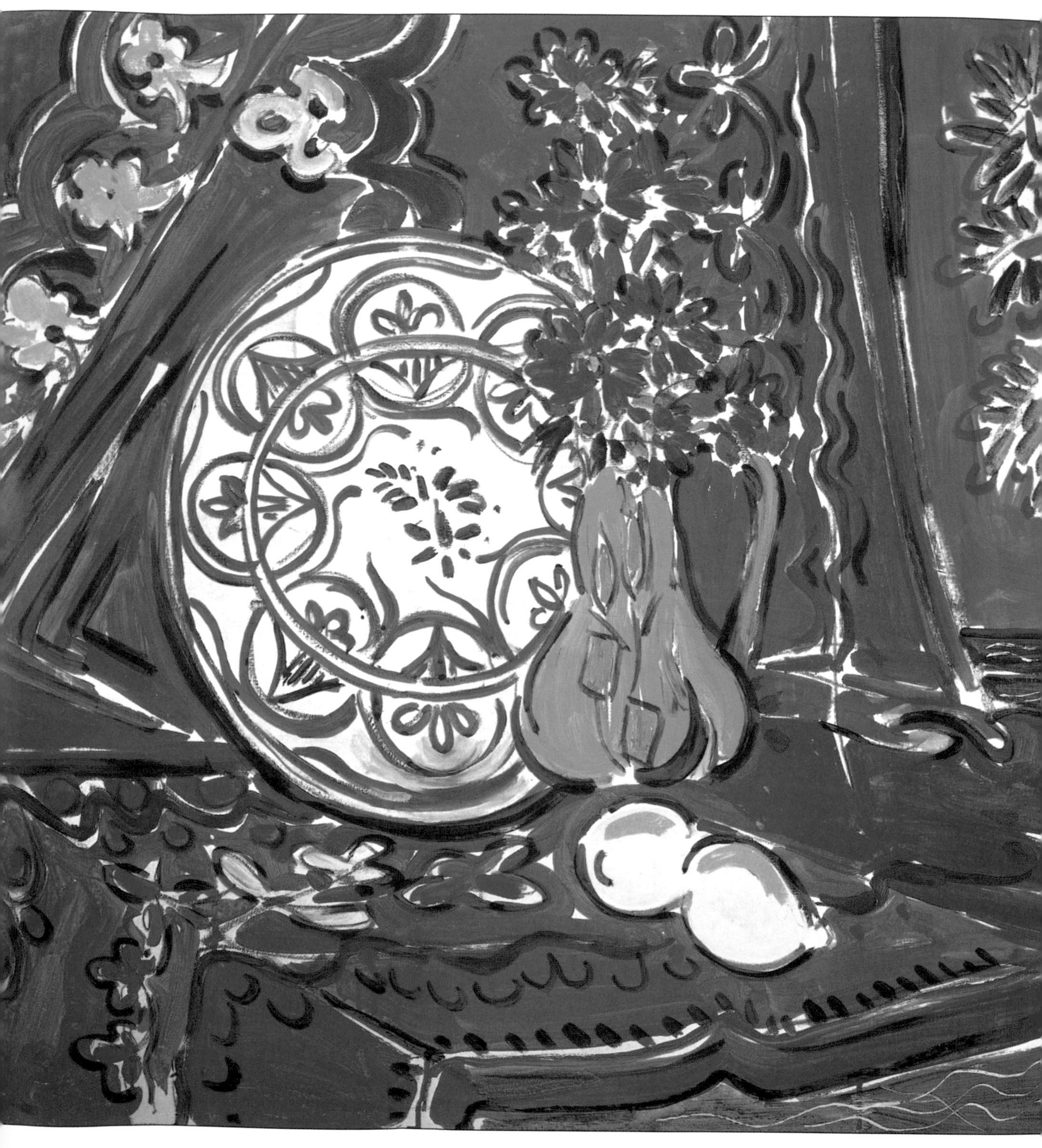

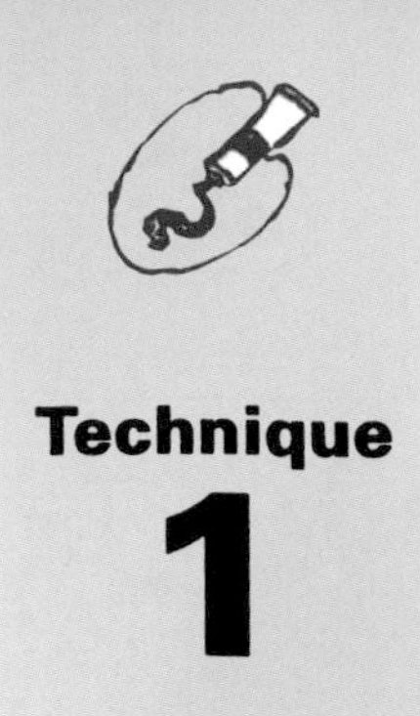

Technique

1

PAINTING "ALLA PRIMA"

The French painter Henri Matisse (1869-1954) once declared that "to copy the objects in a still life is nothing. One must render the emotions they awaken."

Matisse's ideas on the use of colour and design to translate the artist's feelings about a subject are evident in this painting. Speed, fast attack and brilliant colour are the keynotes of this work, which expresses the artist's joy in colour and the very act of painting.

The picture was painted in the alla prima manner – that is to say, completed in one session, without any preliminary underpainting. Working alla prima requires confidence, but it is very liberating – the idea is to work rapidly and intuitively, using the brush freely to express your instinctive response to your subject.

~

Kay Gallwey

Still Life

76 x 76cm (30 x 30in)

~

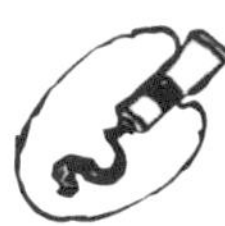

Alla Prima Technique

An Italian expression, *alla prima*, meaning "at the first", describes a painting which is completed in a single session. It also describes a direct method of working, in which each brush stroke is applied decisively and left alone; the colours are applied directly onto the painting surface, often without a preliminary underdrawing or underpainting.

Acrylic paints are ideally suited to this type of painting because they can be used thickly – straight from the tube – or diluted with water for wash-like effects. And because they dry so quickly, you can apply one colour over another within just a few minutes, without fear of disturbing the colour beneath.

An alla prima painting normally has a certain amount of untouched white canvas, because the brush strokes are applied freely without modification or any attempt at precision. (This can be seen in the demonstration painting which follows.) The combination of expressive brushwork and glints of unpainted canvas gives the painting a verve and energy which is very appealing; just as a quick sketch often has more immediacy and vigour than a fully worked drawing, so an alla prima painting can convey the artist's emotional response to a subject better than a more deliberate studio painting.

Alla prima painting requires a confident approach, so it is important to start out with a clear idea of what you want to convey in your painting and dispense with inessential elements which do not contribute to that idea. It is best to stick to a limited range of colours so as to avoid complicated colour mixing which might inhibit the spontaneity of your brushwork.

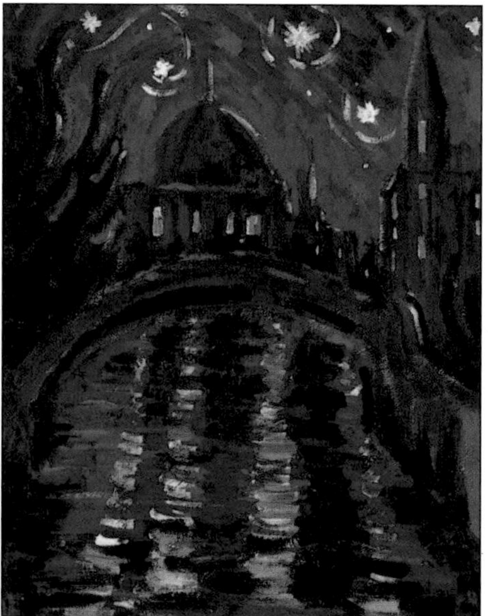

Thick paint and rapid, swirling brush strokes were used to highlight the dreamlike quality of this painting. The fast-drying quality of acrylic paint allows successive layers of colour to be applied without disturbing those beneath.

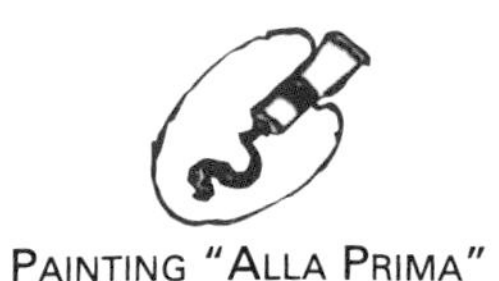

STILL LIFE

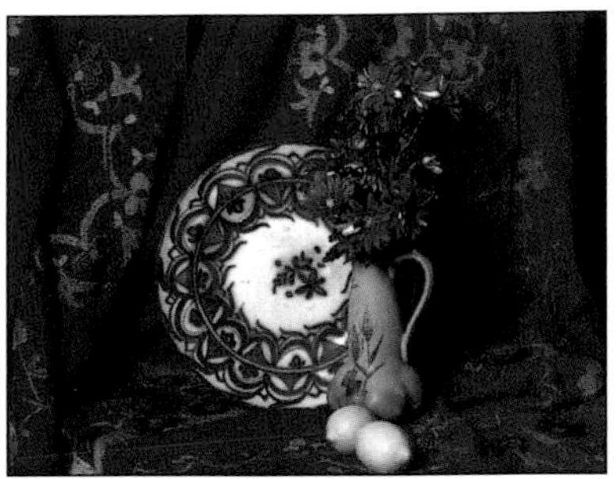

Left: This is a very simple still-life group, but the objects were carefully chosen so that the artist could exploit their bright colours and decorative patterns.

Materials and Equipment

• SHEET OF CANVAS, CANVAS BOARD, OR HARDBOARD (MASONITE) PRIMED WITH ACRYLIC PRIMER • ACRYLIC COLOURS: NAPHTHOL CRIMSON, CADMIUM SCARLET, AZO MEDIUM YELLOW, HOOKER'S GREEN, LIGHT GREEN OXIDE, COBALT BLUE, PRISM VIOLET, CADMIUM ORANGE AND RAW UMBER • SOFT HAIR ROUND BRUSH • BRISTLE BRUSHES: LARGE AND MEDIUM-SIZED

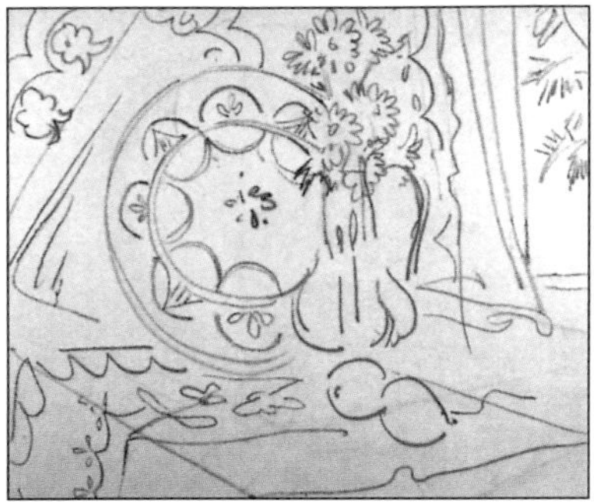

1

Sketch out the main outlines of the composition using either thinned paint and a round soft hair brush, as here, or a stick of charcoal. Soft charcoal allows you to erase mistakes, but you should "knock back" the drawn lines by rubbing away the excess charcoal dust with a cloth to prevent it from mixing with the paint and muddying the colours.

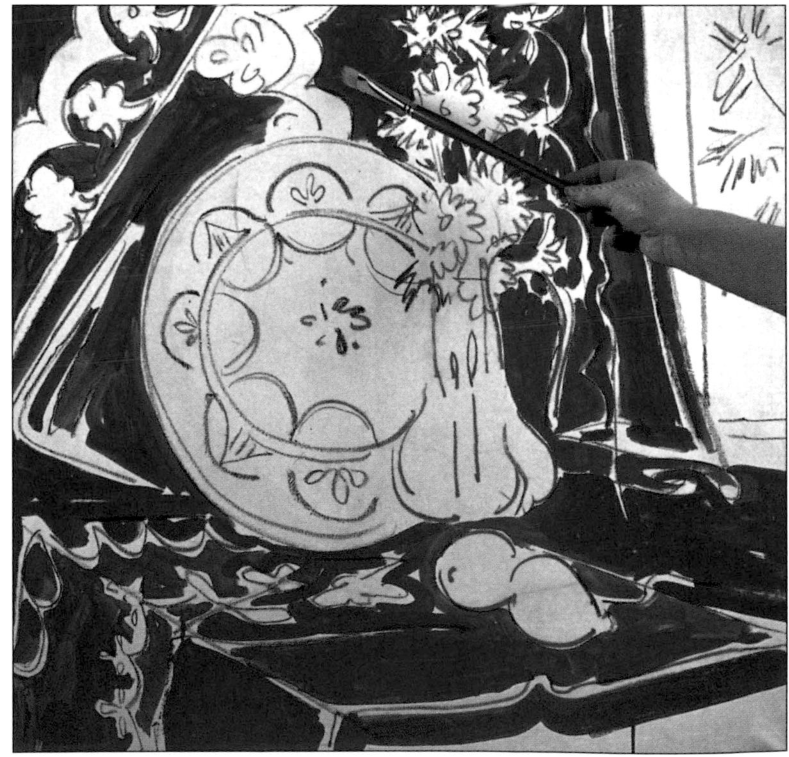

2

Mix together naphthol crimson and cadmium scarlet and dilute to a fairly thin consistency with water. Use a large flat bristle brush to block in the red backcloth. Leave the patterned areas of the cloth, and the "window", unpainted.

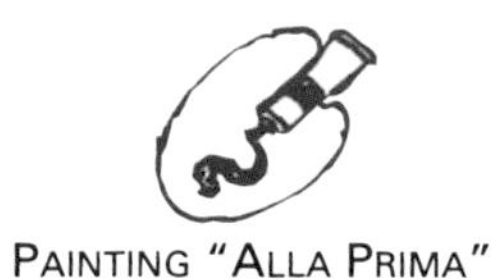

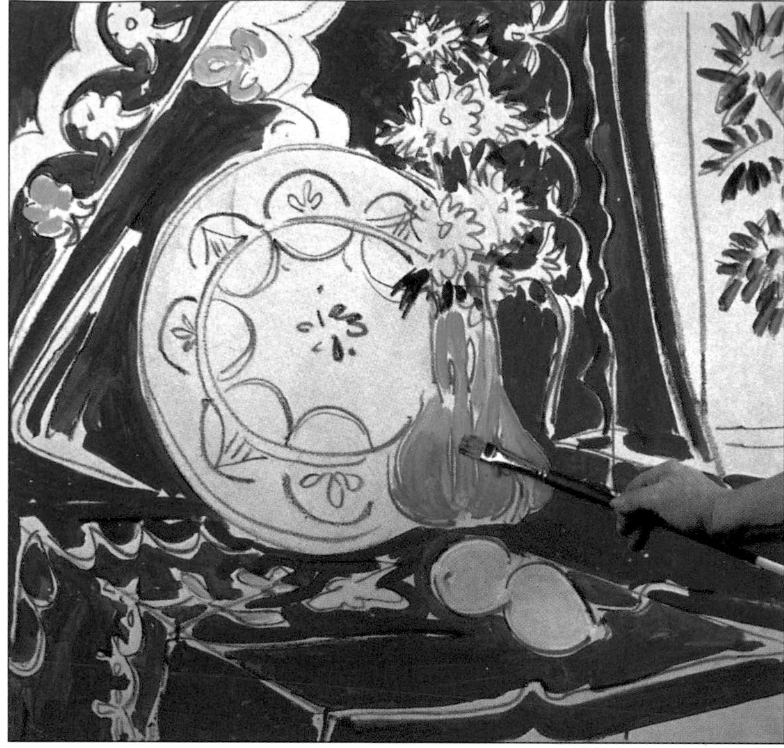

3

Paint the two lemons with azo medium yellow leaving a sliver of white canvas just inside the drawn outlines. With the same colour, block in the yellow floral pattern on the backcloth. Paint the flower foliage and the leaves in the window with Hooker's green. Roughly block in the vase with light green oxide, overlaid with Hooker's green in the darker parts.

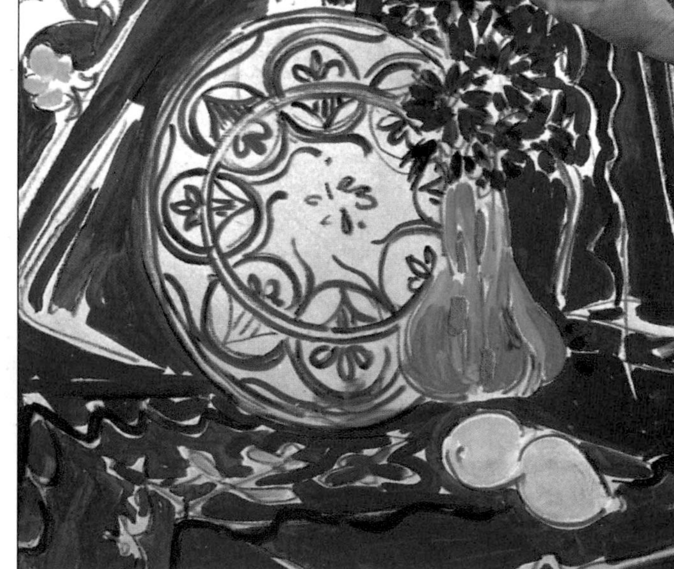

4

Paint the pattern on the plate with thin cobalt blue and a medium-sized flat bristle brush. Quickly wash in the sky outside the window with cobalt blue and white. Mix prism violet and cobalt blue for the flowers in the vase and the blue pattern on the backcloth. Suggest the pattern on the vase with quick strokes of cadmium orange.

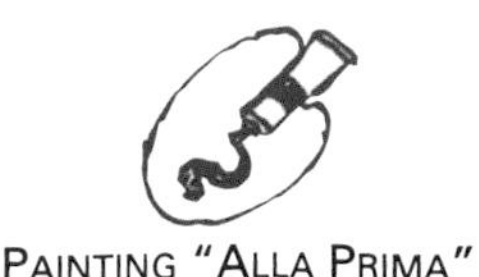

5

Paint the visible areas of the wooden table top with thinly diluted raw umber. Before the paint dries, draw undulating lines into it quickly with your thumbnail. This gives a suggestion of wood grain and also adds to the decorative effect of the painting.

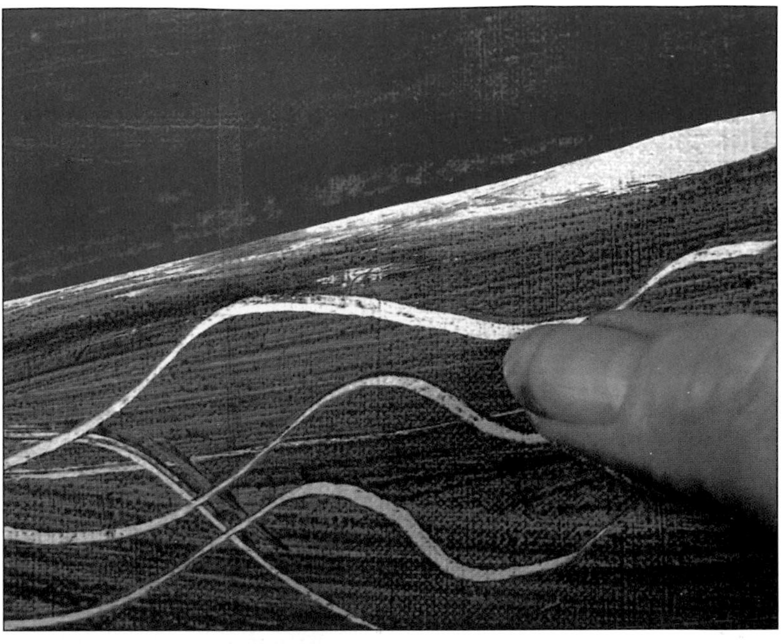

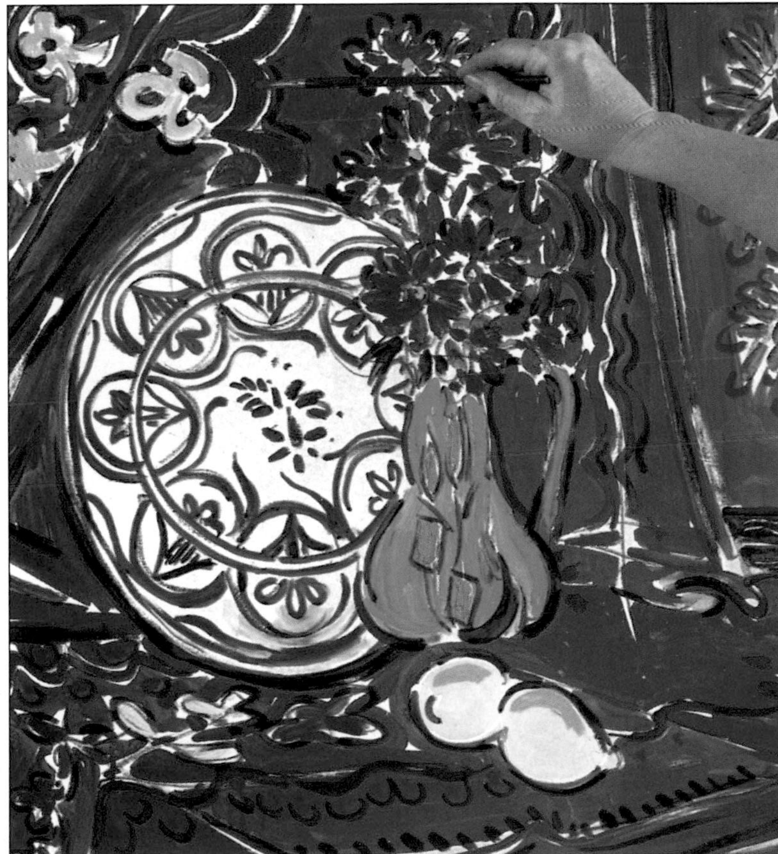

6

Add curving strokes of cadmium orange to the tops of the lemons to give a suggestion of form. Finally, use fairly diluted cobalt blue and prism violet to complete the linear details of the painting such as the pattern on the vase and the linear pattern, folds and creases on the backcloth.

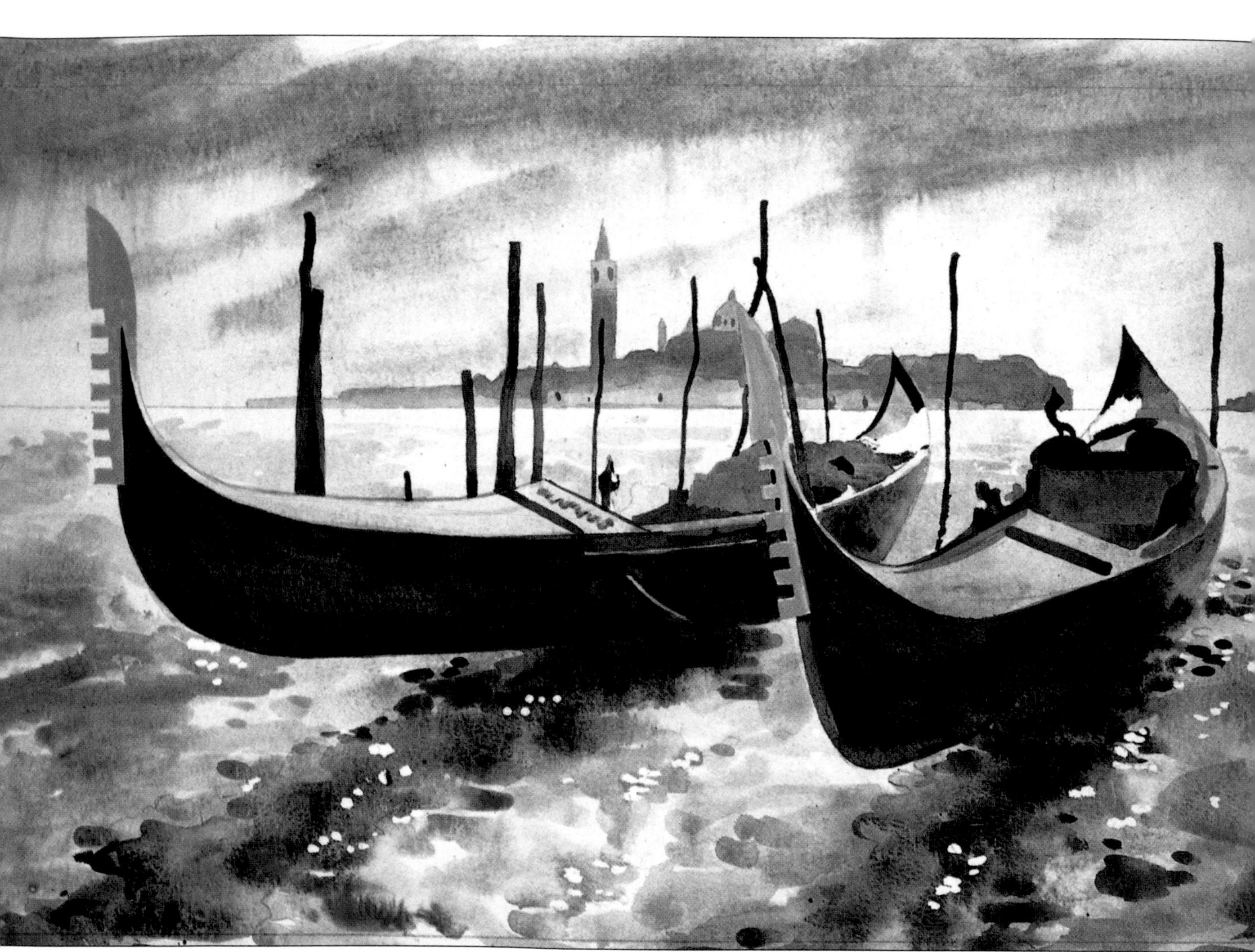

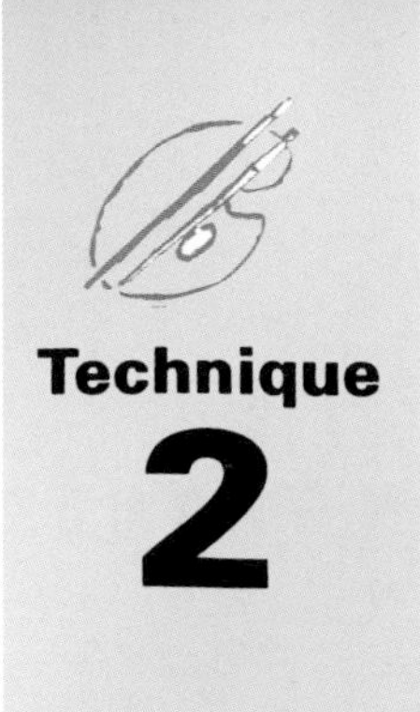

Technique
2

THE TRANSPARENT TECHNIQUE

Acrylic paint can be used in thin washes to produce an effect which is almost indistinguishable from traditional watercolour. In this acrylic painting of gondolas moored in Venice's Grand Canal, the artist has worked on a heavy, rough-textured watercolour paper using typical watercolour techniques. The diffuse colours of the sky are portrayed with wet washes, blended softly together on the damp paper. The water, too, is painted wet-into-wet; the sparkling highlights in the foreground were first stopped out with masking fluid to preserve the white of the paper, allowing the artist to paint freely over them. The finished painting suggests the hazy, watery quality of the light just after a rainstorm.

~

Phil Wildman
Two Gondolas
33 x 51cm (13 x 20in)

~

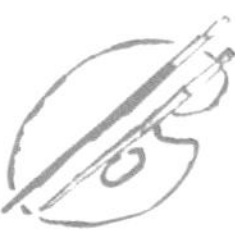

Using Transparent Washes

When acrylic paints are diluted with enough water and/or medium they behave in a way similar to traditional watercolours, producing delicate washes through which the whiteness of the paper or canvas shines, enhancing the luminosity of the colours.

One of the great advantages of acrylic over watercolour, however, is that once the colour is dry, acrylic is insoluble and permanent. This means that successive washes of transparent colour can be applied without disturbing the underlying colours.

Another problem with watercolour is controlling a wash so that the colour is evenly distributed, but when working with acrylics this problem can be solved by adding a brush-load of matt (flat) or gloss medium to a wash. This thickens the paint just enough to help it roll smoothly onto the paper or canvas. Brush strokes hold their shape better when applied with medium and water rather than water alone, and are easier to control.

Some artists might claim that the quick-drying properties of acrylic make it difficult to apply fluid washes wet-into-wet in the watercolour manner. In fact, watercolours, too are quick-drying; the problem – in watercolour as in acrylics – arises when the inexperienced artist fusses and prods at the paint, muddying the colours and ruining the limpid, translucent beauty that is the hallmark of all water-based media. Fluid washes should be applied swiftly and confidently and left alone – so drying times should not be a worry.

When using acrylic as watercolour you can use either soft hair or bristle brushes, but for the best results use soft hair ones as these hold more paint and produce smoother strokes. Acrylic washes can be applied on canvas, canvas board or smooth illustration board, and all the traditional watercolour papers are suitable, though it is best to use heavier papers as the lightweight ones tend to buckle when wet.

It is a good idea to tilt your drawing board at a slight angle so that the colour runs downwards and any excess can be mopped up at the bottom of the area you are covering.

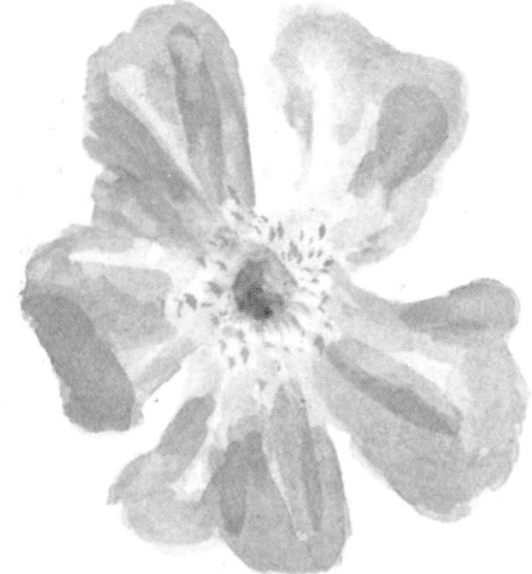

Acrylic paint is often regarded as a bright, brash medium. Yet when thinly diluted and used like watercolour paint it is capable of suggesting even the most delicate flower petal.

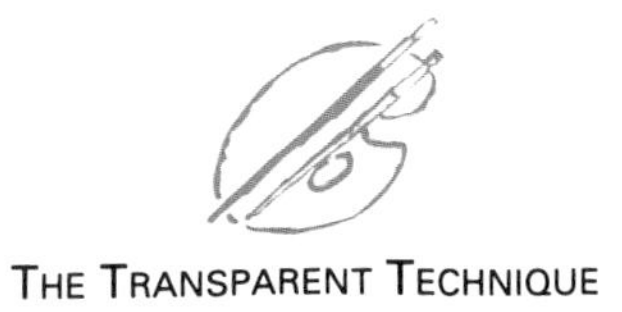

Two Gondolas

Materials and Equipment

• Sheet of heavy grade, rough-surface watercolour paper • HB pencil • Old watercolour brush for applying masking fluid • Masking fluid (liquid frisket) • Soft hair brushes: large flat; medium and small rounds • Acrylic colours: Payne's grey, yellow ochre, lemon yellow, bright green, ultramarine blue, raw umber and burnt sienna • Plastic eraser

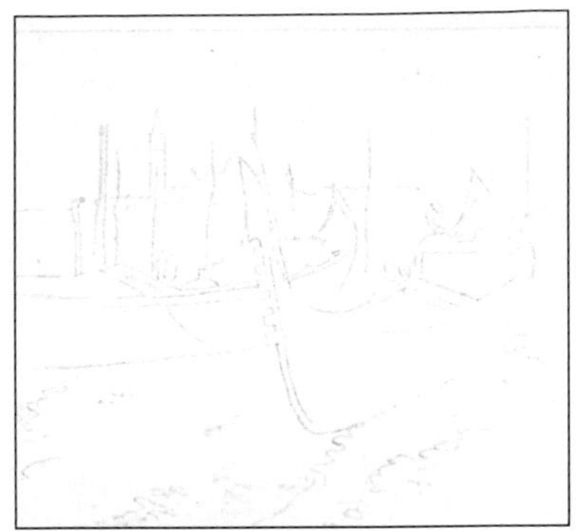

1

Make a light outline drawing of the composition in pencil.

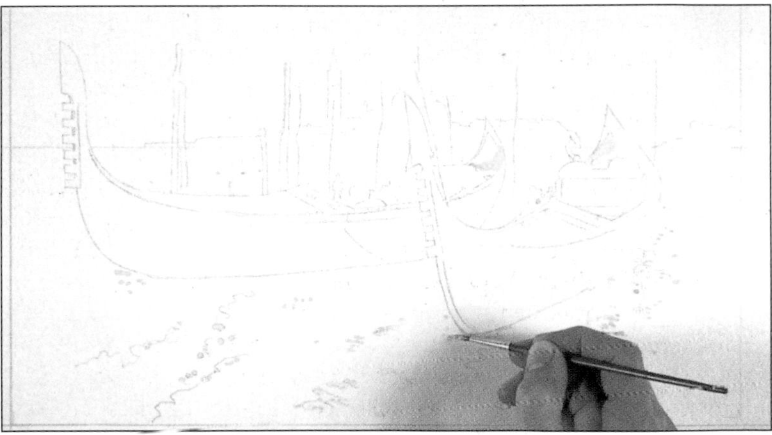

2

As in watercolour, the white of the paper will provide the brightest highlights – the sparkling reflections of the sun on the water's surface. Begin by painting these with small dabs of masking fluid (liquid frisquet), using an old watercolour brush. This water-resistant mask will preserve the white of the paper while allowing you to apply washes freely over the area. Allow a few minutes for the masking fluid to dry.

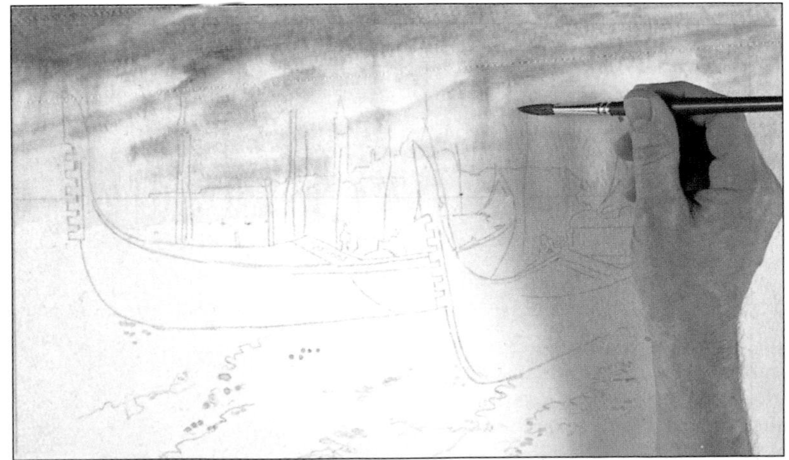

3

Tilt the board at a slight angle and use a large flat soft hair brush to wet the sky area with clean water. Mix Payne's grey with a little yellow ochre and lay in diagonal streaks of this colour with a medium round brush. Then apply strokes of very diluted lemon yellow for the sunlit clouds. Allow the colours to bleed softly together to create a hazy effect. The colour should be strongest at the top of the sky, grading down almost to nothing on the horizon, to give the illusion of the sky receding into the distance.

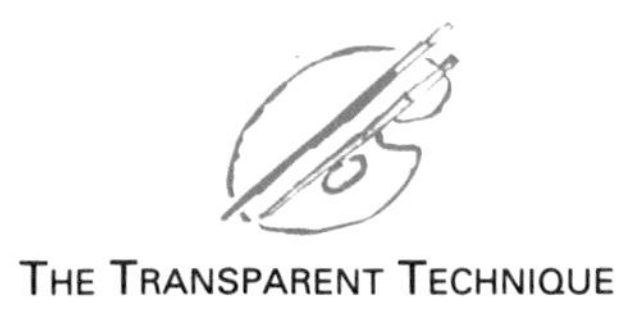

4

Mix bright green, ultramarine blue and lemon yellow and dilute to a pale wash. Quickly brush this over the water. Mix a darker green from Payne's grey, ultramarine blue and lemon yellow and, before the first wash dries, paint the darker parts of the waves. Leave to dry.

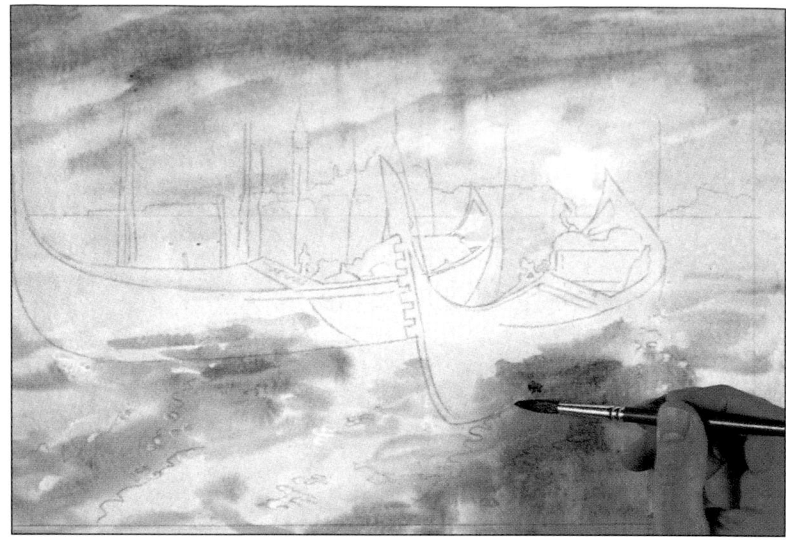

5

Mix ultramarine blue and raw umber to a very pale tint. Using a small round brush, fill in the outlines of the buildings in the distance. Let the paint dry slightly, then apply a wash of diluted burnt sienna over the darker parts of the buildings. Lighten the tone with more water for the buildings in the further distance.

6

Mix a stronger tone of ultramarine blue and raw umber and use this to strengthen the darkest parts of the buildings and dot in a suggestion of windows and doors.

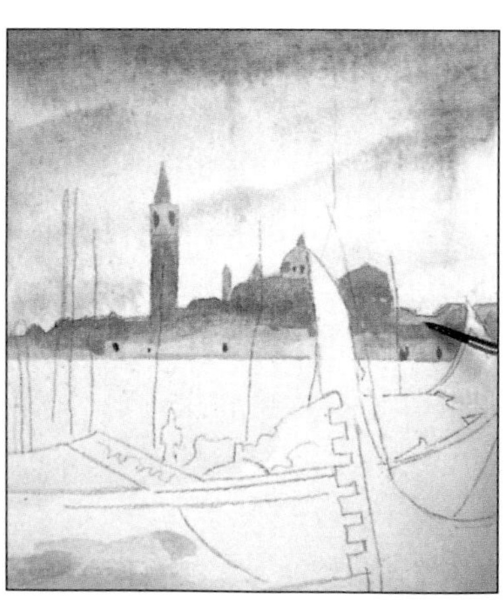

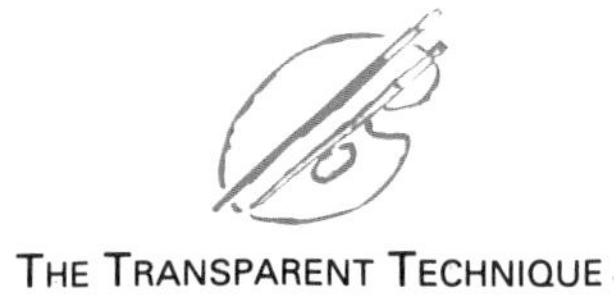

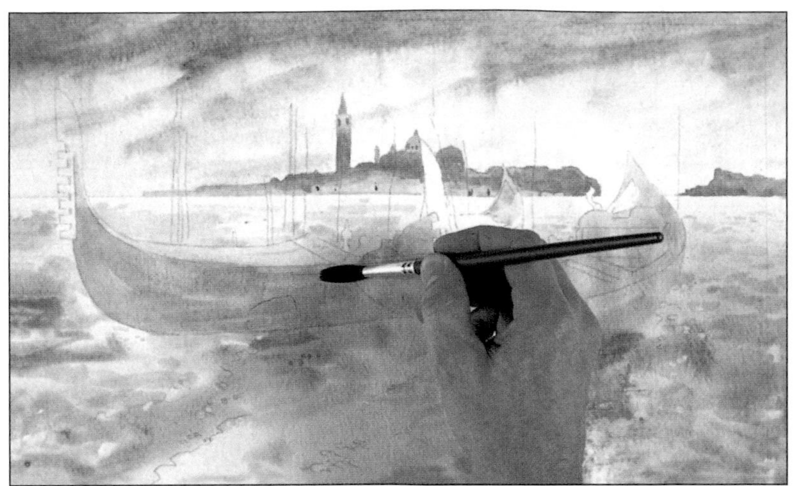

7

Mix Payne's grey and yellow ochre to a pale tint and wash this over the hulls of the gondolas with a medium-sized round brush. Use the same colour to paint the ripples in the water behind the gondolas with small strokes, and strengthen the darks in the water in the immediate foreground.

8

Paint the seat inside the gondola with burnt sienna. Paint the wooden poles in the foreground with a small round brush and a mixture of raw umber and a touch of Payne's grey. Use slightly thicker paint here to create a denser tone.

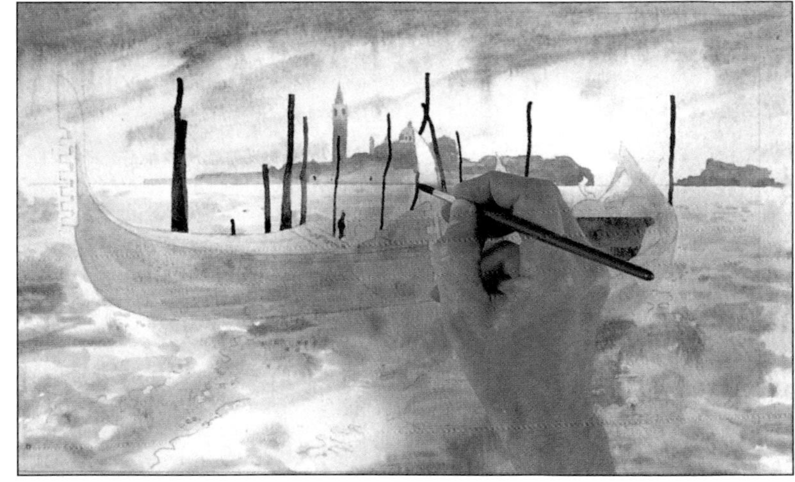

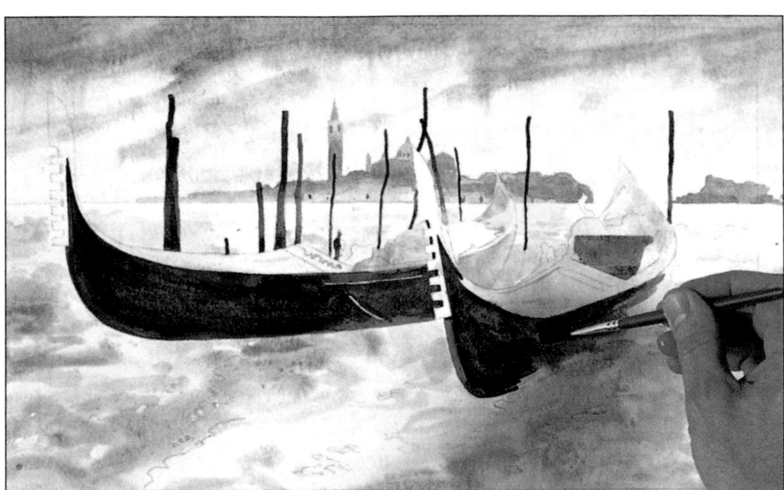

9

Mix Payne's grey and ultramarine to make a very dark tone and paint the hulls of the gondolas with the medium-sized round brush, leaving the tops unpainted as these reflect light from the sky and are much lighter in tone. Model the rounded forms of the boats by graduating the tone from light to dark.

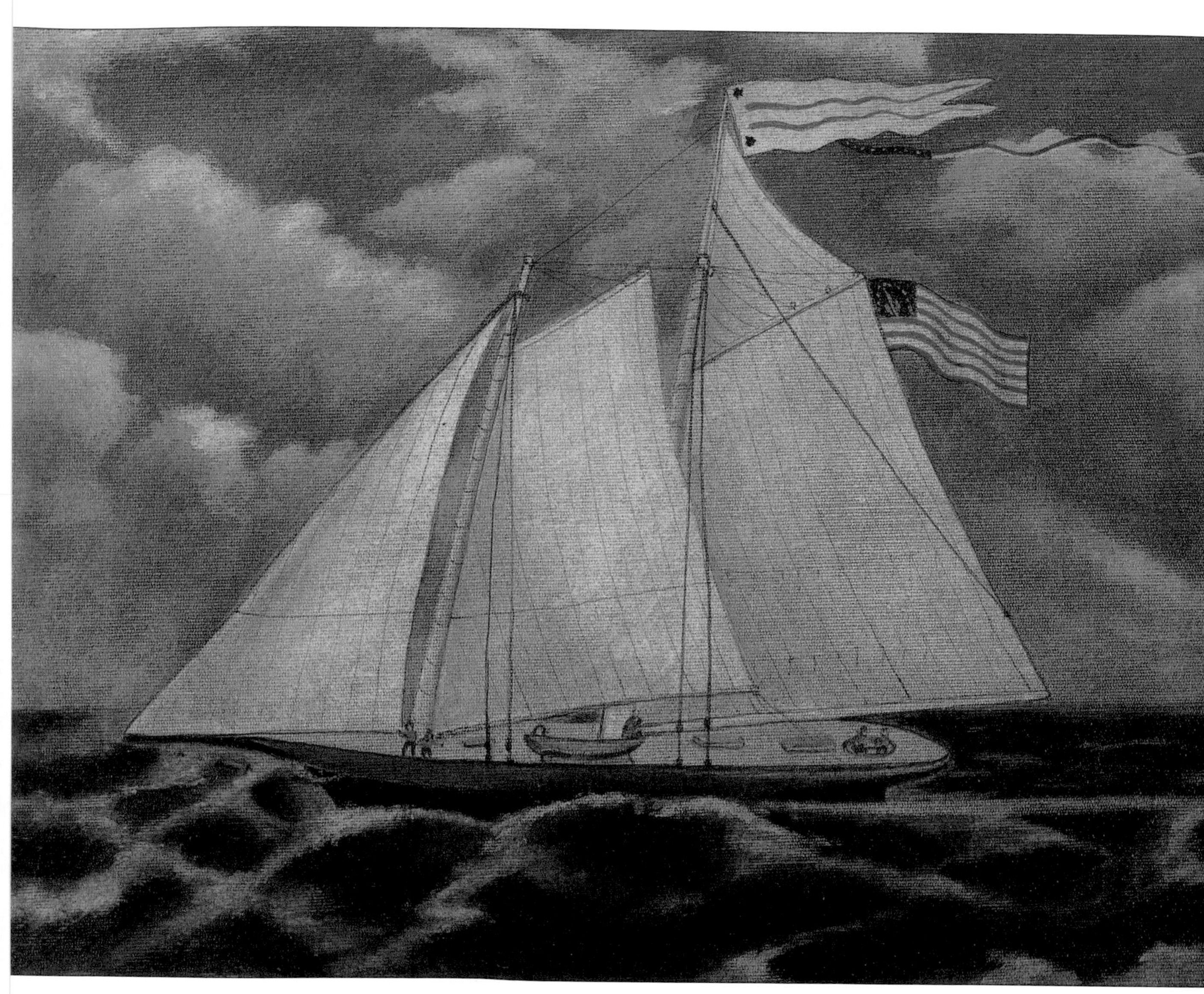

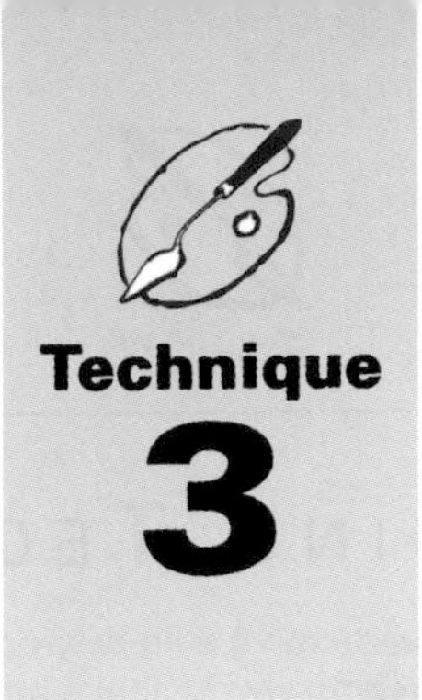

Technique 3

ANTIQUING

Traditionally, oil paintings are varnished to protect the surface from dust and to restore the colours, which tend to darken as the paint dries. Over the course of many years the varnish itself darkens and gives an oil painting that mellow glow which we associate with Old Master paintings.

Acrylic paints do not crack or fade, and the surface can be washed with soap and water, so varnishing is not strictly necessary. However, it is possible to give an acrylic painting an "antique" look – within minutes of completing it – by applying a coat of tinted varnish and then rubbing it off to leave a residue behind.

The effects of making a new painting appear old can be seen in this charming seascape, which is copied from a painting called *The Schooner Yacht America* by the American folk artist, James Baird (1815-1897).

Josephine Whitfield
The Schooner
25 x 36cm (10 x 14in)

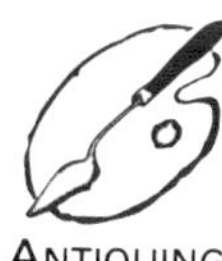

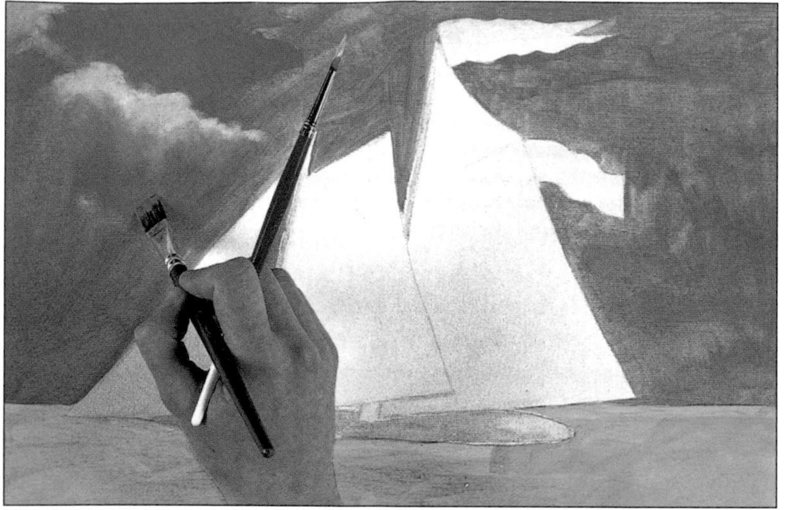

5

Start painting the soft cumulus clouds using thin, dryish paint to create an airy effect. For the dark grey areas use the flat brush and the same mixture as in step 2 but with a thicker, more creamy consistency. For the white tops use a medium-sized round soft hair brush and titanium white. Apply the grey and then the white, then use the brush to softly blend the colours together where they meet to create a half-tone in between.

6

Work on one cloud at a time so that you can blend the colours softly before the paint dries. Also soften the outer contours of the clouds by rubbing them into the weave of the canvas, to create a sense of atmosphere and prevent the clouds from appearing "pasted on" to the sky.

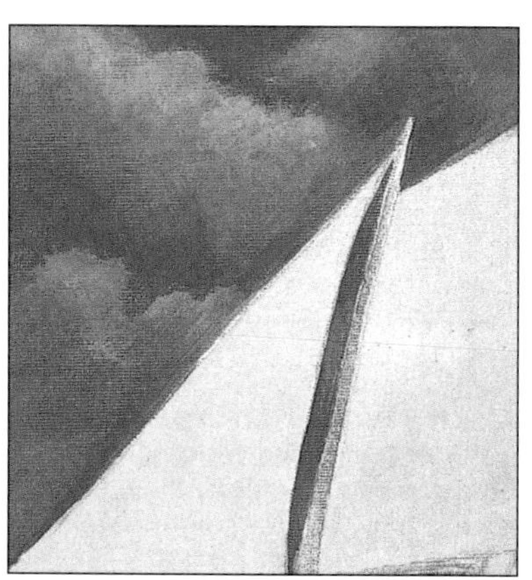

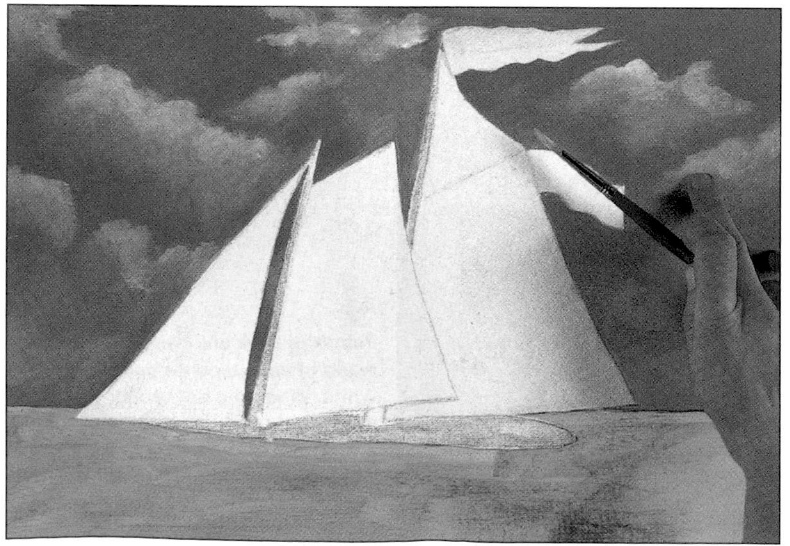

7

Continue working on the clouds, making sure that they are largest near the top of the picture, becoming gradually smaller as they near the horizon so as to give the effect of receding space. To create very soft gradations of tone in the clouds, use a fingertip to blend the greys and whites together.

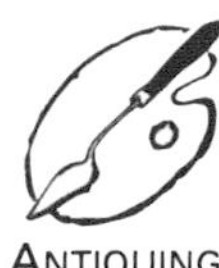

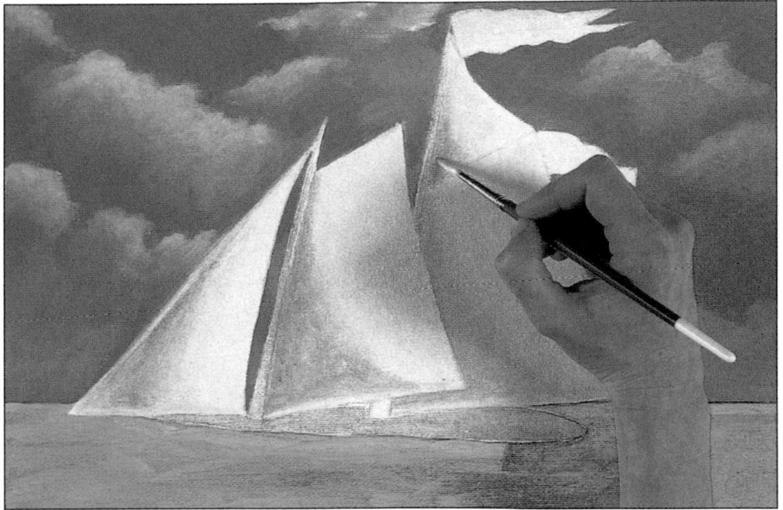

8

Mix a very pale tone of burnt umber and titanium white and paint the shadows on the sails and flags with a medium-sized round soft hair brush.

9

With the same brush paint the lower half of the boat's hull with emerald green darkened with Prussian blue and a little raw umber. Use the same colour to paint the dark areas of the waves with curving strokes.

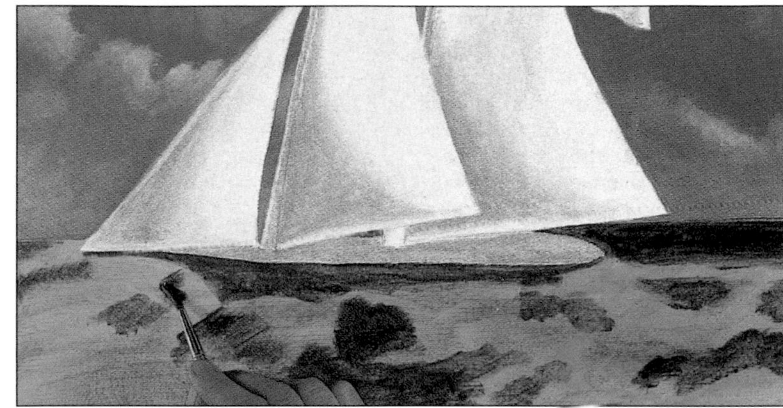

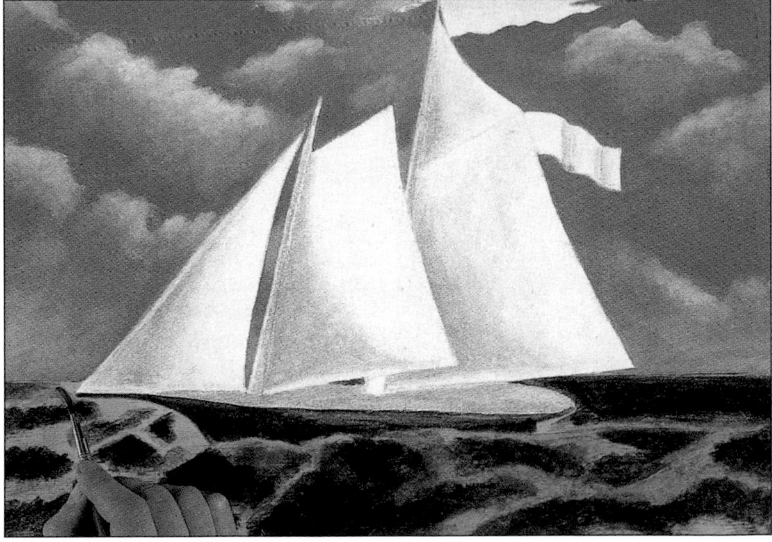

10

While the paint is still wet, quickly block in the mid-tones in the waves with emerald green and a touch of titanium white, blending the dark and mid-tones together in places. Also paint the upper half of the boat's hull.

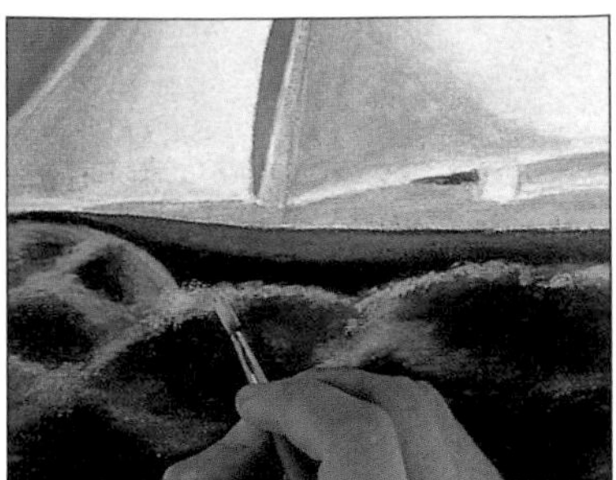

11

Wash the brush, then paint the crests of the waves with tiny strokes of white toned down with just a hint of emerald green, reserving pure white for the highlights.

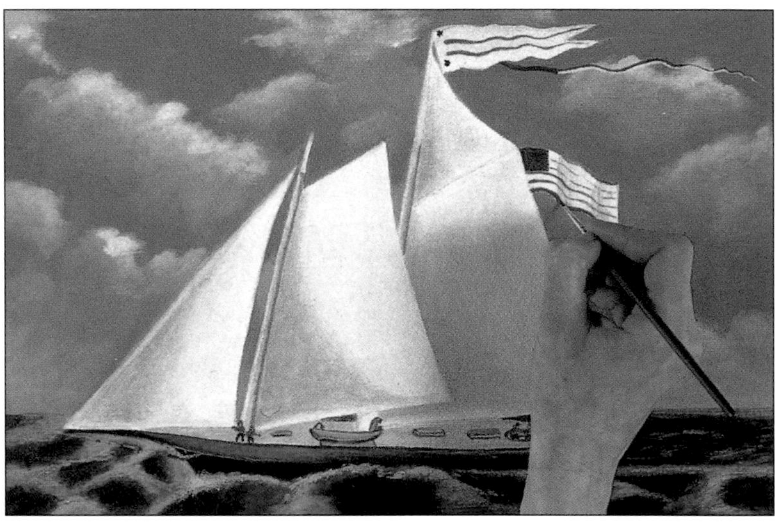

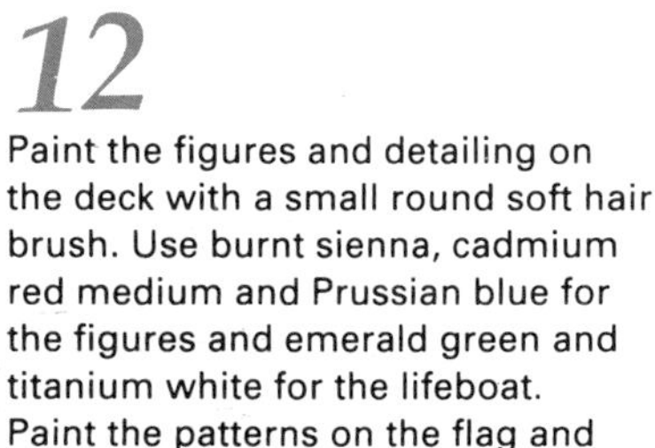

12

Paint the figures and detailing on the deck with a small round soft hair brush. Use burnt sienna, cadmium red medium and Prussian blue for the figures and emerald green and titanium white for the lifeboat. Paint the patterns on the flag and pennant with cadmium red medium and Prussian blue.

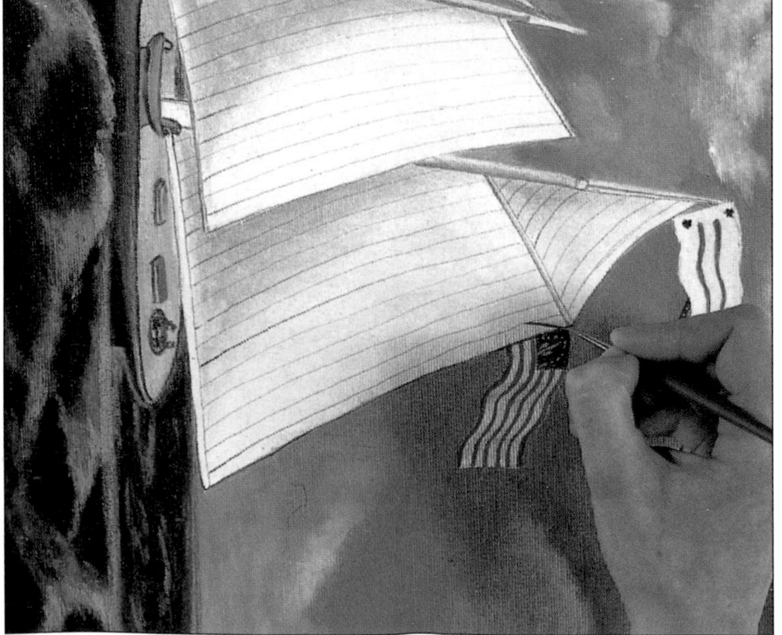

13

Mix burnt umber and titanium white and dilute to a thin consistency. Use a rigger brush to paint the thin vertical lines on the sails. You will need a steady hand for this, but the lines must not be too mechanical so don't use a ruler! You may find it easier to turn the painting around and draw the lines in a horizontal rather than vertical direction.

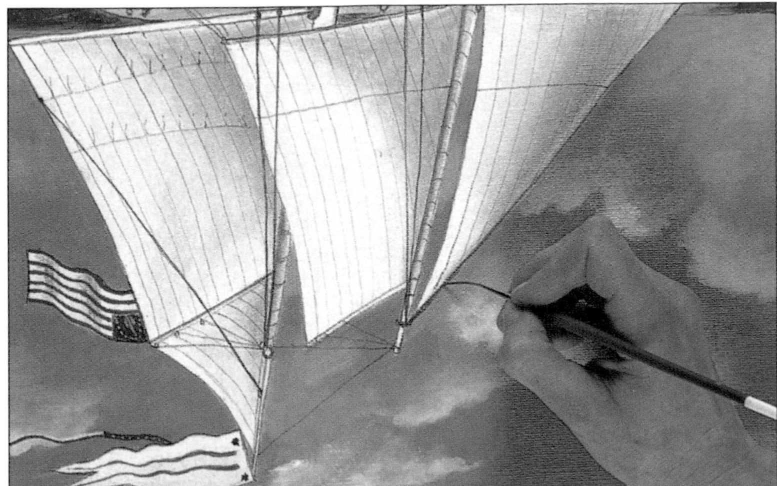

14

Now use the rigger to outline the sails and paint the rigging with slightly thicker lines of burnt umber. Again, turn the painting around if you find it easier to paint the lines in a horizontal direction. Leave the painting to dry thoroughly.

15

Apply a thin coat of dark gloss varnish over the entire painting using a 7.5cm (3in) flat soft hair brush or a household paintbrush. Work quickly because the varnish must remain wet for the next stage.

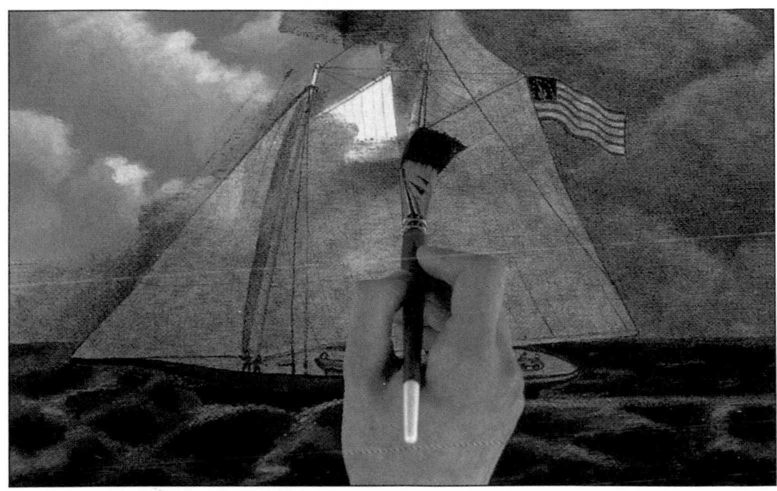

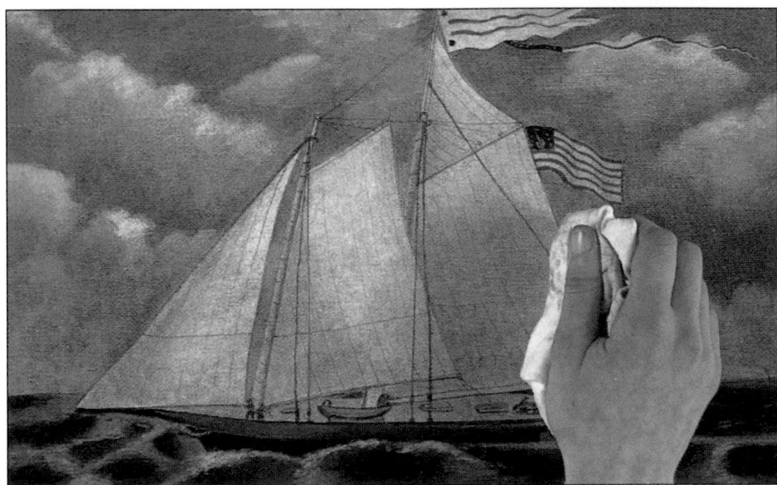

16

Rub vigorously over the entire canvas with a clean, lint-free cloth. This removes most of the varnish, at the same time pressing some of it into the weave of the canvas so as to leave a light stain of warm colour.

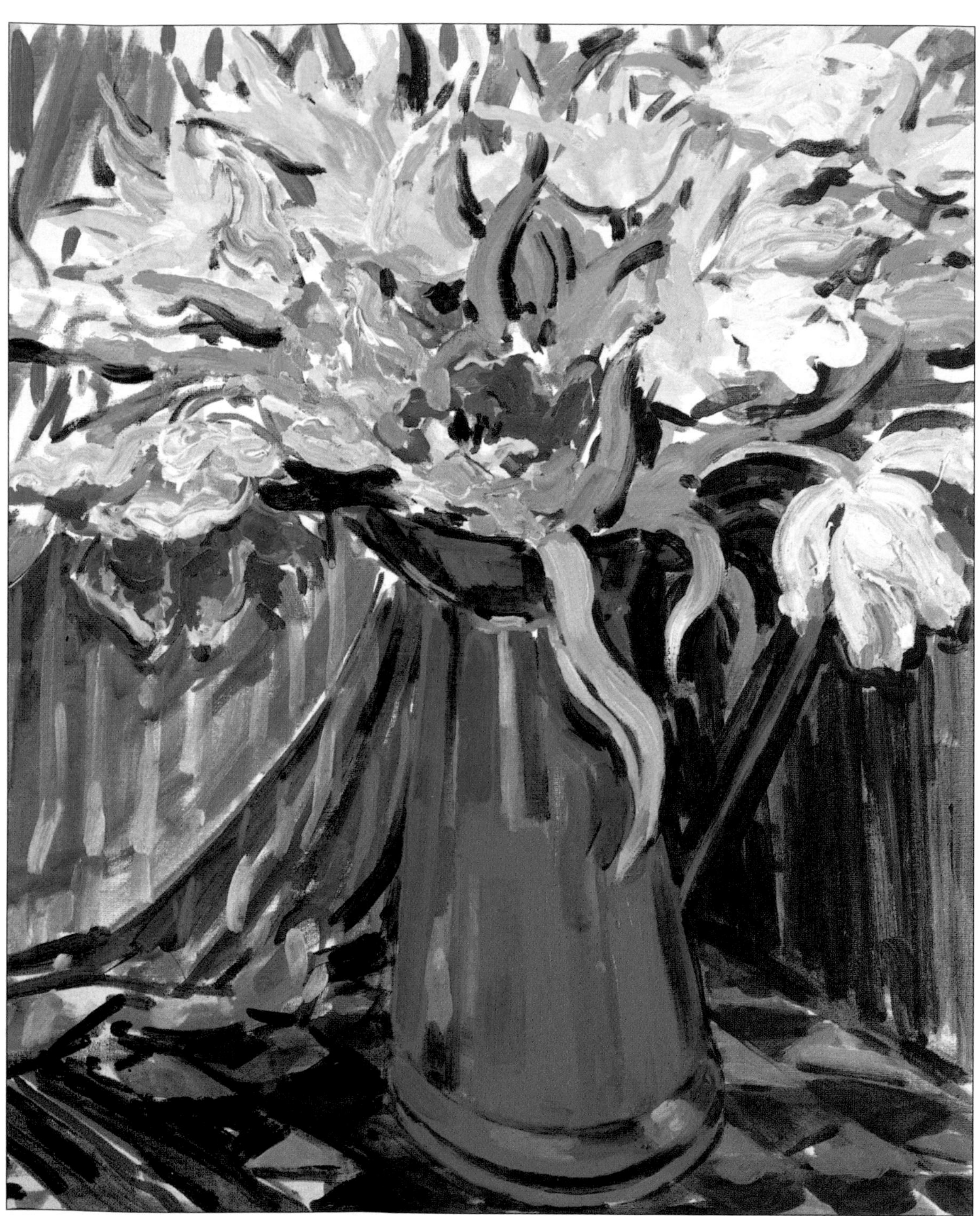

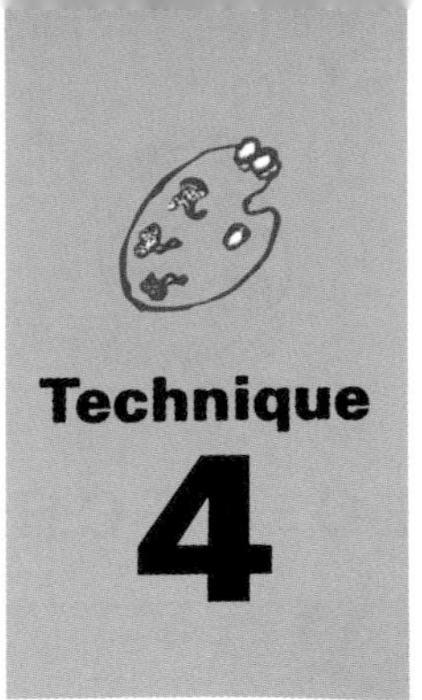

Impasto

Impasto – thick, heavily textured paint – is most commonly associated with the direct, or "alla prima", style of painting, in which a picture is completed in one session, without a preliminary underpainting. Thick paint and rapid brush strokes allow the picture to be built up quickly and in a spontaneous manner, and this approach was adopted by the artist in this painting of a jug full of tulips. Thick layers of undiluted paint were applied directly onto the canvas, "sculpting" the pigment with a bristle brush to heighten its textural quality. The result is a highly tactile painting which emphasizes the strong forms of the flowers and foliage.

Kay Gallwey
Tulips
61 x 51cm (24 x 20in)

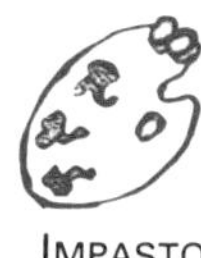

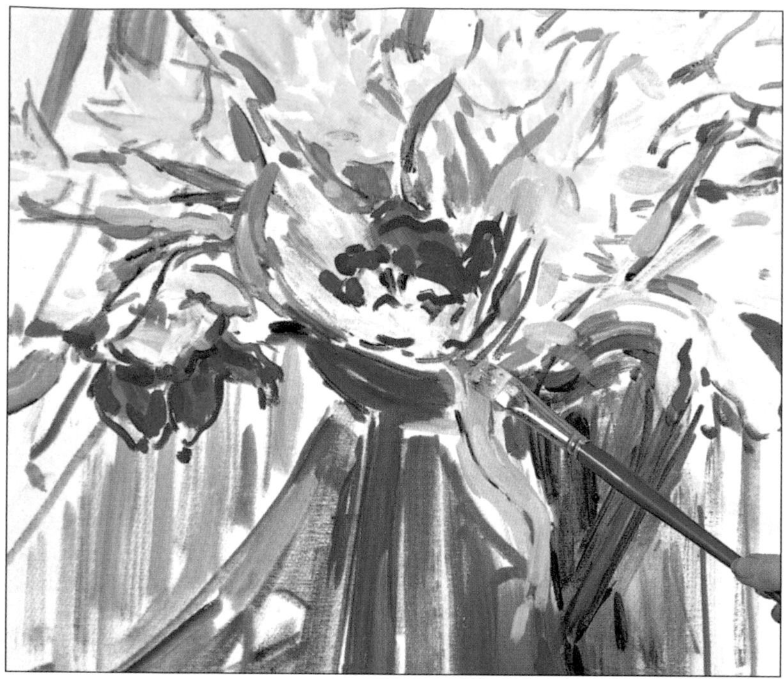

3

Using thicker paint, diluted with just a little water, paint the deepest tones on the orange-red tulips with various reds – cadmium scarlet, naphthol crimson and quinacridone violet. Paint the leaves of the tulips with thick, sinuous strokes using Hooker's green for the darkest tones, light green oxide for the medium tones and citrus green for the lightest tones, mixing all of these colours with titanium white.

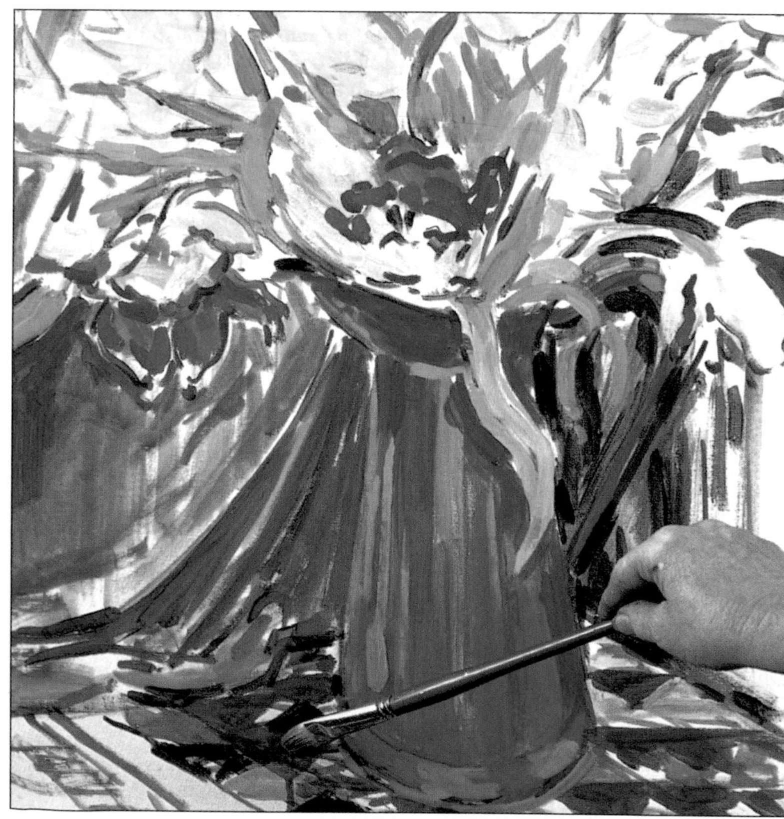

4

Strengthen the tones on the blue jug and backcloth with thick paint, using brilliant blue and titanium white for the lights and cobalt blue for the darks. Paint the diamond pattern on the kilim using quinacridone violet, naphthol crimson, cadmium orange, mars black and brilliant blue mixed with white.

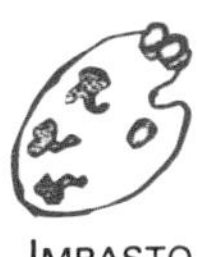

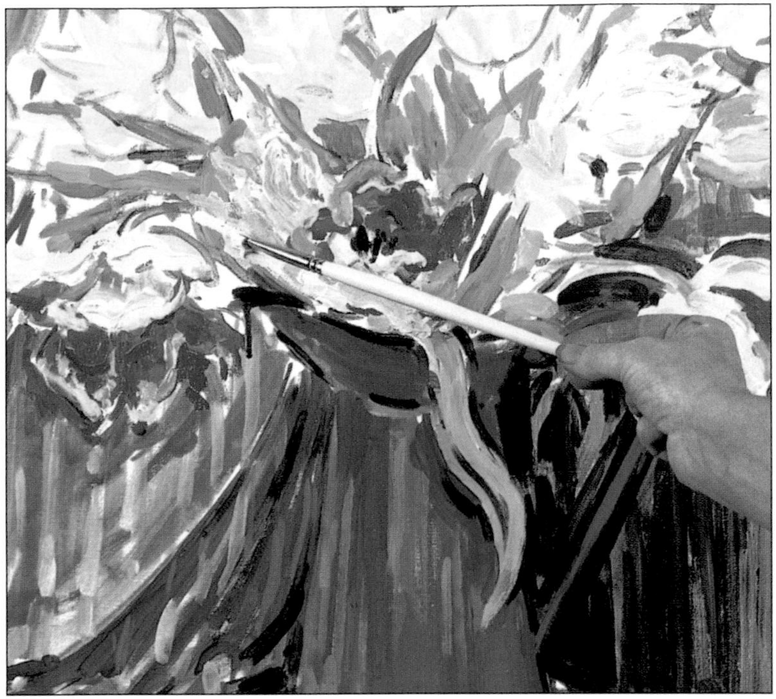

5

Paint the white stripes on the blue backcloth, adding a hint of brilliant blue to the white where the folds create shadows. Block in the dark cloth on the right with loose mixtures of raw umber, cadmium yellow deep and Hooker's green, scrubbing the paint on with vertical strokes of a fairly dry brush. Switch back to the medium-sized brush and paint the pale, creamy-coloured tulips with mixtures of azo medium yellow, titanium white and hints of cadmium scarlet. Use the paint thickly, undiluted, and apply it with prominent, textured brush strokes.

Right: This detail shows how the thick, juicy paint and swirling brush marks define the forms of the flowers and also lend rhythm and movement to the picture. The contrast of thick paint in the foreground, which appears to advance, and thinner paint in the background, which appears to recede, helps to create a sense of depth and three-dimensional space.

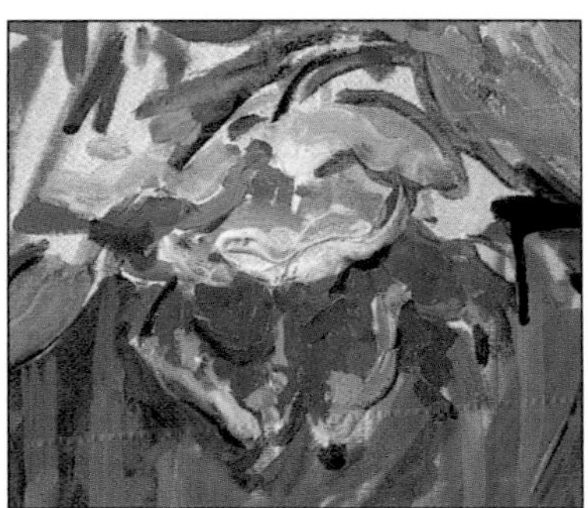

6

Finally, define the shadows on the tulip leaves with strokes of Hooker's green; this also emphasizes the graceful curves of the leaves. Refine the tones in the jug with further strokes of cobalt blue, brilliant blue and titanium white, blending the tones together with feathery strokes of the brush to model the jug's rounded form.

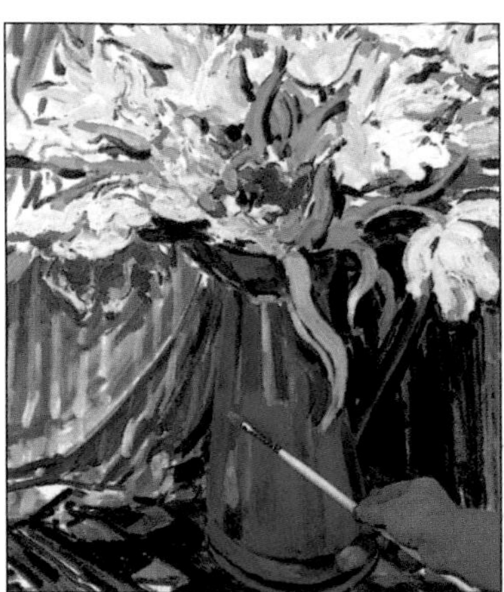

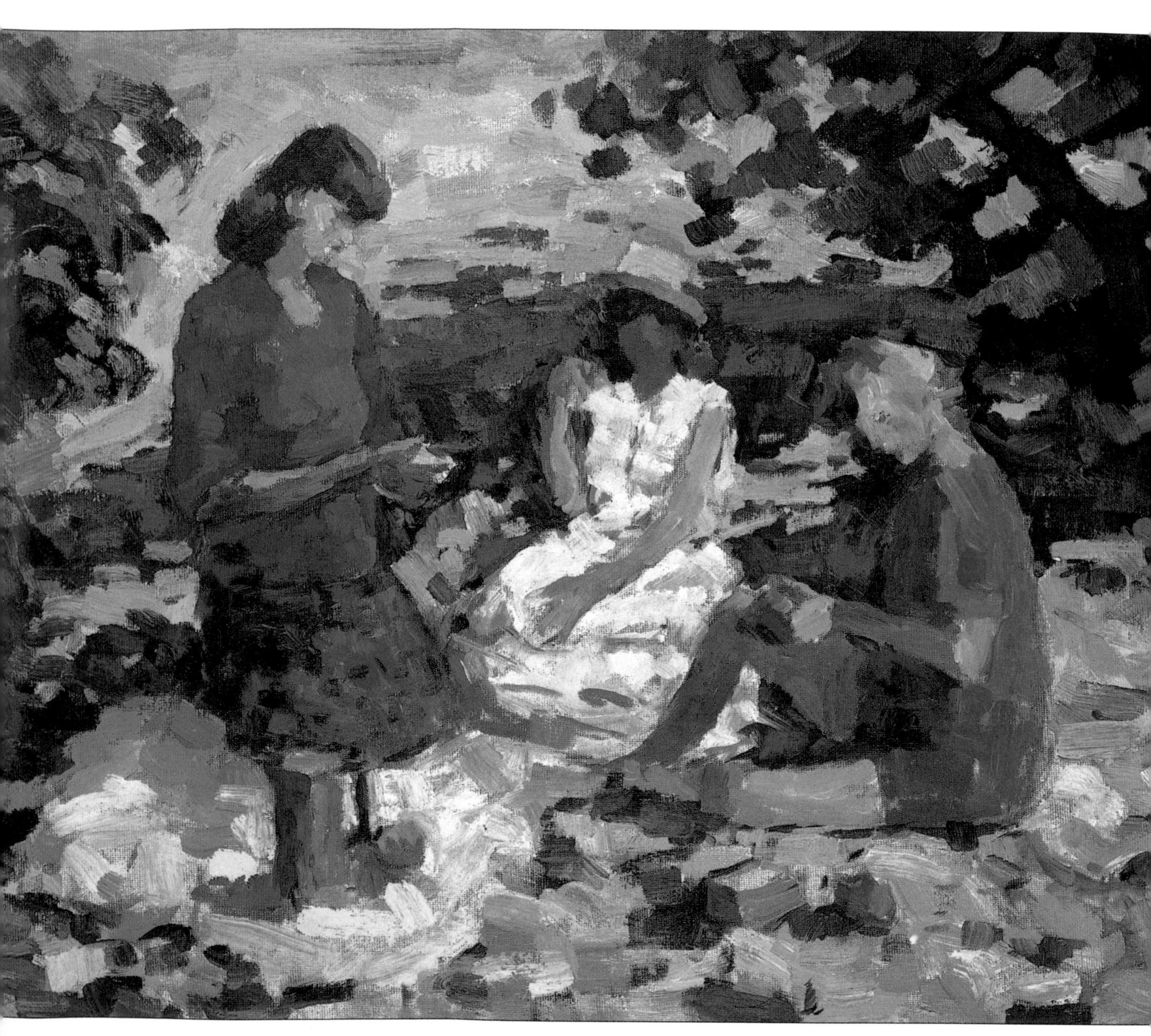

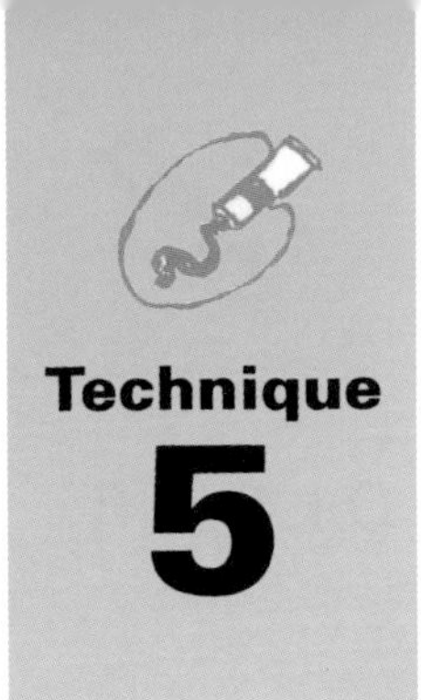

Technique

5

Using Broken Colour

In this painting the artist has adopted the Impressionist technique, using broken brush strokes of thickly applied paint in vibrant hues to create a shimmering web of colour. The paint, which is rich and buttery in consistency, has been applied in separate touches or strokes of a well-loaded bristle brush, building up wet layers over dry with some mixing of colour wet-into-wet on the surface of the painting. The lively dragged, broken and slurred brushwork gives a vital sense of light flickering off and blurring forms, evoking the atmosphere and light of summer.

Ted Gould
The Picnic
41 x 51 cm (16 x 20in)

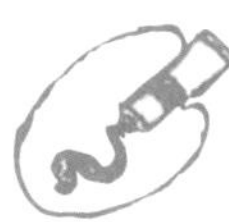

Broken Colour Technique

The term "broken colour" refers to a method of applying small strokes and dabs of different colours next to and over each other, so breaking up the paint surface into hundreds of tiny patches of colour, rather like a mosaic. When seen from the normal viewing distance these strokes appear to merge into one mass of colour, but the effect is different from that created by a solid area of smoothly blended colour. What happens is that the incomplete fusion of the strokes produces a flickering optical effect on the eye and the colours appear more luminous than a flat area of colour.

This technique is usually associated with the French Impressionist painters, who were the first to exploit its full potential. The Impressionists were fascinated by the fleeting, evanescent effects of outdoor light and found that using small, separate strokes of colour was an ideal way to capture the shimmering quality of the bright sunlight of southern France.

Acrylic paints are well suited to the broken colour technique because they dry rapidly, allowing you to superimpose layers of paint without muddying those beneath. Used straight from the tube, acrylics have a stiff, buttery consistency which is ideal for building up thick layers of impasto in which the mark of the bristle brush remains apparent in the raised paint. In general, short-haired flat bristle brushes (known as "brights") give the best results, as they hold a lot of paint and also offer a degree of control over the marks made.

When applying thick strokes of colour in this way, beware of overworking the texture, which would make the painting become clogged and heavy-looking. Apply each stroke decisively to the canvas and leave it alone. It is also a good idea to follow the Impressionists' example and allow the colour of the tinted canvas to show through in places. In the demonstration painting, for example, the artist began by tinting the canvas with a warm, golden colour; unpainted patches of this ground colour were left visible among the thick patches of paint, which not only add warmth but also breathe air into the painting.

Drybrush is another method of creating broken colour effects. A just-damp brush is lightly charged with colour, then skimmed across the dry canvas or paper. The brush leaves a small deposit of colour on the raised grain of the support, letting tiny specks of white sparkle through. The broken, ragged quality of drybrush strokes is very expressive.

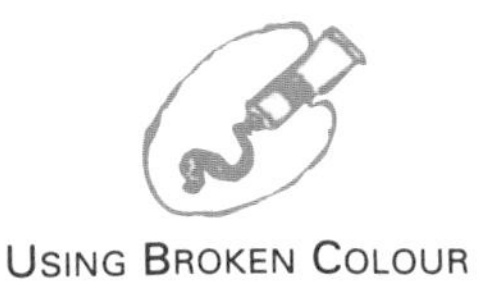

THE PICNIC

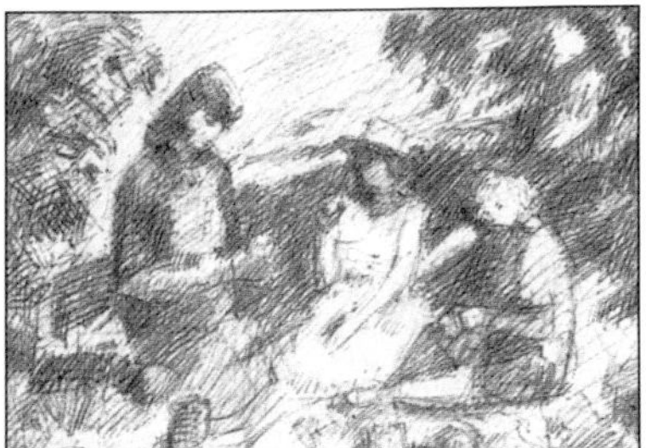

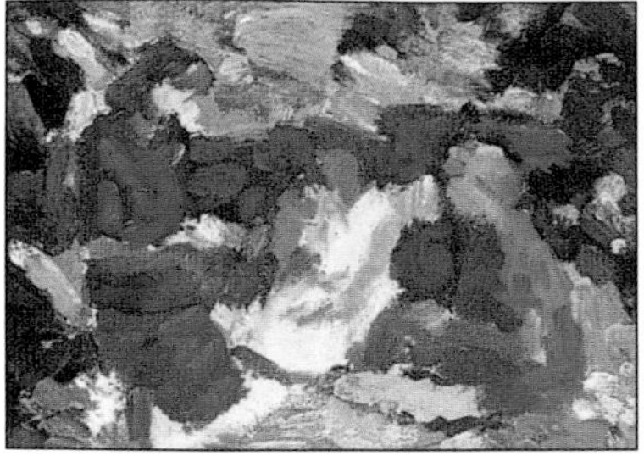

Above: This project painting was based on direct observation of the scene. The artist first made a tonal sketch in ballpoint pen to map out the major lights and darks, then a quick oil sketch to work out the main colour areas before embarking on the painting itself.

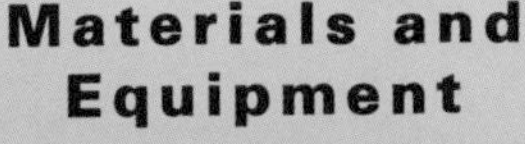

Materials and Equipment

• SHEET OF CANVAS OR CANVAS BOARD • ACRYLIC COLOURS: CADMIUM YELLOW MEDIUM, SAP GREEN, ULTRAMARINE BLUE, PRISM VIOLET, TITANIUM WHITE AND CADMIUM RED MEDIUM • TUBE OF RETARDING MEDIUM • HOG'S HAIR BRUSHES: LARGE AND MEDIUM-SIZED FLATS, SMALL AND MEDIUM-SIZED FILBERTS • COTTON RAG

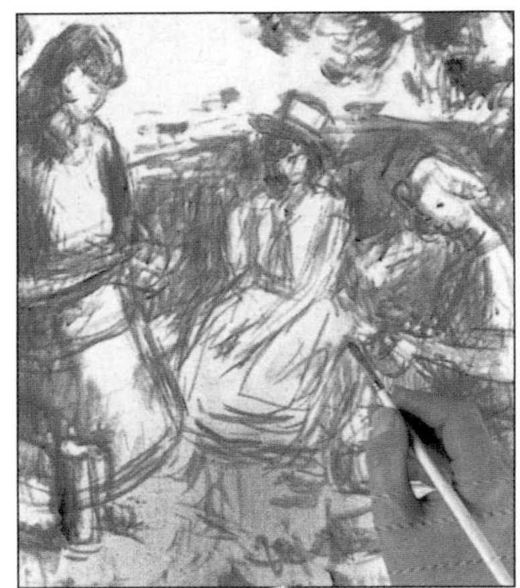

1

Start by staining the canvas with a warm tint mixed from cadmium yellow medium, sap green and a touch of ultramarine blue, diluted with water to a wash-like consistency. Apply the colour with a large flat brush, then rub it into the weave of the canvas with a cotton rag. Leave to dry. With a small filbert brush, broadly block in the main tones and outlines of the scene with a thin mixture of cadmium yellow medium, prism violet and ultramarine. Leave to dry.

2

Block in the lightest tones around the figures with thicker paint. (From this point on, add some retarding medium to your colour mixes to prolong the drying time of the paint and keep it workable.) Mix sap green, cadmium yellow medium and ultramarine blue in various proportions to create a range of warm, yellowish greens and cooler, bluish greens. With a medium-sized flat brush, apply short blocks of colour, varying the direction of the strokes to enliven the surface.

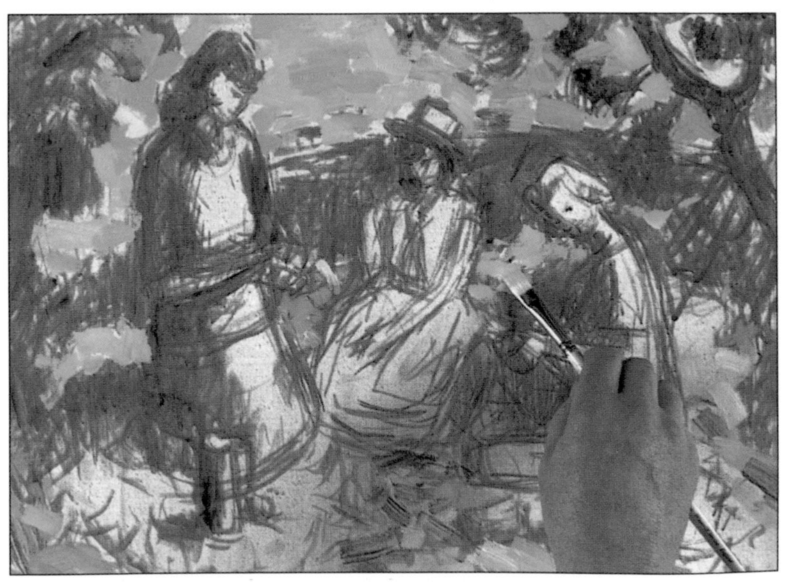

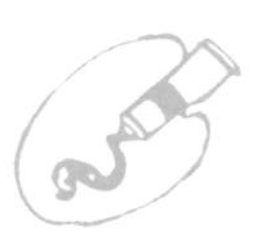

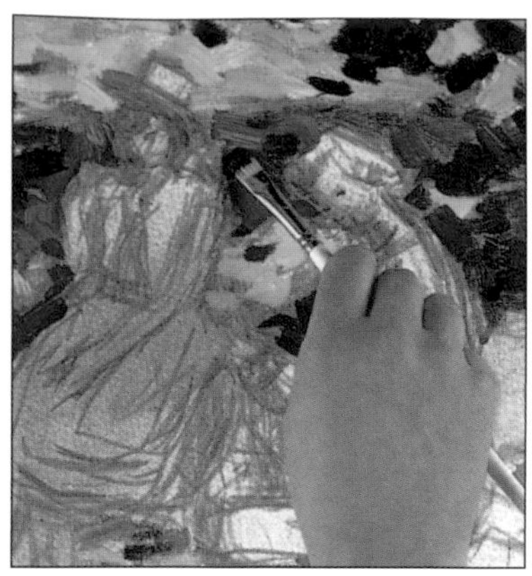

3

Block in the shadows in the grass and foliage using a medium-sized filbert brush and the same mixture, darkened with more ultramarine blue. Apply the paint thickly, using the body of the brush, and allow the brush marks to remain.

4

Rinse the brush and paint the whites of the picnic cloth and the central figure's dress. Use titanium white, modified with cool blues and violets in the shadows and spots of pink and yellow in the highlights. Again apply the colour using the flat of the brush, varying the direction of the strokes to follow the forms. Allow the colour of the stained canvas to break through the strokes and contribute to the feeling of sunlight.

Start blocking in the red areas with cadmium red medium, modified with hints of cadmium yellow medium and titanium white.

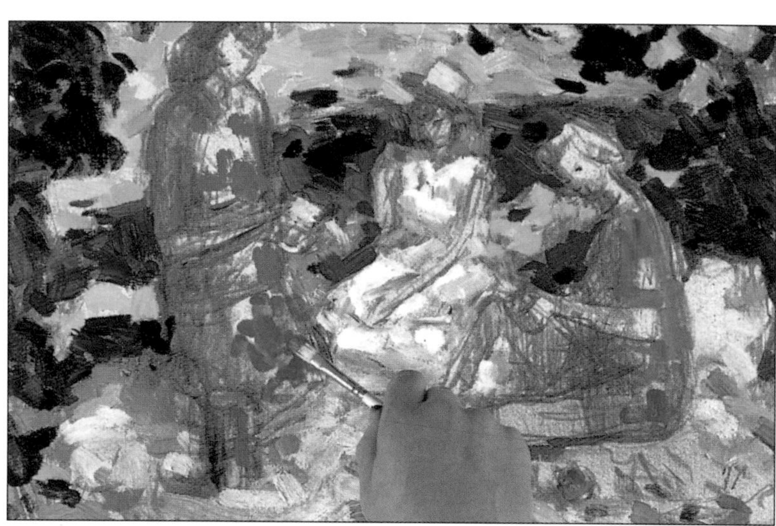

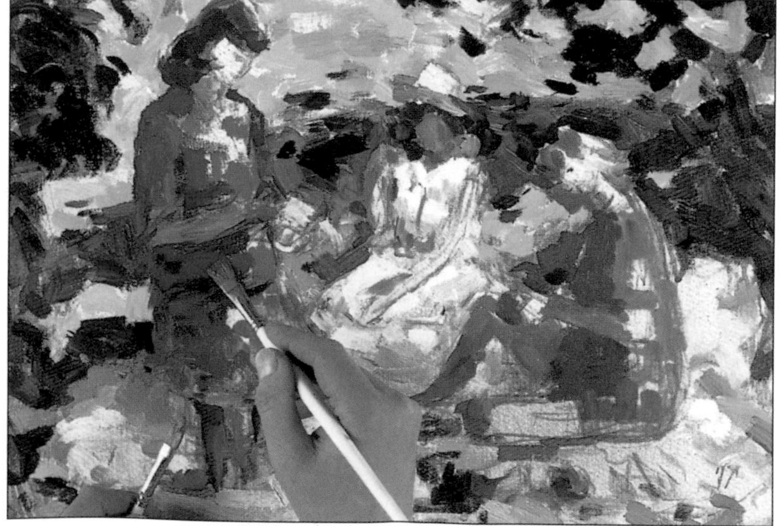

5

Continue working around the figure group, gradually building up a mosaic of thick, luscious colour. It is a good idea to work with two brushes, one carrying warm colours and one carrying cool colours, to avoid having to rinse out your brush too frequently. Paint the blue top of the left-hand figure and the blue vacuum flask with loose mixtures of ultramarine blue and titanium white, darkened with violet in the shadows.

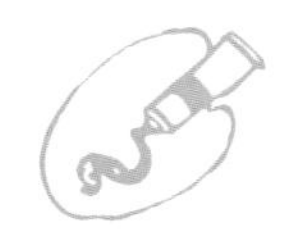

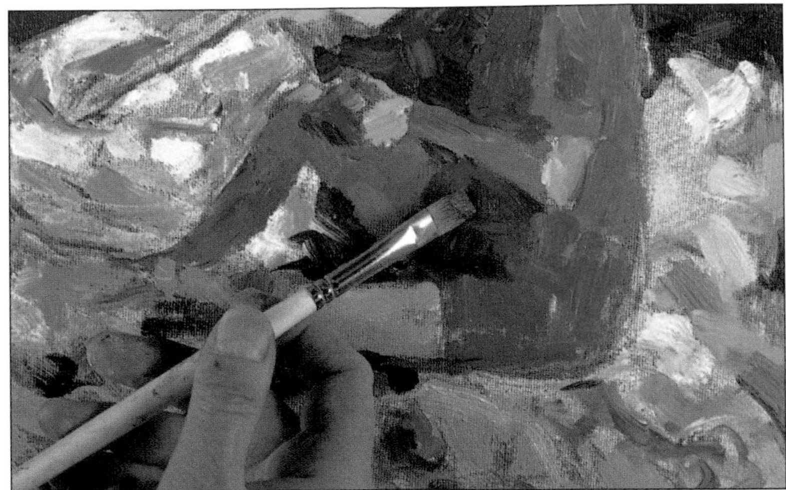

6

Paint the flesh tones of the figures with a small filbert brush and varying proportions of cadmium yellow medium, cadmium red medium and titanium white, adding hints of prism violet and sap green in the cool shadowy tones, such as the right-hand figure's face and her raised leg. Enrich the shadows on the red dress with hints of violet.

7

Use the medium-sized filbert brush and the same flesh tone mixture, lightened with more titanium white, to suggest patches of bare earth in the grass and break up the greens. Paint the hair of the right-hand figure with the same colour. For the dark hair of the remaining figures use rich browns mixed from cadmium red medium, cadmium yellow medium, prism violet and ultramarine blue. Suggest the pattern on the left-hand figure's skirt with strokes of violet and sap green.

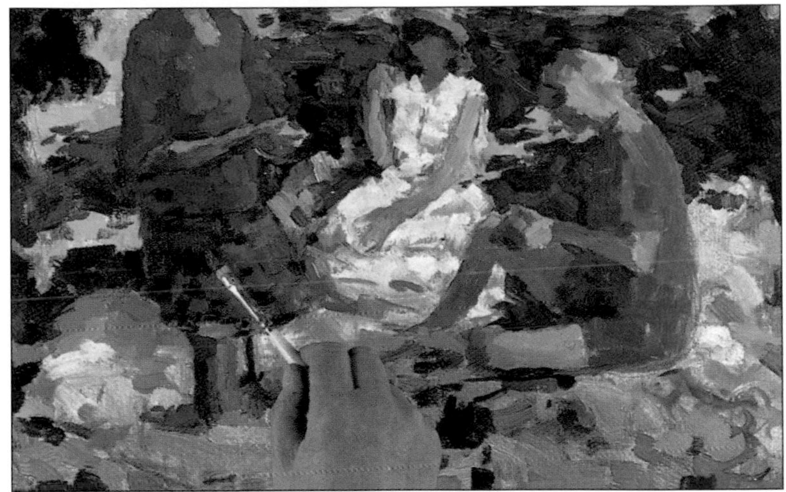

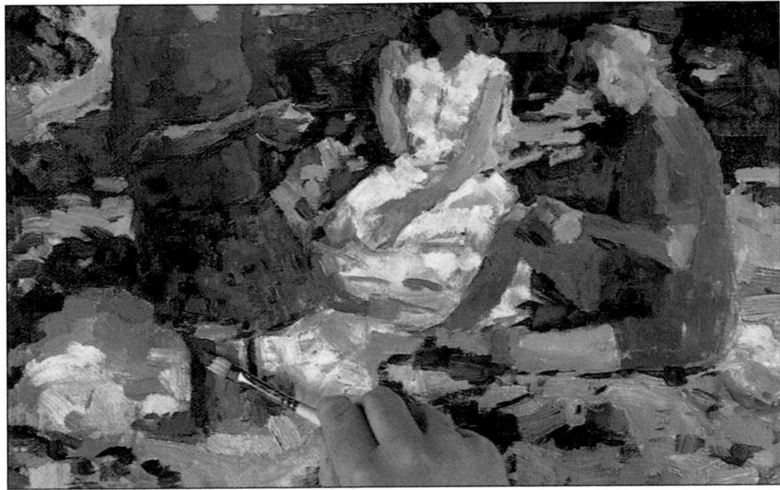

8

Continue working all over the canvas, modifying colours and tones as necessary and adding small touches of pure colour here and there to add luminosity to the picture. Suggest the features very sketchily – otherwise they will look too dominant.

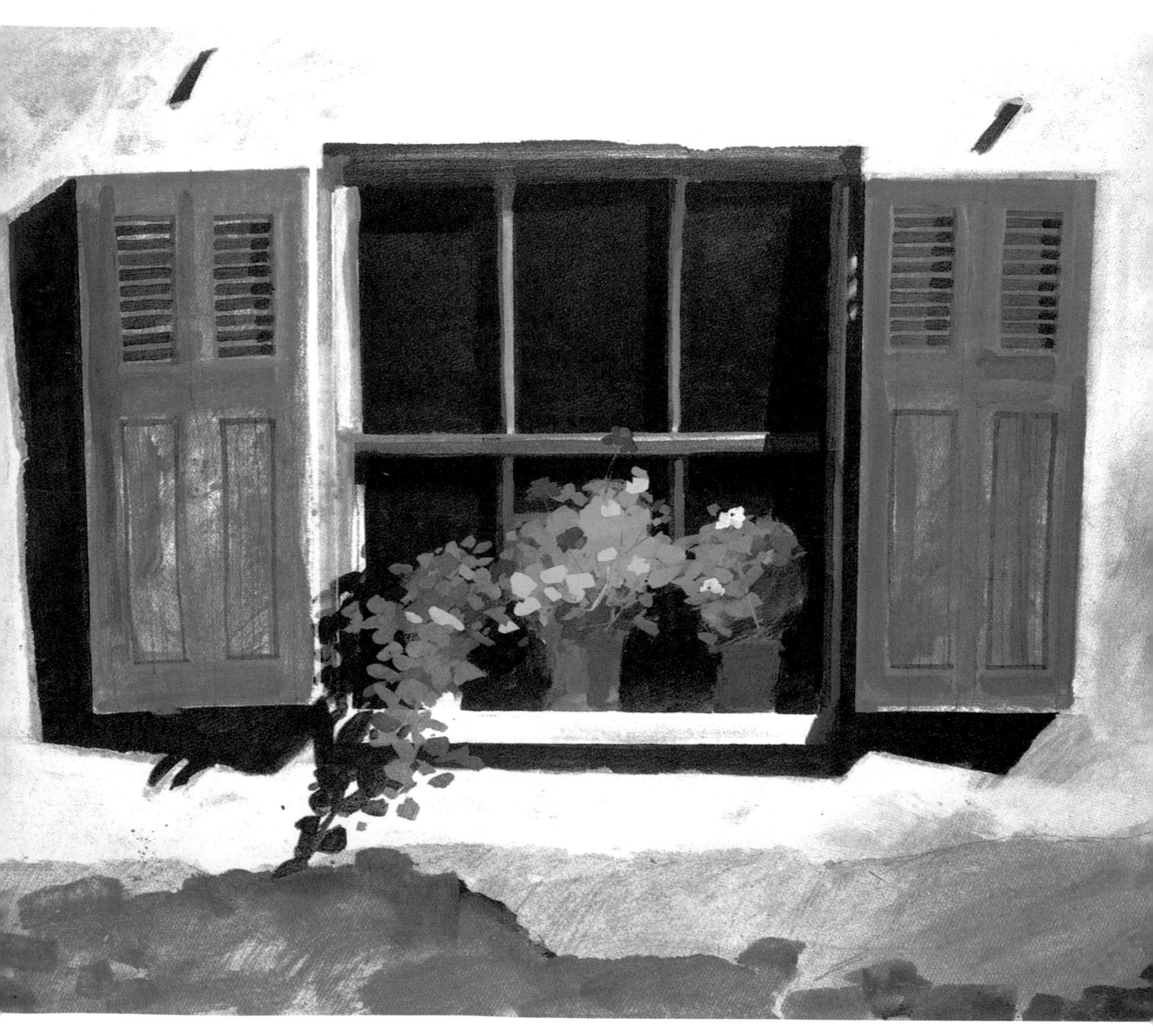

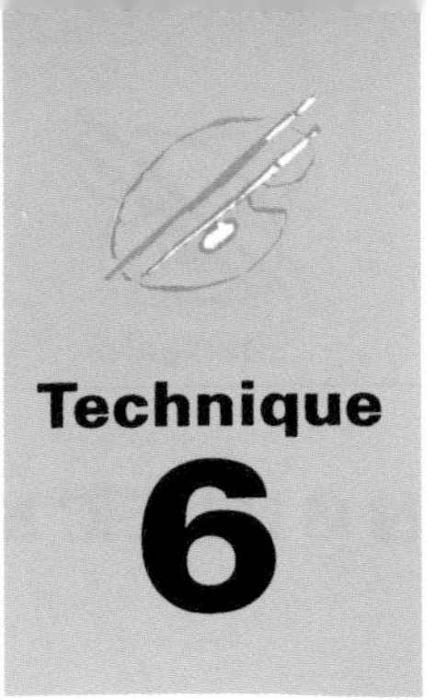

Technique

6

Masking

Old buildings manage to retain their charm, even when in a slightly dilapidated condition, and to an artist with a creative eye they certainly make excellent subjects. This painting was based on a photograph of an old house in a French village. The artist was attracted by the contrast between the organic shapes of the potted geraniums, framed by the stark outlines of the shuttered window.

In the strong afternoon light the lines of the window and shutters, and the areas of light and shadow, were sharp and clearly defined. For these areas the artist adopted a masking technique using strips of masking tape and torn paper. This provided exactly the right degree of crispness to the outlines, which contrast effectively with the freer shapes of the plants.

~

Ian Sidaway
Window, La Garde Freinet
66 x 81cm (26 x 32in)

~

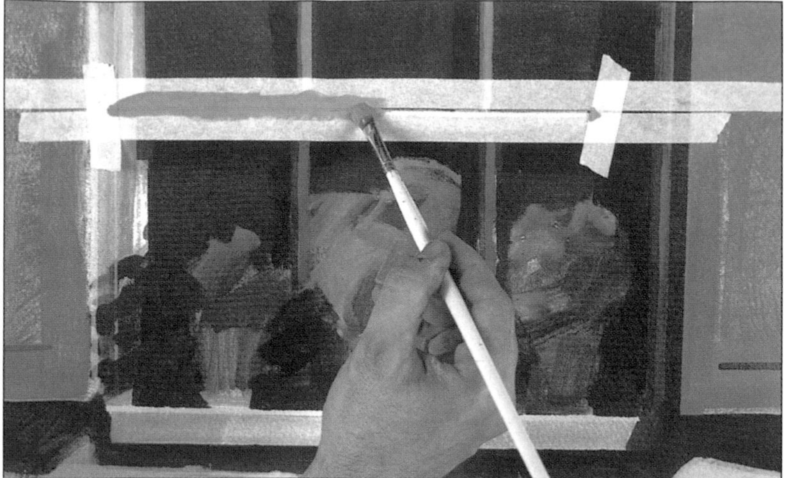

9

Paint the pale highlights on the upper window frames with the large flat hog's hair brush and a mixture of titanium white and a little cobalt blue. As in step 6, use strips of masking tape to achieve crisp, straight lines. When the paint is dry remove the strips of masking tape.

10

Using a medium-sized flat soft hair brush and a medium tone of Payne's grey, paint the linear details on the shutters. Masking tape isn't necessary here as the lines are not absolutely straight.

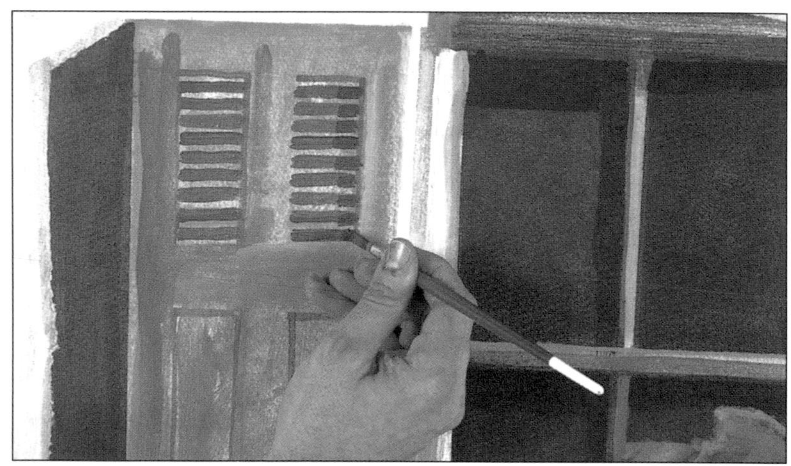

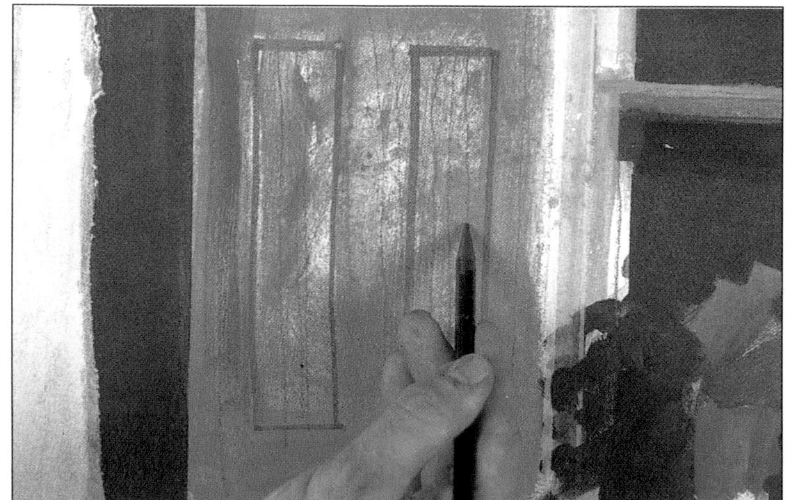

11

When the paint is dry, use a graphite pencil (or an ordinary pencil with a very soft lead) to draw a few lines on the shutters to suggest the texture of ageing wood.

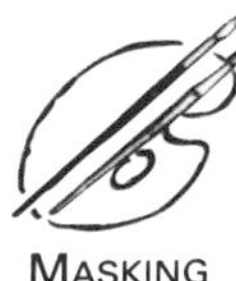

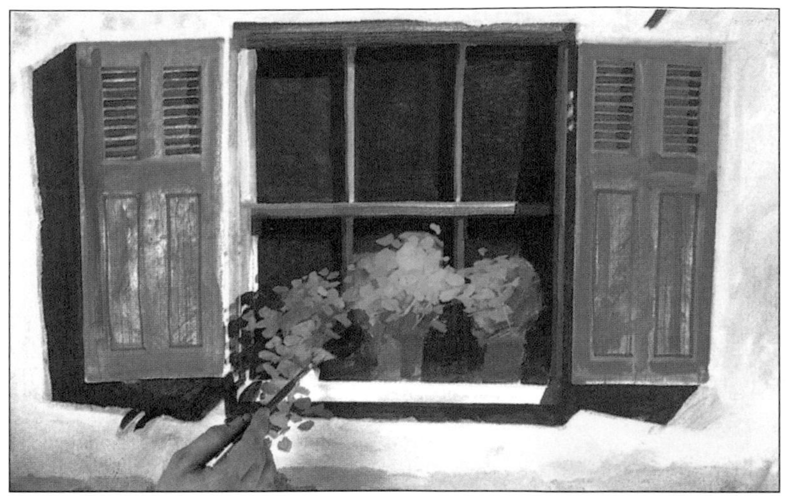

12

Paint the geranium leaves with the medium-sized flat soft hair brush and a basic mixture of phthalo green, yellow ochre and a little cadmium red. Vary the proportions of these colours to create a range of different greens, and add a little chrome yellow for the palest leaves. Leave to dry.

13

Darken the lower part of the wall with a watery wash of Payne's grey and yellow ochre, scrubbed on with loose strokes of the large flat hog's hair brush. Leave to dry, then go over the wall with a few loosely hatched pencil strokes to add textural interest.

Returning to the geraniums, paint the red flowers with neat cadmium red, adding a touch of cerulean blue for the salmon pink ones. For the pale pink flowers use white with a touch of cadmium red.

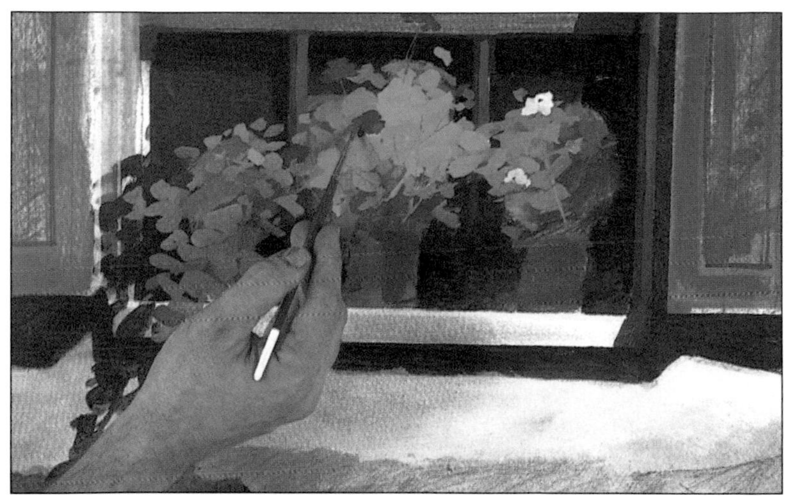

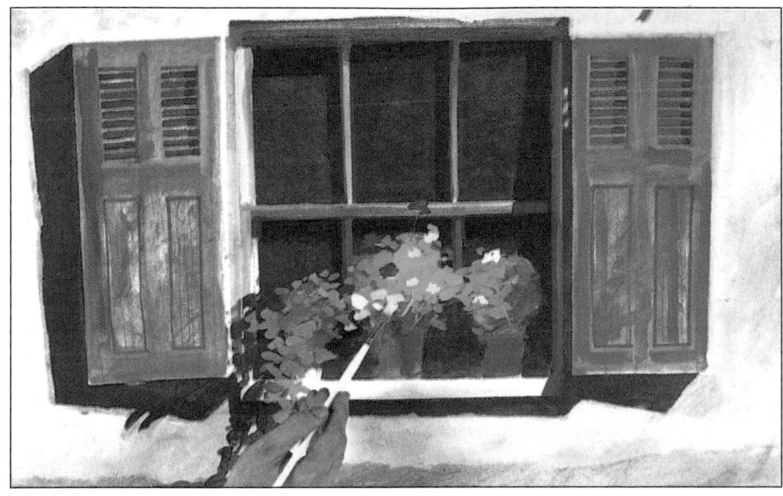

14

Finally, paint a few light-struck leaves with the medium-sized flat brush and a sharp green mixed from phthalo green, a little chrome yellow and white.

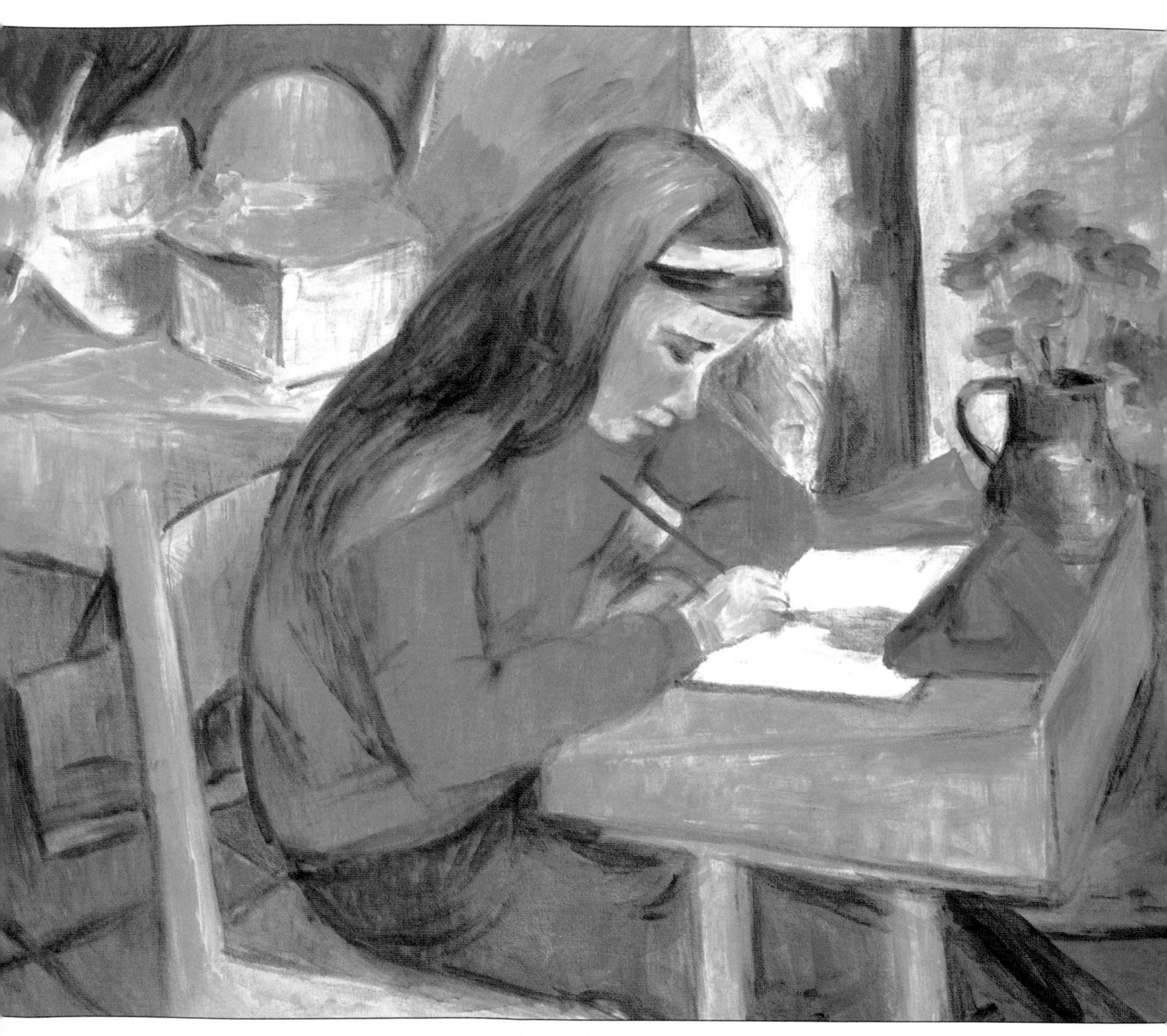

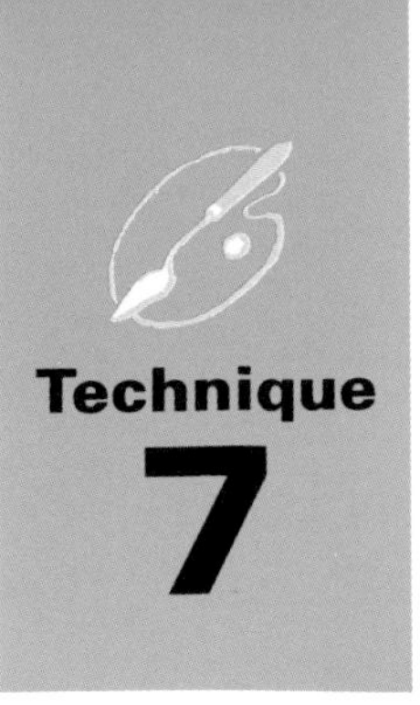

GLAZING

The Renaissance painters "mixed" their colours not by stirring them together on the palette, but by painting one transparent layer of colour over another, like sheets of coloured glass. Through using this method, know as glazing, they achieved the wonderful depth and luminosity of their colours. Glazing with oil paints, however, is a slow process; each layer must be thoroughly dry before the next one is applied – and oil paint takes a long time to dry. Acrylic paint, on the other hand, is perfectly suited to the glazing technique. Because it dries so quickly – and is waterproof when dry – you can paint one transparent layer over another in rapid succession.

This entire painting was built up with delicate glazes of colour applied over a thin underpainting. The artist diluted the paints with acrylic gloss medium. This increases the transparency of the paint while enriching the colour, and also makes the paint more "brushable". The brilliant white of the canvas further enhances the luminosity of the colours.

Ted Gould
Claire Studying
46 x 56cm (18 x 22in)

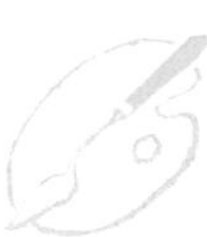

Glazing Technique

A glaze is a thin layer of transparent colour which is applied over another, dry, layer of paint. This produces two important effects. First, the transparency of the glaze allows light to pass through it and be reflected off the underlaying layer, which gives the paint a more luminous quality. Second, the glaze combines optically with the paint below to produce a new colour. For example, a transparent glaze of blue over yellow produces a green, while a glaze of red over yellow produces a warm orange. Colours mixed in this way are quite different in character from colours mixed together on the palette. Glazed colours seem to transmit light from within, whereas with opaque colour the light is on the surface only. In short, glazing modifies the underlying colour and makes it more luminous.

Paint for glazing can be diluted with water and/or acrylic medium. Some manufacturers make a special acrylic glaze medium, which will give a more transparent, even glaze than either of the other two. When diluted with water alone, the glaze dries to a dull, matt finish, which some artists prefer. However, the colours can be enlivened by applying a coat of acrylic varnish or medium to the finished painting.

To make a glaze, mix the paint with water or medium on the palette with a wet brush or palette knife. The paint should have a creamy, fluid consistency. Apply the glaze with either a bristle or soft hair brush and work it into the canvas to form a smooth, even layer. It is best to lay your canvas flat on a table or on the floor, as this prevents the paint from running.

Always begin with the lightest colours and work up to the darkest, so that light is able to reflect up through the colours from the white canvas or paper and makes them more luminous. Never add white to lighten the tone of a glaze; it will turn the colour milky and opaque. It is essential to allow one glaze to dry completely before applying the next, otherwise the clarity of the glaze is lost as the two colours partially mix and become muddy. With acrylics, of course, the colours are dry within minutes.

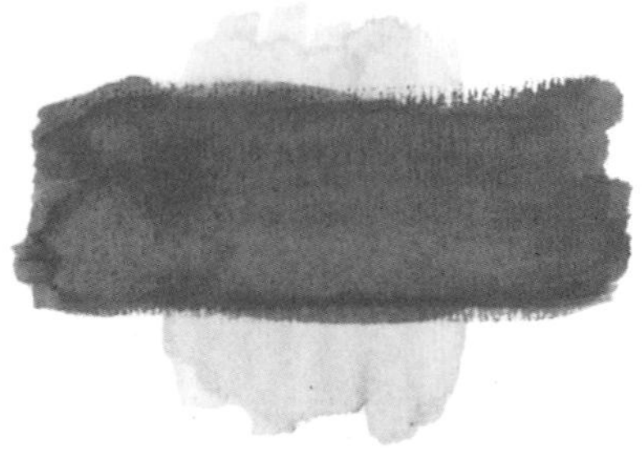

Here a thin wash of cadmium red is applied over a dry layer of cadmium yellow. The two colours blend in the viewer's eye to produce a subtle orange colour. Always apply the lightest colour first, so that light can reflect off the white canvas or paper and enhance the translucency of the colours.

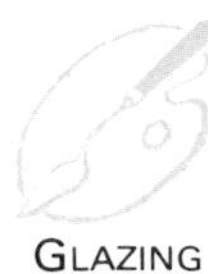

CLAIRE STUDYING

Materials and Equipment

• SHEET OF SMOOTH CANVAS, CANVAS BOARD OR PRIMED HARDBOARD (MASONITE) • ACRYLIC COLOURS: QUINACRIDONE VIOLET, BURNT SIENNA, COBALT BLUE, CADMIUM YELLOW, NAPHTHOL CRIMSON, YELLOW OCHRE, MARS BLACK AND TITANIUM WHITE • HOG'S HAIR BRUSHES: SMALL FILBERT; LARGE AND SMALL FLATS • TUBE OF ACRYLIC GLOSS MEDIUM

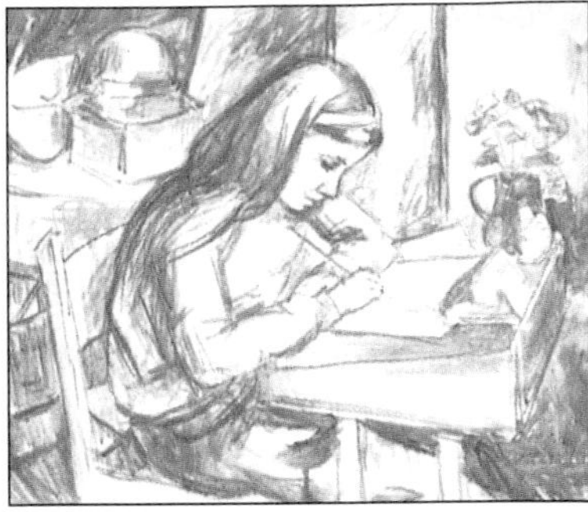

1

Mix quinacridone violet, burnt sienna and a little cobalt blue and dilute to a thin consistency with water. Using a small filbert brush make a loose underdrawing of the composition with this colour, roughly blocking in the dark tones. Allow to dry.

2

From this point onwards, mix acrylic gloss medium into your colours to increase the transparency of the paint. Dilute further with water if necessary. Mix a thin wash of cadmium yellow with a little burnt sienna added. Apply this over most of the canvas, as shown, with a large flat brush. This sets a warm colour key for the succeeding colours. Allow a few minutes for the paint to dry.

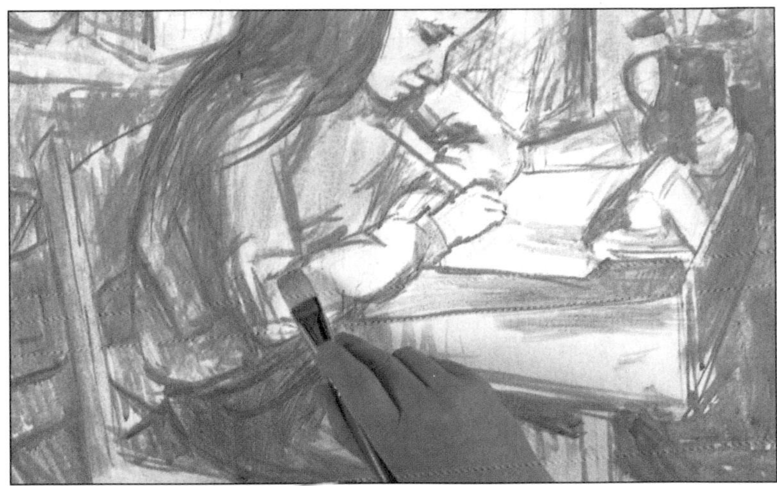

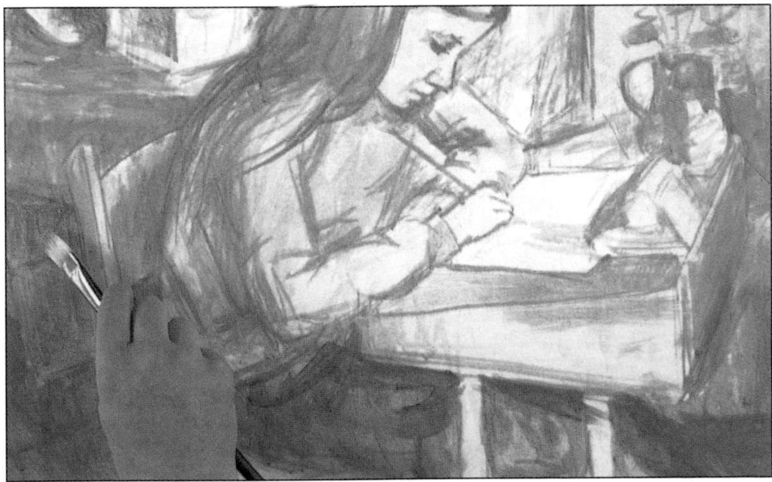

3

Mix quinacridone violet and cobalt blue in the same way and apply this as a base for those areas which are to be violet or blue in the finished painting, such as the girl's trousers, the floor and parts of the background.

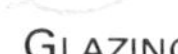

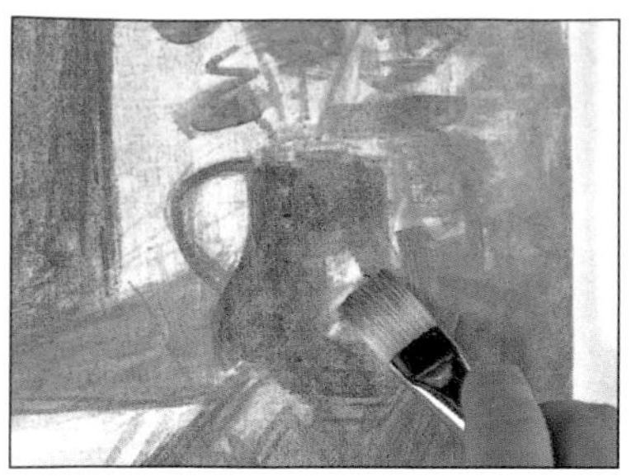

Left: This detail shows how the colours are kept very thin and transparent, allowing the white of the canvas to glow up through them. So that the forms do not dry with a hard edge, quickly blot the brush on a rag and feather over the edges lightly to soften them.

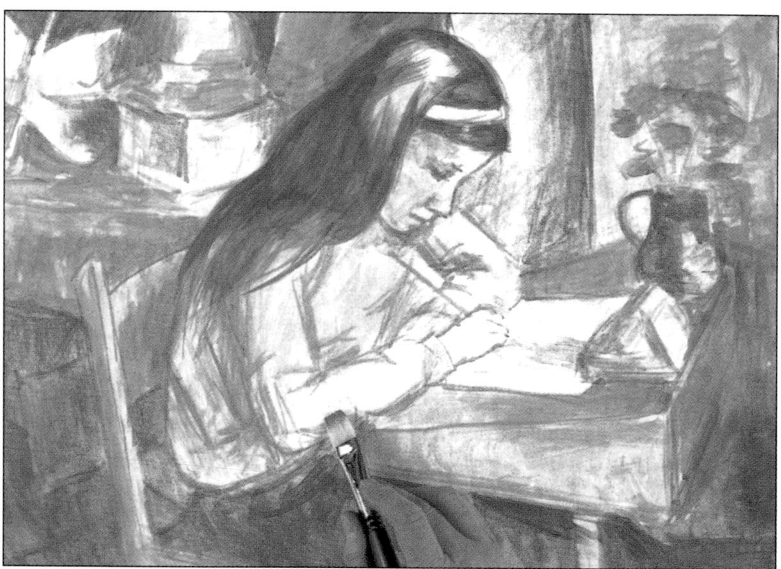

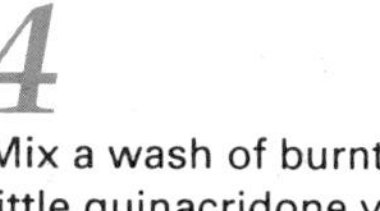

Mix a wash of burnt sienna with a little quinacridone violet and cobalt blue added. Apply this over the girl's hair, leaving the golden highlights and the hair band untouched. Strengthen the warm yellow tones with further glazes of cadmium yellow.

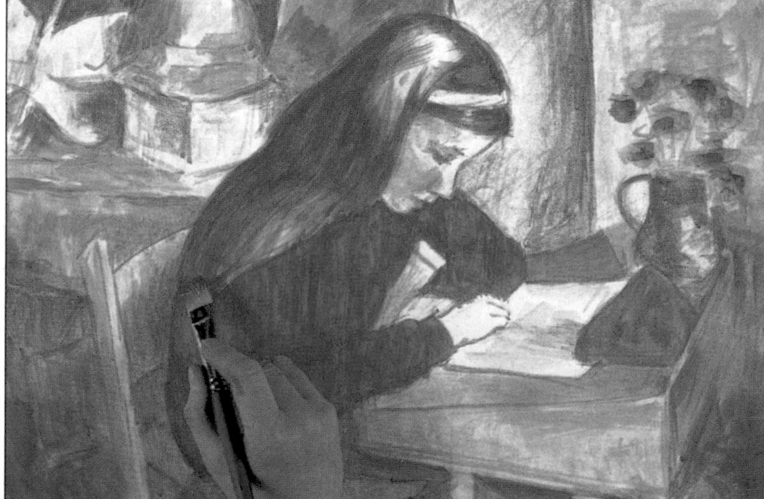

5

Paint the girl's sweater and the telephone with a thin glaze of naphthol crimson with a touch of yellow ochre added. Then work around the painting, adding touches of this warm colour to the background, the flowers in the vase and the girl's hair.

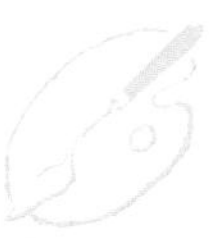

6

Using a small flat brush, define the sleeves and the creases in the sweater with loose drybrushed strokes of very weak mars black. Work up the shadows on the sweater using a large flat brush and thin glazes of violet.

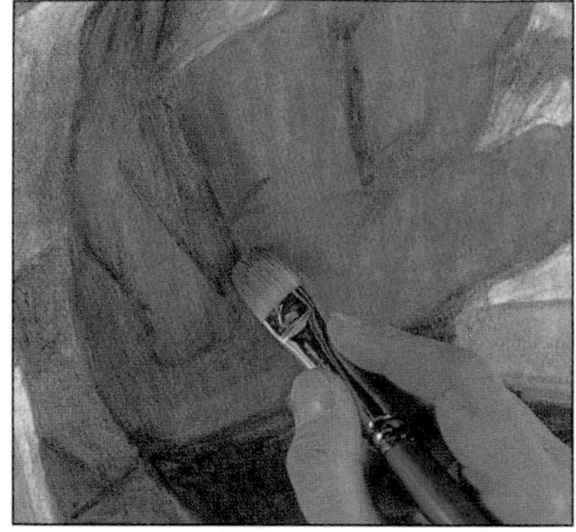

7

Use a small filbert brush to suggest the texture of the girl's hair with light strokes of thin, dry mars black paint, except in the highlights. Use the same colour for the pencil in her hand and to emphasize some of the outlines.

Continue to work all over the canvas adding further glazes of colour to strengthen the image. Add touches of thin titanium white paint in the background and paint the open book with white, adding violet for the cast shadows. Keep the paint wet and thin.

8

Darken the hair with a final glaze of naphthol crimson. Paint the face and hands using a small flat brush and a base mixture of titanium white and naphthol crimson for the light areas. Add more naphthol crimson and some yellow ochre in the cheek and blend the colours together lightly to emphasize the softness of the features. Paint the lips with some of the cheek colour and the eye with mars black and burnt sienna, keeping the colours soft and light. Paint the hair band yellow.

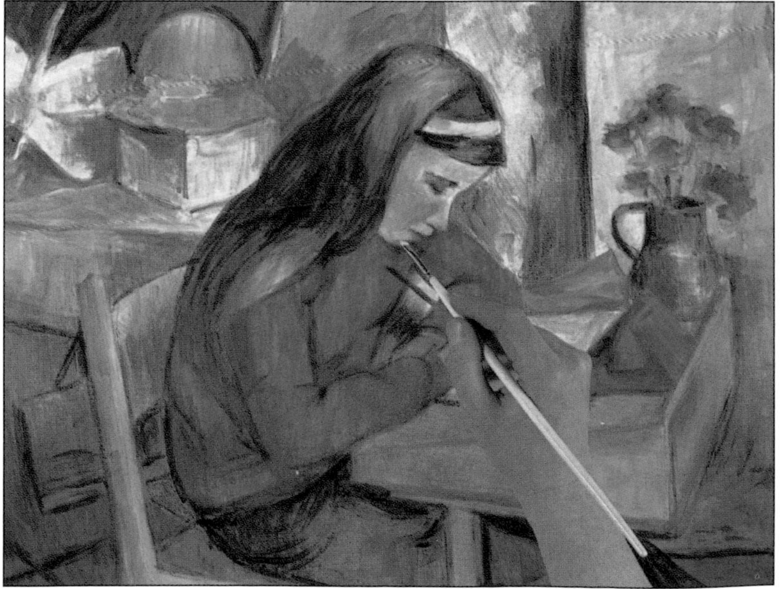

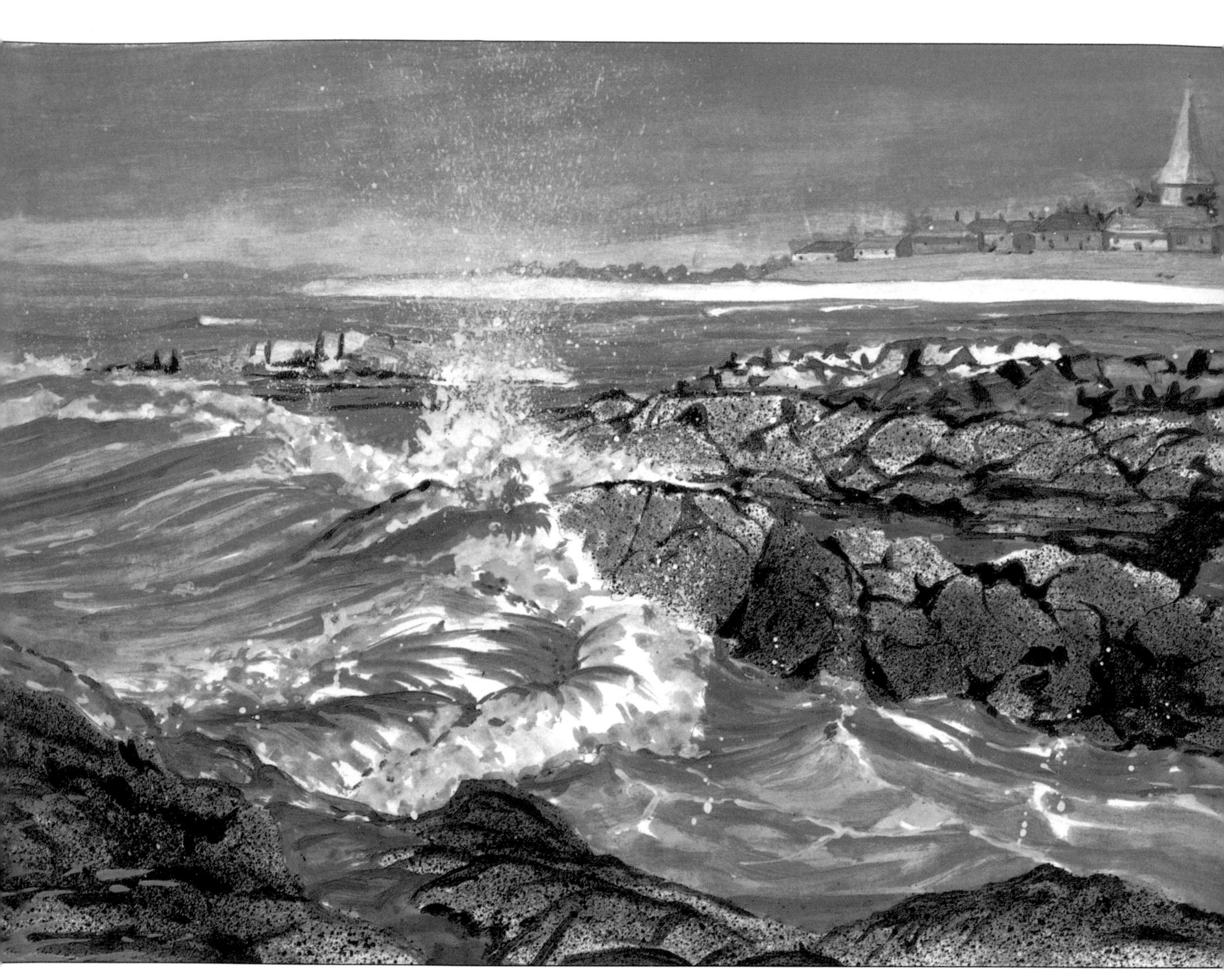

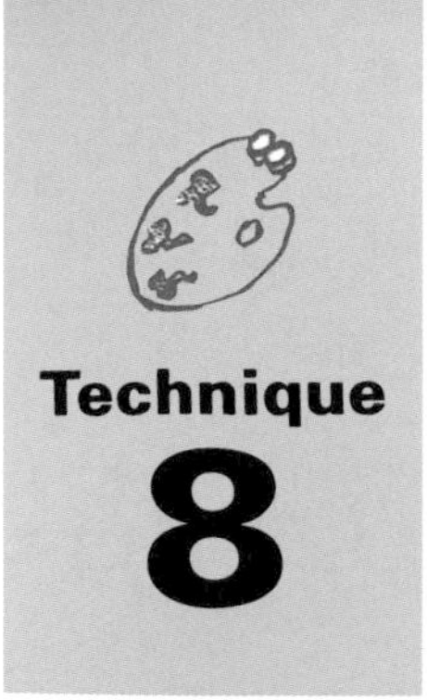

Technique

8

Spattering

This painting contains many interesting contrasts of form and texture. In the foreground the jagged rocks, swirling waves and crashing surf combine to create dramatic tension, while the distant coastline appears tranquil and serene.

To emphasize the rugged texture of the rocks, and to suggest the force of the breaking waves, the artist has used a technique called spattering. A paint-filled brush was held above the painting and tapped sharply, making the paint fall in a mass of tiny, irregular spots. Often used in watercolour painting, spattering is an excellent means of suggesting certain textures and effects without overstating them.

Mark Topham
Seascape
36 x 51cm (14 x 20in)

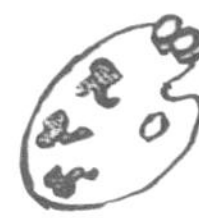

SPATTERING TECHNIQUES

Generally, spattering is used only on small areas of a painting because too much of it can appear mechanical and "tricksy". But when used with discretion it is an excellent technique for simulating rough, pitted textures such as sand, rocks and stones, or for capturing the movement of crashing surf.

When spattering, lay the painting flat on a table or on the floor, otherwise the spattered paint may run down the surface. Use tracing paper to mask off those parts of the painting that are not to be spattered. This allows you to work freely within a specific area. The paint should be wet, but not too runny – the consistency of medium-thick cream.

There are two different methods of spattering. One is to dip an old toothbrush into fairly thick paint and, holding it horizontally a few inches above the painting surface, quickly draw a thumbnail through the bristles. This action releases a shower of fine droplets onto the painting below.

The second method is to load either a stiff bristle brush or a watercolour brush with long bristles, then tap the brush sharply across a finger or across the handle of another brush. This produces a slightly denser spatter with larger droplets. For a slightly finer spatter, gently tap the brush with an extended forefinger.

Spattering is a random and fairly unpredictable technique and it is advisable to experiment on scrap paper to discover the effects it can create before trying it out on a painting. For example, vary the distance between the brush and the painting surface to increase or decrease the density of the dots. Or try spattering onto a damp surface so that the dots become softened and diffused. Finally, spatter with two or more tones or colours.

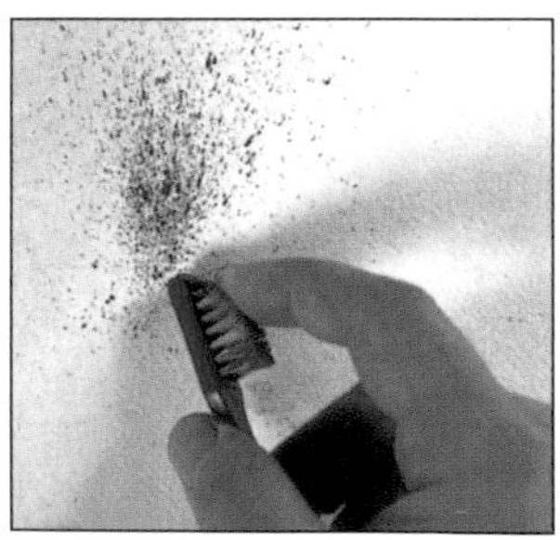

To produce a fine spatter, use a toothbrush and fairly thick paint. Dip the toothbrush into the paint, hold it at an angle to the paper, then draw your thumbnail through the bristles.

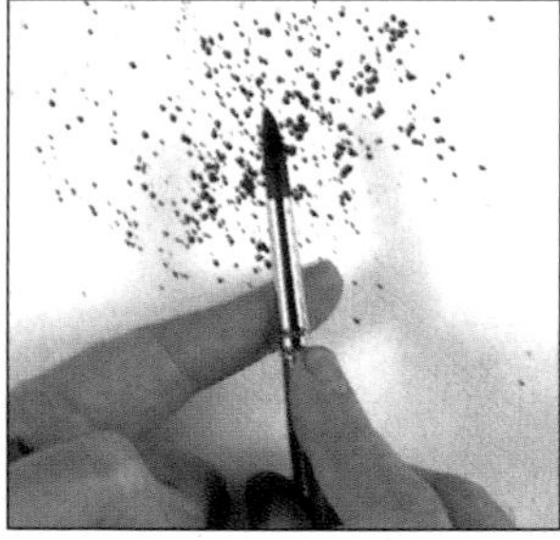

To produce a more random spatter, load a round brush with paint and tap it sharply with your outstretched forefinger.

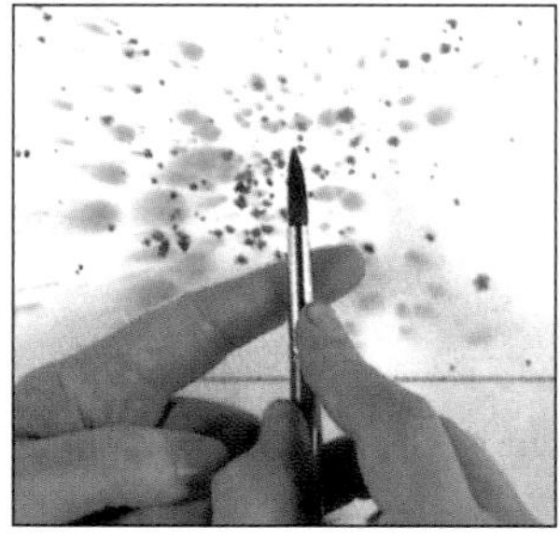

Spattering onto a damp surface produces a soft, blurred effect. Try spattering with two or more colours to create subtle tones and hues.

SEASCAPE

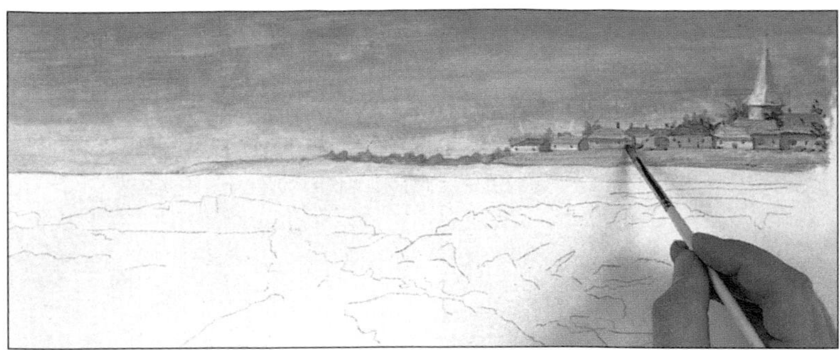

1

Sketch in the main outlines of the composition in pencil. Squeeze out some retarding medium along with your palette of colours; a little should be added to each of your colour mixtures to prolong the drying time of the paint and facilitate smooth brush strokes. With a medium-sized flat bristle brush, mix a pale blue from titanium white with a little cerulean blue and cobalt blue, and dilute quite thinly with a little water. Block in the sky, making it paler towards the horizon so as to give an impression of receding space.

Use a small flat bristle brush to paint the details on the far shore, keeping all the tones pale and hazy.

Materials and Equipment

• SHEET OF SMOOTH CANVAS, CANVAS BOARD OR PRIMED ILLUSTRATION BOARD • HB PENCIL • TUBE OF RETARDING MEDIUM • ACRYLIC COLOURS: TITANIUM WHITE, CERULEAN BLUE, COBALT BLUE, UNBLEACHED TITANIUM WHITE, ULTRAMARINE BLUE, PHTHALO GREEN, RED IRON OXIDE, YELLOW OCHRE, DIOXAZINE PURPLE, PAYNE'S GREY, BURNT UMBER, ALIZARIN CRIMSON, RAW SIENNA AND BURNT SIENNA • BRISTLE BRUSHES: SMALL AND MEDIUM-SIZED FLATS, SMALL ROUND • SOFT HAIR BRUSHES: SMALL AND MEDIUM-SIZED ROUNDS • SHEET OF TRACING PAPER SAME SIZE AS PAINTING • CRAFT KNIFE • OLD WATERCOLOUR BRUSH FOR APPLYING MASKING FLUID • MASKING FLUID (LIQUID FRISKET) • OLD TOOTHBRUSH • SHEET OF SCRAP PAPER OR NEWSPAPER

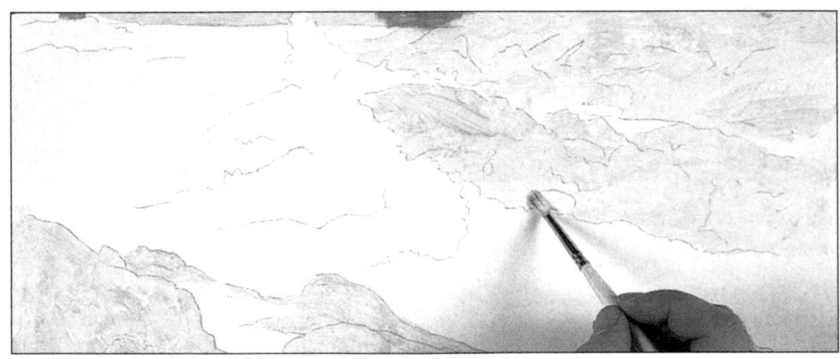

2

Still using thinly diluted colour, paint the narrow area of sea in the background with titanium white, ultramarine blue, dioxazine purple and Payne's grey, loosely mixed. Mix burnt umber and ultramarine blue for the dark rocks jutting into the sea. For the remaining rocks use unbleached titanium white with traces of red iron oxide and ultramarine blue, making the tones increasingly stronger as you work towards the foreground.

3

Paint the dark fissures in the rocks with a dark tone of ultramarine blue and alizarin crimson. Leave to dry, then mix thin glazes of raw sienna, burnt umber and ultramarine blue in varying combinations. Wash these over the rocks to build up their forms, using a medium-sized flat bristle brush. Paint the pools of water with various blues mixed from cobalt blue and raw sienna, and ultramarine blue and dioxazine purple.

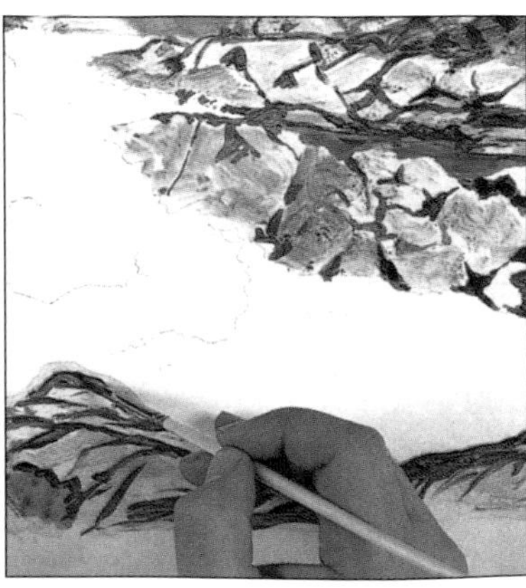

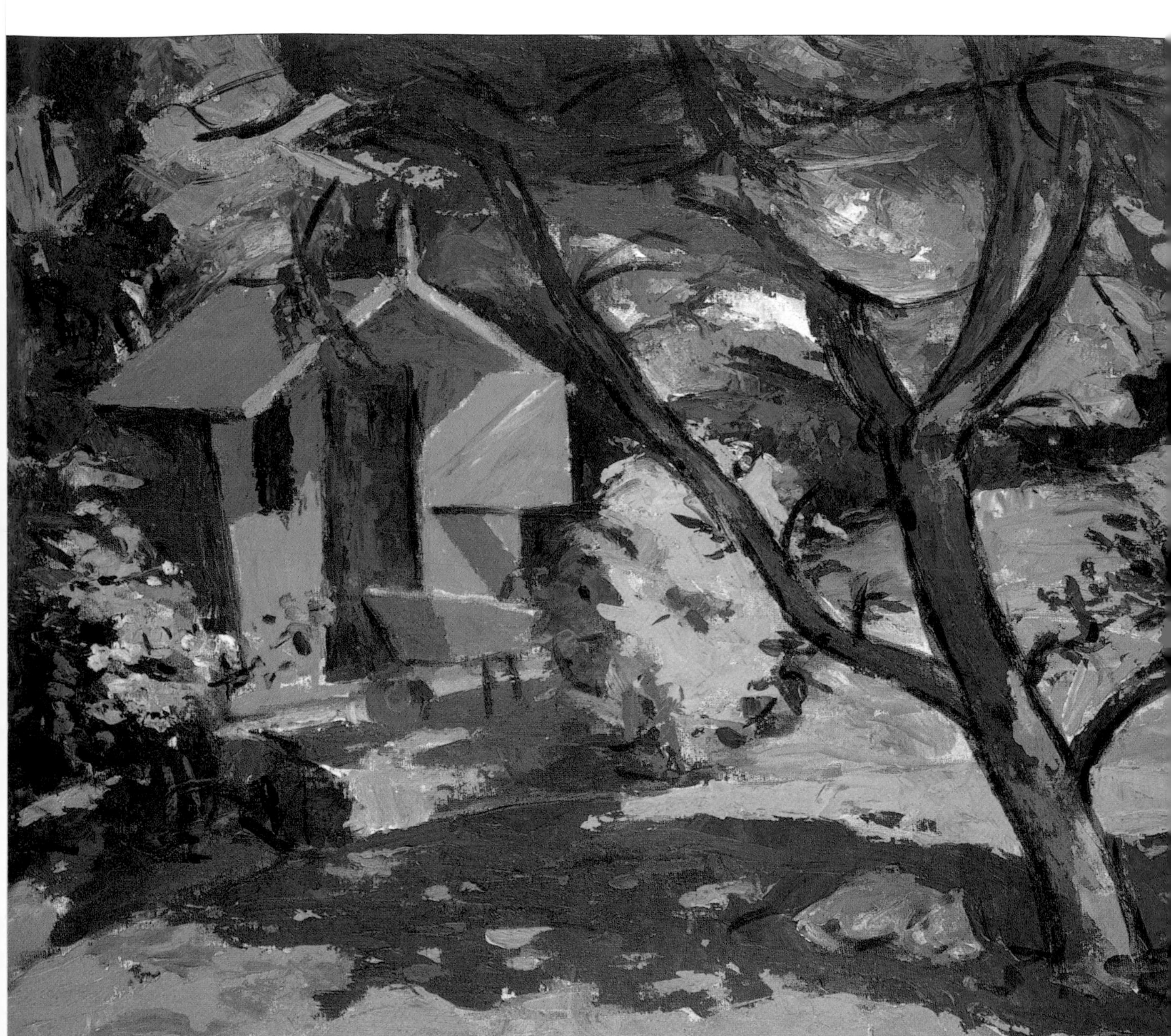

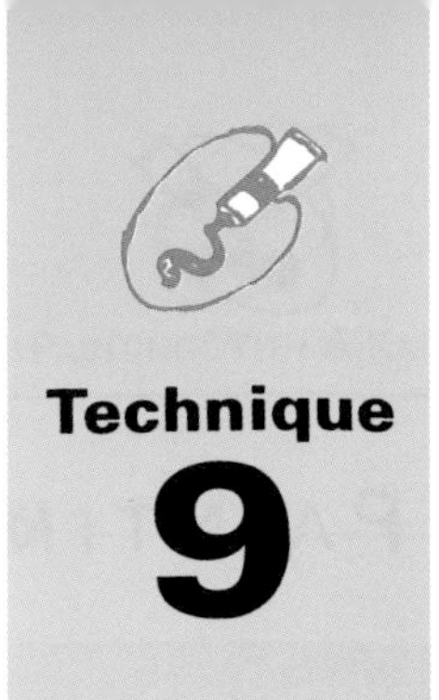

Technique

9

PAINTING WITH A KNIFE

The richly textured surface of this painting has been achieved by applying the paint with a knife. The artist began with an underpainting in thin colour to establish the major tones and colours. Then the image was developed with thick, juicy paint, "sculpting" the textures and forms with the flexible blade of the knife.

No sky is visible in the painting, but the viewer is in no doubt that it was painted on a sunny day. The cool blues and violets of the shadows contrast strikingly with the patches of warm, pinkish brown woven throughout the composition, creating an impression of strong sunlight.

Ted Gould
Summer Garden
46 x 56cm (18 x 22in)

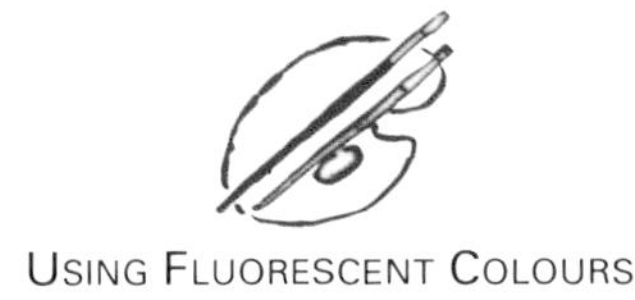

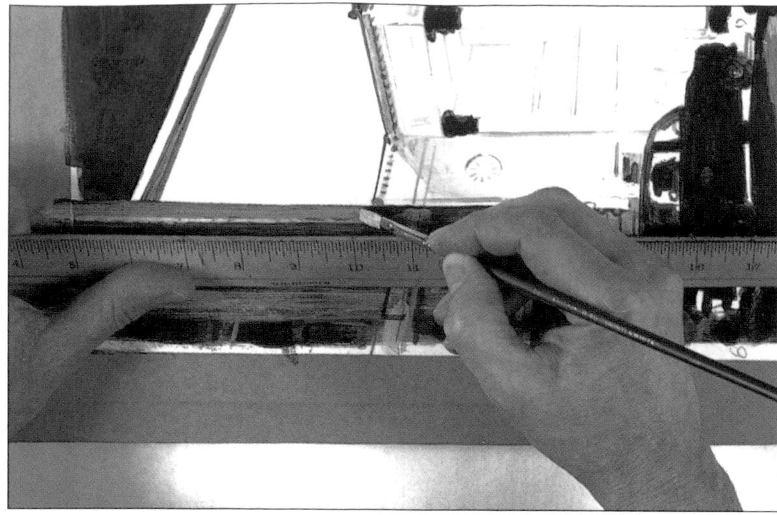

7

To suggest reflected light on the protruding walls of the left-hand building, apply a thin, dry layer of titanium white with a medium-sized flat hog's hair brush.

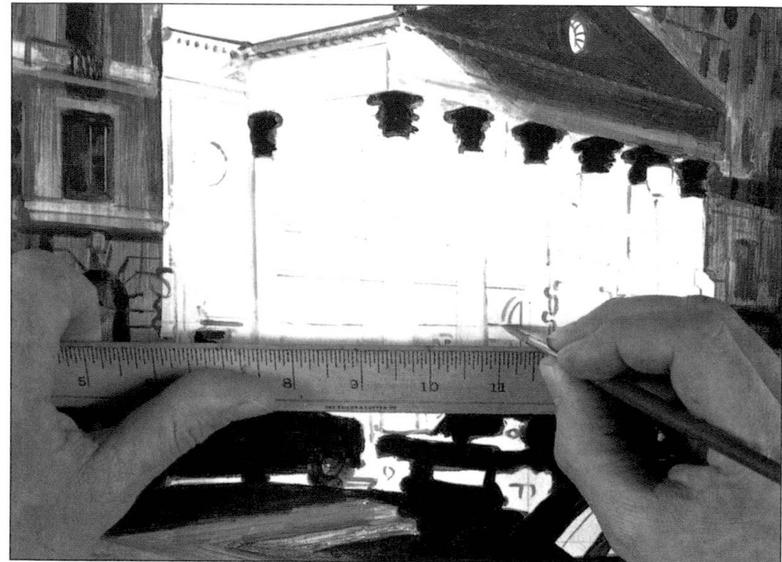

8

Paint the linear details on the theatre building with a small round soft hair brush and a mixture of titanium white and burnt sienna.

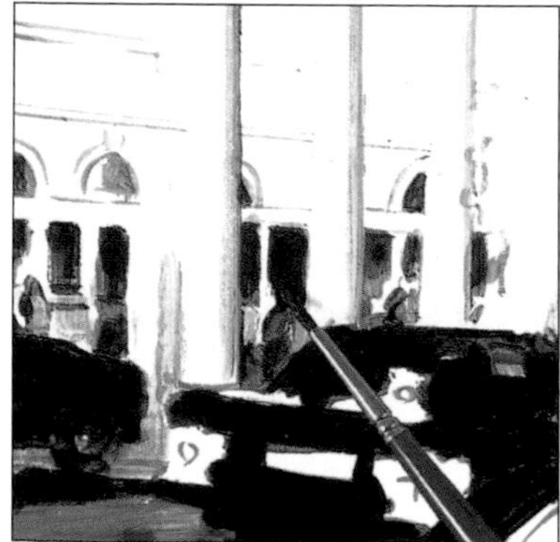

9

Using a small round soft hair brush, paint the doors and windows at the theatre entrance with burnt sienna overlaid with burnt umber and Payne's grey to vary the tones. Paint the shadows on the columns with a pale wash of Payne's grey and yellow ochre. Suggest the dark figures in the street with various tones of Payne's grey, burnt umber and titanium white applied with loose strokes.

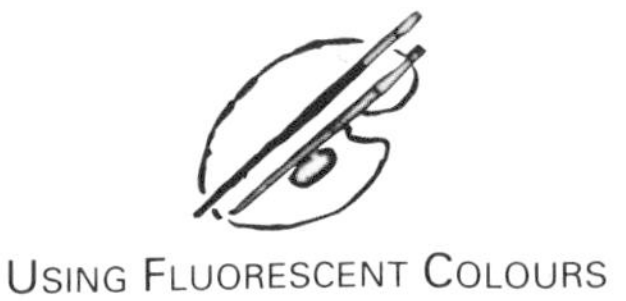

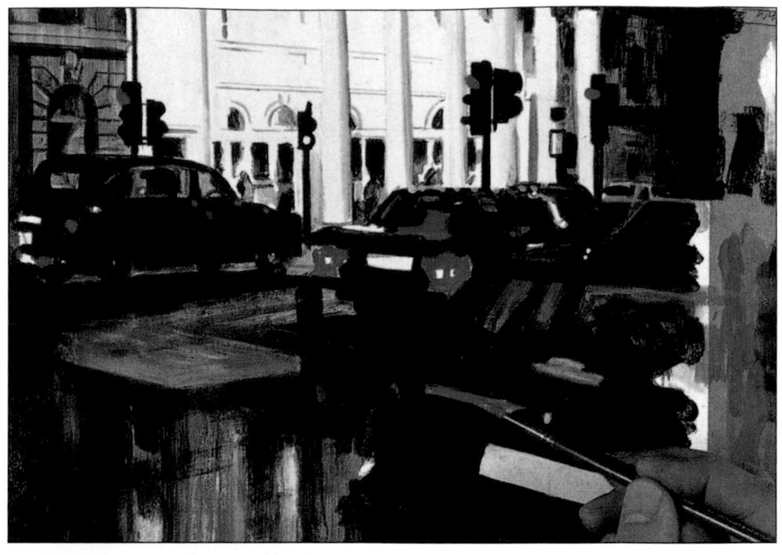

10

Paint the traffic signals with a medium flat hog's hair brush and a dark mix of Payne's grey and burnt umber. Leave to dry. Mix fluorescent red gouache paint with acrylic gloss medium, then deepen the colour with some cadmium red acrylic paint. Use a small round soft hair brush to paint the glowing red lights and their reflections. Dilute the colour to a pale tint and paint the red reflections in the road with vertical strokes of a medium flat hog's hair brush.

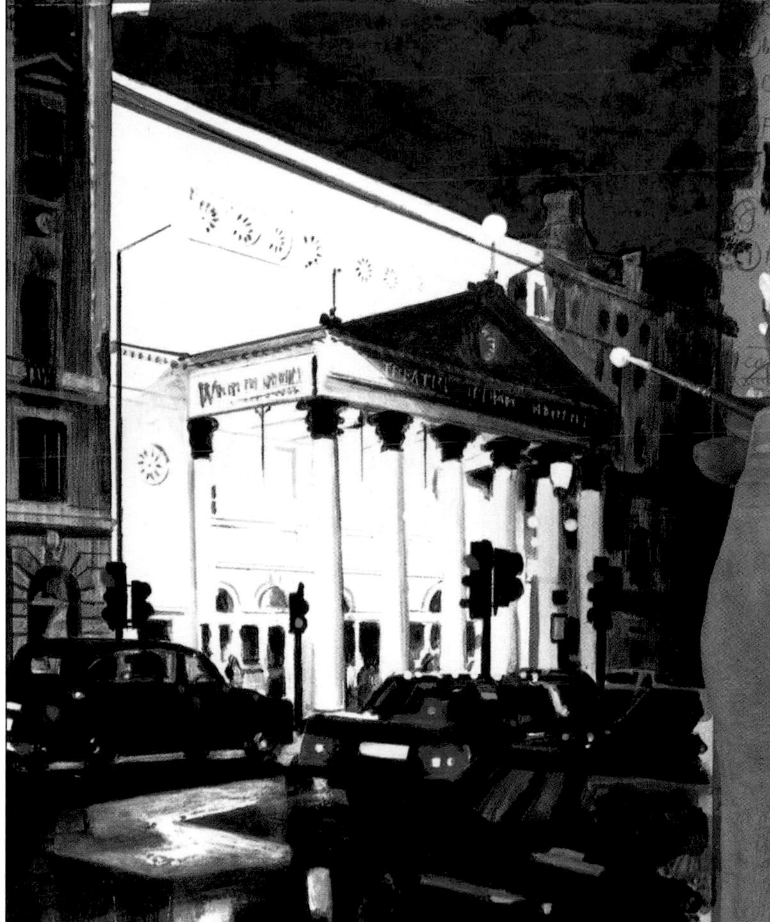

11

Mix fluorescent yellow gouache with gloss medium and add a little lemon yellow acrylic paint. Use this to paint the yellow lights and their reflections as in step 10. Paint the single green traffic signal with fluorescent green gouache mixed with gloss medium. Paint the white reflections in the road with thin, dry titanium white paint. Finally, paint the white lamps above the portico.

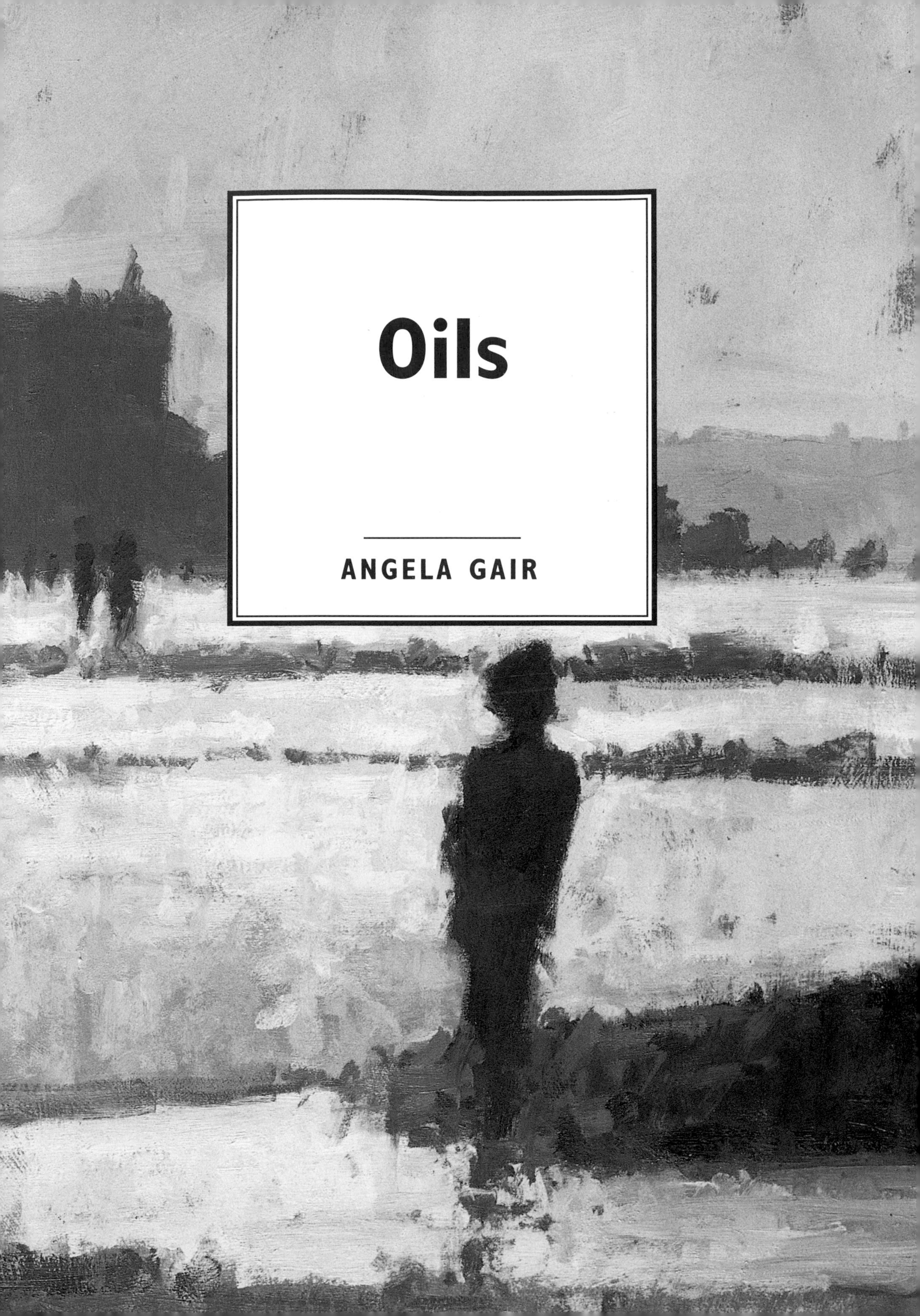
Oils
ANGELA GAIR

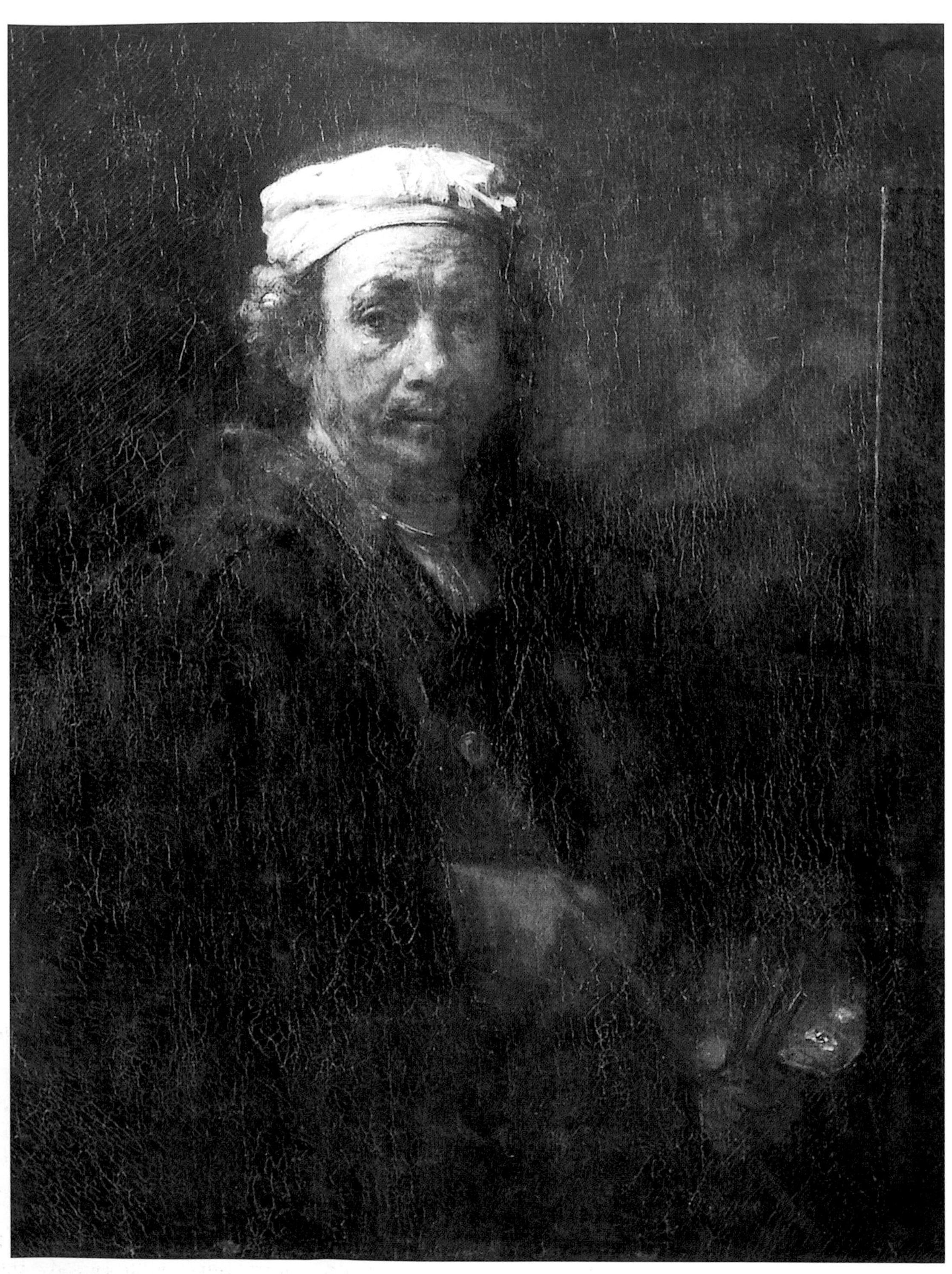

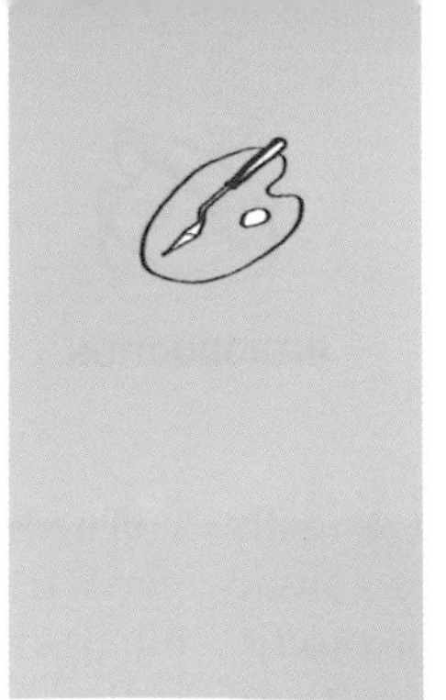

INTRODUCTION

The Flemish painter Jan van Eyck (*c*.1390–1441) has been called the inventor of oil painting. Although this is not strictly true – various oils had been used as paint mediums since the twelfth century – his discoveries and techniques certainly laid the foundations for the art.

Before Van Eyck's innovations, artists painted on wooden panels with egg tempera, which was a difficult medium to use as it dried very fast and thus called for a deliberate and meticulous approach. Around 1420, when van Eyck found that one of his tempera paintings had split while drying in the sun, he determined to "devise means for preparing a kind of varnish which should dry in the shade, so as to avoid having to place the pictures in the sun".

He experimented with raw pigments bound with linseed and nut oils, and found that they dried in the shade to form a hard film without cracking. He also discovered, to his delight, that the oil binder rendered the pigments translucent, at the same time giving them a richly saturated appearance. When applied in thin, transparent layers, the colours took on a depth and luminosity hitherto unknown. Furthermore, the glossy consistency and slow drying of oil paints meant that painters could work more freely than with tempera, applying colours in broad areas and blending tones on the support itself.

Self-portrait at the Easel *Rembrandt van Rijn*

Rembrandt's technical mastery of the oil medium and his profound insight into the human spirit are marvellously combined in this self-portrait. A suggestiveness of mood is created by his use of chiaroscuro *(strong contrasts of light and shadow).*

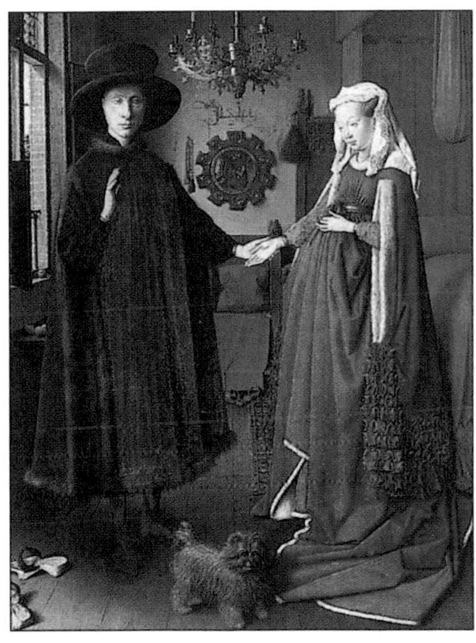

The Arnolfini Marriage *Jan van Eyck*

This tender portrait of a couple plighting their troth is rich in symbolism. The candle flames are emblematic of the ardour of newlyweds; the dog is a symbol of marital faith; and the figure carved on the back of the chair is St Margaret, patron saint of childbirth. Each object is lovingly described with a subtlety and refinement that the oil medium allowed for the first time.

Nevertheless, the early painters in oil, including van Eyck, painted in a style that looks carefully detailed when compared to the freedom of handling that modern painters enjoy. To produce highly polished and realistic paintings, the paint was laid on thinly in flat, separate areas and brushed to produce a smooth satin finish with delicate brushstrokes that are almost invisible to the eye.

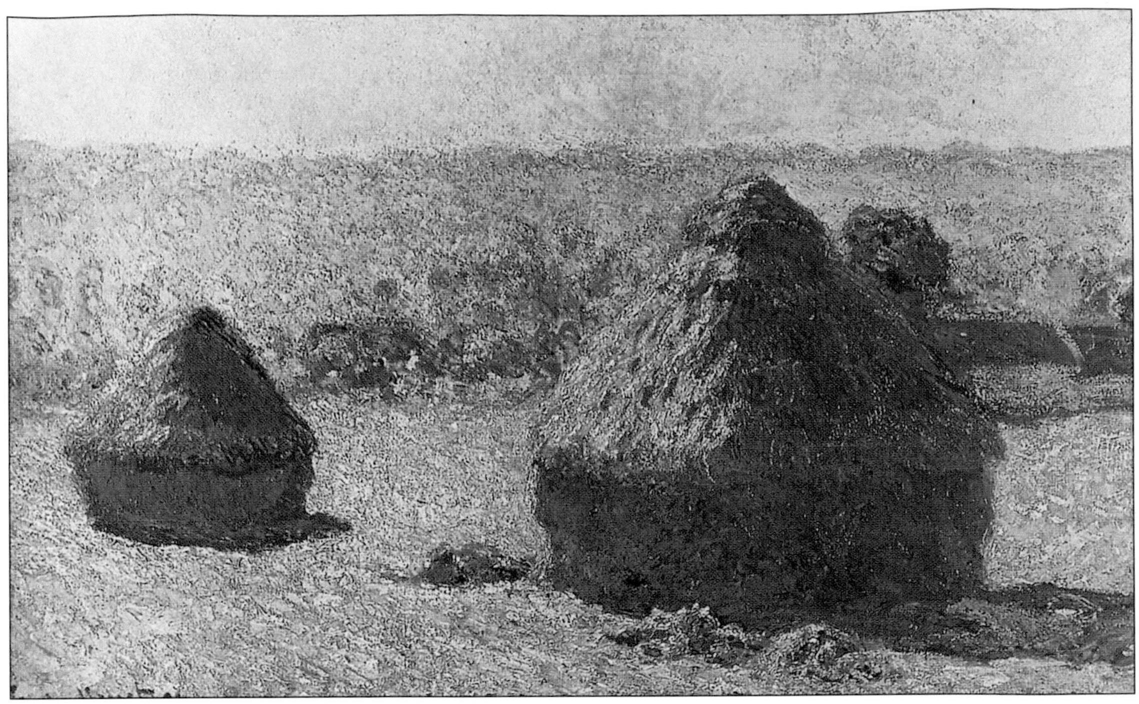

Grain Stacks, End of Summer *Claude Monet*

Between 1889 and 1891 Monet completed a series of over 30 paintings of grain stacks in the field behind his house. Each study captures a brief moment in nature, and Monet worked on several canvases concurrently, dashing from one to the other as the light changed.

collapsible tin tubes of paint in the mid-nineteenth century. This was a boon to landscape painters, for it enabled them to take their paints outside and work immediately in front of nature. Hitherto, oil painting had been largely a studio activity as pigment had to be ground by hand and used instantly.

The biggest revolution in oil painting came in the 1860s and 1870s with the French Impressionists, who perhaps have had the greatest impact on the way that artists approach oil painting today. Monet (1840–1926), Renoir (1841– 1919), Pissarro (1831–1903) and others tried to capture in their paintings the many moods and qualities of light and colour in the landscape as they experienced them directly in the open air.

The Impressionists applied a broken-colour technique in which thick strokes and dabs of opaque colour were laid down separately, side by side, so that they mixed not on the canvas but in the viewer's eye. Rather than a solid, carefully built-up surface, the eye perceives a mosaic of fragmented brushstrokes that only forms a vibrant whole when viewed from a distance.

The Impressionist legacy has spawned a proliferation of art movements during the twentieth century, and artists have felt free to work in whatever way they wish. At one extreme, surrealist painters such as Salvador Dali (1904–1989) used traditional techniques in order to produce a kind of photographic realism. At the other extreme, artists such as the American abstract expressionist Jackson Pollock (1912–1956) have extended the boundaries of oil painting by throwing paint onto the canvas and allowing it to drip.

Despite the arrival of new media such as acrylic and alkyd paints, oil paint has lost none of its attraction – rather, its possibilities have increased beyond anything that could have been imagined by previous masters of the medium.

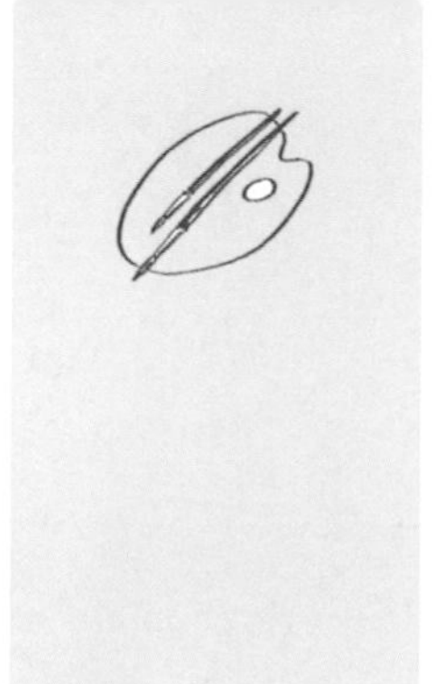

Materials and Equipment

Materials for oil painting can be expensive, therefore it is advisable to start out with the essentials and add extra colours, brushes and so on as you gain more experience.

Paints

Oil paints are sold in tubes and are available in two different grades: artists' and students'. Artists' colours are of better quality and this is reflected in the price. They are made from the finest pigments ground with a minimum of oil so their consistency is stiff, and the colours retain their brilliance well.

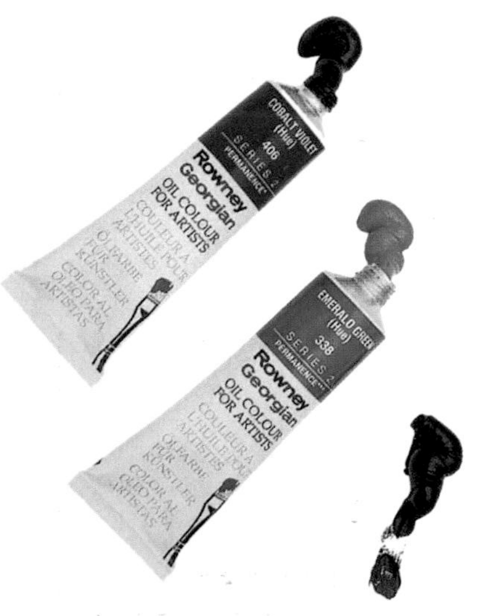

Oil paint consists of dry pigments ground in a natural drying oil, such as linseed or safflower oil.

Students' colours are labelled with trade names such as "Georgian" (Daler-Rowney) or "Winton" (Winsor & Newton). These paints cost less because they contain less pure pigment and more fillers and extenders. They cannot provide the same intensity of colour as the artists' range. They are, however, fine for practising with. Some artists even combine the two types, using artists' paints for the pure, intense colours and students' paints for the earth colours, which are often just as good as those in the artists' range.

Artist-quality paints vary in price according to the initial cost of the pigment. They are classified according to a "series", typically from 1 (the cheapest) to 7 (the most costly). Student colours are sold at a uniform price.

Mediums and Diluents

Oil paint can be used thickly, direct from the tube, but usually it needs to be diluted to make it easier to apply. Paint may be thinned to the required consistency with a diluent such as distilled turpentine or white spirit, or a combination of a diluent and an oil or varnish – what artists call a *medium*.

Diluents

Paint mixed with a diluent alone dries quickly to a matt finish. Always use double-distilled or rectified turpentine – ordinary household turpentine contains too many impurities. If you find that it gives you a headache or irritates your skin, white spirit is a suitable alternative.

Even small quantities of solvents and thinners can be hazardous if not used with care, because their fumes are rapidly absorbed through the lungs.

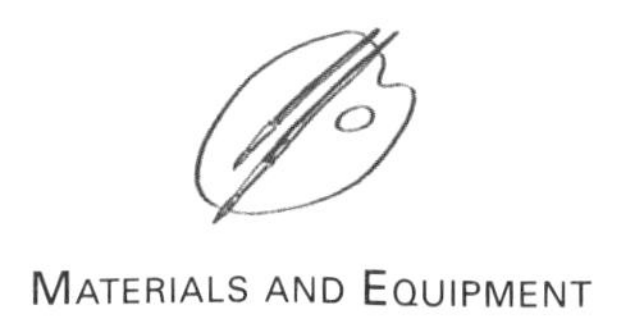

SUGGESTED PALETTE

Cobalt Blue
Greener and paler than ultramarine blue, cobalt is good for skies and cool highlights in flesh tones.

Lemon Yellow
A transparent colour with a cool, pale yellow hue. It forms delicate, cool greens when mixed with blues.

French Ultramarine
This is the best general-purpose blue. A deep, warm blue, it mixes well with yellow to form a rich variety of greens and with earth colours to form colourful greys.

Cadmium Yellow
A bright, warm yellow with good covering power.

Cadmium Red
A warm, intense red. Produces good pinks and purples when mixed with blues.

Viridian
A bright, deep green with a bluish tinge. When squeezed from the tube it appears a "synthetic" green, but is wonderful in mixes.

Titanium White
A good, dense white that mixes well and has excellent covering power.

Cobalt Violet
Though you can make a violet with red and blue, it won't have the intensity of cobalt violet. A very expensive pigment, however.

Raw Sienna
A warm, transparent colour, very soft and subtle. Useful in landscapes.

Permanent Rose
A cool, pinkish red that is similar to alizarin crimson but not quite so overpowering in mixes. It is good for mixing pinks and purples.

Burnt Sienna
A rich, reddish-brown hue, useful for warming other colours. Mix it with ultramarine or viridian to make deep, rich dark tones.

Burnt Umber
A rich, opaque and versatile brown. Useful for darkening all colours.

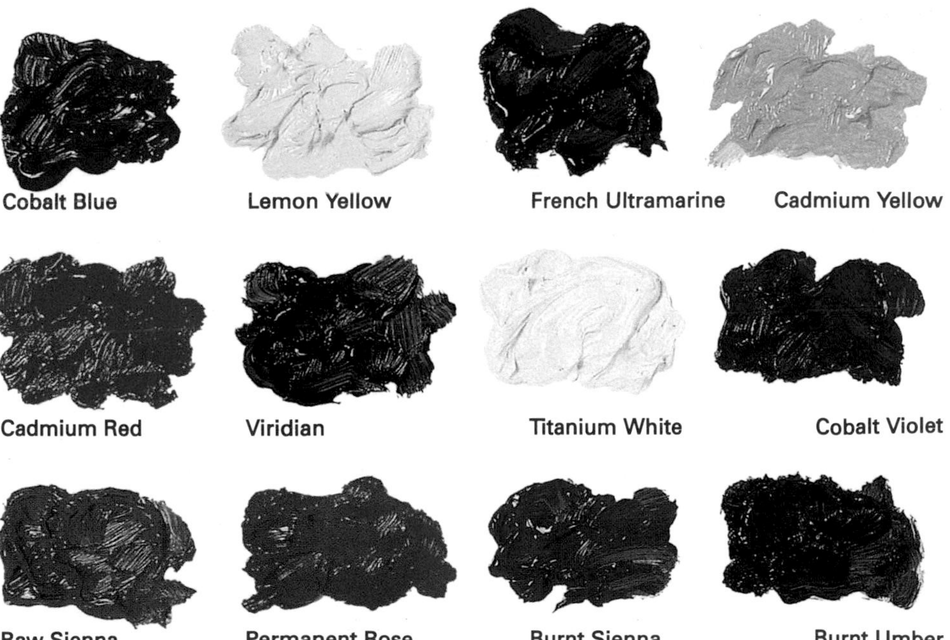

Cobalt Blue — Lemon Yellow — French Ultramarine — Cadmium Yellow

Cadmium Red — Viridian — Titanium White — Cobalt Violet

Raw Sienna — Permanent Rose — Burnt Sienna — Burnt Umber

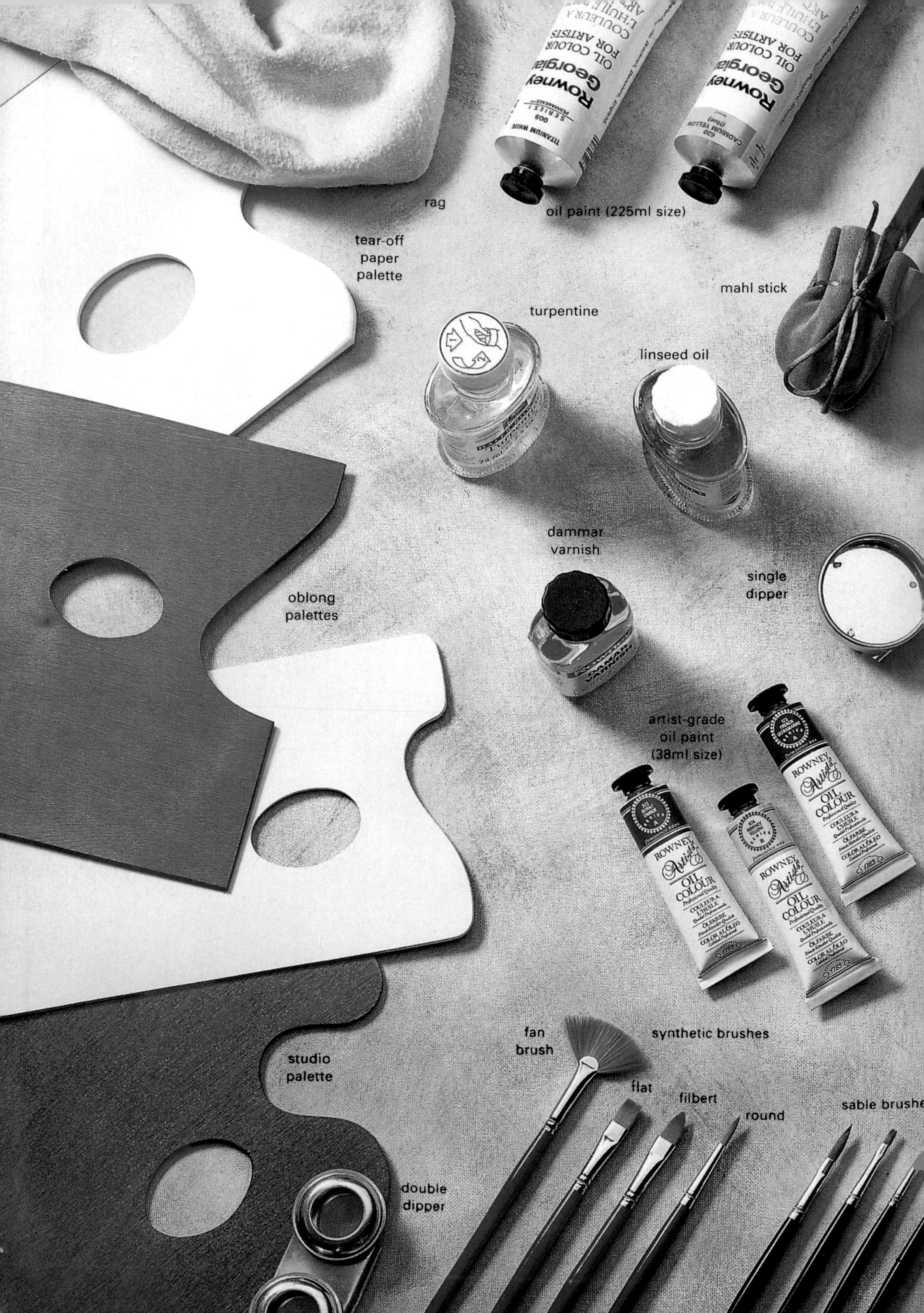
rag
oil paint (225ml size)
tear-off paper palette
mahl stick
turpentine
linseed oil
dammar varnish
single dipper
oblong palettes
artist-grade oil paint (38ml size)
fan brush
synthetic brushes
studio palette
flat
filbert
round
sable brushe
double dipper

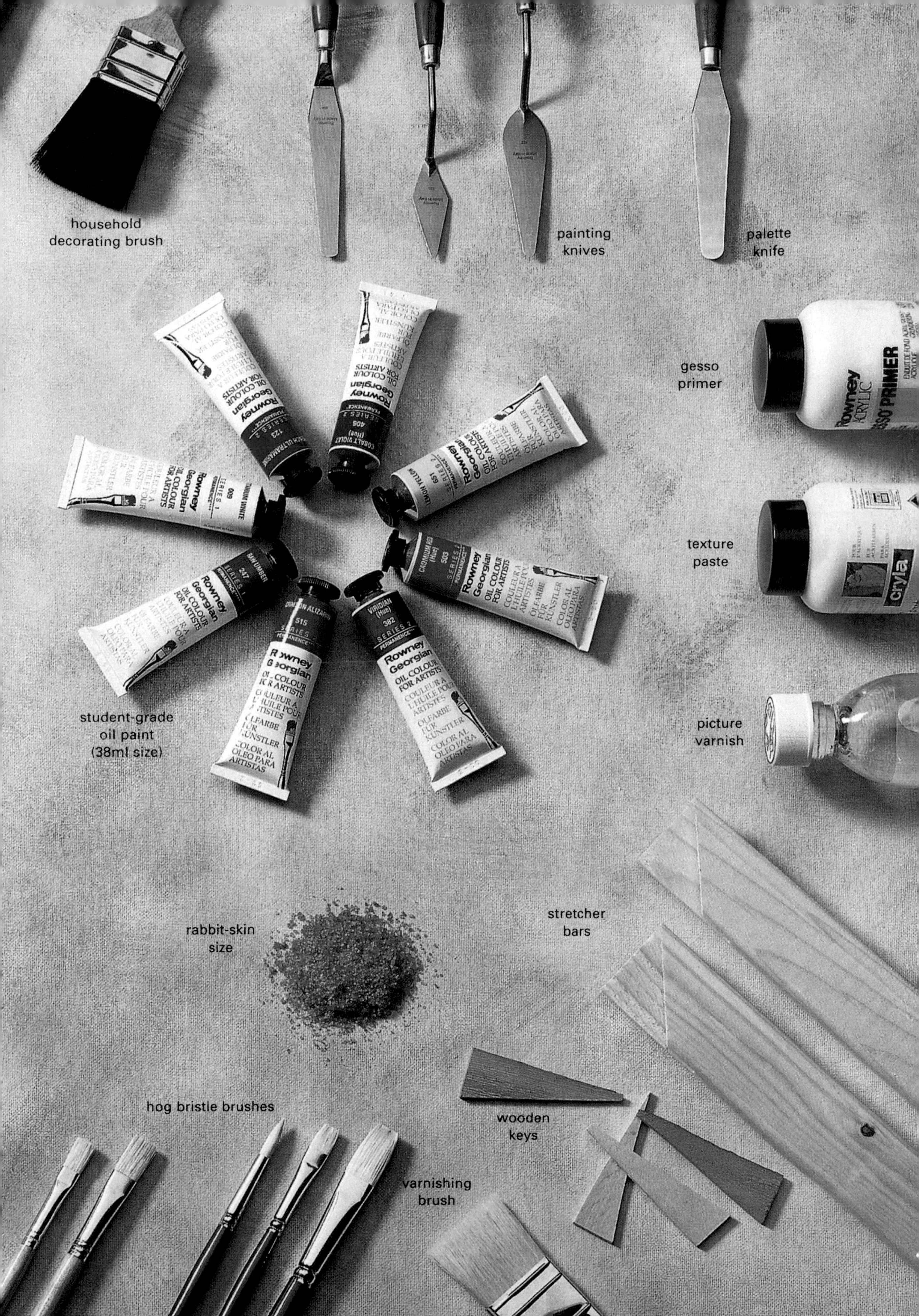
household
decorating brush
painting
knives
palette
knife
gesso
primer
texture
paste
picture
varnish
student-grade
oil paint
(38ml size)
stretcher
bars
rabbit-skin
size
hog bristle brushes
wooden
keys
varnishing
brush

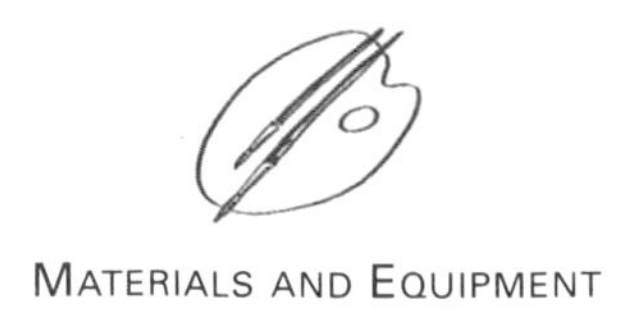

When using solvents, always work in a well-ventilated room and avoid inhalation. Do not eat, drink or smoke while working.

Mediums

Various oils and resins can be mixed with a diluent to add texture and body to the paint. The most commonly used medium is a mixture of linseed oil and turpentine, usually in a ratio of 60% oil to 40% turpentine. Linseed oil dries to a glossy finish that is resistant to cracking – but be sure to buy either purified or cold-pressed linseed oil; boiled linseed oil contains impurities that cause rapid yellowing. Adding a little dammar varnish to the turpentine and linseed oil produces a thicker mixture that dries more quickly.

Ready-mixed painting mediums are available, designed variously to improve the flow of the paint, thicken it for impasto work, speed its drying rate, and produce a matt or a gloss finish.

BRUSHES

Oil-painting brushes come in a range of sizes and shapes. Each makes a different kind of mark, but some are more versatile than others.

Bristle brushes

Stiff and hard-wearing, bristle brushes are good for moving the paint around on the surface and for applying thick dabs of colour. The best ones are made of stiff, white hog bristles with split ends that hold a lot of paint.

Sable brushes

Sable brushes are soft and springy, similar to those used for watercolours, but with longer handles. They are useful for adding details in the final layers of a painting and for applying thinly diluted colour.

Synthetic brushes

These are an economical alternative to natural-hair brushes, and their quality has improved considerably in recent years. They are hard-wearing and easily cleaned.

Brush shapes

Rounds have long, thin bristles that curve inwards at the ends. This is the most versatile brush shape as it covers large areas quickly and is also good for sketching in outlines.

Flats have square ends. They are ideal for applying thick, bold colour and for blending. Use the square end for fine lines and sharp details. So-called "long flats" have longer bristles that hold a lot of paint.

Brights are the same shape as flats, but with shorter, stiffer bristles that make very textured strokes. The stiff bristles are used to apply thick, heavy paint to produce impasto effects.

Filberts are similar to flats, except that the bristles curve inwards at the end. They produce a range of marks. The curved tip is useful for softening and blending edges.

Fan blenders are available in hog bristle, sable and synthetic fibre, and are used for blending colours where a very smooth, highly finished effect is required.

Sizes

Each type of brush comes in a range of sizes, from 00 to around 16. Brush sizes are not standardized and can vary widely between brands. The size you choose will depend on the scale and style of your paintings. In general, it is better to start with medium to large brushes as they cover large areas quickly but can also be employed for small touches. Using bigger brushes also encourages a more painterly, generous approach.

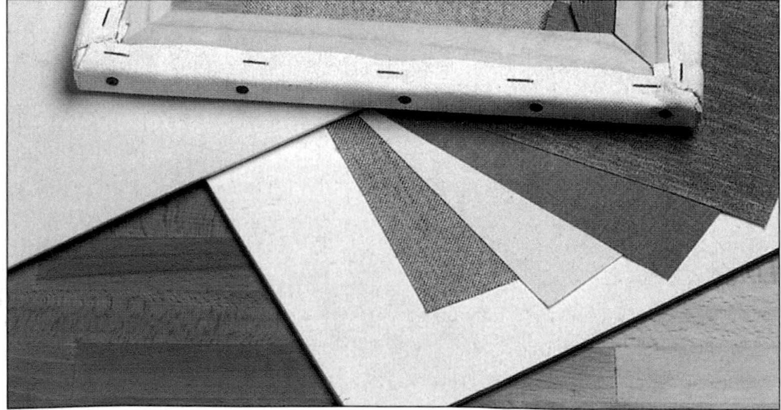

Almost any surface is suitable for oil painting so long as it is properly prepared.

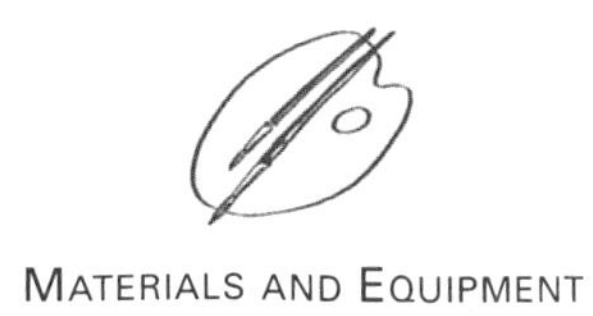

Palettes

Palettes come in a variety of shapes, sizes and materials. The best-quality palettes are made of mahogany ply, but fibreboard and melamine-faced palettes are adequate.

Thumbhole palettes

Thumbhole palettes come in various sizes and are designed to be held while painting at the easel. They have a thumbhole and indentation for the fingers, and the palette is supported on the forearm. There are three main shapes: oblong, oval and the traditional kidney-shaped, or "studio" palette. For easel painting, the curved shape of the studio palette is the best choice as it is well balanced and comfortable to hold for long periods.

Disposable palettes

Made of oil-proof paper, disposable palettes are useful for outdoor work and for artists who hate cleaning up. They come in pads with tear-off sheets.

Improvised palettes

Any smooth, non-porous material is suitable, such as a sheet of white formica, a glass slab with white or neutral-coloured paper underneath, or a sheet of hardboard sealed with a coat of paint.

Supports

Supports for oil painting – whether canvas, board or paper – must be prepared with glue size and/or primer to prevent them absorbing the oil in the paint; if too much oil is absorbed, the paint may eventually crack.

Canvas

The most popular surface is canvas, which has a unique responsiveness and plenty of tooth to hold the paint. It is available in various weights and in fine, medium and coarse-grained textures. You can buy it either glued onto stiff board, ready-stretched and primed on a wooden stretcher frame, or by the metre from a roll.

Canvas weight is measured in ounces per square yard. The higher the number, the greater the density of threads and the better the quality. The two main types are linen and cotton.

Linen is the best canvas. It has a fine, even grain that is free of knots and easy to paint on. It is expensive but very durable.

Cotton Good-quality cotton canvas, such as cotton duck, comes in various grades. It stretches well and is the best alternative to linen – at about half the price. Lighter-weight canvases are recommended for practice work only.

Boards and papers

Prepared canvas boards are inexpensive and are ideal for practice work.

Hardboard is an excellent yet inexpensive support for oils. Plywood, chipboard and MDF (medium-density fibreboard) are also suitable, and can be prepared with primer if you like a white surface, or simply apply a coat of glue size or PVA for a neutral mid-toned surface.

Oil sketching paper is prepared for oil painting and is textured to resemble canvas weave. Sold in pads it is handy for outdoor sketches and practice work.

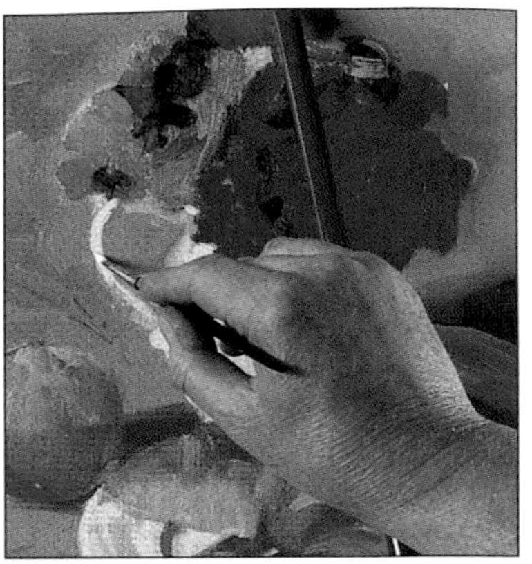

Use a mahl stick to steady your hand when painting details and fine lines. Place the padded end on a dry section of the painting or on the edge of the canvas. Then rest your painting arm on the stick.

Painting Accessories

Painting in oils can be messy, so the most essential accessories are large jars or tins to hold solvents for cleaning brushes, and a supply of cotton rags and newspaper! The following items are not essential, but useful.

Painting knives have flexible blades and cranked handles, and can be used instead of a brush to apply thick paint.

Palette knives have a long, straight, flexible blade with a rounded tip. They are used for cleaning the palette and mixing paint.

Dippers are small, open cups that clip onto the edge of your palette to hold mediums and thinners during painting.

Mahl stick This is used to steady your hand when painting small details or fine lines. It consists of a long handle made of wood or metal, with a cushion at one end.

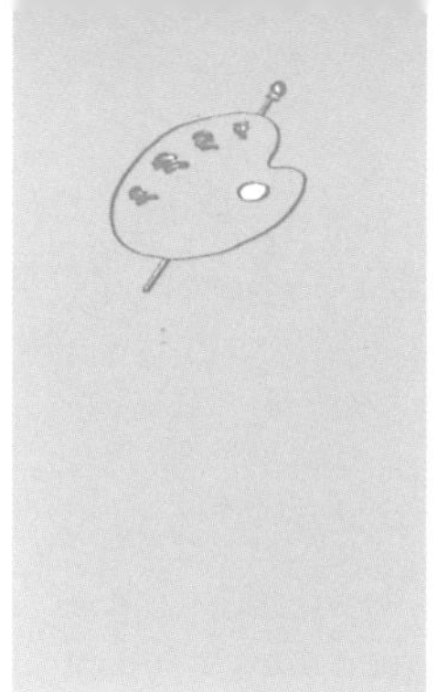

Basic Techniques

Priming the Support

Canvas, board and other supports for oil painting must be sealed before being used, otherwise oils from the paint layer seep down into the canvas, leaving the paint impoverished and eventually prone to flaking or cracking. The traditional method is to apply a "ground" consisting of a layer of glue size and one or more layers of emulsion or gesso primer. The modern alternative is acrylic primer, which can be applied directly to the support without the need for glue size and is ready to paint on in about 30 minutes.

An economical primer that can be used on board (but not on stretched canvas) is ordinary matt white household paint, which provides a sympathetic semi-absorbent ground. However, use only good-quality paint, because cheap emulsions will quickly yellow.

Smooth surfaces such as hardboard (masonite) should first be lightly sanded to provide a key for the primer. Using a household paintbrush, apply two or three thin coats, each one at a right angle to the one before. Allow each coat to dry before the next is applied. If you prefer to work on a more textured painting surface, apply the primer using rough brushstrokes, or mix it with equal proportions of acrylic texture paste, which is available from art supply stores.

Toned Grounds

A pure white canvas can be inhibiting to work on, especially for beginners, and it is difficult to assess colours and tones against white. Most artists prefer to tone the ground with a thin layer of paint, diluted with white (mineral) spirit (see page 271). Subdued earths, ochres and blue-greys are normally chosen for toning because they provide a neutral mid-tone from which you can work out towards the darks and lights. If some of the

Priming Supports

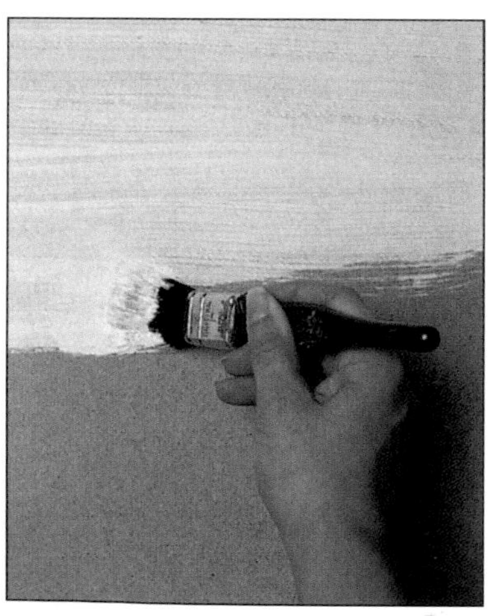

1
Using a decorating brush, apply a smooth coat of primer and leave to dry.

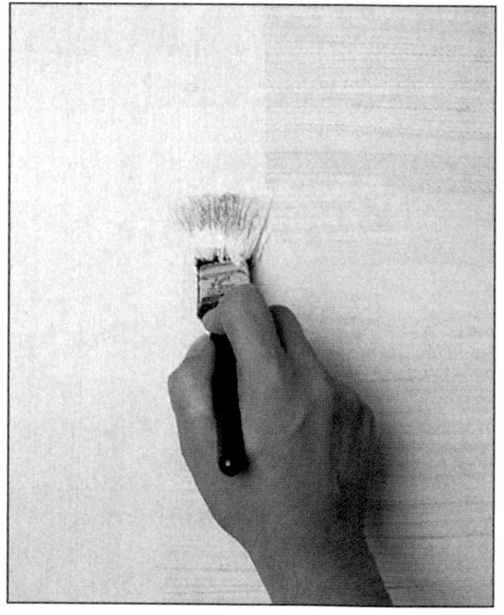

2
Apply the second coat at right angles to the first to give a smooth, even surface.

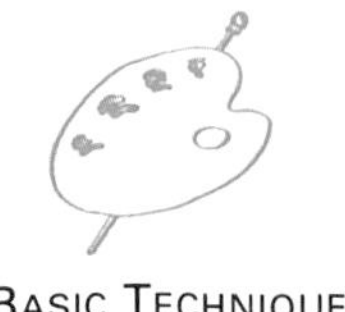

Toned Grounds

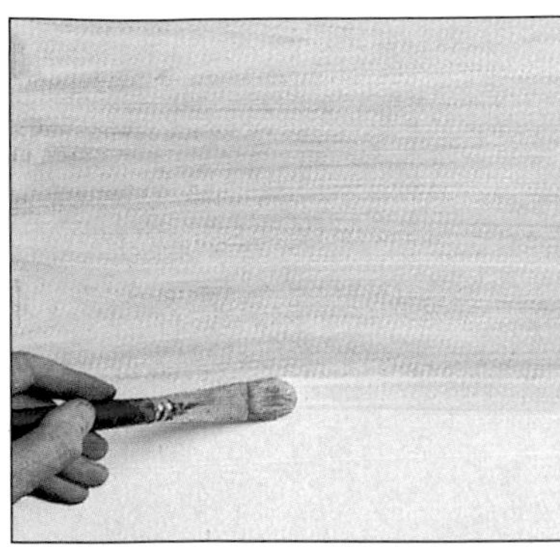

1

Dilute the paint with turpentine or white spirit to a thin consistency and scrub it on vigorously with a large flat brush or a decorating brush.

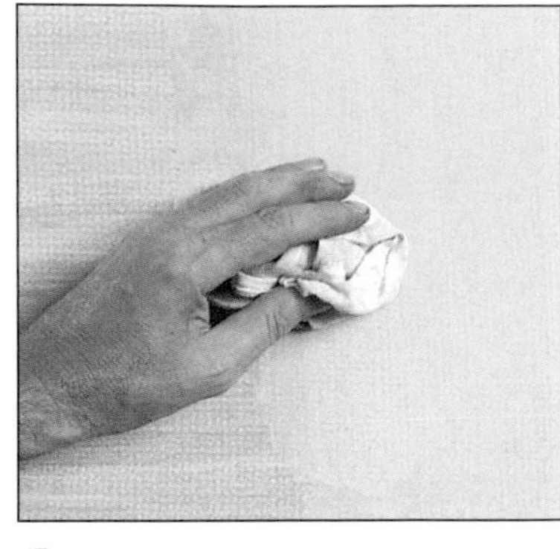

2

If you prefer a smooth ground, work over the wet paint with a soft rag to even out the brushstrokes. The toned ground must be completely dry before you start to paint on it. With oils this can take up to 24 hours.

ground is left exposed it will give an overall sense of unity to the painting.

Palette Layout

It is said that if your palette is messy, your painting will be messy, so it is a good idea to get into the habit of laying out your colours in the same systematic

The colours on this palette are arranged in the order of the spectrum. Clockwise from the bottom, they are: cadmium red, alizarin crimson, burnt sienna, yellow ochre, cadmium yellow, lemon yellow, viridian, cobalt blue, French ultramarine and cobalt violet, with white in the centre.

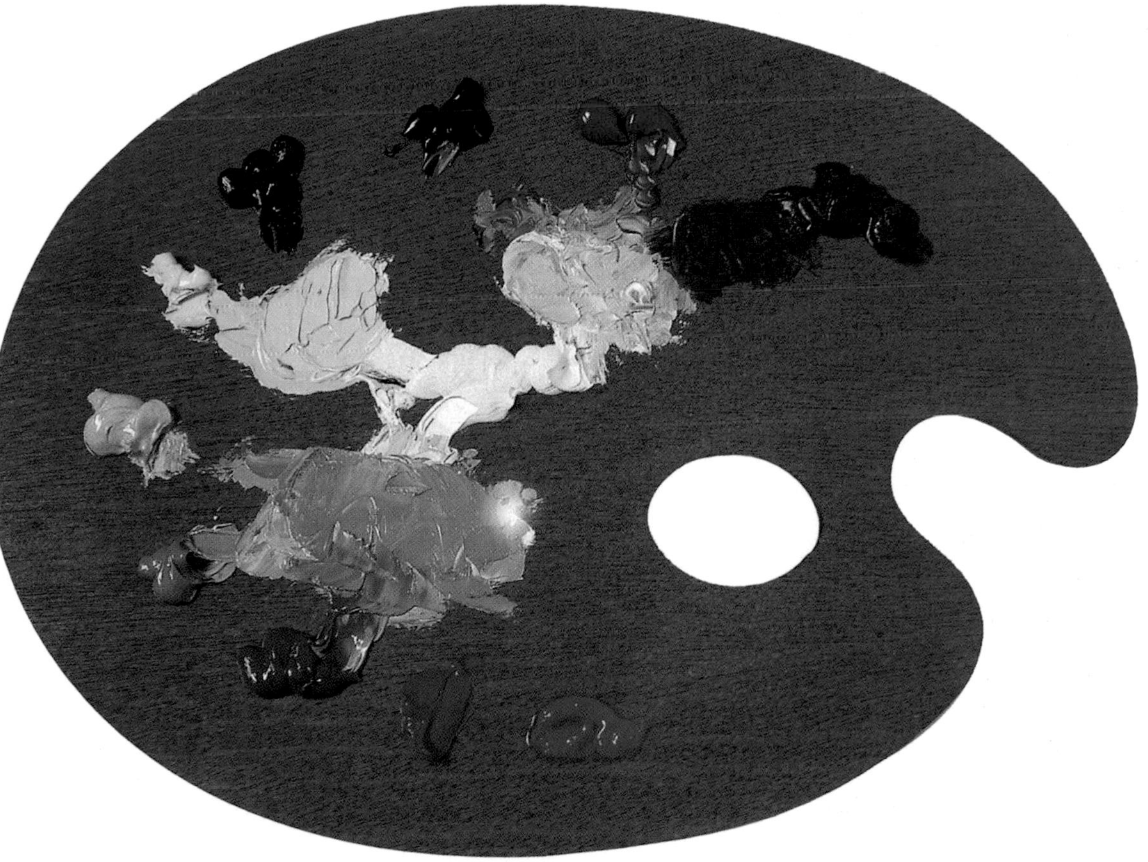

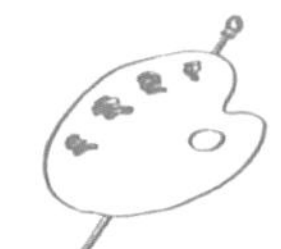

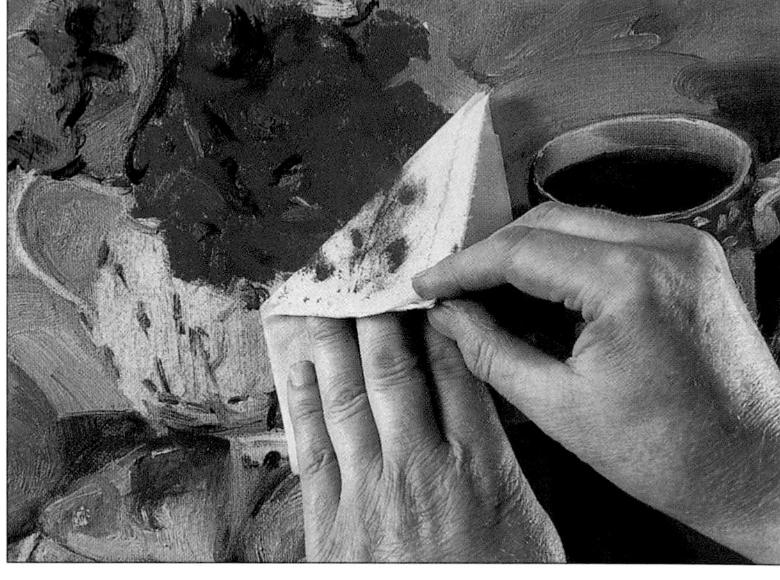

A wet oily surface can be difficult to work over. Use a piece of absorbent paper to blot off the excess paint, leaving a surface with more "grip".

order each time you paint. That way, you will automatically know where each colour is without having to search for it, and you will be able to concentrate on observing your subject. There are several systems for laying out colours. Some painters prefer to arrange their colours along one side of the palette in the order of the spectrum, with white and the earth colours on the other side; others use a light to dark or warm to cool sequence. Whatever system you choose, it's a good idea to put a large squeeze of white paint (used in most mixes) in the centre so the other colours can be easily combined with it.

HOLDING THE PALETTE

The traditional kidney-shaped palette has a bevelled thumbhole for maximum comfort when painting at the easel. The curved indent at the leading edge allows you to grasp several brushes and your painting rag in one hand, while painting with the other. Hold the palette in your left hand (if you are right-handed), resting it on your forearm and fitting it up against your body.

MAKING CORRECTIONS

One of the advantages of painting in oils is that corrections can be made easily while the paint is still wet, or simply painted over when the paint is dry. An unsatisfactory passage can be removed while the paint is still fresh by scraping off the unwanted paint with a palette knife. This will leave a ghost of the original image and will form a helpful base on which to begin again. Alternatively, the scraped area can be completely removed with a rag soaked in turpentine.

If the canvas becomes clogged with thick paint and too slippery to work over, you can remove surface paint with absorbent paper, such as newspaper or tissue. Press the paper over the wet canvas and gently smooth it down with the flat of your hand, then carefully peel the paper away. The paper absorbs the excess oily paint,

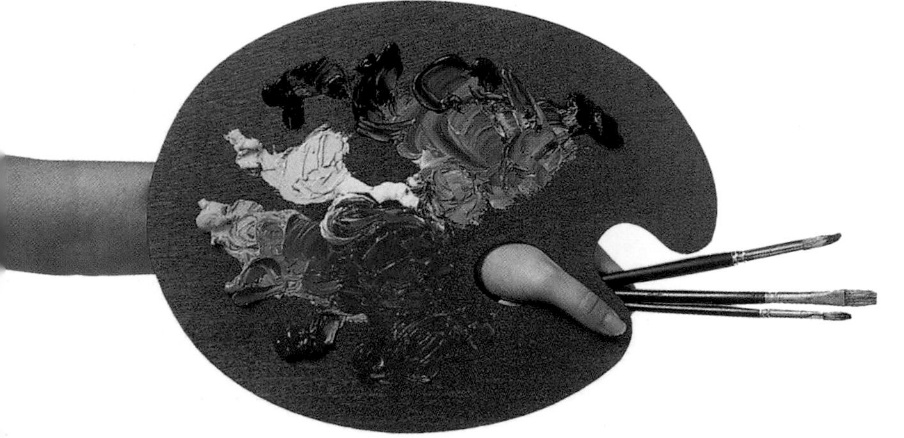

At first when you try to hold your palette and everything else you may find it uncomfortable, but very soon it will become second nature.

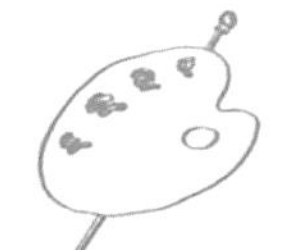

leaving a cleaner surface on which to work. This process is called "tonking", after Henry Tonks, a former professor of painting at the Slade School of Art in London.

Brush Care

Take good care of your paintbrushes and they will give you many years of service. You should clean your brushes at the end of every painting day, and never leave them soaking in solvent with the bristles touching the bottom of the container.

After rinsing the brush in white spirit and thoroughly wiping with a rag, soap the bristles well with plenty of pure household soap (not detergent) and warm water. Then rub the brush around gently in your palm, rinsing now and then. Continue rubbing and rinsing until all the paint is removed. Rinse finally in warm water, shake dry, then smooth the bristles into shape. Leave the brush to dry, bristle end up, in a jar.

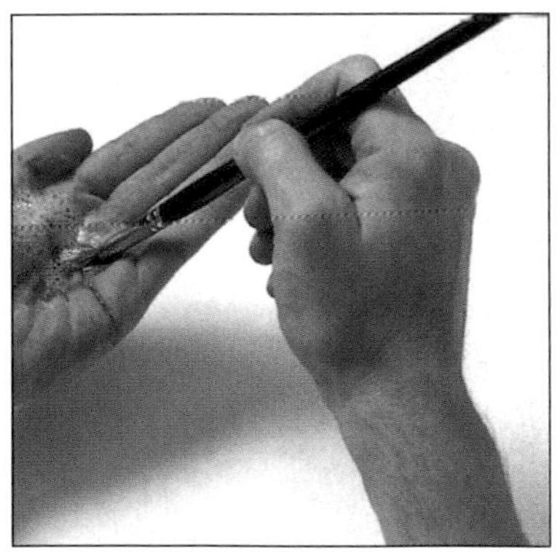

It is essential to remove every trace of paint, especially near the ferule. Repeat the soaping until no trace of pigment appears in the lather.

Squaring Up

You may wish to base an oil painting on a sketch or a photographic image; but it is often difficult to maintain the accuracy of the drawing when enlarging or reducing a reference source to the size of your canvas or board. A simple method of transferring an image in a different scale is by squaring up (sometimes called scaling up).

Using a pencil and ruler, draw a grid of equal-sized squares over the sketch or photograph. The more complex the image, the more squares you should draw. If you wish to avoid marking the original, make a photocopy of it and draw the grid onto this. Alternatively, draw the grid onto a sheet of clear acetate placed over the original, using a felt-tip pen.

Then construct an enlarged version of the grid on your support, using light charcoal lines. This grid must have the same number of squares as the smaller one. The size of the squares will depend on the degree of enlargement required: for example, if you are doubling the size of your reference material, make the squares twice the size of the squares on the original reference drawing or photograph.

When the grid is complete, transfer the image that appears in each square of the original to its equivalent square on the support. The larger squares on the working sheet serve to enlarge the original image. You are, in effect, breaking down a large-scale problem into smaller, more manageable areas.

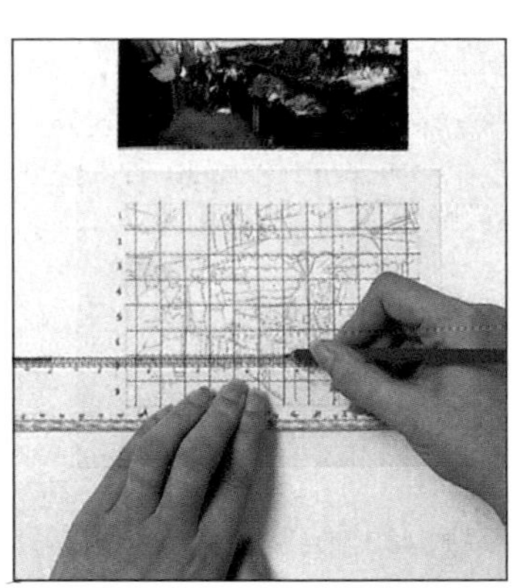

1

Make a sketch from the reference photograph and draw a grid of squares over it.

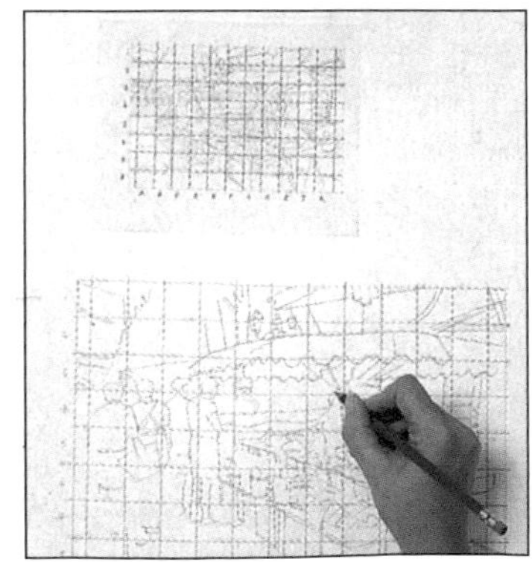

2

Draw a grid of larger squares onto the support and transfer the detail from the sketch, square by square.

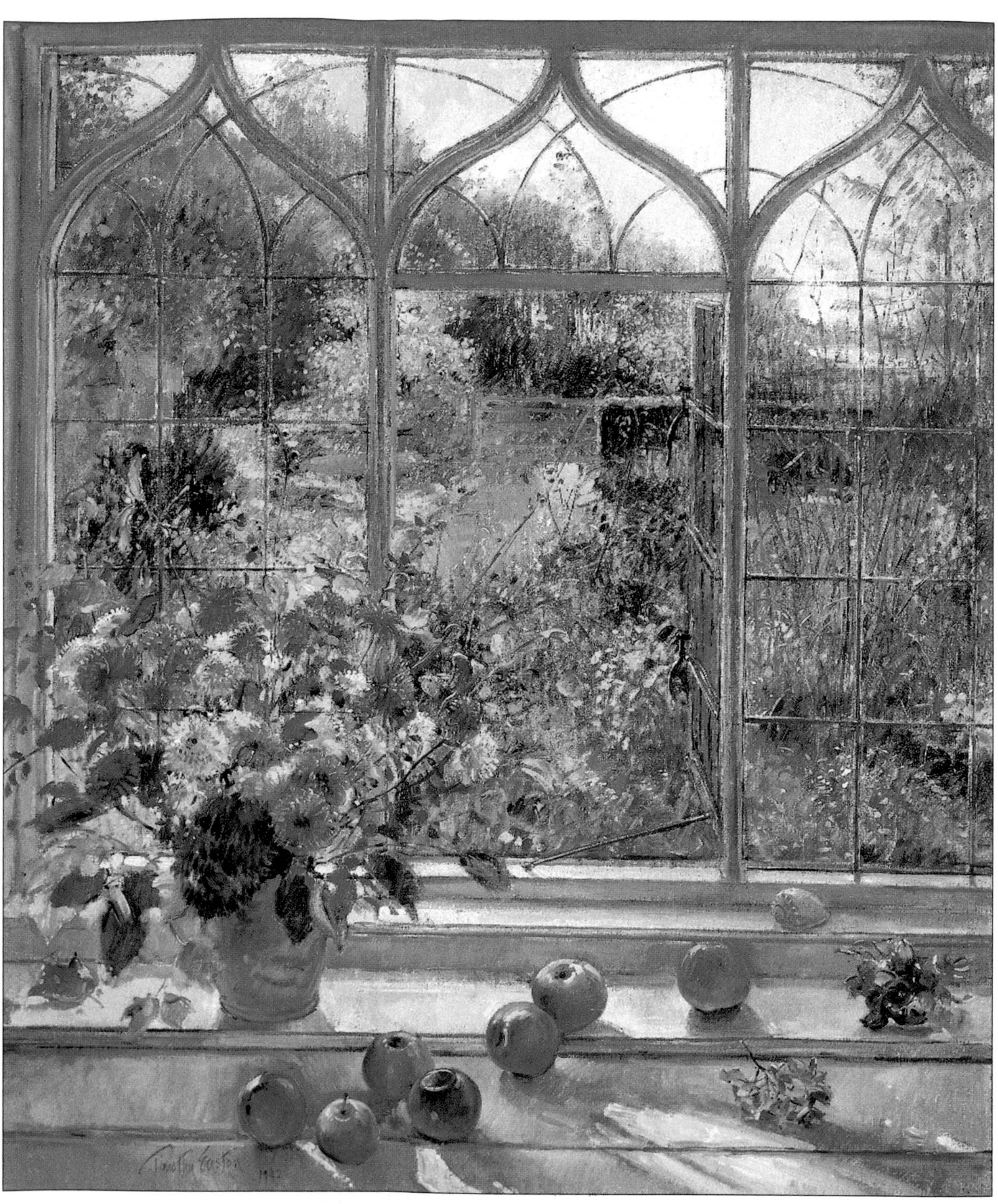

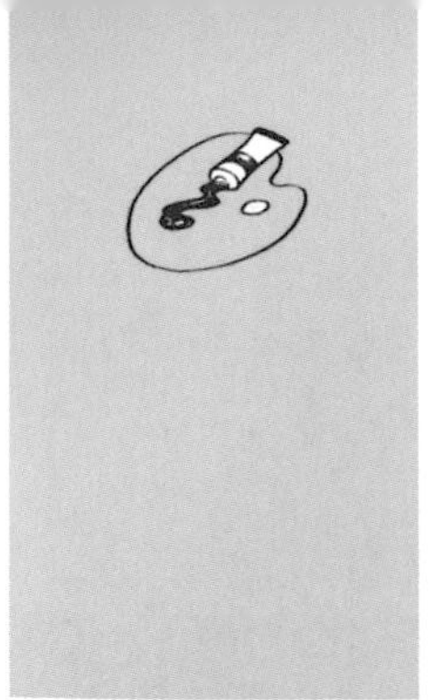

GALLERY

Oil paint is a highly versatile and responsive medium, capable of producing an infinite range of textures and effects. Used straight from the tube it produces thick, rich impastos in which the quality of the paint surface and the mark of the brush become an integral part of the finished image. Thinly diluted it can be used to apply delicate, translucent glazes that seem to glow with an inner light. And there are many fascinating variations between these two extremes.

On the following pages you will find a selection of oil paintings by contemporary artists, revealing a diversity of technique and breadth of imagination which, it is hoped, will inspire you to try out new techniques or to tackle unfamiliar subjects.

Autumn Window
Timothy Easton
61 x 51cm (24 x 20in)

Easton has exploited the richness and lustre of oil paints in conveying the warm glow of autumn sunshine on this scene. The wonderful vibrancy of the picture stems, too, from the use of complementary colours – the predominantly warm, yellowish hues are offset by touches of cool violet.

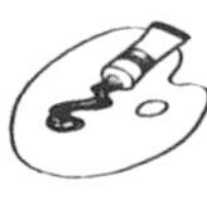

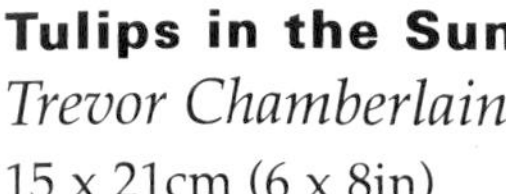

Tulips in the Sun
Trevor Chamberlain
15 x 21cm (6 x 8in)

You don't have to venture far afield to find interesting subjects to paint. To an artist with an inquiring eye, just about anything will make a good picture – much depends on how you crop the subject and compose the image. Here, the artist was taken with the loose informality of a clump of tulips growing in his garden.

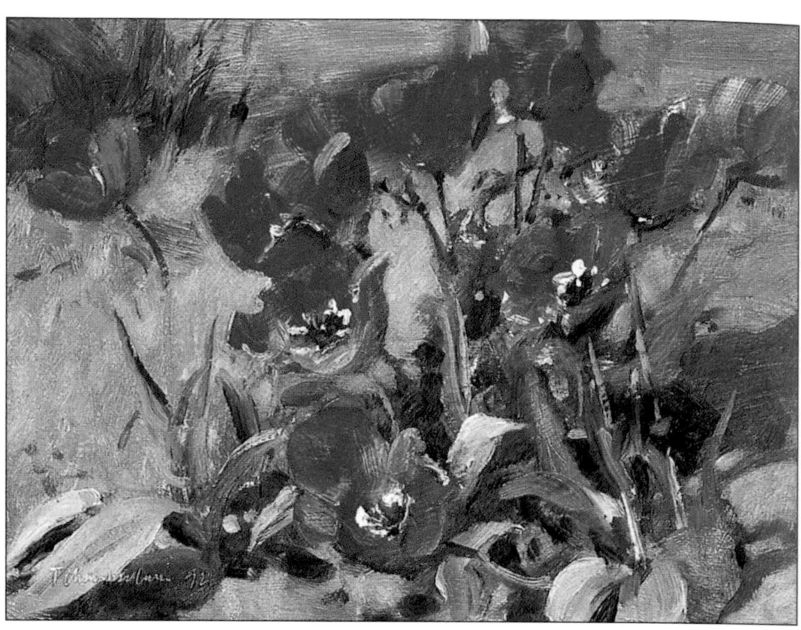

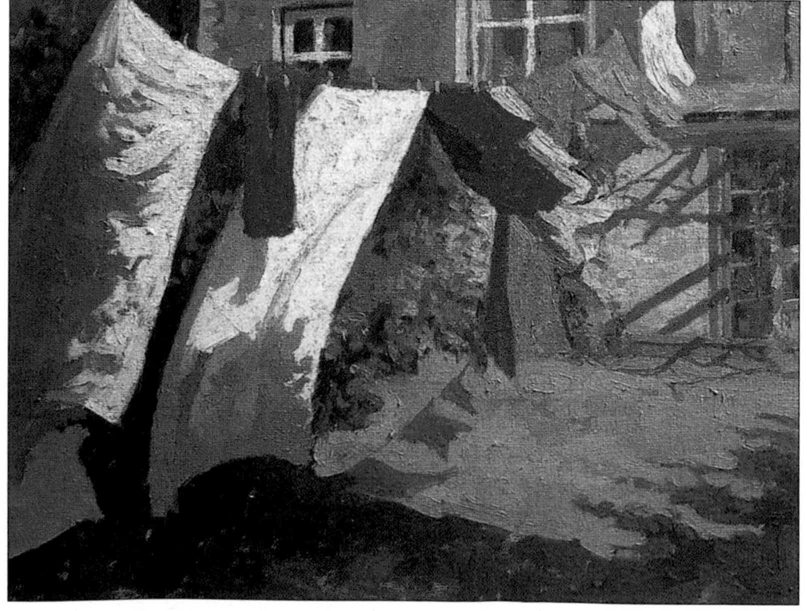

Washing on the Line
James Horton
30 x 41cm (12 x 16in)

Here we have another seemingly mundane subject – a line of washing – which has been transformed into an appealing image through the artist's astute handling of colour and composition. With a moving subject such as this you have to work fast to capture the essence, relying heavily on your visual memory.

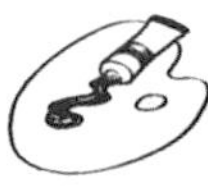

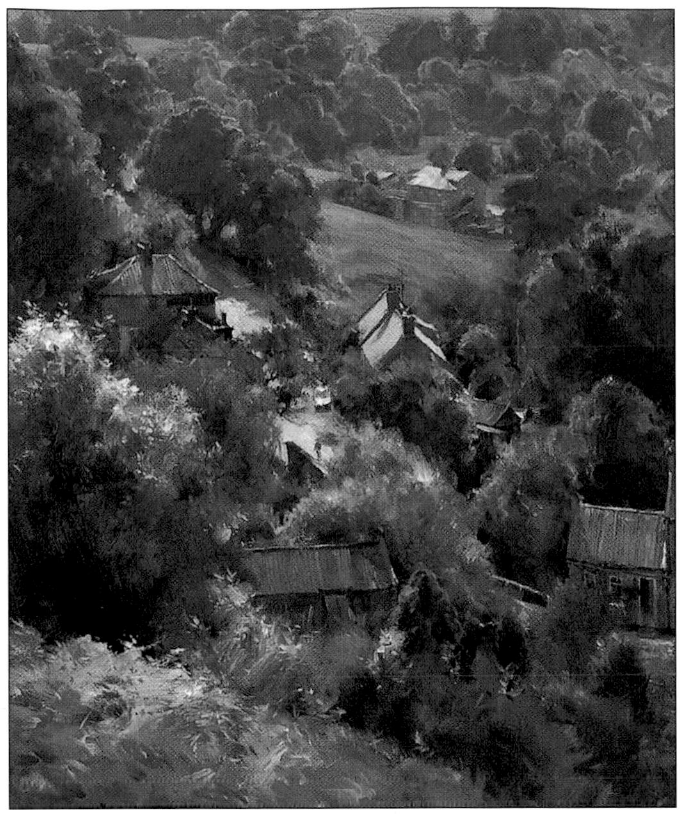

Above Beck Hole, near Whitby
David Curtis
56 x 46cm (22 x 18in)

The high viewpoint here affords an opportunity to convey a thrilling impression of space, light and atmosphere. The painting was executed over two consecutive days, the artist returning at the same time each day when the light conditions were consistent. The finished piece captures the feel of a blisteringly hot day, with the distant landscape enveloped in a bluish heat haze.

Orange Sunshade
Barry Freeman
25 x 36cm (10 x 14in)

The beach is a rich source of imagery for the artist, so make sure you pack your sketchbook along with your suntan cream! Intrigued by the refreshingly simple arrangement of shapes and colours in this little group, Freeman painted it exactly as he saw it, apart from moving the beach ball from the right to the left in order to improve the compositional balance of the image.

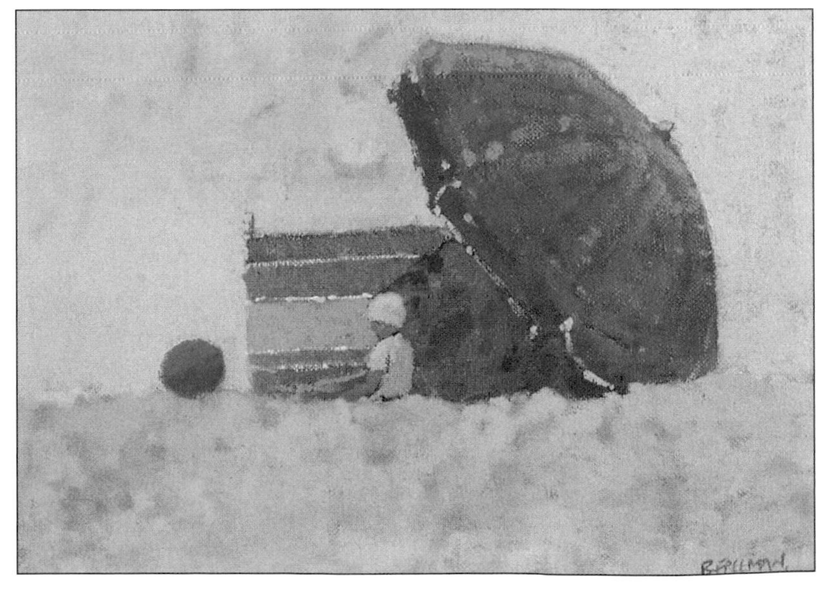

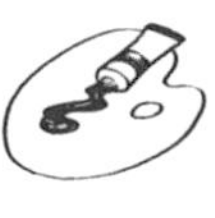

Apollo
Olwen Tarrant
61 x 91cm (24 x 36in)

Tarrant's paintings are carefully designed with an eye to colour, shape and overall pattern. The flat, matt quality of the paint surface and the use of broad blocks of colour accentuate the formal abstract qualities of the image, though it also reads as a collection of recognizable objects. There are many subtle echoes and repetitions that activate the shallow space, leading the eye around the painting and giving it a satisfying harmony.

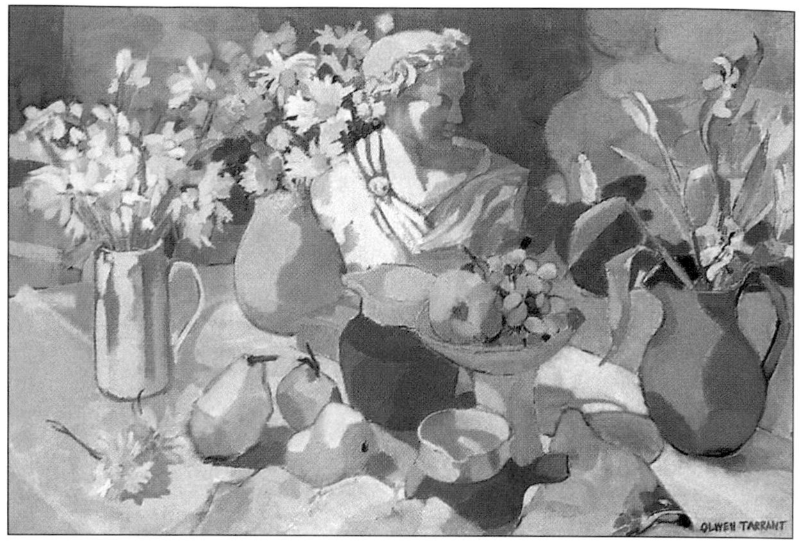

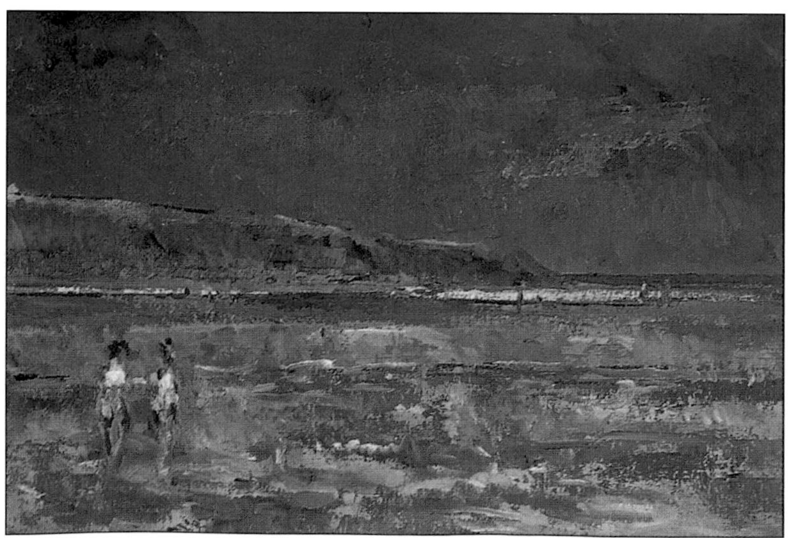

Bathers on the Strand
John Denahy
18 x 27cm (7 x 10½in)

For Denahy the marks and textures of the paint are in themselves an exciting and enjoyable part of the painting process. He mixes his colours with a little white spirit or alkyd medium to a stiff, matt, "chalky" consistency and applies them with brushes, knives and scrapers. Rich and complex interactions of colour are achieved by loosely dragging and scumbling over thinly glazed underlayers.

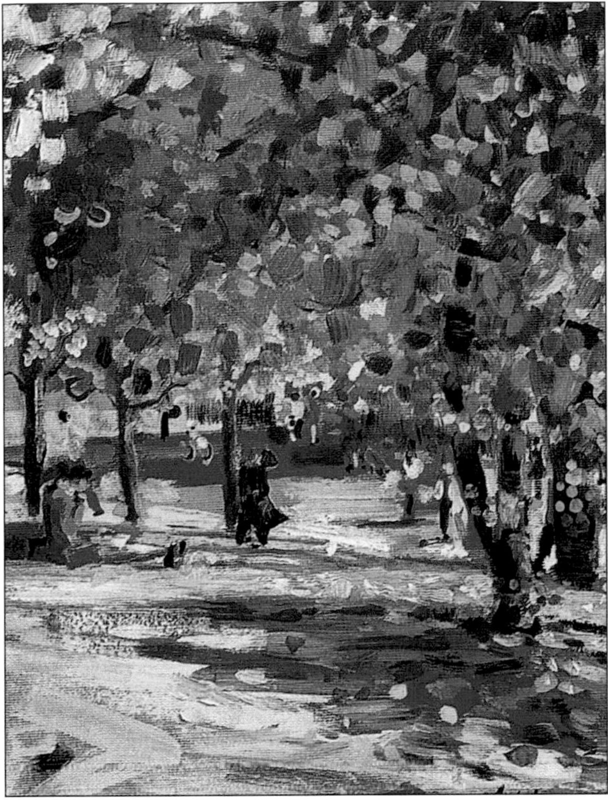

Full Summer
Peter Graham
36 x 25cm (14 x 10in)

This painting was executed rapidly on site in order to capture the mood of the moment. Beneath the apparent careless vivacity of surface, however, lies a carefully thought-out structure; the verticals of the trees are counterpointed by the sweeping curves of paint in the foreground, which lead the eye to groups of figures. These, in turn, are positioned to lead the eye through the picture in a rhythmic way, the tiny dots of red on the clothing acting as visual "stepping stones".

Dusk, San Mario
James Horton
13 x 23cm (5 x 9in)

Painted with dash and bravura, this tiny study effectively conveys the atmosphere of a wet and windy evening in St Mark's Square, Venice. Horton was less interested in recording the physical features of the scene, more with capturing the eerie quality of the light. It was essential to gauge the tonal values accurately, and working on a mid-toned ground enabled him to work out to the lights and darks more easily.

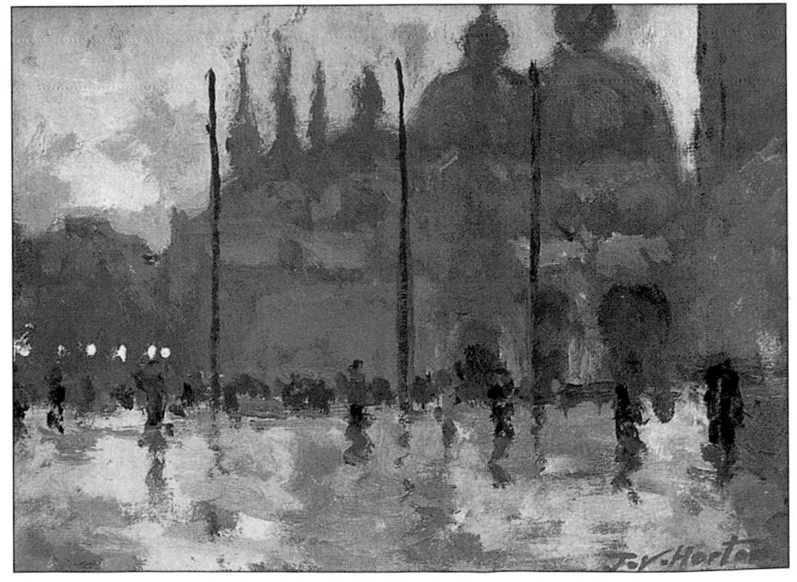

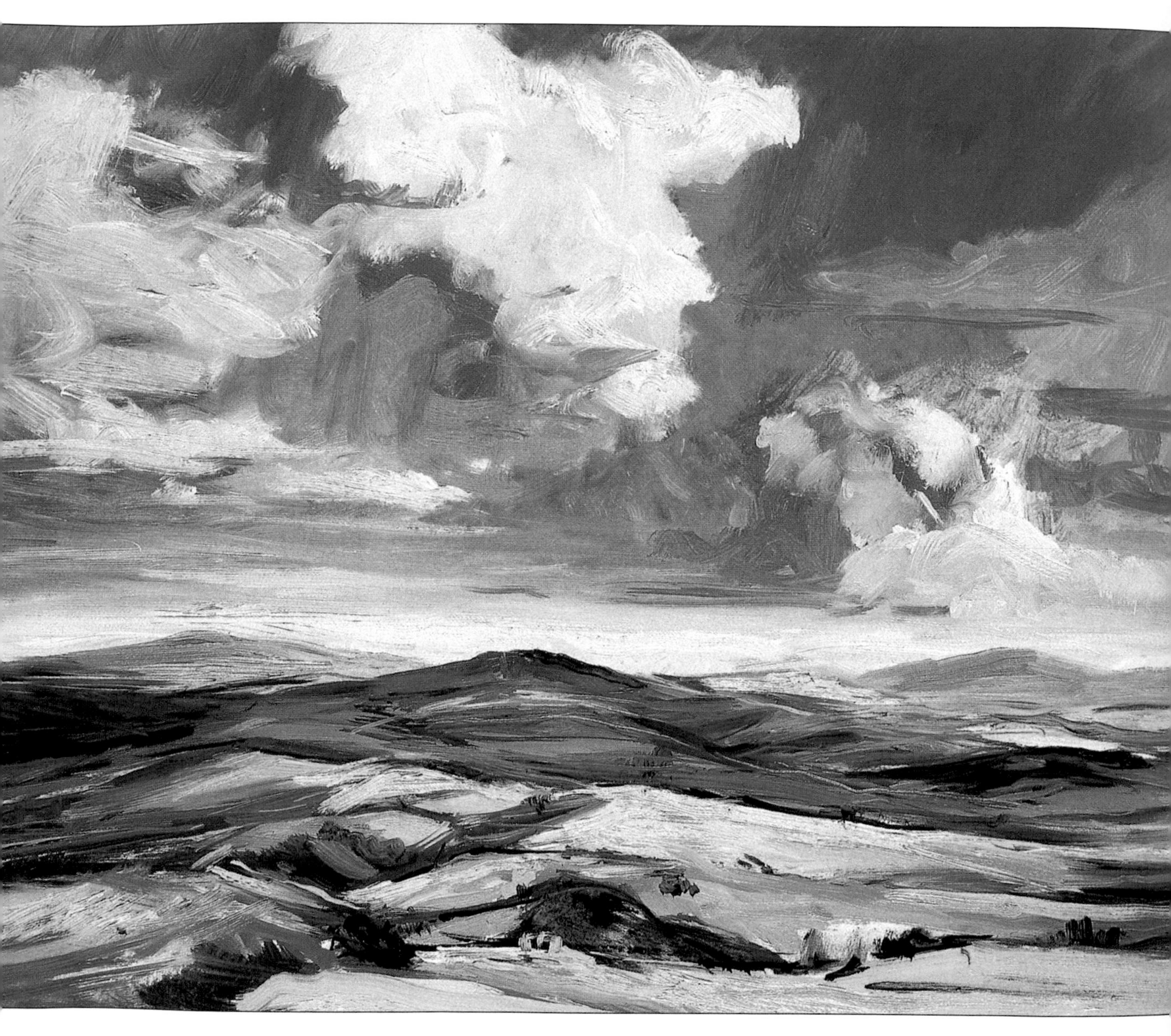

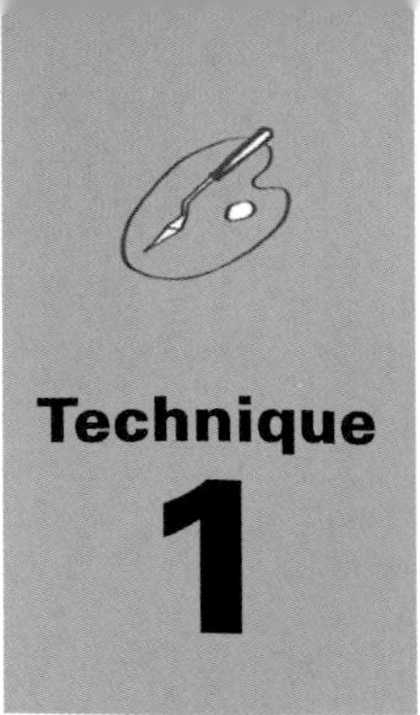

Technique

1

PAINTING "ALLA PRIMA"

This delightful and exuberant landscape was painted on-the-spot in the hills of Tuscany in southern Italy. In order to capture the movement of the scudding clouds and the rapidly changing light, the painting had to be executed quickly, in one sitting – a method known as "alla prima".

The artist started by blocking in the broad areas of the composition with thinned paint, which is easy to manipulate when working fast. He continued building up the colour, applying it in wide sweeps and rapid scumbles that give energy and movement to the scene.

When painting "alla prima" you have to be constantly aware of how the different elements of the image – line, mass, tone and colour – interact. To achieve balance and unity, the artist worked on all areas of the composition at once, rather than painting one area in detail before starting on the next; he kept his brush moving around the canvas, working from sky to land and back again, bringing all areas of the image to a similar level of detail at each stage.

David Carr
Tuscan Landscape
33 x 43cm (13 x 17in)

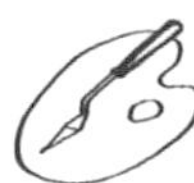

ALLA PRIMA TECHNIQUE

Alla prima is an Italian expression meaning "at the first", and describes a technique in which a painting is completed in one session, instead of being built up layer by layer. The French Impressionists and their forerunners – Constable (1776–1837) and Corot (1796–1875) – were great exponents of this method, which is particularly well suited to painting outdoors.

In *alla prima* painting there is generally little or no initial underpainting, although artists sometimes make a rapid underdrawing in charcoal or thinned paint to act as a guide. Each patch of colour is then laid down more or less as it will appear in the finished painting, or worked wet-into-wet with adjacent colours. The idea with this kind of painting is to capture the essence of the subject in an intuitive way, using vigorous, expressive brushstrokes and minimal colour mixing.

One of the great advantages of *alla prima* painting is that it creates an extremely stable paint surface. Whereas a painting that is composed of several built up layers may be prone to cracking eventually, due to the uneven drying rates of the different layers, a painting completed in one session dries uniformly, even when it is laid on thickly.

The ability to apply paint quickly and confidently is the key to the *alla prima* approach. It is, of course, always possible to scrape away and rework unsuccessful areas of a painting, but in doing so there is a danger that some of the freshness and spontaneity will be lost. It is therefore very important to start with a clear idea in your mind of what you want to convey in your painting, working with a limited palette can sometimes be a good idea, as you will not be tempted to include any unnecessary detail.

TUSCAN LANDSCAPE

Materials and Equipment

• SHEET OF PRIMED CANVAS OR BOARD • OIL COLOURS: CADMIUM RED, CADMIUM YELLOW, CADMIUM LEMON, YELLOW OCHRE, COBALT GREEN, VIRIDIAN, FRENCH ULTRAMARINE, COBALT BLUE, CERULEAN, RAW UMBER, BURNT SIENNA AND TITANIUM WHITE • BRISTLE BRUSHES: LARGE AND SMALL ROUNDS, AND MEDIUM FILBERT • SMALL LETTERING BRUSH OR ROUND SOFT-HAIR BRUSH • TURPENTINE • LINSEED OIL • RAG AND WHITE SPIRIT FOR CLEANING

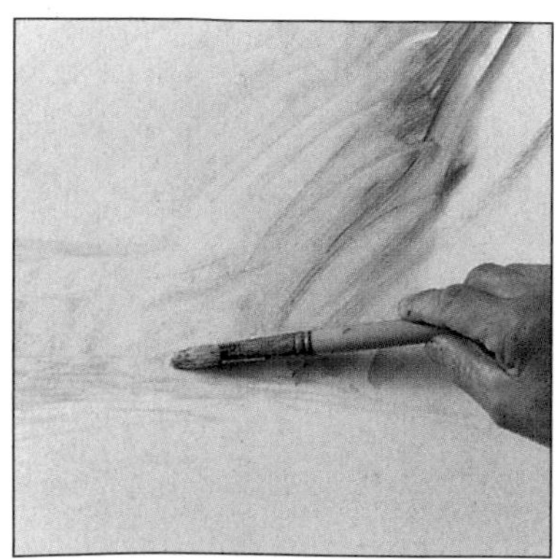

1

First establish the position of the horizon line, then work straight into the sky area. To create a warm base colour for the clouds, mix a soft yellow from yellow ochre and titanium white; for the patch of blue sky, use ultramarine and white. Dilute the paint thinly with a 50–50 mix of turpentine and linseed oil and apply it rapidly with broad, sweeping strokes, using the belly – not the tip – of a large round-bristle brush.

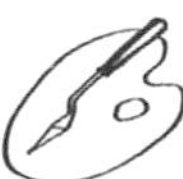

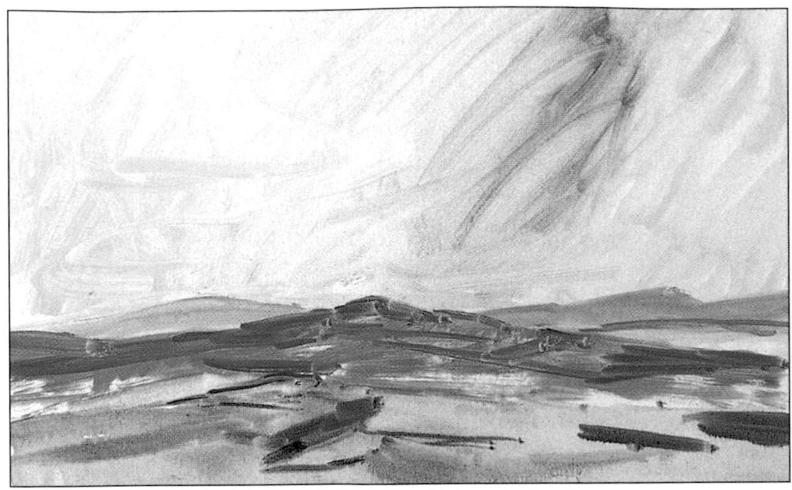

2

To enhance the mellow warmth of the Italian landscape, the greens and yellows of the hills and fields are underpainted in their complementary colours – reds and blues, respectively. Using a medium filbert brush, paint the most distant hills with a thin wash of pale pink mixed from cadmium red, white and a touch of cadmium yellow. Strengthen the mix with more red and less white for the nearer hills. Underpaint the wheat fields with cobalt blue, then map in the dark trees and hedges with a mix of burnt sienna and cadmium red.

3

With a thin mix of ultramarine and white, block in the patches of blue sky and roughly outline the masses of cumulus cloud. Again, use the flattened belly of the bristle head to make broad, energetic strokes, letting the brush marks convey a sense of movement.

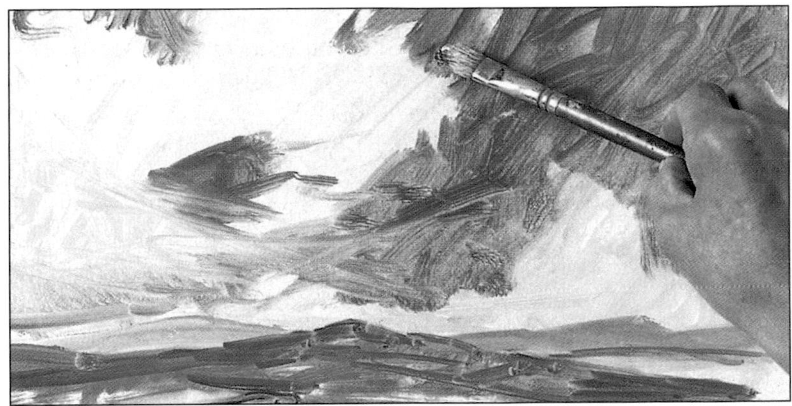

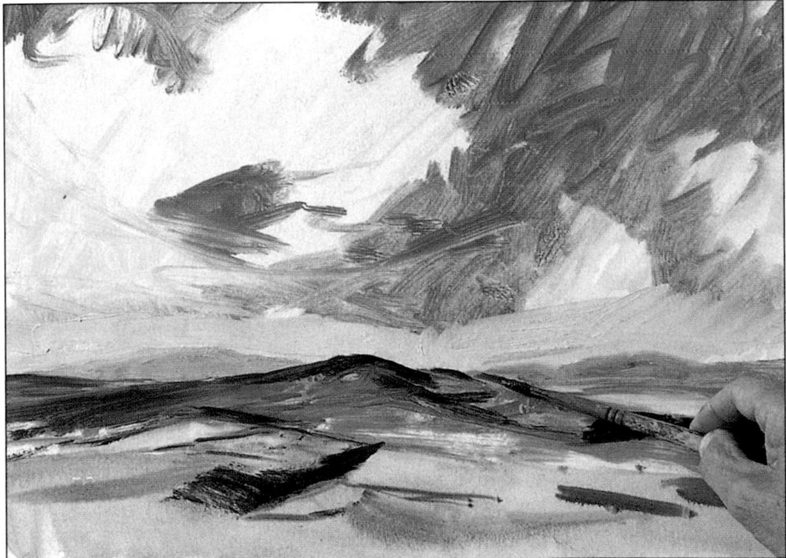

4

Now work on the distant sky and hills to create a sense of the land and sky disappearing over the horizon. Mix a cool, soft green from cobalt green and white. Drag this over the furthest hills, letting the pink undercolour show through the green. Then mix a soft pinkish yellow from cadmium yellow, white and a touch of cadmium red and paint a narrow band of this right along the horizon line, just above the hills, to create the effect of misty light in the distance.

With a small round brush, mix a dark green from viridian and yellow ochre and define the trees and hedgerows between the fields, dragging the paint on with the side of the brush.

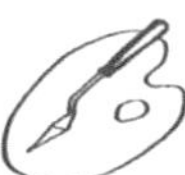

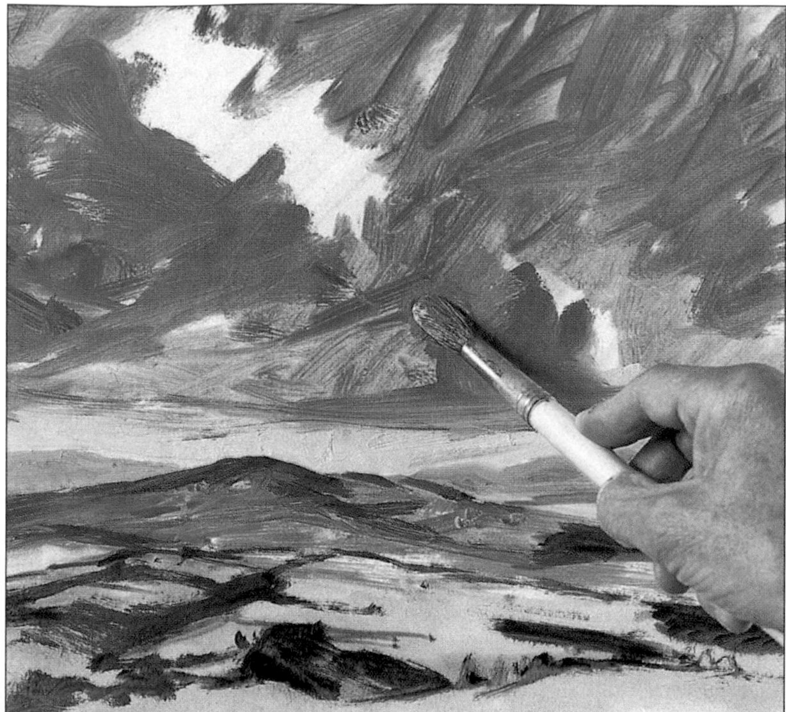

5

Mix ultramarine and white, then add touches of burnt sienna and yellow ochre until you have a warm grey. Paint the shadow sides of the clouds with a large round brush, scrubbing the paint on with vigorous brushmarks that give a sense of movement. Always remember to keep your cloud shadows consistent with the direction of the light – here the sun is at the top right, so the cloud shadows are on the left of the cloud masses.

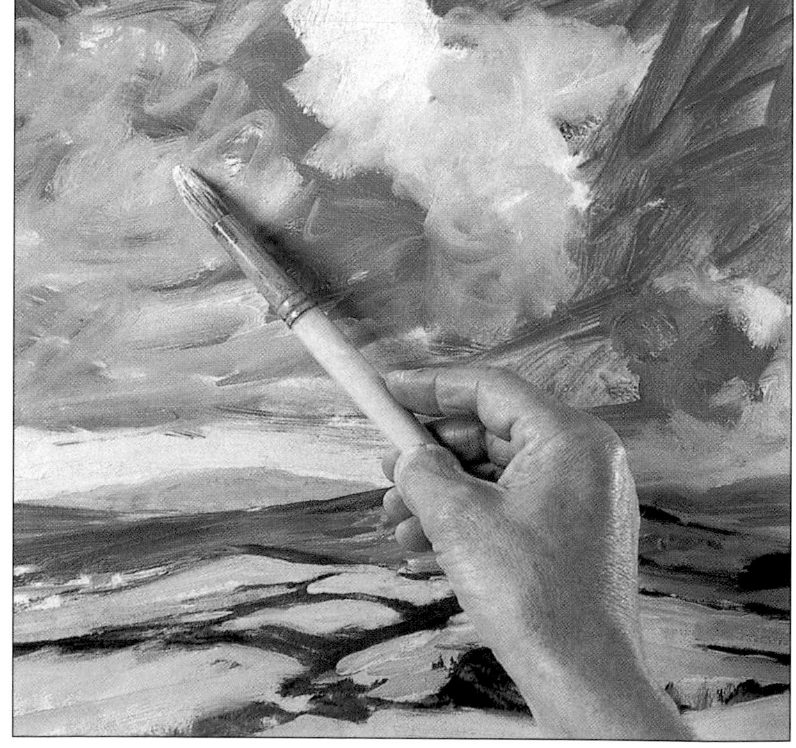

6

Paint the patchwork of wheatfields using a medium filbert brush and varied mixtures of cadmium yellow and yellow ochre, plus cadmium lemon for the brightly lit fields. With a large round brush, paint the lit areas of cloud by working into the grey clouds with a warm, creamy white mixed from white, cadmium yellow, cadmium red and yellow ochre. Use slightly thicker paint and scrubby, scumbled strokes to create the effect of towering heaps of cloud, particularly in the foreground.

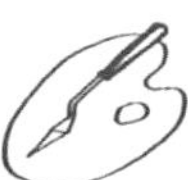

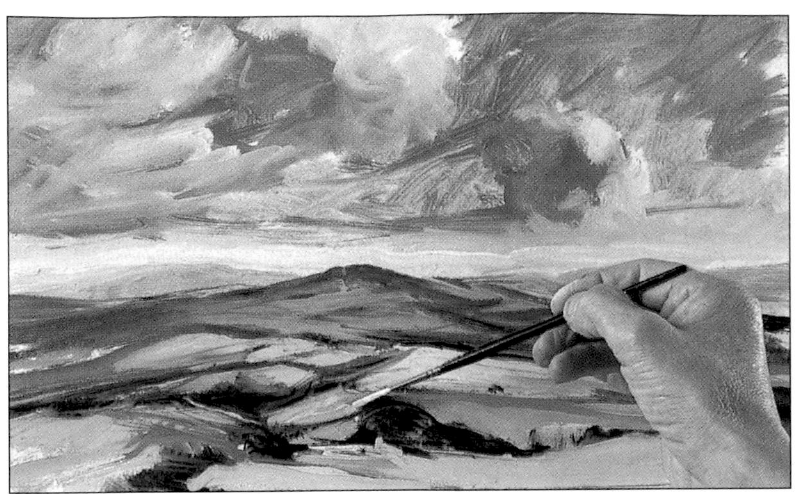

7

Neutralize the yellow mixes with some grey mixed earlier and, with a medium filbert brush, darken areas where the clouds cast shadows onto the land. Add definition to fields and hedgerows using paint that is fluid, but with body. (Here a sable lettering brush, which is round but with a flat point and long bristles is used to give smooth, fluid lines. If you don't have one, a small round soft-hair brush will do.) For the hedgerows, use a dark mix of viridian, ultramarine and raw umber. Bring the nearest fields forward with mixtures of cadmium red, yellow and lemon.

8

The sky appears paler and cooler as it recedes towards the horizon. To recreate this effect, mix three shades of blue on your palette and then blend them together on the canvas with a medium filbert brush so that they merge gently into one another. Start at the top with ultramarine and white, then introduce cerulean and white as you work downwards. Near the horizon, use white with hints of cadmium yellow and red added.

Scumble a mixture of white and a hint of yellow ochre onto the sunlit tops of the clouds with rough, scrubby marks.

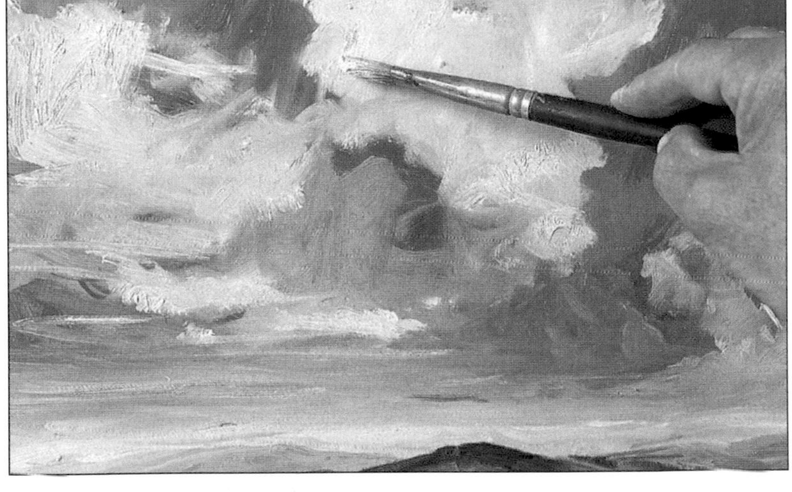

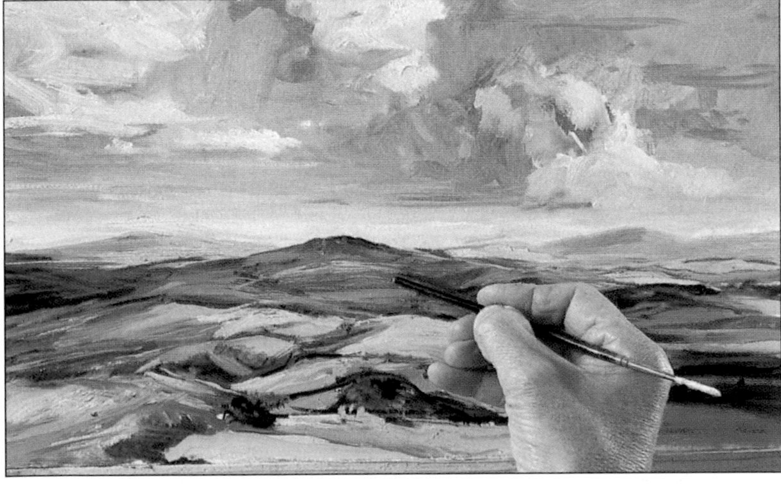

9

Finally, tie the painting together by echoing some of the sky colours in the land below, adding touches of ultramarine and white, and yellow ochre and white to the fields. Strengthen the shadows on the fields with dark greens. Try not to overwork the painting – keep it fresh and lively. If the paint becomes too opaque and dense, you can scratch into it with the end of a paintbrush to reclaim the colour of the underpainting, as shown here.

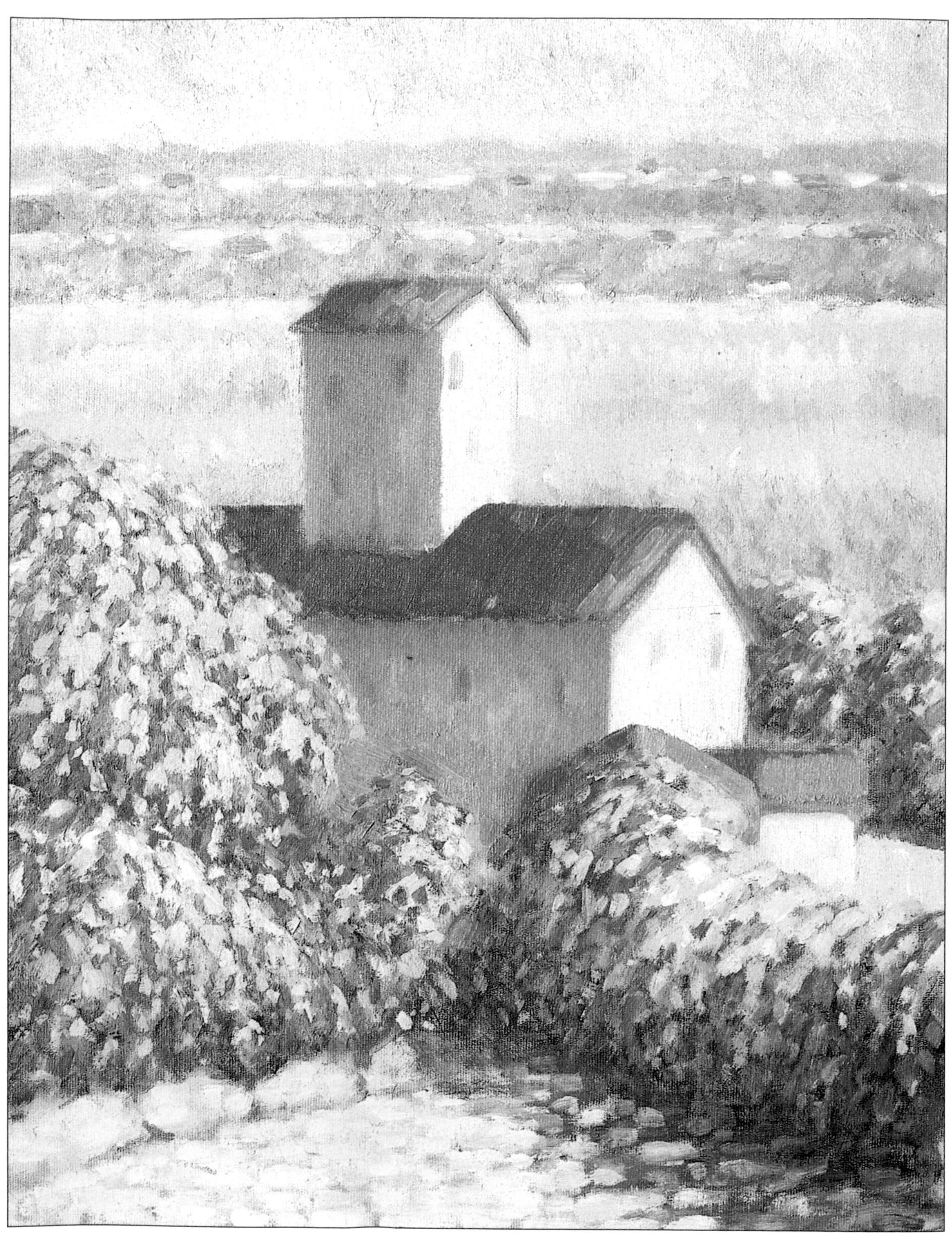

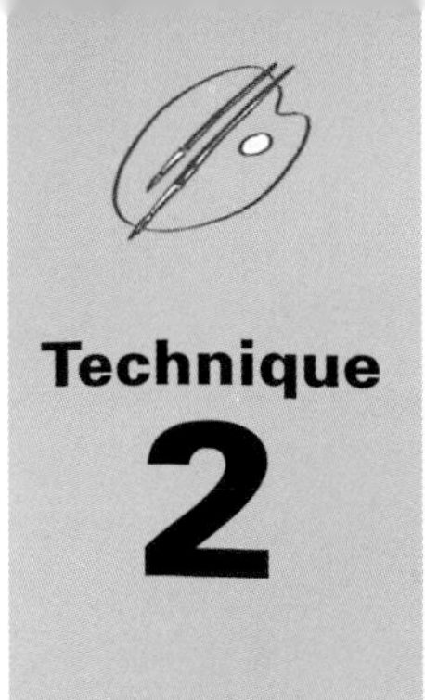

IMPASTO

Impasto painting exploits to the full the rich, buttery consistency of oil paint. Because thickly impasted paint retains the strokes made with the brush or knife, the marks produced are an expressive element in the finished work and help to produce a pleasing, tactile surface.

The impasto technique is often used in direct, "alla prima" painting, as the thick paint and rapid brushstrokes allow the picture to be completed quickly and spontaneously. To capture an impression of intense heat and sunlight on this Italian landscape the artist worked quickly and freely, blocking in the broad forms and areas of colour with thin paint before starting to build up the overall image with thick, rich impastos. With this thicker paint, the marks of the brush can be used to describe and follow form as well as to indicate the texture of particular areas. Compare, for example, the slurred strokes of creamy paint used for the distant fields with the heavier, stippled marks used to suggest the foliage in the foreground. The thicker strokes in the foreground bring that area forward in the picture plane, pushing back the distant landscape and increasing the sense of recession.

Derek Daniells
Monastery, Tuscany
46 x 36cm (18 x 14in)

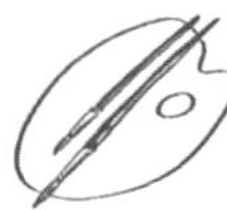

The Impasto Technique

When oil paint is applied thickly and liberally so that it protrudes from the surface of the support and retains the marks and ridges left by the brush, it is called impasto.

Some pictures are painted entirely in impasto, the thick paint and descriptive brushwork creating a lively, energetic surface. In others, impasto is reserved for certain areas such as details and highlights, or it is used to accentuate the focal point of the picture. Vincent van Gogh exploited the expressive potential of impasto in his paintings, often squeezing the paint straight from the tube and "sculpting" it into generous sweeps and swirls. In contrast, Rembrandt mainly used thin paint and reserved small but telling strokes of thick, light-reflecting paint to show the highlights on skin tones, jewellery and clothing in his portraits.

Paint for impasto work can be applied with a brush or a painting knife. The paint should be of a buttery consistency and may be used straight from the tube or diluted with a small amount of turpentine or medium so that it is malleable, yet thick enough to stand proud of the support.

Using heavy applications of oil paint in this way can be expensive, but fortunately thickening mediums specially for use with impasto work are available; they bulk out the paint without increasing the drying time.

Bristle brushes are best for impasto work because they hold a lot of paint. Load the brush with plenty of colour and dab it generously onto the canvas, teasing it into peaks and ridges or spreading it out in luscious bands that reflect a lot of light.

Monastery, Tuscany

Materials and Equipment

• SHEET OF PRIMED CANVAS OR BOARD • OIL COLOURS: CADMIUM RED, CADMIUM YELLOW, YELLOW OCHRE, LEMON YELLOW, NAPLES YELLOW, CERULEAN, PRUSSIAN BLUE, COBALT BLUE, COBALT VIOLET, BURNT SIENNA AND TITANIUM WHITE • SMALL ROUND SOFT-HAIR BRUSH • LARGE, MEDIUM AND SMALL FLAT BRISTLE BRUSHES • PAINTING KNIFE • SOFT CLOTH • DISTILLED TURPENTINE • PURIFIED LINSEED OIL • ALKYD MEDIUM

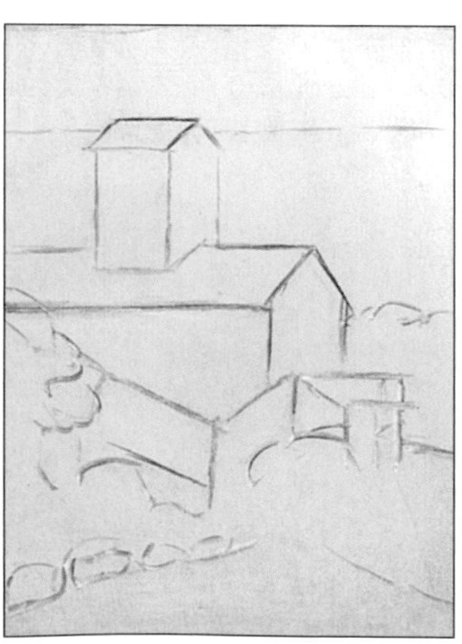

1

Prepare your canvas 24 hours in advance by tinting it with a wash of yellow ochre thinly diluted with turpentine. Apply the paint with a large flat brush, then rub with a soft cloth to eliminate the brushstrokes and leave a smooth surface. When the canvas is dry, use a small round soft-hair brush to sketch in the main outlines of the composition with a thin mix of burnt sienna. (If you feel hesitant about drawing with paint, use charcoal instead.)

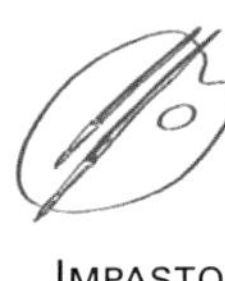

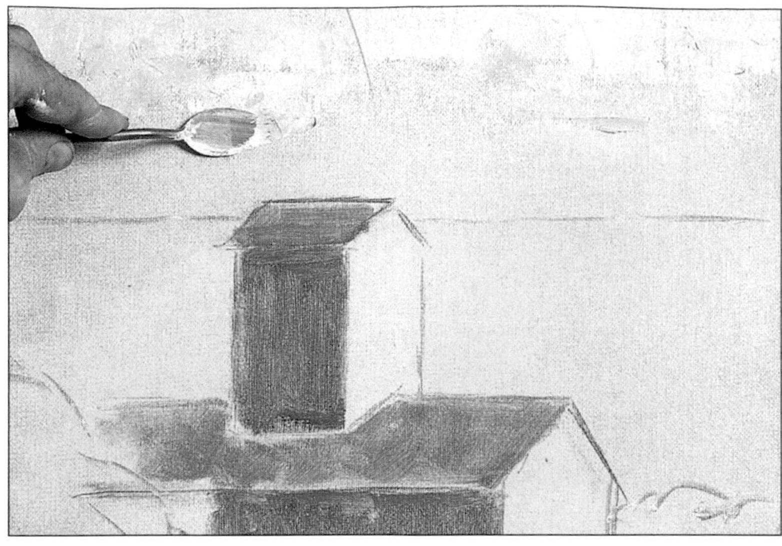

2

Block in the terracotta roofs of the monastery with a thinly diluted mix of cadmium red and cadmium yellow, applied with a medium-sized flat bristle brush. Mix a cool brown for the walls in shadow using yellow ochre, cobalt violet and a touch of cobalt blue. Using slightly thicker paint now, mix a pale blue from cobalt blue and titanium white and block in the sky and distant fields with roughly scumbled strokes applied with a painting knife.

3

Mix a pale, cool green from cerulean, lemon yellow and white. Apply bands of this colour across the background with a medium-sized flat bristle brush to indicate the green fields and trees in the distance. Make the bands narrower and closer together the nearer they are to the horizon, to suggest perspective and distance.

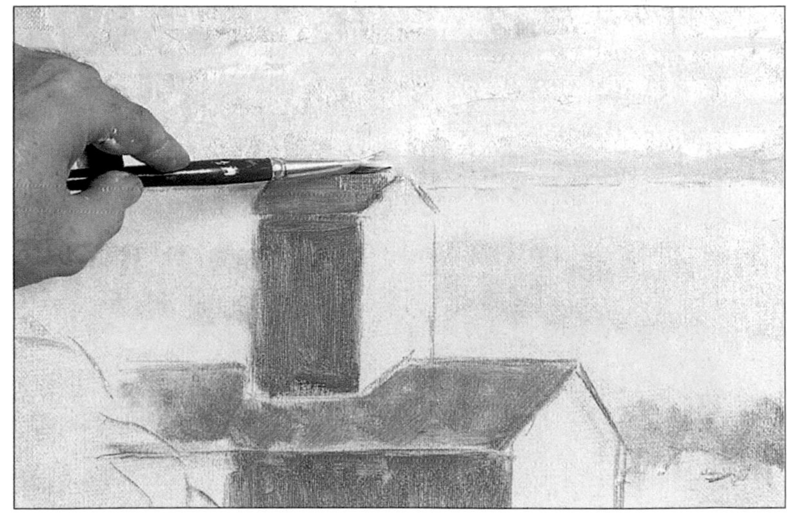

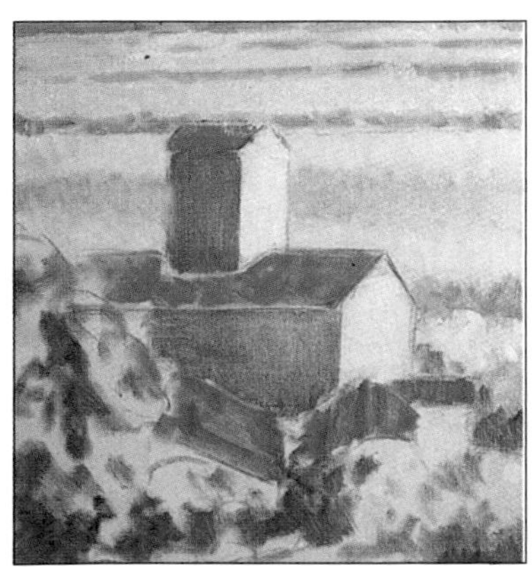

4

Add further bands of colour in the distance, this time using a mix of cobalt blue, cobalt violet and white to suggest the hazy, bluish light on the far horizon. Soften and "knock back" the distant landscape by lightly feathering over the wet colours with a dry brush. Mix a thin wash of Prussian blue and rough in the darks in the foreground trees and foliage. Use a fairly dry brush and scumble the paint on lightly so that it dries quickly.

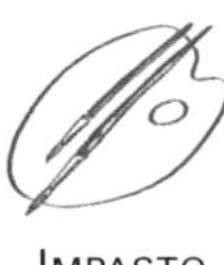

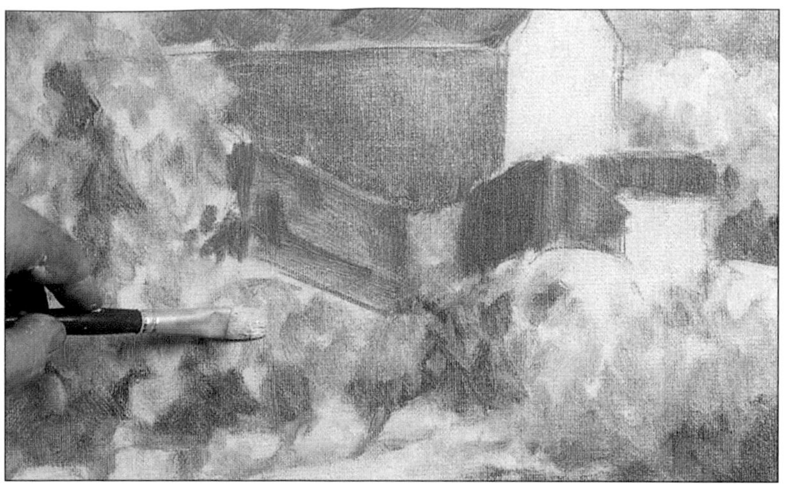

5

Continue blocking in the broad areas of light and shadow in the foreground foliage. Mix cerulean, lemon yellow and white for the warm, sunlit greens and Prussian blue and white for the cool, bluish tints. Use similar colours to indicate the cobbled road. The paint at this block-in stage is still quite thin and "dry"; this will allow you to build up a rich impasto on top in the later stages without creating an unpleasant, churned-up surface.

6

Mix cadmium red, cadmium yellow and a hint of burnt sienna and block in the shadowed parts of the roofs. Work into the outline of the tree on the left with loose, broken strokes using a small flat brush to give the effect of rooftops glimpsed through the foliage.

Mix Naples yellow and a tiny touch of cadmium red and block in the sunlit walls of the monastery. Mix a warm grey from yellow ochre and cobalt violet and indicate the windows, painting each one with a single stroke of the small flat brush.

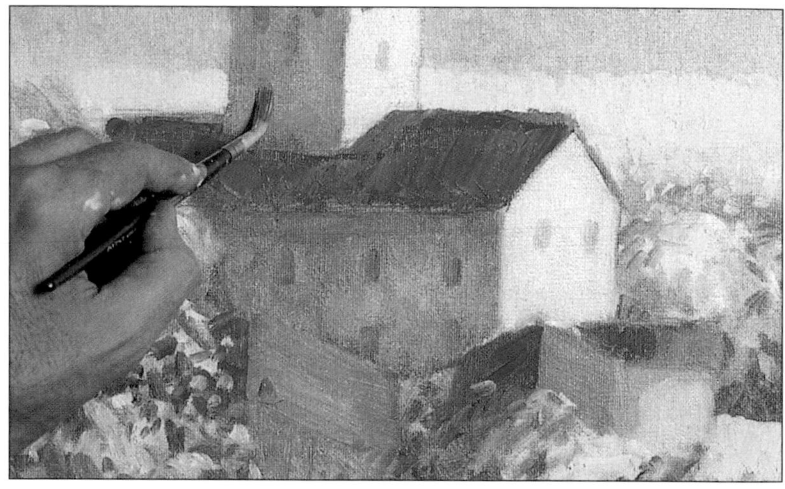

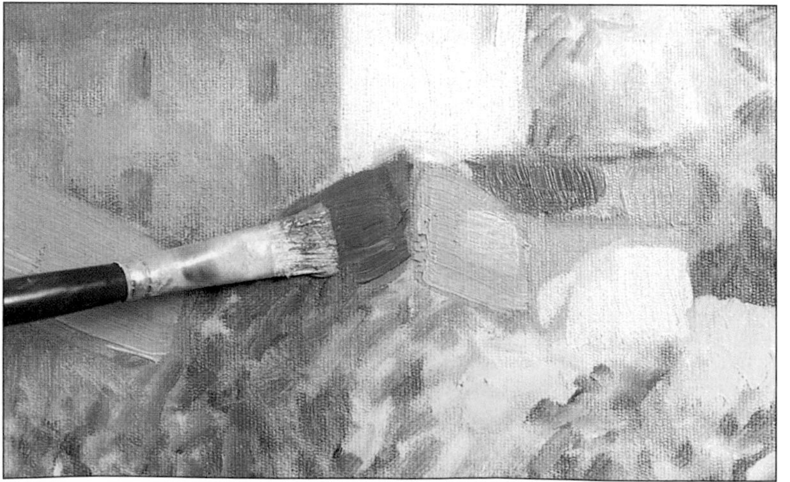

7

Begin to build up a thicker impasto now. Work over the roofs with the same colours used in the thin underlayers, this time mixing the paint with a little medium to give it a buttery consistency that emphasizes the impasto. Lay on the colours with a well-loaded medium-sized flat brush, letting the marks of the brush show so that they add texture and interest to the paint surface.

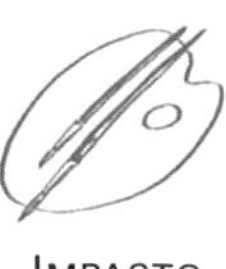

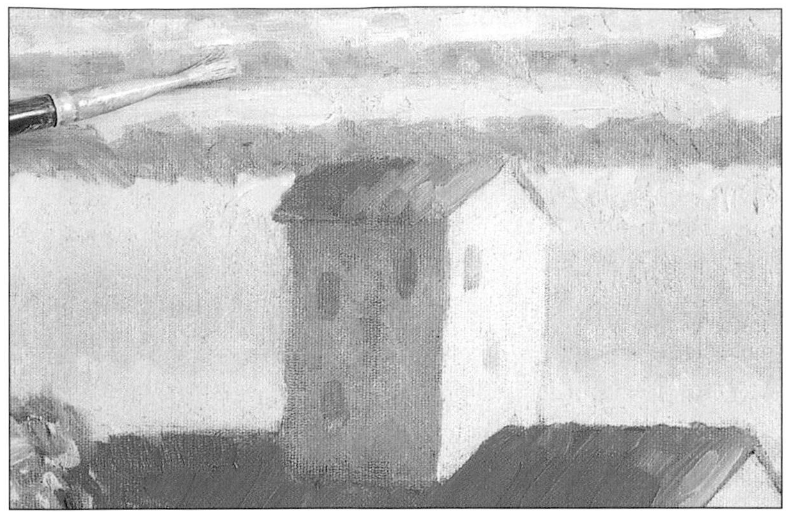

8

Add more detail to the distant landscape, using a small flat brush to apply small, broken touches of thick colour that suggest the shimmering haze around the fields, houses and trees under the hot Mediterranean sun. Mix cerulean and white for the sky, then add touches of cobalt blue and cobalt violet and work over the lines of the trees with lightly scumbled strokes. Paint the corn fields with varied tones mixed from yellow ochre, Naples yellow, cadmium yellow and white. Suggest the rooftops glimpsed between the trees with cadmium red, cadmium yellow and white.

9

Returning to the foreground, continue to build up texture and define the individual clumps of foliage with small strokes and dabs of thick paint worked in different directions. Emphasize the dark, shadowy tones by adding touches of cobalt blue and cobalt violet to the greens. For the sunlit foliage mix lemon yellow and white.

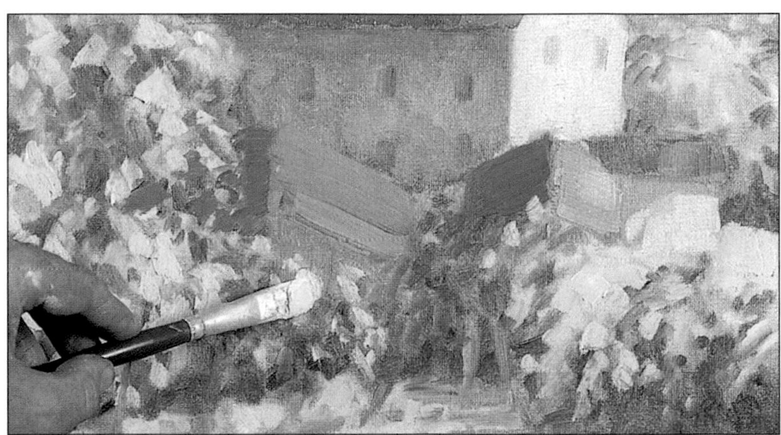

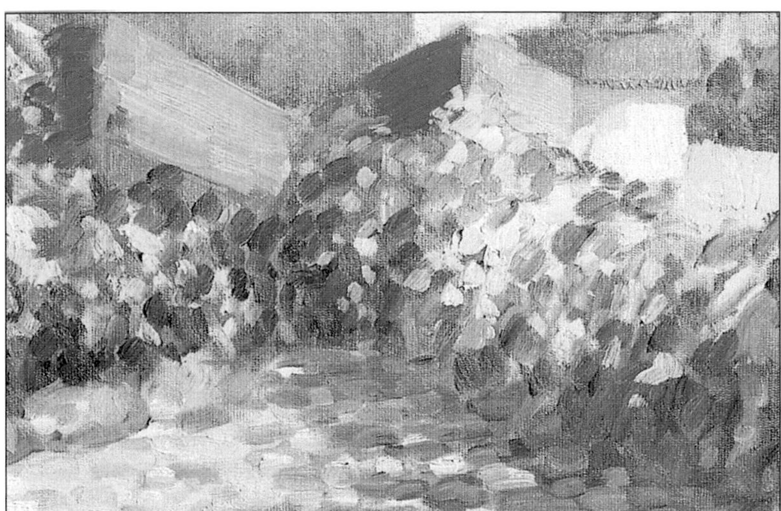

10

Now work on the cobbled road, again using short strokes and dabs of colour but laying them on horizontally. To show dappled sunlight, use mixes of Prussian blue, cobalt blue and cadmium red, with a little white for the shadows cast by the hanging foliage. For the sunlit areas, use varied tones of cadmium red, yellow ochre and white.

If you find it difficult to apply fresh paint over wet paint without muddying the colours, allow the painting to dry off for a day or two. Continue building tones in the foliage with small strokes of broken colour, adding more detail and depth.

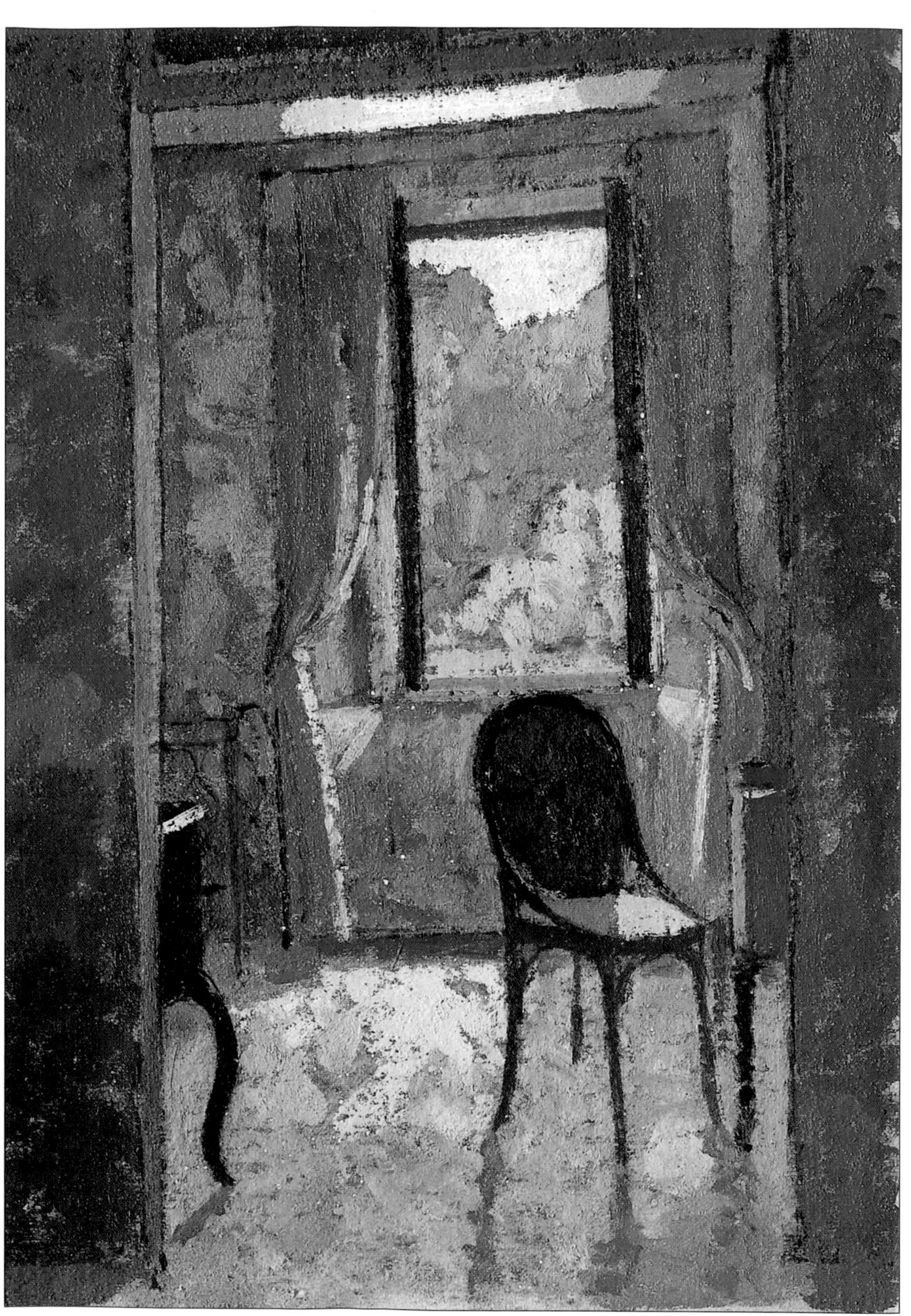

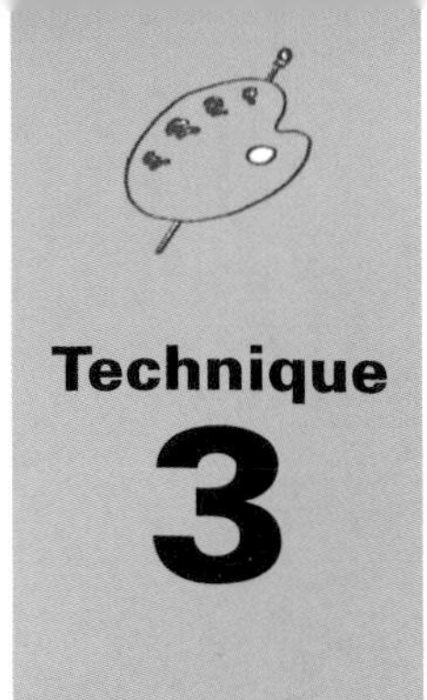

Technique

3

Using a Toned Ground

There are times when it is appropriate to paint directly onto a white canvas, but most oil painters prefer to tint the ground with a colour that sets a key for the painting. In this interior scene small patches of the umber ground remain exposed throughout the picture, their neutral colour helping to unify the composition and enhancing the impression of soft, cool light penetrating the room from the window behind.

It is important that the toned ground is completely dry before you paint over it. An oil ground usually takes around 24 hours to dry thoroughly, but you can save time by using acrylic paint instead. This dries in minutes, allowing you to overpaint in oils straight away. The other great advantage is that acrylic paint acts as both a sealing agent and a primer, so you don't need to size and prime the support as you would for oils. (Never apply acrylics on a ground that has been sized and primed for oils, however, as this may lead to eventual cracking of the paint film.)

~

James Horton

French Interior

25 x 18cm (10 x 7in)

~

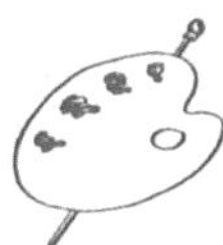

Toning The Ground

A primed white ground can be rather intimidating to begin painting on and can also give you a false "reading" of the colours and tones you apply, especially in the early stages when you've no other colours to relate them to. The way to avoid this problem is by toning the ground with a wash of neutral colour prior to painting.

A toned ground provides a more sympathetic surface to work on, acting as a unifying mid-tone against which you can judge your lights and darks more accurately. Generally it is best to choose a subtle, muted colour somewhere between the lightest and the darkest colours in the painting. Diluted earth colours such as Venetian red, raw sienna or burnt umber work very well, as do soft greys and greens. Some artists prefer to begin with a ground that will harmonize with the dominant colour of the subject; for instance, a soft pink or yellow ground for an evening sky. Others prefer a ground that provides a quiet contrast, such as a warm red-brown that will enhance the greens used in a landscape.

To tone the ground, dilute the paint to a thin, "orange juice" consistency with turpentine or white (mineral) spirit and apply it freely and vigorously over the white priming with a household decorating brush or a rag soaked in turpentine. If you prefer a smooth, more regular effect, work over the wet paint with a damp, lint-free rag to even out the brushmarks.

French Interior

Materials and Equipment

• SHEET OF PRIMED HARDBOARD OR MDF • OIL COLOURS: CADMIUM RED, ALIZARIN CRIMSON, VERMILION, CADMIUM ORANGE, CADMIUM YELLOW, YELLOW OCHRE, LEMON YELLOW, TERRE VERTE, FRENCH ULTRAMARINE, COBALT BLUE, RAW UMBER, BURNT SIENNA, TITANIUM WHITE AND IVORY BLACK • 25MM (1IN) DECORATING BRUSH • OIL-PAINTING BRUSHES: SMALL SABLE OR SYNTHETIC, MEDIUM-SIZED ROUND BRISTLE, SMALL ROUND BRISTLE, SABLE OR SYNTHETIC RIGGER • PURE LINSEED OIL • DAMMAR VARNISH • DISTILLED TURPENTINE

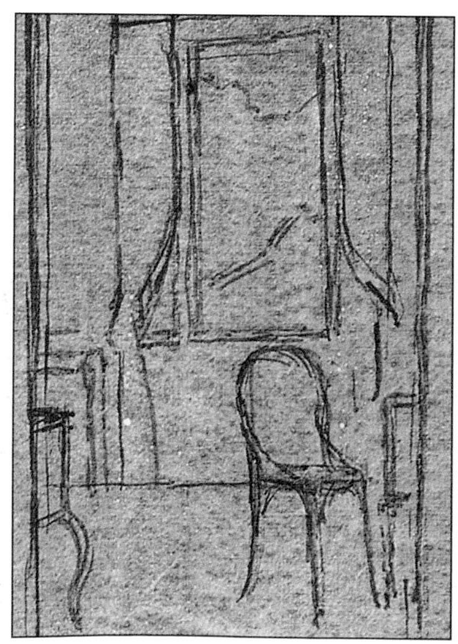

1

Prepare the toned ground about 24 hours in advance – it must be thoroughly dry before starting to paint. Mix raw umber with a little French ultramarine and dilute it to a thin consistency with turpentine. Apply this all over the board using a 25mm (1in) decorating brush.

Sketch in the main outlines of the composition using thinly diluted French ultramarine and a small sable brush.

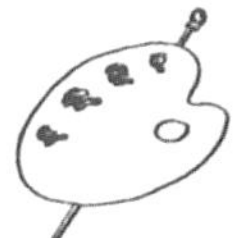

2

From this point, mix your colours with a medium consisting of linseed oil, dammar varnish and turpentine. Using a medium size round bristle brush, rough in the walls around the open doorway with a warm brown mixed from burnt sienna, raw umber and titanium white. Vary the proportions of these colours and add touches of lemon yellow and terre verte to create subtle shifts in tone and temperature. Don't apply the paint in a flat wash but scuff it on with broken strokes, letting the ground colour show through.

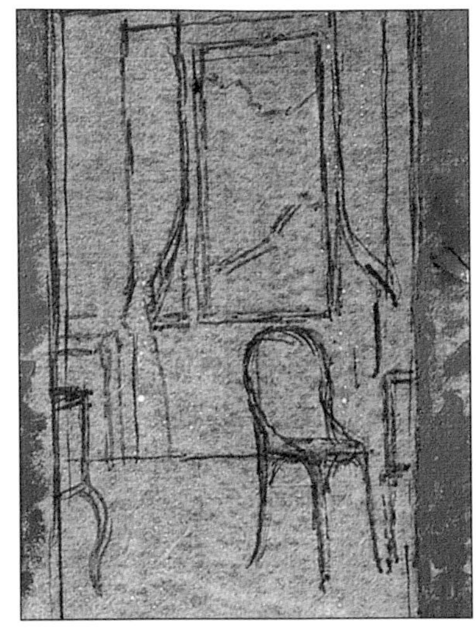

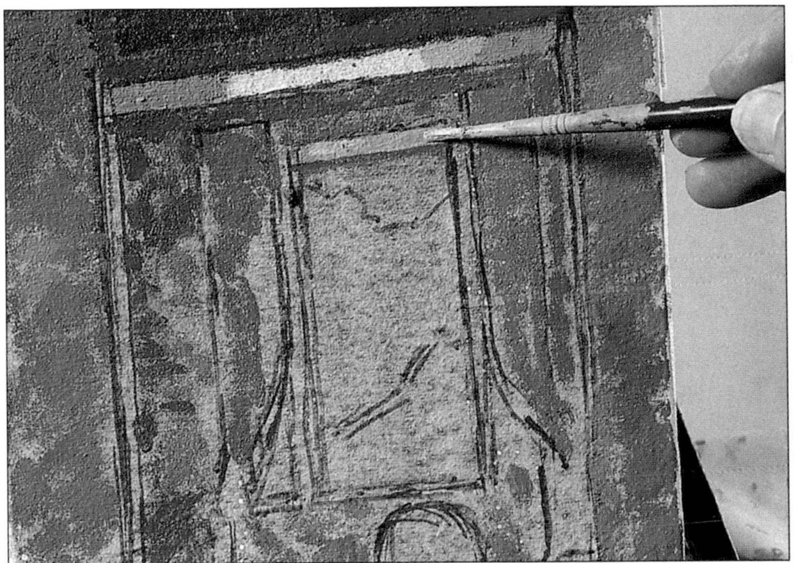

3

Use the same colour and the same technique to paint the curtains at the window. Start to block in the wall around the window using loose strokes of ultramarine greyed with a little yellow ochre, interspersed with strokes of greenish grey mixed from raw umber and yellow ochre. Use a smaller round brush to paint the bright reflection on the ceiling with white and a mix of cobalt blue, alizarin crimson and white. For the pink strip at the top of the window, mix vermilion and white.

4

Now paint the view glimpsed through the window. Mix white and a tiny drop of alizarin crimson for the sky, then suggest the trees with varied mixtures of lemon yellow, terre verte, cobalt blue and white. Use a greater proportion of blue and green for the darker tones and more yellow and white for the lighter tones. Paint the window frame with raw umber and the sill with cobalt blue, alizarin crimson and white.

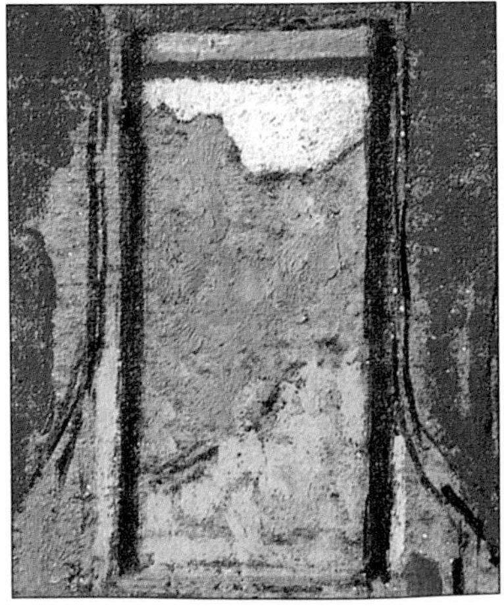

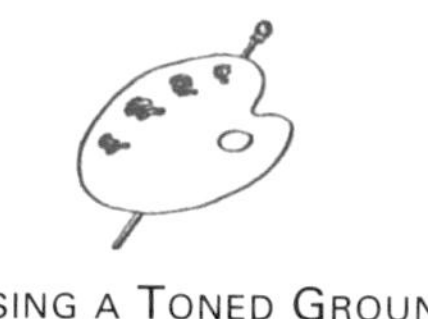

5

Add more colour to the curtains with strokes of raw umber and white. Loosely paint the chair back with a mix of French ultramarine, yellow ochre and a little ivory black. Then suggest the reflective surface of the floor using mainly white, broken with a little burnt sienna and alizarin crimson. Apply the colour in loose patches, letting the ground colour form the mid-tone.

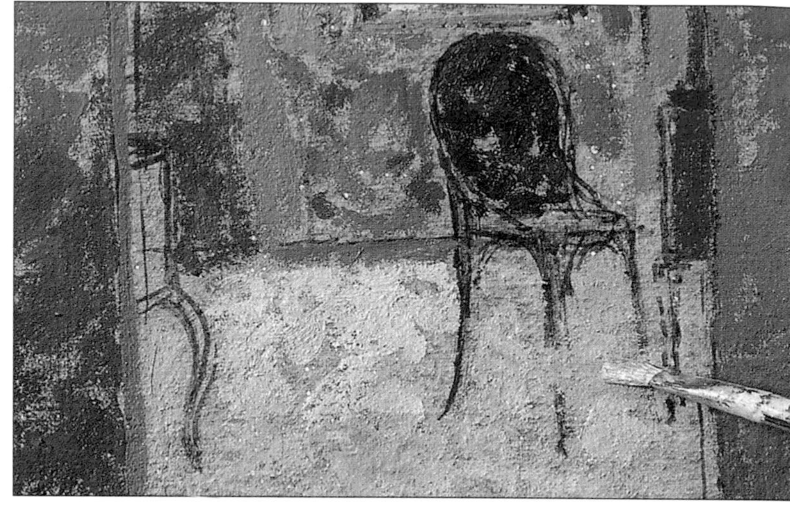

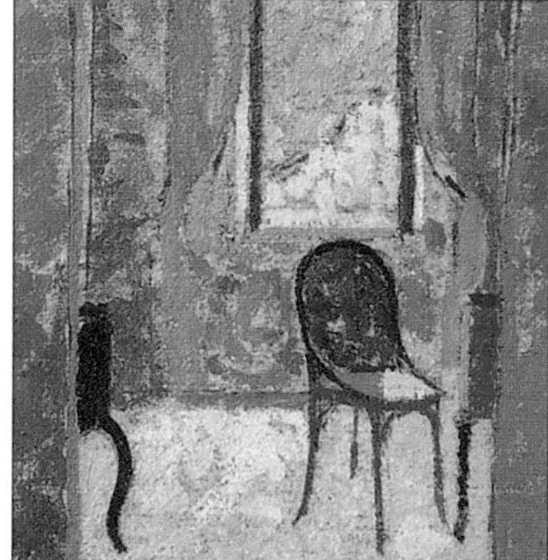

6

Paint the pieces of furniture glimpsed through the doorway, using black, cadmium red and alizarin crimson for the dark wood and burnt sienna and raw umber for the lighter wood of the chair legs. For the chair seat, mix white, ultramarine and alizarin. Use the same mixture used on the back, lightened with more white, for the shadow on the chair seat.

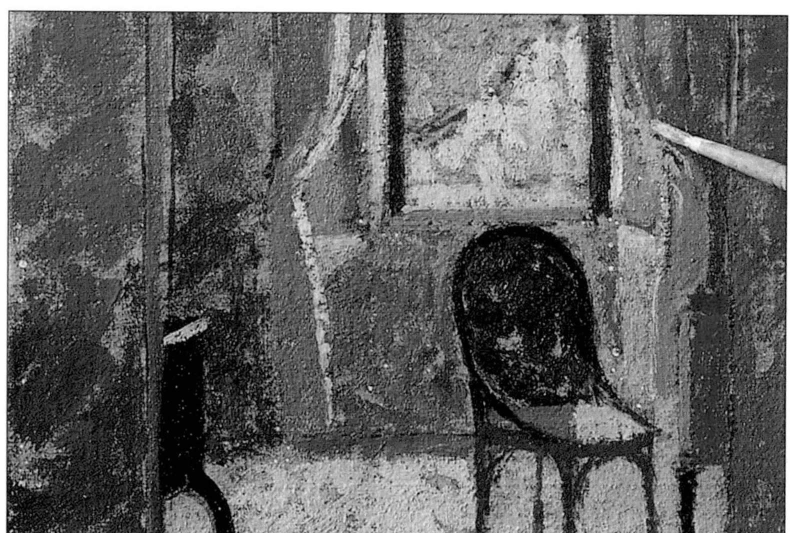

7

Lighten the tone of the wall beneath the window with a warm grey mixed from ultramarine, yellow ochre, white and a hint of black, loosely applied over the underlayer of brown. Block in the base of the shutters with vermilion and white, then add warm highlights on the curtains where the light shines through the fabric, using a small round brush and mixtures of cadmium orange, cadmium yellow and white.

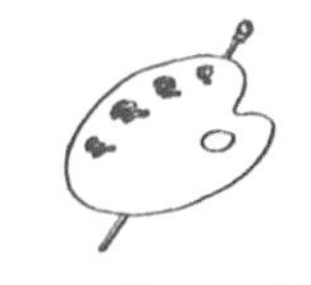

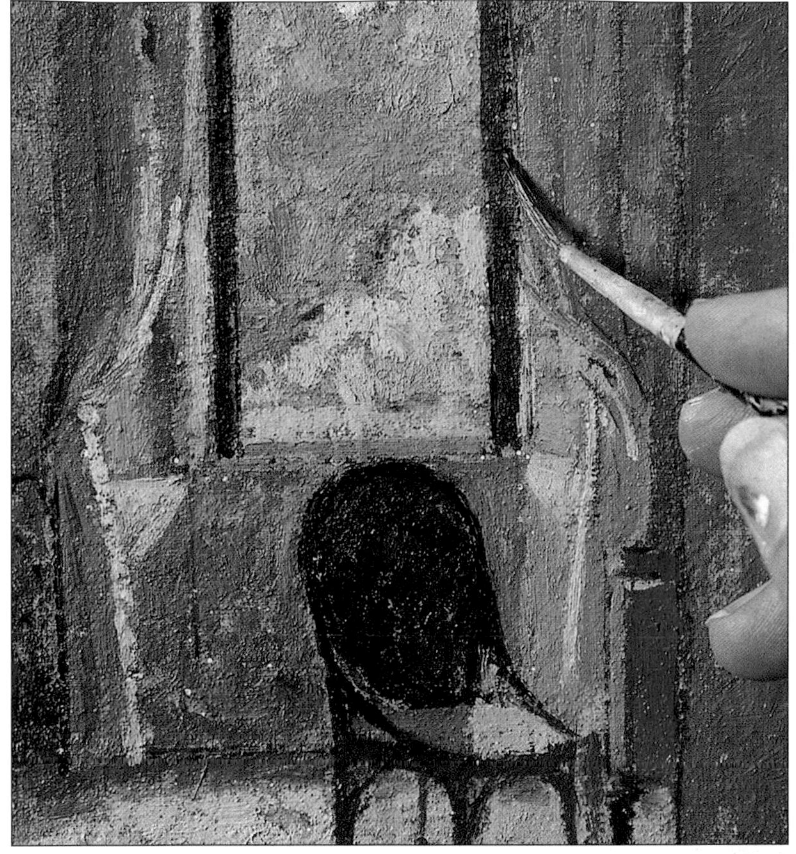

8

Now that the close tones of the interior are established, you can adjust the brighter tones of the sunlit view outside to the correct pitch. Here the greens of the hills and trees need to be lighter and cooler to push them back in space. Mix cobalt, alizarin and white for the distant hills, then block in the medium-toned foliage with varied mixtures of white, lemon yellow, terre verte and a hint of cobalt blue. Use a rigger brush, which has long, flexible hairs, to define the edge of the window frame with a very thin line of black.

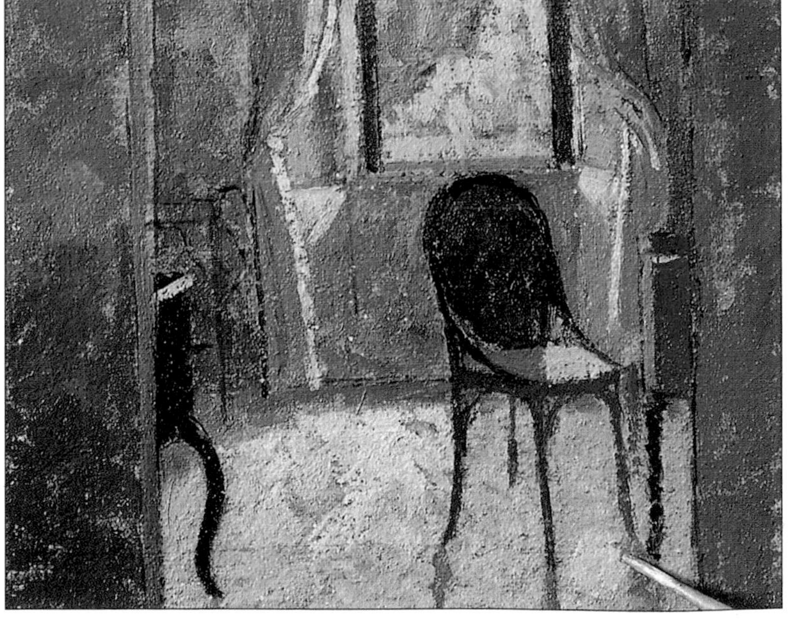

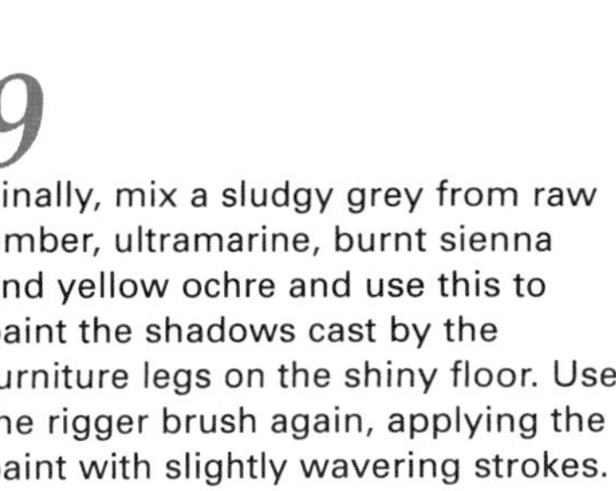

9

Finally, mix a sludgy grey from raw umber, ultramarine, burnt sienna and yellow ochre and use this to paint the shadows cast by the furniture legs on the shiny floor. Use the rigger brush again, applying the paint with slightly wavering strokes.

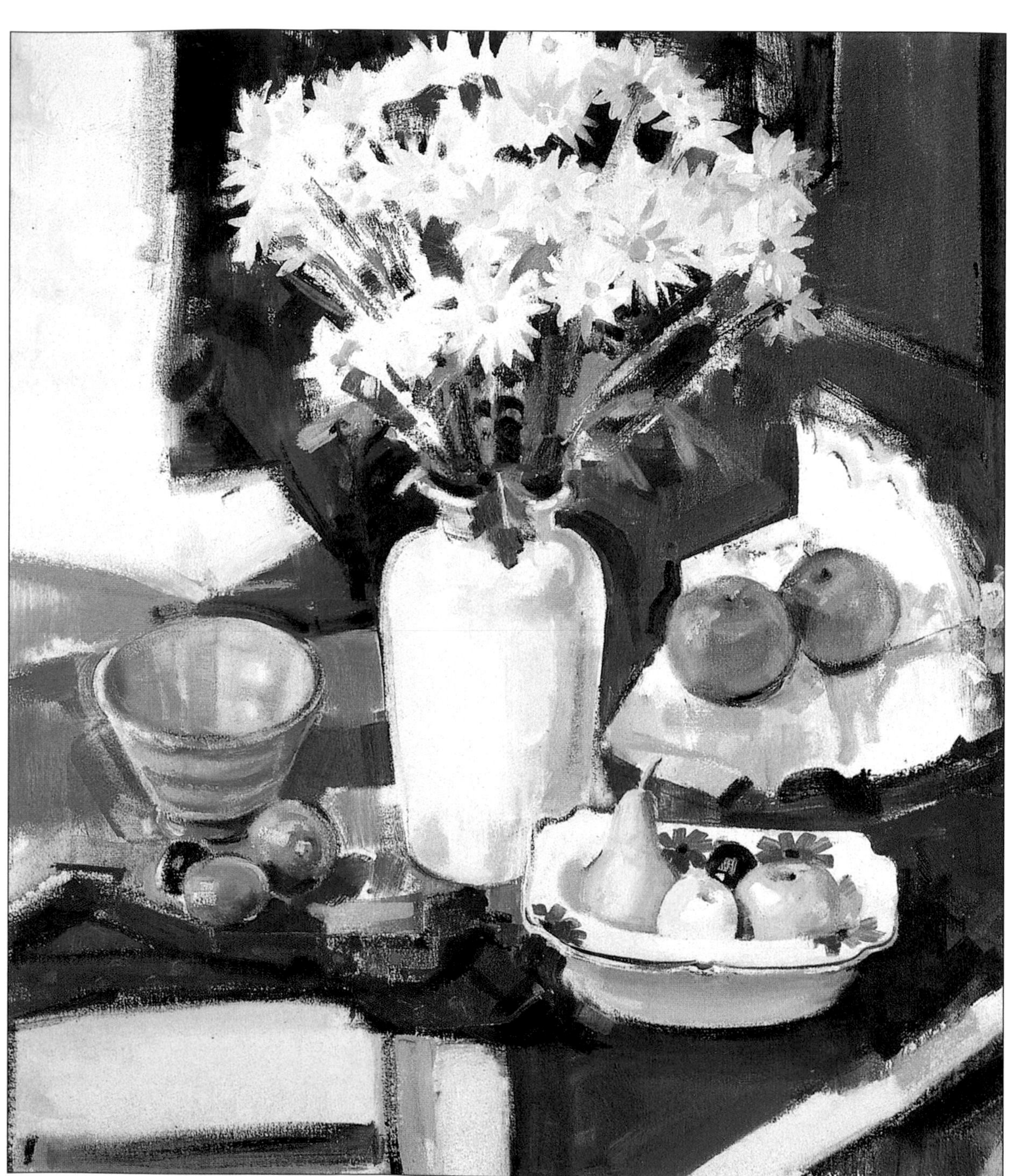

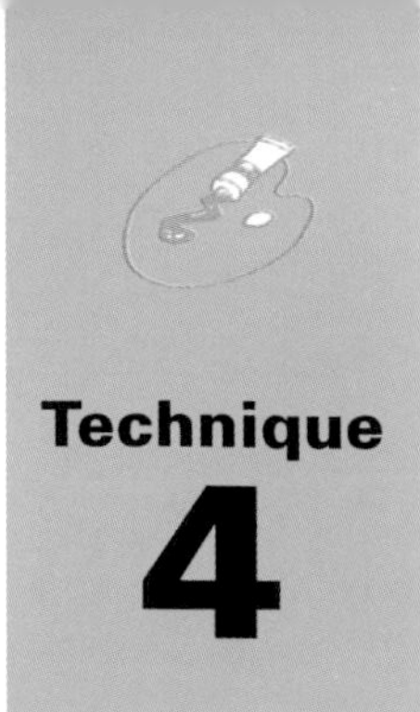

Technique

4

WORKING "FAT OVER LEAN"

Painting "from lean to fat" is the time-honoured method of building up an oil painting in layers, especially when mixing the paint with turpentine and linseed oil. Put simply, this means using thin, "lean" paint in the early stages and gradually increasing the oil content in the upper layers. Along with sound preparation of the canvas or board, this method can prevent one of the problems associated with oil painting – the possible cracking of the paint surface.

For this still-life painting the artist started out with very thin paint diluted to an "orange juice" consistency with turpentine. This allows the white primer to shine through and give luminosity to the succeeding colours. Because the paint was so lean it dried quickly, allowing further layers to be applied almost immediately. The artist then continued working with layers of increasingly thick paint, building up depth and luminosity in the colours.

Peter Graham
Bouquet and Fruit
63½ x 56cm (25 x 22in)

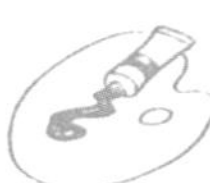

WORKING "FAT OVER LEAN"

"Fat" describes paint that comes straight from the tube or is mixed with an oily medium. "Lean" describes paint that has been thinned with turpentine or white (mineral) spirit. The golden rule in oil painting, particularly when building up a painting in layers, is always to paint fat over lean. If lean paint is applied over fat, you could find that your painting begins to crack eventually – something that may take weeks, months or even years to become apparent.

The reason for this has to do with the way oil paints dry. The oils in the paint do not evaporate; they oxidize and harden on exposure to the air. This process can often take several months, and during this time the paint surface first expands, then shrinks a little. Fat paint is more flexible than lean paint, and takes longer to dry. It follows, then, that if lean paint is applied over fat, the top layer will dry before the lower, more oily one, has finished shrinking. The movement in the lower layers may cause the hardened lean paint on top to crack and even flake off.

Thus, when painting in layers, you should begin with an underpainting that is thinner and faster-drying than subsequent layers. For example, start with paint thinned with turpentine or a fast-drying alkyd medium. The next layer may consist of either undiluted tube paint, or paint mixed with turpentine and a little oil. Any successive layers may contain either the same or increasing amounts of oil, but they should not contain less oil.

Generally speaking, the *alla prima* method – completing the painting in one session with a single layer of opaque paint – presents fewer problems. When paint is worked wet-into-wet, the danger of cracking is considerably less because the paint films dry together rather than at different rates.

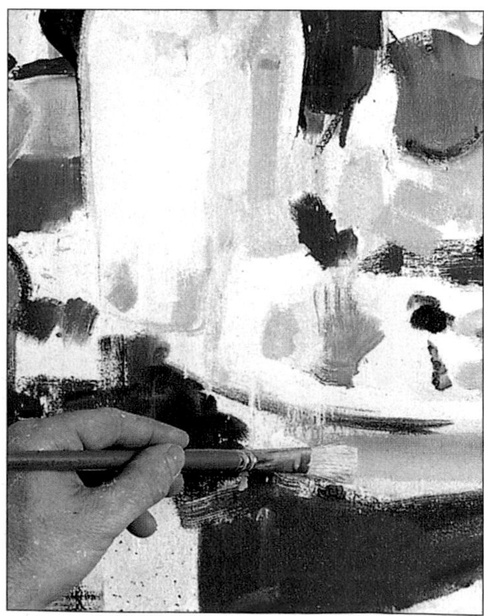

Preliminary underpainting in thin, lean paint provides a basis for the application of subsequent layers of oilier paint.

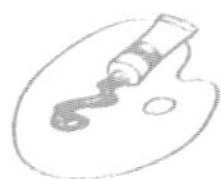

BOUQUET AND FRUIT

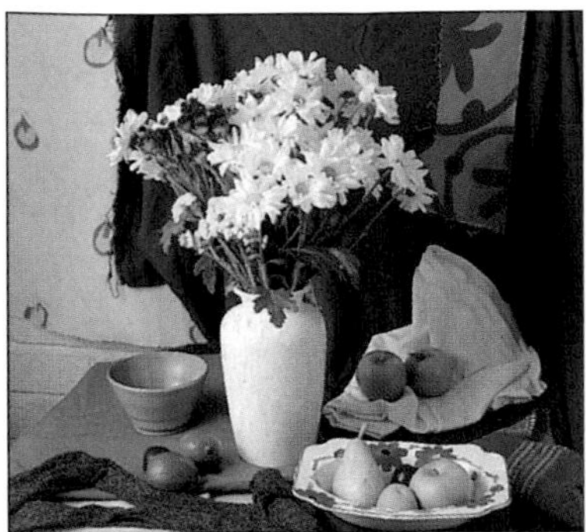

Left: In this still-life arrangement, gaily coloured cloths and scraps of fabric are carefully arranged to break up the picture space in an interesting way. The white flowers and objects act as a foil for the brighter hues.

Materials and Equipment

• SHEET OF STRETCHED AND PRIMED CANVAS • OIL COLOURS: ROSE MADDER DEEP, CADMIUM SCARLET, CADMIUM RED, PERMANENT MAGENTA, MAUVE, ALIZARIN CRIMSON, CADMIUM LEMON, CADMIUM YELLOW, NAPLES YELLOW LIGHT, COBALT TURQUOISE, EMERALD GREEN, PRUSSIAN GREEN, COBALT GREEN, VIRIDIAN, FRENCH ULTRAMARINE, COBALT BLUE, INDIGO, RAW SIENNA, RAW UMBER AND TITANIUM WHITE • BRISTLE BRUSHES: LARGE FLAT, MEDIUM LONG FLAT, SMALL LONG FLAT AND FAN BLENDER • SMALL ROUND SYNTHETIC-HAIR BRUSH • COTTON RAG • PALETTE KNIFE • DISTILLED TURPENTINE • PURIFIED LINSEED OIL

1

Position the main elements of the composition with loose, vigorous strokes, using paint thinly diluted with turpentine and applied with a large flat bristle brush. Use French ultramarine and indigo for the blue backcloth and cobalt turquoise for the small bowl on the left. Block in the limes and apples on either side of the white vase with emerald green, cobalt green and Prussian green and use the same colours for the flower foliage. Block in the vase itself with titanium white mixed with a little cadmium lemon, adding a hint of mauve on the shadow side.

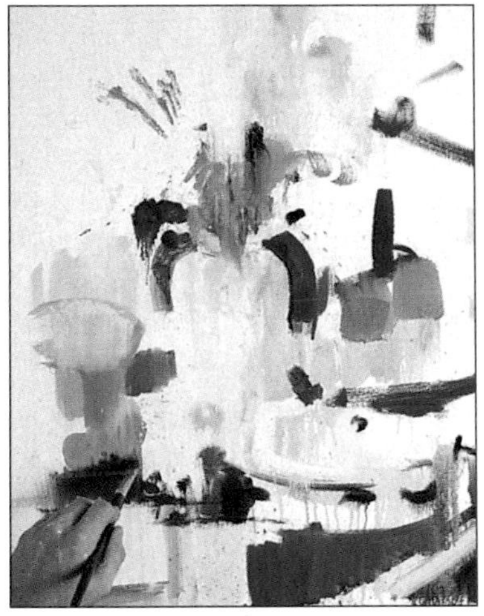

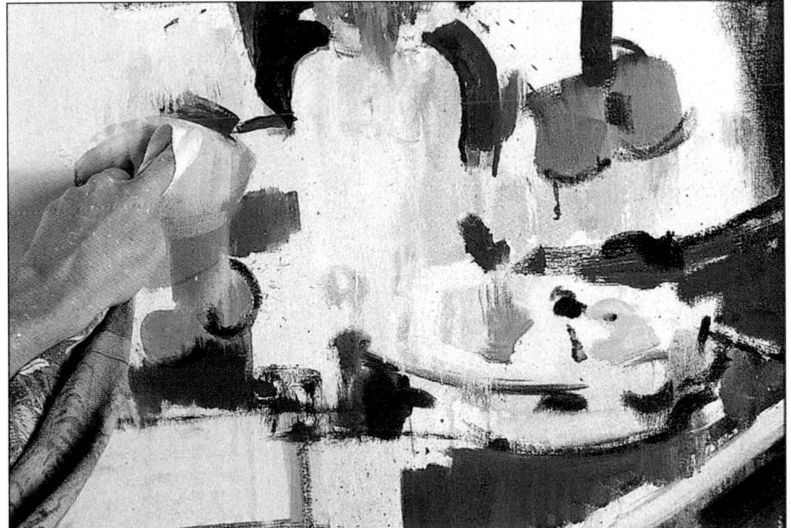

2

Continue painting loosely, developing all areas at the same time. Define the shape of the white daisies "negatively", by painting the blue backcloth behind them. Paint the scraps of red fabric using permanent magenta on the left and cadmium red on the right. Mix cadmium yellow, white and raw sienna for the pieces of yellow fabric. Use raw umber to strengthen outlines and block in shadows, and lift out highlights by rubbing back to the white canvas with a rag. As the paint is thin there will be spatters and runs, but they will be covered up later.

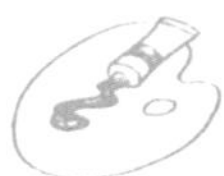

3

With the broad masses of the composition mapped in you can now start to refine and define. Add a little linseed oil to the turpentine in your jar or dipper to thicken and enrich the paint, and go over the shadows on the white vase with soft greys mixed from varied proportions of white, mauve and a little cobalt green. Use the same mixes to paint the shadows on the fruit dish, helping to define its shape.

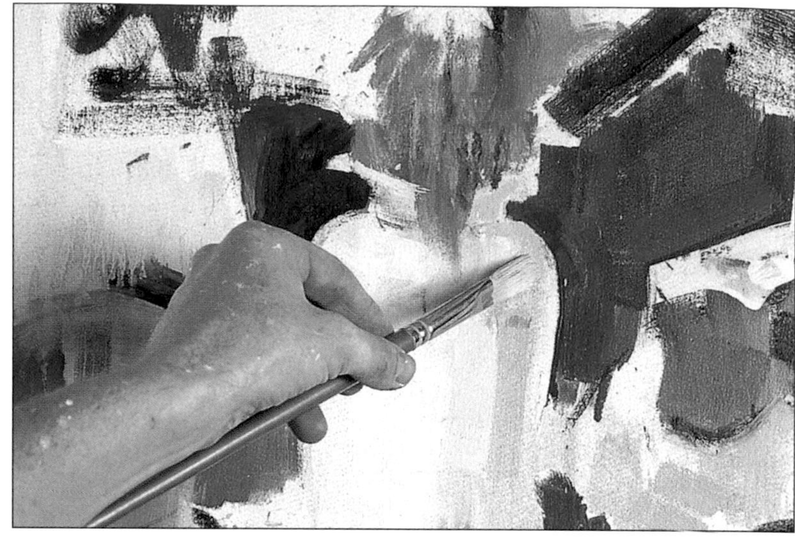

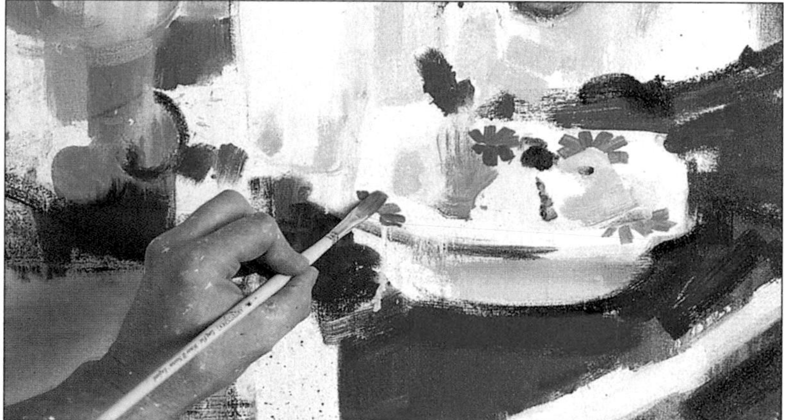

4

Mix a bright orange from cadmium scarlet and cadmium lemon and suggest the floral pattern on the fruit dish. Switch to a medium-sized long flat brush for this, using the body of the brush to paint each petal with a single stroke.

5

Slightly increase the proportion of linseed oil in your painting medium and begin to model the rounded forms of the apples on the right with light, medium and dark tones of green. First block in the mid-tone with viridian, cadmium yellow and a hint of raw sienna. Then put in the darker shadow tones with Prussian green. For the lighter tops of the apples use a mix of emerald green and Naples yellow light, with touches of cadmium lemon for the highlights. Twist and turn the brush as you work, following the forms of the apples with your brushstrokes.

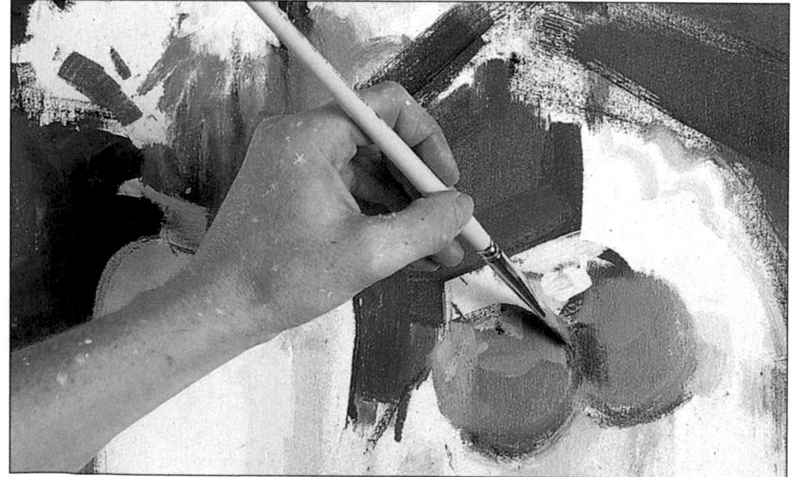

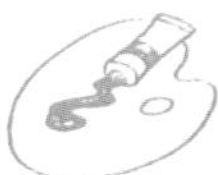

6

Paint the fruit in the bowl. Mix varied amounts of white, emerald green, Naples yellow light and cadmium lemon for the apple and pear, both of which are lighter in colour than the apples farther back. Mix cadmium yellow, Naples yellow light and white for the apricot, and block in the plum at the back with a near-black mixed from rose madder deep and Prussian green.

Block in the shadows cast by the apples on the white cloth with mixes of white, mauve and cobalt green applied with overlaid strokes. Use the edge of a palette knife to scrape out the highlights on the blue backcloth.

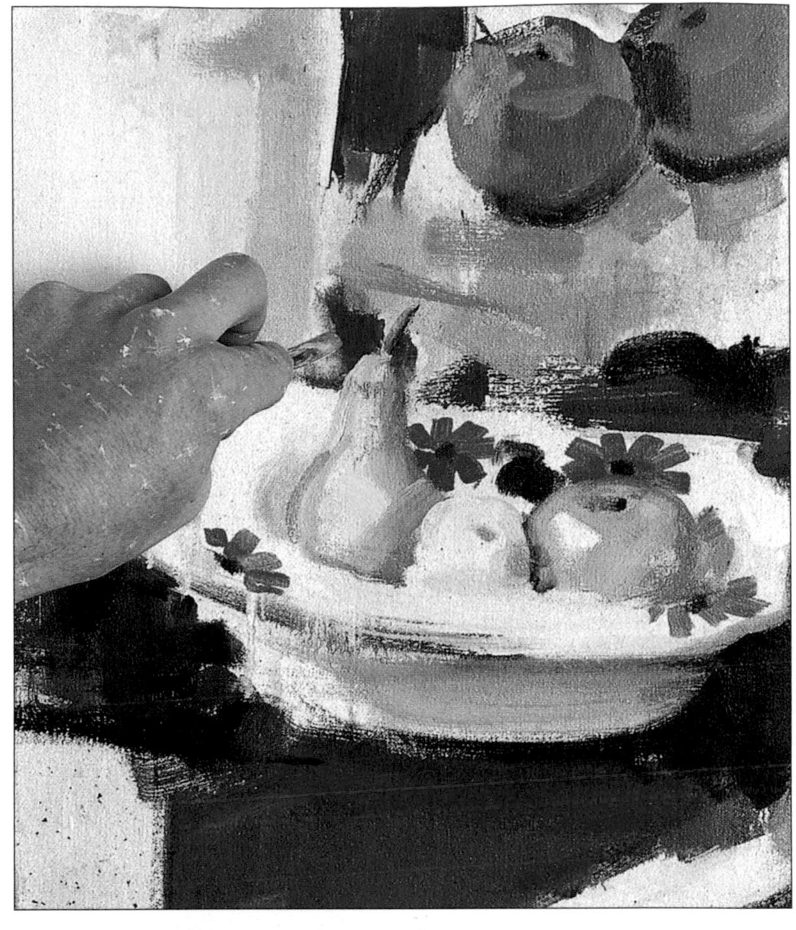

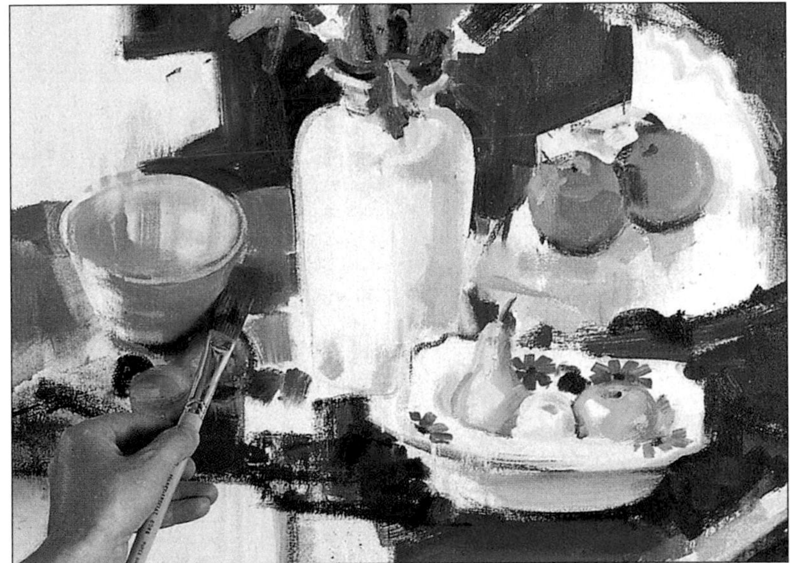

7

Work on the green bowl with softly blended strokes of cobalt turquoise and cobalt green lightened with white. Combine white with hints of viridian and cadmium lemon and use to suggest the shiny highlights. Then use a medium-sized long flat brush to paint the blue-green cloth with varied mixes of cobalt turquoise, French ultramarine, white and indigo.

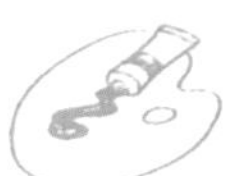

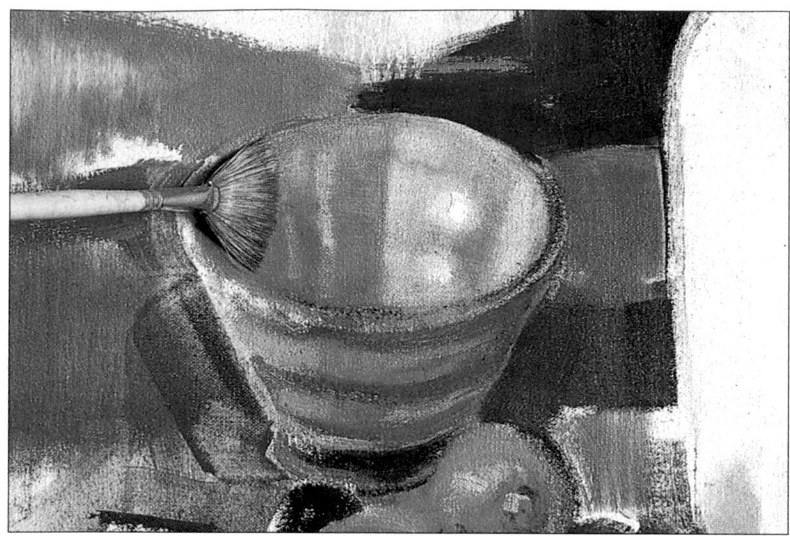

8

Model the forms of the limes using the same mixtures used for the apples but with a greater proportion of emerald green to make the limes slightly more acid in colour. Mix rose madder deep and Prussian green for the plum behind the limes. Use the same colour to define the folds in the red cloth. Paint the stripes on the green bowl with cobalt blue, using a small flat brush. Put in the brightest highlights with small, thick strokes of pure white. Then use a fan blender, with very light pressure, to soften and blend the tones on the inside of the bowl.

9

Now work on the bouquet of daisies. With a medium-sized long flat brush, define the forms of the leaves, using Prussian green for the darkest areas and various mixes of cobalt green, Naples yellow light and viridian for the mid- to light tones. Switch to a small long flat brush and start to define some of the daisy petals. Use pure white for those at the front, and white "dirtied" with hints of raw sienna and cobalt blue for those in shadow near the back. Mix Naples yellow light and cadmium red for the eyes of the daisies.

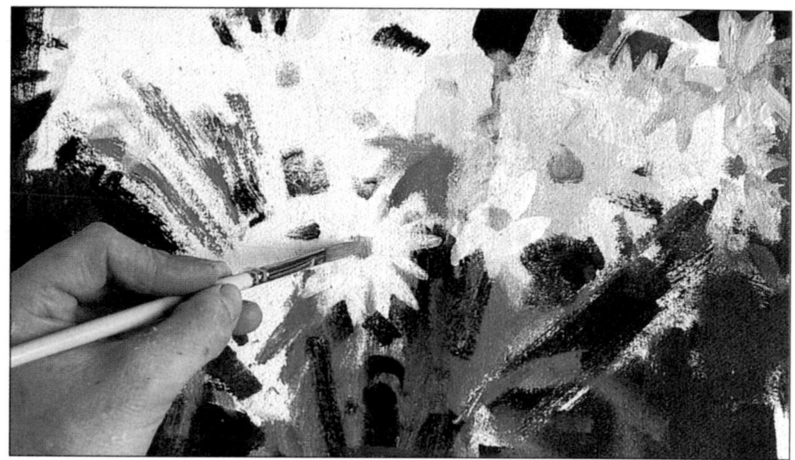

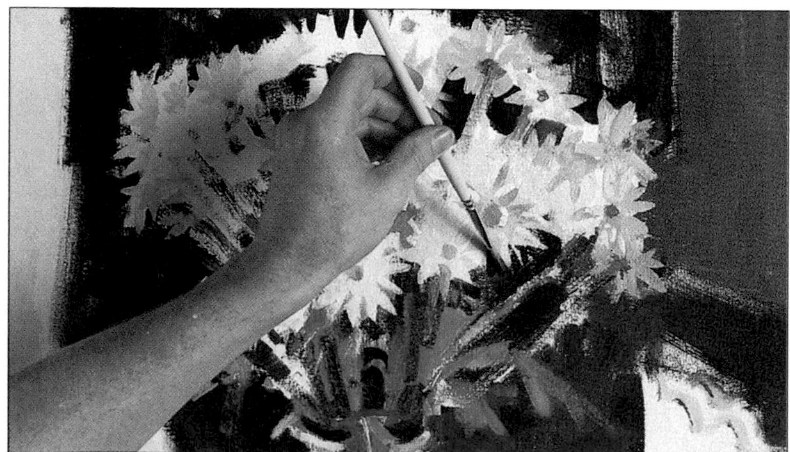

10

Continue describing the forms of the daisies by painting the shadowy petals with warm and cool greys mixed from varying amounts of raw sienna, cobalt blue, mauve and white. Paint each petal with a single mark, using the long edge of the brush to "imprint" the paint onto the canvas. Here the artist is employing the technique to paint the daisies at the front "negatively", using indigo mixed with alizarin crimson to create sharp definition between the white petals and the dark blue background.

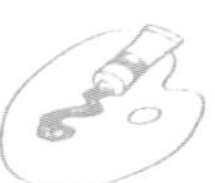

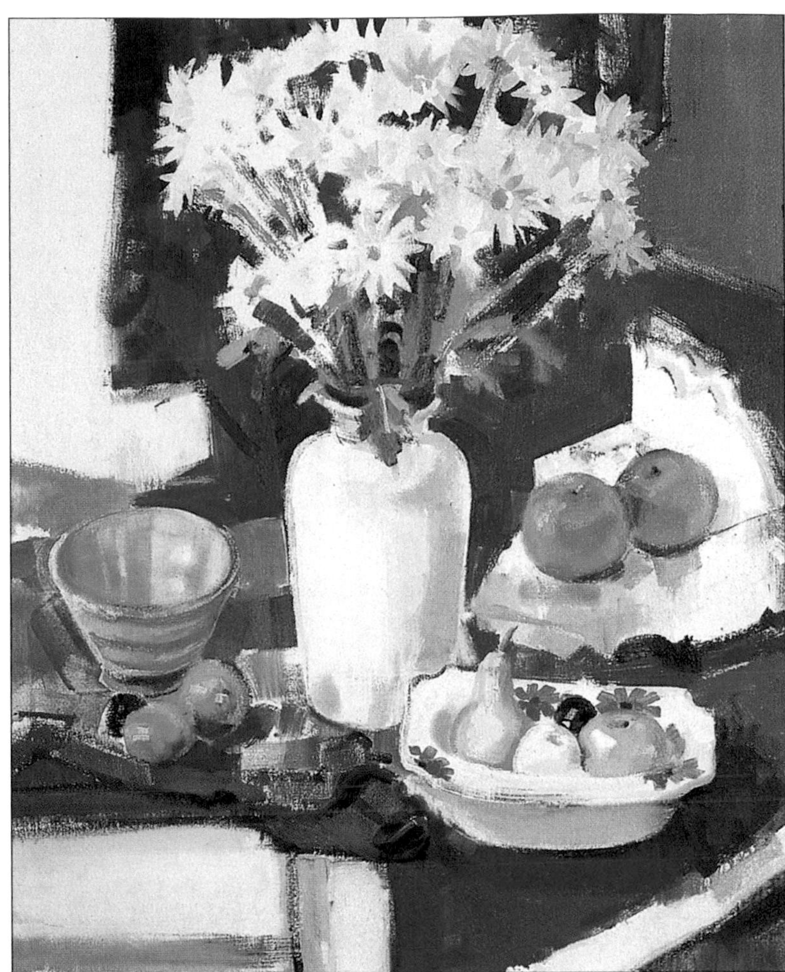

11

Stand back and assess the painting overall, looking for the way tones, colours and shapes relate to each other and making adjustments accordingly. Complete the daisies, adding touches of Naples yellow light here and there to warm up the lighter petals. Add the highlights on the plums with white and a touch of the rose madder deep/Prussian green mix. Deepen the tone of the yellow cloths on the left of the picture with cadmium yellow.

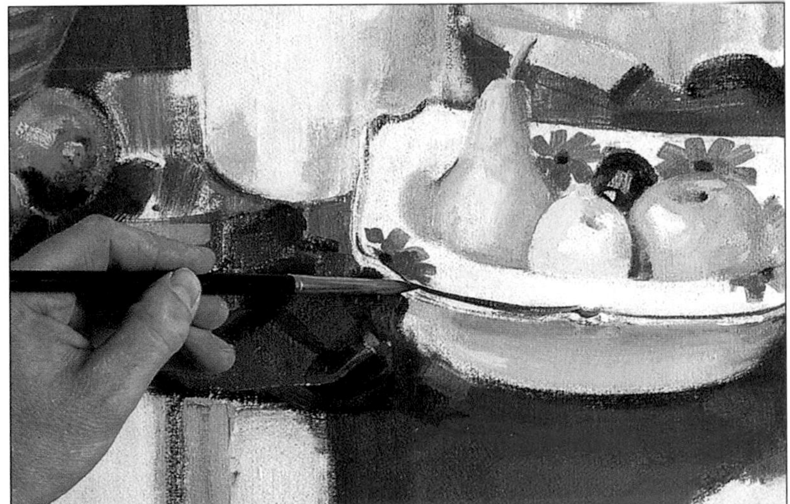

12

To complete the picture, use the tip of a small round soft-hair brush to paint the decorative edging on the fruit dish with a near-black mixed from indigo and alizarin crimson.

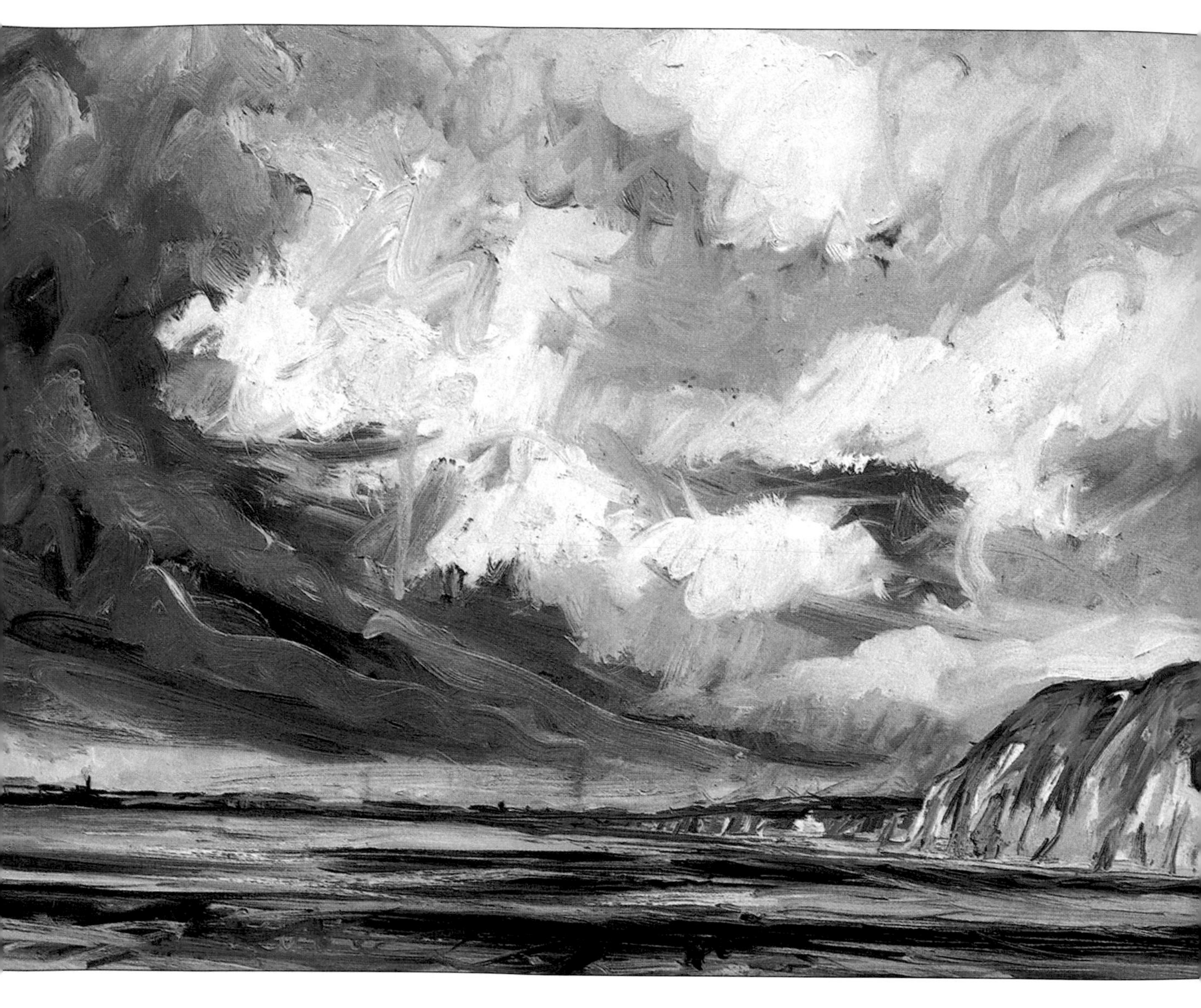

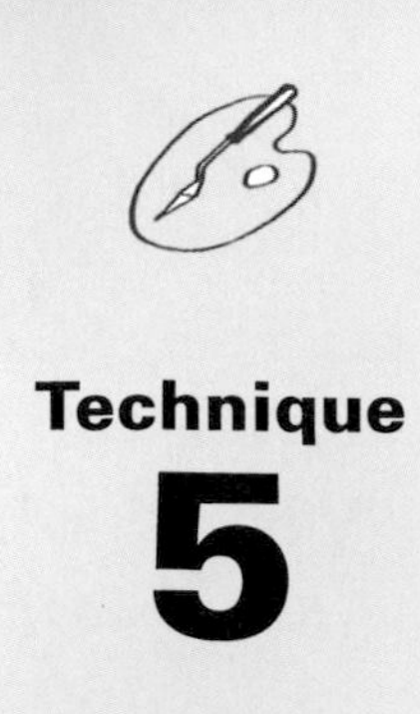

Technique

5

Expressive Brushwork

One of the greatest pleasures of oil painting is the way the paint responds to the brush, and for most artists the actual use of the paint and the resulting marks and textures are in themselves an exciting and enjoyable part of the painting process. In addition, the visible sign of the brush becomes an outward mark of the artist's individuality – a personal calligraphy, as unique as his or her handwriting.

This stormy coastal scene was painted on-the-spot, and the artist's excitement about the subject is reflected in the way he has handled the paint with great freedom and inventiveness. The rapid, expressive brushstrokes, plus the use of both thick and thin paint, convey a marvellous feeling of movement and changing light.

By using paint thinly diluted with a mixture of turpentine and linseed oil the artist was able to work at great speed and with considerable freedom. This approach is particularly useful when working outdoors where the light and weather are liable to change at any moment.

David Carr
Storm Approaching
33 x 44½cm (13 x 17½in)

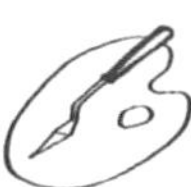

Expressive Brushwork

Inexperienced painters often make the mistake of applying the paint with uniform, flat strokes, as if painting a door, but this can render the painting somewhat flat and lifeless.

As you gain more experience, start to think of your painting as a two-dimensional surface in its own right, as well as a recreation of a scene. In other words, think about ways to exploit the expressive possibilities of the paint itself. Not only do different techniques and kinds of brushstrokes help to define forms and suggest the textures of objects, they also give the finished painting a pleasing tactile quality, the character of which is as unique to you as your handwriting.

It is well worth experimenting with a variety of brush shapes – rounds, flats and filberts – as well as bristle brushes and soft-hair brushes, to find out what kind of marks each one can make (see page 268 for more information on brushes). Try making rapid, sweeping strokes and slow, deliberate ones. Hold the brush at various angles to see how this affects the weight of the stroke. Stipple thick paint on with the tip of the brush, or lightly drag it over the surface so that the colour is broken up by the textured weave of the canvas – a technique called drybrush.

Hold the brush where it feels naturally balanced, but not too near the ferule as this limits movement to the fingers and encourages monotonous, restrictive brushmarks. Think of the brush as an extension of yourself. The movement of the arm from the shoulder, through the elbow and wrist, should be fluid, confident and controlled.

Storm Approaching

Materials and Equipment

• SHEET OF PRIMED CANVAS OR BOARD • OIL COLOURS: CADMIUM RED, ALIZARIN CRIMSON, YELLOW OCHRE, LEMON YELLOW, CERULEAN, VIRIDIAN, FRENCH ULTRAMARINE, COBALT BLUE, BURNT SIENNA, BURNT UMBER AND TITANIUM WHITE • BRISTLE BRUSHES: LARGE AND MEDIUM-SIZED FILBERTS AND LARGE ROUND • SOFT-HAIR RIGGER BRUSH • PURE LINSEED OIL • DISTILLED TURPENTINE

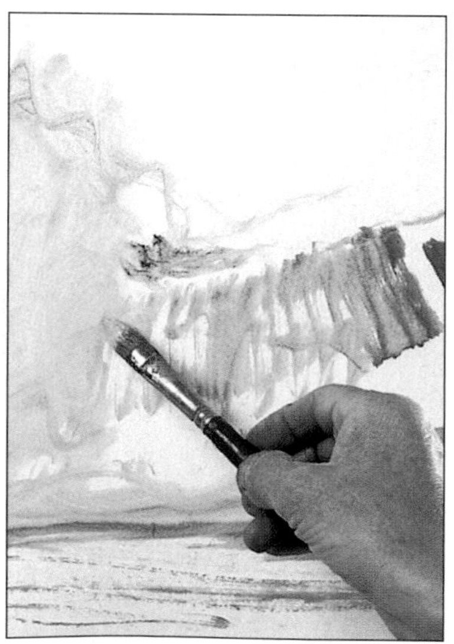

1

Take a deep breath and plunge straight into the painting without making an underdrawing. Mix yellow ochre with a little cadmium red, dilute thinly with turpentine medium, and draw in the low horizon line using the chisel edge of a large filbert brush. Then mass in the main shapes in the sky with thin paint, using varied tones of the yellow ochre/cadmium red mix. Add touches of cerulean and cobalt blue in the upper sky. Work vigorously, using the body of the brush for the broad masses and the edge to make linear marks.

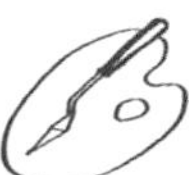

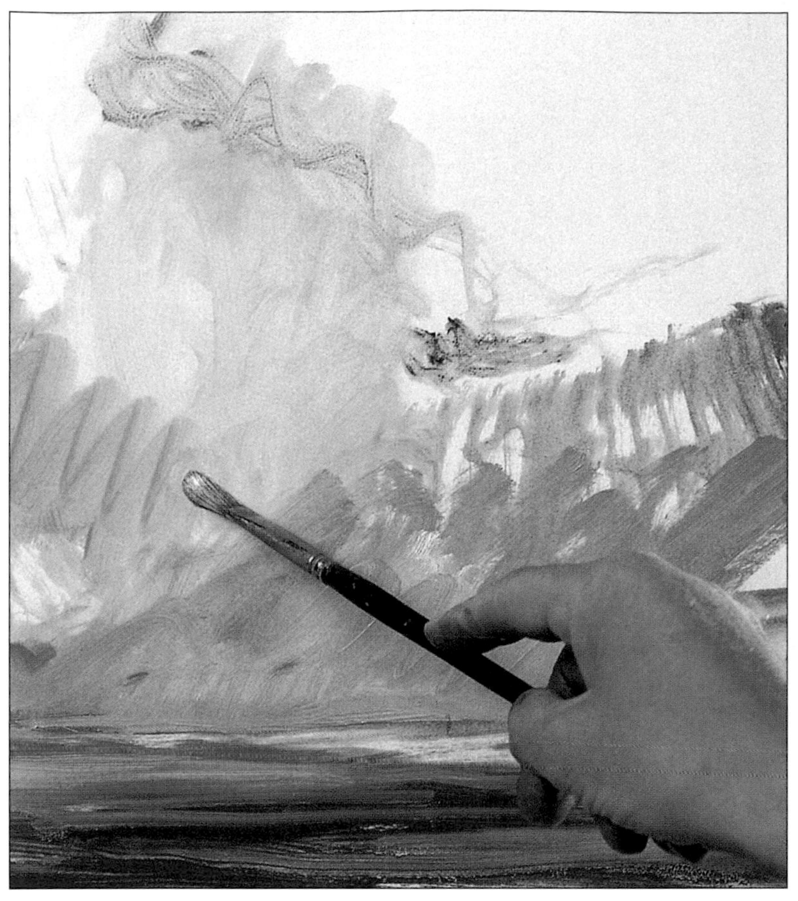

2

Paint the sea with long horizontal strokes of variegated colour – cerulean, lemon yellow, French ultramarine, and violet mixed from alizarin crimson and ultramarine. Continue blocking in the main shapes, masses and lines in the sky, scrubbing the paint on with lively, vigorous brushstrokes to establish a sense of the towering heaps of storm cloud.

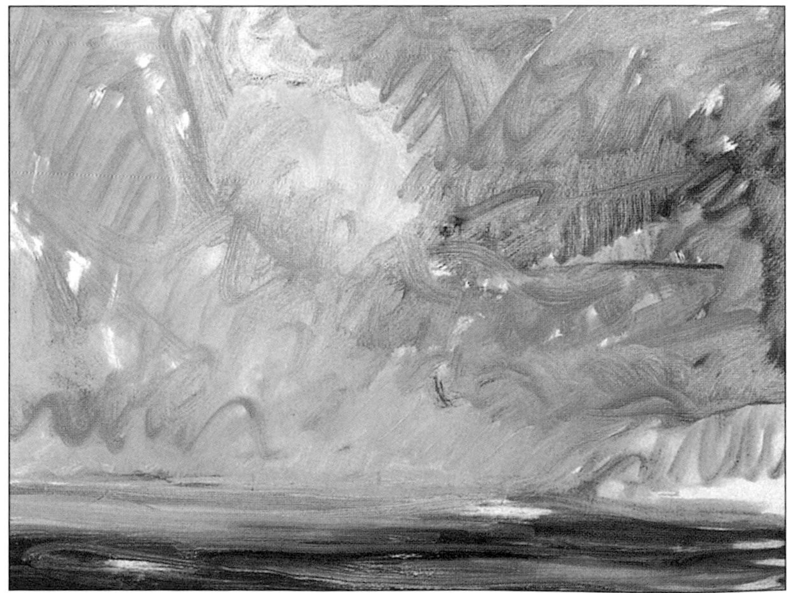

3

Rough in the cliffs on the right with thinly diluted cadmium red, then complete the underpainting of the sky with warm blue-violets mixed from alizarin crimson, ultramarine and lots of titanium white. Here you can see how the artist has worked the brush in various directions, leaving the brushmarks visible so that they contribute a feeling of energy and movement.

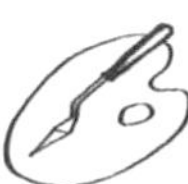

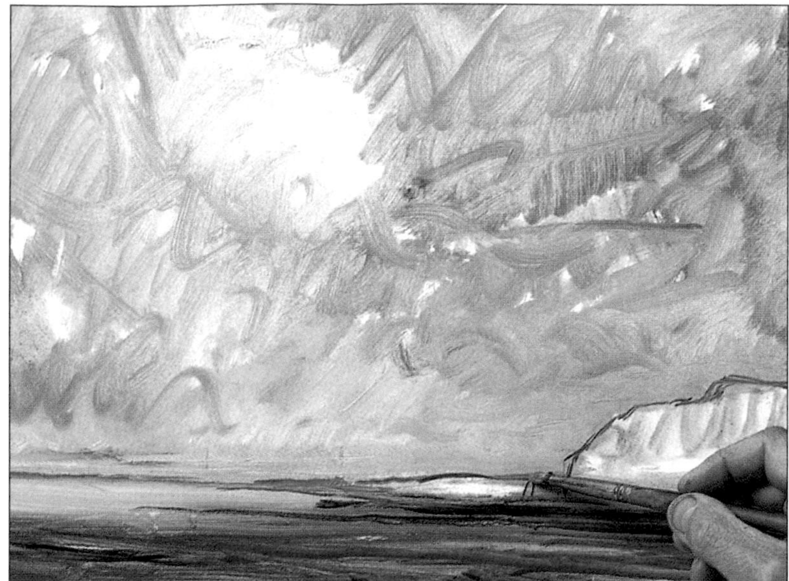

4

Make a creamy mixture of viridian and a hint of yellow ochre and white. Switch to a medium-sized filbert brush and use the tip to define the horizon line, the cliffs and the dark patches of sea.

5

Fill in the cliffs with reds, greens and yellows. Modify the colours in the water, lightly stroking pale greys and earths over the wet colours beneath so that they blend and streak. Mix a dark, inky grey from ultramarine, burnt sienna and a little white and paint the dark sweep of storm cloud using a large round brush. Use broad, expansive strokes, but keep the paint fairly thin so that the warm colours in the underpainting show through in places. Leave a narrow sliver of light just above the horizon.

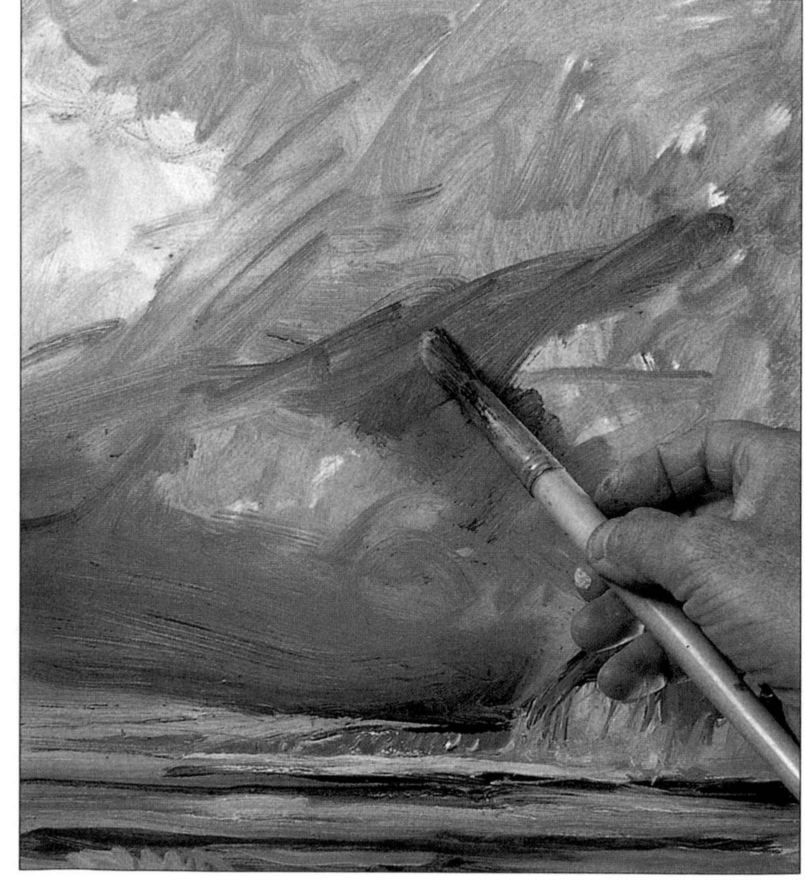

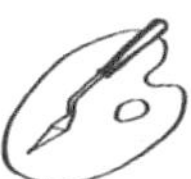

6

Switch to a large filbert brush and paint the patches of blue sky using cerulean, cobalt blue and white. Paint the light cumulus clouds with white warmed with a hint of yellow ochre. Use thicker paint now, applied with plenty of gusto to give the clouds form and movement. Make the clouds smaller and flatter as you near the horizon, to emphasize the illusion of receding space.

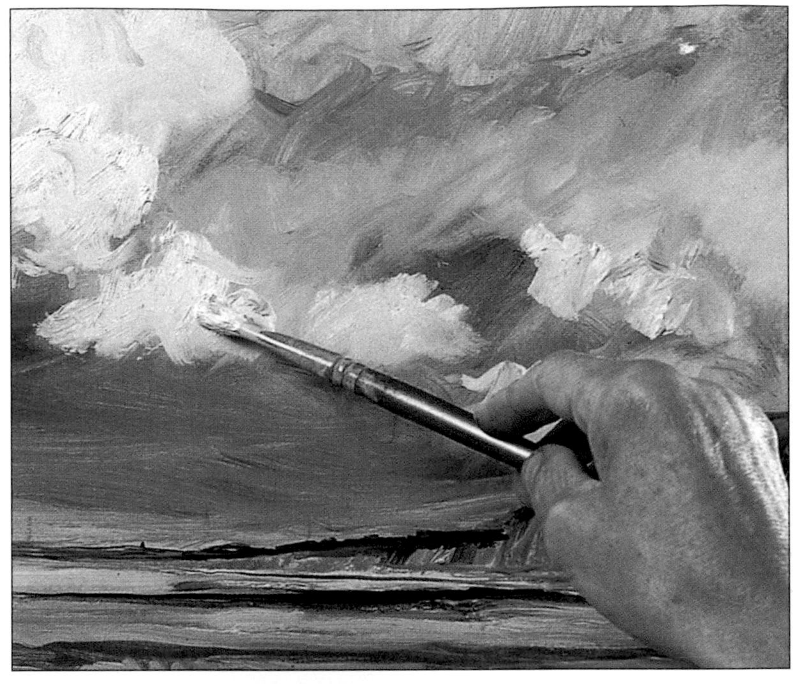

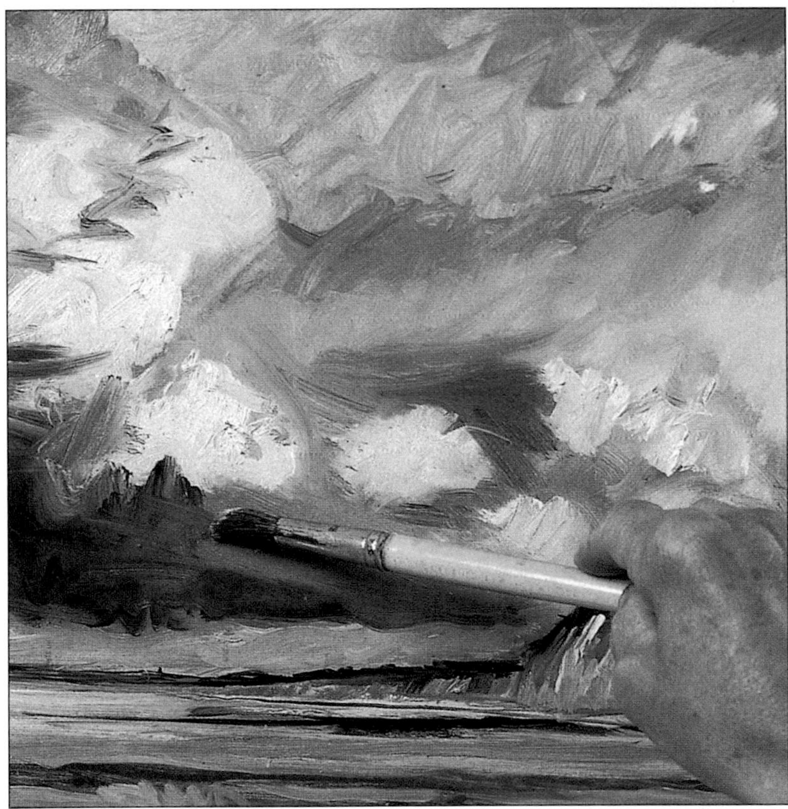

7

Streak some of the white cloud mixture across the distant sea, which reflects light from the sky. Now use the large round brush to build up the form of the dark storm cloud with thicker paint, using a cooler grey mixed from ultramarine, burnt umber and a touch of alizarin crimson. Bring some yellow ochre into the clouds at top left, to suggest the sullen light of a stormy day.

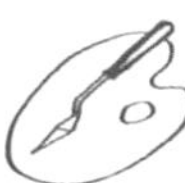

8

Mix up some white and add a tiny hint of yellow ochre and cadmium red to warm it. Paint the chalky cliff face with this colour, using a well-loaded soft-hair rigger brush. Use the same brush to work some streaks and wisps into the sky to recreate fragmented clouds being blown by the wind.

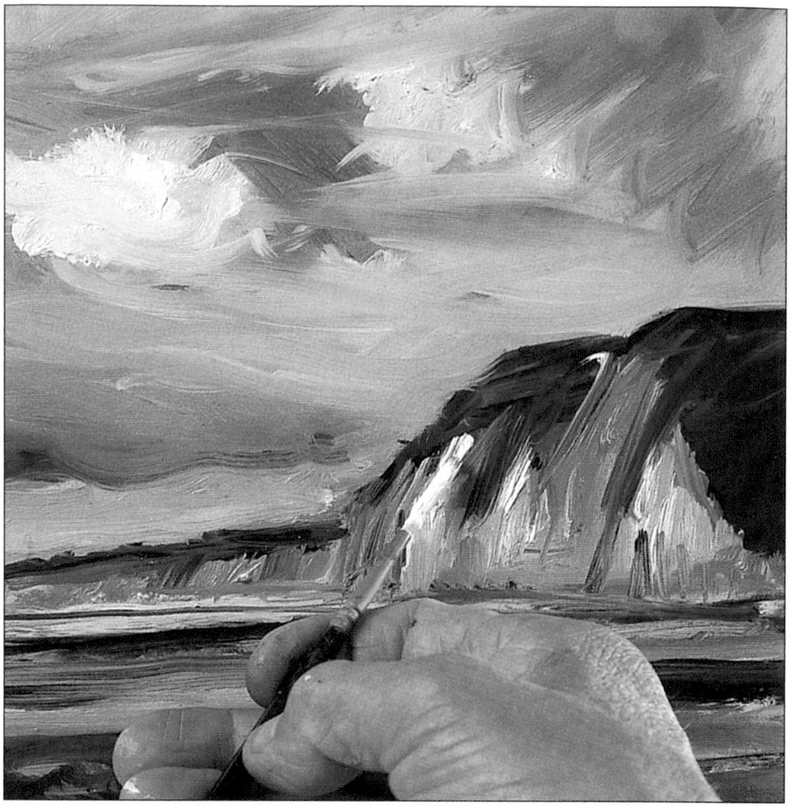

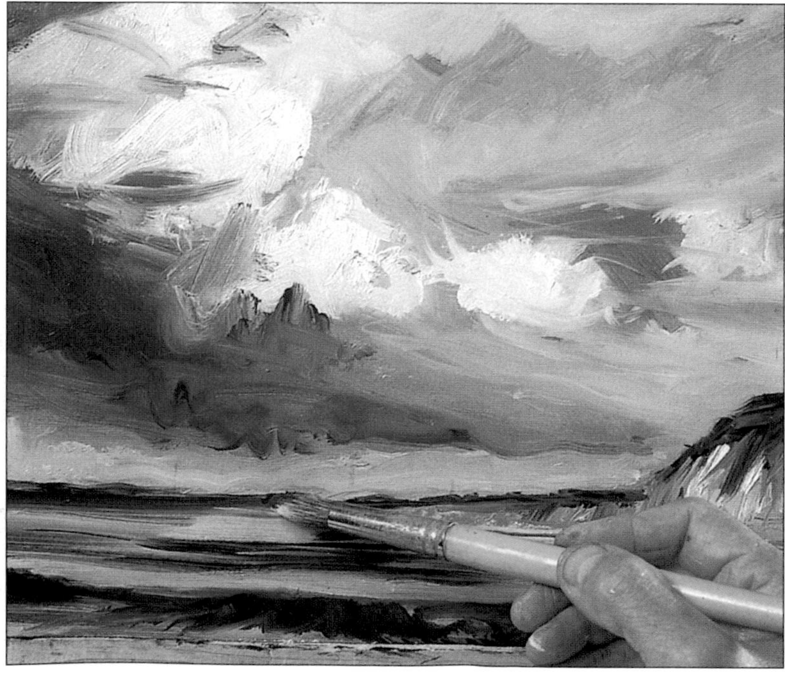

9

Mix a dark grey with burnt sienna and ultramarine and paint the dark patches on the water reflected from the clouds above, using the tip of a large round brush. Feather the colour on lightly, letting it pick up some of the wet colours beneath to create streaks of variegated colour.

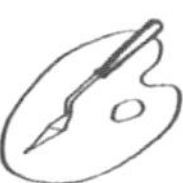

10

Use the same mixture to emphasize the dramatic sweep of the dark storm clouds with vigorous diagonal strokes. Then switch to the rigger brush again and suggest the waves breaking on the shore with a mixture of white and lemon yellow applied with drybrushed strokes: flick the brush on a rag to remove most of the paint, then drag the brush lightly across the surface to make thin, broken lines.

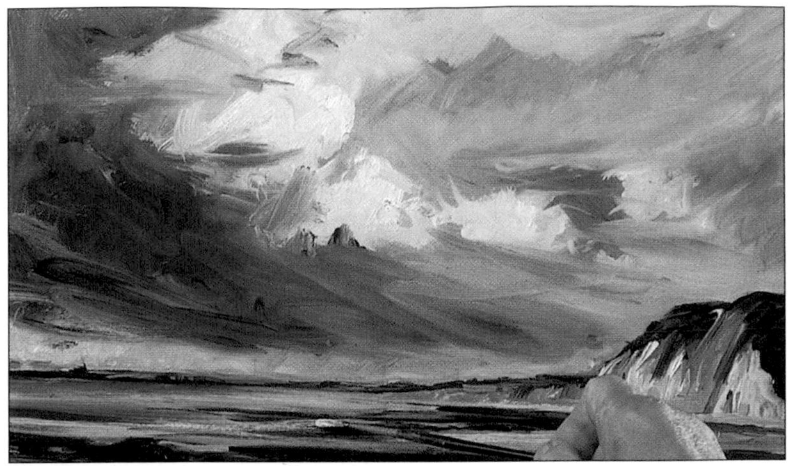

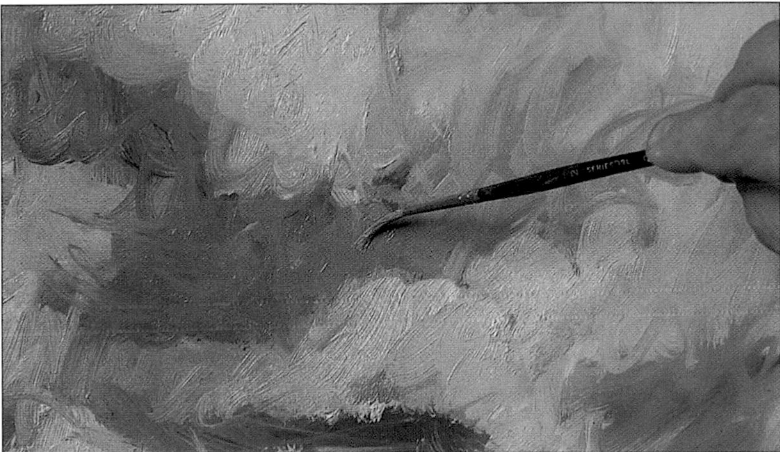

11

Now use the rigger brush to soften some of the brushstrokes on the light clouds to give them a more fluid, vaporous appearance. Blend some of the cloud edges into the surrounding blue to prevent the clouds appearing "pasted on" to the sky.

12

Add a final dramatic touch to the picture by putting in a long, diagonal sweep of storm cloud that leads the eye from the foreground into the distance. First, mix two colours: yellow ochre, and a grey mixed from yellow ochre, cadmium red and a white. Dip a large round brush, first into one mix and then into the other so that you have two colours on the brush. Then drag it through the paint already on the surface, depositing the two colours at once and letting them blend with the colours beneath. As you drag the brush down to the horizon, make a slightly wavering stroke to give movement and energy to the clouds.

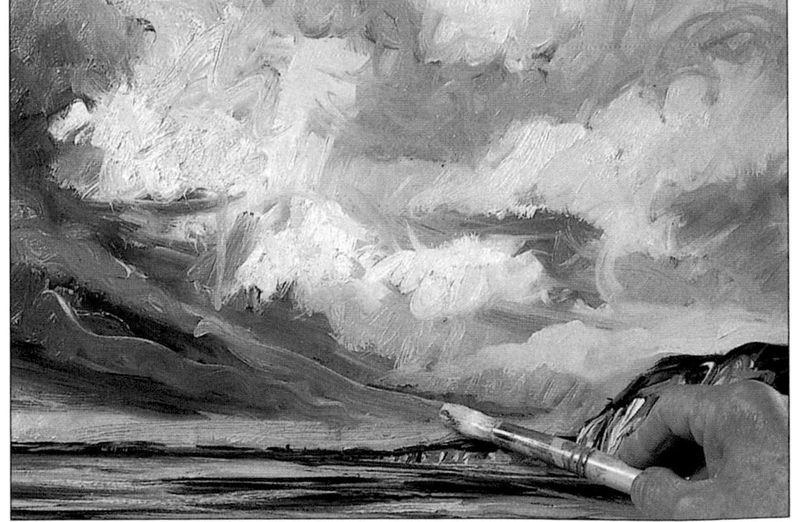

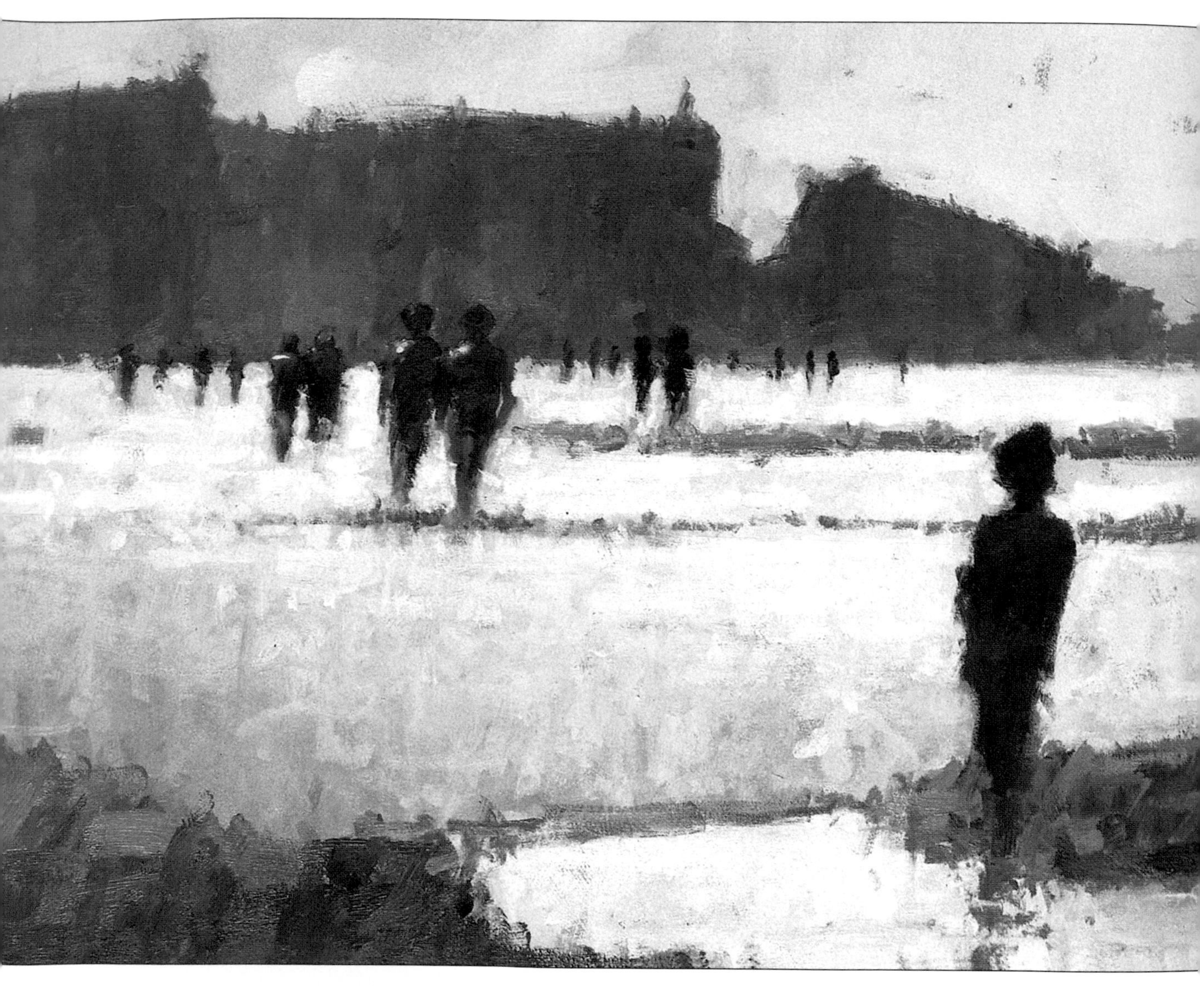

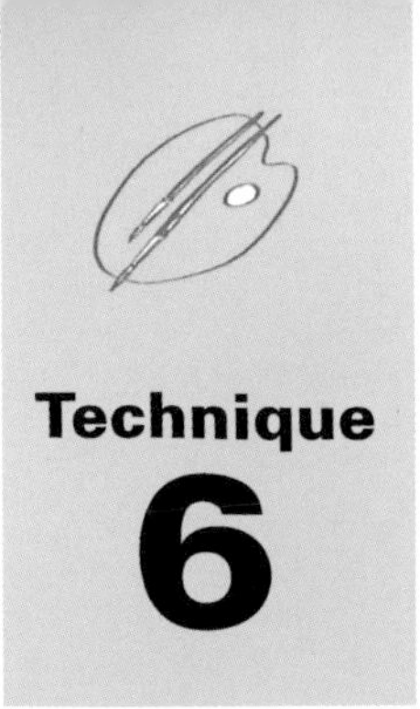

Technique
6

Scumbling

One of the most beautiful effects in oil painting, scumbling involves brushing thin, dry paint over another layer of colour with a rapid scrubbing motion. Because the colour is applied unevenly the underlayer is only partially obscured and shimmers up through the scumble, creating an "optical" colour mix with extraordinary depth and richness. Scumbling also produces a lively, unpredictable texture in which the marks of the brush are evident.

The technique is used to good effect in this painting to capture the shimmer and the reflective quality of a beach at low tide when viewed directly into the setting sun. The artist worked over the whole canvas with thin veils of stiff, chalky paint scumbled and dragged over a red ground. The warm tone of the ground glows up through the overlaid colours, capturing the pearly, luminous quality that is characteristic of early evening light on the coast.

Barry Freeman
Evening Sun, Portugal
41 x 51cm (16 x 20in)

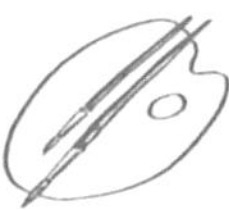

Scumbling

A scumble consists of short, scrubby strokes of thin, dry, semi-opaque colour applied loosely over previous layers of the painting. Because the colour is applied unevenly the underlayer is only partially obscured and shimmers up through the scumble. The interaction between the two layers creates a pleasing effect – the colours mix optically and have more resonance.

Scumbling is also a good way to modify an exisiting colour. A red that is too strident can be subtly "knocked back" by scumbling over it with a cool green, and vice versa. Similarly, passages that have become too "jumpy" and fragmented can be softened and unified by working over them with scumbled colour.

Use stiff bristle or synthetic brushes for scumbling. Pick up some paint on your brush, then flick it across a rag to remove excess moisture. Lightly scrub the paint on with free, vigorous strokes, leaving the brushmarks. The aim is to produce a semi-transparent overlayer, like a haze of smoke, through which the underlayers can be glimpsed. The paint can be worked in various directions. You can also scumble with a rag or a painting knife.

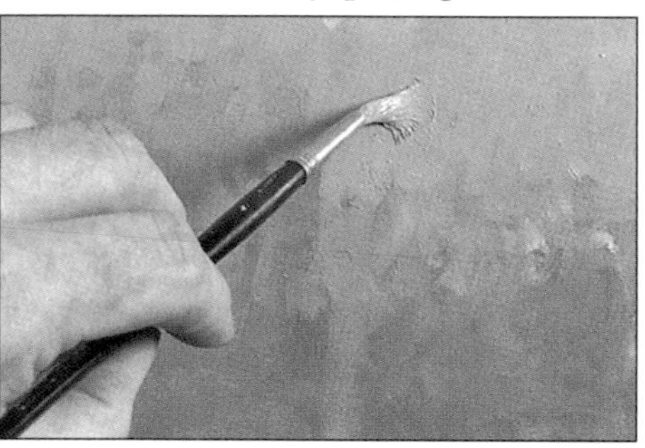

It is important to build up scumbles thinly, in gradual stages. If the paint is applied too heavily, the hazy, veil-like effect will be lost.

vening Sun, Portugal

Materials and Equipment

- SHEET OF PRIMED MDF BOARD
- OIL COLOURS: CADMIUM RED, ROSE MADDER, ALIZARIN CRIMSON, CADMIUM LEMON, CADMIUM YELLOW, FRENCH ULTRAMARINE, COBALT BLUE, CERULEAN AND TITANIUM WHITE
- SMALL ROUND SOFT-HAIR BRUSH
- MEDIUM ROUND SYNTHETIC BRUSH
- SMALL DECORATING BRUSH
- LINT-FREE RAG
- DISTILLED TURPENTINE
- PURE LINSEED OIL

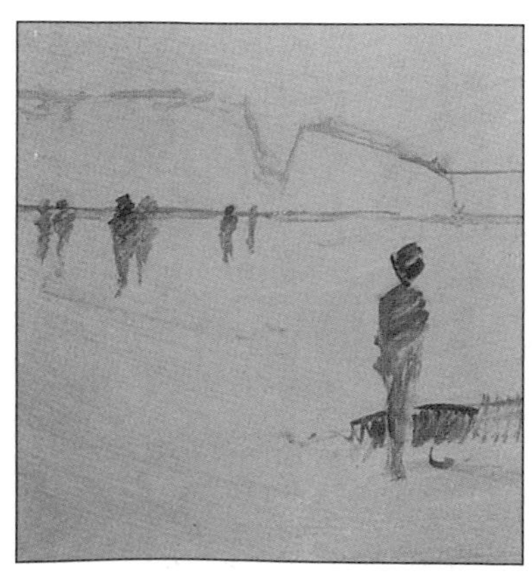

1

Prepare your board by tinting it with a thin, turpsy wash consisting of roughly 70% cadmium red and 30% cerulean. Apply this with a small decorating brush, then wipe over the wet paint with a clean rag to unify the surface. Leave to dry overnight.

Sketch in the main elements of the composition with a small round soft-hair brush, using varied tones of French ultramarine and cadmium red. Indicate the figures with brief, sketchy marks at this stage.

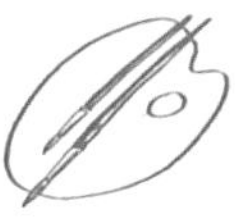

2

Mix the paint with a little oil-painting medium to give it more body. Don't add too much though – paint for scumbling should be fairly "dry" in consistency. Block in the sky using titanium white "dirtied" with small amounts of cadmium red, cobalt blue and a touch of cadmium yellow. Apply the scumbling paint with lively strokes worked in different directions, using a medium-size, round synthetic brush.

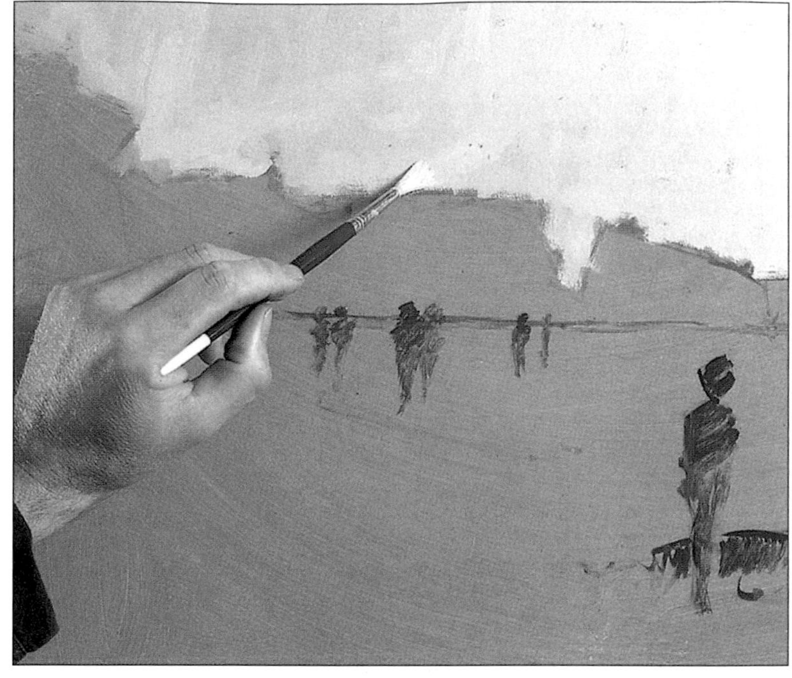

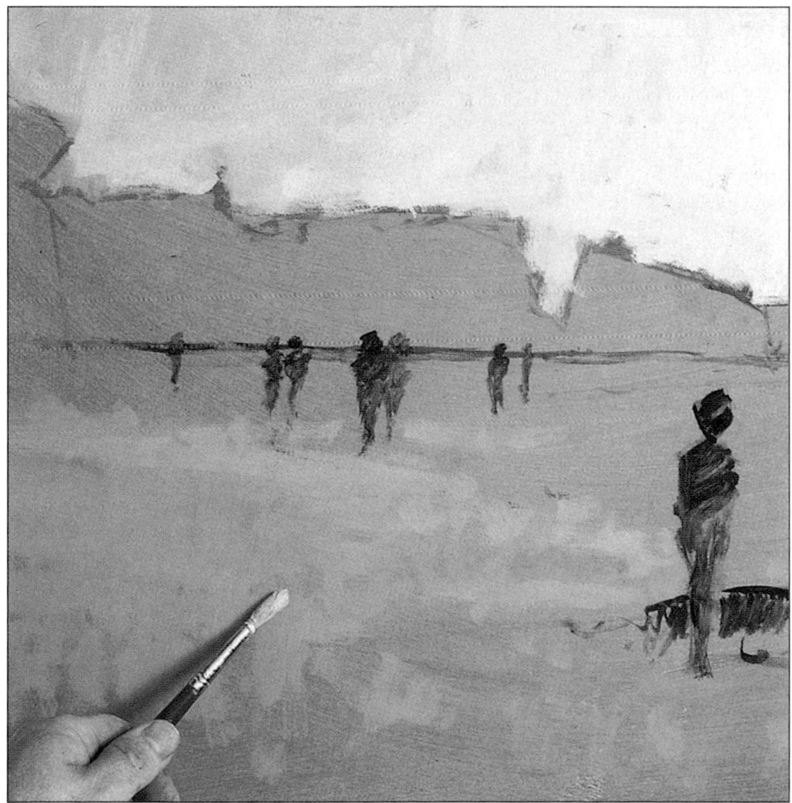

3

Now darken the mixture with more cadmium red and a touch of alizarin crimson and start to paint the sand in the foreground. Apply the paint with loose, scrubby strokes, letting plenty of the warm red of the tinted ground to show through. Modulate the tone and temperature of the sand colour as you work, adding more cobalt to cool the mix, or more cadmium yellow to warm it.

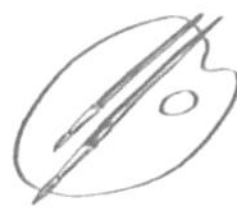

4

Add French ultramarine, plus more cadmium red and cadmium yellow to the mix on the palette to make a dark grey. Paint the cliffs in the background, again modulating the colour from warm to cool by adding more blue or more yellow to the basic mix. Work your brush in different directions to suggest the craggy surface of the cliffs.

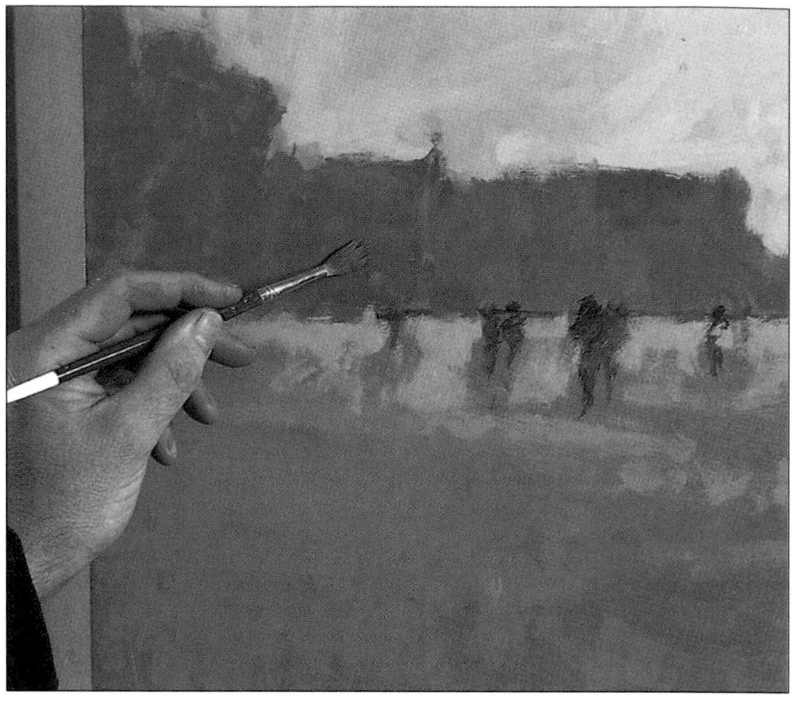

5

Lighten the grey mixture with more cobalt blue and titanium white to make a cooler, lighter grey for the headland glimpsed on the right, in the far distance. Now lighten the mix even more, adding plenty of white plus hints of rose madder and cadmium yellow to make a silvery grey. Use this to paint the sea and the rock pool in the foreground, scumbling the paint on loosely with small brushmarks worked in horizontal and vertical directions. Where the shallow water meets the sand, use a thirsty brush and dryish paint, dragging it lightly across so that the strokes break up on the rough surface of the canvas.

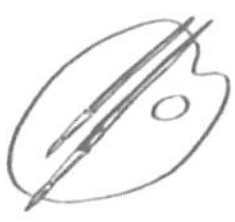

6

Mix a soft, neutral tint of cadmium red, cadmium lemon, a little cobalt blue and lots of titanium white. Apply this with lightly scumbled strokes to soften the edge where the water and sand meet and link them naturally together. Then mix varied amounts of cobalt blue, cadmium red and white and paint the cast shadow in the foreground and the rock on the right, letting flecks of the toned ground show through the scumbled strokes.

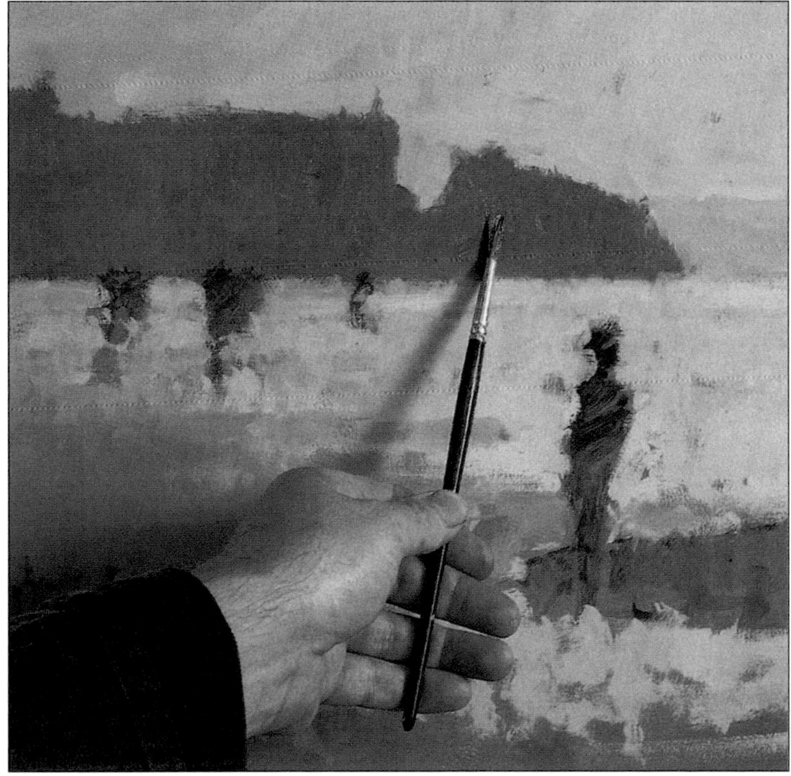

7

Build up more colour on the cliffs, mixing varied tones of ultramarine, cadmium red and touches of cadmium yellow and white for the dark cliff on the left. Work over the lighter cliffs with varied tones of rose madder, cobalt blue and cadmium yellow mixed in varied proportions. Scuff the paint on lightly so that some of the pink ground glows through and lends a luminosity to the colours.

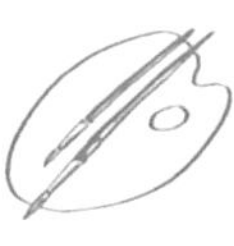

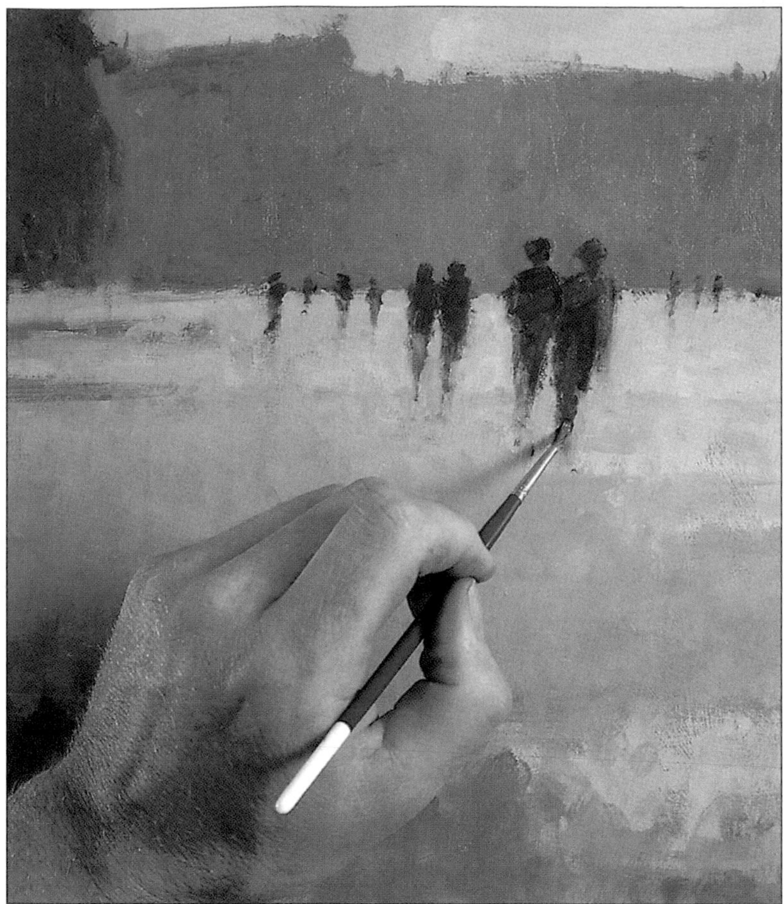

8

Switch to a small round soft-hair brush and define the figures on the beach using a soft, bluish grey mixed from ultramarine, rose madder and a bit of cadmium yellow. Use the tip of the brush to suggest tiny figures in the distance, beneath the cliffs. The figures should not be too dark as the evening light is soft and hazy.

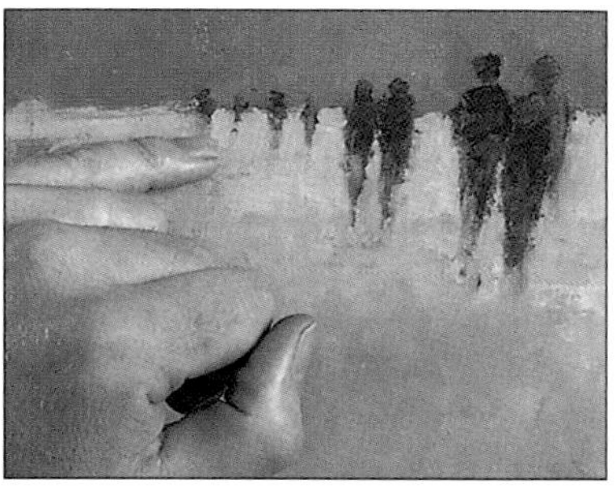

9

Avoid defining the figures too sharply and making them appear wooden and "pasted on" to the picture. Here the artist has "lost" edges on the figures by smudging the paint. By lightly dragging the colour down from the base of each figure, he also suggests their reflections on the wet sand.

10

Stand back from your painting – or even take a break from it – so you can assess any modifications that need to be made before continuing. Here, for example, the artist realized that the figures form a straight line going into the distance, so he added two more figures, a little to the right, to break the monotony. He also altered the shape of one of the figures, which was too heavy and square. Finally, he warmed the colour of the distant figures with a mix of cadmium red and cobalt blue, and added highlights using white mixed with cobalt blue and a little alizarin.

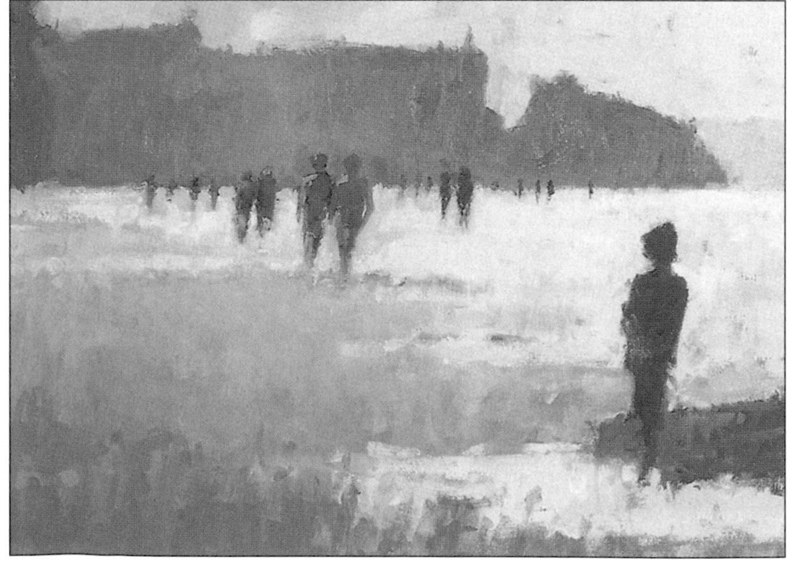

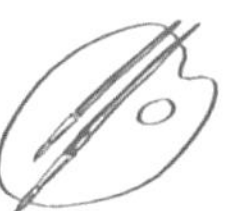

11

Build up the tones on the sand with varied mixes of white, cadmium lemon, cadmium yellow and a hint of alizarin. Then paint the seaweed-covered rocks in the foreground using scumbled strokes. Start with a violet mix of cadmium red and cobalt blue, then mix cobalt, cadmium yellow and a little cadmium red for the seaweed. Add French ultramarine to the mix for the darker greens, and more yellow and white for the lighter greens on the top of the rock. Lighten the mixes with white to paint the rocks and seaweed in the background.

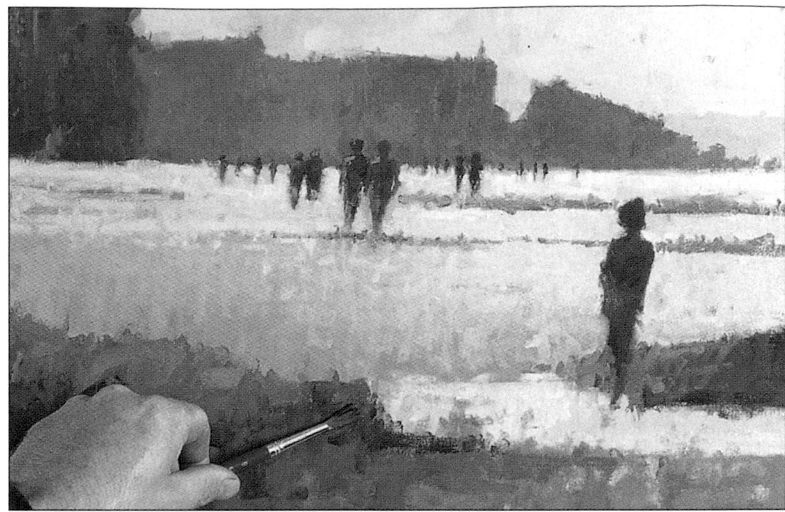

12

Mix a warm grey with cobalt blue, white and a touch of alizarin and use this to grey down the water in the rock pool. Darken the mix and suggest the figure's reflection in the water. Then mix cadmium red, cadmium yellow and a touch of cobalt and scumble this over the sand in the immediate foreground to deepen its tone and bring it forward.

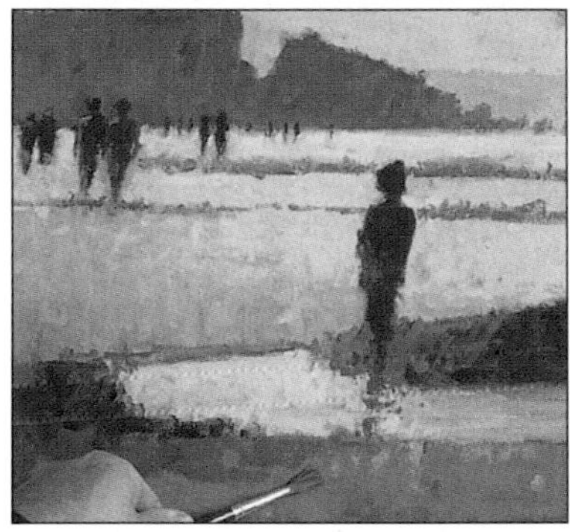

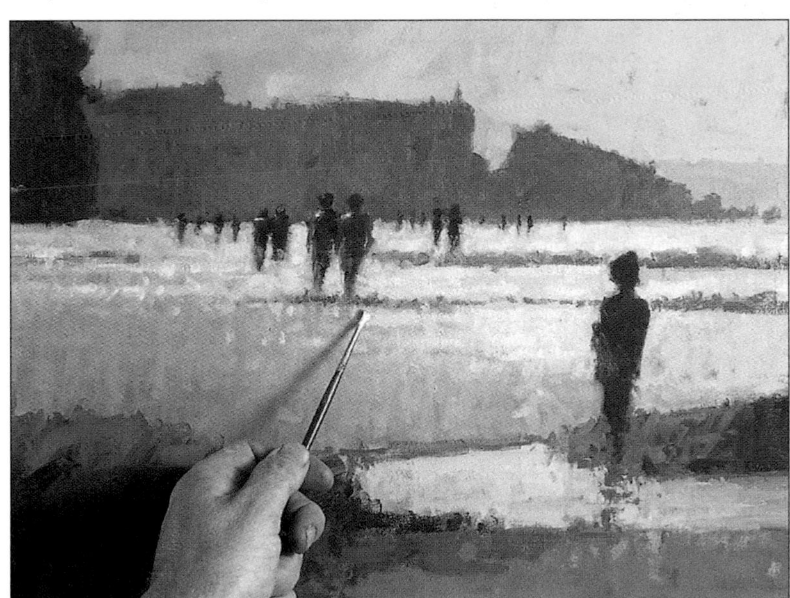

13

Step back and assess your painting once more, and make any final adjustments to the tones and colours. Use a small round brush to scumble on the sparkling highlights on the water using white tinted with a hint of rose madder and ultramarine. To complete the painting, mix white with cadmium red and yellow and add tiny highlights on the shoulders of some of the background figures lit by the setting sun.

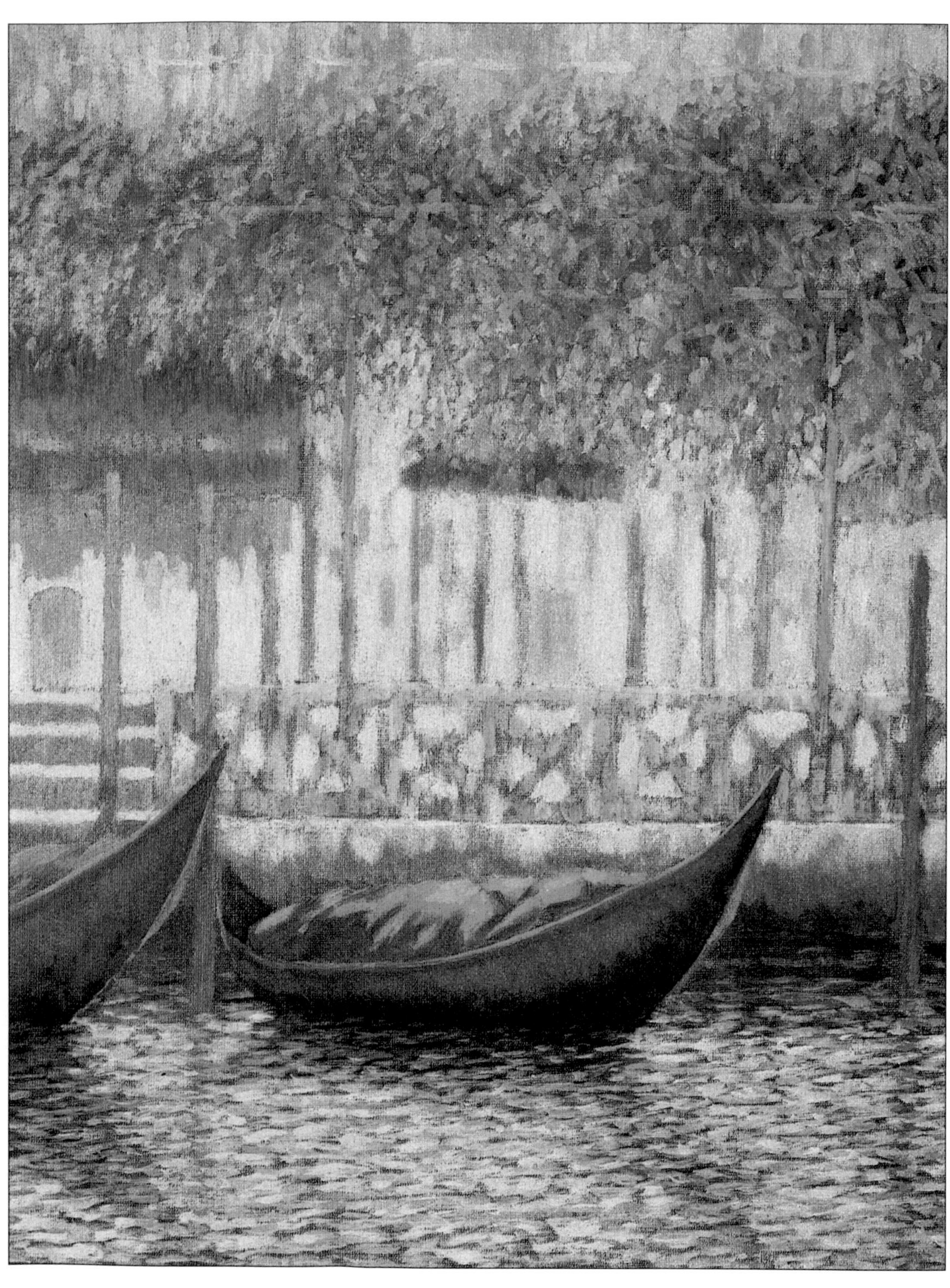

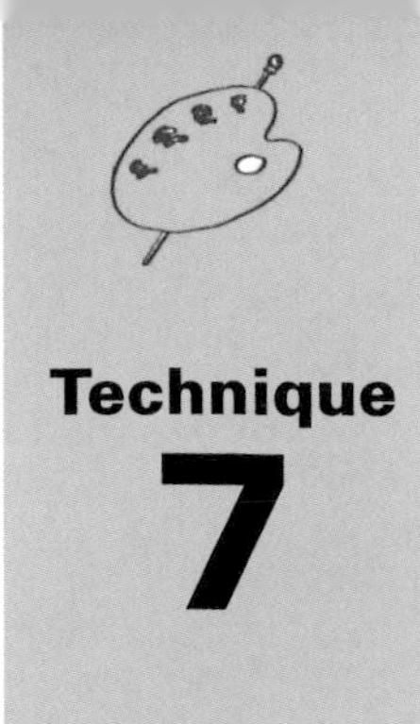

Technique

7

DEVELOPING THE PAINTING

No area of this painting is flat or monotonous – all the tones and colours have been built up with an intricate network of small, separate brushstrokes reminiscent of the French Impressionist painters. The artist developed all areas of the composition at the same rate, moving from one part of the painting to another. Inevitably colour is picked up on the brush and taken from one area to another and these recurring colour notes give the painting an underlying coherence that pulls otherwise disparate elements together and results in a pleasing whole.

When tackling a complex subject such as this, it is good to keep in mind the advice of Cézanne: "Start with a broom and end with a needle." Begin by blocking in the broad areas, then attend to the intermediate shapes and tones, and finally, apply the details and finishing touches.

~

Derek Daniells

Gondolas, Venice

56 x 46cm (22 x 18in)

~

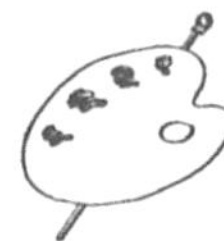

Developing the Painting

A mistake that is sometimes made by inexperienced painters is to work on one small area of a painting until it is "finished", and then to move on to the next section. This technique can result in a confused and disjointed image because each area of tone and colour is unrelated to the neighbouring sections of the work.

Instead of working in piecemeal fashion, try to work over all areas of the canvas simultaneously, moving from foreground to background and letting the composition weave itself into a whole. The image should emerge gradually, rather like a photograph in a developing tray. Keep your eyes moving around the subject, looking for the way tones, colours and shapes relate to each other and making necessary adjustments as you go. You will need to do this because the tones and colours you apply to your canvas will not work in isolation – they will all be influenced by the tones and colours surrounding them. For example, a tone that appears dark on its own will take on a much lighter appearance when it is surrounded by darker tones. Painting is a continuous process of balancing, judging, altering and refining – which is what makes it so totally absorbing.

By building up the tones and colours gradually you will also avoid overworking the surface and churning up the paint, so that when you come to paint in the detail with linear marks and thicker colour towards the final painting of the picture, the colours will remain fresh and the brushstrokes distinct.

Gondolas, Venice

Materials and Equipment

- SHEET OF CANVAS OR BOARD
- OIL COLOURS: CADMIUM RED, YELLOW OCHRE, CADMIUM YELLOW, NAPLES YELLOW, LEMON YELLOW, VIRIDIAN, CERULEAN, PRUSSIAN BLUE, COBALT VIOLET, COBALT BLUE AND TITANIUM WHITE
- LARGE FILBERT BRISTLE BRUSH
- SMALL ROUND SOFT-HAIR BRUSH
- TURPENTINE
- ALKYD MEDIUM

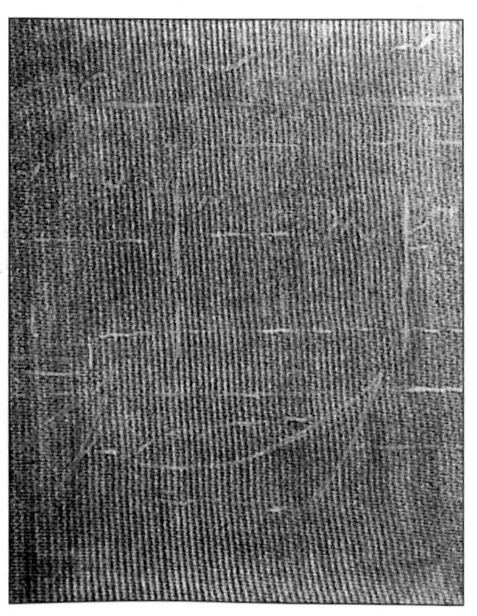

1

Before starting to paint, tone the ground with a thin wash of yellow ochre. Leave to dry for 24 hours, then mix a thin wash of Prussian blue and a little cobalt violet and apply this loosely so that the yellow underlayer gleams up through the blue, creating a lively base colour for the painting. Leave to dry for 24 hours, then mix titanium white and cobalt blue and draw the main elements of the composition with a small round soft-hair brush.

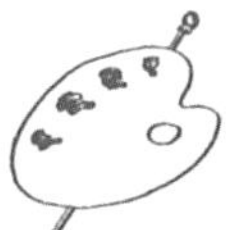

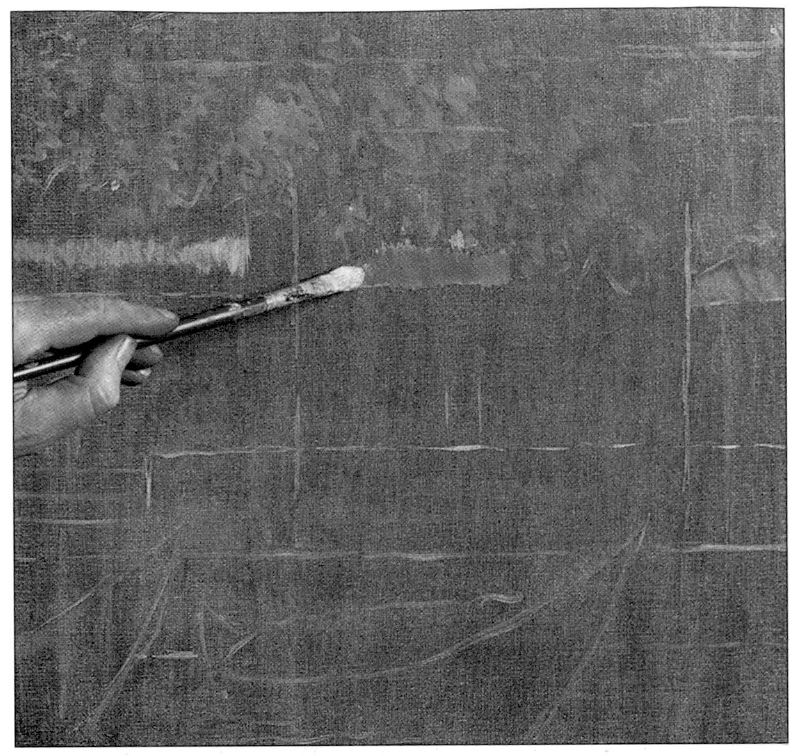

2

Start to block in the main colours using thin paint diluted with turpentine. Mix cerulean, cadmium yellow, yellow ochre and a touch of white and rough in the overhanging vine using a large filbert brush. Vary the proportions of the colours to give variety to the greens. Paint the pink awning with cadmium red, cobalt violet and white; for the blue awning use cerulean and white; add more yellow to the foliage mixture for the green awning. Mix a soft creamy colour from cadmium red, yellow ochre and white and scumble this thinly over the buildings and the steps leading down into the water.

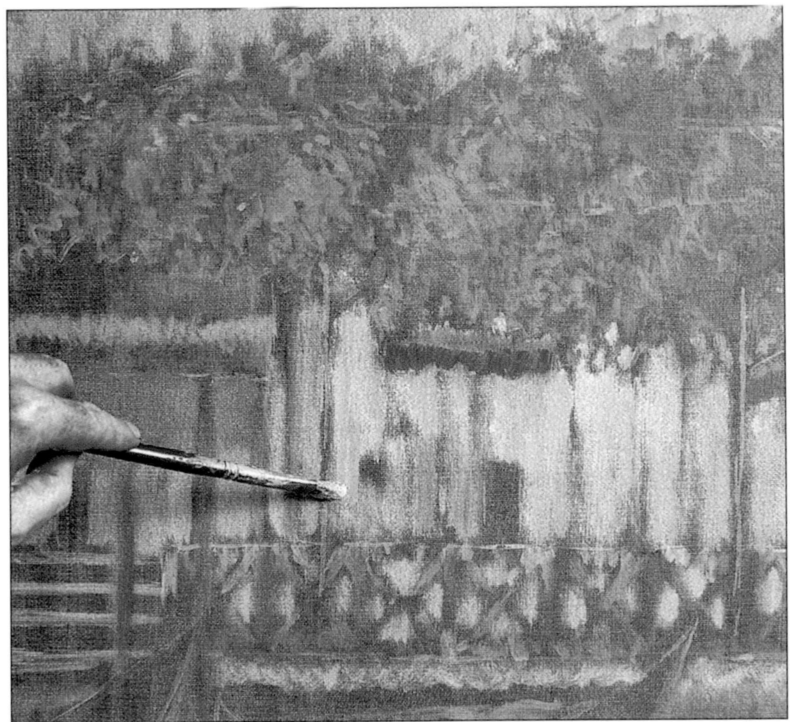

3

Use a small filbert brush to build up tone and texture in the foliage with tiny curved strokes. Mix viridian, Prussian blue and yellow ochre for the darker greens and cerulean, yellow ochre and a touch of cadmium yellow for the lighter greens. Paint the wooden posts with yellow ochre and violet. Mix viridian, cerulean and white and paint the railings of the green balustrade. Then mix a pinkish brown from cadmium red, violet, white and a little cadmium yellow and scumble this over parts of the buildings to give an impression of light and shadow. Work the same colour into the spaces between the railings on the balustrade.

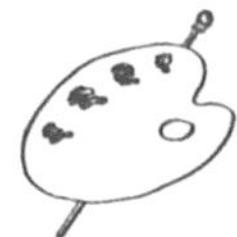

4

Paint the tarpaulin covers on the gondolas with viridian, cerulean and a little white. Now start to paint the water using a small round soft-hair brush to apply small flecks and dashes of broken colour, allowing the dark ground colour to show through. Mix cobalt violet and white for the dark reflections of the gondolas. Then apply loosely spaced strokes of viridian and white over the rest of the water interspersed with soft pinks, yellows and oranges mixed from varying proportions of Naples yellow, cadmium red, yellow ochre and white.

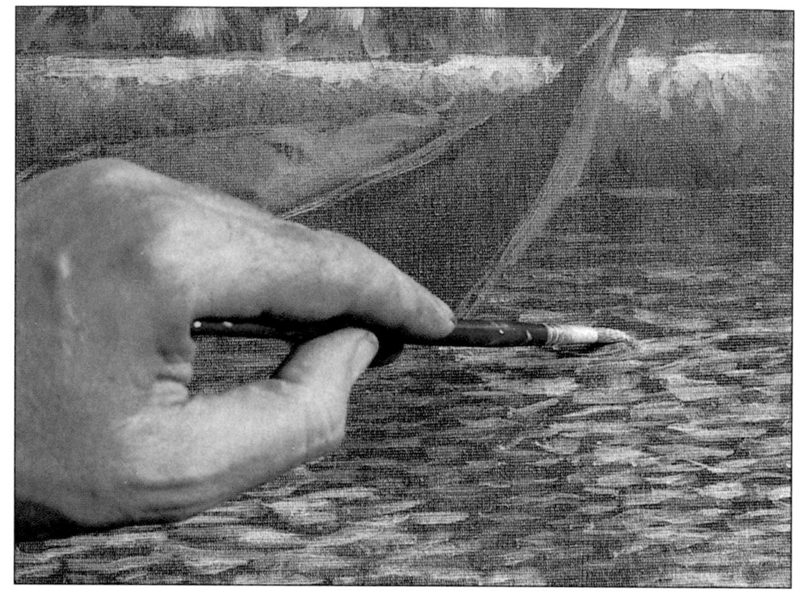

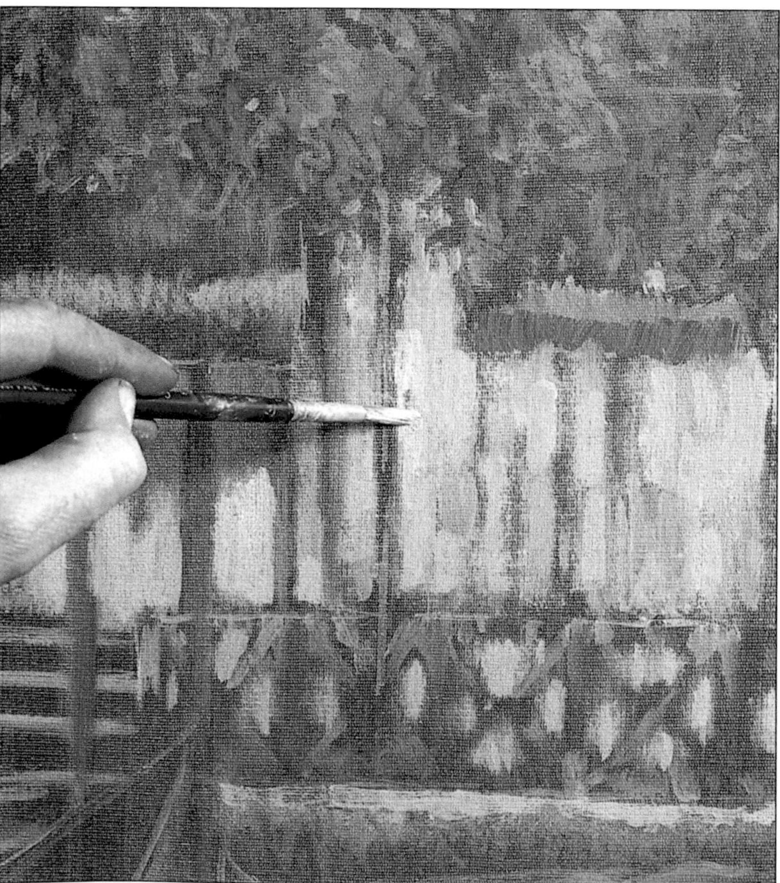

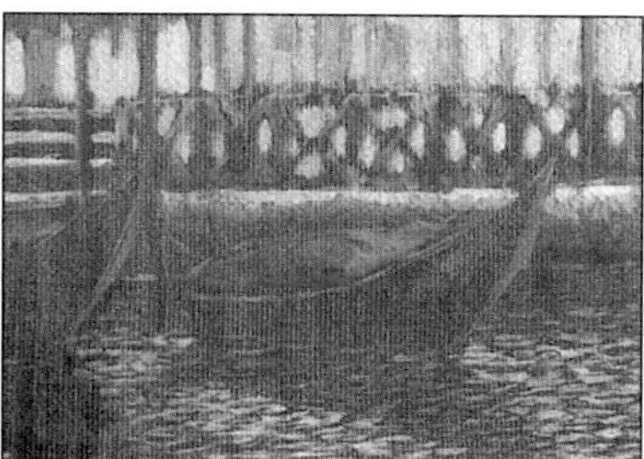

5

Use a network of tiny strokes and dabs of colour to create a shimmering surface that suggests the flickering quality of the light.

6

Don't work on one area in isolation but add touches of colour over the whole image. Scumble greens onto the vine, then add strokes of cadmium red mixed with varying amounts of yellow ochre and white to the buildings. Mix yellow ochre, cadmium red, cobalt violet and a hint of white for the shadow beneath the green awning. Indicate the doors and windows with cerulean and white, and the poles supporting the vine with viridian and white.

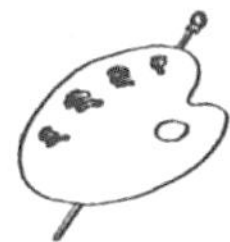

7

Paint the boat hulls with Prussian blue, viridian and a little white, adding more Prussian blue for the shadowed parts. Indicate the shadowy folds on the tarpaulins with Prussian blue, cerulean and white. Lighten the tone of the balustrade with tiny, broken strokes, using varied mixes of viridian, white and yellow ochre. Continue building up the highlights and reflections in the water with broken strokes of pink, green, violet and soft yellow. Mix cadmium red, cadmium yellow and white for the pinks; viridian, lemon yellow and white for the pale greens; yellow ochre and white for the creams, and cobalt violet and white for the violets.

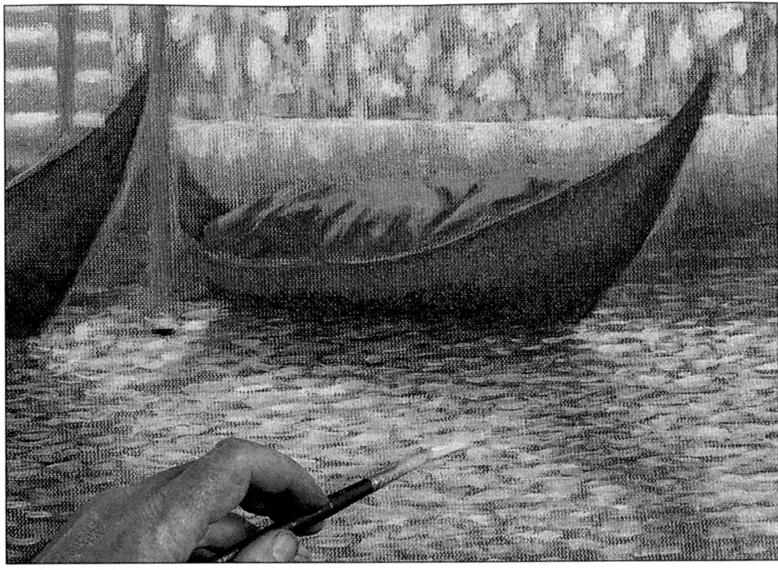

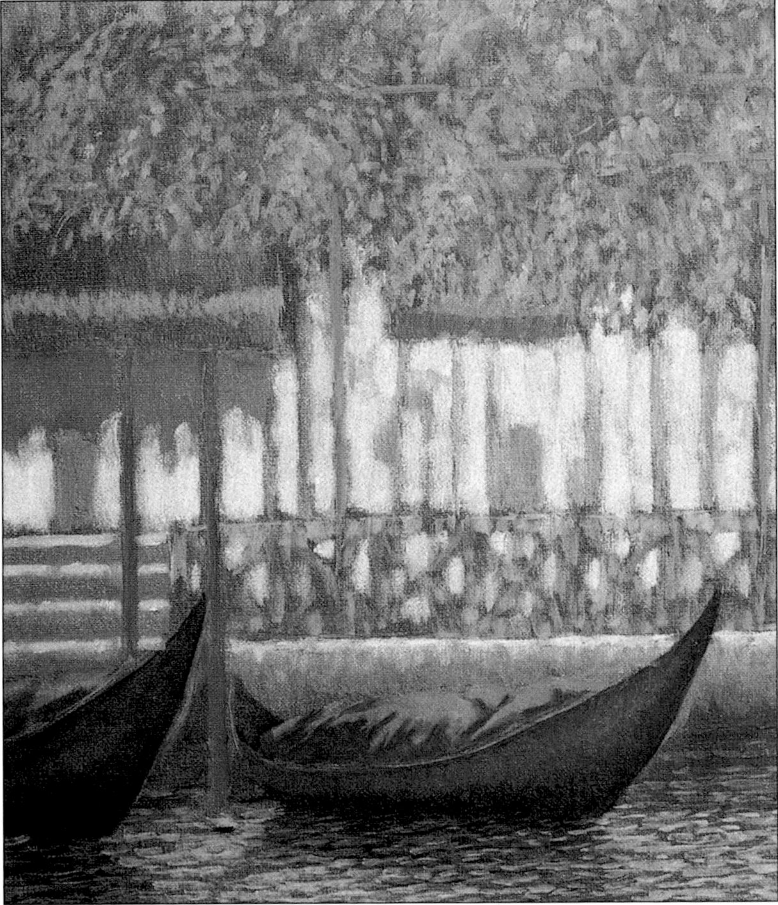

8

Continue working all over the canvas, gradually modifying the colours you have put down to bring the picture into focus. Use a small round brush to complete the foliage, defining the darks with Prussian blue, yellow ochre and a touch of violet and the lights with yellow ochre, cerulean, white and a touch of viridian. Build up the colours in the water, and don't forget to define the reflections of the boats and the mooring poles.

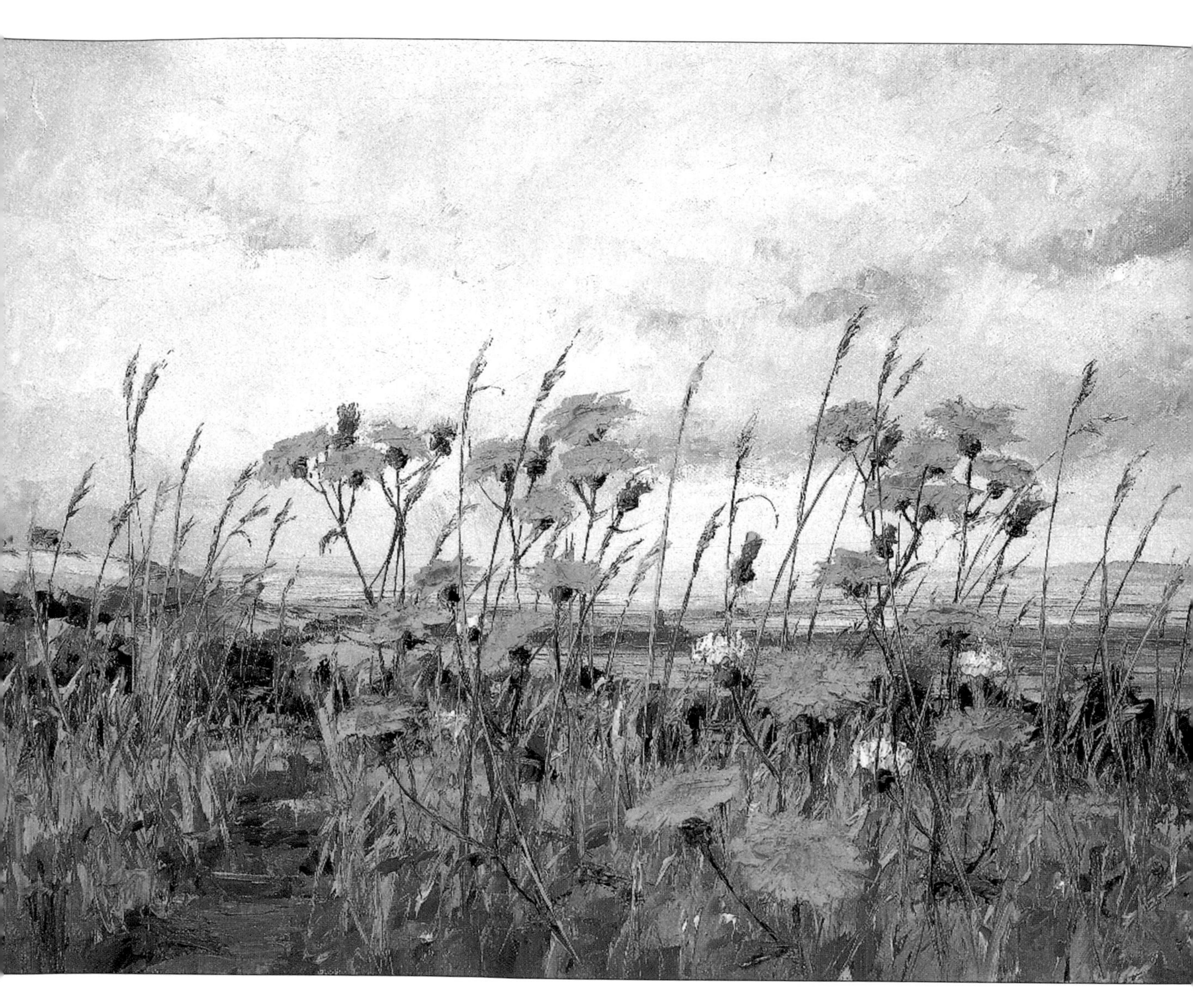

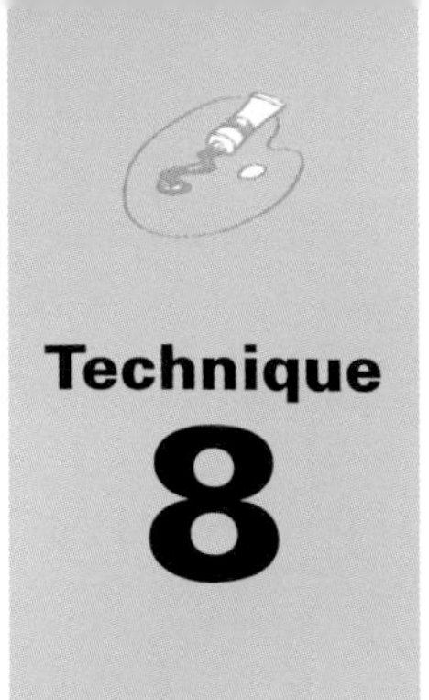

Technique
8

Knife Painting

Essentially, the painting knife is a miniature "trowel" and may be used alone, or in conjunction with brush painting, to apply oil paint to the canvas in a direct and spontaneous manner. Knife painting is ideal for the artist who enjoys the tactile sensation of applying thick, buttery paint to the canvas, moving it around and partially scraping it off with the edge of the blade, or scratching into the wet paint to suggest details and texture.

This striking composition was executed entirely with a painting knife, the colours applied in a thick impasto over a thin underpainting. The ridged texture of the paint stands out in relief and casts tiny shadows that enhance the texture of the grasses and thistles and give a suggestion of movement and changing light.

The artist chose a high viewpoint, looking out over a valley, but crouched low so that the flowers and grasses dwarf the landscape behind. Such an exciting contrast of scale adds greatly to the impact of the picture.

~

Brian Bennett
Sowthistles and Grasses
41 x 56cm (16 x 22in)

~

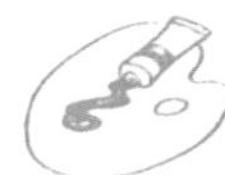

Knife Painting

Knife painting is a versatile and expressive method of building up layers of thick impasto to create a richly textured paint surface.

Painting knives are not the same as palette knives, which have a straight handle and a long straight blade and are used for mixing paint on the palette and for cleaning up. A painting knife has a very springy, responsive blade and a cranked handle to prevent the knuckles accidentally brushing against the canvas when applying the paint. Knives are available in different sizes and in trowel, diamond and elliptical shapes, for creating a range of textures and effects.

Painting with a knife is initially trickier than painting with a brush, so it is wise to practise until you get the feel of it. You can apply the paint in broad sweeps with the flat of the knife, or use the tip to get sharp, angular marks. "Printing" with the edge of the blade produces fine linear marks, useful, for example, when painting the rigging on boats. You can also skim paint off the canvas with the edge of the blade to leave a translucent stain of colour.

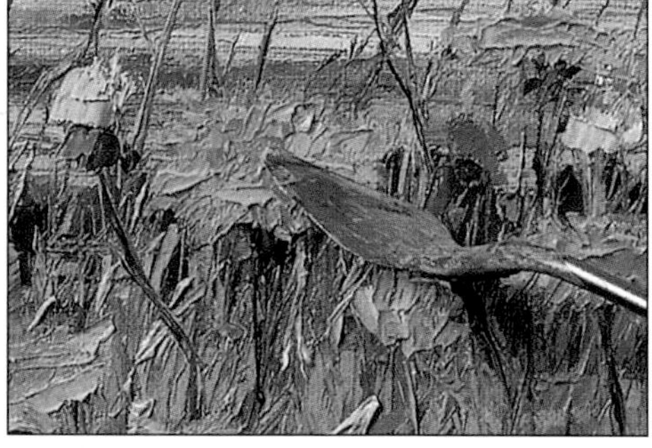

Painting knives encourage a lively and impressionistic treatment, yet are capable of achieving fine detail.

Sowthistles and Grasses

Materials and Equipment

• SHEET OF CANVAS OR CANVAS BOARD • OIL COLOURS: ALIZARIN CRIMSON, FLESH TINT, YELLOW OCHRE, CHROME YELLOW, LEMON YELLOW, CADMIUM YELLOW PALE, WINSOR GREEN, FRENCH ULTRAMARINE, COBALT BLUE, INDIGO, VANDYKE BROWN AND TITANIUM WHITE • LARGE FILBERT BRISTLE BRUSH • TROWEL-SHAPED PAINTING KNIFE • REFINED LINSEED OIL • DISTILLED TURPENTINE

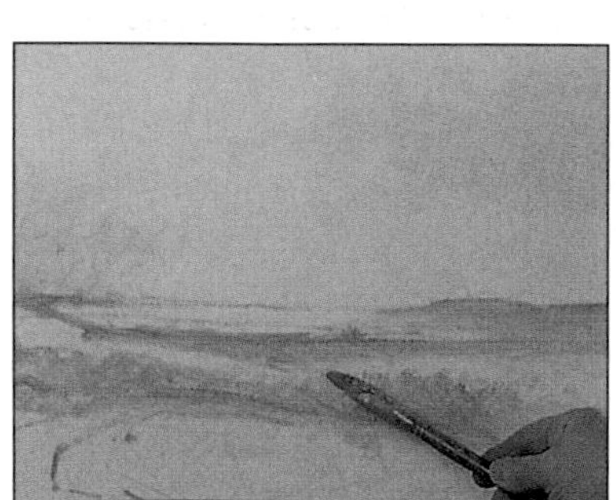

1

Mix a brownish grey from cobalt blue, Vandyke brown and titanium white and dilute to a thin consistency with oil-painting medium. Use this to plot in the main compositional lines and the broad areas of light and dark, scrubbing the paint on quite dryly with a large filbert bristle brush.

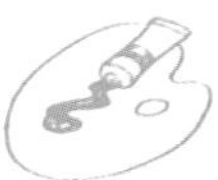

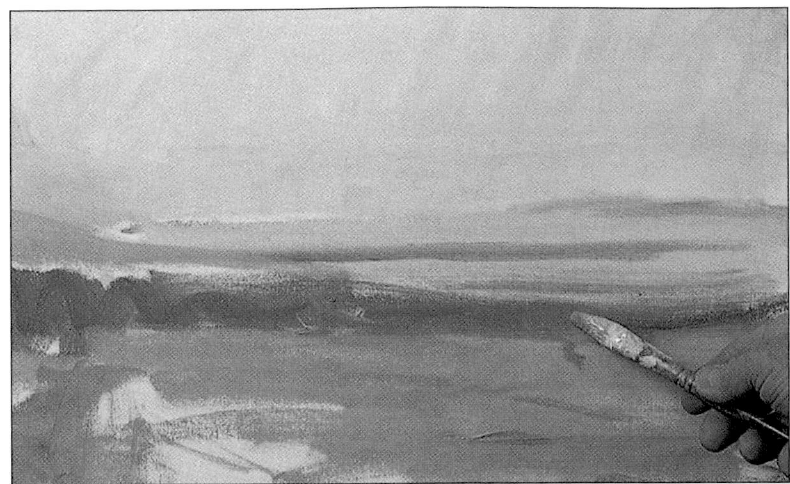

2

Still using the brush, build up an underpainting in thin colour using broad, sweeping strokes. Block in the sky with a pale mix of white, indigo and a little alizarin crimson. Then establish the light and dark tones in the landscape, mixing warm and cool greens from varied proportions of indigo, yellow ochre, chrome yellow and touches of the colours already mixed on your palette.

3

Start to overpaint with the knife, using thicker colour mixed with a little medium. Mix French ultramarine, white and a little alizarin for the upper sky, changing from ultramarine to cooler cobalt blue as you work downwards. Introduce warmer tints (flesh tint, yellow ochre and white) near the horizon. Mix indigo, ultramarine, white and a touch of Vandyke brown for the dark clouds. Touch the colour on with the edge of the blade and then smooth it out with the flat, working the colours into each other, wet-in-wet.

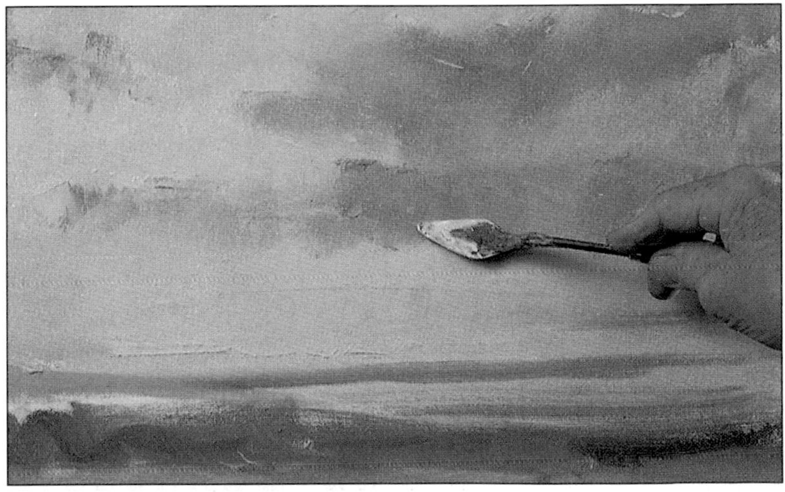

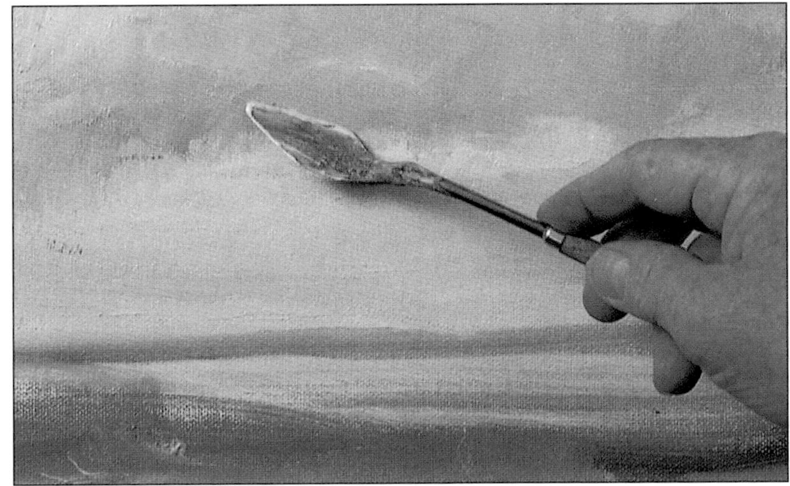

4

Continue building up the massed heaps of storm cloud with thick, creamy paint. For the warmer tops of the clouds, mix yellow ochre, flesh tint and white, softly blending the colour into the grey beneath. Use the back of the knife to drag colour down from the base of the clouds to give the impression of distant rain. This also creates subtle rhythms that lead the eye down to the landscape.

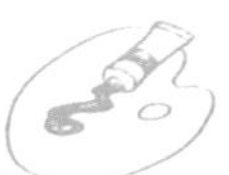

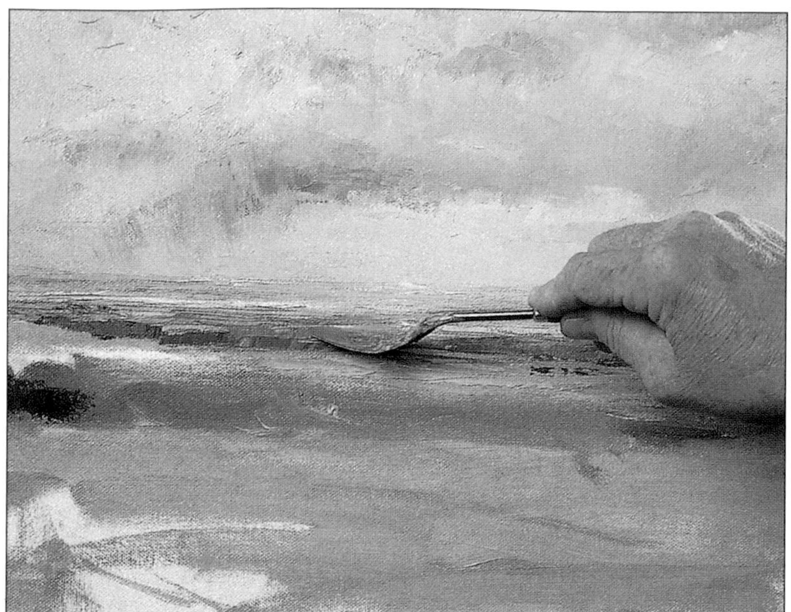

5

Add the fields in the far distance by applying narrow bands of thick paint. For the darks, mix indigo, alizarin and a little white; for the lights, mix cadmium yellow pale, chrome yellow and a little white warmed with yellow ochre in places. Then draw the edge of the knife through the paint to create a series of delicate lines and ridges suggesting fields and hedgerows in the background.

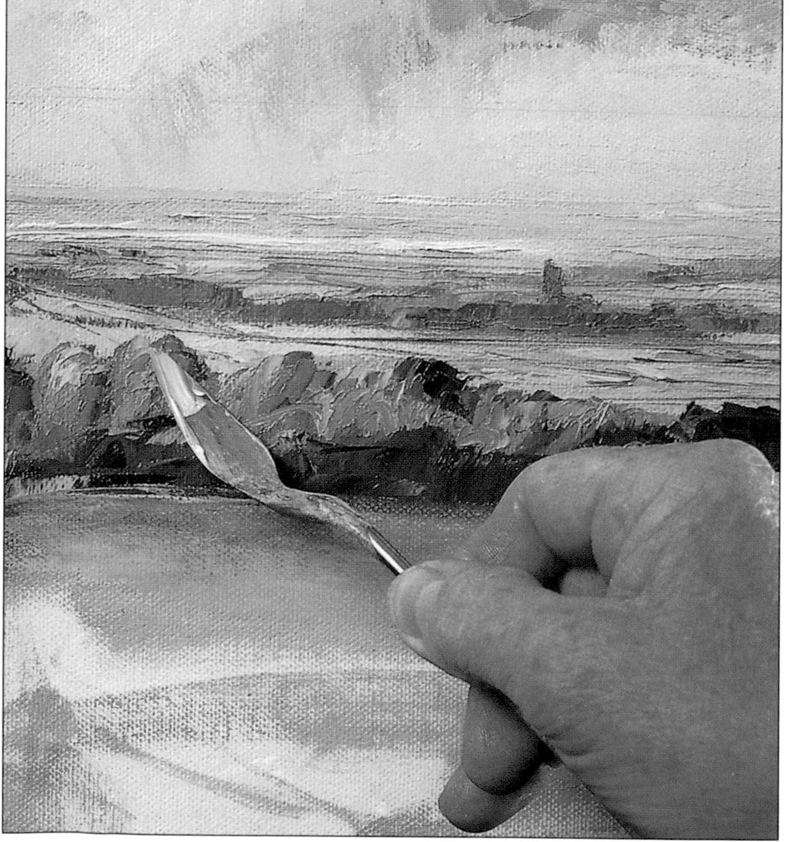

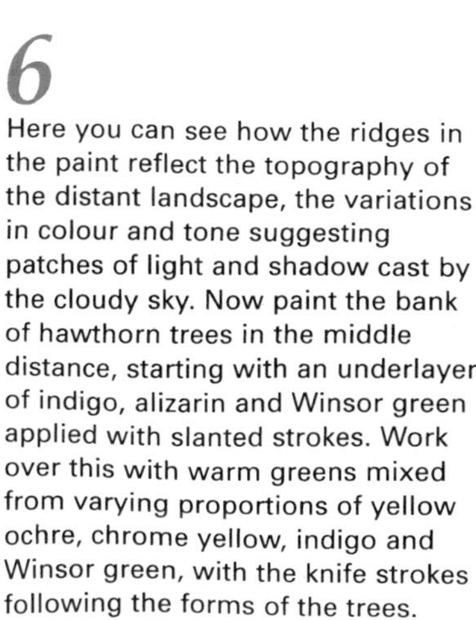

6

Here you can see how the ridges in the paint reflect the topography of the distant landscape, the variations in colour and tone suggesting patches of light and shadow cast by the cloudy sky. Now paint the bank of hawthorn trees in the middle distance, starting with an underlayer of indigo, alizarin and Winsor green applied with slanted strokes. Work over this with warm greens mixed from varying proportions of yellow ochre, chrome yellow, indigo and Winsor green, with the knife strokes following the forms of the trees.

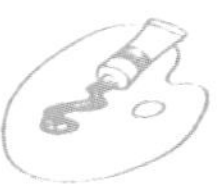

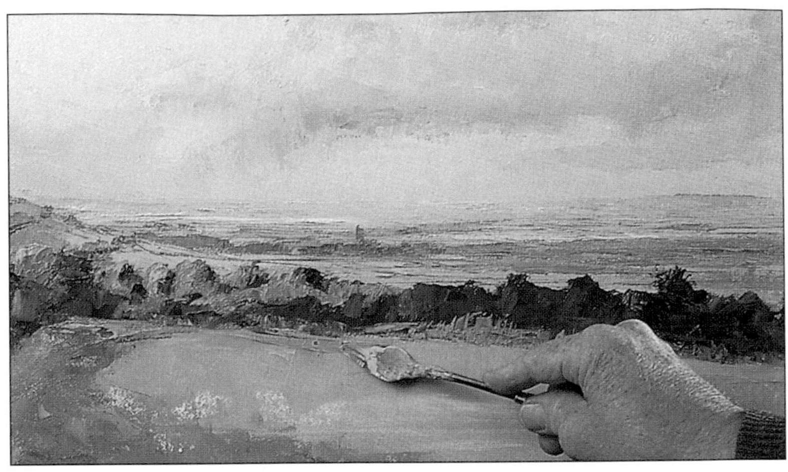

7

Define the curve of the dirt track leading into the distance with Vandyke brown, yellow ochre and white mixed in varying proportions to create a variety of warm lights and cooler darks. Notice how the curve of the track and the shapes of the clouds both help to lead the eye into the picture.

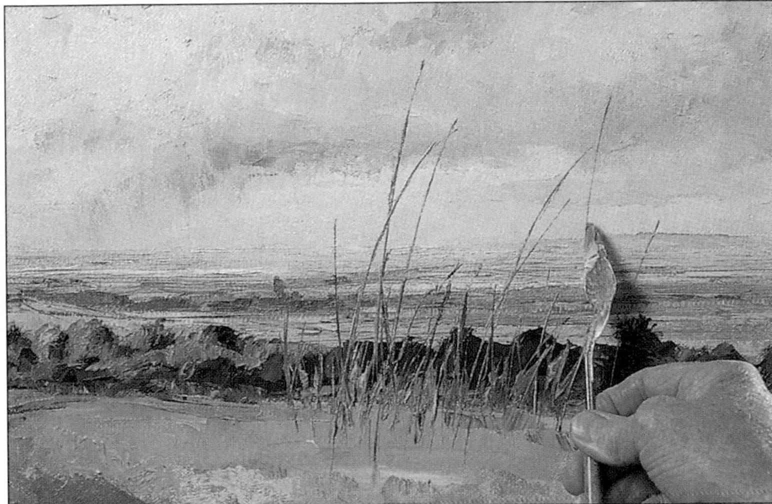

8

On your palette, mix a dark brown from yellow ochre, Vandyke brown and a touch of flesh tint, and a warm yellow from yellow ochre, white and a little lemon yellow. Pick up some dark brown on the edge of the knife and use it to "draw" a series of fine, gently curved lines suggesting stalks and grasses, altering the pressure on the knife as you drag it downwards. Now go over the lines with the yellow mixture; this creates a convincing three-dimensional impression, giving the stalks a lit side and a shadowy side.

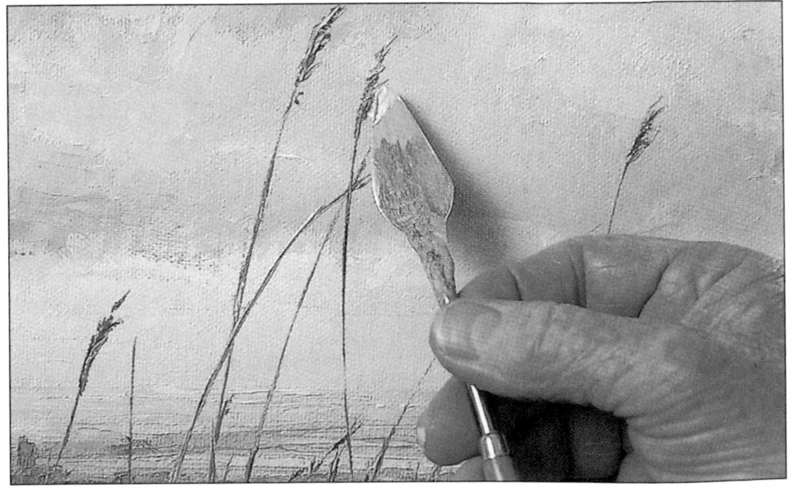

9

Paint the seed heads using delicate upward flicks with the tip of the knife. Again, apply the dark brown first and then add the yellow for the highlights. Paint the grasses dark against the light parts of the sky, and vice versa; this tonal contrast – called "counterchange" – not only creates visual interest but also helps to create space and distance between the foreground and the background.

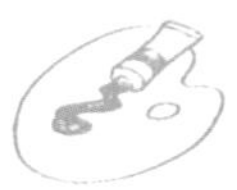

10

Continue painting the stalks and grasses. Avoid creating a "barrier" across the picture by making some grasses taller than others and by varying the density of the clumps so that they appear natural. The dirt track on the left is a useful device, creating a break in the foreground that invites the viewer into the picture. Mix various warm and cool greens from yellow ochre, indigo, Winsor green, chrome yellow and white and apply these with broad knife strokes in the foreground.

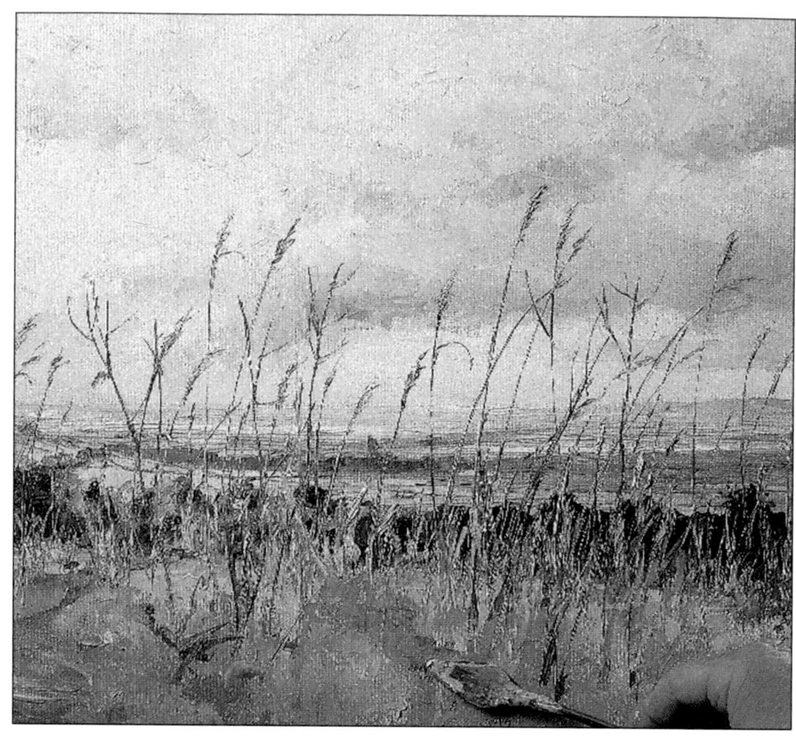

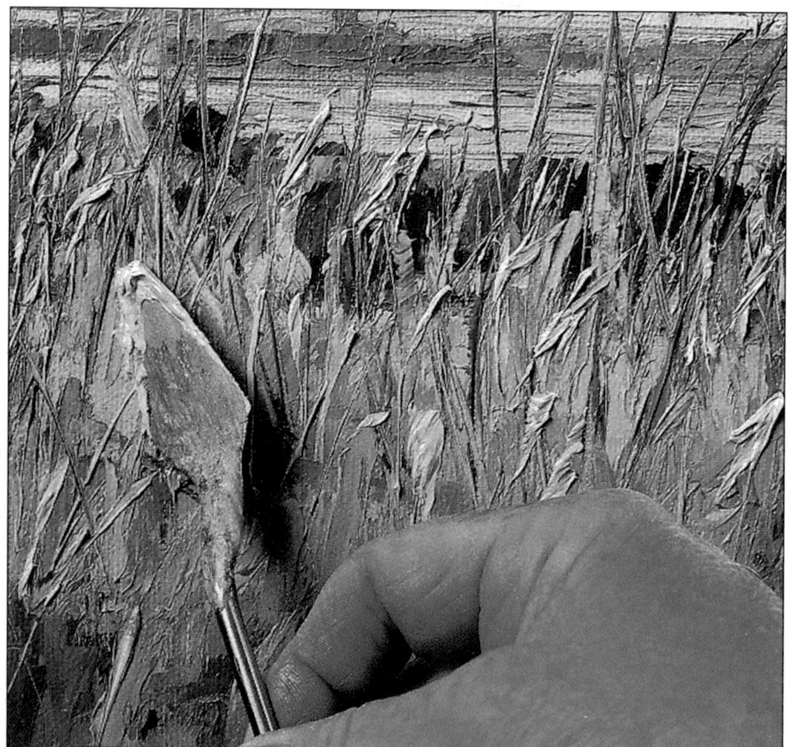

11

Combine yellow ochre, white and a little lemon yellow and fill in some shorter grasses in the immediate foreground of the painting. Merge the bases of the stems into the greens applied in step 10 so that they appear to emerge naturally from the ground. This detail clearly shows the three-dimensional effect of the thick, raised knife marks. You can almost hear the dry grasses rustling in the breeze!

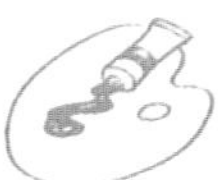

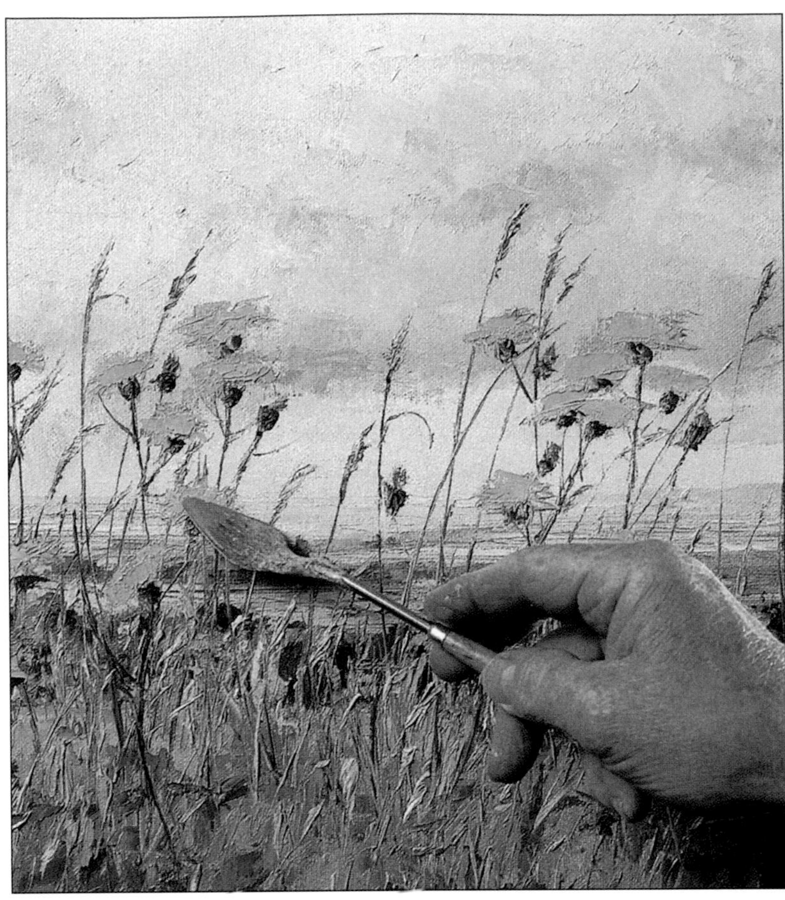

12

Now paint the bright yellow sow thistle flowers using chrome and cadmium yellows "dirtied" with a touch of grey from your palette (first scrape away some of the underlying paint so that the yellow doesn't pick up the blue of the sky). Vary the size, shape and direction of the flower heads – and resist the temptation to put in too many. Suggest some flowers further back amongst the grasses with little touches and smears of paint – don't outline them too clearly otherwise they will jump forward.

13

This close-up reveals how the daisy-like flowers are suggested by applying thick strokes of paint with the tip of the knife, and then feathering them to create ragged edges. Paint the pods under the flowers using warm and cool greens mixed from indigo and chrome yellow. Finish off by painting in the darker centres on some of the flowers with yellow ochre and by touching in one or two white flowers to offset the bright yellows.

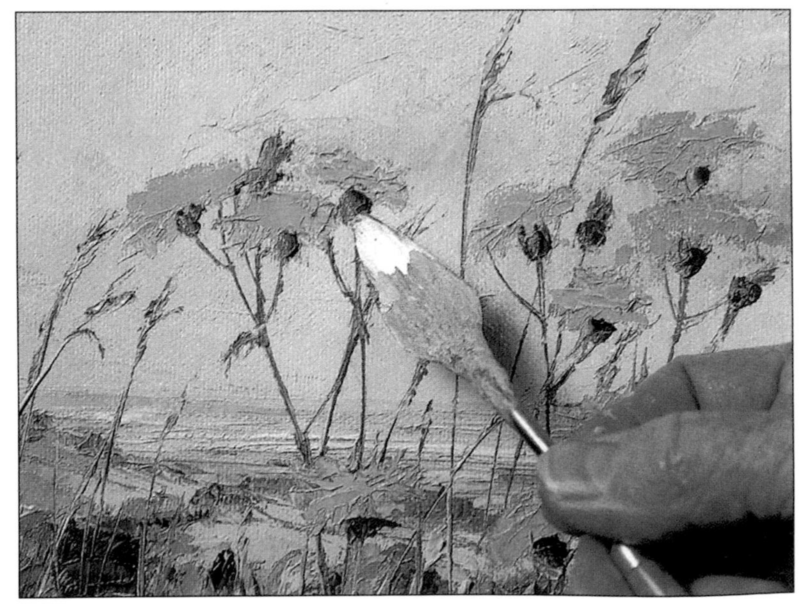

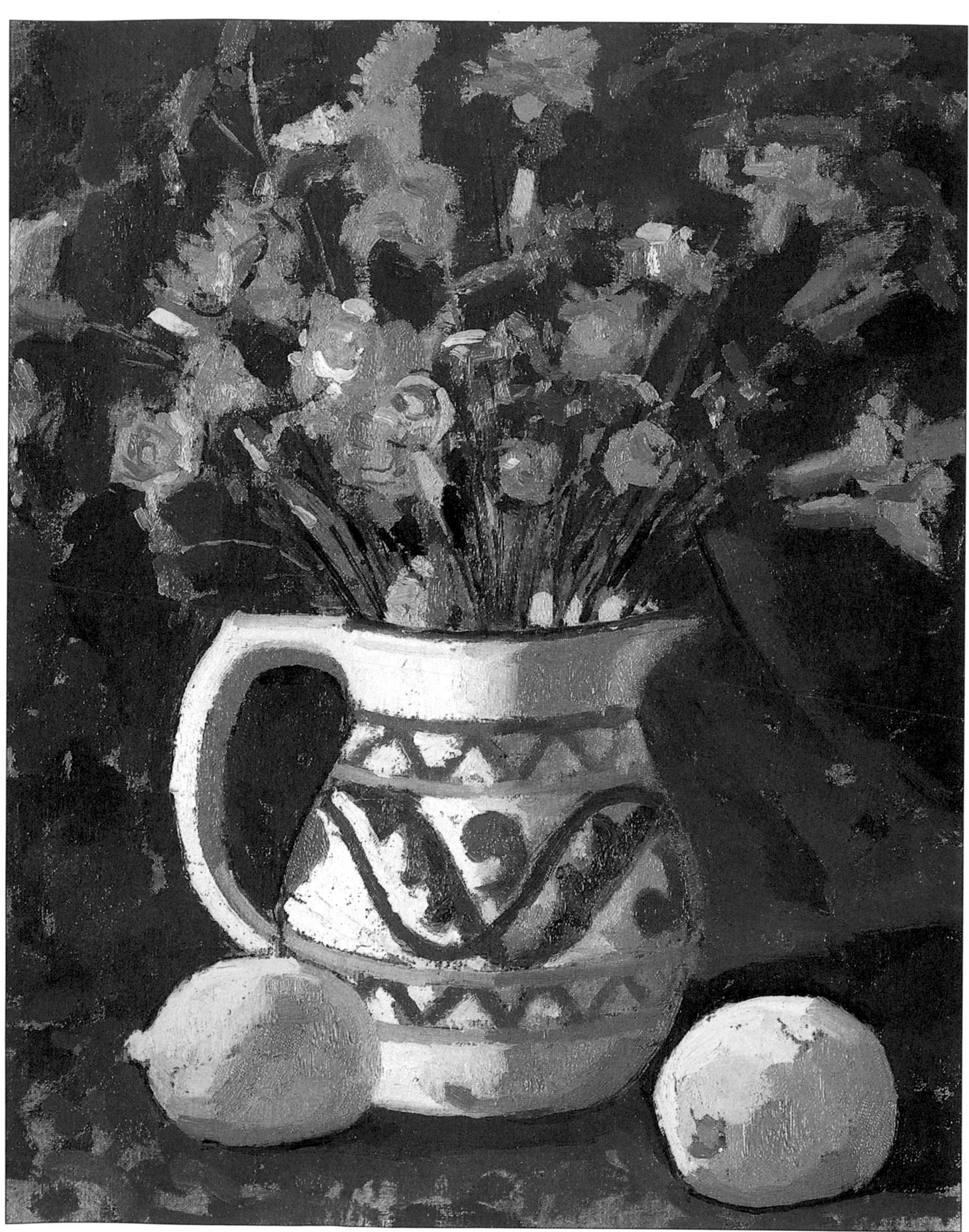

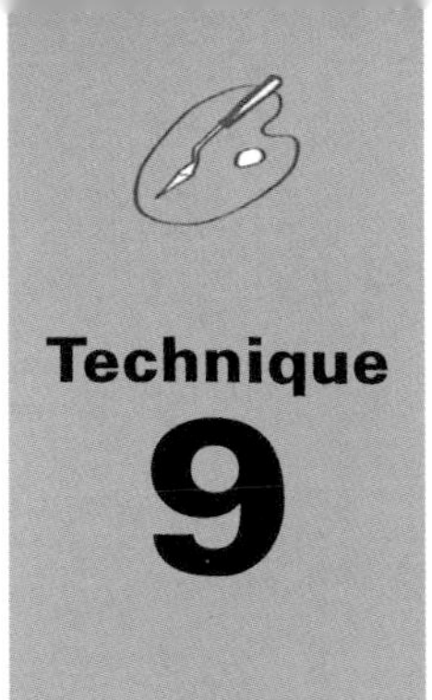

Technique

9

Blending

Oil paint lends itself readily to the blending technique because its soft, buttery consistency and slow drying time allow it to be extensively manipulated on the canvas.

In this still-life study colours are applied over and into one another while still wet, producing subtle gradations of tone and colour that describe the rounded forms of the jug and lemons and give them solidity and weight. The artist was careful, however, to retain the liveliness of the brushmarks, as overblending can make the surface look monotonous.

The standard oil-painting medium (two-thirds turpentine and one-third linseed oil) will give the paint the right amount of body and fluidity for blending wet-into-wet. However, as you gain more experience you should experiment with different mediums as some may be better suited to your way of working than others. In this instance, the artist has used a medium consisting of equal amounts of linseed oil and dammar varnish plus twice the volume of turpentine. This medium holds the marks of the brush well and gives the paint surface an attractive, matt and airy quality.

James Horton
Jug and Lemons
25 x 21cm (10 x 8in)

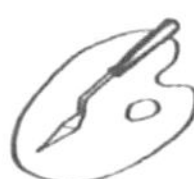

Blending Technique

Blending is a means of achieving smooth gradations between adjacent tones or colours by brushing them together wet-into-wet. It is used to render soft materials and surface qualities such as fabrics, skin tones, flowers and the reflective surfaces of metal and glass. It can also be used to describe certain atmospheric impressions found in the landscape, such as skies and clouds, fog and mist, and reflections in water.

The techniques of blending colour fall between two extremes. On the one hand you can blend the colour with your brush so smoothly and silkily that the brushstrokes are imperceptible even when viewed close-up. At the other extreme it is possible to knit the colours together roughly so that the brushmarks remain visible at close quarters; when viewed at a distance the colours appear to merge together, yet they retain a lively quality because they are only partially blended.

Any type of brush can be used for blending, depending on your style of painting. Some artists use stiff-bristled brushes so they retain the liveliness of the brushstrokes. Others prefer to use soft-hair brushes to achieve very smooth gradations. Brushes called "fan blenders" – they have long hairs arranged in a fan shape – are specially adapted for smooth blending; work over the edge between two tones or colours using a gentle sweeping motion until a smooth, imperceptible blend is achieved.

Jug and Lemons

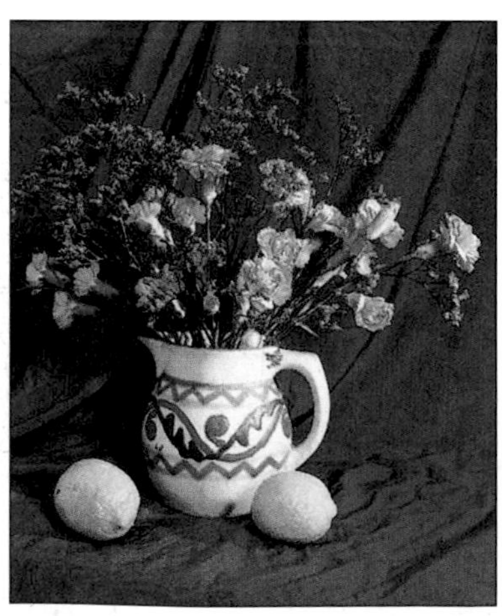

Left: The items in this still life were chosen for their gently rounded forms, which are ideally suited to the technique of blending colour wet-in-wet. Bright complementary colours – blues and purples, oranges and yellows – enliven the composition.

Materials and Equipment

• SHEET OF PRIMED HARDBOARD OR MDF • OIL COLOURS: ALIZARIN CRIMSON, YELLOW OCHRE, CHROME YELLOW, LEMON YELLOW, CADMIUM ORANGE, VERMILION, TERRE VERTE, FRENCH ULTRAMARINE, COBALT BLUE, BURNT SIENNA, RAW UMBER AND TITANIUM WHITE • 25MM (1IN) DECORATING BRUSH • MEDIUM AND SMALL ROUND BRISTLE BRUSHES • SMALL ROUND SABLE OR SYNTHETIC BRUSH • RIGGER BRUSH • REFINED LINSEED OIL • DISTILLED TURPENTINE • DAMMAR VARNISH

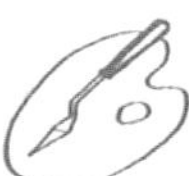

1

Start by tinting the board with a neutral mid-tone to eliminate the stark white of the priming. Mix burnt sienna and a little French ultramarine with lots of turpentine to a thin consistency. Apply this freely across the board with a 25mm (1in) household brush. Leave to dry overnight.

Sketch out the main outlines of the composition using a small round sable or synthetic brush and French ultramarine diluted with turpentine to make it flow easily.

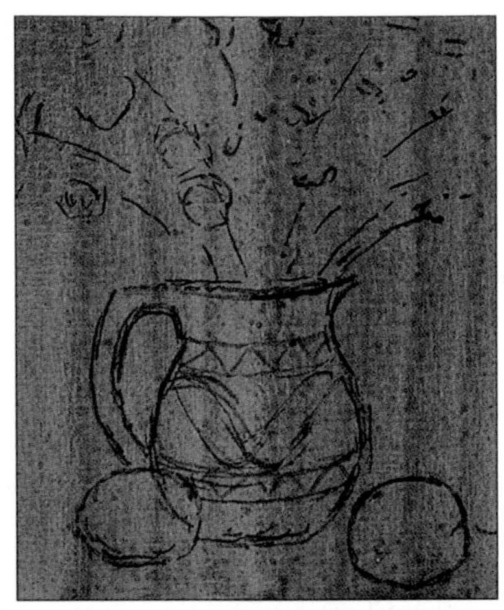

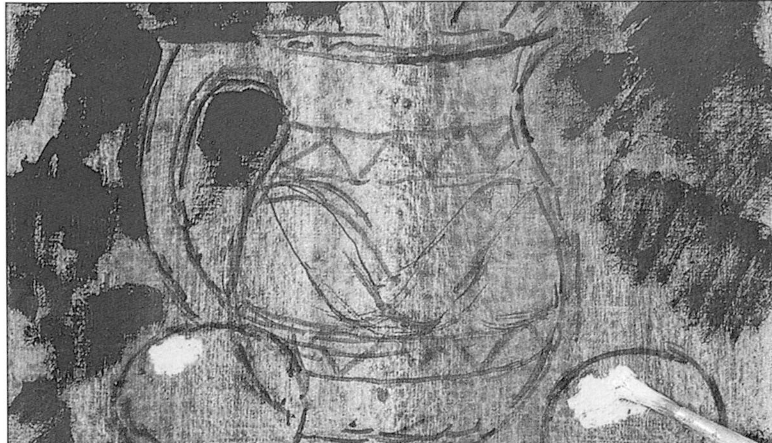

2

It is often a good idea to plot the lightest and darkest tones early on, as they provide a useful reference for the mid-tones. Rough in the darks in the blue backcloth with a mixture of ultramarine, alizarin crimson and titanium white applied with a medium round bristle brush. Scrub the paint on with loose, open strokes that allow the tinted ground to show through. Apply dabs of neat chrome yellow on the tops of the lemons to establish the lightest tones in the image.

3

Block in the shadows on the lemons with a mix of lemon yellow, ultramarine and a drop of cadmium orange. Start to work on the jug, establishing the broad tones of light and shade. For the lighter tone, mix white with a touch of cadmium orange; for the shadow side, mix a warm grey from yellow ochre, ultramarine, white and terre verte. Roughly block in the tones. Make no attempt to blend at this stage.

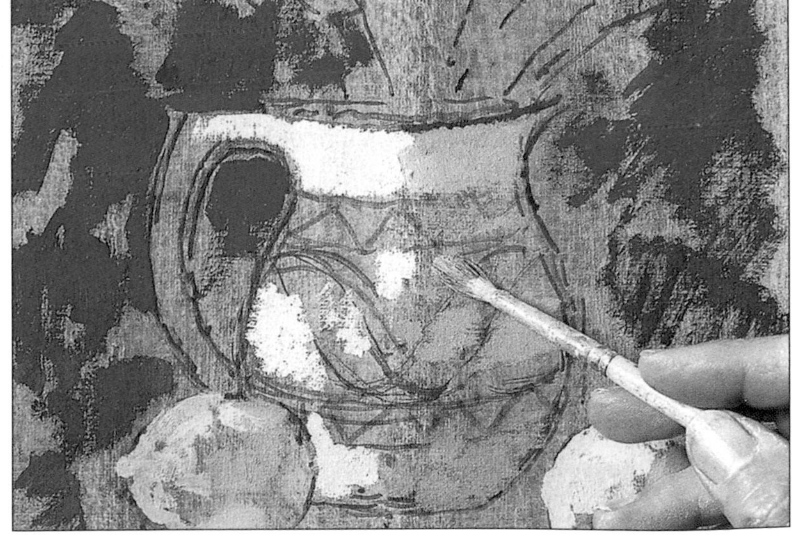

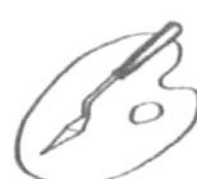

4

Use the dark blue mixed in step 2 to put a shadow under the jug and lemons to give them a feeling of solidity and weight. Then add more white to the mix and rough in the lighter blue of the cloth in the foreground. Switch to a smaller round bristle brush to paint the decorative pattern on the jug. For the dark blues, mix ultramarine, cobalt blue and alizarin crimson. For the greenish blues mix ultramarine, cobalt and lemon yellow. And for the greens mix ultramarine and lemon yellow. Remember to darken the tone of each colour as the jug turns into shadow, graduating the tones by blending them wet-in-wet.

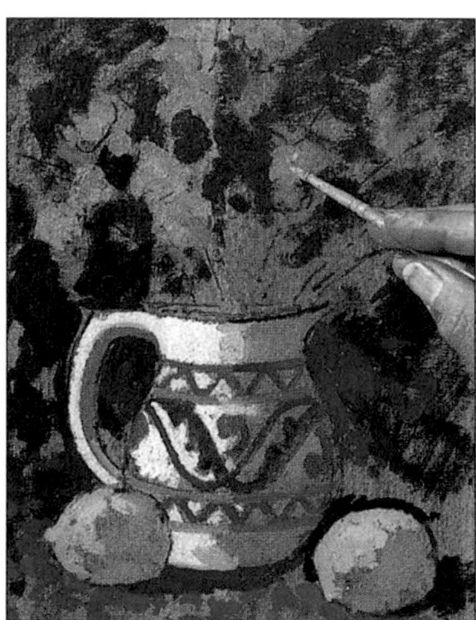

5

Paint the brown patterns on the jug with burnt sienna and white. Then start to work on the flowers, mixing cadmium orange, vermilion and white for the carnations, and ultramarine, lemon yellow and white for the foliage. Vary the proportions of the colours used in each mix to create a range of warms and cools and lights and darks.

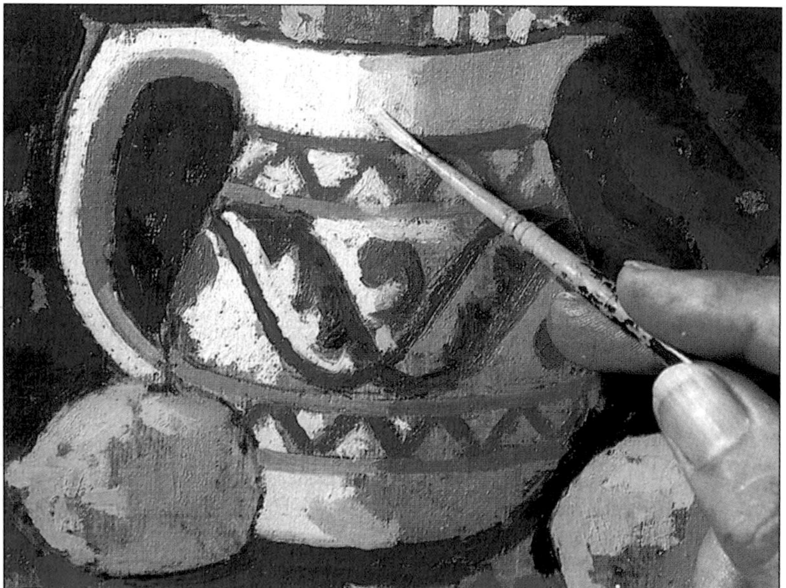

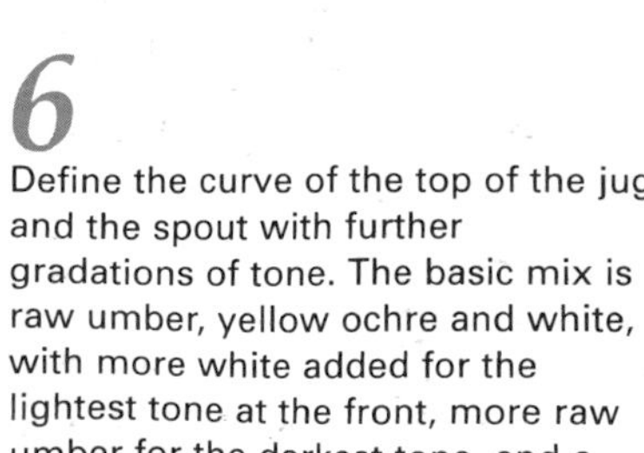

6

Define the curve of the top of the jug and the spout with further gradations of tone. The basic mix is raw umber, yellow ochre and white, with more white added for the lightest tone at the front, more raw umber for the darkest tone, and a touch of cadmium orange added for the darker, warmer tone in between.

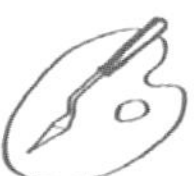

7

Now use the medium round bristle brush to describe the light folds in the backcloth, using a mixture of ultramarine, alizarin crimson and white. Vary the tones by adding more white in the lighter folds.

Use the small round bristle brush to develop the forms of the flowers, adding touches of vermilion to define the petals. Paint some of the statice flowers with a mix of ultramarine and alizarin, adding a hint of white in the lighter areas. Mix white with a touch of cadmium orange to add warm tints to the lit side of the jug and its handle.

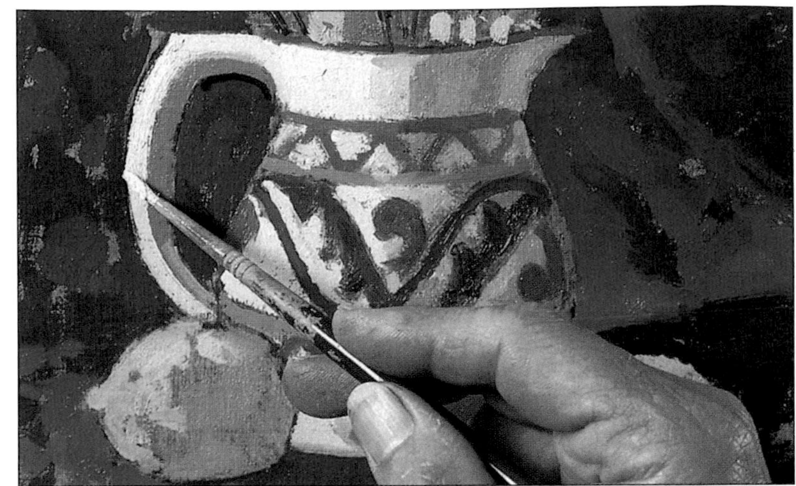

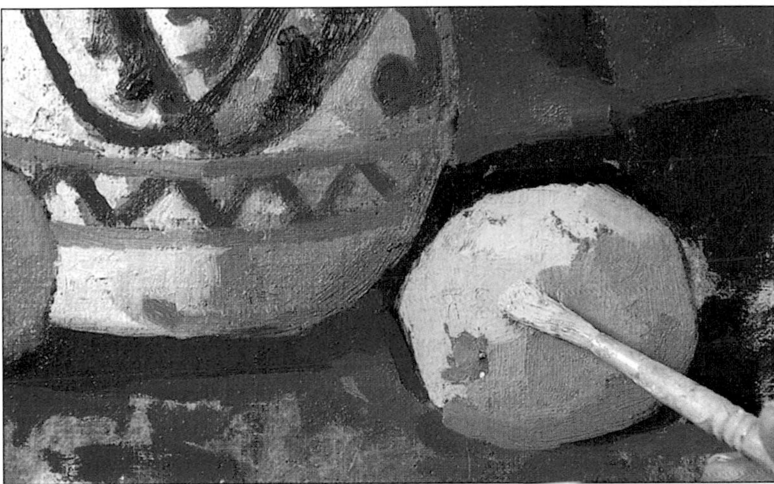

8

Define the rounded forms of the lemons with tonal gradations from light to dark. Using the medium round brush, work over the highlights with a mix of chrome yellow and white, then add a little raw umber to the mix for the mid-tones. Finally, add more raw umber and a little cadmium orange for the warm shadows at the base of the lemons. Use thick, juicy paint and lively brushmarks that follow the forms of the fruits, blending the tones together where they meet to define the different planes.

9

Feather over the different tones on the jug with a dry brush to soften them. Give definition to the carnations at the front, adding swirls of vermilion and picking out the light petals with vermilion, lemon yellow and white. Add more of the purple statice flowers using ultramarine, alizarin and white.

Stand back and decide on any final adjustments. Add pale highlights along the tops of the lemons using white and a little lemon yellow. Use a rigger brush to redefine any edges that have become ragged, such as on the handle of the jug.

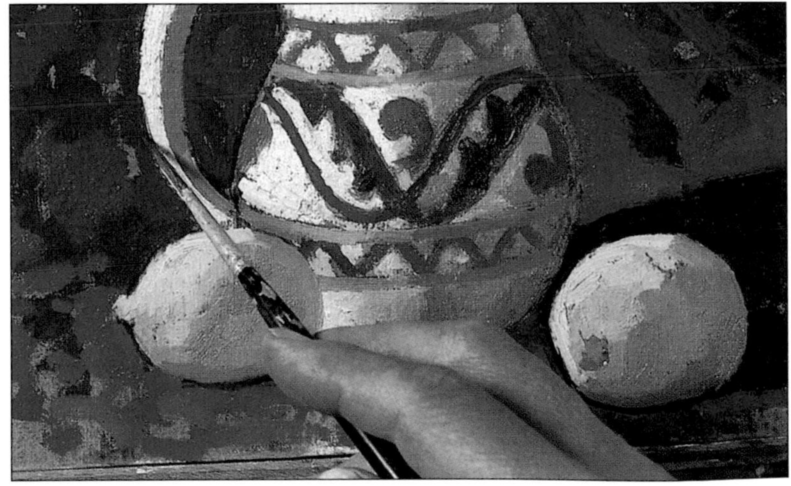

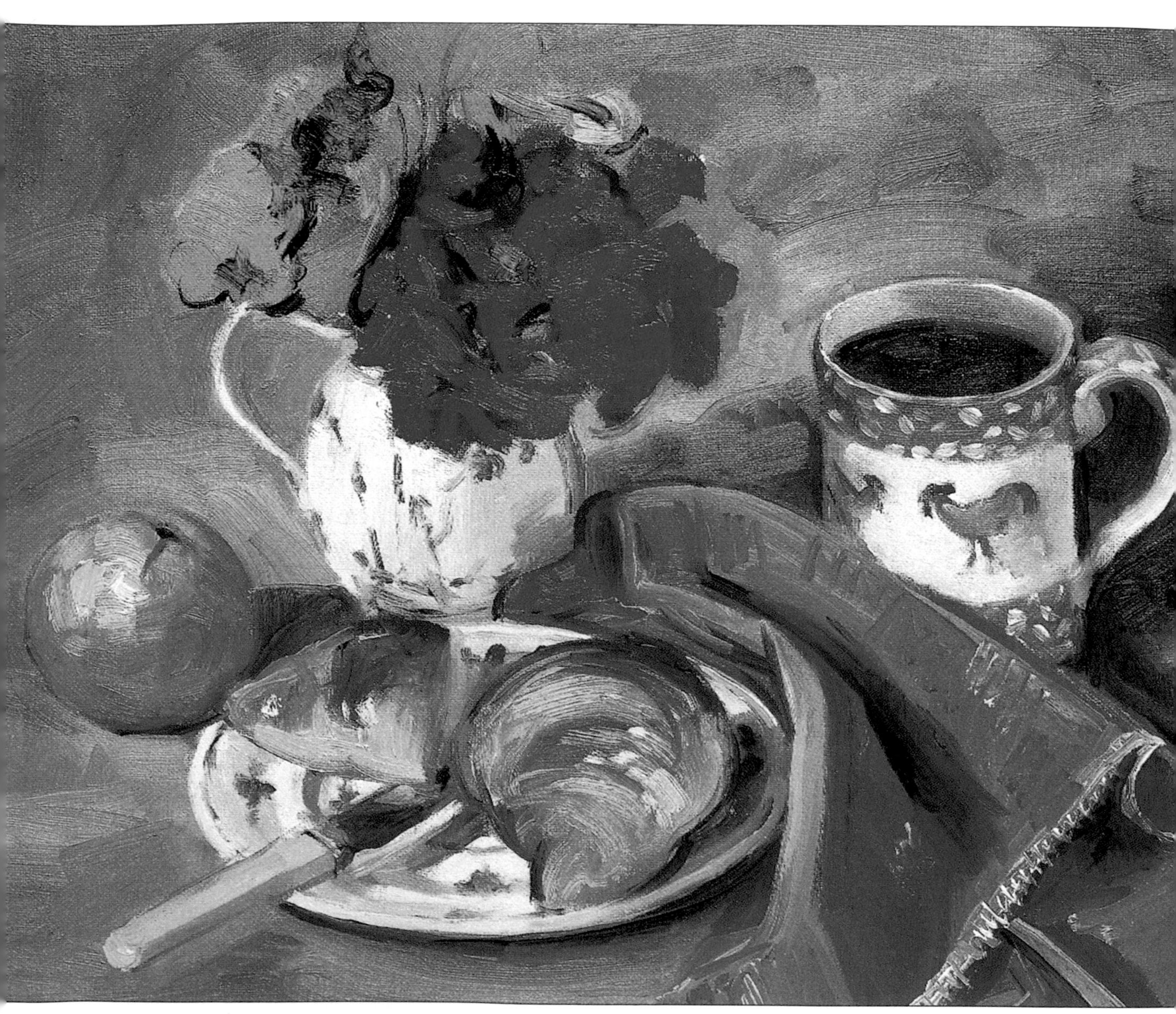

Technique 10

Underpainting

Many painters like to start a complex oil painting by brushing in the broad areas of the composition in thin colour in order to help them organize the picture in terms of shapes and tones.

Making an underpainting is, in effect, a way of "starting before you've begun". The intimidating white of the canvas is quickly covered, and at a very early stage the picture already reads as a whole. The underpainting may be completely covered as the picture is built up, or it can play an active role in the final painting if parts of it are left visible. This creates a pleasing contrast between thin and thick applications of paint, as well as breathing air into the painting and injecting a lively, working feel.

Underpainting is traditionally done in a monochrome grey or earth colour, which acts as a guide for the light and dark tones in the image. In this painting, however, the artist chose to underpaint in light colours approximating those of the subject. Thus the succeeding colours, as well as tones, are more easily judged against the underpainting.

Ted Gould
Coffee and Croissant
36 x 46cm (14 x 18in)

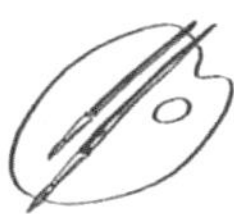

Underpainting

The traditional way of starting an oil painting is to block in the broad shapes and masses with thin paint before adding the details and surface colour. The underpainting gives you the opportunity to organize the composition and the distribution of light and dark values at the outset, and to resolve any problems before starting to paint. Because the paint is thin, corrections are easily made at this stage by wiping with a rag.

The result is a practical division of labour; once the underpainting is complete you can concentrate on colour and detail, confident that the composition and tonal values are sound.

Traditionally, neutral greys, blues or earth colours are used to underpaint. The darks and mid-tones are established with tones of one colour, leaving the white or tinted canvas to act as the highlights. Underpainting may also be done in colours that either complement or contrast with the overall colour values of the subject. For example, an underpainting in warm browns or reds will give resonance to the cool greens of a landscape. The underpainting can also be laid in several colours that relate to those used in the final painting.

Colours for underpainting should be thinly diluted with turpentine or white (mineral) spirit. The underpainting must also be thoroughly dry before you start the overpainting. To save time, you can underpaint with acrylic colours (thinly diluted with water) and then overpaint in oils. Acrylics dry within minutes, allowing you to apply the next layer in oil almost immediately.

Coffee and Croissant

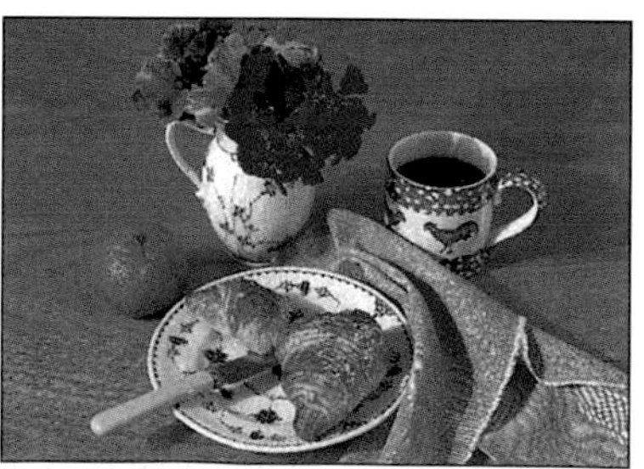

Left: A pretty and informal breakfast setting is the subject of this still life. Although the objects appear casually arranged, they are in fact carefully composed to create a strong, cohesive group.

Materials and Equipment

- SHEET OF CANVAS OR BOARD
- ACRYLIC COLOURS: BRIGHT RED, CRIMSON, LEMON YELLOW YELLOW OCHRE, BRIGHT GREEN, FRENCH ULTRAMARINE AND BURNT SIENNA
- OIL COLOURS: INDIAN RED, VENETIAN RED, SCARLET LAKE, ALIZARIN CRIMSON, YELLOW OCHRE, WINSOR YELLOW, WINSOR GREEN, FRENCH ULTRAMARINE AND TITANIUM WHITE
- SMALL ROUND SYNTHETIC BRUSH
- SMALL, MEDIUM AND LARGE FLAT BRISTLE BRUSHES
- TURPENTINE
- LINSEED OIL
- JAR OF WATER

1

Start by drawing the main outlines using acrylics. Mix yellow ochre with a touch of French ultramarine and dilute with water to a thin consistency. Sketch loosely with a small round synthetic brush. Horizontal and vertical axes lines will help you to draw the round and elliptical shapes accurately. Leave to dry – this will take only a few minutes.

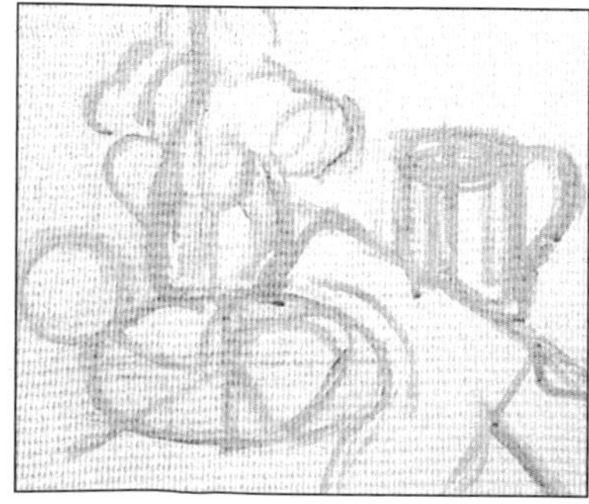

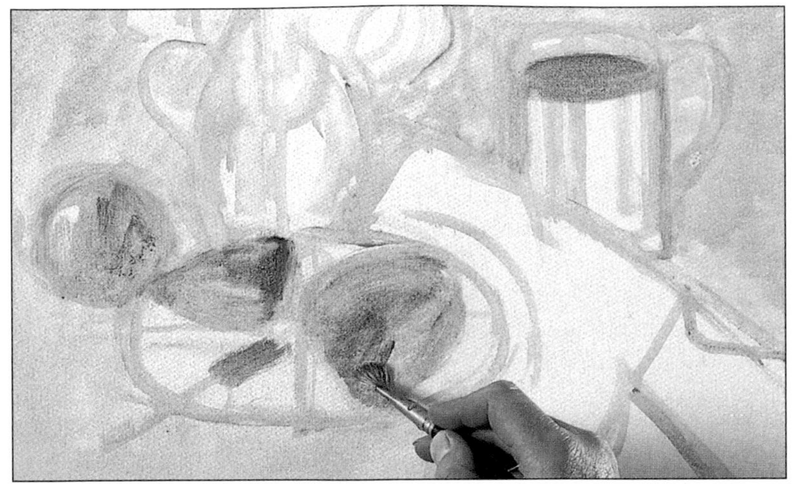

2

Now establish the underpainting, again using fast-drying acrylic paints. Mix a thin, watery wash of yellow ochre warmed with a little burnt sienna, and use a large flat synthetic brush to loosely block in the background. Darken the mix with ultramarine and touch in the coffee in the mug using a medium-sized flat brush. Mix yellow ochre and bright red for the orange, then add a touch of burnt sienna to the mix and block in the split croissant and the knife blade. Work thinly and rapidly, not worrying about details at this stage.

3

Continue underpainting with colours approximating those of the actual objects. Use very thinly diluted crimson for the napkin, darkened with ultramarine for the shadows and creases. Block in the geranium flowers with crimson mixed with lemon yellow for the warmer reds and ultramarine for the cooler, darker reds. Use bright green for the geranium leaves, adding lemon yellow for the warmer greens and ultramarine for the cooler greens. Paint the blue cockerel pattern on the mug with ultramarine, then add burnt sienna for the cast shadows.

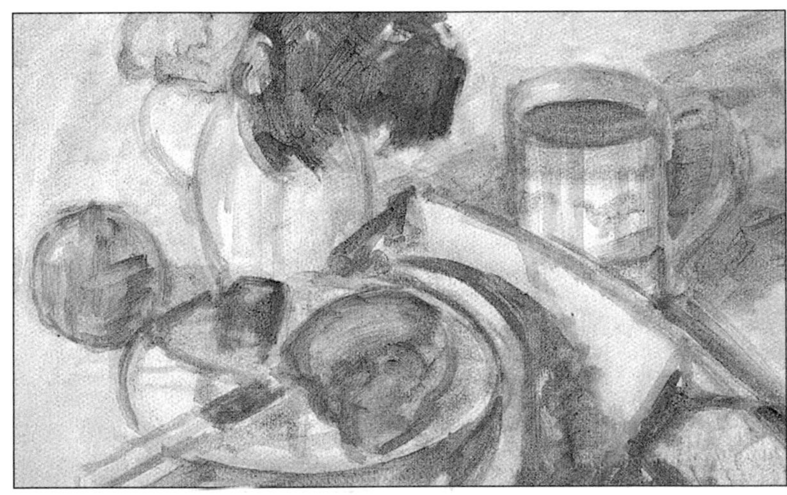

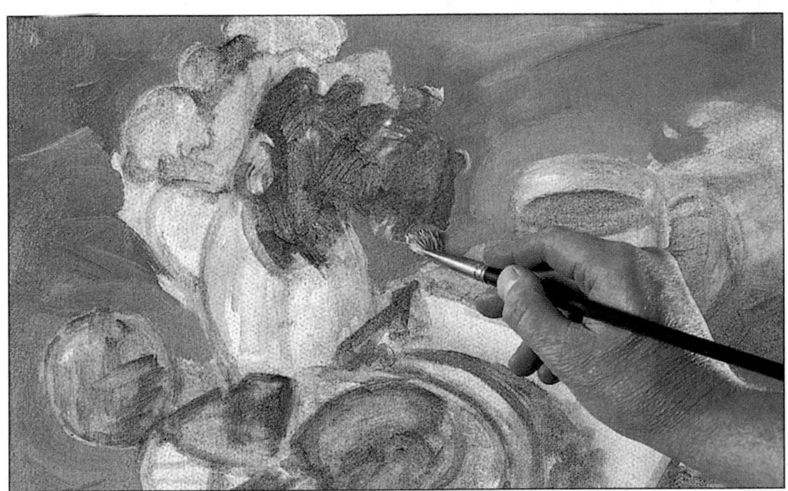

4

Once the acrylic underpainting is dry you can start to overpaint in oils, thinning the colours with turpentine and linseed oil medium. First, block in the background with loosely mixed Indian red, yellow ochre, Winsor yellow and titanium white. Use a large flat bristle brush and sweep the paint on quite vigorously, working the brush in different directions and letting the marks of the brush show. Paint up to the still-life forms, then cut into them to begin to define them.

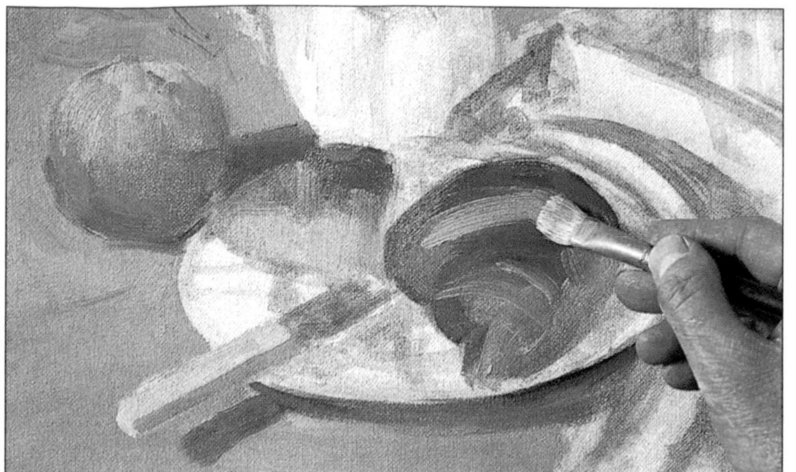

5

Use a medium-sized flat brush to define the orange with Winsor yellow and Indian red, adding more yellow for the light tones on top and more red for the shadows. For the deeper shadow near the base, darken with a little alizarin. Mix yellow ochre, white and a touch of ultramarine for the knife handle. Paint the shadows on the table with a mix of yellow ochre, Indian red and ultramarine. Define the croissant halves using Indian red broken with yellow ochre, Winsor yellow and white. Add more Indian red for the crusty tops. Follow the forms with your brushstrokes.

6

Paint the coffee in the mug with a mix of Indian red, ultramarine and yellow ochre. Mix a warm grey from ultramarine, yellow ochre and a touch of Indian red and put in the shadows on the plate and the blade of the knife. Define the flower jug with pale greys mixed from ultramarine, yellow ochre, a touch of Indian red and plenty of white. Create different subtle tones, adding more blue for the shadows on the jug. Mix alizarin and Winsor yellow and block in the geraniums with strokes in different directions. Add ultramarine for darker reds.

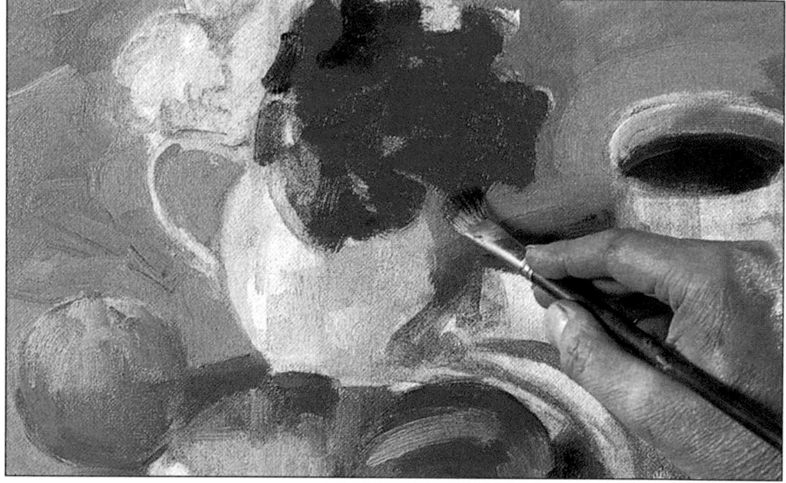

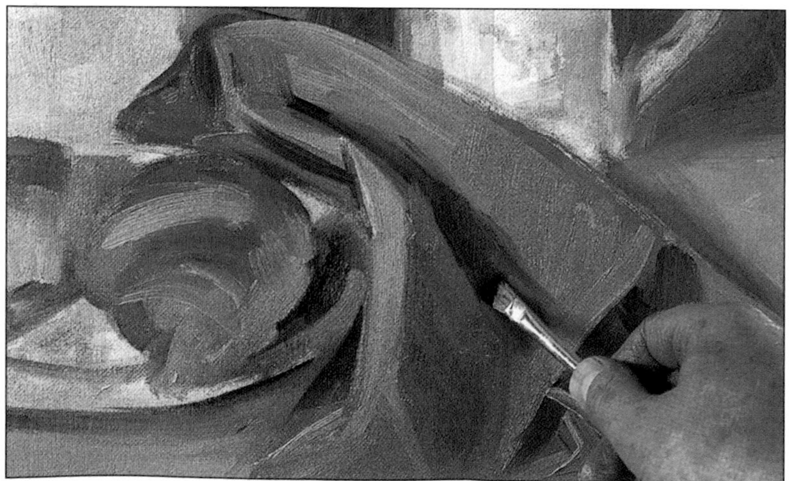

7

Now work on the pink napkin, first blocking in the local colour with a medium-toned mix of alizarin crimson, white and a touch of ultramarine. Then define the creases and folds with thick, creamy paint applied with a small flat brush. Mix alizarin crimson and ultramarine for the shadowy folds, and white with a touch of alizarin for the highlights along the tops of the folds.

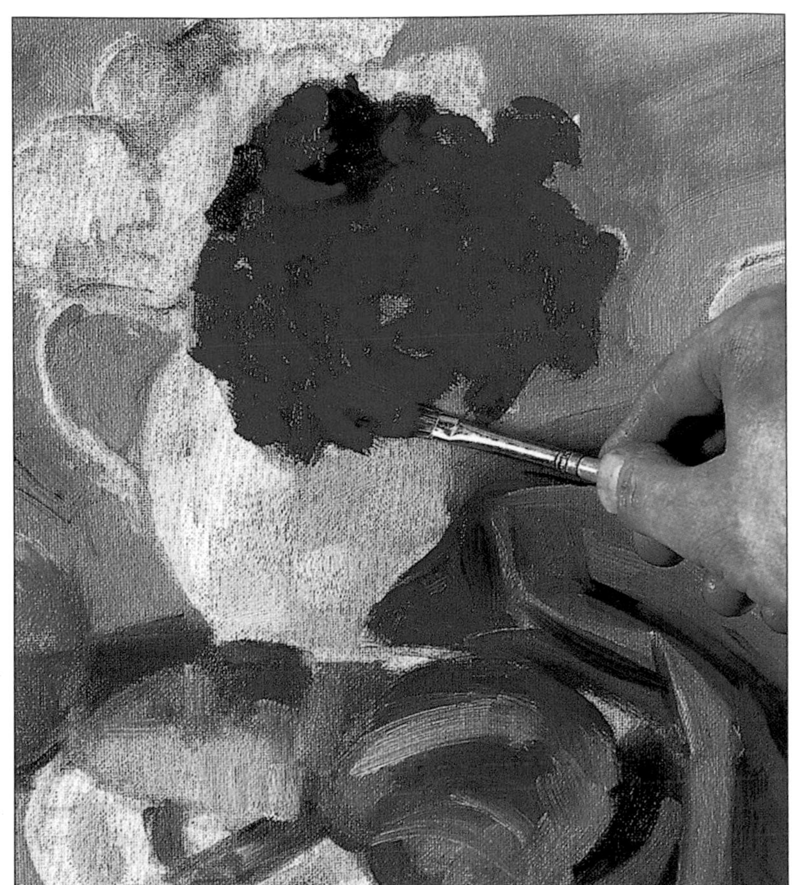

8

Return to the geranium flowers and start to define the petals with short strokes of thick, juicy paint, letting the individual brushstrokes form the shapes of the petals. Mix some scarlet lake and a touch of titanium white for the lightest petals, and alizarin crimson and ultramarine for the darker, cooler petals. Add touches of Venetian red for the warm shadows between the blooms.

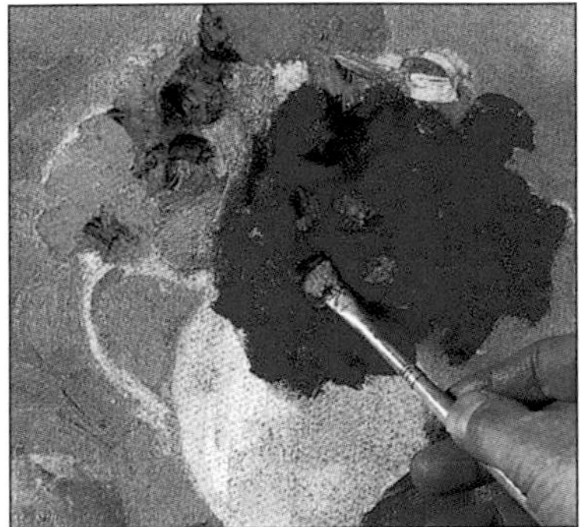

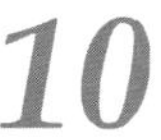

9

Now paint the geranium leaves in the same way, pivoting from the wrist to follow their curved forms with blocks of colour and tone. Use pure Winsor green for the darkest tones, adding Winsor yellow for the bright greens and a touch of yellow ochre for the warm mid-tones. Cut into the flowers with small strokes of green to indicate the gaps between the blooms.

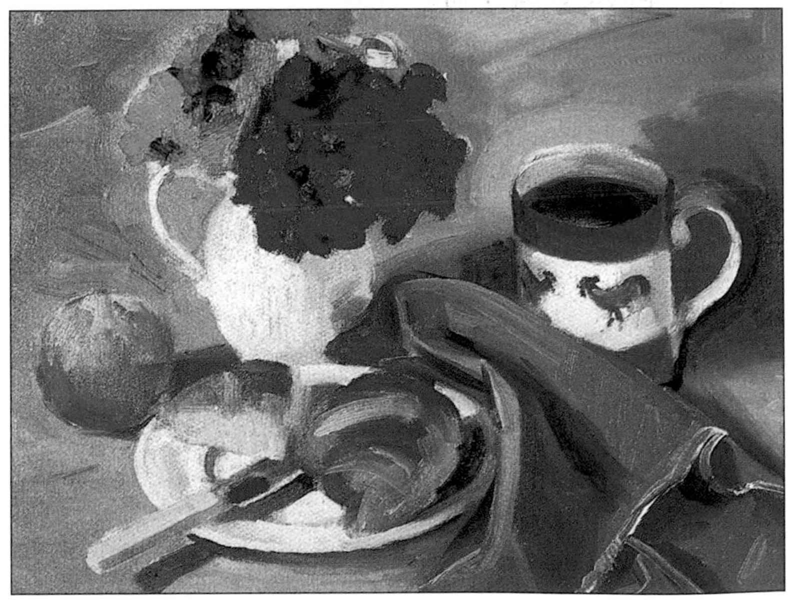

10

Refine the tones on the jug and plate with smooth strokes of white, broken with hints of alizarin and ultramarine blended into the greys applied earlier. Suggest the napkin's reflection on the jug with a hint of alizarin and white. Define the blue and white pattern on the coffee mug with ultramarine and white.

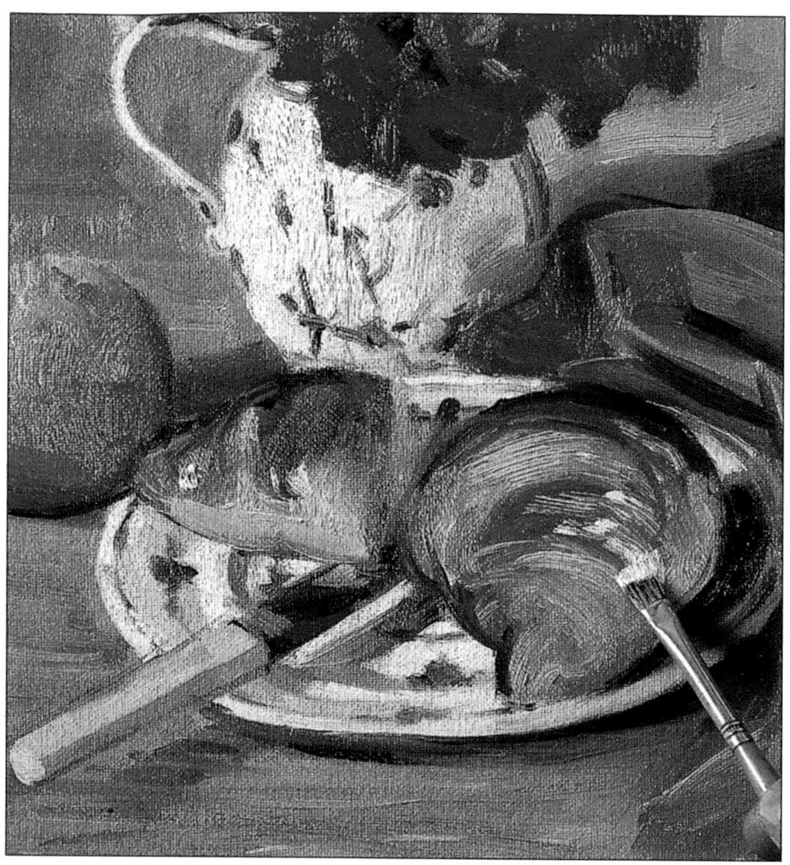

11

Mix ultramarine with a hint of Indian red and paint the decorative blue pattern on the jug and plate with the tip of a small round soft-hair brush. Paint the reflections on the knife blade with strokes of ultramarine, Indian red and yellow ochre. Switch to a small flat bristle brush and suggest the grain of the wooden table with loose drybrush strokes of white and yellow ochre mixed with ultramarine and Indian red. Enrich the colours on the croissant with thick strokes of Indian red and Winsor yellow. Then use white greyed with hints of ultramarine and Indian red to suggest the sugar-frosting on the top of the croissant with feathery strokes of thick paint applied with a thirsty brush.

12

Develop light and shade on the orange with thickly impasted strokes of alizarin crimson, Winsor yellow, white and a touch of scarlet lake, with more yellow ochre for the greenish shadow on the right. Paint the dimple with ultramarine and Indian red, and add the bright highlights with thick dabs of pure white. Mix ultramarine, Indian red and yellow ochre for the dark shadows on the surface of the coffee. Finally, add more texture and movement in the background with loose mixtures of Indian red, yellow ochre, Winsor yellow and white applied with vigorous strokes of creamy paint.

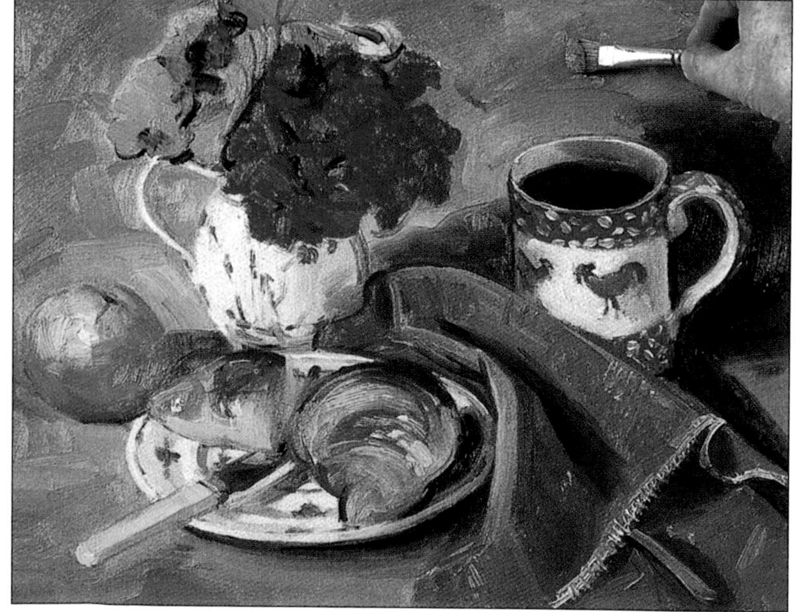

Suppliers

UK

The Arthouse
59 Broadway West
Leigh-on-Sea
Essex
SS9 2BX
Tel: 01702 071 2788
Wide range of art supplies

Cass Arts
13 Charing Cross Road
London WC2H 0EP
Tel: 020 7930 9940
&
220 Kensington High Street
London
W8 7RG
Tel: 020 7937 6506
www.cass-arts.co.uk
Art suppliers and materials

L Cornelissen & Son Ltd
105 Great Russell Street
London WC1B 3RY
Tel: 020 7636 1045

Cowling and Wilcox Ltd
26-28 Broadwick Street
London
W1V 1FG
Tel: 020 7734 9556
www.cowlingandwilcox.com
General art supplies

Daler-Rowney Art Store
12 Percy St
London
W1T 1DN
Tel: 020 7636 8241
Painting and drawing materials

Daler-Rowney Ltd
PO Box 10
Southern Industrial Estate
Bracknell
Berkshire
RG12 8ST
Tel: 01344 424621
www.daler-rowney.co.uk
Painting and drawing materials
Phone for nearest retailer

T N Lawrence & Son Ltd
208 Portland Road
Hove
BN3 5QT
Shop tel: 01273 260260
Order line: 0845 644 3232
www.lawrence.co.uk
Wide range of art materials
Mail order brochure available

John Mathieson & Co
48 Frederick Street
Edinburgh
EH2 1HG
Tel: 0131 225 6798
General art supplies and gallery

Russell & Chapple Ltd
68 Drury Lane
London
WC2B 5SP
Tel: 020 7836 7521
www.russellandchapple.co.uk
Art supplies

The Two Rivers Paper Company
Pitt Mill
Roadwater
Watchet
Somerset
TA23 0QS
Tel: 01984 641028
Hand-crafted papers and boards

Winson & Newton Ltd
Whitefriars Avenue
Wealdstone
Harrow
HA3 5RH
Tel: 020 8424 3200
www.winsornewton.com
Painting and drawing materials
Phone for nearest retailer

SOUTH AFRICA

Cape Town

Artes
3 Aylesbury Street
Bellville 7530
Tel: (021) 957 4525
Fax: (021) 957 4507

George
Art, Crafts and Hobbies
72 Hibernia Street
George 6529
Tel/fax: (044) 874 1337

Port Elizabeth

Bowker Arts and Crafts
52 4th Avenue
Newton Park
Port Elizabeth 6001
Tel: (041) 365 2487
Fax: (041) 365 5306

Johannesburg

Art Shop
140a Victoria Avenue
Benoni West 1503
Tel/fax: (011) 421 1030

East Rand Mall Stationery and Art
Shop 140
East Rand Mall 1459
Tel: (011) 823 1688
Fax: (011) 823 3283

Pietermaritzburg
Art, Stock and Barrel
Shop 44, Parklane Centre
12 Commercial Road
Pietermaritzburg 3201
Tel: (033) 342 1026
Fax: (033) 265 1025

Durban

Pen and Art
Shop 148, The Pavillion
Westville 3630
Tel: (031) 265 0250
Fax: (031) 265 0251

Bloemfontein
L&P Stationary and Art
141 Zastron Street
Westdene
Bloemfontein 9301
Tel: (051) 430 1085
Fax: (051) 430 4102

Pretoria

Centurion Kuns
Shop 45, Eldoraigne Shopping Mall
Saxby Road
Eldoraigne 0157
Tel/fax: (012) 654 0449

NEW ZEALAND

Auckland

The French Art Shop
33 Ponsonby Road
Ponsonby
Tel: (09) 376 0610
Fax: (09) 376 0602

Studio Art Supplies
81 Parnell Rise
Parnell
Auckland
Tel: (09) 377 0302
Fax: (09) 377 7657

Gordon Harris Art Supplies
4 Gillies Ave
Newmarket
Auckland
Tel: (09) 520 4466
Fax: (09) 520 0880
&
31 Symonds St
Auckland Central
Tel: (09) 377 9992

Takapuna Art Supplies
18 Northcroft St
Takapuna
Tel/fax: (09) 489 7213

Wellington

G Webster & Co Ltd
44 Manners Street
Wellington
Tel: (04) 384 2134
Fax: (04) 384 2968

Affordable Art
25 MacLean Street
Paraparaumu Beach
Tel/Fax: (04) 902 9900

Littlejohns Art & Graphic Supplies
170 Victoria Street
Wellington
Tel: (04) 385 2099
Fax: (04) 385 2090

Christchurch

Fine Art Papers
200 Madras Street
Christchurch
Tel: (03) 379 4410
Fax: (03) 379 4443

Brush-N-Palette Artists Supplies Ltd
50 Lichfield Street
Christchurch
Tel/Fax: (03) 366 3088

Dunedin

Art Zone
57 Hanover St
Tel/Fax: (03) 477 0211
www.art-zone.co.nz

AUSTRALIA

NSW

Eckersley's Art, Crafts and Imagination
93 York St
SYDNEY NSW 2000
Tel: (02) 9299 4151
Fax: (02) 9290 1169

Eckersley's Art, Crafts and Imagination
88 Walker St
NORTH SYDNEY NSW 2060
Tel: (02) 9957 5678
Fax: (02) 9957 5685

Eckersley's Art, Crafts and Imagination
21 Atchinson St
ST LEONARDS NSW 2065
Tel: (02) 9439 4944
Fax: (02) 9906 1632

Eckersley's Art, Crafts and Imagination
2-8 Phillip St
PARRAMATTA NSW 2150
Tel: (02) 9893 9191
Fax: (02) 9893 9550

Eckersley's Art, Crafts and Imagination
51 Parry St
NEWCASTLE NSW 2300
Tel: (02) 4929 3423
Fax: (02) 4929 6901

VIC

Eckersley's Art, Crafts and Imagination
97 Franklin St
MELBOURNE VIC 3000
Tel: (03) 9663 6799
Fax: (03) 9663 6721

Eckersley's Art, Crafts and Imagination
116-126 Commercial Rd
PRAHRAN VIC 3181
Tel: (03) 9510 1418
Fax: (03) 9510 5127

SA

Eckersley's Art, Crafts and Imagination
21-27 Frome St
ADELAIDE SA 5000
Tel: (08) 8223 4155
Fax: (08) 8232 1879

QLD

Eckersley's Art, Crafts and Imagination
91-93 Edward St
BRISBANE QLD 4000
Tel: (07) 3221 4866
Fax: (07) 3221 8907

NT

Jackson's Drawing Supplies Pty Ltd
7 Parap Place
PARAP NT 0820
Tel: (08) 8981 2779
Fax: (08) 8981 2017

WA

Jackson's Drawing Supplies Pty Ltd
24 Queen St
BUSSELTON WA 6280
Tel/fax: (08) 9754 2188

Jackson's Drawing Supplies Pty Ltd
Westgate Mall, Point St
FREEMANTLE WA 6160
Tel: (08) 9335 5062
Fax: (08) 9433 3512

Jackson's Drawing Supplies Pty Ltd
108 Beaufort St
NORTHBRIDGE WA 6003
Tel: (08) 9328 8880
Fax: (08) 9328 6238

Jackson's Drawing Supplies Pty Ltd
Shop 14, Shafto Lane
876-878 Hay St
PERTH WA 6000
Tel: (08) 9321 8707

Jackson's Drawing Supplies Pty Ltd
103 Rokeby Rd
SUBIACO WA 6008
Tel: (08) 9381 2700

Index